Presidential Politics

Due Return	Due Return
Date Date	Date Date

Presidential Politics

Readings on Nominations and Elections

EDITED BY

James I. Lengle
Georgetown University

Byron E. Shafer
Russell Sage Foundation

ST. MARTIN'S PRESS / NEW YORK

Library of Congress Catalog Card Number: 80–50145
Copyright © 1980 by St. Martin's Press, Inc.
All Rights Reserved.
Manufactured in the United States of America.
43210
fedcba
For information, write St. Martin's Press, Inc.,
175 Fifth Avenue, New York, N. Y. 10010

cover design: *Tom McKeveny*
typography: *Leon Bolognese*

cloth ISBN: 0–312–64045–5
paper ISBN: 0–312–64046–3

PREFACE

This collection of readings on the politics of presidential selection grew out of a series of discussions between the editors about change in American presidential politics. Our enthusiasm for the project grew as we encountered a fair degree of success in finding materials bearing upon the presidential nominations and elections of the recent past. The book is offered to anyone who classifies himself as a student of presidential politics, with the hope that its general outline will help to organize the topic and that the specific readings will stimulate more rigorous thought, and perhaps even some additional work, on crucial questions in the field.

In organizing the collection, we have started with an overview of recent reforms and then followed the politics of presidential selection in roughly chronological fashion—running from the day after one presidential election to the day of the next. In selecting the readings, we have generally favored articles and extracts that remain at a fairly concrete level and show how the process works rather than how it fits into larger trends, other institutional developments, or abstract social theory. When we have moved beyond this concrete and chronological approach, we have focused on the interaction of three fundamental elements: the *social base,* American society, within which presidential politics is largely played out; the *institutional structure* which rests upon that base and which converts public desires into decisions about presidential selection; and the *actions of relevant elites,* especially presidential candidates and their supporters, who try to respond to the first two factors in order to secure the Presidency.

By *social base* we mean the characteristics and desires of the diverse individuals who make up American society, as well as their levels of attention to politics and willingness to participate in it. By *institutional structure* we mean especially the formal arrangements by which nomination campaigns are conducted, delegates allocated, and candidates nominated, on the one hand, and by which campaigns are conducted and Presidents elected on the other. Such rules, structures, and procedures are never neutral: each requires certain resources and devalues others; each favors certain strategies and makes others unproductive. These two central concepts, social base and institutional structure, are then linked by the *actions of the relevant elites*—namely, the candidates and their strategists. These groups attempt to apply their perceptions of the nature of American society, and of the institutional environment through which their goals must be attained, to the task of nominating and electing a President.

In order to sketch even the rough outlines of this process, we had to range fairly far afield. Where there were classic works in political science which provide generalized knowledge, we snapped them up. But in areas such as campaign finance, or nomination campaigns *before* the first primary, in which there has been comparatively little systematic inquiry, we searched newspapers and other journalistic sources for pieces which could shed light on the topic.

In all of this, we were aided by a small but crucial supporting cast. In New York, Peter Lemos helped pull some of the early material together, so that we could see whether the project was practical. In Washington, Mary O'Gorman chased down critical "hole-fillers" in the late stages. And all along the way Marjorie J. Laue kept the enterprise moving. When we needed a piece on a given topic, she was the one who conducted the more detailed search. When the entire project had to be assembled, she managed this technical process as well. In short, if the outline and ideas are ours, the largest share of expended energy is surely hers. In the final stages of manuscript preparation, she was aided by Anne Stillwaggon and Judith Ditzel, and their efforts helped to ensure that deadlines were met. Finally, Bertrand W. Lummus, Ruth Anderson, and Mary Barnett of St. Martin's Press not only encouraged the project, but encouraged us to do it our way.

All these individuals have our thanks. For ourselves, if the project helps readers to develop an interest in, and to think systematically about, the politics of presidential selection, we shall have received all the thanks necessary.

James I. Lengle
Byron E. Shafer

CONTENTS

Presidential Politics

Introduction

The justification for any book of readings on the politics of presidential selection lies largely with the existence of change in that politics. If there were very few elements in flux, there would be far less room for improvement on earlier readers. On the other hand, efforts to make anything intelligible of such change must still be rooted in those elements which have remained stable, or at least in some readjustment of previously stable ways of thinking about the presidential selection process. Fortunately, there are both indications of change and aspects of continuity nearly everywhere. The former are more evident at the nomination stage, the latter at the general election stage, which remains more stable, predictable, and hence open to concise summary. This difference between the two stages has been present throughout the period following World War II. Of late it has become even more noticeable, as much of the formal nomination process has been self-consciously reformed.

The most familiar elements of variation from one presidential election to the next, of course, are the *principal candidates* for nomination and election, along with the *issues* which they want (or need) to address in order to reach their goals. At the most basic level, this means that when the aggregate of contenders changes, the available personalities change as well—and personal attributes are often substantial factors in nomination and election outcomes. But beyond that, when the individual candidates change, so does the way in which various social interests—their constituencies—are tied into presidential politics, and so does the blend of issues available to the electorate. Candidates have their own personal bases in specific groups and organizations, and they cannot simply recombine these at will. By the same token, they bring with them certain issue identifications which are peculiarly their own, and these, too, cannot be mixed or matched to suit one particular campaign. Finally, the *field* of these contestants, apart from the characteristics of any one member or members, often has an independent effect; aspirants may succeed or fail because of the presence of some other contender(s), not because of any attribute of their own.

Less visible, but no less real, are alterations in the overall *party system* through which presidential candidates are nominated and elected, and alterations in the forms of organization which are found within the individual parties or which run parallel to them on the outside. Since World War II the balance of party identifiers has shifted to increase the proportion of Democrats to Republicans and the ratio of "independents" to both groups. The nature of the parties as organizations has changed as well. The inability to mount campaigns and control nominations has clearly declined; substitute organizational bases are clearly on the rise.

More visible, if less often consciously considered, are innovations in the *means of communication* about presidential politics—innovations which continue up through the present. The coming of the electronic media, and especially television, is the most obvious example. Actual televised presidential debates show this increasingly critical factor at its most dramatic, but the changes which televised news has wrought on reporting and on the availability (and character) of political information are surely much larger and more encompassing.

Enveloping all these developments are changes in American society itself, that is, evolutions in the *social base* upon which presidential politics is played out. Some trends, such as the gradually rising level of mass education, seem general and continuing. Others, such as the growing organization of particular ethnic or racial minorities, are both more limited and more subject to further redirection as the status of these groups shifts. Both types of change, however, alter the kinds of candidacies which can be mounted, the forms of campaigns which might be successful, and the range of issues which are likely to enter presidential politics.

Finally, in the last dozen years there have been a large number of major *institutional alterations* affecting presidential selection, all of which have been deliberately undertaken, though not always with their actual results as the goal. At the nomination stage, two types of structural change are particularly important: reform of the delegate-selection process, and reform of campaign financing. At the general election stage, the change in campaign financing arrangements is again striking.

All such formal changes, in turn, are either exaggerated, redirected, or contained by shifts in the aspects of presidential-selection politics—in candidates and issues, in parties and party systems, in media of communication, and in the social base of politics generally. Together these create sufficient elements of change to prevent the results of the presidential-selection process from being highly predictable. At the same time, the more stable elements of nomination and election politics still offer some hope that change can be analyzed in a fashion which will illuminate the present and help understand the future.

PART I

Reform

For most of the twentieth century, the institutional framework within which presidential nominations occurred—party structure, rules, and procedures—could be taken as a constant by presidential candidates, rank-and-file participants, and even academic analysts. Delegate-selection mechanisms were changed from time to time by individual states, but largely in response to peculiarly local pressures, and the cumulative shifts rarely provided advantages for any particular contender. Campaign finance reforms, when they did occur, were simply ineffective.

After 1968 all this changed. In the aftermath of the 1968 election, the national Democratic party undertook a thorough revision of its nomination process. In the course of that effort, most Republican nomination procedures were revised as well, courtesy of democratic state legislators who did not confine themselves to their own party's business. In the aftermath of the 1972 election, the U.S. Congress joined in and sharply altered the laws governing nomination and election finance. And this time, these new laws had a clear and substantial impact.

In the area of delegate selection, the five basic institutions which had previously been used to create delegates were scrutinized by Democratic party reform commissions and either banned, limited, or expanded in some restructured form:

Party Caucuses. In party caucus systems, the bottom level of party officers—usually precinct committeemen and committeewomen—meet to select delegates to some higher-level convention, which eventually chooses the national convention delegation. This is the oldest and most widely used delegate-selection device in American history, but the Democratic party nonetheless banned it outright. The Republicans still permit its use, but it has declined within that party too, as many states (in response to Democratic party rules) have switched to presidential primaries.

3

Participatory Conventions. The structure of a participatory convention system is similar to that of a party caucus, with one crucial exception: the bottom level is open to any party member—and usually to anyone who claims to be a member. This became the sole permissible convention arrangement within the Democratic party after 1968, and it is not uncommon on the Republican side as well.

Committee Selection. Under a committee selection system, the party's state central committee—or occasionally just its state chairman or sitting governor—selects the national convention delegation. This device was never very prevalent outside the South, but the Democratic party has cut it back everywhere, so that it now serves mainly as a means of complying with other delegate-selection requirements. The Republican party has historically relied very little on committee selection, although the procedure today is comparatively more common among Republicans because the Democrats have curtailed it so severely.

Delegate Primaries. In a delegate primary all candidates for national convention delegate appear on the ballot under their own names only. They may campaign for election by publicizing their loyalty to a presidential candidate, but they may also campaign by emphasizing community ties, celebrity, or whatever. The Democratic party has banned the device entirely; the Republican party still uses it in several states, including a few of the largest.

Candidate Primaries. In candidate primaries the name of the presidential candidate, rather than the potential delegate, is featured. In some states the delegate merely puts his presidential preference after his own name, but in many others only the name of the presidential candidate appears, and the individual delegates whom he wins are actually selected through some other mechanism. In the wake of the Democratic party's reform drives, candidate primaries have become by far the most common delegate-selection instrument in both parties.

The changes in the rules for *allocating* the delegates created by these mechanisms are also substantial. Previously there had been three permissible formulas:

Winner Take All. In a winner-take-all primary, the candidate who receives the most votes receives all the state's delegates. In a winner-take-all convention, either a convention majority allocates all the delegates, or that majority binds all delegates to its wishes. The Democratic party has banned all such arrangements; the Republicans have retained a few major winner-take-all primaries, like the one in California.

Districted. In a districted primary or convention, delegates run in geographic subunits within the state, and the candidate who receives the most votes wins all of that particular district's delegates. The Democrats permitted such systems through 1976 but have outlawed them for 1980. The Republicans have left the arrangement alone and will presumably retain it in states where a Democratic legislature does not take more sweeping action.

Proportional. There are a variety of proportional systems, but all divide delegates among presidential aspirants according to some explicit mathematical standard. Some divide on a statewide basis; more use proportionality within districts. For both groups the crucial internal consideration is the threshold percentage, the cutoff below which a candidate is no longer entitled to share in the delegate division. The Democrats have made some version of proportionality a requirement for 1980; the Republicans have left the matter to state option.

Finally, the rules for *raising and spending money* in nomination and election campaigns have undergone extensive alterations, this time at the hands of the U.S. Congress rather than the parties or their reform commissions:

Sources. In the prereform era, sources for financing a nomination campaign were limited only by fund raisers' imaginations or by their candidates' individual fund-raising potentials, although large amounts from large givers were surely the easiest way to handle the problem. By the late 1970s, however, the federal government had provided "matching funds" from the public treasury for all nomination aspirants who agreed to raise their money in a certain way, and only Republican John B. Connally has since refused this subvention (and its attendant restrictions). For the general election campaign, Congress went even further by providing a flat sum for each major-party nominee if he consented to even more stringent limits. Once again, no one has yet refused.

Limitations. The same reform specified that, to qualify for matching funds, a candidate for nomination had to raise $5,000 in each of twenty states in single contributions of no larger than $250. Thereafter the federal government would "match" every such contribution dollar-for-dollar. However, individual givers would still be permitted to contribute up to $1,000 to any individual candidate, with the dollars above $250 going unmatched. Similarly, for the general election campaign, major-party nominees would receive a sizable subvention directly from the public treasury ($25,000,000 in 1976), if they agreed that neither they nor the national party would spend *any* additional amount.

The cumulative effect of all this reform continues to be the subject of extensive argument, but a few preliminary areas of consensus are emerging. Clearly, the sweeping changes in permissible delegate-selection devices have decentralized the process of assembling a nomination majority. Previously, a candidate had to perform well in a small number of contests and then use that performance to bargain with the leadership in other states. Now the same candidate is almost compelled to seek a campaign presence in most of these states, and the bargaining blocs which he encounters there or elsewhere are very much smaller.

By the same token, the state parties themselves have been greatly reduced in importance, even within "their own" nomination process. This began when the delegate-selection devices which are most favorable to regular party organizations were replaced with others which gave them no automatic role, and it continues with the newer rules which emphasize the role of presidential contenders and which break state delegations down into smaller, even single-delegate, pieces.

The finance reforms have, at the very least, changed the character of the campaign organizations which seek these delegates. The matching-funds provision has made its initial statutory requirement ($5,000 in twenty states, etc.) into a preliminary threshold which all campaigns that hope to be taken seriously must pass. Beyond that, the more general finance rules and limitations have almost compelled creation of a separate and substantial "financial campaign." By so doing, they have also made the finance tacticians and their assistants, the lawyers and accountants, a much larger part of the nomination campaign generally.

The continuation of this reform process has had one other, slightly perverse consequence: it has meant that the ability to guess correctly about the impact of the latest round of reforms has become an independent asset in its own right. When delegate-selection arrangements and finance laws are stable for a generation or more, they produce a generalized understanding to which all candidates have equal access. But when such rules and procedures are in flux, they distribute a new form of advantage—quite separate from the effect of any given reform—to anyone who is able to discern how the revised framework will actually work.

In Chapter 1 Austin Ranney's "Putting the Parties in Their Place," from his book *Curing the Mischiefs of Faction: Party Reform in America,* places nomination reform in its full historical perspective, from the highly centralized and relatively impermeable "King Caucus" of the early 1800s to the decentralized and highly permeable system of today. Jeane J. Kirkpatrick, in a section from her monograph *Dismantling the Parties: Reflections on Party Reform,* discusses some major effects of the most recent round of delegate-selection changes on the traditional party functions of recruiting candidates, conducting campaigns, aggregating public desires, and structuring voters' decisions. Finally, in "The Drive for Reform: Pre- and Post-Watergate" from his book *Financing Politics,* Herbert E. Alexander reviews the history of the more specialized financial reforms and covers the lingering issues which the recent round of such activity has raised once again.

CHAPTER 1

Reform and the Rules of the Game

A. Overview: Presidential Nomination Reform

B. Delegate-Selection Reform

C. Finance Reform

· A ·

Overview: Presidential Nomination Reform

Putting the Parties in Their Place

BY AUSTIN RANNEY

Any effort to understand the politics of one time from the perspective of another is hazardous, and our own survey of the theory and practice of party reform in America is no exception. One hazard is that, as we review and evaluate what Americans in earlier times have said and done about party reform, we assume that they saw what they were doing as just as important as we see it, and for the same reasons.

But the fact is that until well after the Civil War most Americans—even those most involved in the early conflicts over party reform—thought they were dealing with passing matters of practical necessity rather than with matters eternally central to the life of the Republic. To be sure, many reforms were adopted which we now regard as highly important: for example, the end of nominations by legislative and congressional caucuses in the 1820s, the creation of the national nominating conventions in the 1830s, and the establishment of the national committees in the 1840s. But the people who instituted those reforms did so almost casually, believing them to be useful solutions to practical problems, not matters of high principle. And their ideas and actions received no attention whatever from James Kent, Theodore Parker, Alexis de Tocqueville, Henry David Thoreau, or the period's other leading commentators.

There is no mystery about why this was so. Until well after the Civil War parties were not generally thought to be either permanent or impor-

Excerpted from Austin Ranney, *Curing the Mischiefs of Faction: Party Reform in America* (Berkeley: University of California Press, 1974), pp. 58–74. Most footnotes deleted. Copyright 1975 by The Regents of the University of California; reprinted by permission of the University of California Press.

tant features of the nation's political life, and there seemed no reason why serious men should pay serious attention to sordid little intraparty squabbles. On the rare occasions when the organization of parties was mentioned in the course of official government business, most respectable people found the topic demeaning to the dignity of the forum. For example, in March, 1824 there was some discussion on the floor of the United States Senate about whether the Republican party's congressional caucus should continue to make presidential nominations. Almost every Senator present had personally participated in making such nominations, but most who spoke regretted that so unsuitable a topic had been raised in official debate. Walter Lowrie of Pennsylvania said, "It is with a sensation of pain that I observe the situation in which the Senate is . . . placed by introducing the subject." John Henry Eaton of Tennessee declared that the topic was "altogether improper" and "ought not to be permitted to remain any longer before the Senate." It was, he said, "unbecoming the dignity of the body," and would "place the members in no very elevated view before the public." And William Findlay of Pennsylvania ended the embarrassment by declaring that "as this [is] the most unpleasant discussion . . . [I] have ever heard since [I] have had the honor of a seat in the Senate, [I will] endeavor to terminate it"—which he did by successfully moving to adjourn. So it seems that in the Era of Good Feelings political necessity might occasionally force one to *practice* party politics, but simple etiquette required one at least not to *talk* about it in the Republic's highest tribunals.

By the 1870s, however, most politicians and political commentators accepted the fact that, for better or worse, parties had become an established part of the nation's political life. One consequence was a veritable quantum jump in the volume of comment about how the parties operated and might be purified. Another was the rapid growth of a notion that has profoundly affected the parties ever since: the idea that they will not voluntarily mend their ways and so must legally be forced to behave. When that notion became widespread in the 1880s, conflict over party reform became highly visible and discussion of it even respectable. It has remained so ever since.

Rules, Stakes, and Outcomes in Party Reform

The immediate object of dispute over party reform in all epochs has been the *rules*—the party rules, public laws, or both governing the status, organization, membership, and operations of the parties. As in all conflicts over rules, most of the debates have consisted of arguments over normative issues of what values should be maximized in the political system, and over empirical issues of what institutional arrangements are likely to maximize the preferred values. The debaters have touched on many of political theory's most ancient and difficult questions, and we shall pay full heed to what they have said.

While doing so, however, we should bear in mind the truism that decisions on rules are never politically neutral. Any rule governing the conduct of conflict is bound to make the competition easier for some contestants and more difficult for others. So any proposal to change a rule is in part a proposal to alter each contestant's chances for success. Thus the politics of party reform, like any other kind of politics, is bound to be, in Harold Lasswell's famous phrase, a contest over "who gets what, when, how."

We shall review many arguments about the merits of particular party reforms as judged by the standards of democracy, representativeness, participation, and other abstract ideals. What I said a moment ago does not mean that these arguments have been uttered only by knaves or fools. It does mean that in each dispute there has been more at stake than the logical proximity of words in a rule to words in a statement of high principle. And it also means that to understand fully any particular conflict over party reform we must consider not only what the contestants said but also who they were and what they stood to gain or lose by the reform in dispute. For, as Paul David and his colleagues concluded in their massive survey of the national nominating conventions:

> Changes in party rules seem most likely to occur when a proposal of seeming general merit happens to coincide with the factional interests of a potential majority group that needs an issue.

The relevance of this observation for party reform can be shown by a brief review of battles over reforms in the parties' procedures for nominating presidential candidates.

DEVELOPMENT OF NOMINATIONS BY LEGISLATIVE AND CONGRESSIONAL CAUCUSES

(1) The State Legislative Caucus System. In America's preparty days, prior to the early 1790s, most nominations of candidates for elective offices were made by self-presentation: the aspirant simply announced through the newspapers or on the town bulletin board that he was seeking the office. In a few areas, nominations were occasionally made by mass meetings and even by primitive delegate conventions; but self-presentation was by far the most common method. This was the Golden Age looked back on so longingly by those commentators . . . who condemned nominations by parties on the ground that no self-selected body should intervene between the sovereign people and their choice of public officials.

But the Golden Age did not last very long. When the parties began to emerge in the early 1790s their prime object was to concert their strength behind selected candidates so as to maximize their chances of winning elections. Hence each party's first organizational need was a procedure for selecting its candidates, identifying them to the voters as the party's standard-bearers, and uniting the party's adherents behind them in the campaign. They generally settled upon what was called a "caucus" or "primary": the terms were used interchangeably to mean a general meeting of all of a town's or county's party supporters who cared to attend. Such meetings were called "primaries" not only because they occurred earlier in time than the general elections but also because they were thought to be closest to the parties' members.

At first the parties' nominees for such statewide offices as governor and lieutenant governor were chosen by caucuses held in the state's capital city, to which partisans from all parts of the state were nominally invited. But the difficulties of eighteenth century transportation prevented most non-residents from attending, and the primaries were dominated by residents of the capital. This struck most nonresidents as highly unfair, and some unsung Solon thought up a solution: the party's members in the state legislature came from all parts of the state; their nomination and election proved they had the confidence of the people in their districts; and they were already resident in the capital. Therefore, they should pick the party's nominees for statewide offices on behalf of the party's members in the whole state. This suggestion made good sense to most partisans, and by 1800 both parties' nominations for governor and lieutenant governor in most states were made by their legislative caucuses.

Soon thereafter a number of the party faithful in legislative districts held by the opposition party complained that since they had no legislator to speak for them they were unrepresented in the nominating machinery. Thus the parties for the first time faced the issue of the apportionment of party assemblies which has plagued them ever since, as we shall see later. In the early 1800s the parties dealt with it by instituting what came to be known as "mixed caucuses." These were gatherings in the capital not only of the party's legislators but also of delegates elected by caucuses in those districts that had no party legislator. As we shall see, the mixed caucuses were the precursors of the delegate conventions which became the dominant nominating method a generation later.

(2) Origins of the Congressional Caucus Nominating System.   From the mid-1790s on the Republican and Federalist members of Congress met together occasionally in caucuses to discuss issues and plot legislative strategy. It is not clear just when these bodies first began to nominate their parties' presidential candidates, but most historians agree that both parties held nominating caucuses in 1800. Ironically, the first appears to have been called by Alexander Hamilton, the archenemy of the whole idea of organized party competition. Whatever his feeling about parties, Hamilton

had a practical problem needing an immediate solution. He felt that John Adams would make a feeble showing against Thomas Jefferson, and he calculated that Charles Cotesworth Pinckney could beat Adams for the nomination and perhaps also Jefferson in the election. But Adams was the incumbent President and thus the likely choice of most Federalist electors. Since at that time, prior to the adoption of the Twelfth Amendment, each member of the Electoral College voted for two persons, Hamilton's strategy was to persuade the Federalists to concert their strength behind Pinckney as well as Adams—in the hope that Pinckney would ultimately get more votes than Adams and be elected Vice President if not President. So he persuaded the Federalist members of Congress to meet secretly in the Senate chamber and recommend—"nominate," we would say—Adams and Pinckney.[1] The Republicans met in the same year in less formal surroundings—Marache's boarding house in Philadelphia—and endorsed Jefferson for President and Aaron Burr for Vice President.

After the election of 1800 the Federalists tried various nominating devices to recoup their sagging fortunes. In 1804 their congressional caucus nominated Pinckney and Rufus King, but they were swamped in the election. In 1808 the Federalists abandoned the congressional caucus and tried a secret delegate convention in New York which some historians have dubbed the first national nominating convention. They held another secret convention in New York in 1812, but by 1816 they had given up making presidential nominations altogether.

As the Republicans advanced from being the dominant party to being the only party, they continued to use their congressional caucus to pick their nominees. In 1804 they were so confident of success that they held a public caucus to renominate Jefferson, and in the succeeding three election years they continued the practice. In 1820 everyone knew there would be no Federalist nominee and therefore no contested election. And since President James Monroe, the Republicans' leader and certain nominee, believed that the mischiefs of party competition had at last been cured by the elimination of the Federalists, it would not be appropriate to hold a caucus. So none was held.

CAUCUS TO CONVENTION

(1) Death of the Congressional Caucus, 1824.   We have seen that the congressional caucus nominating system was born as an incident in intraparty factional struggles in 1800. It died in 1824 as a casualty of another factional struggle. After the election of 1820 there was no Federalist party

---

[1]Hamilton's strategy failed. All 65 Federalist Electors voted for Adams, but one voted for John Jay instead of Pinckney; so the Federalist electoral vote was: Adams 65, Pinckney 64, Jay 1; Republicans Jefferson and Burr each received 73.

and no chance of a Federalist candidate in 1824. So choosing the Republican nominee would amount to choosing the President. Like Jefferson, Monroe intended to respect the two-term tradition; but, unlike Jefferson, he had not groomed a political heir apparent. So by 1823 at least five serious contenders for the nomination had emerged—John Quincy Adams, John C. Calhoun, Henry Clay, William H. Crawford, and Andrew Jackson—and none of the five had put any great distance between himself and his rivals.

Most of the politicos in all camps recognized that *how* the nomination would be made would do much to determine its outcome. If the party reverted to its traditional congressional caucus system, it looked as though each candidate would get some votes, but Crawford would get the most and, even with only a plurality, would win the nomination and the election. So how people felt about the proper nominating method was correlated very highly indeed with which candidate they supported. The legislature of Crawford's home state of Georgia expressed their support for him *and* declared that the congressional caucus was the only legitimate nominating procedure. The legislature of Jackson's home state of Tennessee formally nominated Jackson and added a resolution condemning the congressional caucus system as unrepresentative and unconstitutional. Henry Clay's home state legislature in Kentucky nominated him, and supporters of all four anti-Crawford candidates held public meetings denouncing "King Caucus" and calling on members of Congress not to attend.

The Crawford faction, now led by Martin Van Buren, nevertheless believed the caucus was their best chance, so eleven pro-Crawford congressmen issued an invitation to all their colleagues to attend a public caucus in the chamber of the House of Representatives on February 14, 1824. When the day arrived, only 66 of the 216 Republican congressmen attended. In a brief session they nominated Crawford for the presidency and Albert Gallatin for the vice presidency. In the subsequent Senate debate referred to earlier, Samuel Smith of Maryland, a Crawford supporter, put his finger on the main source of the attacks on the congressional caucus method:

> May we not, without offence, believe that men are much governed by the consideration of whether the caucus will or will not support their favorite candidate? And must we not believe that those who have heretofore attended caucuses, will find it difficult to assign any other reason for absenting themselves from what they now censure?

But winning the argument is not, then or now, the same as winning the election: Crawford finished third in the electoral college count with 41 votes to Jackson's 99, Adams' 84, and Clay's 37. Since then no party's congressional caucus has ever nominated a presidential candidate.

(2) Emergence of the National Convention. In the period from 1825 to 1828 presidential candidates were put forward by a variety of state-based devices: official acts of state legislatures, unofficial declarations by state legislative caucuses and mixed caucuses, and endorsements by state conventions. But no national agency immediately replaced the defunct congressional caucus. This jumble of local systems worked very well for the Jacksonians, who used it to nominate and elect their leader in 1828. But the anti-Jackson faction, now hardening into a separate party calling themselves first "National Republicans" and then "Whigs," decided that the only way they could hope to defeat "King Andrew" in 1832 would be to unite all their forces in one national movement behind one *nationally* selected candidate. For that purpose they needed some kind of national nominating mechanism, and the best one around seemed to be the national delegate convention pioneered by the minor Anti-Masonic party in 1830. They decided to hold their convention in Baltimore, the nearest big city outside the national capital; and, to avoid offending local sensibilities, they designated the National Republican caucus of the Maryland legislature to issue the call for the convention for December, 1831. The convention met as scheduled, with 167 delegates from 17 states, and nominated Henry Clay.

These proceedings caused the Jacksonians no loss of sleep. But they had other problems to which calling a national convention also seemed the best solution. Jackson and his chief lieutenant, Martin Van Buren, had decided that John C. Calhoun had to be dumped from the ticket and the vice presidency in 1832, but they knew it would not be easy. Calhoun had many supporters in the state legislatures and state parties, and it seemed possible that if the decentralized nominating methods of 1828 were used again they would be saddled with Calhoun for four more years. So the pragmatic Van Buren, who had been one of the chief defenders of the congressional caucus system in 1824, persuaded Jackson that a national nominating convention dominated neither by congressmen nor by state leaders was the solution. The Jacksonian caucus of the New Hampshire legislature was chosen to issue the call for a Democratic Republican convention to meet in Baltimore in May, 1832. The delegates who came balloted only on the vice presidential nomination and chose Van Buren. Thus America's second great party reform was accomplished, not because the principle of nomination by delegate conventions won more adherents than the principle of nomination by legislative caucuses, but largely because the dominant factional interests of 1824 decided that the caucus system made things harder for them, and the dominant factional interests eight years later decided that national conventions would make things easier for them.

(3) Later Conflicts, Interests, and Outcomes. Since 1832 the national parties have nominated their presidential and vice presidential candidates by national delegate conventions. However, the rules governing the con-

duct of those conventions have often been hotly disputed, and in most such contests the candidate and factional interests underlying the pronouncements of principle have been both clear and decisive.

For example, prior to the Whig convention of 1839 some leaders, notably Thurlow Weed of New York, decided that Henry Clay, the party's leader and defeated candidate in 1832, was too unpopular with the voters to be elected but so popular with the party's convention delegates that he was likely to be nominated again. So the trick was to keep the convention from choosing him without totally alienating him and his supporters. As Weed dryly commented later, "The organization of the convention and the mode of proceeding occasioned much solicitude among the friends of different candidates." Well it might. Weed's faction persuaded the convention to drop its customary direct balloting procedure and replace it with a complicated indirect system. Each state delegation chose a committee of three, which canvassed the preferences of its own delegates and reported them to the other delegations through their counterpart committees. Each delegation then balloted secretly, and its committee carried the results to a general meeting of all the committees. The general committee added up the results and reported them to the delegations. The delegations then balloted again, this time under the unit rule, and the votes were aggregated by the general committee. If no candidate received a majority, the procedure would be repeated. In this way, the Weed faction hoped, the delegates would be able to vote against Clay secretly and thus avoid any reprisals from his enthusiasts back in their states. It worked perfectly: the general committee announced that William Henry Harrison had received 148 votes to Clay's 90 and was the nominee.

In 1832, the first Democratic National Convention adopted, with Martin Van Buren's strong approval, a rule requiring a two-thirds majority for the nomination. In the 1844 convention this rule cost him the nomination. His majorities on the early ballots were not enough to win, and he was finally passed over for James K. Polk, history's first "dark horse" winner. The convention's rules, which had seemed suitable and just to the Van Buren men in 1832 and in the two subsequent conventions, suddenly struck them as grossly unfair: they issued a statement denouncing the 1844 convention as

> the first instance of a body of men, unknown to the laws and the Constitution, assuming to treat the American Presidency as their private property, to be disposed of at their own will and pleasure; and, it may be added, for their own profit.

The legitimacy of the two-thirds rule, it seemed, depended on whose ox it gored.

Many subsequent Democratic and Republican conventions have witnessed credentials fights over the seating of rival delegations from particular states. In most, the debates over the merits of the cases have not concealed the fact that what was really at stake was votes for or against particular candidates. The most recent instance was certainly no exception. The hottest fight in the 1972 Democratic Convention was over the issue of whether all 271 pro-McGovern delegates chosen in California's winner-take-all primary should be seated or only the 120 delegates that would be proportional to his 44 per cent of the popular vote. Both sides filled the debates in the Credentials Committee and on the convention floor with appeals to democracy, fair play, the spirit of reform, not changing the rules in the middle of the game, and so on. But these lofty principles were not the only stakes. As *The New York Times* told it:

> The formal arguments were heavy with irony. The anti-McGovern lawyers, representing in fact the more conservative branch of the party, argued that the California law violates "the spirit of reform," as exemplified in the same guidelines their committee members had largely been voting down in other challenges. . . . The question was clearly decided on political, not substantive, grounds. . . . Almost no one who supported Mr. McGovern voted for the challenge; almost no one who supported anyone else voted against it.

Both sides also exuded a moral indignation reminiscent of the Van Buren pronouncements in 1844. McGovern denounced the Credentials Committee's decision to split the delegation as "an incredible, cynical, rotten political steal" and hinted that he might not support Humphrey or any other candidate nominated "by crooked and unethical procedures of the kind that were used in this committee room." The anti-McGovern coalition were equally indignant when the Convention Chairman, Lawrence O'Brien, ruled that the 120 California delegates whose credentials had not been challenged would be allowed to vote and that the majority required to win would be only a majority of the delegates qualified at the time of the vote. The indignation of both sides was certainly genuine, but it stemmed mainly from their correct understanding that the outcome of these procedural fights would decide who won the nomination.

George McGovern's own changing views of party reform provide another striking illustration. From 1969 to 1971 he chaired the commission that wrote the party's new delegate-selection rules. Two of their innovations became especially controversial. One was the rule requiring representation on each state's delegation of women, young people, and minority groups "in reasonable relationship to their presence in the population of the State." The other was the rule prohibiting a presidential candidate or any other party leader from determining which individuals would make up any slate of candidates for delegate, whether pledged to a presidential candidate or not.

No one was more enthusiastic about the new rules than McGovern. He praised them repeatedly during his campaign for the 1972 nomination, and often attacked other candidates, especially Edmund Muskie, for trying to get around them. When he won the nomination he declared it was "all the more precious in that it is the gift of the most open political process in our national history." But soon after his disastrous defeat in the November election he expressed a different view. Testifying before the party's new commission on party organization, he declared that the quotas for population groups should be dropped, and that presidential candidates and other party leaders should be guaranteed the right "to protect the integrity of the method that chooses delegates in their name." The wire service account added: "Asked why McGovern did not take the views then that he now espouses, an aide said, 'We were running for president then.'"

Does this sort of thing show that McGovern and his opponents were hypocrites, knaves, or fools? I think not. McGovern and his supporters certainly believed he would be a better candidate and President than any of his rivals, and those who supported the other aspirants believed the same of them. Surely one need not be a hypocrite, knave, or fool to believe that rules which make it easier to nominate a good candidate are preferable to those likely to saddle the party and perhaps the nation with a bad one. Speaking more generally, to say that some people advocate some party reforms and oppose others because they believe that changing the rules will help or hurt the candidates and policies they believe in is to say that, in politics as in all other forms of human conflict, the rules make a difference in determining who wins and who loses. Not *all* the difference, but enough to force the prudent to pay them heed.

·B·

Delegate-Selection Reform

Dismantling the Parties: Reflections on Party Reform
BY JEANE J. KIRKPATRICK

Recruitment, Screening, and Socialization of Political Leaders

Two types of political leadership are traditionally recruited, screened, and developed through the political parties: candidates for public office and persons who will staff the party. In other democratic nations, leadership recruitment and candidate nomination are the exclusive business of the party organization (that is, leaders) at national and local levels. American parties have always had less control over candidate selection than their European counterparts because that distinctive American institution, the direct primary, gives voters rather than party leaders the last word, and also because legislators and judges have claimed a uniquely large role in the nominating process—by regulating the conduct of primaries and by asserting jurisdiction over questions of the fairness of other party processes. In the past decade changes have occurred that further decreased the parties' already limited control over the presidential nominating process. Most important among these has been the dramatic proliferation of presidential primaries.

As long as primaries were one among several equally or more important methods of choosing a presidential nominee, control over the ultimate decision could be retained by party leaders. However, as the number of primaries increased from seventeen in 1968 to twenty-two in 1972, to thirty in 1976, the impact of primaries grew more profound and pervasive. In 1972, for the first time ever, a majority of the delegates to the national

Excerpted from Jeane J. Kirkpatrick, *Dismantling the Parties: Reflections on Party Reform* (Washington: American Enterprise Institute, 1978). Most footnotes deleted. Copyright 1978 American Enterprise Institute.

conventions was chosen in primaries; in 1976 the proportion chosen by primaries was nearly three-fourths of all delegates and was still climbing. It is almost impossible to overstate the impact of primaries on the nominating process. They affect the character of delegates, candidates, campaigns, conventions, and parties. Convention delegates chosen in presidential primaries are selected because of their relationship to a presidential candidate instead of their relationship to the party. Since a national convention is the highest decision-making body for a party, choosing delegates without regard to their knowledge of or commitment to the party means vesting control over a party in persons who may have little concern for it. That is not all. Because candidates can go directly to the voters in search of the nomination, primaries permit candidates as well as delegates to be selected without having ever served an apprenticeship in the party, without ever being screened in or socialized by the party. In addition, the absence of any role for party organizations encourages a focus on personality and at the same time communicates to voters and activists alike a sense of the party's irrelevance to this most important decision process. Primaries force on candidates functions which have historically been party functions. To compete successfully in primaries, candidates need an elaborate personal organization capable of performing diverse tasks in diverse states. The existence of these organizations reduces a nominee's dependence on a party organization.

Primaries have other effects on the outcomes of nominating contests. The capacity to appeal directly to voters makes it possible to bypass not only the party leadership, but the dominant political class, their standards and their preferences. The campaigns of George Wallace and Ronald Reagan could not have gotten off the ground without primaries. Nor could the campaign of George McGovern. Most observers believe that primaries give extremist candidates a better chance than they would otherwise have, though it should be noted that McGovern did better in nonprimary than in primary states and that Barry Goldwater won his party's nomination before primaries had achieved their contemporary importance.

Primaries also tend to personalize politics by focusing attention on disagreements within parties and on individuals who compete not as their parties' nominees but as persons with distinctive characteristics. Because the competing candidates often share most ideological orientations, personal attributes such as appearance, style, and wit attain new importance. (Presidents today must be fit and not fat, amusing not dull, with cool not hot personalities.)

What caused the proliferation of primaries? Primaries are the institutional embodiment of the persistent American suspicion of organization. They reflect the conviction that in passing through the web of personal ambitions and structural complexities that compose a political party the voice of the people is distorted beyond recognition. In the American tradition the populist instinct and the distrust of organization go hand in hand. Robert M. LaFollette and the early reformers advocated the direct primary as an antidote to bossism and corruption and as a mechanism for achieving greater democracy. The proliferation of primaries since 1968 is also closely related to determined reform efforts to purify the political process by reforming those practices that inhibited expression of the people's will. Unlike the LaFollette Progressives, however, the reformers on the McGovern-Fraser Commission did not believe that it was necessary (or desirable) to resort to primaries. Nonetheless, most observers agree that the recent proliferation of primaries occurred largely as a response to the McGovern-Fraser reforms, even though a majority of that commission's members did not desire the result and "preferred a reformed national convention to a national presidential primary or a major increase in the number of state presidential primaries." Following the promulgation of the reform commission's report, some states adopted primaries as a way around the complex demands of the new rules. Elsewhere primaries were adopted because state party leaders preferred to let voters make decisions in primaries rather than compete with "new politics" activists in caucuses. The spread of presidential primaries, then, has been stimulated by reformers who sought to break the control of bosses, by reformers who made the alternatives too unattractive, by advocates of direct democracy who believe that the most legitimate judgment is that which flows most directly from the people, and by boosters seeking to attract publicity, jobs, and money to their states.

In nonprimary states, candidate selection has traditionally been carried out by "the organization." Party regulars and bosses (whether a traditional machine, a courthouse gang, or a reform clique) met in caucuses and conventions to select candidates and make other important decisions. But at least in the Democratic party, new rules have fundamentally altered the character of caucuses and conventions and further weakened the role of the party in the nominating process. The McGovern-Fraser Commission was determined to "open" party meetings to all interested persons; they adopted rules to achieve that purpose. New requirements governing public notice, slating, and "timeliness" effectively diminished organizational control over caucuses and removed these meetings from the control of organization leaders and regulars. Instead of being meetings of persons with experience in the party and demonstrated commitment to it, caucuses have become assemblages of persons interested in particular candidates or issues. Under the new rules anyone willing to state that he is a Democrat (at least for the evening) can join the small group making decisions about the party's presidential nominee. The dynamics of participation (about which a good deal is known) insures that turnout at these meetings will be relatively low and made up mainly of persons whose interest in politics is much more intense than that of the ordinary voter, and whose views are probably also more extreme. Opening the caucuses, in sum, has made them vulnerable to manipulation by candidate or issue enthusiasts who may or may not have a broad or long-term concern with the party. Opening the caucuses coincided with the emergence of ever stronger candidate organizations capable of turning out supporters. Because anyone can participate, open caucuses dilute the influence of party leaders. Though the easy manipulability of the caucus system has been overlooked by many academic observers, it was well understood and described by Senator McGovern's manager for the nonprimary states, Richard Stearns, in his Oxford thesis. The caucus victories of McGovern in 1972 and of Carter in 1976, at a time when neither candidate had significant support from party leaders and regulars, were evidence of the changed character of caucuses and conventions.

Open caucuses are a clear-cut example of party reform drastically weakening a party. The transformation of caucuses was a direct consequence of rules changes that opened the Democratic party, transferring control over the composition and decisions of delegations from party leaders to ad hoc assemblages of candidate and issue enthusiasts. It illustrates the continuing tendency of many American reformers to find ad hoc groups less sinister than institutionalized ones, just as they find enthusiasm for a candidate or, better still, an issue, a more elevated motive for political activity than loyalty to an organized party—in spite of clear evidence of the crucial importance of party to democratic processes.

Not only have party leaders lost a large part of their influence over recruitment of presidential candidates, they are also less able to control the recruitment and socialization of the leaders and volunteers who work in the party's name. Association with a successful candidate's organization has become an acceptable substitute for organizational apprenticeship and service. After 1964, the Republican party was dominated in many areas by persons whose influence had grown with Goldwater's; the post-1968 and 1972 Democratic party included even larger numbers of "peace" Democrats who had entered politics with McCarthy and McGovern movements. And in 1976 everyone understood that the composition of both the Republican and Democratic National Committees would be determined by the outcome of the parties' nominating contests. An important consequence of the inability of parties to control access to their organizations is that it becomes possible for persons with little concern about the organization to achieve influence over its policies. This is a matter of capital importance to the polity because a long-range concern for the American type of party breeds habits of compromise, inclusiveness, and moderation. My study of delegates to the 1972 Democratic convention confirmed the presence there of large numbers with weak, instrumental attachments to the party, who were opposed to many of the practices necessary to preserving an organization—such as compromising conflicts, building coalitions, and rewarding the faithful. In the 1976 Democratic convention, there were fewer delegates than in 1972 without prior party experience, more who had held party and public office, fewer who were indifferent to winning, more who expressed generalized concern for the party. But the cumulative evidence indicates that the new type of activists drawn to politics by candidate or issue enthusiasm had by no means disappeared from the national scene. In 1976, as in 1964, such activists were more numerous at the Republican than at the Democratic convention. In that year, "new right" intellectuals encouraged conservative activists to abandon Republican loyalties, and the behavior of a good many (but not all) disappointed Reagan supporters demonstrated lack of concern about their party's prospects for persistence. Barry Sussman's survey (undertaken for the *Washington Post*) established that a majority of Ford's backers were pragmatic and party oriented, while 57 percent of Reagan's delegates preferred ideological agreement to electoral victory.

In 1976, then, it was possible for the highest decision-making levels of either party to be penetrated by persons without seasoned, reliable ties to the parties. The outcomes of the preconvention primaries and caucuses—which of course were beyond the control of party—determined the kind of people attracted into party roles. Both parties remained vulnerable to penetration by people without a strong, generalized attachment to the party. Such people, should they become influential, can be expected to adopt policies (concerning, for example, compromise, victory, and party structure) that leave already weak parties still weaker.

The inability of American parties to control the recruitment and socialization of their cadres is in part a result of the same efforts to reform political life that have stripped the parties of control over nominations. But there are also other sources. The fact that American parties are dependent on volunteers and that more volunteers are needed than are available makes parties more permeable than most organizations. Reliance on volunteers, for whom politics is a hobby and a leisure-time activity, causes rapid turnover of party office holders and makes it easier for newcomers to achieve influence in a political party than in most other institutions. Therefore, brief apprenticeship and socialization prevail.

Primaries and candidate organizations contribute to the problem by providing activists an opportunity—outside the parties—to demonstrate skills and accumulate influence. Lack of prior experience and reputation in national politics mattered little to the future of Hamilton Jordan, Jody Powell, or Rick Hutchenson once their candidate had achieved the nomination and won an election. Commenting on this relationship, Leon Epstein noted that although direct primaries make it possible for a candidate to win control of a party label without gaining control of a statutory (or extralegal) party, "Generally control of the label and of the statutory party will go together since even an organizational shell is likely to be taken over by those who secure the party label (if they did not control the statutory party to begin with)."

An interesting question, rarely raised, is *why* American parties depend so heavily on volunteers to conduct their most important ongoing activities. This question leads, I believe, back to the theory and practice of party reform. In this country material incentives to political participation are not well regarded. An important reason for the disappearance of paid precinct captains, for example, was the widespread feeling that buying the service of precinct leaders is, if not exactly corrupt, somehow gross, and that the volunteer who donates his service as precinct leader is to be preferred— politically and probably morally—to one who can be "bought." This ethos, which conflicts sharply with the practices and moral codes of democratic politics elsewhere, becomes more curious in view of the range of services that *are* regularly bought and paid for by the most morally sensitive candidates. Instead of paying ward heelers "walking around money," today's candidates pay much higher fees to consultants who are knowledgeable about mass media, public relations, and direct mail to get out the vote. Like the traditional "pol," professional campaign managers, political pollsters, and a host of media and direct mail specialists make their living out of politics by mobilizing and delivering support. There are some interesting differences between past and present types of persons who get paid for political activity, but these are not differences in function. The most important differences are in the skills and the social backgrounds of the different types of experts. Unlike the professionals of earlier times, those who receive lucrative fees in presidential politics today are usually highly educated professionals skilled in market research or communications technology. Could it be that the high fees of these paid professionals are more acceptable than the lower fees of traditional "pros" because the former closely resemble in background, skills, and style the educated, upper income, high status professionals who have come to dominate both national parties? Apparently, the reform spirit that deprived low status, lower-middle-class pols of jobs abetted the incomes as well as the influence of persons much like the reformers. At the same time, it weakened party organization, because, although the professional of yesterday was dependent on, and identified with, the party organization, the contemporary professional is fundamentally independent of party. His income depends less on the party than on his skills, which are useful to different kinds of organization.

The rise of the new professionals is paralleled by the ascendance to political power of the "new class," a development which also contributes to the growing weakness of the parties. In 1976 as in 1972, there were enormous, apparently increasing discrepancies between the social backgrounds of the delegates to the two conventions and those of the parties' rank and file. The elite and mid-elite of the national parties had much more education, much better jobs, much higher incomes than most people. As in 1972, delegates were heavily drawn from the professions, especially from law, teaching, and government employment. About half the Democratic delegates were highly educated professionals: nearly 90 percent had been to college and over 40 percent held graduate degrees; about a third had incomes of at least $30,000. More important, there was a marked tendency for these socially privileged political influentials to have very different opinions from those of ordinary voters on many subjects.

It was not always thus. The urban boss and his lieutenants, the county courthouse gangs, often had financial interests that diverged from those of their constituents. Usually, however, they shared their constituents' religion, values, mores, and political preferences. The rise of the new class to political influence has brought with it a growing distance between party (and political) elite and mass. This trend, which is fraught with pitfalls for any party afflicted by it, and for the society more generally, has been accelerated by changes in the processes through which party leadership is recruited. Technological and social change produced a larger, educated, middle class with the leisure and the inclination to participate in volunteer politics, and parallel cultural changes heightened the prestige of the communications skills this group possessed, but without the adoption of rules hospitable to its skills and proclivities the new class could not have achieved its current dominance of national politics. There can be little reasonable doubt that the reform rules of the Democratic party, which stress persuasive skills, self-presentation, ideological motivation, and such nonpolitical characteristics as sex, race, and age, have greatly aided the rise to political influence of the new class and at the same time dramatically decreased the political value of such traditional assets as local ties, organizational skills, and team loyalty. Party reform, especially the Democratic variant, advanced the class interests of the reformers in the sense that it rewarded persons with the skills, styles, and values of the reformers at the expense of others. At the same time, these reforms tended to weaken party organization because they gave power to "disinterested" persons whose careers were not tied to the future of the party and increased the gap between elite and rank and file. Reform has advanced the class interests of the reformers.

Conducting Campaigns

Electoral campaigns are structured competition, carried on in the name of parties, which links candidates to voters and relates government policies to the consent of the governed. Historically, presidential campaigns have relied heavily on national parties to plan strategy and on state and local party officials to extract such needed resources as money and services, to

less likely than ever before to identify with either major party, more likely to think of themselves as independents, less likely to think well of parties, less likely to relate their party identification to an evaluation of candidates or party positions, and all voters more ready to defect from their party.

The causes of the parties' declining ability to structure the electorate are less clear than the fact of the decline. Verba, Nie, and Petrocik emphasize the generational aspects of the phenomenon, noting that the surge of independents—who now compose approximately two-fifths of eligible voters—comes more from younger voters entering the electorate than from older voters who once identified with a party, and also that the intensity of party identification among young voters is low as compared with that among older voters. It seems clear that the declining extent and intensity of party identification is also associated with such phenomena as the increasing salience of issues and issue constituencies in the electorate. Not only do the new cultural and social issues—abortion, amnesty, welfare, busing—have a great capacity to engage the voters' attention, but the social and cultural upheavals associated with their rise have made voters more aware of the connections between questions of public policy and have left them much more disposed to see themselves as "liberal" and "conservative." American politics, then, are simultaneously becoming more ideological and less institutionalized.

This whole process of cultural-social-political polarization and deinstitutionalization was not caused simply by policies adopted to regulate nominations and elections. But the effects of formal processes on the structure of partisanship have been shaped by rules that favored persons with leisure, high education, highly developed persuasive skills, and extreme views on issues. The processes have thus affected the capacity of parties to represent voters. It is doubtless significant that party identification has declined precisely when the strength of party organization was diminishing, just as it was no accident that party organization developed and expanded alongside an expanding electorate. If there is a causal relation between strong organization and party identification then policies which weaken the former should also tend to weaken the latter.

But the major causes of the declining extent and intensity of party identification probably lie beyond policies and rules—in the emergence of the new issues, the decreased confidence in social and political institutions, the increased use of television which enables candidates to establish a direct, personal relationship with voters unmediated by parties, and, perhaps especially, the progressive ineffectiveness of the family and other agencies of vertical socialization. Previous research has established that in political systems such as Britain and the United States, party identification is largely hereditary, that it is acquired at an early age in the family and persists through life, that it functions to screen communications, focus attention, and structure affect, that it persists in spite of disagreements on particular candidates and policies. Because socialization into a party system normally occurs in the family, it is necessarily weakened by the weakening of the family structure, by the de-emphasis on the transmission of explicit norms and identifications from one generation to the next, and by the increased role of peer groups and media in the socialization process. Since familial socialization is the principal means for recruiting new party identifiers (and activists), any lessening of the extent or effectiveness of this intergenerational transmission would produce more independents who identify with neither party and more weak identifiers for whom party identification lacks the power to order the political world.

The declining capacity of the parties to attract and hold the loyalty of masses results from the interaction of broad social processes and deliberate decisions. It is quite clear that no one planned or intended it and that no one is quite sure how to reverse the trend.

·C·

Finance Reform

The Drive for Reform: Pre- and Post-Watergate

BY HERBERT E. ALEXANDER

For decades, official apathy toward serious reform of political finance was a Washington habit. The federal and state laws that were enacted tended to be predominantly negative—their chief purposes were to prohibit and restrict various ways of getting, giving and spending political money.

From the early 20th century, when President Theodore Roosevelt proposed disclosure laws, a prohibition on corporate political giving and government subsidies, until 1961, several Presidents went on record in favor of reform, but none took vigorous action. President Kennedy was the first president in modern times to consider campaign financing a critical problem, and he showed this concern in 1961 by appointing a bipartisan Commission on Campaign Costs. This started a chain of events which began to falter in the late 1960s. Then, in the short space of two months, efforts to reform our antiquated system of political finance came to a sudden climax when Congress passed two measures—the Federal Election Campaign Act of 1971 (FECA), which replaced the 1925 Federal Corrupt Practices Act, and the Revenue Act of 1971.

Until the time the Kennedy Commission was appointed, most of the laws affecting political finance were devised to remedy or prevent flagrant abuses. It was evidently assumed that honest politicians could afford to pay their campaign expenses with their own money or with "untainted" gifts. Efforts to free candidates from dependence upon any one person or interest group usually took the form of restricting or prohibiting contributions from presumably dubious sources. Moreover, arbitrary ceilings were set to prevent excessive spending. The rationale was that ceilings would

Excerpted from Herbert E. Alexander, *Financing Politics* (Washington: Congressional Quarterly Press, 1976), pp. 131–141 and 149–154. Footnotes deleted. Reprinted by permission of Congressional Quarterly Press.

prevent dollars from dominating and unwisely influencing elections and would tend to reduce undue advantages held by wealthy candidates or the party with the most funds.

As restrictive laws were passed, however, new methods of raising and spending money were soon devised. When the assessment of government employees was prohibited, attention swung to corporate contributions. When they in turn were barred, gifts from wealthy individuals—including many stockholders or officers in corporations—were sought. When direct contributions from the wealthy were limited by law, ways to circumvent the limitations were shortly found.

Early Efforts at Regulation

After the 1904 election—during which it was charged that corporations were pouring millions of dollars into the Republican campaign to elect Theodore Roosevelt—a move for federal legislation that would force disclosure of campaign spending led to the formation of the National Publicity Law Association (NPLA). Under the banner of the NPLA were gathered such prominent figures as Charles Evans Hughes (later Chief Justice), William Jennings Bryan, Harvard President Charles William Eliot and American Federation of Labor President Samuel Gompers.

The first federal prohibition of corporate contributions was enacted in 1907. The first federal campaign fund disclosure law was passed in 1910; the following year, an amendment required primary, convention and pre-election financial statements and limited the amounts that could be spent by candidates for the House and Senate. The law was contested in a famous case in 1921 in which the U.S. Supreme Court overturned the conviction of Truman Newberry—a candidate for the Senate in 1918 who defeated Henry Ford in the Republican primary in Michigan—for excessive campaign spending. The court held that congressional authority to regulate elections did not extend to primaries and nomination activities (most of the questionable expenses in Newberry's campaign had preceded the Republican primary). This narrow interpretation of congressional authority was rejected in 1941 in another Supreme Court case relating to federal-state powers, but Congress did not reassert its power to require disclosure of campaign funds for prenomination campaigns until 1972.

CORRUPT PRACTICES ACT

Relevant federal legislation was codified and revised, though without substantial change, in the Federal Corrupt Practices Act of 1925. That act remained the basic law until 1972. Essentially, the law required disclosure of receipts and expenditures by candidates for the Senate and House (not for President or Vice President) and by political committees which sought to influence federal elections in two or more states. The Hatch Act of 1940 also limited to $5,000 the amount an individual could contribute to a federal candidate or to a political committee in a single year and set a $3-million limit on committee expenditures. The former provision, however was interpreted to mean that an individual could give up to $5,000 to numerous committees, all supporting the same candidate. A more significant factor in limiting individual contributions was the federal gift tax which imposed progressive tax rates on contributions of more than $3,000 to a single committee in any year. But again, individuals could give up to that amount to multiple committees working for the same candidate. Thus, $25,000 or $100,000 or larger gifts from one individual to one candidate were legally acceptable. The bar on corporate giving that had been on the books since 1907 was temporarily extended to labor unions in the Smith-Connally Act of 1944 and then reimposed in the Taft-Hartley Act of 1947.

The post–World War II years witnessed a series of congressional gestures, usually no more than congressional committee reports, toward reform. In 1948 and again in 1951, special House committees on campaign expenditures recommended that substantial revisions be made in the Corrupt Practices and Hatch Acts. But no legislation passed. In 1953 the Elections Subcommittee of the Senate Committee on Rules and Administration proposed that the limit on spending for national political committees be increased from $3-million to $10-million a year. It also proposed increases in permissible spending for congressional campaigns. The Senate did not act. In 1955, a comprehensive bill requiring all committees active in campaigns for federal office to file financial reports, even if their activities were confined to one state, was introduced and reported out of committee, but it never was called up for debate on the Senate floor.

The 1956 disclosure by Sen. Francis Case of South Dakota that he had been offered a $2,500 campaign gift if he would vote for the Harris-Fulbright natural gas bill led to three congressional investigations. None of them produced reform legislation. President Eisenhower, however, vetoed the gas bill on the grounds that "arrogant lobbying" had been exercised on its behalf.

POST-WORLD WAR II

Presidents Truman, Eisenhower, Kennedy and Johnson all voiced concern about the methods used to raise money to pay for political campaigns. Truman favored government subsidies. He and Eisenhower both endorsed the recommendations of the Kennedy Commission on Campaign Costs.

Commission on Campaign Costs

Kennedy had expressed much concern about campaign finance before he became President. He was sensitive to the advantages wealth gave a candidate. Having himself been accused of buying public office, he was aware of the public's cynicism. Before his inauguration, he set in motion the activities which led to the creation of the Commission on Campaign Costs.

Kennedy asked the commission to recommend suitable ways to finance presidential general election campaigns and to reduce the costs of running for the presidency. When he submitted legislative proposals based on the commission's report, he invited Congress to extend the proposals to all federal offices. Among those endorsing the report were the chairmen of the Republican and Democratic national committees, former Presidents Truman and Eisenhower and Richard Nixon, Adlai Stevenson, and Thomas Dewey—all the living presidential candidates of both major parties in the preceding quarter century.

Taken as a whole, the report presented a model and comprehensive program for reforming the financing of the political system, covering not only federal legislative remedies but also bipartisan activities, certain party practices and state actions. Few innovations were included in the report's recommendations; most of the proposals had been suggested before. An exception was one alternative presented for the first time: matching funds (or matching incentives). The proposals were not to be adopted for more than 12 years, but the report's purpose was more immediate: to get things moving in the field by detailing a comprehensive program for reform of political finance, covering all aspects of regulation—disclosure, publicity, limitations, corrupt practices, tax incentives and political broadcasting.

One of the commission's recommendations was carried out promptly by the Treasury Department. The Internal Revenue Service authorized taxpayers to deduct from income their expenditures in connection with federal, state or local elections, if the money was used for the following purposes: buying advertising to encourage the public to register and vote and to contribute to a political party or campaign fund; sponsoring a political debate among candidates for a particular office; granting employees time off with pay for registration and voting; and maintaining a payroll deduction plan for employees wishing to make political contributions.

The recommendations were less than enthusiastically received on Capitol Hill, where certain members of Congress were distrustful of a presidential initiative in a field traditionally considered a legislative prerogative. Nor was there applause from such groups as the U.S. Chamber of Commerce, which was concerned that the tax incentive features would erode the tax base, and the labor movement, which objected to proposals on public reporting and tax incentives. Press comments, however, were favorable.

JOHNSON ADMINISTRATION

Understandably, the new Johnson administration had other priorities. During his first two years in office, President Johnson failed to support any legislative reform of political finance and ignored representations to act made by former members of the commission. The program was one of the few Kennedy creations to suffer seriously in the transition that followed his death. Publicity about Texas oil money and the Bobby Baker case may have turned Johnson against opening the political financing issue in the 1964 election. The White House gave the subject no public attention until 1966 when reports of criticism about the President's Club (a group composed of contributors of $1,000 or more, including some government contractors) and other political fund-raising activities moved Johnson to act. In his State of the Union address in 1966, he stated his intention to submit an election reform program. His proposals, however, were not transmitted until too late for passage by the 89th Congress. During this period, 1962–66, the cause of campaign finance reform had also been dormant on Capitol Hill.

ASHMORE-GOODELL BILL

In 1966, the censure of Sen. Thomas Dodd of Connecticut for using political funds for personal purposes helped spark new interest in reform, and the House subcommittee on elections produced the bipartisan Ashmore-Goodell bill, the most comprehensive bill considered in Congress up until then. The bill was a mixture of the stronger portions of the Johnson and Kennedy proposals and of other bills and proposals. Most importantly, it called for a bipartisan Federal Election Commission (FEC) to receive, analyze, audit and publicize spending reports by all candidates and committees in federal elections. A weakened version of the bill, eliminating the FEC as the single repository, passed the Senate the following year by a surprising 87–0 vote.

Both the Baker and Dodd cases no doubt contributed to the Senate's major step forward. Another factor was pressure growing out of extended debate over the Long Act.

LONG ACT

The Long Act was enacted by the Congress in 1966 largely as the result of the persuasion and parliamentary skill of its sponsor, Sen. Russell Long of Louisiana, chairman of the Senate Finance Committee. The bill provided a federal subsidy for presidential elections, a scheme contrasting sharply with the Johnson administration's plan to provide tax incentives for political contributors who were taxpayers. The bill passed on the last day of the second session of the 89th Congress without drawing much attention from the public, press or opinion leaders. It caught the Johnson administration off guard but, at the last hour, the White House chose to support it, shelving its own recommendation for tax incentives.

In the spring of 1967, Sen. Albert Gore of Tennessee and Sen. John Williams of Delaware cosponsored an amendment to repeal the Long Act. Passage of the bill had met with a negative reaction. One of the leaders of the floor fight for repeal was Sen. Robert Kennedy, who argued that the subsidy put a dangerous amount of power into the hands of the national party chairmen. Through promises of distribution of money in the general election, Kennedy argued, the chairmen would be able to influence the delegations of the large states to support the presidential candidate of the chairmen's choice. The Long Act was not formally repealed, but its provisions were no longer in force after May 1967.

Federal Election Campaign Act of 1971

But the Long Act and the Ashmore-Goodell bill might be termed the parents of the two pieces of legislation passed by Congress four years later that constituted a major turning point in the history of campaign finance reform: the Federal Election Campaign Act of 1971 (FECA), which replaced the Federal Corrupt Practices Act of 1925, and the Revenue Act of 1971. The latter provided tax credits, or, alternatively, tax deductions for political contributions at all levels and also a tax checkoff to subsidize presidential campaigns during general elections. The FECA of 1971, which passed in January 1972, a month after the Revenue Act, required fuller disclosure of political funding than ever before—a factor that was to play a key role in the Watergate affair. Among its provisions, the FECA:

- •Set limits on communications media expenditures for candidates for federal office during primary, runoff, special or general election campaigns. This provision was replaced in the 1974 Amendments with candidate expenditure limitations on total spending (which were then in part declared unconstitutional by the Supreme Court in 1976).
- •Placed a ceiling on contributions by any candidate or his immediate family to his own campaign of $50,000 for President or Vice President, $35,000 for senator and $25,000 for representative, delegate or resident commissioner. This provision was later ruled unconstitutional by the Supreme Court, but it was reinstated in the 1976 Amendments for presidential elections because public funding is provided.
- •Stipulated that the appropriate federal supervisory officer to oversee election campaign practices, reporting and disclosure was the Clerk of the House for House candidates, the Secretary of the Senate for Senate candidates, and the Comptroller General for presidential candidates and miscellaneous other committees. This provision was partially changed by the 1974 Amendments which established the Federal Election Commission (FEC).

•Required candidates and their committees for the Senate and House to file duplicate copies of reports with the secretary of state, or a comparable officer in each state, for local inspection. This provision was designed to help provide information about the funding of campaigns to local voters.

•Required each political committee and candidate to report total expenditures, as well as to itemize the full name, mailing address, and occupation and principal place of business of each contributor, plus date, amount and purpose of each expenditure in excess of $100; to itemize similarly each expenditure for personal services, salaries and reimbursed expenses in excess of $100.

•Required candidates and committees to file reports of contributions and expenditures the 10th day of March, June and September every year, on the 15th and fifth days preceding the date on which an election is held and on the 31st day of January. Any contribution of $5,000 or more was to be reported within 48 hours if received after the last pre-election report. The dates of these filings were changed in the 1974 Amendments to include quarterly disclosures as well as one 10 days before an election and 30 days after an election.

•Required a full and complete financial statement of the costs of a presidential nominating convention within 60 days of the convention.

REVENUE ACT OF 1971

The Revenue Act of 1971 provided that political contributors could claim a tax credit against federal income tax for 50 per cent of their contributions (to candidates for federal, state or local office and to some political committees), up to a maximum of $12.50 on a single return and $25 on a joint return (increased to $25 and $50 in the 1974 Amendments). Alternatively, the taxpayer could claim a deduction for the full amount of contributions up to a maximum of $50 on a single return and $100 on a joint return (increased to $100 and $200 in the 1974 Amendments).

The tax credits and deductions had an easy passage, but the accompanying tax checkoff provisions have had a long and stormy history. The checkoff represented a revival of a provision of the Long Act of 1966 but was revised to provide money directly to presidential candidates, not to the political party committees on their behalf. The checkoff provided that every individual whose tax liability for any calendar year was $1 or more could designate on his federal income tax form that $1 of his tax money be paid to the Presidential Election Campaign Fund; married individuals filing jointly could designate $2. The money it raised was to be paid directly to the candidates, not the parties.

The Watergate events brought new pressures for reform. In May 1973, President Nixon proposed creation of a nonpartisan commission to study campaign reform. Nixon was by no means "out in front" on the issue. A week earlier, a House Republican leader, John B. Anderson of Illinois, had introduced a bill that he cosponsored with Democrat Morris K. Udall of Arizona calling for an independent Federal Election Commission. Nonetheless, it was almost two years before a new election law became fully operative. This happened in April 1975, when President Ford swore in the six members of the FEC established by the 1974 Amendments. Less than a year would pass before their method of selection (some by Congress, others by the President) would be declared unconstitutional by the U.S. Supreme Court.

1974 Amendments

Along with creation of the commission, the other major "firsts" in the 1974 Amendments were the establishment of overall limitation on how much could be spent on political campaigning and the extension of public funding to campaigns for the presidential nomination and to the national conventions.

Despite impetus given reform by the Watergate scandals, consideration of the measure was drawn out. Movement toward enactment in 1973 came only in the Senate where, on July 30, a reform bill designed to improve the FECA was adopted by an overwhelming 82–8 margin. As has been the pattern with most campaign finance legislation in the Senate in the past decade, the version reported out of committee was then strengthened on the floor of the Senate.

In the fall, the scene had moved to the House, where the greater frequency with which its members must face re-election has traditionally made it a more conservative body when dealing with campaign reform. There the bill faced Rep. Wayne L. Hays of Ohio, chairman of the Committee on House Administration, a vocal opponent of reform and of public financing of elections. Referred to his committee's Subcommittee on Elections, it remained there throughout the remainder of the first session of the 93rd Congress.

When the 93rd Congress reconvened in January 1974, campaign reform was a major item on its agenda. In his State of the Union message, President Nixon noted the congressional delay on reform and announced he would submit an administration proposal. When the Nixon proposals arrived, they pleased almost no one in Congress, and members of his own party made that clear publicly. The Nixon proposals were viewed by many as combining "safe" reforms with others that were unpassable. Nixon called public finance "taxation without representation."

In the House itself, Rep. Hays kept pushing back the date of his promised bill; his committee did not begin markup sessions until March 26. In April, the Senate, by a 53–32 vote, passed a reform bill that combined parts of the original bill with a call for public funding of presidential and congressional primary and general election campaigns. Among the amendments offered was one by Sen. James Buckley, New York Conservative-

Republican, requiring an immediate certification by the federal court of appeals of any court test of the constitutionality of the bill's provisions— an opportunity of which he and other opponents availed themselves when the bill became law and which led to the Supreme Court's *Buckley* v. *Valeo* ruling.

On Aug. 8, 1974, a few hours before Nixon announced his resignation as President, the House version of a campaign reform bill was approved 355–48. The House version differed sharply from the Senate bill. While it was much more limited in scope, it did call for public funding for presidential elections and added public financing of presidential nominating conventions.

After further delaying tactics by Hays, the conference committee began meeting in September. The impasse on the public finance issue was not settled until early October. As finally passed by large margins in both houses, the bill included public funding only for presidential elections. It did not change significantly the flat grant provisions for the general election, but it extended government financing to include both matching funds for the presidential prenomination period and flat grants to the political parties for their national nominating conventions.

President Ford signed the bill Oct. 5, 1974, in a White House ceremony to which all members of Congress were invited. A long-time opponent of public funding, the President expressed doubts about some sections of the law but said, "the times demand this legislation."

. . . .

CONSTITUTIONAL CHALLENGE

In addition to its early liaison and communications problems with Congress, the new FEC's future was clouded almost immediately by a legal suit challenging not only the constitutionality of most of the major provisions of the 1974 Amendments but also the commission's very existence.

The 1974 Amendments invited legal challenge because Congress failed to take seriously the warnings of experts and others that important constitutional issues were involved. Reformers were so enthusiastic that they pushed to the outer bounds of strict regulation. They urged and Congress agreed to a tight system of limitations, arguing that as long as private independent expenditures were permitted, limitations could be placed on them as well as on contributions. Overall candidate expenditure limits were thought to be constitutional because they were considered necessary for an effective system of regulation that would restrain excessive spending. Traditionally, excessive spending had been unfair to candidates without personal wealth or access to large contributions. A system of regulation with low and effective limitations was the goal also of some reformers and others who sought to "starve" electioneering by reducing the money available to a point where Congress would enact public funding of senatorial and House as well as of presidential campaigns.

In *Buckley* v. *Valeo,* the courts confronted a difficult judicial task. There were dilemmas to be resolved that made the issue one of appropriate debate for the decade in which the United States marked its bicentennial. The problem, in its simplest form, was for the courts to balance the First Amendment rights of free speech and free association against the clear power of the legislature to enact laws designed to protect the integrity of the election system. Involved were questions of public discussion and political dialogue. Basically, the plaintiffs sought to ensure that the reforms, however well-meant, did not have a chilling effect on free speech or on citizen participation.

An unusual provision of the law had authorized any eligible voter to start federal court proceedings to contest the constitutionality of any provision of the law. The amendment had been designed to speed along any case by permitting questions of constitutionality to be certified directly to the federal court of appeals, which was obliged to expedite the case. A case was brought a few days after the law became effective on Jan. 1, 1975. Plaintiffs covered a broad spectrum of liberals and conservatives, individuals and organizations and included Sen. James L. Buckley, New York Conservative-Republican, Eugene J. McCarthy, former Democratic senator from Minnesota, Stewart R. Mott (a large contributor), the Conservative Party of the State of New York, the New York Civil Liberties Union, the Mississippi Republican Party, the Libertarian Party and the Conservative Victory Fund, among others. Defendants included, along with the Attorney General, the FEC, the Secretary of the Senate and the Clerk of the House, and three reform groups, Common Cause, the Center for Public Financing of Elections and the League of Women Voters.

The case was argued before the U.S. Court of Appeals for the District of Columbia, which in an Aug. 15, 1975, opinion sustained most of the law's provisions. Appeal was then made to the U.S. Supreme Court, the arguments were heard, and on Jan. 30, 1976, a little over a year after the case was initiated, the Supreme Court ruled in a *per curiam* opinion that was joined in all aspects by three justices and joined in part by others. (There was one major dissent.) The Supreme Court decision reversed many major points that had been considered and upheld by the court of appeals. The impact of the decision has been great not only on the regulation of federal elections but also on state and local law.

The central question was posed by Justice Potter Stewart during oral arguments: Is money speech and speech money? Or stated differently, is an expenditure for speech substantially the same thing as speech itself because the expenditure is necessary to reach large audiences by the purchase of air time or space in the print media? The decision resolved the conflict by asserting the broadest protection to First Amendment rights to assure the unrestrained interchange of ideas for bringing about popular political and social change. Accordingly, the court majority concluded that individual expenditure limitations imposed direct and substantial restraints on the quantity of political speech. This applied to limits on both individuals and on candidates in their personal expenditures on their own behalf as well as on spending by or on behalf of a candidate. However, an exception was made with reference to overall candidate expenditure limits, with the court holding that candidates who accepted public funding when provided by the government could also be obliged to accept campaign expenditure limits as a condition of the granting of the public money. The court made clear that independent spending by individuals and groups could be considered as a protected form of free speech only if the spending were truly independent. Independent spending could not, then, be coordinated with the candidate or his campaign organization nor consented to by the candidate or his agent.

On the other hand, the court upheld the limits on individual and group contributions to campaigns, asserting that these constitute only a marginal restriction on the contributor's ability to engage in free communication. Saying that free expression rests on contributing as a symbolic act to help give a candidate the means to speak out with views congenial to those of the contributor, the court also asserted that the quantity of speech does not increase perceptibly with the size of the contribution. Hence limits on contributions were constitutional. The Supreme Court found that there was a real or imagined coercive influence of large contributors on candidates' positions and on their actions if elected, leading to corruption or the appearance of corruption, and it said that contribution limits were acceptable because they serve to mute the voices of affluent persons and groups while also restraining the skyrocketing costs of political campaigns.

The Supreme Court sustained all the disclosure requirements of the law, sanctioned the forms of public funding provided by the federal law, and upheld the concept of a bipartisan regulatory commission to administer and enforce the law so long as the agency was within the executive branch of the government and its members were appointed by the President. These are the three main directions in which regulation of political finance will proceed, perhaps modified to some extent by efforts to retain contribution limits (though the limits may be increased to help provide more seed money to mount campaigns and to offset unlimited spending by wealthy candidates on their own behalf) and by expenditure limits when candidates accept government funding (though their effectiveness is offset by unlimited independent spending by individuals and groups).

1976 Amendments

When the Supreme Court required appointment of all members of the commission by the President within 30 days, the Congress began the process of revising the law. The reconstitution of the FEC took 111 days.

The proposed revision was complicated by the suggestion of controversial changes in the law. Among the proposals was one to extend public funding to senatorial and House campaigns. When the Congress failed to act within the 30-day period, an additional stay of 20 days was granted by the Supreme Court. When Congress again failed to act promptly, the FEC on March 22, 1976, lost its executive functions, without which it could not certify payments of matching funds to candidates then seeking their party's presidential nomination. Until the law was revised, government funds could not be paid out, causing the candidates to economize while relying solely on private funds. The commission also officially lost its powers to render advisory opinions, promulgate regulations, process complaints, initiate civil enforcement actions and refer criminal cases to the Attorney General.

Much of the delay occurred because Congress was unable or unwilling to act promptly. President Ford requested a simple reconstitution of the FEC in order to permit the FEC to continue to operate through the 1976 election. He argued against becoming bogged down in other controversial changes. Instead, Congress undertook significant revisions dealing with compliance and enforcement procedures, the issuing of advisory opinions and the role of corporate and labor political action committees.

Some observers thought the delay was purposeful, designed by Democratic congressional leaders to help the nomination prospects of Sen. Hubert H. Humphrey (who was not an active candidate but was thought by many to be a potential one if other candidates failed) and to hurt the candidates actively contesting in the primaries, and by Republican congressional leaders to assist President Ford's prospects against Ronald Reagan. The suspension of matching funds came at a critical time, forcing candidates to rely wholly on private funds and loans during the Pennsylvania, Texas and other crucial primaries.

The Senate and the House initially passed substantially different bills. A conference committee finally reached agreement on a substitute bill, but Congress by then was in spring recess, and with the presidential primary season in full sway, seven remaining contenders for their parties' nominations—six Democrats and one Republican, Ronald Reagan—asked the Supreme Court to permit the matching funds to be paid out immediately, before the court-ordered reconstitution took place. The court denied the plea but left the way open for the appeals court to modify its ruling. The court of appeals turned down the request, as did the Supreme Court twice upon further appeals. The appeals were made on grounds of violation of

First Amendment rights to speak effectively, compelling candidates to raise money under tight contribution limits while running crucial campaigns without expected funds. In effect, the rules had been changed in mid-campaign, but the courts failed to find grounds to intercede.

Key Senate Republicans delayed final approval of the conference committee report until early May. Then the focus shifted to the White House, where President Ford took a week to sign the bill, while the Nebraska primary went by. Ford refused to say that he would sign the bill, while the other candidates sought his assurances he would sign it in order to make it easier for them to borrow money against the promise of matching funds.

After signing the law May 11, Ford took another six days to reappoint five commissioners and name former Rep. William L. Springer to replace Chairman Curtis, who had resigned. This held up matching money for the Michigan and Maryland primaries. The Senate promptly reconfirmed the reappointed commissioners. Within hours of being sworn in, the renewed FEC certified $3.2-million due for various candidates and $1-million to the major party national conventions. The FEC had continued to process submissions for matching funds while certifications were suspended.

The Ford campaign was relatively healthy financially throughout the hiatus. Reagan charged that President Ford benefited from "interest-free credit" from the government, which billed the President Ford Committee while other candidates needed advance money before their chartered planes would fly. Ultimately the delays did not especially help Ford, nor did Humphrey become an active candidate. The effect on Ford's campaign was not clear, because Reagan went into debt in this period of time yet won primaries in Texas, Indiana, Georgia and Alabama, while Ford's cash advantage was slowly dissipated. The delays did not hurt Carter seriously, though he lost nine of the last 14 primaries in a winning campaign for the nomination; given his momentum, prompt matching funds could have helped him in the later primaries.

PART II

Nomination Campaigns

It is ordinarily difficult—and rather pointless—to seek out the date at which the field of contenders for a given presidential nomination began to form. There have been major-party nominees who were more or less selected by the convention itself, without much more than a little prior home-state activity. There have been others whose campaigns for a nomination really began well before the *preceding* one had been concluded. Most contenders, of course, fall somewhere in between. Since World War II, variety has also characterized the "fields" for presidential nominations, that is, the number of aspirants and their campaign patterns. Even the reasons for being in those fields vary considerably in a normal year. Some contenders begin with every intention of reaching the nomination, but others are there for motives, ideological or personal, having little to do with that goal per se. Finally, some of these candidates start as recognized possibilities; others break into prominence from a near-total lack of public recognition; and most fall quickly by the wayside.

In the current postreform era, the average campaign for a major-party presidential nomination begins much earlier than it once did. Because delegate selection has been decentralized, and because almost all delegates can indeed be won or lost through activities in the states, aspirants are encouraged to get out onto the hustings as early as possible. Nonetheless, the trend should not be overstated. Prospective candidates have always accepted a stepped-up schedule of engagements in the period leading up to a possible nomination campaign; they have always gone out into the country at large to "test the waters"; and their agents have always scurried hither and yon to check for "ground swells" of support.

In Chapter 2 Robert L. Peabody and Eve Lubalin survey these patterns for the entire period since the Civil War in "The Making of Presidential Candidates," from a collection of essays on *The Future of the American Presidency*. Arthur T. Hadley offers more detail on two aspirants from the contemporary era—Walter Mondale and Elliot Richardson—from his book *The Invisible Primary*. Both Mondale and Richardson campaigned actively during the pre-delegate-selection stage, yet never made it to the first primary. By contrast, Christopher Lydon provides an early analysis of another hopeful, Jimmy Carter, whose activities appeared every bit as bootless, but who managed to collect the ultimate prize.

Beyond the diverse candidacies and time periods which these authors cover are the different aspects of prenomination campaigns which they choose to emphasize. Peabody and Lubalin look at candidates' careers before a presidential nomination and underscore the predominance of the U.S. Senate as a presidential launching pad. (This raises the question of whether the 1976 success of former Governor Jimmy Carter, and the near-success of former Governor Ronald Reagan, are exceptions to the rule or harbingers of a new era.) Hadley concentrates instead on the detailed tactics by which aspirants try to improve their positions during this early phase of the nomination campaign, and on the personal drives that keep them going when there are no obvious delegate successes (or failures) to help them measure their progress. Lydon, finally, notes the range of motives which can lead *other actors* to rally behind such a candidate—motives which may have little to do with simple ideological or personal preference.

While the field for the next round of nomination politics is still forming, the institutional matrix within which that field will operate—the aggregate of delegate-selection devices which, collectively, will produce a winner—is also taking shape. In the past, participants needed to devote comparatively little attention to this institutional complex. In the postreform era that is no longer true. The single largest cluster of major alterations was concentrated between 1968 and 1972, but for each election since then, a sizable number of states have continued to change the basic institution through which they create delegates and/or the basic formula by which they allocate them. And while the trend shows signs of slowing, its end is not in sight.

Beyond that, the basic delegate-selection institutions and allocation arrangements mask a huge variety of subrules, many of which can also have consequences for the outcome of the delegate hunt. Such matters as filing dates, for example, and the procedures for entering slates of delegates, require the careful attention of the candidates' staffs. Then too, the matter of scheduling for this delegate-selection process, of deciding *when* a state will have its convention or primary, can be of serious consequence to each candidate's campaign. The mere placement of a primary or convention may convert it into a key element in the contest and may thereby benefit some contestants and disadvantage others. State parties are fully aware of that fact, although the predictability of key contests remains low in spite of their efforts to capitalize on it.

In Chapter 3 "Democratic Delegate Rules Influencing Candidate's Strategies" by Michael J. Malbin summarizes this institutional framework for the presidential nomination of 1976 and describes some preliminary efforts to cope with it. Charles Mohr's look at battles over party rules in Wisconsin, "Democrats Alter Wisconsin Vote," offers a concrete example of institutional jockeying during the campaign itself. Joseph Lelyveld in "U.S. Fund Cutoff Slows Campaign" covers a parallel but far more sweeping shift in the basic finance laws while a campaign was in progress. And Theodore H. White's review of the 1972 Democratic "Confrontation at Miami," from *The Making of the President 1972,* shows just how far such rules combat can go.

Malbin's piece also suggests why recognized "rules experts" have become an important part of nomination campaigns. With thirty or more primaries, and with twenty or more party conventions of varying degrees of permeability, each with its own particular ground rules, someone who can attend to their mechanics—and, even more, who can envision the way they will work *as a group*—is an essential part of any developing campaign. Such rules specialists are hardly unaware of the potentials in their role, but they rarely go as far as to try and manipulate the rules in order to make their predictions come true, though one such attempt is described in the Mohr article on Wisconsin. The Lelyveld piece, by contrast, shows the extent to which other national political institutions—the U.S. Supreme Court, in this case—may enter party rules battles and shape subsequent delegate contests in crucial ways. White provides a final corrective in his description of the Democratic rules fights at the 1972 convention, for he shows that they were not all that different from, for example, the Republican battles over party rules at the 1952 convention, or indeed, from party credentials contests since the rise of the national party convention.

Sometimes such institutional tinkering matters a great deal; other times, when the nomination has finally been awarded, it becomes clear that it mattered very little. The timing of individual state primaries or conventions, when it interacts with the field of contenders at any given point, may determine which are the key contests. Similarly, the kind of delegate-allocation rules, when coupled with basic state characteristics, may enhance or dissipate the role of any given contest. Some candidates are much more susceptible to institutional peculiarities than others. A weak and unknown aspirant may be mortally damaged, or rocketed into the limelight, by the interaction of the field of contenders and the rules of the game at one or two critical points. Initially stronger contenders probably suffer less (and reap less) from the same circumstances.

All this suggests that some careful planning and a dollop of good luck might convert a given candidate's original resources into a presidential nomination. At the very least, most potential contenders develop a general plan for reaching the nomination, a scenario under which they can attain a delegate majority by some point in their national convention. This may involve entering all state contests, or only a carefully selected sample. It may involve stressing national or local issues and national or local supporters. It may require concentrating on fund raising, personal appearances, media, activist networks, or state or national policy making. All such plans contain a general goal (usually, but not always, a presidential nomination) and specify the steps by which it might be reached, the locales in which those steps can be accomplished, and the organizational mechanics by which to move through them.

All such plans, on the other hand, are revised continually as the campaign progresses, at least if the contender remains a serious nomination possibility. The field of candidates itself shrinks more or less steadily, but otherwise changes in only partially foreseeable ways. By the same token, the institutional tinkering through which state parties establish their delegate-selection mechanisms does not halt when the first state contest begins, but continues throughout the succession of contests. Perhaps there are only two things which can safely be said about the original nomination scenarios. First, some are evidently better than others. The best contribute to a nomination; the adequate ones at least roughly predict subsequent developments. And second, even the most successful will be changed substantially along the way—and will look more impressive afterwards if their original content is not recalled too accurately.

In Chapter 4 Irwin Ross and Theodore H. White review two successful plans: the Truman reelection scenario in "Backdrop for 1948," from Ross' *The Loneliest Campaign,* and the Kennedy nomination scheme in "The Democrats: First Stirrings," from White's *The Making of the President 1960.* Joseph Lelyveld and Christopher Lydon separately demonstrate how one candidate, Hubert Humphrey, tried to parlay an "announced noncandidacy"—which certainly did not involve any lack of activity—into a convention deadlock and subsequent nomination. And Lucinda Franks and Linda Greenhouse cover the way in which various nomination hopefuls and their agents can fight, not over delegates per se, but rather over particular subrules which might eventually influence the disposition of those delegates.

Together these pieces suggest another aspect of nomination politics, namely, the extent to which nearly everything, from alterations in the rules to outcomes in this week's primaries, can shift more or less simultaneously as a campaign moves along. A candidate's grand scenario may have to be changed not just because another candidate's supporters succeed in changing the rules in State A, or because the candidate himself succeeds in winning a primary or state convention there, but because a second candidate *fails* to win in State A. That failure may remove the second contender from the race when the first candidate had counted on his presence, or it may cause the loser in State A to withdraw from State B when the first candidate had not anticipated such a move.

A candidate with a general plan for a nomination must also generate the machinery necessary to support that plan. Because most nomination campaigns do indeed fold up quickly, and because all are jerry-built, there is relatively little written about their mechanics. Campaigns tend to evolve their own individualized style for scheduling, advance work, advertising, issue presentation, contacts with the formal news media, and so on. And they usually maintain that style for only a very short time before it becomes necessary either to adapt it for the general election or to dissolve it and go home.

With the passage of serious campaign finance reform, "financial campaigns" have also sprung up alongside the more specifically delegate-oriented efforts. Because funds must now be raised in a limited and decentralized fashion, there must obviously be some specialized organization to accomplish that task. Like delegate campaigns, however, finance campaigns tend to be built in stages and tailored to the individual candidates, with perhaps a trifle more uniformity because they must all respond to the same federal law.

In Chapter 5 Jonathan Cottin and Andrew J. Glass' article, "Democrats Depend on Speechwriters for Their Ideological Images" provides detailed insights on one task of these nomination campaign organizations: the creation of things for the candidate to say. Xandra Kayden summarizes a conference of campaign finance organizers in a selection from her *Report on Campaign Finance: Based on the Experience of the 1976 Presidential Campaigns*. Nicholas M. Horrock discusses the specific elements in one such financial effort—the Carter finance campaign of 1976. And Christopher Lydon and *The New York Times* staff delve into a comparatively new *form* of campaign fund-raising—computerized mailing-list solicitation—through profiles of two masters of this emerging art, Richard Viguerie and Morris Dees.

All these pieces highlight the role of *staff* in any attempted nomination conquest. As a group, the pieces on finances also suggest increased roles for *campaign technologies* and, once again, for the *formal rules* governing nomination politics this time, the rules of campaign financing. They indicate that such rules and technologies have elicited numerous changes in political behavior and in campaign politics, any number of which were *not* necessarily in the minds of those who drafted the laws or imported the techniques in question.

CHAPTER 2

The Candidates: Formation of the Field

A. Overview: Strategies, Tactics, and Routes to a Nomination

B. Campaigns before the Delegate Race

Overview: Strategies, Tactics, and Routes to a Nomination

The Making of Presidential Candidates

BY ROBERT L. PEABODY
& EVE LUBALIN

As the Ninetieth Congress drew to a close in 1967, William S. White, the long-time chief congressional correspondent for *The New York Times* and a Washington columnist, noted a nostalgia, and even bitterness, among senior members of the Senate that was provoked by the irreverent behavior of their younger colleagues. Lamenting on a decline in the chamber's dignity, White reported that senior and "more responsible" Senate members attributed this decline to " . . . the vastly harsh and abrasive climbing techniques of younger members who plainly regard the Senate as not an end in itself but only a transitory holding place on the way up to a Presidency or Vice Presidency." Commenting further, White concluded,

> Among the first termers, and sometimes among the second termers, too, ambition's strident call is almost perceptibly thrumming at Senatorial ears. Practically everybody under 50 years old is running for something he hasn't got; and running with a lack of grace and savoir faire that would have been quite shocking in the Senate of only a few years ago.

These impressions represent more than the ruefulness of an acknowledged admirer of the Senate of Russell, Taft, and Johnson, the Senate of the 1940s and 1950s. They constitute a pungent, even agonizing, outcry about the changing role of the contemporary Senate in presidential

Excerpted from Robert L. Peabody and Eve Lubalin, "The Making of Presidential Candidates," in Charles W. Dunn, ed., *The Future of the American Presidency* (Morristown, N.J.: General Learning Press, 1975), pp. 26–57. Reference notes and some tables deleted. Reprinted by permission of the authors, Robert L. Peabody and Eve Lubalin.

nominating politics. For White, the Senate was and should remain a citadel—an insular body, but one with a sense of grandeur and proper perspective on its true role in the national political scene. In the mid-1950s he described the Senate as an instinctively conservative body, resistant to change, dominated by senior members with little or no ambition outside its walls, and governed by a set of informal norms stressing civility, institutional pride, legislative specialization, reciprocity, and deference to one's elders. Even the most cursory knowledge about presidential recruitment patterns since 1960 makes one aware of the extent to which the chamber's insularity has been breached and the career aspirations of its members deflected outward beyond its red carpets, Victorian snuff boxes, and hand-crafted desks.

The pattern from 1960 on is deceptively simple—the presidential nominating conventions of both major parties have consistently granted their highest prize—the presidential nomination—to either incumbent senators or vice presidents who served in the Senate immediately before ascending to the vice presidency. Kennedy and Nixon in 1960, Goldwater and Johnson in 1964, Humphrey and Nixon in 1968, and McGovern and Nixon in 1972—this systematic choice of individuals from one major governmental institution reveal a consistency in presidential recruitment patterns by both parties unmatched at any time in the history of the republic. Moreover, it represents a rather drastic, if not radical, departure from the political backgrounds of almost all other presidential nominees of the last century.

Before the Civil War, when the nominating process was heavily influenced by Congress, nominees often had congressional experience. Of the twenty-two pre-Civil War major party presidential nominees (1789–1860), nineteen, or 86 percent, had prior congressional experience, and five of these were incumbent senators. However, in the post–Civil War period, as nominating procedures became increasingly independent of Congress, the tendency for the major political parties to reach out to members of Congress progressively diminished. Between 1868 and 1956, only eleven, or 37 percent, of the thirty presidential nominees had served in Congress before receiving the nomination, and only three were incumbents. Two were senators and one was a member of the House of Representatives.

Despite this post-Civil War diversification in nominating processes, the overall contribution of Congress as an important training ground for future presidents remains impressive. Twenty-five of the thirty-six men who have occupied the White House have a prior record of service in one or both Houses of Congress. Of the eleven exceptions, five have been governors (Cleveland, both Roosevelts, Wilson, and Coolidge); three came from a military background (Taylor, Grant, and Eisenhower); two were essentially administrators (Arthur and Hoover); and one, William Howard Taft, emerged from primarily judicial experience.

The last Democratic nomination of an incumbent senator prior to John

F. Kennedy's selection was the choice of Stephen A. Douglas in 1860, a procedure that took fifty-nine ballots and two conventions to achieve. Historically, senators have seldom been favored by the Republicans either. Only two Republican senators have received their party's nomination in the post–Civil War period, Benjamin Harrison in 1888 and Warren G. Harding in 1920. Both emerged as compromise choices—Harrison's nomination took eight ballots and Harding's ten. In contrast, all senatorial nominations since 1960 have been gained on the first ballot, generally flowing out of front-running presidential primary experiences. Beyond the nominations of incumbent Senators Douglas, Harrison, and Harding, only two other post-Civil War presidential nominees have even had senatorial experience. James G. Blaine, nominated in 1884 by the Republicans, served for five years in the Senate after a long and distinguished career in the House of Representatives and just before a short stint in President Garfield's cabinet. Vice President Harry S. Truman, nominated by the Democrats in 1948, who succeeded to the presidency following Roosevelt's death, had served in the Senate from 1935 until 1945.

Perhaps even more revealing than the clear Senate monopolization of recent presidential nominations is the fact that serious contenders for the nomination, for the Democrats at least, have almost exclusively been limited to those serving in the Senate. In 1960 Senator Kennedy met serious competition for the nomination from three other colleagues, Lyndon Johnson, Stuart Symington, and Hubert Humphrey, with ex-Governor and former nominee Adlai Stevenson the only strong potential nonsenatorial candidate. In 1968, the next open Democratic nominating situation, their presidential aspirants again came exclusively from the Senate, with Senators Humphrey, McCarthy, Robert Kennedy, and McGovern seriously considered for the nomination. The third party and protest candidacy of George Wallace, the former governor of Alabama, was, of course, the important exception.

In 1972, no less than ten Democratic senators, comprising almost one-fifth of that party's Senate members, were either announced or frequently discussed aspirants for the nomination. In contrast to this veritable horde of Senate hopefuls, only six other contenders of varying credibility offered themselves publicly. Former Governor Wallace was the standout once again. Once he was eliminated by an attempted assassination, no others survived the ordeal of the primary contests to emerge as serious contenders for the nomination. Only Senators McGovern, Humphrey, Muskie, and Jackson stayed in the race late into the preconvention period. Despite Chappaquiddick and his declared intentions not to run, Senator Edward Kennedy also remained an outside possibility as a compromise draft choice.

Recent Republican presidential aspirants clearly have been a more varied group, despite the party's ultimate reliance on senators or ex-senatorial vice presidents as nominees. In the three presidential election years since 1960 when the Republican nomination was at least nominally open, governors have been as conspicuous in their efforts to secure the nomination as have senators (Rockefeller in 1960; Rockefeller, Romney, and Scranton in 1964; Rockefeller, Reagan, and Romney in 1968). In addition, Mayor Lindsay (1968), Lieutenant General James Gavin (1968), and Ambassador Henry Cabot Lodge (1964) contributed diversity to the backgrounds of recent Republican hopefuls.

What can one expect in 1976 and beyond? We will return to such speculations in the conclusion. Suffice it to point out here that, at least so far, 1976 promises to replicate this recent pattern of Democratic reliance on the Senate as a source of presidential nominees in contrast to Republican dependence on both governors and senators.*

For the moment, let us withhold any attempt at explanation of these partisan differences in recent presidential recruitment patterns. First, it will prove helpful to bring together more systematically some longitudinal data on the past political careers of presidential nominees in order to set contemporary patterns in a comparative context. This will help to illustrate the magnitude of change in recruitment patterns in the recent period, as well as highlight their relative simplicity.

Post–Civil War Patterns of Presidential Nominations

. . . .

Of the seven major paths that have been followed in securing the presidential nomination between 1868 and 1956, three of them account for 70 percent of all nominees. These three, in their order of importance, are gubernatorial office (40 percent), federal appointive office (20 percent) and succession to the presidency from the vice presidency following presidential death in office (10 percent). In addition, both parties have relied on prominent nonpoliticians, mostly military heroes and businessmen, as nominees when they were out of power. These four paths combined account for 83.4 percent of all nominations. The remainder of the nominations were scattered between two Congressmen—Garfield and Bryan (6.7 percent), two Senators—Harrison and Harding (6.7 percent), and one former elected state judge (3.3 percent).

Generally, the two parties have not exhibited radically different recruitment patterns in the past, with one exception. The Democrats have relied most heavily on governors, while the Republicans have scattered their

Editors' note: These remarks raise the question of whether the 1976 success of former Governor Carter and the near-success of Governor Reagan—events which occurred after publication of this article—are exceptions to the rule or harbingers of a shift in the pattern Peabody and Lubalin identify here.

nominations more liberally and chosen those holding high federal appointive office as frequently as they have chosen governors. Probably the most straightforward explanation for this discrepancy is the fact that prominent federal appointees were more available to the Republicans than to the Democrats. This is true because the latter party controlled the presidency for only sixteen of the sixty-four years preceding Franklin Roosevelt's presidency. Thus, few Democrats could hope to have continuous careers as federal appointive officers as, for example, did William Howard Taft, Charles Evans Hughes, and Herbert Hoover, all of whom received the Republican party's nomination.

Relative use of these different paths to presidential nominations remained fairly consistent throughout the period, with the major changes reflecting decreased preference for federal appointees and an increased willingness to renominate presidents who had automatically succeeded to the presidency from the vice presidency because of presidential death. Table 1 summarizes the data.

In table 1, the longer time period has been broken into three smaller segments that correspond to changes in the electoral bases of the parties and that, additionally, consist of approximately the same number of nominations and elections. This breakdown should permit us to see if our aggregated frequency trees hide change over time and, if so, if such changes are associated with changes in the party system.

It is clear from table 1 that no dramatic changes in the career patterns of nominees emerge over time. Gubernatorial office has not only been the most frequent route to the presidency in the past, but also the most consistent. It is the only office of the seven "steppingstones" that ranks or ties for first place in each of the three time periods. In contrast to this consistent turning toward governors, a federal appointee has not won the nomination since 1928 (Hoover), and the last member of Congress before 1960 to receive a presidential nomination was Warren Harding in 1920.

The nomination of nationally prominent nonofficeholders shows no time trend, but probably indicates that such nominees are favored by parties when out of office. Under such circumstances, the Democrats nominated former Republican Horace Greeley, noted journalist and lecturer, in 1872 and General Winfield Hancock, a military hero, in 1880. In 1940, the out-of-power Republicans nominated Wendell Willkie, who mounted an unusually successful last-minute preconvention campaign based on the newly emerging mass media and his prior commercial contacts, and in 1952, General Eisenhower.

Probably the most meaningful trend has been the increase in nominating success exhibited by vice presidents who succeeded automatically to the presidency upon the death of the directly elected incumbent. This trend is not dramatized by the table because so few nominations were gained this way and because data have not yet been presented on the denial of

Table 1 · Last Office Held Before Presidential Nomination
by Period—Two Major Parties

	1868–1892	*1896–1924*	*1928–1956*
	N	N	N
Vice president succeeded to presidency		18.1% (2)	11.1% (1)
Senate	10.0% (1)	9.1% (1)	
House of Representatives	10.0% (1)	9.1% (1)	
Governor	40.0% (4)	27.3% (3)	55.6% (5)
Federal appointive	20.0% (2)	27.3% (3)	11.1% (1)
Statewide elective		9.1% (1)	
None	20.0% (2)		22.2% (2)
	100% (10)	100% (11)	100% (9)

nominations to vice presidents who became presidents and subsequently were nominated for an additional term in their own right. However, twentieth-century adherence to this tradition, starting with Theodore Roosevelt and continuing with Calvin Coolidge, Harry Truman, and Lyndon Johnson, represents a sharp contrast to nineteenth-century practices. Of the four nineteenth-century incumbent presidents who succeeded automatically to the presidency, all sought renomination and none achieved it. In this century we have seen a complete reversal of this pattern.

More recently, the vice presidency has become important for the presidentially ambitious in yet another way. Since 1956, each time a presidential incumbent has not sought renomination, the incumbent vice president—Nixon in 1960 and Humphrey in 1968—has received the nomination of the party in power. Polls showed that while President Ford was still vice president, he was the preferred candidate of Republican and independent voters for the 1976 Republican nomination.

It is clear from these data on pre-1960 presidential recruitment patterns that the aggregate congressional contribution to the major parties' pool of presidential candidates has been quite negligible. Altogether the House and Senate have contributed only four nominees (13 percent), and none of these congressmen were first ballot nominations. Of all thirty nominations during this period, two-thirds have required less than five ballots to achieve, but all four congressional nominations required more.

Two of the congressional nominations, Congressman James Garfield's (R., Ohio) and Senator Warren G. Harding's (R., Ohio), were the results of deadlocked conventions, and both candidates can be characterized as proverbial "dark horses." Neither nominee received any delegate votes in the initial convention balloting, and Garfield's nomination required thirty-six ballots, while Harding's required ten. Of the two, only Garfield can appropriately be called a career congressman. He served in the House for eighteen years before his nomination and had been elected to the Senate by the

Ohio state legislature several months before his nomination. Harding served one full term in the Senate before his nomination and held minor state elective offices prior to that.

The other two congressional nominees during this period, Congressman William Jennings Bryan (D., Neb.) and Senator Benjamin Harrison (R., Ind.), were clearly more serious contenders for their party's nomination than either Garfield or Harding were initially. Both nominees received substantial support in the early convention balloting and both clearly represented factions within their parties. However, neither of them had made Congress the major focus of their careers. Bryan served in the House for only two terms prior to his first nomination and had been out of office for over a year before receiving it in 1896. After losing this election he remained politically active as a journalist and lecturer rather than as an officeholder. He was renominated in 1900 and 1908. Harrison served one term in the Senate immediately before his nomination, but had not held formal office for thirteen years before his appointment to the Senate in 1881. That prior office was a minor state elective one. In the interim he was very active in the Indiana Republican party and attended national conventions regularly as a delegate. His political roots clearly lay in the Republican state political organization and not in the Senate.

Thus, it would seem that these past presidential recruitment patterns contrast vividly with those of the years 1960 through 1972. . . .

The contrast with the past is especially interesting because senators seem to have been consistent, though less frequent and successful, contenders in the earlier period. Aggregate data collected on governmental positions held by presidential contenders since 1832, when nominating conventions were first used, indicate that senators were active candidates for the nomination in the years between 1832 and 1956. Senators constituted 35 percent of all losing contenders for major party nominations in both halves of the 120-year period.

Having established this historical contrast in recruitment patterns over time, we turn now to attempts at explanation. The major burden of our argument will be that changes in the nature of the presidential nominating process over the last thirty years have dovetailed with changes in the post–World War II Senate in such a way as to favor ambitious senatorial presidential aspirants over their traditional gubernatorial rivals, especially for senators of the congressional partisan majority.

The Evolving Nature of Presidential Nominating Processes

MOTIVES IN THE NOMINATING PROCESS

Historically, the major criterion used in selecting presidential nominees in national party conventions has been their perceived ability to win. Held together by neither ideology nor organization, political incentives have constituted the major reason for disparate party leaders to cohere at all at a national level. Examples of such incentives are the expected help of a presidential coattail in state and local elections, the exchange of patronage and other material benefits for political support, and the likely satisfaction of individual ambitions through cabinet and other federal appointments that a new president might have to dispense.

The direct association of American presidential nominating politics with election outcomes distinguishes American executive recruitment patterns from those of other Western nations. This distinctive political characteristic has led one recent observer of British and American practices to characterize the American system as an "entrepreneurial" one. What this designation is meant to convey is the premium placed in the American system on the ability of a presidential aspirant to creatively manipulate current partisan balances, political resources, and public images and preferences in such a way as to mobilize the political interests of others in his behalf. This twentieth-century view closely parallels that of a well-known nineteenth-century British observer of American presidential politics. "Who is the man fittest to be adopted as candidate?" James Bryce asked rhetorically in the 1880s. "Plainly," he answered, "it is the man most likely to win."

One consequence of this motive force in nominating politics has been that the field from which American presidential nominees have been chosen has been comparatively flexible, wide-ranging, and inclusive. Prominent steppingstones, to the extent that they exist, have varied over time as changing political contexts established different opportunities and liabilities for the ambitious politician. What seems to have remained constant is the high probability that presidential nominations will go to aspirants, or entrepreneurs, who can combine political resources and opportunities in such a way as to gain support from a wide range of party leaders and, ultimately, from rank-and-file voters.

This interpretation of American nominating politics presupposes that major party conventions are composed of professional politicians and grassroots activists primarily motivated by political rather than ideological concerns. Undoubtedly, this assumption does not apply equally in every case. For example, it is not helpful in explaining the Goldwater candidacy in 1964 or the McGovern candidacy in 1972. The Goldwater and McGovern nominations, especially the latter, were made possible by the presence of a large number of issue-oriented grassroots amateurs within the delegate ranks. In both cases, amateur politicians stressed the importance of ideology rather than the more traditional concerns as a basis for candidate support, and in these two cases, the "amateur politicians" were able to capture the presidential conventions. This orientation contrasts rather sharply, for example, with the concerns of John F. Kennedy's supporters in 1960, most of whom stressed the senator's ability to win in their states.

These grassroots challenges to traditional party leadership may constitute nothing more than historical anomalies. On the other hand, they may signal the emergence of a new motive force in nominating politics. Recent changes in local party organization and reforms in the presidential nominating process may facilitate the future takeover of conventions by similarly motivated amateurs.

Despite the possibility of such future grassroots challenges, a fundamental assumption of this paper is that a candidate's ability to persuade convention delegates that he can win the presidential election will remain crucial to his successful pursuit of the nomination. Our attempts at explaining contemporary changes in American presidential recruitment patterns flow from this perspective.

CHANGES IN THE NOMINATING PROCESS

Over the past thirty years the American presidential nominating process has been transformed by three major developments that have had a pervasive impact on both delegate and aspirant behaviors: (1) an increase in popular influence, (2) a revolution in the American communications system, (3) the nationalization and increasing competitiveness of American presidential politics. We shall try to indicate briefly how these developments have altered the parameters of presidential nomination contesting.

Prior to the advent of mass means of communication, such as national news magazines, radio, television, and public opinion polls, the network of political contacts that made up state and local party organizations constituted the major source of political information for political leaders. Given this primitive communication system and the relative isolation of party leaders from one another, national party conventions represented unique opportunities for political leaders to meet, exchange information, cement bargains, and drum out a national ticket with a chance of winning.

Convention interaction was also important because presidential candidates traditionally limited their involvement in election campaigns, did not travel extensively, and had limited means of reaching the public directly. Thus, the support of state and local party organizations was often more important for election outcomes than personal candidate appeal. As a result, the criterion of "winnability" dictated that convention delegates find a candidate acceptable to most, if not all, major party factions who could be supported enthusiastically by established local party organizations.

As a consequence of these needs, national party conventions were truly deliberative bodies that exercised considerable discretion in the nominating process. Usually, convention deliberations were dominated by the search for a safe, "available" candidate who could win—a politician of white, Anglo-Saxon Protestant background whose personal life was uncompromised and who had not, during his political career, irrevocably offended any major party faction or interest. Beyond these criteria, one other major consideration, related to the sectional nature of American politics prior to the New Deal, seems to have been important in the selection process. This was a candidate's geographical origin. Because presidential politics in the post–Civil War period was, in contrast to recent contests, relatively partisan and sectional, the selection of a nominee from a competitive, and possibly swing, state with a large number of electoral votes had unusually high strategic value. The typical result of convention deliberations in this period was the choice of a rather noncontroversial candidate, acceptable to all party factions, whose major asset was his ability to carry a large swing state. As we have seen earlier, these candidates were often governors.

These patterns in the nominating process, patterns that obtained as recently as forty years ago, seem almost quaint in light of contemporary preconvention campaigns. The vast changes that have occurred in the interim seem to be a result of the increasing importance of finding a candidate with national appeal and of the interactive effects of polls, primaries, and television on both presidential aspirants and convention delegates.

The presidential elections of 1928 and 1932 considerably eroded the sectional and intensely partisan patterns in American politics that had prevailed throughout most of the post–Civil War period. Outside the South, the impact of the Depression and the combined political campaigns of Alfred E. Smith and Franklin Delano Roosevelt led to a redistribution of partisan preferences in the electorate in such a way as to focus political contests around national rather than sectional concerns. This political realignment of the electorate, combined with the growth of national mass media as the major source of political information, resulted in the spread of competitive party politics to a relatively large number of pivotal states, compared to the past, and increased the frequency of uniform national trends in presidential voting behavior.

Given these political developments, the weight placed upon the geographical origins of presidential candidates in convention decision making has been drastically reduced, if not entirely eliminated. The likelihood that a presidential candidate will carry one or two swing states as a result of his geographical identification has paled in significance compared to the question of whether or not a candidate will have national appeal. This, in turn, has led to the heightened importance of opinion polls, primaries, and national television coverage—all crucial components of recent preconvention campaigns.

The combined impact of these forces has significantly altered the nature of preconvention campaigning and decentralized the nomination process. Pursuit of presidential nominations has become markedly more open, and lengthening preconvention campaigns have progressively focused on the cultivation of a popular national constituency as an indirect means of securing delegate support. The discretion exercised by the conventions has been reduced, and nominations have been increasingly determined before the conventions meet. Nomination is won as a result of decentralized bargaining between aspirants and delegates during which the former seek advance commitments from the latter on the basis of their poll showings.

This brief description of changes in the nominating process should make clear the major contrasts between recent presidential nominating contests and those conducted in the past. These modifications have confronted aspiring presidential candidates with new opportunities and liabilities in their quest for the presidency. In the words of one student of the nominating process, the traditional standard of "availability" has given way to that of "prominence."

The Senate as an Incubator of
Presidential Candidates

Several familiar, if not fully persuasive, arguments have been advanced to explain senatorial failures to win nomination contests over the last century. First, it has been alleged that, in contrast to governors, senators were infrequently "safe" candidates, acceptable to disparate party factions, since their legislative responsibilities required that they take public stands on the whole gamut of issues that came before a Congress. Governors seldom established much of a public record, unless they had previously served in Congress, since in their role as state chief executives, they were rarely required to take positions on national issues.

Second, at a time when presidential responsibilities were largely administrative, the legislative experience of senators was not seen as directly relevant to the skills required of the president. In comparison, the experiences of governors, especially those of large states, who dealt with state legislatures, and administered the affairs of an important executive office, seemed more appropriate training for the presidency than that of senators.

Third, governors usually had more influence in state party organizations than did senators and, therefore, often controlled their states' delegations to national conventions. Thus, if they themselves wanted to run for the presidency, governors were in a good position to launch their own candidacy.

Finally, senators were not popularly elected until 1914 and, therefore, usually lacked campaign experience and popular testing in their own states. Because of the special importance of nominees carrying their own states in a period of closely contested national elections, senators were seen as riskier candidates than governors fresh from one or more election victories.

Explanations for the relative failure of governors, as compared to senators, in recent conventions have often focused on many of the same dimensions but with a different twist. Governors now appear to be isolated from national policy-making, and their immersion in parochial state concerns is considered more of a liability than an asset. Moreover, the purely administrative aspects of the president's job have contracted in comparison to presidential responsibility for formulating complex national economic and social policies, conducting American foreign affairs, and leading national public opinion.

Further, governors are seen as handicapped by their state executive responsibilities because of the ostensibly unhappy political plight of most contemporary governors. Faced with increasing public demands for services and inadequate sources of revenue, governors have either had to delay improvements in public services or raise taxes to cover state expenditures. In addition, it is maintained, their effectiveness in dealing with these problems has been further reduced by antiquated state constitutions, independent state administrative agencies, and malapportioned, hostile state legislatures. Since they are the most visible state politicians and handiest scapegoats, incumbent governors are seen as increasingly vulnerable politically and as failing in progressively larger numbers to win their attempts at reelection. Thus governors are perceived by some as having lost most of the solid base they once possessed for launching nomination campaigns.

The final interrelated set of liabilities said to plague contemporary governors is their relative anonymity and the public's image of them as parochial figures. With the growth of national mass media centered in Washington and the shifting of political resources and responsibilities from state capitols to Washington, governors have been at a disadvantage in attracting the attention of the national media. Increasingly, because of the nationalization of American politics and disproportionate media coverage of the president and members of Congress, the latter political officials have become most familiar to the public and provide much of what national and partisan leadership of public opinion now exists.

Given the changes in the nominating process that we have outlined above, this last argument, in tandem with one other rarely mentioned gubernatorial liability—that of relatively short tenure—seems to us to be one of the most compelling explanations for recent gubernatorial failures in nomination contesting.

Recent research on the political vulnerability of governors, as reflected in actual election outcomes, contradicts the assumption that governors are in a markedly more tenuous political position now than they were earlier in this century. Although gubernatorial elections were unusually competitive during the 1950s, governors were not more vulnerable as a group in the 1960s than they had been in earlier decades. In fact, their electoral fortunes, compared to those of Congressmen, actually improved.

Rather than being a recent phenomenon, relative gubernatorial vulnerability appears to be a constant attribute of state executive office compared, for example, to national legislative office. Comparison of the aggregate political fortunes of governors and senators in the 1900s reveals that during this century gubernatorial races have been more competitive than House or Senate contests. Additionally, there has been a higher rate of turnover of gubernatorial nominations and elections during this period than of senatorial ones.

These political characteristics of senatorial and gubernatorial career patterns are reflected in data that have been collected on office tenure of presidential and vice presidential nominees. Between 1848 and 1968, 79 percent of all governors winning either of these nominations served four years or less in that office before winning their nomination. In contrast, 57 percent of senatorial recipients served eight years or more before winning their nominations, and 39 percent served 12 years or more.

Thus, a marked recent increase in the political vulnerability of governors does not seem to be a fully persuasive explanation for recent gubernatorial failures. However, increased gubernatorial competition in the 1950s may have constituted a temporary liability that was further aggravated by the failure of any gubernatorial nominee to win a presidential election subsequent to Franklin Roosevelt's victories. What seems a more plausible explanation in light of changes in contemporary nominating processes—or at least a necessary complement to possible perceived gubernatorial political vulnerability—is that the traditionally short office tenure of governors and long office tenure of senators, combined with the different national roles currently played by these officials, have placed senators in an advantageous position vis-à-vis their gubernatorial rivals.

It is only about a decade since one student of political recruitment, Joseph Schlesinger, argued that because gubernatorial tenures were short, governors were likely to have progressive ambitions and orient themselves toward higher, that is, federal, office. In contrast, Schlesinger noted that because senatorial tenures were typically extended, senators were more likely to have static ambitions and not aim for higher office. Rather, he argued, senators would view the Congress as a permanent resting place and abide by institutional norms in order to advance quietly within its walls.

Two considerations now seem to mitigate against the force of this argument. First, the short tenure typically associated with gubernatorial office has become a distinct liability for ambitious governors because of long preconvention campaigns, the reduced frequency of open nominations, and nomination strategies based on the gradual development of a national constituency. As David Broder has noted: "A Senator can lay siege to the Presidency; a Governor must seize it on the run." Contemporary patterns in presidential nominating politics and the decreasing frequency of open nominations have made this last strategy increasingly difficult.

Second, the relative paucity of senatorial nominations in the past stemmed not so much from a lack of senatorial ambition as from the liabilities intrinsic to a Senate career in relation to the criterion employed in selecting presidential nominees. As we have noted, senators frequently did contest for presidential nominations in the past, but failed to obtain them. We have already presented a number of reasons why senators seem to have fared poorly in the post–Civil War period in contests for the presidential nomination. Now we shall try to explain why recent changes in the Senate have proved to be advantageous to the presidentially ambitious senator.

THE CITADEL VERSUS THE CONTEMPORARY SENATE

The Senate of the 1940s and early 1950s was an unlikely incubator of nationally prominent political leaders. In trying to convey a sense of Senate life during this period, we need not dwell overly long on the familiar folklore of William S. White, or the more empirically grounded contributions of Donald R. Matthews and Ralph K. Huitt.

"The Inner Club," as White described it, was an elusive construct at best, and one whose utility has been debated. Still, it represented the essence of the body for White, and he has since lamented its passing. Constituted of "Senate types" drawn from all sections, but dominated at its core by senior Southern members, White argued that this oligarchical assemblage ruled over the Senate through a combination of personal skills and a monopoly of the institutional bases of power within the chamber.

White's portrait of the Senate was supplemented by Donald Matthews in 1960 when he published his famous description of Senate folkways, gleaned from semistructured interviews with various participants in the Senate legislative process. Matthews' enumeration of six norms that guided Senate behavior—apprenticeship, concentration on legislative work, specialization, courtesy, reciprocity, and institutional patriotism—did not diverge appreciably from the code of conduct described by White. Rather, it seemed to make it more explicit as well as to undergird it with an empirical base. The writings of Ralph K. Huitt partially mitigated these interpretations by pointing up the range of alternative behaviors or roles available to individual senators, party leaders, and committee members.

The Senate as "Citadel" or "Establishment" contrasts vividly with characterizations of Senate behavior, influence, and function offered recently by congressional scholars, as well as by a number of White's fellow journalists. Several feature newspaper articles that appeared during the middle and late 1960s questioned the continued validity of the old model of the Senate, noting an increase in activity and initiative on the part of junior members, a decrease in the power of Southerners and committee chairmen, an erosion of traditional voting blocs premised on regional and/or economic homogeneity, and an increase in the number of senators dependent on their public image rather than a party organization for election.

These journalistic assessments have been reinforced by Nelson W. Polsby and Randall B. Ripley in their recent writings on the contemporary Senate. Both of these scholars have argued that the Senate can no longer be accurately portrayed as a body dominated by a limited number of powerful committee chairmen or bloc leaders engaging in habitual reciprocity on important policy questions and armed with sanctions to punish deviant members. Rather, they have submitted that changes in Senate personnel and committee structure, especially the proliferation of subcommittees, combined with the size, visibility, and rules of the chamber, have resulted in a decrease in conservative, Southern influence and a concomitant dispersion of power among individual members.

Polsby, especially, has emphasized that the opportunities available to senators in the policy-making process have made the Senate a launching pad for the presidency and a more innovative institution. In contrast to its earlier conservative, deliberative functions, Polsby notes that the Senate's main activities now consist of seizing policy initiatives, defining new issues, and cultivating national constituencies in support of them through publicized hearings, investigations, speeches, and legislative sponsorship. Given these opportunities, he finds individual senators less dependent on their senior elders for political advancement, less insular in orientation, and less willing to accept the traditional "Senate type" as an appropriate model for their own behavior.

Several other changes in internal Senate operations and institutions exogenous to the chamber may also be singled out as contributors to change in the Senate in the postwar period. Of prime importance, and probably unanticipated at the time, were the long-run consequences of stronger Democratic and Republican party leadership in the 1950s and 1960s. Elected minority leader in 1953 and majority leader in 1955, Lyndon B. Johnson reduced the power of the old Senate Inner Club in a number of ways. First, by building a formidable information network and welding together a band of diverse senators predisposed to help out their leader, Johnson placed himself at the center of coalition building efforts in the chamber and thus deprived Senate elders of one of their important functions.

Second, in his search for available resources to cement his power, Johnson, with the approval of Senator Russell and other Southern dignitaries, modified the seniority rule by instituting the practice of awarding choice committee assignments to junior senators before permitting senior members to occupy more than one influential committee seat. This practice was also adopted by the Republicans in 1959, and since has been codified in the Legislative Reorganization Act of 1970. This breach in the strict application of seniority, as well as changes in personnel, is commonly cited as having been advantageous for Senate liberals. For although it gave more discretion to the parties' Committees on Committees, it also meant that the dispersion of leadership roles made theoretically possible by the proliferation of subcommittees could take on further significance.

Finally, the changes Johnson instituted in the daily operation of the chamber, complemented by Senate Minority Leader Everett Dirksen's consolidation of power, further reduced many of the advantages that senior members had enjoyed as a function of their mastery of chamber rules and monopolization of debate. By employing aborted quorum calls and the unanimous consent procedure extensively to control Senate proceedings, and by scheduling either stop-and-go legislative activity or continuous night sessions, Johnson reduced the role of debate and debaters in the Senate's operations and more or less controlled its business. While Johnson's successor, Mike Mansfield, has not used equally dramatic ploys to maintain control of the chamber, scattered observations on his leadership style suggest that the formal Democratic leadership has maintained control over scheduling and has supported junior members' efforts to take an active role both within the congressional party and in the larger chamber.

A number of factors, exogenous to the internal operations of the chamber, may also be construed as contributing to change in the postwar Senate, although none have been systematically studied in that context. The first of these is the increasing degree of political competition at the state level. Donald R. Matthews predicted that increasingly competitive two-party politics would lead to greater deviance from Senate folkways or even to their modification, as senators with marginal victories acted to decrease their political vulnerability by making a record early in their careers. Similarly, Tom Wicker of *The New York Times* has argued that a reduction in the political homogeneity of Senate constituencies and the national salience of new political issues has made reciprocal relationships between cohesive economic or regional blocs more difficult.

In addition to changing constituency pressures, the ramifications of the growth of national mass media and polling agencies have probably had far-reaching consequences for the Senate. As political resources and activity have shifted from state capitols to Washington, national television coverage of political events also has shifted public attention to national policy makers and away from state and local politicians. Aside from the presidency and vice presidency, the Senate has been the only national institution that has shared in this publicity through its use of televised hearings and investigations.

This technological change has made it possible for relatively junior senators to use their subcommittee chairmenships to develop national standings probably unmatched in earlier eras. Some evidence exists that politically ambitious senators have done just this in their quest for the nomination. Data collected on nine publicly announced Democratic senatorial presidential aspirants and nine "controls" matched for seniority, ideology, and constituency characteristics in 1971, the year before the

Table 2 · Senate Subcommittee Structure Between 1950 and 1970

	1950	1960	1970
Number of Standing Committee Subcommittees	60	93	116
Number of Special Committee Subcommittees	0	0	7
Number of Select Committee Subcommittees	0	6	6
Number of Joint Committee Subcommittees	0	10	15
Total Number of Subcommittees	60	109	144

Source: Congressional Index, 81st, 86th, and 91st Congresses (Commerce Clearing House).

onset of the 1972 presidential primaries, reveal that presidential aspirants held twice as many hearings, on the average, as their counterparts. These group differences could be expected by chance only three out of 100 times.

Drawing together these observations on the contemporary Senate, several major interrelated trends can be set forth as to why senatorial incumbency seems to facilitate successful nomination contesting. First, and perhaps most important, is the apparent increasing dispersion of influence and initiative to a larger number of senators, made possible by the small size of the chamber combined with postwar dilution of the seniority principle and proliferation of subcommittees. The proliferation of subcommittees from 1950–1970 is documented in table 2. In addition to the gross quantitative increase in the number of subcommittees, the reorganization of the Senate committee structure reduced the relative number of unimportant subcommittees, such as those under the jurisdiction of the Committees on the District of Columbia, Post Office and Civil Service, and Rules and Administration, and increased the number falling under the jurisdiction of more politically salient and prestigious committees, such as the Committees on Armed Services, Foreign Relations, Judiciary, Labor and Public Welfare, and the nonstanding investigatory committees. In 1950 subcommittees of the three former committees constituted 38 percent of all subcommittees while in 1970 they constituted only 10 percent of all subcommittees.

By the time of the Ninety-third Congress (1973–1974) fully fifty-five of the fifty-seven Democratic senators were taking advantage of the staff assistance and other benefits flowing from the incumbency of at least one subcommittee chairmanship. Similarly, only one Republican senator did not hold at least one ranking minority position on either of his several committees. This relatively quick absorption of junior senators into the power structure is especially advantageous for Democratic newcomers who enjoy the prerogatives of subcommittee chairmanships as a result of their membership in the majority party.

This diffusion of organization responsibility has probably been an important contributor to another aforementioned trend in the postwar Senate—the erosion of traditional institutional norms as, for example, apprenticeship. Compared to their forerunners, junior senators of the late 1960s and early 1970s have not hesitated to speak out. Instead, incoming members have taken an immediate and active role in legislative matters and sought to establish a visible and public record from the start. This relative independence of incoming freshmen has been further enhanced by the recent formation of active bipartisan class clubs oriented toward collective lobbying of more senior colleagues on various housekeeping matters and rules changes. Composing nearly 40 percent of the Senate membership, these clubs, if they continue to be active, represent a potentially strong force for the continuation of reforms that facilitate the exercise of initiative by individual members.

These attempts by junior members to exercise more initiative in Senate affairs have been facilitated by a third change in the Senate—the reorientation of the current party leaders, Democratic Majority Leader Mike Mansfield and Republican Minority Leader Hugh Scott. While Johnson and Dirksen, when in analogous roles, contributed to the erosion of the Inner Club in the 1950s and 1960s by centralizing party leadership, Mansfield and Scott have facilitated individualism in the Senate by reverting more to a shared pattern of leadership. Mansfield, for example, has described his role as being that of a servant to other senators.

These modifications in Senate structure, norms, and leadership style over the last few decades have removed a number of constraints that previously limited individual senatorial initiative and have created new opportunities for relatively junior senators to actively participate in Senate life. By enhancing such opportunities to lead public opinion on new issues through the use of nationally broadcast hearings, nightly news coverage, and guest appearances, presidentially ambitious senators, especially those of the majority party, have exploited the potential for national leadership now inherent in Senate incumbency.

The opportunities offered senators by virtue of membership in the contemporary Senate give them unique advantages in the nominating process, shared or surpassed, perhaps, only by the vice president. Politicians holding these high federal offices, if they wish, can have access to a degree of national media coverage that gubernatorial tenure rarely merits. The popular awareness developed in this manner by senators and vice presidents often snowballs by spurring speaking engagements that further increase their political contacts and public recognition.

In addition to the publicity attendant on office, senators have an advantage, as compared to governors, in rarely being unwilling captives of specific and troublesome issues. Rather, as a result of their membership in a collective body and their relatively large number of committee and subcommittee assignments, senators have considerable discretion in allocating their energies and can develop public images and national constituencies in a calculated fashion. These tasks are facilitated by their extended tenure. Similarly, vice presidents who enjoy the respect of their presidents can expect to assume, at least formally, national and international responsibilities that permit them to develop the image of responsible, experienced statesmen. Skillful exploitation of television is especially effective. Research on the political impact of television indicates that beyond serving informational needs, this medium has been most influential in its indirect effect on public images about politics and politicians.

Before hazarding a few predictions about the likely future of presidential nominating patterns, the importance of precedence in the nominating process should be underscored once more. Each time a senator or vice president receives the presidential nomination, the legitimacy of these officials becoming future nominees increases. The gradual elevation of senatorial and vice presidential office to the status of presidential steppingstones, in turn, reinforces such recruitment patterns. The combination of regular interelection media coverage and the public's perception of senators and vice presidents as appropriate presidential candidates gives those incumbents who are politically ambitious an advantage over governors in the preconvention period. While governors may still make a try for the nomination by entering primaries, their assets give senators and vice presidents a headstart in nomination contesting and probably increase the likelihood that they will gain the nomination and/or win the subsequent election. Recent precedents in presidential recruitment, while shortlived, strongly condition speculation about likely future nominating patterns.

· B ·

Campaigns before the Delegate Race

Walter Mondale

BY ARTHUR T. HADLEY

The second Democratic candidate formally to quit the invisible primary—though like Kennedy he had never officially entered the race—was Senator Walter "Fritz" Mondale of Minnesota. For Mondale, as for Kennedy, the decisive track turned out to be psychological, though by the time he finally dropped out Mondale had not shown the strength of Kennedy on a number of other tracks.

Fritz Mondale entered the invisible primary about as early as possible, the evening of Nixon's reelection, November 7, 1972. That was when Hubert Humphrey stood beside Mondale, who had just been elected to his second Senate term, and told a television audience he thought Mondale would make a great President. Humphrey ended his fulsome endorsement by saying: "If it isn't being too sacrilegious, I don't mind being John the Baptist for Walter Mondale."

Mondale hadn't expected this peal on the Democratic shofar. But as a result invitations to speak began to come in. He found he had the beginnings of a constituency on the liberal left of the Democratic party. "I'd mortgage my house if it would help him," said Joseph Rauh, former ADA chairman. (Is it possible that a liberal is now a man so wealthy he doesn't have a mortgage on his house?) Friends rallied round and offered to help Mondale get organized. He was off and running before he realized what campaigning would entail, his feet moving before he decided to be in the race.

Significantly Mondale could not put his finger on the moment when he decided to try for the presidency. "When did you decide?" I kept pressing him.

Excerpted from Arthur T. Hadley, *The Invisible Primary*, (Englewood Cliffs, N.J.: Prentice-Hall, Inc., 1976), pp. 29–38. © by Arthur T. Hadley. Published by Prentice-Hall, Inc., Englewood Cliffs, New Jersey 07632, and reprinted by their permission.

"We were talking it over," he answers.

"When?"

"After the last election."

"Can you be more specific?"

"I don't think so."

"Who was 'we'?"

"A bunch of us."

Mind you, he wasn't giving the impression, sitting there in shirt sleeves and puffing a cigar as if it were a seldom enjoyed sin, that he was ducking questions. His happy round face—reminding one of Orr in *Catch 22*—looked genuinely puzzled and troubled that he couldn't remember, and that the interview wasn't on some safe ground like his energy policy.

"Who was in the bunch?"

"Dick Moe and Mike Berman and myself, I think. [That is, his two aides and himself.] We sat down and said 'Why not?' "

After Mondale withdrew in December, I talked to his wife, Joan, about the personal side of deciding to run for President. We sat before a bare fireplace because the Senator was away campaigning in Minnesota and had forgotten to order wood. "We had him home for a week after he announced he wasn't running for President; and after he drained the air out of the radiators we didn't know what to do with him," said Joan with a laugh.

"I don't think," she said, "that he ever did make the decision to run. Hubert [Humphrey] said those nice things about him on television and the invitations started to come in. . . . We got to travel and went to so many wonderful places. . . . He always talks over major decisions with me and we never talked about his running. I think you're right. The decision never was made."

She paused for a moment, then added: "But he enjoyed campaigning."

"His aides say he'd come back awfully down."

"Sometimes. Sometimes he'd go to bed the whole next day."

On the evidence, I'd say Mondale enjoyed being on the road some of the time, but less and less as the campaign went on.

Privately Mondale used a poignant metaphor to describe how it felt to run week after week in the invisible primary.

"I don't want to be a rent-a-car; that's what I'm becoming in this campaign. You get into me at some airport, whoever wants to, they drive me as fast as they want as far as they want, and then return me to the airport and just forget about me."

The son of a traveling Norwegian Methodist minister (his great-grandfather changed the family name from Mundal to Mondale on friendly advice from an immigration officer), Mondale was brought up strictly, in rural isolation. The result is a character that seems a strange, even uneasy, mixture of conservative habit and cast of mind, combined with liberal beliefs and solutions. Mondale himself is conservative, upright, and un-swervingly moral. He brings his children up strictly, likes to hunt and shoot, believes in strong family ties, and is deeply, not just politically, religious. All these are conservative values. As state attorney general he was a strict law-and-order man, cracking down on utilities and ordinary criminals with vigorous impartiality. To hear him talk about the need for alternative life-styles in America and massive aid to starving nations causes one to wonder where his beliefs arise and why.

Mondale's campaign, like the candidate, was full of contradictions: a strange mixture of the haphazard and the totally programmed. Mondale was a planner in rigid control of himself who yet had a campaign without strategy or basic idea. "Except perhaps not to peak too soon," he said with a laugh about a month before he decided to quit the race. "I'm just going around the country drilling for oil, seeing where it gushes up." I reminded Mondale that several months before, late one night on the road, Robert Boyd, the multilingual, poetry-quoting genius who masquerades as the Knight newspaper bureau chief in Washington, had pushed him about what issues he thought were most important to his campaign. Mondale had answered then: "I am not sure I am in a position to give you a definitive answer yet," because he had not had time to do all the research.

That must have been because he was tired (being tired was a continual Mondale problem, probably reflecting the psychological tension induced by his campaign). Mondale said, "I really am an issues man." His face, which habitually wears the look of a surprised owl, assumed the alarming expression of a senator winding up to give you his half-hour "where-I-stand-on-the-issues speech."

I cut in hastily: "Would you be happier running for the presidency as a governor or a senator?"

"Oh, from the Senate. I've learned so much here. . . . I am an issue man. I really don't like administration." He did a Bob Hope double take as the implications of his words that he doesn't like administration hit presidential candidate Mondale. "I mean, I mean, I'm keen on administration, too."

"I really don't think he thought too much about the presidency," says his wife.

. . . .

"Let's hear a big one for Senator Mondale," screams the loudspeaker system at the Carbondale, Illinois, shopping center. There is no big one. Not even a small one. No response at all. Indeed the parking lot is deserted in the bright noon sun, the asphalt empty beneath the twisting gasoline sign burning energy as it spins against the wind. Inside the restaurant where Mondale is speaking, the couples, some twenty of them, listen dully while they sip their beer. Mondale does not turn people on. He has been campaigning for a year and still only 4 percent of the voters know his name.

In the editorial office of the Chicago *Tribune* Mondale talks about the need for "an open and law-abiding presidency." No viewer of *The Front Page* would recognize the men listening. Respectability has hit the upper reaches of journalism. These bankerlike men smoke expensive cigars and wear white shirts. The editor sits behind a polished, dark, antique desk and behind him are a pair of encased fencing foils. Mondale tells the editors how much his father hated Colonel Robert McCormick, the deceased *Tribune* owner. Then he talks about the need to have compassion and move the country forward.

The senator seems to have trouble finding enough breath to push out the last words of his sentences. On the *Tribune*'s office couch, the head of the reporter from the Washington *Post,* a gung-ho guy who helped nail Spiro Agnew, sinks slowly to his chest. His breathing changes to a soft snore. Out of respect for the integrity of our craft, I nudge him gently awake. Besides, I might need help myself in a few minutes.

In her lakeside living room, Mrs. Benton rises to ask Mondale if he favors income redistribution to aid the poor. Mondale has been briefed that she always asks this question and that a "sock-it-to-the-rich" answer would unlock bank vaults for him. Instead, he gives a thoughtful and straightforward exposition of the problems and difficulties of welfare reform. "I won't stand there in a two-million-dollar house and do a liberal two-step for them," he tells his staff later.

On the media track, Mondale got a divided reception. In May 1973 a gushing profile appeared in the *New Yorker,* eight pages long, mostly lengthy quotes by the senator. The piece began, "Walter Frederick Mondale, a forty-five-year-old Democrat from Minnesota, is an increasingly important member of the United States Senate," and built him up from there with a series of soft questions. "Do you think the Congress is really capable, institutionally, over the long run, of acting effectively . . . ?" Not surprisingly Mondale found Congress okay in some 490 words. However, elsewhere the organs of the liberals, who are his natural constituency, muted their enthusiasm. Their themes were usually the same. He has been a good, if not too effective, senator. But he has always been appointed to the jobs he has held, first as attorney general of Minnesota, then to the United States Senate (though he won reelection to both offices in his own right). Can he find the fire within himself to turn people on and stay the course?

In former years the *New Yorker* article by itself would have been tremendously important to Mondale on the money track. Liberals respond to the *New Yorker.* The favorable mention there would have guaranteed several large donations, financed further a more active campaign. But under the new rules where no one person could give more than one thousand dollars to any one candidate, those funds weren't available. To the surprise of all but a few, the first hurt by the new campaign financing laws were the liberal Democrats who had done the most to pass the measure. Middle-of-the-road Republicans and Democrats have many supporters who can give five hundred to one thousand dollars. The conservative Republicans and liberal Democrats had been the two groups relying on the largess of millionaires—the millionaires of the far right giving out of greed; the millionaires of the far left, out of guilt.

Discouraged by the lack of money, political support, media inattention, and by the small size of most of his audiences, Mondale planned to withdraw from the invisible primary in 1973. He told no one but his staff; and they talked him out of the decision. Their argument in effect was: Look, you don't know your strengths yet. As the '74 elections approach, you'll get more invitations to speak, draw bigger crowds, begin to move. You don't really know how effective a campaigner you are yet because you haven't been fully committed. Press the test further. We believe in you. We think you'll become good at campaigning and find it a joy. Mondale said, all right, he'd continue to campaign, see what happened.

The same criticism leveled at Mondale—that he'd had things too easy in politics, never had to face the tough ones—was also charged of his staff. Everyone liked and respected Mike Berman, the Falstaffian leader of Mondale's drive, but they pointed out that though he was an old Hubert Humphrey political operative, he'd left Hubert's disastrous and bloody '68 campaign for President to manage the winning campaign of Wendell Anderson for governor of Minnesota.

"They've never been shit on in a tough fight," a rival politician noted with understandable bias. "Had to turn the nut and kick ass in a losing campaign. That's what makes you or breaks you as a manager."

Convinced by his staff, Mondale went back on the road in 1974—the dinners, the speeches, the cocktail parties, the names: August 17, Dubuque, Iowa; August 19, New York City; September 2, Oakland, California; September 4, Minneapolis; September 7, Great Falls, Montana; September 8, Chicago; September 14, Elk Grove, Illinois; September 16, Phoenix.

Then in the second week of September, Senator Edward M. Kennedy made his Sherman-like statement and withdrew. The press immediately reported that Mondale's campaign was the chief beneficiary. Mondale's staff talked happily about the great benefits now that Kennedy had withdrawn. They pictured their candidate spending hours on the phone taking pledges of support from all over America. "Mondale's '76 Presidential Campaign Gets Lift from Kennedy Withdrawal," headlined *The New York Times* on October 10.

"I'm 99.44 percent sure I'll seek the nomination," Mondale said publicly.

The problem for Mondale was that the shift in support to himself after Kennedy's withdrawal was only a media event. Much of the Kennedy strength—by no means all, but much—had been a press creation. Other parts of that strength like the blacks, first-time voters, and some older labor leaders had been drawn to Senator Kennedy out of memory and the appeal of his life-style, rather than for political convictions. Those groups had no reason to move into the Mondale camp. Nor did the hard-eyed professional politicians, who had joined Kennedy to get in early with a winner, wish to transfer to a man with only a 4 percent favorable recognition factor.

Having created a semi-mythical body of liberal support for Kennedy, the press, with help from Mondale's staff, transferred that nonexistent strength to Mondale. That was all very heady for two weeks; but when Mondale tried to collect from the myth, no one was at home to sign the checks. It was widely reported that the week after Kennedy withdrew, forty thousand dollars came into the Mondale coffers. Mondale's figures filed with the Government Accounting Office show a jump, but nothing like the money coming to Senators Jackson and Bentsen in the same period. Mondale's staff kept on talking about the Kennedy supporters who were beating the doors to enter the senator's campaign. But they never gave specific names. And sitting in their offices listening, I never heard a barrage of knocks.

In fairness to Mondale, other candidates were also insisting that Kennedy's withdrawal had given their campaigns a shot in the arm. I finally pinned down Terry Bracy, the cuttingly honest thirty-year-old who is one of two masterminds behind the Udall campaign.

"Hadley, stop bugging me," said Bracy. "You know nothing has changed. But the press thinks it's changed so it has changed. What do you want me to do? Tell the press the Kennedy support is a myth they created? You want to kill us? Besides there will be a change. The press is looking for one; so all the candidates will scramble hard and produce one."

Mondale's problem was that he believed the withdrawal of Teddy Kennedy would result in increased support for himself. The other candidates merely talked as if they believed it. When that support didn't arrive, Mondale was upset; they were not.

The next blow to hit Mondale's invisible primary race was New Hampshire. Mondale had planned to build up an organization in New Hampshire so that he could do well in that primary and make a spectacular leap forward, as Gene McCarthy had done in 1968 and George McGovern in 1972. But here Mondale's lack of strategy hurt him. While he was out campaigning more or less without plan, Udall's staff sewed up Mondale's planned liberal constituency in New Hampshire.

The taking of New Hampshire by Udall, a classic piece of invisible primary maneuvering, is worth considering in detail. Terry Bracy, who had worked New Hampshire for Muskie against McGovern in '72, had been impressed with McGovern's magnificent media campaign, orchestrated and designed by Merv Weston, head of Weston Associates and a liberal power in the state. Bracy arranged a trip in April '74 for Udall, the ostensible reason to campaign for Norman d'Amours, the Democrat running for Congress. Weston threw a cocktail party for Udall and invited the deans of the New Hampshire liberal establishment. "We were favorably impressed," said Weston, though some of the leaders remained on the fence between Udall and Mondale.

Then in September, Mondale's supporters in the teachers' union engineered him a speaking engagement before all the state's Democrats at a fund raiser in Manchester, New Hampshire, on October 5. Mondale said yes, but after Kennedy's withdrawal he ducked out of the New Hampshire engagement because his staff felt he had a better offer from Florida. The Udall people zeroed on New Hampshire and grabbed the speaking date for Udall. Mondale's Florida trip blew up—the mythical Kennedy strength transfer again—and Mondale's staff tried to get the October 5 date back. Mondale and Udall's staff went into negotiation, which is rather like one of the boys from the Saturday night poker game sitting down against Amarillo Slim. Mondale ended up speaking after Udall and without a proper introduction.

On that fateful Friday evening Udall got up, looked out over the roomful of bored Democrats, and began: "You may think Senator Mondale and I are here because there is a presidential election in 1976. That is not true. We are here to visit museums and the habitat of the purple finch." The audience broke up. Udall went on to tell about the politician back in his state of Arizona who was wooing the votes of the Indians on a reservation. He was promising the moon, new schools, paved roads, hot and cold running water in the tepees, two tepees for every brave and a brave in every tepee. Each promise was greeted by enthusiastic cheers of "Goomwah! Goomwah!" The politician thought he was doing real well till he went down to the corral to accept the gift of a pony and the chief warned him not to step in the goomwah.

Udall slipped in some serious bits about conservation, energy, and the economy and his record on these, but mostly he kept the audience rocking. Then Mondale got up and delivered a head-nodder about his record in the Senate. After the meeting was over, Mondale's staff had him scheduled to leave in a hurry, while Udall stayed around until one in the morning shaking hands and making friends. The next day Marie Carrier, the Democratic National Committeewoman and one of the handful of de facto Democratic leaders in New Hampshire, got on the phone with her other activist friends. They decided to unite behind Udall. It was that simple. And that deadly for Mondale.

In late October Mondale paced his office as he described how unfair it was that a man's fate should be decided in a small state like New Hampshire. It was an atypical state, he complained, small and conservative; why should it play such a large influence in the campaign? His own staff was already recommending that he avoid the New Hampshire primary, much as Kennedy's staff had done.

The second week in November '74 Mondale visited the Soviet Union. This trip supplied the final ingredient in his decision to withdraw. It broke the rhythm of his campaigning, removed him from the grinding bustle and excitement of politics, and let him reflect on how much he wanted the presidency, how much he wanted to lose control over major parts of his life. When he returned from Moscow on November 17, Mondale found the emotional strain of gearing himself up to campaign again nearly intolerable.

The Russian visit may have done more than unravel Mondale's already strained ties to presidential politics. On previous trips to the Soviet Union the Russians had treated Mondale well. Mondale inclines to the belief that the Russians are just like us, only they lace their shoes up a bit differently. This time the Russians, unhappy over Senate pressure to ease the restrictions on the immigration of Jews to Israel, gave Mondale a thorough hosing. Just as Nikita Khrushchev had done to President Kennedy when he thought he detected signs of softness, the top officials of the Soviet Union now showed Mondale just how rough they could be. While his staff say otherwise, friends who saw him right after the trip report him profoundly shaken.

In any event Mondale went through a period of depression on his return. This coincided with the moment at which it became necessary to hire campaign staff. Up to the end of November, Mondale's effort had been run by three men, Mike Berman, Dick Moe, and Sid Johnson. All of them had been with Mondale since his early campaigns for attorney general in Minnesota. He felt he could ask them to help him out early in the invisible primary without imposing great hardships on their lives if he withdrew later. Now it would be necessary to bring others on board, ask them to give up jobs, chances for promotion, money, family, personal life, all in a cause that appeared a long shot at best. In asking people to take such a risk, Mondale felt that he had to reevaluate his own purpose. Could he ask people for a binding commitment when he himself was not sure of his own?

Overshadowing the political and personal issues was the psychological fear that he was losing control over his life. "He felt he was changing," says Johnson. "He didn't like what campaigning was doing to him," says Berman.

The impression that his life was out of control must have been quite frightening as Mondale moved deeper into the campaign. He felt his extremities were beginning to disappear into the political embrace of strangers.

"All the week before, he'd go to bed with his mind made up one way and wake with it decided on the other," said his wife. "We talked it over and over."

"Which way did he seem to be leaning?"

"I couldn't tell."

Mondale called his wife up shortly before noon on Wednesday, November 20, and told her to come down to the Senate because he was going to make an important statement at four P.M. She still wasn't sure which way he was going to decide, "though something in his choice of words made me think he would withdraw."

He surprised his staff also. Sid Johnson had just sold his house in Minnesota and taken an apartment in Washington. He was down at the Democratic governors' conference at Hilton Head, South Carolina, the Monday before the announcement, trying to line up support for Mondale when he got the indication from Berman that withdrawal was possible. I was standing in front of the phone booth door as he came out and assumed he had just learned of a death in his family or had been thrown over by his girl, he looked so white and glazed.

A letter to all the delegates to the Democrats' midterm convention at Kansas City was in the mail, urging them to drop by and meet Mondale. Berman had been talking to an advertising agency in New York about handling the campaign on Monday and was still negotiating with the phone company for office phones on Tuesday.

"I found I did not have the overwhelming desire to be President which is essential for the kind of campaign that is required," said Mondale in his public announcement." . . . I don't think anyone should be President who is not willing to go through the fire. . . . I admire those with the determination to do what is required to seek the presidency, but I have found I am not among them."

The statement dealt with the race almost exclusively in psychological terms. In it there was practically no mention of politics. Would he have continued running if he had found himself more politically successful? His wife and friends are not sure, but, on the whole, they think not. For Mondale, as for Kennedy, the try for the White House had been primarily an interior voyage.

And what did he do upon leaving the invisible primary? He went ice fishing in the far north of Minnesota in January. Two months later he looked more relaxed and happy than I had seen him in two years.

———————————

Elliot Richardson

BY ARTHUR T. HADLEY

Percy's campaign ended because of Watergate. The campaign of the other early-starting Republican, Elliot Richardson, was created by Watergate. In the invisible primary the two men ran a totally different type of race. Percy spent $200,000 and had the power, staff, and prerequisites of his Senate office. Citizen Elliot Richardson, late attorney general of the United States, late secretary of defense, late secretary of health, education, and welfare, late undersecretary of state, former lieutenant governor of Massachusetts, financed himself from his lecture fees, and had a two-person office and no job. Richardson hadn't intended to run for President or be attorney general. In fact, when summoned to Camp David after Nixon's '72 triumph to learn his fate—there were rumors he would be asked to leave the administration because of his constant pressure for welfare reform—"The one job I planned to refuse was attorney general." His preference was "to stay in health, education, and welfare, complete the work started." But he had become too controversial in that job; and Nixon shifted him to secretary of defense.

Then under the dogged probing of the Washington *Post* the "third-rate burglary" of Watergate slowly bubbled bigger into national scandal. On the last day of April, the then attorney general, Richard Kleindienst, resigned because of his "close personal and professional relationship" with some of those being investigated. Less than three months after becoming secretary of defense, Richardson accepted the job he had no intention of taking. "To restore the integrity of Justice itself. . . . 99 and 44/100 percent pure is not now, if it ever was, good enough." He hung in there for half a year: quite a half year, Watergate and Agnew.

In the end President Nixon ordered Richardson to fire Watergate Special Prosecutor Archibald Cox, who was insisting on his right to hear more White House tapes. At the time Richardson had hired Cox, his friend and former law professor, he had pledged publicly before the Senate Judiciary Committee that he would give Cox a free hand. After trying hard to compromise the differences between Cox and the White House, Richardson resigned. In so doing he became a presidential candidate. He also picked up the respect of the press; and since he had always dealt fairly, if somewhat distantly, with reporters, he had established a firm position on the media track.

His resignation and the press conference that followed showed Rich-

Excerpted from Arthur T. Hadley, *The Invisible Primary* (Englewood Cliffs, N.J.: Prentice-Hall, Inc., 1976), pp. 47–52. © by Arthur T. Hadley. Published by Prentice-Hall, Inc., Englewood Cliffs, New Jersey 07632, and reprinted by their permission.

ardson at his best. The times were passionate, partisan, and confused; Richardson with his intellectual coolness and dramatic act of integrity showed to advantage. He is a lot better at remaining calm in the eye of a storm than in stirring up a storm, a fact at once both his personal strength and his political handicap. Richardson tends to look uptight. He wears conservatively cut, single-breasted gray suits and shirts with high collars held firm and semistarched about his neck by a retaining device—the tight knotted tie cinching the collar even tighter. As he talks informally, he weaves back and forth as if battered by conflicting pressures. He pauses now and again, puts his head to one side as if listening to the echoes of what he has just said, and finding it both brilliant and unsatisfactory at the same time, smiles.

Beneath this controlled Boston exterior is a passionate subsurface. " I always feel I have Italian blood in me," says Richardson. This stream erupts now and then in temper, humor, and, I suspect, private tears (also in some professionally acceptable watercolors). Richardson seems at times perplexed by the buried romantic, which probably accounts for the tight rein on which he holds himself and his opinions. He appears to have stepped out of a late Tintoretto portrait of some leader of the Serene Venetian Republic: patrician, politically calculating, wise past the point of cynicism, but still passionate.

"Honesty is the best policy. It is important to remember that honesty is not enjoined by morality alone but by the benefits it confers on the practitioner. Honest politics are the best politics. Undoubtedly this reason for proper behavior is not quite as good as a genuine moral conversion but the behavior that results is liable to be quite similar." That's quintessential Richardson. Hardly the stuff to cause the troops to leap from the trenches and storm the presidency. Compare this to Senator Birch Bayh explaining he should win the invisible primary because "I can tell a bad man from a good."

Richardson, starting his campaign in the unseen race nine months after Percy, and from his vantage point as a just-retired attorney general, still made the same assumption about Nixon and Ford. "I thought the odds on Nixon not finishing his term were less than fifty-fifty," said Richardson. He was relaxing while campaigning in Indiana in November '74, the day before the midterm congressional elections—the last day of his own campaign. Richardson felt at the time he resigned that Nixon was innocent of any criminal wrongdoing. "I came slowly to the conclusion over the next three months that there was damaging evidence on the tapes." From the assumption that Nixon would finish his term, Richardson drew the same conclusion as Percy's staff: that Ford would be so tarnished by Watergate as to be defeatable in selected primaries.

So the ex-attorney general set out. He was trying to find "those little random currents of air that successful politicians look for to get up, stay up and get where they want to go." He was also writing a book and delivering a series of lectures to pay his way and cover the office expenses of a secretary and one-man staff, Richard Mastrangelo, who had been with him since his first campaign in Massachusetts. (Does the Italianate subsurface of Richardson account for the number of his close associates who are Italian?)

Even as he entered the invisible primary, Richardson made two decisions, one personal, the other public, as to his degree of commitment. Personally he decided not to say, "Yes, I'm running" because "I wanted to remain my own man . . . not take that psychological step." Too often he felt the decision to run robbed the candidate of all objectivity. He could no longer tell how his campaign was going, whether he should or should not be in the race.

On the psychological track, Richardson was displaying his usual precise caution. All the candidates and their staff talked about this judgmental problem. Most often they cited the example of George McGovern, whom they saw as a prisoner of his staff and his own ego. Seeing the world out of focus through the eyes of admirers, he was unable to muster his staff to his will.

The second reason for Richardson's tentativeness about his presidential race was political: "to increase my attractiveness as a candidate." He believed more people would be interested in him as a candidate as long as he was not a candidate. He could also be of more help to those GOP candidates for the House and Senate who asked for his aid, and because he was not a candidate but a crusading ex-attorney general, he would draw a bigger audience on the lecture circuit, which was important both financially and politically. This also says something about how the public regards the pride of presidential candidates who are on the prowl for votes through the political veldt.

Throughout his race, Richardson was very careful never to cross that line he had set for himself and become more of a candidate than he intended. Here are a series of his public responses to probings on whether he was a presidential candidate:

"Mr. Richardson, do you want to be President?"

"The only honest answer I can give is that when I've thought about it, which is not often, I don't honestly think I don't want to be President."

"Do you have any plans to run?"

"No, I don't."

"Well, would you like to run if things broke right?"

"I could be persuaded over my natural reluctance; but this does not mean that I am a candidate."

Richardson was asked to speak often; not as often as he had hoped, but enough to keep him out of Washington three or four days a week. If a wise Republican candidate for the Congress wished to divorce himself from President Nixon without kicking the Republican party in the slats, Richardson as featured speaker at a rally was the ideal way. Richardson had remained a loyal Republican. He obviously had no desire to march forward by the light of bridges burning behind him. He always went out of his way to say he couldn't comment on whether the President should or would be impeached since he had been part of the process. "I think impeachment is a matter on which I cannot afford to indulge in personal feelings. It should be approached on the evidence with as little tinge of partisanship as possible." Only the most ardent Nixon partisan could ask for more. Yet he was the man who refused to fire Archibald Cox, who believed: "No man should be above the law," and "we all should live our lives so we would not be afraid to sell our parrot to the town gossip."

On all his campaign swings Richardson kept himself highly organized. In the three hours between an Indianapolis TV appearance and his flight back to Washington, Mastrangelo had arranged a room so Elliot could finish a chapter in his book. Richardson boasts that one night while secretary of defense, he came back to his house overlooking the Potomac at seven, put on his waders, walked a quarter mile to the river, caught a large bass, saw three blue heron, came home, recorded seeing the heron, showered, shaved, got into a black tie for dinner at the Danish embassy, and was in the car with his wife at precisely eight. Traveling with Richardson, I am both jealous and reminded of the nursery rhyme: "How doth the busy little bee, improve each shining hour."

With the degree of noncandidacy that he had chosen for himself, Richardson did not seek commitments of support when out on the road. He was energizing his constituency for future action but not signing up individual members. Candidates and their staffs differ completely on how to go about obtaining political commitments: "pitch and wait" versus "grab and twist." For example, though Senator Jackson is a tough political operator in the Senate, on the road he and his staff believe that only the names of those who volunteer to work should be taken. To twist arms for a commitment, they feel, merely signs up many people who will later only work halfheartedly or perhaps not at all.

On the other hand, Richardson, like Senator Bentsen, is a convinced "grab and twist." Based on his campaigns for attorney general and lieutenant governor of Massachusetts, he is convinced that after you make your speech you have to force those in the audience you want with you to make a public declaration of support. "The average amateur politician," Richardson holds, "once they have made a public commitment, will stick with you even at some detriment to themselves." (Terror kept me from asking what the average professional politician would do after publicly pledging himself.) But for this noncampaign, while Richardson would accept the names of volunteers who offered to help, he made no arm-twisting grabs.

Richardson claims that he enjoys campaigning, pressing the flesh, meeting different people. Well, maybe. He doesn't exactly radiate bonhomie. Asked for some moments of joy during one year of the invisible primary, he cited a fund raiser in Salem, Massachusetts, where he got to dance with a great many beautiful women in evening dresses. He is a superlative dancer—the Italian in the Brahmin again? Probably Richardson enjoys in the abstract the idea of campaigning as part of his concept of "being of service."

. . . .

Successful politician that he was, Elliot Richardson managed to stay airborne on the winds of his Watergate firing for some time. But his lack of political base made him vulnerable on many of the invisible primary tracks, even on media, where he was at his best. Between 1936 and 1972, 90 percent of those rising high enough in public esteem to be considered by the polls as possible presidential candidates have been political office-holders, or else linked to public affairs in some fashion by their job, such as a military officer. Richardson had no job. This handicapped him on the staff and psychological tracks as well as with the media.

Without a political base a man has to be continually careful not to cross that thin dividing line between serious candidate and kook—a line quite a few of the candidates crossed in the period 1972–76. After all, any one of us could call up our local TV stations and newspapers tomorrow and announce that we were running for the presidency. This might disturb our families, but it would not cause much disturbance on the body politic. Constituency, media, and public must perceive the candidacy as reasonable.

For example, in 1968, before either Senator Gene McCarthy or Robert Kennedy had decided to challenge President Lyndon Johnson's Vietnam policies, General James M. Gavin, then chairman of the board of Arthur D. Little, Inc., courageously planned to campaign in New Hampshire as an antiwar candidate. Gavin, because of his past public life and candor on vital issues, enjoyed, like Richardson, a credibility with the press that was close to unparalleled for a private figure. The media were anxious to find someone of stature who opposed the Vietnam War. Yet there were actions Gavin could not take—such as leaving his job to campaign for a month in New Hampshire—that would have come naturally for a political figure.

Running for President, a private individual has to be very careful not to fracture his credibility. And if broken, like Humpty Dumpty's shell, all of Madison Avenue's horses aren't going to be able to put it back together again. ("That Van Lingo Wombatt is nothing but a nut.") Richardson would joke about the strain this need for constant caution caused him, referring to the Doonesbury cartoon which had him refusing to rake leaves around his house because he is going to look for a job tomorrow. However, his laughter didn't always successfully mask the genuine effects of his problem.

Toward the end of his campaign Richardson felt the batterings of depression. "I don't know where I'm going to live, much less what I am going to do," he said, flying into Indianapolis. "For the first time in my life I am in doubt." He talked about how hard and tiring the work had been. "The crucial and most exhausting moment in any campaign is when the candidate is trying to get his campaign off the ground and that is usually in the preprimary stage."

He also talked in those last weeks a great deal about death and about chance, which he felt had played a crucial part in his life. "I'm trying to live each day as if this very minute were my last. . . . I don't know what it's like to have nothing to do. I mean nothing I have to do." He felt each time that he got onto an airplane that the flight might well end in death. Dropping out of the icy turbulence of the ILS approach to Cincinnati brought into view a large billboard which asked: "Are you ready for Jesus?"

"Hardly reassuring," said Elliot, cinching his seat belt tighter.

Speaking on the political chaos that lack of trust in government creates, he began to repeatedly use a new, and unusual for him, highly personal metaphor. "Have you ever thought to wake in the middle of the night and wonder if the floor between the bed and the door will hold your weight?"

"Have you recently, Elliot?"

No reply, just a slight pause and inclination of the head. As one who now and again wakes in terror not knowing where I am, I sympathize.

In the end his absence of a constituency, plus the chance he so believed in, combined to make the continued Richardson campaign impossible. Once Ford became President and appointed Nelson Rockefeller as Vice-President, Richardson felt that in continuing in the invisible primary he would merely be splitting the liberal Republican vote and so opening the party up to Ronald Reagan. He withdrew. Only for him there was a final irony.

Belatedly realizing that his staff, which had been barely marginal for a Vice-President, was totally inadequate for a President, Gerald Ford called NATO Ambassador Donald Rumsfeld back from Paris to be his chief of staff. The two men had been friends when Rumsfeld had been a Republican congressman from Illinois. Having no place to stay when he first got back to Washington, Rumsfeld moved in with another old friend, Senator Charles Percy. One can only guess what they talked about late at night, two gung-ho midwestern liberal Republicans, either of whom might replace Nelson Rockefeller in '76 as Vice-President. But there was that other guy around, Richardson.

On December 6, Richardson, at his desk working on his book, was called on the phone by Kissinger and offered the post of ambassador to Great Britain. Surprised, Richardson said he would think it over. Four days later the two men met again late at night. Richardson meanwhile had checked around and found that none of the jobs he would have preferred—like being reappointed attorney general—was open to him. So after being reassured by Kissinger that he would have a "substantive effect on policy" and not just sit around and entertain, Richardson took the ambassadorship. He felt that seemed preferable to "marginally trying to keep alive a candidacy."

A year later, as the invisible primary was drawing to its close, Richardson would return to Washington and a new cabinet post. By that time it would be too late to revive what was left of his candidacy. He would, to be sure, remain a Republican vice-presidential possibility, and that could be important for the future. But there was now no hope that history would remember 1976 as the Year of Elliot Richardson.

Democratic Hopefuls Live Off the Land

BY CHRISTOPHER LYDON

Money is a "real problem," Jimmy Carter concedes cheerfully. With a campaign payroll grown suddenly to 18 men and women, Mr. Carter has to raise $2,000 a day, on the average, to stay even. He is managing to do just that, but he has no cash reserve yet. He got only $30,000 back on his first $50,000 investment in direct-mail fundraising, so he makes a lot of personal appeals for money these days and misses no opportunity in his travels to schedule paid lunches and receptions.

Then again, money has *always* been a problem for candidates. The more surprising news of midsummer 1975 is probably the ability of underdog, "have-not" candidates like Jimmy Carter, the peanut-farming former Governor of Georgia, to hustle, improvise, live leanly off the land and survive.

A many-winged coalition of plaintiffs—from Human Events, Inc. and Senator James L. Buckley of New York on the right, to former Senator Eugene J. McCarthy and liberal "angel" Stewart Mott on the left—is still hoping to overturn in court the multitude of new restrictions Congress has

Christopher Lydon, "Democratic Hopefuls Live Off the Land," *The New York Times*, July 13, 1975, Section IV, p. 3. © 1975 by The New York Times Company. Reprinted by permission.

placed on political fundraising. One of the central arguments against the new law is that its $1,000 limit on individual contributions to a candidate makes it tough for any unconventional candidate to get started. However, among the numerous candidates, conventional or otherwise, in the Democratic field already, none are complaining about the new rules of the game.

Jimmy Carter, typically, expresses some philosophical sympathy with the constitutional arguments against the new law, including the charge, for example, that a $1,000 limit on contributions abridges the "free speech" of people who want to give more. But as a practical matter, he is delighted with the new arrangements, with the promise of Federal matching funds, in reach if not yet in hand, and with the limit on what the "have" candidates can get from their private backers.

The conspicuous "haves" are Senators Henry M. Jackson of Washington and Lloyd M. Bentsen Jr. of Texas, the former with more than $1-million in the bank at the moment. Governor George C. Wallace of Alabama claimed months ago to have raised the $1,000 in small, scattered contributions to qualify for public matching funds at the start of next year. Representative Morris K. Udall of Arizona celebrated passing that qualifying mark a few weeks ago. Completing that first round of fundraising— $5,000 in gifts of $250 or less in each of 20 states—is the new pseudo-event in Presidential politics. It is a threshold of credibility. Or as former Governor Terry Sanford of North Carolina, far back in the money race, commented sourly several weeks ago, the event confers "a kind of license to practice" in the big time.

A Set of Tactics

But rich, poor or in-between, the candidates all say they welcome the new rules and can adapt to them. Former Senator Fred Harris of Oklahoma, a relative pauper, illustrates the process best. Bankrolled by Wall Street but quickly busted in his first "populist" campaign for the Presidency four years ago, he has lasted longer in his second effort, toward 1976, on what amounts to nickels and dimes. "We're not hurting for money," he says, "because we're not paying people much. And I've got the best staff now I've ever had."

Beyond that more studied focus on money, two important tactical processes mark the Carter campaign following the end of its first six months— just a year now away from the Democrats' nominating convention.

The first is decentralization. Five young men, nearly a third of the Carter staff, are now based outside the Atlanta headquarters area, dropping pebbles in far-flung waters and trying to turn ripples into waves. Knox Pitts, for example, an idealistic soldier of fortune from Nashville, took an apartment in Greenwich Village last month; his mission is to start soaking up Manhattan money and, by testing well-wishers with practical assignments, to turn a loose file of 600 nominal supporters into a cadre of perhaps 50 local captains of the Carter campaign in New York State. His full-time counterparts are working from Tallahassee, Albuquerque, Los Angeles, and Concord, N.H.

The second is a strategic concentration of political energies being invested in three early states in the delegate-selection process: Iowa, New Hampshire and Florida, where Jimmy Carter will either lick his obscurity problem early next year or start a fast, final fadeaway.

Selecting the right testing grounds can be critical: then-mayor John V. Lindsay of New York gambled everything on the Florida primary in 1972—and lost. But Jimmy Carter thinks Iowa's January caucuses were made for his organizers. Winning the New Hampshire primary, says Knox Pitts dreamily, "might get you on the cover of *Time* magazine." The Florida primary will be Armageddon against Mr. Wallace, who won that round big against a split field in 1972.

Jimmy Carter has survived this far without benefit of a platform or a definable "issue." Yet for most of the Democratic party the "politics of character" has displaced the politics of issue positions, and Mr. Carter fares well by the new standard among people who have met him. An interesting variety of Democrats keep saying they are impressed and a little surprised by Jimmy Carter.

The Rev. James Wall, editor of *The Christian Century* and an insurgent member of Illinois' Democratic State Central Committee, says that "issue-oriented" suburbanites around Chicago have found him "anything but a Southern politician." At one meeting this month, Mr. Wall said, "Scientists from the Argonne National Laboratory were pressing him on energy and nuclear warfare—questions I didn't even understand—and they were very much impressed with his answers. We don't want a pure left candidate this time," he said, "as much as we're looking for ability and character. The fact that Jimmy Carter has run a state as big as Georgia counts for something."

Max Palevsky, the Xerox millionaire from Los Angeles who backed George McGovern in 1972, says, "I'm impressed. He's intelligent; he's hard working. I learned the hard way that a politician's character is more important than his issue positions." Matthew J. Troy, the finance committee chairman of New York's City Council, was surprised how well Jimmy Carter was received in Queens.

But there is a catch and perhaps a warning behind each of those fairly typical endorsements: Supporters are drawn to a candidate for their own purposes, and their purposes are not exactly Mr. Carter's.

Mr. Wall, whose local interest is bucking the organization of Chicago Mayor Richard J. Daley, is looking for a candidate daring enough to spearhead a challenge against the mayor's slate of delegates. Max Palevsky feels that liberals are compelled to support any plausible alternative to George Wallace in the Southern primaries, but it is unclear whether he sees Jimmy Carter as a serious candidate for the Presidency or as cannon-fodder against the Alabama Governor. Matty Troy says openly that he sees Jimmy Carter as Vice Presidential material—as a Southern consolation prize to Wallaceites who might inevitably be disappointed at the Democratic convention.

Those are hardly evil reasons for encouraging Jimmy Carter. But they suggest why it is much too soon to say how Jimmy Carter is doing. It is still too soon to say even that he—or any candidate—is the master of his own destiny.

CHAPTER 3

The Institutional Environment

·A·

Delegate-Selection Rules: Primaries and Conventions, New and Old

Democratic Delegate Rules Influencing Candidates' Strategies

BY MICHAEL J. MALBIN

After 1972, no one can dispute the potential importance of party rules to presidential nominations. By the time the cigar smoke had cleared away and the hot television lights had been turned off on the opening night of the Democratic National Convention, delegates supporting the candidacy of Sen. George McGovern, D-S.D., had won two critical credentials challenge votes that set the tone for the days that followed.

First, the convention overturned a credentials committee vote to strip McGovern of 151 of California's 271 votes by imposing proportional representation on the winner-take-all primary a month after the vote.

The convention then voted to uphold the credential committee's unseating of 59 Illinois delegates controlled by Chicago Mayor Richard J. Daley because Daley had violated 1972 guidelines prohibiting slate-making behind closed doors and because he did not have "enough" women, youth and minorities in his delegation.

Democratic Rules Changes.   Reforms in the Democratic delegate selection rules since 1972 have made such slate-making legal again. They also outlaw mandatory quotas and prohibit winner-take-all primaries.

Excerpted from Michael J. Malbin, "Democratic Delegate Rules Influencing Candidates' Strategies," *National Journal,* June 6, 1975, pp. 1664–1672. Reprinted by permission of the *National Journal.*

In other words, if the 1976 party rules had been in effect in 1972, McGovern might have had 210 fewer delegates from Illinois and California. In addition, if the 1976 primary schedule had been in effect—with the New York primary coming early instead of last—it is unlikely that McGovern would have captured nearly the entire state delegation without opposition.

Add McGovern's 252 New York delegates to the contested ones from California and Illinois and the total reaches 462, almost one-third the number needed for the nomination. Without these delegates, McGovern might not have been his party's nominee. It is no wonder then that this year's candidates are paying close attention to the details of the rules and to the calendar in planning their preconvention campaigns.

GOP.   The Republican Party had much calmer conventions in 1968 and 1972 than did the Democrats, and it has been far less deeply affected by the trend toward party reform. While the Democrats between 1972 and 1976 set up a national body, the Compliance Review Commission, to enforce national standards on state delegate selection procedures, Republicans refused to reverse the long-standing view of the party as a federation of state organizations that largely can set their own rules.

Nevertheless, Republican candidates are not unaffected by the new rules procedures. The new primary dates affect both parties equally. Similarly, the increased number of primaries—many of which were instituted by states wanting to sidestep the intricate Democratic rules for convention systems—affects President Ford and Ronald Reagan every bit as much as it does the 10 declared Democratic candidates.

. . . .

Primaries

The most significant by-product of the Democratic rule changes has been the rapid increase in the number of primaries. Twenty-nine states are holding primaries in 1976, compared with 23 in 1972 and 17 in 1968. The Democratic parties in two additional states, Connecticut and Louisiana, will run primaries of their own in 1976. According to information compiled by the Compliance Review Commission, approximately 75 per cent of the delegates to the 1976 convention will be chosen in primaries.

Numbers.   The number of primaries has different effects on the chances of different candidates. Most people active in presidential politics agree that the emphasis on primaries helps those candidates who are relying on a devoted following, frequently a minority, to run against a party organization or an incumbent. McGovern in February 1972 said that Sen. Edmund

S. Muskie of Maine would have the Democratic nomination sewn up if the choice was up to the party leaders. Similarly, the supporters of former Gov. (1967–75) Ronald Reagan, R-Calif., and Wallace feel that the proliferation of primaries is what gives their campaigns life. Wallace's campaign slogan, "Trust the People," is meant to emphasize this. "I have never met a Wallace supporter who ever has been to a party function, let alone a caucus," Wallace aide Griffin said. "They're literally afraid, they don't know what to expect, and they don't know parliamentary procedure."

Proportional Representation.   While the number of primaries has increased, the importance of any one primary to Democratic candidates has been decreased by the abolition of winner-take-all primaries. "California no longer is the big mother delegation" since it dropped its winner-take-all Democratic primary for proportional representation, Siegel said. But California kept its winner-take-all Republican primary, which it could do under that party's rules. It remains the "big mother delegation" for the GOP, as Ford's frequent trips to the state show.

Most campaign workers are unwilling or unable to say whether their chances are helped or hindered by proportional representation, "loophole" or winner-take-all primaries. The Wallace campaign was an exception. Wallace's campaign manager, Charles S. Snider, said he thought proportional representation "put him [Wallace] in the ball game. We think he's good for a portion of the vote in all 50 states, and obviously this will give him more delegates than he would have had." Snider said Wallace would lose some delegates in a state like Florida, where he was able to win all but two of the delegates in 1972 with 42 per cent of the vote, but he expects that he will more than make up for the loss in California.

Timing.   Most other candidates are more concerned about the timing of the primaries than the types. They see the primary season as a time for building momentum in the public eye from one primary to the next, and they see this as being more important to their success than any marginal differences in the number of delegates they may take out of any given state.

This is especially true of the four Democrats competing to be the candidate of the party's liberal wing—Sen. Birch Bayh of Indiana, former Oklahoma Sen. (1967–73) Fred Harris, 1972 vice presidential candidate Sargent Shriver and Rep. Morris K. Udall of Arizona.

"To a curious extent," Bayh's political coordinator Ann F. Lewis said, proportional representation "hasn't mattered yet." Harris's national coordinator agrees. "I don't think it makes much of a difference in terms of his chances," James A. Hightower said. "You can end up outsmarting yourself" if you worry too much about these things.

Impact.   Others who are not associated with a campaign are more than willing to comment on the likely impact of proportional representation.

"Wallace is stronger under proportional representation," Alan Baron said. "But generally, whatever rules help Wallace help Harris, [Eugene J.] McCarthy [in 1968] or McGovern [in 1972]. The conflict over the rules is not between liberals and conservatives, but between majorities and minorities. And who knows who's establishment and who's insurgent? In half of the states this year, Jackson is an insurgent."

One effect of proportional representation may be to keep candidates in the race longer, especially if they can get federal funds to keep their campaigns alive. "Proportional representation is cheap and it encourages candidates to stay in," Siegel said. "A lot of these candidates are looking to be kingmakers or number two." Lewis partly confirmed this by saying that proportional representation means that "I don't want to close the door on any state. I want to keep a much wider range of options open."

Despite this, Fraser said, "I think the impact of proportional representation is likely to be relatively small" because of the party's acceptance of the loophole primary. Siegel agreed, saying that "a majority of the primaries are proportional, but not a majority of the delegates selected."

Caucuses.   The Democratic proportional representation requirement extends to caucus-convention systems as well as primaries. Under the party's 1976 rules, the preferences of those who participate at every level of the process, from the precinct level on up, must be reflected fairly at the next higher level.

Party activists are divided in their estimates of what proportional representation will do to party organizations. "Regulars" tend to think it forces unnecessary confrontations by requiring potential delegates to declare their presidential preferences at precinct meetings, which may occur too early for them to form solid opinions. "It just creates unnecessary divisions," John Perkins of the AFL-CIO's Committee on Political Education said.

Fraser, on the other hand, thinks proportional representation can help strengthen local party organizations by lowering the stakes. "It doesn't create mortal enemies," Fraser said, "and it helps create a modest degree of cohesion."

In either case, there is general agreement that proportional representation in a caucus-convention system is likely to produce votes for fewer minority candidates than it will in a primary. "It's the intensity of feeling. You have to have strong feelings to go to a caucus," Siegel said.

Changing the Rules during the Campaign: Delegate Selection

Democrats Alter Wisconsin Vote

BY CHARLES MOHR

The Democratic Party stretched its own rules today to make the Wisconsin Presidential primary election on April 6 a binding test that will select 68 national convention delegates as well as serving as a popularity contest for Presidential candidates.

The move could help Representative Morris K. Udall of Arizona, a leading liberal candidate, by giving him a chance to win a meaningful primary on the same day that New York State holds a primary election in which Senator Henry M. Jackson of Washington is believed to have a strong position.

But one disturbed Democrat called the Wisconsin decision an example of "selective enforcement" of party rules and said it could prove to be a "Pearl Harbor" for the entire liberal wing of the party if Mr. Udall's strength in Wisconsin has been overestimated.

The Democratic Compliance Review Commission voted 18 to 5— against the advice of its own staff and legal advisers—to reverse an earlier ruling that the Wisconsin primary would be a so-called "beauty contest." The earlier ruling was based on the state Legislature's refusal to pass a law bringing the primary into compliance with Democratic Party rules.

Crossover Voting Stays

The Wisconsin Assembly voted 60 to 36 today to comply partly with Democratic Party rules by allotting national convention delegates proportionally to candidates on the basis of their popular vote rather than letting the winner take all delegates as in the past. The State Senate is expected to act on the bill next week.

But the Assembly did not vote to end the traditional Wisconsin practice of crossover voting in which a Republican can vote in the Democratic primary and vice versa.

Today's decision could have a direct, perhaps major, impact on the contest for the Democratic Presidential nomination.

In the New Hampshire and Massachusetts primaries Mr. Udall emerged as the apparent leader among liberal contenders. Senator Jackson, former Georgia Gov. Jimmy Carter and Alabama Gov. George C. Wallace are strong among the moderate and conservative voters.

Liberals on the rules compliance body voted to make the Wisconsin primary binding—but were joined by supporters of Governor Wallace and Mr. Carter.

"It is very difficult to justify what we did today," said one Democratic source. "Udall needed a primary he could win and there is no question that some liberals voted the way they did today in the hope of getting a headline in Wisconsin on April 6 to mitigate a Jackson victory in New York the same day."

The liberal expectation could backfire, however. A Milwaukee Journal poll published Wednesday showed Mr. Wallace ahead with 25 percent of those polled, Mr. Jackson second with 18 percent, and Mr. Udall fourth with only 9 percent.

Udall Camp Hopeful

The same poll indicated that total conservative and liberal sentiment was about equally divided at the time the polling was done in early February.

A spokesman for Mr. Udall said, "Our organization in Wisconsin is the best we have any place in the nation" and expressed the hope that Wisconsin could serve again as a liberal springboard as it did in 1972 for George McGovern.

Mr. Udall said in a statement that "progressive Democrats across the nation should be heartened" by today's decision and that without it a "bastion of Democratic Party progressivism would have lost much of its significance."

However, some other analysts thought Governor Wallace, who got 22 percent of the vote in 1972, might win Wisconsin and that it was not impossible that Mr. Jackson could do so. If the latter happened, it would virtually kill liberal hopes to select a nominee this year, one Democrat said.

Gov. Patrick J. Lucey, who came to Washington to argue for the move, said that Mr. Udall "has a lot of work to do" to win Wisconsin.

Until today's vote the plan had been for the primary to be a beauty contest only, with the state's 68 delegates to be selected in county and Congressional district caucuses. Mr. Udall might have won many more delegates in caucuses than he could win in a binding primary, but a victory now would have greater psychological impact.

·C·

Changing the Rules during the Campaign: Finance

U.S. Fund Cutoff Slows Campaigns

BY JOSEPH LELYVELD

Despite the talk of "momentum" in Presidential politics, the campaigns of nearly all the leading candidates have been slowing since the last Federal matching funds were paid out three weeks ago.

Senate and House conferees agreed today on extensive changes in the law governing the 1976 campaign, but the action came too late to permit the restoration before mid-May of Federal subsidies for Presidential candidates.

The one campaign that appears to be proceeding without severe money problems is that of President Ford, whose approval of new legislation is required before his challengers can again get funds from the Federal Election Commission.

With two weeks to go before the Pennsylvania primary, the three leading Democrats are barely meeting operating expenses. None of them have the money to buy significant amounts of television and radio time to influence Pennsylvania voters.

"It's really incredible to think that anyone who can come up with $150,000 now has a good shot at the nomination," said Harold Pearson of Lois Holland Callaway Inc., a New York advertising agency that handles Senator Henry M. Jackson's account.

But, with the $1,000 limit on campaign contributions by individuals still in force, it is necessary to find a minimum of 150 donors to raise that kind of money. Increasingly, the candidates are being diverted from the campaign trail to help with fund-raising. Senator Jackson's schedule, for instance, calls for him to spend most of Thursday in a hotel room in Philadelphia making appeals to likely contributors.

The Senator once said that his financial resources would enable him to pull ahead of his rivals at this stage of the campaign. But this evening he was scheduled to spend 2 hours 15 minutes traveling by car from Wilkes-Barre to a Philadelphia suburb because he could not afford a chartered plane for his party.

Money problems have also led to a second reorganization in less than three months of Representative Morris K. Udall's campaign. Until this week his campaign was managed by a Boston consulting firm headed by John Marttila. The firm, which also prepares Mr. Udall's television and radio ads, has been urging that the Arizonan concentrate his resources on a media campaign in Pennsylvania.

Its argument is that Pennsylvania is so large a state that a major organizational effort would not be effective in a short campaign.

But Stewart L. Udall, the candidate's brother who holds the title of campaign manager, said today that the extent of the Pennsylvania advertising effort was likely to remain an open question until the campaign's final week.

"If we can't do anything else," he said, "we'll use a radio commercial that Julian Bond has recorded for us." Mr. Bond, a member of the Georgia legislature, has repeatedly questioned the liberal credentials of Jimmy Carter, the state's former Governor who is also seeking the Democratic Presidential nomination.

Cash Needed for Telecasts

The Carter campaign is the only one that has prepared new television commercials for Pennsylvania and set up a schedule for broadcasting them on local stations. But the money to pay for that television time has yet to be raised, and if it is not on hand by the end of the week, the commercials will have to be canceled, since no stations give credit to candidates.

Gerald Rafshoon, the head of the Atlanta advertising firm that prepares the Carter material, said that three new 60-second commercials were shot in Atlanta today. Each was designed to give the candidate's detailed stand on an issue to overcome the accusation that his position is fuzzy. Mr. Rafshoon said that it would cost $160,000 to televise the full schedule he had drawn up.

The campaign spending law removed a number of options that were available to candidates four years ago. Senators George McGovern and Hubert H. Humphrey both borrowed heavily to sustain their campaigns when funds were short. Now loans from individuals are subject to the same $1,000 limit as contributions; loans from banks, the election commission has ruled, have to meet the standards of ordinary commercial transactions; that is, they must be secured by collateral or related to a candidate's credit rating.

Cost of Carter Jet

The Carter campaign obtains a bank loan every month to keep the candidate's chartered 727 jet in the air. The loans are secured by payments anticipated from the news organizations whose correspondents regularly travel with Mr. Carter and from the Secret Service. Further loans would have to be secured by Mr. Carter's own property.

The difference between 1972 and 1976 is seen in a comparison of the spending by candidates. Senator McGovern spent $440,000 to win the Wisconsin primary in 1972, according to figures compiled by Herbert E. Alexander for a forthcoming book, *Financing the 1972 Election.*

Mr. Udall, who was the big spender in Wisconsin this year, spent $300,000, roughly twice what Mr. Carter spent. Prices have risen about 50 percent in the intervening four years, so the contrast is even sharper than it appears at first glance. In all, Senator McGovern spent $12 million on his way to the Democratic nomination; it now appears unlikely that any of the Democrats will spend even half that amount in 1976.

Friction and Competition

As funds dwindle, plans are canceled and egos hurt, and friction in campaign organizations tends to increase. Yesterday, for instance, the Jackson effort almost came to a standstill as a result of long-simmering personality and policy differences between members of the Senator's campaign staff and members of his Senate staff. After a day of meetings, the campaign staff reportedly won the authority that it had sought, to make the basic decisions on the allocation of scarce resources.

Cuts in advertising budgets force the candidates to compete more aggressively for exposure on local and network TV news shows. The result is that the candidate's time is largely used up in the pursuit of "visuals"— that is, settings—that will attract the TV cameras.

"I think you'll see a lot of people going down coal mines in Pennsylvania next week," a Jackson staff man said.

·D·

Changing the Rules after the Campaign

Confrontation at Miami

BY THEODORE H. WHITE

The central problem of the critical dispute is to decide what makes a majority of this 1972 convention. The convention counts 3,016 votes. Specifically, however, what will be a majority when the convention roll-call comes to California? If McGovern can vote all the 271 delegates he won in California, then he is virtually assured of nomination by the absolute majority of 1,509 on the first nominating roll-call. But if the rip-off decision of the Credentials Committee is sustained by the convention, then he will be stripped of the 151 California votes handed over to the coalition and now in dispute. Thus the question: How large a majority will it take to reverse the Credentials Committee by appeal? Should it be an absolute majority of all delegates—1,509? Or should it be a majority of those eligible to vote on the floor? And does this phrase "eligible to vote" exclude the 120 certified California McGovernites as well as the 151 in dispute?

The arithmetic of this inside story, on which may hang the nomination, is immensely complicated. But not at Stearns's desk. He has for weeks been computerizing all delegates to the convention by nineteen variable personal characteristics. He knows how many McGovern has for certain; how many of the coalition delegates are wavering because the California steal is too raw for their stomachs; how many more delegates can be reached if McGovern makes specific details with their leaders. Stearns is quite confident. On his yellow pad he has marked in blue 1,442 votes frozen for McGovern, another 187 coalition votes disturbed by conscience, a possible 106 more than can be reached by deals.

All weekend the pressure on these elastic numbers has been building

Excerpted from Theodore H. White, *The Making of the President 1972* (New York: Atheneum Publishers, 1973), pp. 170–176. Copyright © 1973 by Theodore H. White. Reprinted by permission of Atheneum Publishers.

and pulsing at the Doral-Fontainebleau pivot. At the Fontainebleau, National Committee Chairman Larry O'Brien must decide how he will arrange the arithmetic—who votes on which challenges, what constitutes a majority, what sequence of parliamentary maneuvers he will accept on Monday night for the sudden-death balloting on the credentials of members in dispute.

It is a moment of passage. What is about to follow is the final maneuver of the McGovern army, a virtuoso exercise in parliamentary tactic, the final investment prior, some would say, to the sacking of the Democratic Party. There are few real professionals in the battlefield of national conventions. The experience of a county or state party chairman in no way prepares him for the forces deployed, the maneuvers required or the overwhelming pressure of public attention at a quadrennial national convention. National conventions are like moon landings—there are too few contested conventions in a lifetime to train operational masters. Young men who devote themselves exclusively to a study of such conventions can achieve a grasp on their dynamics easily as complete as that of the so-called pros; and if rare opportunity offers them a chance to practice their study, they can make old pros look like stumblers. This opportunity was now offered Rick Stearns—and he was to mount a classic of convention warfare, a Battle of Tannenberg in which he was to be the young Hindenburg.

At 4:30 in the afternoon of Sunday, July 9th, the day before the convention is to meet, the command gathers in Gary Hart's suite on the seventeenth floor of the Doral. They are seven: two women, Ann Wexler and Jean Westwood; two of the field commanders, Eli Segal and Harold Himmelman; one black, Congressman Walter E. Fauntroy; Hart himself in gray denim pants, high cowboy boots, flower-blue open-necked shirt; and Rick Stearns. They are waiting for Frank Mankiewicz, who is attending the decisive meeting at the Fontainebleau Hotel in the bedroom of party counsel Joseph A. Califano, who is telling the staffs of all the contenders how Larry O'Brien, the chairman, plans to rule on votes, majorities, disputes.

Mankiewicz, in rumpled gray seersucker suit, bustles in, a smile erasing the fatigue lines of his face, ebullient. He starts reportorially, "Unless my brains have left me, we've just won California." Then, being unable to resist coloring the scene he has just left, " . . . it broke up with twenty-three out of twenty-four guys in the room rushing to the phone, all of them in a rage at Califano and Max Kampelman [Humphrey's spokesman] shaking his finger. Kampelman was trembling with anger, saying to Califano, 'Joe, my principal instructs me to say that yours is a hostile act in response to intimidation and pressure.' "

Then to business, for no time can be wasted. Mankiewicz explains: O'Brien will rule that McGovern's 120 certified California delegates will be allowed to vote on the California challenge; but the 151 coalition Californians, under challenge themselves, will not. On all challenges, a majority will mean a majority of those present, eligible and voting. So far, simple. But the parliamentary complications are mind-boggling. The coalition will certainly appeal this ruling of the chair, and McGovern's people must be ready to sustain the chair. Their point of maximum strength will be on the California challenge—on that vote the 151 coalition Californians will be barred. But California is to be fifth on the agenda of appeals; and so strategy evolves. Nothing must give the coalition an opportunity to appeal or overturn the chair's ruling, and set a precedent, before the convention gets to California. The team must find a way to scuttle, compromise or eliminate all other challenges until California comes up.

Which raises the matter of South Carolina. South Carolina is not only first on the agenda of seating challenges, but it is the chosen battleground of the Women's Political Caucus, whose leaders wish to challenge the Credentials Committee's seating of 20 of 32 delegates from South Carolina. By the chair's ruling which Mankiewicz has just explained, a majority of those eligible to vote on this challenge is a majority of 1,499 (i.e., total delegate votes = 3,016; minus 20 disputed = total eligible, 2,996; divided by two for majority = 1,499). But supposing the floor majority for the women falls between this figure of 1,499 and the absolute majority of 1,509? And supposing then there is an appeal of the chair's ruling on what constitutes an absolute majority? What then? Has the coalition enough votes to overturn the chair's ruling on South Carolina and set a precedent for the later challenge on California—that decision must come by an absolute majority of all 1,509? The higher mathematics of the parliamentary conversation approaches Einsteinian complexity. But one point is clear: If the voting on South Carolina falls somewhere in the mystery zone of 1,499 to 1,509, there is peril.

"We can't afford to fall in that magic number zone," says someone. Comment, mutter. Nor can they afford to risk an appeal on the black-caucus challenge in Alabama or Georgia. It is obvious that the women's cause must be betrayed on the South Carolina challenge; all know that this will infuriate them. "We have 150 women out of our 1,500 votes who love women more than they love McGovern," warns Rick Stearns. "You mean," comes another voice, "we risk losing the blacks on Alabama, the women on South Carolina?" Another voice: "Our narrow interest is to see that we win California and Daley loses Illinois." Then Eli Segal, summing it up: "This means we've got to balance the psychological cost of losing South Carolina against the need of carrying California."

The meeting moves easily, smoothly, to decision: How strictly can control of vote be exercised? How many McGovern votes can be persuaded to vote *against* the women's caucus in South Carolina so as to make sure, by defeat, that the critical challenge does not come up until California? "Let's get at least one delegation that can go both ways," says someone; then it becomes two or three delegations, four delegations they need that can go both ways. The Humphrey people are smart, they'll be tossing votes our way, we have to toss votes their way—we can't risk a floor appeal until California.

"This whole thing is bottomed on floor discipline," says Hart to Stearns, who is in command of the floor controls and floor captains. Stearns nods, quite unworried, like a wing commander confident of his flight's performance in combat. "Rick," repeats Hart quietly, "this means you'll be under intense pressure tomorrow night—we have to field a team with nineteen sophomores out of twenty-two on the squad, and we go up against Nebraska." Stearns nods again. They are all now giving advice to Stearns, who will be calling signals from the command wagon as his floor captains play basketball with the votes against Humphrey's men. "They've got to be drilled, Rick—in California they've got to follow Willie Brown, in New York they've got to follow Crangle."

So they are going to plan to lose on South Carolina, and the conversation turns to the politics of the outside world, and of television. "Well, if we're going to stake the organization on South Carolina, what'll we do if Walter Cronkite says on CBS it's a test of strength for McGovern and we're losing? What do we do about tipping Walter off?" and they play the game of how fully television should be informed of the maneuver. At this point, this observer decided to leave the room, being caught in a conflict of interests which might require him to spoil in public on air the game that was theirs to play.

Walking down from the Doral, back to the Fontainebleau, reflection on the meeting began to pucker into a question. There could be no doubt that the staff command was right—if McGovern was to be nominated, then the California vote was critical and the outcome on South Carolina would determine that. Besides, the women's caucus had no real case to present on South Carolina, except the case of power. Right was right, wrong was wrong; in scuttling the women on South Carolina the McGoverns were morally clean, just as they were in fighting for their rights in the battle on California. Yet, on the other hand, McGovern had promised the Women's Political Caucus just the day before that we would support them all the way on South Carolina. The women would be furious at the unfurling of events tomorrow and would scream betrayal—but who betrayed them? No answer to that one except, in retrospect, thinking of other leaders like Richard Nixon or John F. Kennedy, it was curious that at this meeting no one had asked what McGovern himself wanted to do about the problem. The staff was making his decisions for him. Nixon or Kennedy would have controlled such a decision, one way or another, and Lyndon Johnson would have imposed himself down to the tiniest detail of the lady-sticking, with relish at the art of vote-manipulation. All three—Kennedy, Johnson, Nixon—knew how to play dirty; *their* staffs knew their leaders sometimes had to play dirty; but when a major dirty was under way, they usually made sure the leader knew of it. This evening McGovern had been absent; he would approve, of course, later. But the operation was under way.

As planned, so it happened the next evening, Monday, July 10th, opening night of the convention—the votes cast, recast, switched and planted; and the Women's Political Caucus challenge to the South Carolina delegation, which McGovern had pledged himself to support, went down in public view, to the mystification of most reporters and public commentators. So, too, was the black challenge on Alabama and Georgia compromised and swept from the agenda. Now, at midnight Monday, it was time for the California challenge which would determine the nomination. And I wandered back from the hall to the McGovern command wagons.

As I came in, they were still chuckling at the public ruse, the private triumph, the hidden-ball tricks of the game; Gene Pokorny was recapping, as after a good hard-fought game, "They threw forty votes our way in Ohio, so we had to toss in a few others. . . . " Frank Mankiewicz was still there, enjoying the scenery, watching the television sets, observing the floor, then, distressed by a McGovern demonstration he viewed on screen, he ordered, "Cut that demonstration." At which all eight young men at the telephones rose, seized their white instruments and passed the command to the floor. "Listen, Irving, this is Harold Himmelman. Two things: stop the demonstrations right now. And no adjournment until after Illinois."

When Mankiewicz had left, to be on the floor when his native California was voted on, one could observe that this operation center contained no one over the age of thirty. Four tables set in U-shape in the air-conditioned trailer wagon bore eight white phones, manned by eight young men. One had seen most of them operate all over the country—Pokorny, Segal, Smith, Clinton, O'Sullivan, Swerdlow, Himmelman. At the floor end of their phones now were much older people, of more presence and larger prestige, Governors, Senators, Congressmen, captains of a floor area of the convention. But the power to manipulate was here.

The master of the ballet is Stearns, as always relaxed and gently smiling, his sheet of projections before him, his vote count sure as, a few minutes before one o'clock in the morning, O'Brien's face on television says, "The clerk will call the roll."

California leads the roll this time—its 120 McGovern votes vote to unseat the 151 coalition votes. But the South Carolina delegation, seated by McGovern tactics, votes with the coalition ("Who cares?" says one of the table lieutenants). Stearns's sheet of estimates is the measure now, the lieutenants counting pluses or minuses from his estimate. Rhode Island is a break upward of 2 over their projection—all 22 to unseat the coalition ("Son of a bitch, got them all!"). Wyoming comes in at 4.4 ("Up one"). Indiana comes in at 33 ("Up one"). At Wisconsin's 55, the cry is "We're on our way, baby." Vermont comes in at 11 to unseat the coalition ("Up two," says someone, "we're going to cream them"). Then comes the second call of the roll for delegations which had passed. By Virginia, which comes in at 38½, it is all over. Stearns says: "We're going over 1,550. Get the word out, we're 38 ahead of absolute majority, the psychology is starting, get the word to the floor." The phones work; the command wagon presses the floor captains to stampede the rest of the balloting; the final vote is 1,618 to 1,238 to unseat the coalition's 151 California delegates and restore the seats to McGovern; which means that on Wednesday night's balloting the nomination of McGovern is assured.

There comes the anticipated after-test—the appeal to the chair on the nature of the majority just established, as Norman Bie, Jr., of Florida shouts, "This entire vote is contrary to the rules and done in contravention of two points of order." Stearns listens, comments, "Who would have thought that Hubert Humphrey's last hurrah would be a Wallace delegate from Florida making a point of order?" Then he snaps as commander, "Keep everybody in the hall, don't let anyone drift away." He is watching television, commanding the performance. "Get them ready to sustain the chair." Then, watching television, a minute or two later, "Turn them on."

Again comes the sense of ballet. The eight young men rise from their chairs as if drilled to rhythm; each puts a knee on his folding chair and lifts a white phone in a swooping motion. Each speaks to a floor captain who patrols one part of the floor to pass the word to other deputies. And it is all over. The chair is sustained—all California's 271 votes are seated for McGovern. One of the lieutenants snaps to his floor section: "Keep them there, keep them there, we're gonna seat Bill Singer's people in Illinois—all out!"

The smoothness of the performance is reminiscent of something past— of what? The phone in the backroom is ringing, someone leaves to answer, then reports: George McGovern has just called from the Doral before going to sleep: "I just want to thank you. I want to thank everyone, Gary and Rick and Frank and Gene, for the magnificent job you've done. Well, it's been a great night for me, and we just had a little celebration, and I think I'll go to bed." The words are different, but the echo brings reminder. Back there in 1964, in San Francisco at the Cow Palace, Clifton White and Goldwater's argonauts had performed exactly the same ballet, exactly the same exercise, in a trailer wagon laid out on the same floor plan—and had received the same courteous message of thanks from the then prophet in his tower suite at the Mark Hopkins. Goldwater too had confused the politics of a nomination with the politics of American life.

A rule had now been demonstrated twice in a single decade: When a determined and intelligent group of people, energized by moral conviction, sets out to seize control of a major American national party at its convention, it can generally do so. But the impression the rest of the American people get of this seizure, and of its purpose, is as important as the control itself. This the Miami convention was to demonstrate once more.

CHAPTER 4

Strategies and Tactics

A. Planning for a Nomination Campaign

B. Planning during the Campaign: Responses to the Field of Contenders

C. Planning during the Campaign: Responses to the Institutional Environment

·A·

Planning for a Nomination Campaign

Backdrop for 1948

BY IRWIN ROSS

It was one of the ironies—perhaps one of the public relations triumphs—of the 1948 Democratic campaign that it generally gave the impression of being an improvised, desperate effort of an embattled President fighting single-handedly against overwhelming odds. There was no doubt about the desperation of the Democratic campaign, but it was not improvised. Careful planning preceded every step, with the general lines of strategy being articulated as early as the autumn of 1947.

The basic blueprint was contained in a lengthy memorandum on "the politics of 1948," for which Clifford began to gather intelligence and sift ideas in the summer of 1947. The President was all for the project and suggested a variety of individuals to be consulted. When Clifford began his soundings, Truman was hardly the underdog that he became the following year. As already mentioned, his popularity had begun to rise; no one had any reason to predict a revolt in the South and Henry Wallace had not yet declared his candidacy. On the other hand, none of the people around Truman suffered from an excess of optimism. The 1946 debacle was too fresh in memory, the Republicans had many able candidates—Dewey, Stassen, Taft, and Warren being the most prominent—and Henry Wallace, while not an avowed candidate, was certainly a threat.

During 1947, Wallace had been traveling around the country, collecting large audiences for his denunciations of Truman's foreign and domestic policies; many disaffected Democrats had rallied to his cause and he had behind him the not inconsiderable apparatus of the Communist party and the support of those unions in the CIO which the Communists con-

Excerpted from Irwin Ross, *The Loneliest Campaign* (New York: New American Library, 1968), pp. 29–34. Footnotes deleted. Copyright © 1968, by Irwin Ross, reprinted with permission. Reprinted by permission of Russell & Volkening, Inc. as agent for the author.

trolled. Many of Wallace's followers were urging him to run for President in 1948 and he freely scattered hints that he might lead the first major third-party effort since Robert La Follette ran in 1924. A Wallace candidacy was understandably a nightmare to the Truman strategists; many of them refused to believe that in the end he would take the leap.

In mid-November, Clifford presented Truman with a 43-page double-spaced memorandum on legal-size paper. It was a remarkable political document—bold and unambiguous in its analysis of present trends, surprisingly accurate in treating of the future, courageous and not a little cynical in proposing a vigorous course of action for the President in the twelve months leading up to the election.

The memorandum predicted that Thomas E. Dewey would be the Republican candidate, though the contest for the nomination had barely gotten under way; that Henry Wallace would run on a third-party ticket; that President Truman could win even with the loss of the populous states of the East, so long as he held the support of the South and of the West and recaptured the labor vote which F.D.R. had always commanded. Events eventually confirmed each of these judgments.

Clifford was wrong in one prediction: that there would be no break in the South, no matter what program the President presented. "As always, the South can be considered safely Democratic," he wrote. "And in formulating national policy, it can be safely ignored."

He argued that "If the Democrats carry the solid South and also those Western states carried in 1944, they will have 216 of the required 266 electoral votes. And if the Democratic party is powerful enough to capture the West, it will almost certainly pick up enough of the doubtful Middle-western and Eastern states to get 50 more votes. . . . We could lose New York, Pennsylvania, Illinois, New Jersey, Ohio, Massachusetts—all the 'big' states and still win." While Clifford was mistaken in assuming no southern breakaway—the Dixiecrat rebellion in the end lost Truman 39 electoral votes—he was quite correct in stressing the importance of winning the West and in arguing that a victory there presupposed sufficient strength to win some Midwestern states; in the end Truman took Idaho, Iowa, Minnesota, Missouri, Wisconsin—as well as Ohio and Illinois.

Clifford went on to provide a shrewd analysis of the various special interest groups which the Democrats had to attract. Only the farmer "was presently favorably inclined towards the Truman administration"—a judgment which continued to be correct throughout 1948, but which the Republicans somehow failed to appreciate. The farmer's crops were good, Clifford pointed out; he was protected by parity and would be aided by the Marshall Plan. Should he be inclined to defect in 1948, nothing more could be done by way of "political or economic favors" to win back his support. The implication was that only rhetoric could be employed—an exercise in which Truman was never deficient throughout the campaign.

The labor vote was a great imponderable. Clifford flatly asserted that Truman "cannot win without the *active* support of organized labor. It is dangerous to assume that labor now has nowhere else to go in 1948. *Labor can stay home.*" Labor had been "inspired" to vote for Roosevelt, but had largely abstained in the 1946 congressional elections. "The labor group has always been politically inactive during prosperity," Clifford wrote. "The effort to get out the labor vote will thus have to be even more strenuous than in 1944." Much would also have to be done to attract independent liberals, who were not important numerically but exerted a considerable leavening effect on public opinion. "The liberal and progressive leaders are not overly enthusiastic about the administration," Clifford commented with tolerable understatement.

He warned that the Republicans would make a strong appeal for the Negro vote, which had been Democratic since 1932, and foresaw that the Negroes might hold the balance of power in states like New York, Illinois, Pennsylvania, Ohio, and Michigan. "The Negro voter has become a cynical, hard-boiled trader," Clifford suggested, and the Republicans were likely to appeal to his self-interest by offering an anti-poll-tax bill and Fair Employment Practices legislation in the next Congress. Clearly, the Democrats would have to outbid the Republicans in order to hold the Negroes. Truman's civil rights message in February 1948 followed logically from this premise.

Clifford's appraisal of the Catholic vote, which had begun to defect from the Democrats in 1944, turned out to be prophetic: "The controlling element in this group . . . is the distrust and fear of communism. . . . The attitude of the President and the administration toward communism should exert a definite appeal."

Turning to the issues in the campaign, Clifford saw "considerable political advantage to the administration in the battle with the Kremlin." Relations with Russia would probably continue to deteriorate and, as in all times of crisis, the average citizen would tend to rally to his President. As for Republican attacks on the administration's foreign policy, "President Truman is comparatively invulnerable to attack because of his brilliant appointment of General Marshall who has convinced the public that as Secretary of State he is nonpartisan and above politics." On the other hand, the Republicans would probably intensify their efforts to make an issue of Communist infiltration in government. In this area, however, "The President adroitly stole their thunder by initiating his own government employee loyalty investigation procedure."

In the domestic field, Clifford saw high prices and the housing shortage as the most pressing issues to the average citizen. He urged that the President call upon the next session of Congress to enact a maximum anti-inflation program, including mandatory price controls, an ambitious housing program, and tax revisions favoring lower-income groups. The President would offer his program in full awareness that the Republicans would reject it and thus be politically vulnerable. Clifford's strategy could hardly have been more forthright or candidly phrased (this was, after all, a private memorandum): " . . . the Administration should select the issues upon which there will be conflict with the majority in Congress. It can assume it will get no major part of its own program approved. Its tactics must, therefore, be entirely different than if there were any real point to bargaining and compromise. Its recommendations—in the State of the Union message and elsewhere—must be tailored for the voter, not the Congressman; they must display a label which reads 'no compromises.' "

This strategy was designed not only to embarrass the Republicans but to steal Henry Wallace's thunder, for if Wallace drew enough votes, especially in the West, he would defeat Truman. Clifford pointed out that in 1924 the third-party candidate, Robert La Follette, polled more votes than the Democratic candidate in eleven western states. To undercut Wallace's appeal, Clifford urged that at the psychologically correct moment the Communist inspiration behind Wallace's campaign should be denounced by "prominent liberals and progressives—*and no one else.*" But denunciation would not be enough; Truman had to move to the left in order to attract Wallace's followers. An ambitious program of economic measures and civil rights reforms was only part of the strategy which Clifford proposed, for he was worried by Wallace's calling the roll of the many Wall Street figures in the Truman administration—such men as Averell Harriman, Robert Lovett, James Forrestal and William Draper. Clifford saw Wallace appealing "to the atavistic fears of all progressives—the fear of 'Wall Street.' " Clifford urged the President to make "some top level appointments from the ranks of the progressives—in foreign as well as domestic affairs." It was important to make the effort, he argued, even if some of the appointees should not be confirmed by the Senate.

The memorandum deplored the decay of the Democratic party organization, urged that a new chairman be soon appointed to rebuild the party, and that a small working committee be established to coordinate the political program of the administration, provide monthly estimates of the political situation, and begin the drafting of memoranda for the 1948 platform and major campaign speeches. Clifford also stressed the need for close liaison with the labor movement and with independent liberals. In these sections Clifford's memorandum became a fascinating manual on the practical arts of politics at the Presidential level. He urged President Truman personally to cultivate labor leaders, who of late had rarely been seen in the White House. "It is easy for the incumbent of the White House to forget the 'magic' of his office," Clifford explained. But he cautioned that in such private colloquies the President ask advice on "matters in general," for "it is dangerous to ask a labor leader for advice on a *specific* matter and then ignore that advice."

Clifford spent a good deal of space on the problem of refurbishing what he called the President's "portrait" ("image," as a public relations term, had not yet come into general use). He pointed out that most people get their impressions of a President from his activities as Chief of State, but that Truman had been notably reticent in this area, with the consequence that he was largely thought of as a politician. Clifford made a number of proposals whereby the President might correct this distorted view. One of them was to exploit the social resources of the White House, by inviting one or two "nonpolitical personages" for lunch each week; the newspapers would inevitably give these encounters great publicity. Henry Ford II, who was receiving an excellent press as the young head of the Ford Motor Company, was an obvious candidate; Clifford saw considerable popular appeal in "this picture of the American President and the Young Business Man together."

Equally impressive would be a lunch with Albert Einstein, with the President explaining at his next press conference "that they talked, in general, about the *peacetime* uses of atomic energy and its potentialities for our civilization. He can then casually mention that he has been spending some of his leisure time getting caught up with atomic energy"—which would doubtless have acted as a corrective to the common impression that Truman spent much of his leisure time at the poker table. Another way to display his more reflective side to the public would be for the President to suggest to the newsmen "that it would do them no harm at all to read such and such a book (as long as he picked the right one) which he has just read." His staff would have presumably provided the President with an appropriate list.

Clifford also suggested that Truman repeat the nonpolitical "inspection tours" which Roosevelt employed in the 1940 campaign. The problem was that a President could not campaign openly until after the party conventions, yet there was urgent need for him to carry his case to the voters long before the late summer of 1948. F.D.R.'s inspection tours had been marvelously effective. "No matter how much the opposition and the press pointed out the political overtones of those trips," Clifford wrote, "the people paid little attention because what they saw was the Head of State performing his duties." The people were to show a similarly tolerant attitude toward President Truman on his "nonpolitical" coast-to-coast train tour the following June.

Truman read the document carefully and discussed it at length with Clifford. He was in general agreement with the analysis and proposed strategy, although he had little sympathy for the public relations gimmickry to sell the President to the American people. He was not about to turn the White House over to labor leaders with whom he felt little personal rapport or to invite Albert Einstein or Henry Ford to lunch or to nominate prominent liberals to high office in the knowledge that the Senate would knock them down. He found these gestures too obviously synthetic and out of character. On the other hand, the concept of a bold, uncompromising political offensive appealed to him. He subsequently agreed that it would start with the State of the Union message on January 7.

The Democrats: First Stirrings

BY THEODORE H. WHITE

The roots of this meeting lay deep. For three years now, ever since the defeat of Adlai E. Stevenson in 1956, the Kennedy strike for the Presidency had been underway. In the beginning, there had been but two men involved—Kennedy himself, and Ted Sorensen, his alter ego, Sorensen doubling as thinker, writer, contact man, field agent, political fingerman. After the Massachusetts Senatorial victory in 1958, more elaborate machinery had been required and staff began to grow. First Smith had opened Washington base offices. Then O'Brien had transferred to Washington from Massachusetts; then Harris had been launched and Salinger retained; local committees were quietly established everywhere that a possible regional Kennedy base might be of value.

A first survey meeting had taken place long since, in Palm Beach, Florida, on April 1st of 1959. Headquarters space and clerical help had been set up in ten rooms at the Esso Building in Washington in the spring, a quarter of a mile from the Senator's legislative chambers. By fall, Robert Kennedy, having resigned as counsel to the Senate Committee on Legislative Oversight and having also finished his own best-selling book, *The Enemy Within,* was ready to come aboard full time as campaign manager.

This was the meeting that was to see the final assault plans laid; it was to be a meeting for precise definition of functions. At its close, Sorensen, the effective campaign manager up to then, was to become national policy chief, and Bobby Kennedy, operational and practical campaign manager. All these men had been meeting week after week, traveling and reporting to the voluminous files and index system of headquarters for months now. But this was the first time all had gathered at one time away from Washington or New York or Boston or Hartford, away from telephone calls, away from press attention, to consider for a full day not the Yes or No of

Excerpted from Theodore H. White, *The Making of the President 1960* (New York: Atheneum House, Inc., 1961), pp. 53–58. Footnotes deleted. Copyright © 1961 by Atheneum House, Inc. Reprinted by permission of Atheneum Publishers.

the Presidential strike, but the HOW: which levers, in what manner, must be pressed in the American structure of influence and control to bring about the occupation of the White House.

Each of those present remembers one fragment of the meeting, and no one can recall it all. Perhaps Sorensen's memory, for he has an historic memory, is best.

"Meetings are good for information," said Sorensen several months later, "for exchanging information, for clearing the air. Meetings are rarely the source of major decision. The fundamental note that morning, as of earlier meetings down in Palm Beach and in Washington, was the note of confidence. We were confident we knew how it would turn out, that we could meet them and lick them.

"There are no hard-and-fast, dramatic, black-and-white decisions that come out of a meeting like that. What comes out is a firming up of missions, after you decide from the top down what the problems are.

"Now the basic difficulties always boiled down to the facts that the country had never elected a Catholic, that the country had never elected a forty-three-year-old, that the country had only selected one Senator to be President in this century.

"This being true, you had to examine the nominating process, which is not a free open popular vote, but a process which is dominated and influenced by all the groups in the Democratic coalition—the farmers, labor, the South, the big-city people, etcetera. These groups are more influential in a convention than they are in the country as a whole. Therefore he had to prove to them that he could win. And to prove that to them, he'd have to fight hard to make them give it to him, he couldn't negotiate it. If the Convention ever went into the back rooms, he'd never emerge from those back rooms. So it evolved from the top down that you had to go into the primaries."

"From the top down" meant from the lips of the candidate to the attention and obedience of his staff, there assembled.

John F. Kennedy opened the meeting from where he stood, his back to the fireplace, facing the others as they sat, dressed in a sports jacket (which he later doffed), slacks and loafers, looking thoroughly boyish. (His hair was then still cut in the youthful brush cut with which the public was then familiar, later replaced by the more mature side cut of the present President.) He then proceeded to amaze them all by a performance that remains in the memory of all those who listened. Kennedy, who speaks from the platform in a high, resonant, almost melancholy tone of voice, is, in private, one of the more gifted conversationalists of politics, second only to Hubert Humphrey in the ease, simplicity and color with which he talks. On this morning he was at his best.

Now for three hours, broken only occasionally by a bit of information he might request of the staff, he proceeded, occasionally sitting, sometimes standing, to survey the entire country without map or notes. It was a tour of America region by region, state by state, starting with New England, moving through the Atlantic states and the Midwest, through the farm states and the mountain states, down the Pacific Coast, through the Southwest and then the South. "What I remember," says O'Brien, director of organization and keeper of the political ledgers, "was his remarkable knowledge of every state, not just the Party leaders, not just the Senators in Washington, but he knew all the factions and the key people in all the factions."

"We had," says Sorensen, "not only the best candidate there, but the best campaign manager, too. He knows the facts, who likes him and who doesn't, he knows where he should go and where he shouldn't, he has this incredible memory of places, names, dates, who should be written to and who shouldn't."

"He can still drive down an avenue in Boston," adds another, "and remember which stores put up his campaign posters ten years ago."

Now and then Kennedy would pause, ask for comment on a local political situation where one or the other of his staff men had particular knowledge, invite corrections, then go on. By the time he had finished and the group broke for lunch, the strategy had been clarified from the top down, as he saw it and meant to take it.

The nomination had to be won by the primary route. Not until he showed primitive strength with the voters in strange states could he turn and deal with the bosses and the brokers of the Northeast who regarded him fondly as a fellow Catholic but, as a Catholic, hopelessly doomed to defeat. And all the while the primary campaigns were being mounted, attention must be paid to the other states—contacts with the bosses in machine states, citizen committees in states where citizens were effective; and all of this with a projection beyond the Convention, with the organization so tooled that on the day after the Convention it could be converted into election machinery.

There were in all sixteen states of the union that were to hold primaries in 1960 for the choosing of delegates to the national Convention. Some should not be entered for fear of offending favorite sons; some should not be entered because they were unimportant. But of the sixteen, a broad enough number had to be chosen to give a national cast to the campaign, and those chosen had to be of value for their impact on neighboring states and on the big bosses who would be watching. And every primary had to be won—there could be no stumbling. "It has to come up seven every time," said Kennedy later, on the evening of the first contested primary in Wisconsin.

No hard-and-fast decisions on primaries were made at the morning meeting—except for New Hampshire. That had to be entered as the nation's first and as a matter of course. Ten of the other states were put on a list for consideration as opportunity and politics developed during the next few months.

Wisconsin was uppermost in the minds of all at the moment—a big victory there would destroy Hubert Humphrey for good; but Wisconsin was dangerous. Disagreement about Wisconsin was to divide the Kennedy staff for the next two months, until Kennedy, supported only by his father and Lou Harris, overrode his brother and all the others and entered there. There was Maryland, a strong possibility (later accepted); Indiana—interesting (if Stuart Symington could be lured to challenge in the Indiana primary and be wiped out there, it would be worth the effort; Symington, realizing the trap, briefly considered Indiana in the spring and then dodged it); Oregon was unavoidable, for the Oregon laws forced all candidates, willy-nilly, onto the primary ballot; West Virginia was vaguely discussed— no one at the moment could foresee the impact West Virginia would later have; Ohio and California were both special situations—they would depend on Kennedy's own relations with their favorite-son governors, Mike DiSalle and Pat Brown. Kennedy reviewed each of the sixteen primary states; explained the differing primary laws of each state; discarded the hopeless states or states where victory would not be worth the effort; and the morning meeting broke up.

The gathering now trooped across the lawn to the home of old Joseph Kennedy, where the usual hearty Kennedy board offered lunch—roast turkey and several sorts of pie, baked two thicknesses high by the Kennedy cook.

When the meeting reassembled in the afternoon, it reassembled under the chairmanship of brother Bobby. This, too, is a characteristic of Kennedy campaigning. The candidate is not only a flag bearer and leader, he is also a person and a resource. His energy is not to be over-used, as one does not drain a battery more than is necessary. ("We used the candidate perfectly in '58," said one of Kennedy's lieutenants, commenting on the technique of that campaign. "Some days we'd run him through fifteen towns and fifteen speeches and still have him in bed by eleven in the evening. It was perfect use of a candidate—we never wore him out."

The morning's meeting had been analytical and strategic. Now, under Bobby's chairmanship, it was operational, for assignments were to be distributed and the nation quartered up by the Kennedy staff as if a political general staff were giving each of its combat commanders a specific front of operations:

• New England and upstate New York went to John Bailey. New England's 114 Convention votes had to be absolutely solid for the home candidate, and there were slight ripples of disturbance in both Maine (Symington strength) and New Hampshire (Stevenson strength). In addition to New England, Bailey was assigned upstate New York—this was to be a covert over-the-border raid on delegates north of the Bronx county line, to round up all that was loose in the

Empire State before the flabby downstate Tammany leadership realized what was happening.

- New York City and northern New Jersey were not so much assigned as left, by silent understanding, to be worked out by the personal contacts of the candidate, the operations of John Bailey and the private resources of Joseph Kennedy.
- Raskin was to be responsible for the Western states and his native Iowa. Raskin had first come to national prominence in the two Stevenson campaigns. His citizen and organizational contacts in the West were extensive and particularly valuable in the mountain states, Oregon, and California.
- Young brother Ted Kennedy was to join Raskin in scouting the Rocky Mountain states.
- Wallace was to survey and sound out West Virginia, preparing the ground if it were necessary to enter, later, the West Virginia primary.
- Brother Bobby Kennedy, in addition to his general duties, undertook to establish contact with Southern leaders and seek out what friendship he could there as soon as possible.
- O'Brien was to be responsible for drawing up a general master plan of organization and procedure for all states, to insure a standard operational procedure everywhere. In addition, he was to watch Maryland, Indiana and Wisconsin.

This left out such crucial states as Ohio, Pennsylvania, Michigan, California—but these were all states where negotiations had to proceed on a summit basis, between the candidate himself and their "favorite sons." Salinger's work, O'Donnell's work, Harris' work, was general across-the-board staff work. All had taken notes at the long session—detailed notes on their specific assignments, general jottings on the over-all shape of the campaign. Harris, leaving that weekend for a vacation in the Virgin Islands, mentioned his trip casually—he was immediately given two contact men to look up there; after all, the Virgin Islanders had four votes at the Convention. Sorensen, now relieved of the detailed bookkeeping of political contacts and opportunities he had handled for three years, was to mobilize the thinking, the ideas, the speeches and issues of the campaign.

When at 4:30 in the afternoon the meeting finally ended, all were tired. They went out on the lawn and breathed the cold fresh air gratefully, watching the breeze blow the bay into whitecaps. They chatted in groups of twos and threes about their assignments and about the minutiae of politics until the cars came to pick them up and bring them to the Kennedy plane that would drop them off in New York and Washington ready for their new work. It had been a bread-and-butter day, a day of discussion of the nitty, gritty stuff and substance, names and places from which politics in America move; no one remembers any talk of greatness, or any drama, or of any of the perils of the outer world and America. That had happened long since or would come later and was locked in the mind of the candidate.

So, in the darkening afternoon, they were carried away, men with precise, deputized marching orders. Two months and six days later, on January 2, 1960, to the surprise of no one, John F. Kennedy announced to the press that he, too, was a candidate for President of the United States.

· B ·

Planning during the Campaign: Responses to the Field of Contenders

Humphrey's '76 Stance: Willing, But Not Running

BY JOSEPH LELYVELD

Diffidence has never been an obvious political flaw in Hubert Horatio Humphrey. Even now, as a declared noncandidate for the Presidency after three futile tries, he remains an irrepressible and unabashed aspirant.

He is highly and openly delighted by the political handicapping that portrays him as an early frontrunner for the Democratic nomination on the strength of his standing in the polls and gleefully repeats a quip by his Democratic colleague, Senator Gaylord Nelson of Wisconsin, that Mr. Humphrey seems to do better when he is not campaigning than when he is.

But, as a matter of inclination and calculation, Mr. Humphrey appears resolved to hold back from the scramble in the primaries, although it is there that the overwhelming majority of delegates to the Democratic convention will be chosen.

His inclination is to avoid a bruising fight for the nomination in which his Democratic opponents could be expected to discount him as shopworn.

His calculation is that the best chance he has is to stay on good terms with all the active candidates so that in the event of a convention deadlock, they and their delegates will be inclined to turn to him not only as a proven campaigner but also as a unifier and healer.

His strategy—which is, essentially, to be everyone's second choice—

puts him in a special category: He is available as a candidate but is not running.

He has been enjoying a resurgence not only in the polls but also in his influence in the Senate, where he has become, once again, a leading Democratic spokesman on economic issues. Vietnam, a Humphrey albatross in the past, won't figure. Still, a Humphrey candidacy would be the ultimate test of the view that the voters, in a mood of general frustration and alienation, are searching for new faces and leadership styles.

"It may be," Senator Humphrey speculates, "that the best politics for a man in my position is absolutely no politics." Loosely translated, that seems to mean he has little room for maneuver.

In the far-flung circle of friends, backers and Senate colleagues in which he discusses his prospects, there are those who argue that the former Vice President will have to plunge into the primaries at some point in order to have any chance at all.

Some friends sense that his mind is not firmly made up, that he is waiting for the results of the early primaries. Others, who believe that he can't afford to wait that long, are starting to sound discouraged.

"I don't think his present role will lead to the nomination and I don't think he'll change," said Governor Wendell R. Anderson of Minnesota, a Humphrey protegé. "If he's playing a waiting game, he has waited long enough."

The timing of the primaries and their filing deadlines tend to bear out the Governor's analysis. The California primary will be on June 8, but the filing deadline is March 14, five days after the Florida primary, which is only the third primary.

Senator Humphrey knows that if he moves before Florida, he can expect to be castigated as a "spoiler"—as he was four years ago by followers of Senator Edmund S. Muskie—rather than hailed as a unifier. He says he feels morally bound not to play that role.

Humphrey supporters who see the possibility of his entry into the race in early March suggest that his way could be smoothed by appeals from prominent Democrats calling on him to run. Such appeals would be especially effective, they say, if Gov. George C. Wallace of Alabama runs even stronger in Massachusetts and Florida than is now expected, or if a bandwagon for Ronald Reagan gathers momentum on the Republican side.

If Mr. Humphrey waits for the Florida results, he will have already passed the deadlines for New York and Pennsylvania, two states in which he might figure on doing well.

And if he lets the California deadline go by to wait for the results of the New York primary on April 6, he will have time left to file for only four of the 29 primaries now scheduled: Idaho, Kentucky, South Dakota and New Jersey, which together account for barely 12 percent of the number of delegates needed for nomination.

The Senator concludes that running in these late primaries wouldn't make "a bit of difference" to his chances. If he were to go the primary route at all, he says, he would do best to start early and if that were his intention, he goes on, he would need to be laying the groundwork for an organization and fund-raising drive now. That, he points out, is precisely what he has not been doing.

On the contrary, he has made himself available for fund-raising functions so far for six of the announced candidates. A number of his own most dependable financial backers are now formally committed to other candidates. If he tried now to reclaim their loyalty, said S. Harrison Dogole, an old Humphrey loyalist in Philadelphia who is serving as a finance chairman for Senator Henry M. Jackson of Washington, he might find that they have been "pre-empted."

The campaign spending law, with its $1,000 limit on contributions, makes a late start all the more difficult. "In the past, all you had to do was get 50 guys to put up $20,000 each," a wealthy Humphrey backer in California observed, "and you had yourself a candidate. Now with the limit, you've got to go to a lot of people. There's no way you can do that in secret and if you don't have the money, how are you going to blitzkrieg?"

Still Settling Debts

When the conversation reaches this point, it becomes evident that Senator Humphrey's resistance to a race in the primaries is at least as visceral as it is a matter of political judgment.

Money has always been the bane of his quests for the Presidency. In 1960, he ran out of funds in West Virginia where he was running against John F. Kennedy. The same thing happened in California in 1972 in his race against Senator George McGovern. He is only now settling nearly $900,000 in campaign debts left over from 1972, at a rate of about four cents on the dollar.

In addition, he has had the embarrassment of having to deny knowledge of illegal contributions made to his campaigns by Associated Milk Producers, Inc., Ashland Oil Inc. and, allegedly, the Gulf Oil Corporation. His 1972 campaign manager, Jack L. Chestnut, was sentenced last year to four months in jail for accepting illegal contributions from the milk producers during Mr. Humphrey's 1970 race for the Senate.

Now when the subject of political money comes up, Mr. Humphrey flushes angrily. "It's a monster roaming in the forest that no one can control," he fumes. "I'm not going out asking anyone for one damned dollar for anything except the Red Cross and the Community Chest. No way. I've had a bellyfull of that."

Soliciting funds is not the only indignity that he associates with the primaries. Others may forget, but he obviously hasn't, the old cries of "Dump the Hump" and the abusive, even contemptuous, things that were said about him by hostile Democrats and skeptical commentators in 1968 and 1972.

"It's not romance, it's not theory for him at all," said Senator Walter Mondale, one of those who has urged Mr. Humphrey to think seriously about the primaries. "He knows how it hurts and cuts."

Little Dazzle in Polls

As a noncandidate, he has the satisfaction of having old opponents urge him into the race. As a candidate, he senses, he would be caricatured once again as a political throwback and campaigner addict.

The polls don't seem to dazzle him as much as they do some of his friends. In the Gallup Poll, when Senator Edward M. Kennedy's name is omitted, Mr. Humphrey now leads the Democratic pack, with 30 percent of all Democrats listing him as their first choice for the nomination. A year ago, he was getting 11 percent.

Buoyed as he is by the rise, he is detached enough to point out that 30 percent is "not overwhelming" and to wonder aloud, as no confirmed candidate would, whether it is really support for him as a candidate or an index of regard for someone who is well known.

It is a shrewd question, for pollsters generally say that the prospect of another Humphrey candidacy stirs more ennui than enthusiasm among younger voters. Humphrey support is most noticeable among voters over 35, they say, and not especially intense.

The polls measure responses to Mr. Humphrey as a known quantity. They reflect only dimly, if at all, the strong showing he has lately been making in the Senate. In his own mind, his restored effectiveness is traceable to a period of enforced introspection in 1973, when he underwent surgery for growths on his bladder that were described as precancerous.

He illustrates his sense of having experienced important inner changes by alluding to an essay by Woodrow Wilson, a boyhood hero, which he keeps in his desk drawer, tucked away in a loose-leaf sampler of inspirational writings. The essay's title, "When a Man Comes to Himself," describes what he thinks has happened to him.

Aging But Bouncy

A man comes to himself, Wilson wrote, "when he has cleared his eyes to see the world as it is, and his own true place and function in it." His own true place, Mr. Humphrey concluded when the White House seemed permanently out of reach, was the Senate.

Mr. Humphrey still finds it hard to let go of an audience that does not seem wholly mesmerized, but he now recognizes his tendency to oratorical excess and the limitations in what he calls "the capability of others to tolerate me."

In 1968, campaigning in the shadow of Lyndon B. Johnson, he wanted to show that he was his own man. In 1972, having gone through defeat and a painfully awkward return to the Senate, where his party's leadership treated him like any other freshman, he felt a gnawing need to vindicate himself. Now, he insists, "I don't want anything so much that I'll risk anything to get it." As he says them, the words do not sound coy. Indeed, they seem to be more for his own benefit than his listener's.

He is nearing 65 and, when he is not wearing television makeup, his years are plainly evident in the puffiness under his eyes, the deep lines at the corners of his mouth and the sagging flesh beneath his lantern jaw. His hair, less conspicuously tinted than it was four years ago, is now white in front, shading to blond and then to auburn.

But he has the bounce, stamina and straight-backed posture of a man years younger.

"Clearly, he is the most energetic member of the Senate," Senator Richard C. Clark, an Iowa Democrat 18 years his junior, asserted. "He just barrels ahead all the time."

The range of his legislative enthusiasm is so broad—from school lunches to Sinai, solar research to health care for the elderly—that even his admirers tend to regard him as hyperactive. It is not his knowledge or effectiveness that is questioned, but rather his steadiness and readiness to concentrate on the details of a problem in a disciplined way.

If anything, it is said, he is too open to ideas. "He moves around a lot on issues—in all honesty," a colleague said.

Still technically a freshman Senator, Mr. Humphrey is chairman of the subcommittee that deals with foreign aid and foreign agricultural policy and now that the Vietnam war is over, has re-emerged as a key member of the Foreign Relations Committee, managing most of its legislation on the Senate floor.

On foreign policy issues, he regularly seems torn between his strong instincts as a cold warrior, nurtured over more than two decades, and his latter-day conclusion that the United States must avoid entangling foreign adventures. This leaves him in the middle of the road on most foreign policy matters—where he is most comfortable—and makes it possible for him to retain the confidence of Congressional liberals and Secretary of State Henry A. Kissinger.

As a result, his role in foreign policy debates is that of a compromiser.

In addition, last year he inherited the chairmanship of the Joint Economic Committee, which he has used to promote schemes for a national development bank, full employment and national economic planning.

None of these are likely to be enacted soon. Senator Humphrey says he has brought them forward to stimulate debate on economic priorities.

This gadfly function is traditional with the committee, but it is also congenial for a potential candidate looking for a forum. This month and next, as the political campaign starts to heat up, Senator Humphrey will take his forum to Los Angeles and Boston for public hearings.

He will spend four days in Los Angeles, where a crowded program of public and private appearances has been arranged by Joseph Cerrell, who was Mr. Humphrey's campaign manager in the 1972 California primary. Of course, the Senator will deny that he is testing the water for another go in California, but the speculation on his plans and prospects will be helpful in maintaining his standing in the polls—a necessity if he is to profit from a deadlock among the active candidates.

Meanwhile, scattered efforts by Humphrey supporters—all formally disavowed by the Senator—will test the sentiment for a draft. The future of these efforts is to be determined next week by the Federal Election Commission, which will rule on a petition from Representative Paul Simon, Democrat of Illinois, who has asked to be allowed to raise funds for a draft-Humphrey committee.

The campaign spending law limits expenditures by committees on behalf of candidates to $5,000; it says nothing about noncandidates. If Mr. Simon's effort is allowed to get off the ground, there is sure to be a move to secure write-in votes for Senator Humphrey in the New Hampshire primary on Feb. 24, and possibly the Massachusetts primary on March 2.

Mr. Humphrey has formally disavowed the draft effort in a letter to the election commission, and his office has told Mr. Simon not to expect any assistance from the Senator. What he has not done is to suggest that Mr. Simon call off the draft effort.

Commenting on plans by Percy Sutton, the Manhattan Borough President and Harlem political leader, to run in the New York primary as a delegate pledged to support him, Mr. Humphrey cheerfully struck a pose of helplessness. "Now, what can I do about that?" he asked. "I can't go up there and hogtie him."

He is taking the same benign, hands-off attitude to a drive in his home state by Governor Anderson and the state A.F.L.-C.I.O. to send a slate of Humphrey delegates to the convention. One Democrat, Representative Donald M. Fraser, has already started to run for his Senate seat on the theory that its occupant will be moving on to bigger things.

In the Senator's own estimation, a Humphrey nomination is still "not a top prospect," but it is noticeable that his judgments on that score have gradually been getting weaker. He now acknowledges the possibility of a deadlock, and says that the chance of a brokered convention turning to him is "about as good as any other."

In a campaign against President Ford or former Gov. Ronald Reagan of California, Mr. Humphrey would probably be denounced as a typical example of one who promotes Federal intervention and big government. "I'm more than ready for that," he replies, starting the counter-attack he would aim at Mr. Reagan. "I would come into his audience and charge him with being against Medicare."

A Humphrey campaign would stress unemployment and economic mismanagement as key issues, finding in these problems the root cause of budgetary deficits, crime and lack of faith in government.

In what was conceivably a preview, the Senator met Mr. Reagan in a debate here a few months ago on the subject of "deregulation." The former California Governor was explaining how the marketplace would see to air service for small towns when Senator Humphrey broke in and attacked Mr. Reagan's free market concepts with a single sentence.

"Governor, you're blowing bubbles," Mr. Humphrey said. Looking back on it now, he does not think there was any contest.

Primaries Put Humphrey in New Democratic Focus

BY CHRISTOPHER LYDON

Senator Hubert H. Humphrey of Minnesota, the ever-buoyant noncandidate for the Presidency, looked to many studious leaders of the Democratic Party today like the passive centerpiece of a "stop everybody" movement. More than ever, he looked very much afloat as a compromise candidate himself.

"All his people are very happy today—and they should be," said a ranking Democratic official, reflecting on the Florida primary returns that seemed to leave four active competitors in the next phase of the primary season but no front-running claimant to the broad middle of the party.

Publicly resolved to stay out of the primaries, the 64-year-old Minnesotan has taken less direct action on his own behalf than some observers suspect, and less than many of his supporters have urged. Mr. Humphrey's refusal to step forward as the substitute captain of Senator Birch Bayh's delegate slates in New York and his rejection of invitations to make a late

Christopher Lydon, "Primaries Put Humphrey in New Democratic Focus," *The New York Times*, March 11, 1976, p. 30. © 1976 by The New York Times Company. Reprinted by permission.

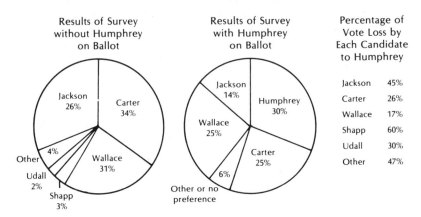

Figure 1

The New York Times, March 11, 1976

entry into the Michigan primary have convinced a variety of skeptics that he will play a waiting game until June.

A See-Sawing Trend

Yet the see-sawing trends of the early primaries, combined with the budding of favorite-son and "uncommitted" movements in big states like California, Illinois, Ohio and New Jersey, seem to many delegate-counting Democrats to work together toward a deadlocked convention and a Humphrey nomination.

And for those who look beneath the early primary scores and see the Democratic Party in a lurching search for its real center of gravity in 1976, the persistent interest in Mr. Humphrey is neither an accident nor the fruit of a conscious conspiracy.

In numerous surveys Mr. Humphrey remains a popular favorite among the Democratic rank-and-file. A New York Times/CBS News sampling of Florida primary voters as they left the polls yesterday suggested that if Mr. Humphrey's name had been on the ballot, he would have led the field with a comfortable plurality. Similar election-day polling of primary voters in New Hampshire and Massachusetts indicated that he would have run strong, and probably first, in those contests, too.

In the last national poll of Democrats by the Gallup organization, completed on March 1 before the Massachusetts and Florida primaries,

Mr. Humphrey ran well ahead of all the active candidates, the choice of 27 percent of his party—ahead of Gov. George C. Wallace of Alabama, in second place with 19 percent; former Gov. Jimmy Carter of Georgia with 16 percent; and Senator Henry M. Jackson of Washington with 6 percent.

Humphrey Consensus Choice

Mr. Humphrey, moreover, still appears to be the consensus choice of several groups that form the central leadership of the Democratic Party. Increasingly, it appears in dozens of interviews this week, that establishment is ambivalent about Mr. Carter, divided over Mr. Jackson, unconvinced by the early returns on Representative Morris K. Udall of Arizona and broadly opposed to Mr. Wallace.

Concretely, the latest view of Mr. Humphrey arises from the anxiety in the center and left of the party about Senator Jackson's emergence in the Massachusetts primary, and from the same factions reading that Mr. Udall does not have sufficient working-class appeal to stop the Senator from Washington.

"Udall looks terribly weak," commented Frederick G. Dutton, a lawyer here long associated with Kennedy family campaigns. "I'm not exactly a Humphrey fan, but compared to Jackson he looks better every day."

Richard N. Goodwin, the liberal strategist and writer, saw Democratic liberals today busily but happily erasing their memories of Mr. Humphrey as a onetime champion of the war in Vietnam and the leader of the more conservative party forces that tried to block Senator George McGovern's nomination in 1972.

'Reconstructing Hubert'

"They're reconstructing Hubert as the liberal leader of the 1950's," Mr. Goodwin observed. "If the Jackson bandwagon starts to roll, Humphrey will be forced into the race. He's the safest nominee: Nobody in the party has to be afraid of him, and he may be the only one who could be reasonably sure of winning the election in November."

"I don't think the party has begun to imagine the polarization ahead on the Jackson question," said Anne Wexler Duffey, another veteran of liberal Democratic politics. "I think you're going to see a lot of people of my stripe looking at Jimmy Carter," she remarked in an interview, "and if Jackson does well in New York and Pennsylvania, you're going to hear people yelling 'Humphrey, Humphrey,' no matter what Humphrey does."

Jackson 'Not Nominatable'

"What most people haven't realized," an avowedly neutral Democratic official said today, "is that the so-called front-runner, Jackson, is not nominatable. The left is not dead, but it will take Humphrey."

Among adherents of the Humphrey strategy, the problem is to keep any active candidate from gathering the roughly 900 votes needed to create bandwagon momentum toward the 1505 convention votes needed for the nomination.

There are ways to keep any front-runner from emerging: a division of labor endorsements between Mr. Jackson and Mr. Carter in the Michigan primary, for example, would keep them battling for minority blocks of delegates; a favorite-son race by Gov. Edmund G. Brown Jr. in California would probably prevent anyone else from winning a dominant share of the largest delegation at the convention.

Mr. Humphrey, who probably understands the process better than he admits, observed with satisfaction this morning that several good candidates were showing strength in the first cluster of primaries. Discussing further divisions with a smile, he told a reporter he expected Mr. Udall to win the Wisconsin primary on April 6.

·C·

Planning during the Campaign: Responses to the Institutional Environment

Signature Argued on Complex Petitions

BY LUCINDA FRANKS

For 30 minutes the other day, the forces of Jimmy Carter and Representative Morris K. Udall picked over the attributes of an innocent and unwitting voter named Selma Stern.

It was not what she had said or done that interested them, nor even who she was. It was how she signed her name.

Was the middle initial included? Did it look legible? Was the "t" properly crossed?

The answers to the questions were crucial. They could even determine whether Mr. Carter's delegates on the West Side of Manhattan were knocked off the ballot for the New York primary April 6.

So it goes in the Byzantine political subculture of New York, a state with perhaps the most bizarrely complicated political system of any in the nation. Its Board of Elections alone is responsible for enforcing laws so minutely technical that only the most machine-wise New York politician can understand them.

Signature Requirement

And one of those laws is that a designating petition bearing 1,250 signatures must be gathered by a candidate for every slate of delegates he puts

Lucinda Franks, "Signatures Argued on Complex Petitions," *The New York Times*, March 20, 1976, p. 12. © 1976 by The New York Times Company. Reprinted by permission.

on the primary ballot in each of the state's 39 Congressional districts. And every signatory must be a registered Democrat who signs the petition exactly, to the letter, as he signed it on the card he filled out when he registered to vote.

Any deviation disqualifies him. And rival politicians do not hesitate to mount challenges, investigating every signatory of their opponent's petitions.

Thus, at a recent court hearing at the City Board of Elections, the names of ordinary citizens like Selma Stern were closely examined and then either allowed to remain on the petition or removed.

The hearing—held at the board's office rather than a courtroom so that election files could be referred to—was at the behest of the Carter camp which was appealing to the State Supreme Court a ruling of the Board of Elections that threw out its slate of delegates in the 20th District—Manhattan's West Side.

Around a chipped formica table sat a referee appointed by the court, inkstains on his plaid pants; a stenographer, balancing her machine on her lap and chewing cough drops; five Carter lawyers, lost in a mass of Xeroxed petitions, and the challenger, a bulky young Udall supporter who kept pushing back his stringy black hair.

Petition Combed

They went over the petition, signature by signature, the challenger seeking to knock out enough to bring the Carter petition below the 1,250 name requirement.

It looked and sounded more like a poker game than a courtroom.

"I got a blank here," mumbled the challenger, Gerard Flanagan, referring to the fact that the card of one signatory showed her as not registered in any party.

"I'll call you on that," said one of the lawyers, producing evidence that the Board of Elections records were wrong—the woman was a registered Democrat.

"O.K.," said the referee, Donald Slamond, who was keeping a running tally of how many signatures on the petition were passing muster. "I'll give you plus one on that." Selma Stern's name stayed on the petition.

"Line five, page 74," barked the challenger. "He's illegible."

"Get the G book over there," ordered a Carter lawyer, pointing to the endless shelves of big black books containing the cards.

"He signs his name illegible," said the referee, looking at the signatory's card with a bored expression. "He's got a European hand—bet he was educated in Europe. Plus one."

"All right, lines 6 and 7," said the challenger. "Husband and wife, both in same hand. Wife obviously signed for husband."

The referee leafed through the couple's cards. "The wife signed for him every year since 1969. Maybe the guy can't write. I'm not going to disenfranchise him for that. Plus one."

It was not the last time that the scrawl of these unsuspecting Carter signatories—many of whom were probably accosted in supermarkets or on the street—would be so exposed. Both candidate and challenger can appeal to three successive courts—a labyrinth of litigation that can last until four days before the primary and tie up dozens of campaign workers for 10 and 12 hours a day.

System under Attack

The Board of Elections laws, originally devised to protect against wholesale forging of petitions but now often used as a weapon by political professionals against insurgents, have come under attack by both Mr. Carter and Gov. George C. Wallace of Alabama. Mr. Carter has lost nine delegate slates because of challenges and Mr. Wallace lost all but about six, effectively taking him out of the New York race.

"The whole thing is a mine field," said Mark Alcott, a volunteer lawyer with the Carter team. "And any nonclub member, such as the kids we brought in who had never before passed a petition, is going to step on mine after mine."

Delegate slates have been entered in 35 Congressional districts for Senator Henry M. Jackson of Washington, in 37 for Mr. Udall, the Arizona Democrat; and in at least 26 for Mr. Carter, former Governor of Georgia. Former Senator Fred F. Harris of Oklahoma has slates in nine districts; Mr. Wallace in six, and there are unauthorized but covert slates in for Senator Hubert H. Humphrey of Minnesota, who is not competing in the primaries, in three districts. Ellen McCormack, the antiabortion candidate, has a slate in one district.

The Carter camp has been particularly critical of Senator Jackson, who has the backing of a large number of the state's Democratic organizations and has thus been able to mount most of the challenges against Mr. Carter's petitions.

"In any case, the whole thing is an invisible process," said Mr. Alcott. "If the average voter could see what was happening in here they'd think it was something out of Kafka."

Jackson Backers Upheld by Court

BY LINDA GREENHOUSE

The State Supreme Court ruled here today that 33 contested delegates in the state's April 6 primary election could still be identified on the ballot as supporters of Senator Henry M. Jackson of Washington even though they missed last Saturday's deadline for filing their "certificates of preference" with the Secretary of State.

The 33 had been challenged by Mario M. Cuomo, the Secretary of State, and by the campaign organization of Representative Morris K. Udall of Arizona on the ground that since they missed the deadline for identifying themselves with a candidate, they should be forced to run as uncommitted delegates.

Suit Is Dismissed

Justice Ellis J. Staley ruled that because the Legislature had been so late in rewriting the state's election law—setting the new deadline only six working days after passage of the bill—flexibility was required to "accomplish the true purpose and intent of the statute, which has a worthwhile objective"—letting voters know which Presidential candidate they are voting for.

The Udall forces announced that they would appeal the decision. Arguments will be heard in the Appellate Division here tomorrow afternoon.

The change in the state's election law, allowing the names of Democratic Presidential candidates to appear on the ballot, was widely hailed as a good-government reform. But its belated enactment has caused confusion, lawsuits and an administrative nightmare at the New York City Board of Elections.

In another legal test to arise from the new law, the State Court of Appeals dismissed today a suit brought by delegates running in support of Senator Hubert H. Humphrey of Minnesota.

The delegates had challenged a provision of the new law that requires them to run as "uncommitted" because Senator Humphrey, as an undeclared candidate, has refused to file the required statement authorizing them to run in his name.

Will Accept Certificate

In a unanimous decision, the state's highest court ruled that the delegates' quarrel should be not with the law, but with Senator Humphrey, and that no constitutional questions were involved in their claim.

"It is inaction on the part of their candidate, rather than the statutory provisions, which frustrates the accomplishment of their objective," the court said.

Last night, a previously uncommitted slate in the 39th Congressional District along the state's Southern Tier announced its support for Senator Humphrey. Slates in three Congressional districts in the Buffalo area had announced their support for him earlier.

Senator Jackson said that he was pleased by today's decision upholding his delegates. An opposite ruling, the Democratic Senator said, "would have denied people of the Empire State the opportunity to vote for delegates of their choice, whether they were mine or anybody else's."

Mr. Cuomo, the Secretary of State, said that in the light of the ruling he would accept certificates of preference filed up to four days later by delegates supporting other candidates, to save them "needless litigation and expense." Nineteen delegates are in this category, 17 supporting former Senator Fred R. Harris of Oklahoma and two supporting Jimmy Carter, former Governor of Georgia.

Despite the court decision, the number of Jackson delegates that will appear on the ballot is still lower than the number that will appear either as uncommitted delegates or as pledged to Mr. Udall.

The latest count this afternoon showed 207 uncommitted delegates scattered among 50 states; 37 Udall slates with 192 delegates; 35 Jackson slates with 181 delegates; 28 Carter slates with 139 delegates; 18 Harris slates with 91 delegates; 3 slates with 15 delegates for George C. Wallace, Governor of Alabama, and one slate with 5 delegates supporting Ellen McCormack, the antiabortionist.

Eight Filed on Time

Beyond protecting the 33 Jackson candidates, today's decision was important for Senator Jackson because the 68 at-large New York State delegates will be divided in proportion to the candidates' showing in the primary.

Originally, there were 42 Jackson delegates, led by Sandra L. Berg of Queens, who went to court to challenge the Secretary of State's decision that they would have to be listed as uncommitted. The most prominent in the group was Daniel P. Moynihan, the former United States representative at the United Nations, who is running at the top of a Jackson slate in the Bronx and whose "certificate of preference" arrived at the Secretary of State's office two days after the deadline and without a postmark.

Upon re-examination, eight of the 42 were found to have filed their certificates on time. One, an alternate in the 16th Congressional District in Brooklyn, was found not to have filed a certificate at all and so will run as uncommitted.

In deciding that the 33 who did in fact miss the deadline should be reinstated, Justice Staley cited "an earlier state court decision that said that the election law "should not be so interpreted as to defeat the very object of its enactment."

Twenty-two of those reinstated are delegates; the 11 others are alternates. Most of them are from Long Island, Queens and Brooklyn.

The various last-minute changes on the ballot, meanwhile, have wreaked havoc on the city's Board of Elections.

A state law requires the board to rotate candidates' positions on the ballot, so a candidate whose slate is on the bottom in one Congressional District is guaranteed the favored top position in another.

But last night Bea Dolen, the board's executive director, decided that the printing schedule for the ballots was already so complicated that she could not obey the law, and positions in each Congressional District were determined by lot.

Carter Suing to Upset Results in Areas Ousting His Delegates

BY LUCINDA FRANKS

Jimmy Carter's New York campaign organization said yesterday that it would sue in Federal District Court to invalidate results of the state primary here next month in 10 Congressional districts where the Democratic Presidential aspirant's name had been stricken from the ballot because of technical irregularities.

William vanden Heuvel, state chairman of Mr. Carter's campaign, said that the technical objections raised by New York's Board of Elections against delegate-designating petitions in the 10 districts violated the Federal Voting Rights Act.

Lucinda Franks, "Carter Suing to Upset Results in Areas Ousting His Delegates," *The New York Times,* March 29, 1976, p. 20. © 1976 by The New York Times Company. Reprinted by permission.

"The New York election laws exclude the average voter in New York," said Paul Rivet, a lawyer who plans to file the suit in Manhattan's Southern District court next week. "The people who signed our delegate petitions have been effectively disenfranchised because they forgot to dot their i's."

Mr. Rivet said that the loss of Carter delegates in the 10 districts had hurt the campaign. Mr. Carter, former Georgia Governor, still has delegate slates in 29 of the 39 Congressional districts in the state.

Most of the challenges were brought by a rival, Senator Henry M. Jackson of Washington. According to Carter backers, their delegate slates had been stricken because the registered voters who had signed the petitions supporting the delegates had made trivial errors such as putting down their election district incorrectly or omitting their middle initials.

Mr. Rivet cited provisions of the voting act that provide that "no person shall deny the right of any individual to vote in any election because of an error or omission on any record or paper relating to any application requisite to voting, if such error is not material in determining whether such individual is qualified under state law to vote in such election."

The Carter organization is fighting through the state appeals courts to get some of the 10 delegate slates put back on the ballot. They are in the 3d, 4th, 5th, 11th, 13th, 15th, 22d, 27th, 31st, and 33d Congressional Districts, in New York and in Nassau, Suffolk, Ulster, Tioga, Onondaga, Oneida and Herkimer counties.

The suit asks that the Carter delegate slates be put back on the ballot in the 10 districts, that the primary election in those districts not be held or that the results be invalidated.

If his suit is successful, Mr. Carter would not be the only candidate in the April 6 primary to benefit. Nearly all of George C. Wallace's delegate slates were stricken from the ballot.

CHAPTER 5

Campaign Dynamics: Organization and Finance

A. Organizing a Nomination Campaign

B. Financing a Nomination Campaign

·A·

Organizing a Nomination Campaign

Democrats Depend on Speechwriters for Their Ideological Images

By JONATHAN COTTIN
& ANDREW J. GLASS

The art of Presidential politics demands that candidates speak their own minds in public and that their speechwriters do their work in private.

Yet in the race for the Democratic Presidential nomination, a candidate's top speechwriter ranks with his media consultant and fund raiser in importance to the campaign.

The difference is that writing campaign speeches can be a highly ego-deflating affair, particularly if the candidate possesses strong ideas of his own on what he wants to say. It is not uncommon for speechwriters to regard the candidate who employs them as an author might regard a particularly demanding editor.

The Hidden Factor.   Again, the difference is that the speechwriter must forever remain in the background while the candidate receives maximum publicity. In any event, the matter of who came up with an inspiring concept or a ringing phrase is usually a closely kept secret among campaign insiders. So far as the voter is concerned, the candidate is responsible for it all.

When a candidate becomes President, the speechwriting function becomes institutionalized.

Jonathan Cottin & Andrew J. Glass, "Democrats Depend on Speechwriters for their Ideological Images," *National Journal*, February 26, 1972, pp. 350–359. Charts and pictures deleted. Reprinted by permission of the *National Journal*.

But among the Democratic hopefuls now battling each other for the right to oppose Mr. Nixon in November, relationships with speechwriters tend to reflect individual needs, abilities and personalities.

Frustrations. As a group, however, campaign speechwriters share some qualities in common.

They work long hours under high pressure. This is why most speechwriters for Presidential candidates are in their 20s and 30s. It is not a business that yields many veterans.

For similar reasons, speechwriters tend to switch candidates between campaigns.

Sometimes, accumulated personal tensions or emerging ideological differences drive a candidate and his speechwriter apart. At other times, talented speechwriters are lured away by the prospect of working in a successful campaign or enjoying a higher status than they did previously.

More than is generally known, speechwriters are called upon to sell their own ideas to the candidates who employ them.

In short, writing speeches for Presidential candidates cannot help but be a frustrating occupation.

Press. Often, these frustrations are directed at the press—particularly when a speechwriter finds that his ideas, as refined and transmitted by the candidate, are being widely ignored.

Many speechwriters feel that newspapers, magazines and television networks cover a political campaign without giving due emphasis to the issues raised by their respective candidates.

In the 1972 Presidential campaign, these specific patterns have emerged among the Democratic contenders:

- Sen. Edmund S. Muskie of Maine has developed an elaborate speech preparation apparatus in which his chief speechwriter also acts as a salesman of ideas to the candidate.
- Sen. Hubert H. Humphrey of Minnesota has tapped the brains of both veteran political chums and bright, young writers to sustain his campaign drive and curb his verbosity.
- Sen. Henry M. Jackson of Washington, aware that his delivery of written addresses lacks zip, uses texts as reference points for his ad-libbed remarks. Yet he too challenges his staff to come up with fresh ideas.
- Sen. George S. McGovern of South Dakota, uneasy about mouthing the words of others, uses his staff primarily as an intellectual sounding board, while preferring to speak from notes.
- Mayor John V. Lindsay of New York, pulling ideas from universities and foundations, often requires a speech to be rewritten four times before it meets his goals of precision and substance.

Muskie

While the main speechwriting chores are the responsibility of one man, the Muskie high command has established an elaborate backup system to insure that the candidate is never at a loss for words. Supporting the main speechwriter, Robert M. Shrum, 29, are more than 30 task forces, each manned by volunteer experts. They research and develop proposals on foreign and domestic matters.

In addition, Muskie is accompanied on his travels by an "idea man," whose job is to provide fast intellectual input on issues that are developing too rapidly for a Washington-based writer to anticipate—but on which Muskie must be ready to comment.

PROCESS

Muskie's over-all speech co-ordinator is John T. McEvoy, the Senator's administrative assistant. McEvoy joined Muskie in 1970 and was charged with the task of streamlining the Senate staff. But he was later assigned additional duties as liaison man with the campaign operation at 1972 K Street NW, in downtown Washington. He explained his responsibilities this way: "I'm simply Muskie's administrative assistant and he's asked me to make sure that the intellectual side of his campaign reflects the best ideas he can find and that they get to the speechwriter."

Ideas. McEvoy calls himself a "talent coordinator," arranging for the easy and fast exchange of ideas between the task forces and Muskie's chief speechwriter, Shrum.

There are between 12 and 15 task forces at work at any one time on foreign policy issues for Muskie, while another 25 are at work on domestic initiatives.

"The speechwriter (Shrum) relates directly to the task force" at work on any given issue, McEvoy said. McEvoy said he is an "expediter," making certain that "each group comes in on time" with its research and policy proposals. Many of these are later translated into speeches.

Muskie "has to be convinced before he will go with something," McEvoy said. McEvoy must therefore see to it that there is substantial supportive documentation accompanying each task-force report. McEvoy said Muskie wants to have enough "backup" information on any issue so that he can develop legislation on the topic, as well as raise the issue in a speech.

McEvoy cited as an example of this process a 60-page research paper on the formation of self-sustaining local health maintenance organizations. The report was the basis for a speech the Senator delivered to an apprecia- tive audience Feb. 14 in Miami Beach at a gathering of the Dade County

Senior Citizens Council. It also served, in part, as a data base for draft legislation.

Writing. Shrum, who joined the Muskie campaign in May 1971, after serving as a speechwriter for Lindsay, is regarded by McEvoy as being "very, very good" at his craft.

Shrum's abilities were acknowledged by Thomas B. Morgan, Lindsay's press secretary. In an interview, Morgan, who worked with Shrum, said of him: "I feel I've created a Frankenstein."

McEvoy and Shrum hold similar views on what the role of Muskie's speechwriter should be, but their emphasis differs. McEvoy stresses Shrum's importance as an idea salesman to the candidate while Shrum is more concerned with the service aspects of his job.

According to McEvoy, Shrum plays a dual role in the campaign. First, "he translates task-force work into reality." But, even more importantly, Shrum shows Muskie how these ideas are "interesting, exciting and worthy of the campaign."

As McEvoy explained, Muskie "not only needs to be convinced an idea is good. He is interested in making it of interest to the audience. If he is not excited by a speech, he won't give it."

On the other hand, McEvoy said, if Muskie has a good speech and an approving crowd, the event provides "a real entertainment for Muskie."

McEvoy said Shrum was sent to Florida Feb. 19 to join Muskie and fly with him to Boise, Idaho. The main purpose of Shrum's trip was to sell two speech ideas to the candidate.

Shrum, on the other hand, says his job for Muskie "is to serve him as best I can, not to try to euchre him into saying things he doesn't want to say." McEvoy said no one on the Muskie staff seeks to "cast Muskie in their image." Moreover, if anyone tried, he said, they would quickly find the task impossible since the candidate has such an independent mind.

With McEvoy directing the movement of task-force reports to him, Shrum meets with Muskie or McEvoy, or both, to talk over speech ideas. Normally, Shrum will then write a draft speech which, whenever possible, is "circulated widely within the staff" for comment. It is also distributed to outside experts. Then, Shrum said, Muskie will make changes, sometimes substantial ones, and ask "tough questions" about the proposed remarks.

REACTION

Whenever important speech drafts are prepared for him, "Muskie reads the whole thing—including all supporting documents" before authorizing a final version, Shrum said.

The speechwriter noted that as he prepares each Muskie address, he keeps in mind that "we're running a national campaign. . . . With everything Muskie has to ask the question, can this stand up nationally? You may emphasize different things in different places. But there is never an occasion that is not national. He must take his beliefs to other places."

Shrum also attempts to adopt Muskie's natural choice of words. "The speeches he gave before [Shrum began work for Muskie] sound very much like the speeches he gives now. I try to write in his style."

He said there is no formula for writing a Muskie speech. "I suspect speeches written according to rule books come out sounding pretty much like rule books," he said.

Traveling Aides. Since Shrum spends most of his time in Washington, while the candidate is mostly on the road, additional speechwriting assistance must be available in the field.

This assignment alternates between Milton S. Gwirtzman and Donald E. Nicoll, Muskie's policy director and veteran aide.

Gwirtzman is a partner in the Washington law firm of Dutton, Gwirtzman, Zumas, Wise & Frey. He has written for former President Harry S. Truman as well as for the late Sen. (1965–68) Robert F. Kennedy, D-N.Y.

Gwirtzman, said McEvoy, "is a guy who Muskie feels particularly comfortable with on the road as a last-minute idea man. We rely heavily on his judgment."

Gwirtzman joined Muskie on board Muskie's campaign plane, the *Josephine,* Feb. 14 as the candidate began a week's tour of Florida. During an airborne interview, Gwirtzman said that "I'm sort of a counsel on substantive issues."

In addition, he said, he will sometimes "refresh" a speech that was prepared a few days earlier and needs updating because of late-breaking events. To keep track of news developments, Gwirtzman carries a radio.

Gwirtzman does considerably less writing than Shrum. He estimated that "85 to 90 per cent of what he (Muskie) says in his total campaign is extemporaneous. He will take ideas and suggestions; argue and debate . . . but the formulations are his own."

Muskie, said Gwirtzman, "was a speechwriter himself. For years and years, he wrote his speeches without any help. He'll often get ideas that no one on his staff thought of . . . one of the reasons he has a comparatively light schedule is because he insists on having time to think through questions and come up with his own ideas."

Crisis. Nonetheless, he added, at times of stress, Muskie is grateful to be given fresh insights. As Gwirtzman put it: "Throwing an idea then is like throwing a life preserver."

Gwirtzman also follows events by staying in touch with the Muskie campaign headquarters in Washington. He keeps track of developments in the area Muskie is headed for by telephone contact with advance men in the field. With last-minute intelligence on local developments fed him by Gwirtzman, Muskie can make informed judgments about what his presentation should be when he arrives.

When something develops which Gwirtzman knows will require a response from Muskie, "we just stop what we're doing and work on that crisis. In that sort of emergency situation, we are acting as a conduit of the facts to him and a conduit to him of what questions might be asked."

VIETNAM

The Muskie speechwriting system was put through its severest challenge after President Nixon's Jan. 25 television broadcast in which he outlined U.S. peace proposals and called on Hanoi to negotiate a settlement of the war.

Although Muskie's initial public reaction to the President's peace plan was positive, his Senate and campaign staffs were simultaneously beginning to weigh the substance of the proposals in greater detail.

Although "the pundits seemed to be shell shocked" by the Nixon address, and assumed it had eliminated the war as an issue, "staff-wise, we didn't buy that," McEvoy said.

Internal Debate. "Muskie had outside advice to hit Nixon hard. The more we looked at the [President's] offer, the closer it was to what had been on the table for 90 days," McEvoy said in an interview.

There were differences in the Muskie camp over when to attack the President. Some advisers warned against making a statement during the Tet New Year holiday. Others on the Muskie staff and some loyal outsiders "thought we shouldn't do it politically," McEvoy recalled. Meanwhile, Shrum, after checking with outside as well as in-house advisers, drafted a speech on the President's peace plan. He completed the first draft on Jan. 30—four days after the Nixon broadcast. It was a Sunday.

"Shrum took the speech to Orlando [where Muskie was then campaigning] Sunday night," McEvoy recalled. There, he worked with Muskie on a final draft. Numerous telephone calls were made. "Muskie needed to be convinced. He wanted further checks made to insure that Hanoi had rejected the offer."

Satisfied that it had, "he made numerous revisions personally in the speech draft," said McEvoy.

Speech. Shrum prepared the final draft, as he had the first, and Muskie read it Feb. 2 to a convention of Church Women United in Washington.

In the speech, Muskie attacked Mr. Nixon for attempting to "win at the conference table what we have not won and cannot win on the battlefield." He said the peace plan was little more than "reissued" points "that have failed for six years."

Using short sentences for their dramatic effect, Muskie was clearly aiming his remarks at an audience far larger than the 150 or so women gathered before him. Some examples:

"America's leaders have been carried along on a tide of illusion, convinced at first that we were right, committed still to making right a war we know is wrong. We fight for a make-believe victory in a real place and real people die each day. . . .

"Surely when we look into our own consciences, we must know that saving lives is more important than saving face. . . .

"We have no right to take for our own the awful majesty of God over life and death, destroying land and people in order to save them."

It was to be the candidate's most controversial speech of the campaign to date.

It stirred a bitter Republican counterattack from Capitol Hill as well as from Secretary of State William P. Rogers, who usually refrains from entering into political debates.

There was some criticism from Democrats as well. Former Sen. (1959–69) Eugene J. McCarthy, D-Minn., contrasted Muskie's remarks with Muskie's earlier staunch support of President Johnson's Vietnam war policies. And Sen. Jackson termed Muskie's rejection of the Nixon proposals "a disservice to his country."

The address, Shrum concluded, "opened up the biggest debate of the campaign" and demonstrated that the war was still an issue.

It also proved once more that even before the first Presidential primary votes were counted, speeches do count in the race for the White House.

Humphrey

In early 1972, Humphrey's campaign strategy requires, above all, that he stay alive politically in order to be in contention at the finish line.

Humphrey feels he must place among the top three Democratic contenders in selected early primaries—Florida, Wisconsin, Pennsylvania and Ohio—to remain a viable candidate. If he can do so, Humphrey thinks he can in time sway enough delegates to his cause at the party's nominating convention in Miami Beach.

Thus, Humphrey is putting the premium on winning primary votes and delegate support. He is paying relatively little attention to producing fine rhetoric. This is why Humphrey's current speechwriting effort is both Spartan in scope and informal in style.

OLD MODEL

For those who had been involved in the last Humphrey Presidential campaign, the contrast between 1968 and 1972 is dramatic.

One veteran of 1968, speaking privately, recalled: "At that time, we had a real honest-to-goodness campaign, with Ted Van Dyk Jr. on the [campaign] plane. Toward the end, John Bartlow Martin was aboard.

"There was a lot of fine editing with Humphrey of key drafts. Now, I really wonder whether the routine stuff even gets through to Humphrey for review."

Today, neither Van Dyk nor Martin is writing political speeches for Humphrey.

(Ted Van Dyk was Hubert Humphrey's chief speechwriter from 1964 to 1968; he prepared most of Humphrey's important drafts on domestic concerns while Humphrey was Vice President. Van Dyk left to serve briefly [1968–69] as vice president of Columbia University in New York. He is now managing a Washington-based political consulting firm and acting as a senior adviser in the McGovern campaign.)

(Martin, a well-known freelance writer, was U.S. Ambassador to the Dominican Republic from 1962 to 1964. In 1970, he drafted speeches for Adlai E. Stevenson III's successful senatorial campaign in Illinois.)

NEW MODEL

An adviser to the small and tightly woven 1972 Humphrey Presidential operation, who declined to be quoted by name, said: "We don't try at this stage of the campaign to get out—I don't know quite how to put it—great prose. Our objective now is to get out issues—to talk about them, to clarify them and to communicate them.

"So we're really not getting out many speech texts. For the most part, we're getting out material for press releases rather than complete texts.

"Anyway, Hubert Humphrey is a better speechmaker than any of us are speechwriters. He thinks about it ahead of time. He knows the issues. This is why we don't try to write finished talks for him. We simply set forth the facts and get them to him.

"He knows as well as anybody else what he should say. In speaking, he may not limit himself to the text. The only thing he wants to do is to keep his speeches brief—and he *is* keeping them brief. He's doing it well."

"KIDDIE CORPS"

Humphrey's reputation of speaking at length is a sensitive matter within his present campaign staff; they are trying to bury the Senator's long-winded image.

More often than not, Humphrey is now speaking briefly and to the point, much to the gratification of Daniel Spiegel, 26, who joined the Humphrey Senate staff as a legislative assistant in July 1971.

Spiegel graduated from Washington University in St. Louis and subsequently earned a master's degree in public administration from Harvard University's John F. Kennedy School of Government and Politics in Cambridge, Mass. After leaving Cambridge in 1969, Spiegel became a legislative assistant to Sen. Alan Cranston, D-Calif.

"I was still in school during the 1968 [Presidential] campaign and played no part in it at all," Spiegel recalled in an interview. "Since I was out of politics in 1968, I don't know anything about the *old* Humphrey."

On Jan. 1, Spiegel left Capitol Hill and moved into cramped quarters on the fifth floor of 1225 19th Street NW, where Humphrey maintains his national Presidential campaign headquarters.

Spiegel writes the Humphrey drafts in a room whose walls are covered with the Senator's speaking schedule, written on plastic sheets with red crayons. Spiegel says he often leaves "early"—at half-past seven in the evening—has his dinner and continues to work at home.

Working alongside Spiegel is Mark G. Epstein, 24, who joined the Humphrey staff when the Presidential drive of Sen. Fred R. Harris, D-Okla., collapsed last year. Epstein graduated from Cornell University and from Princeton's Woodrow Wilson School of Public Affairs.

The lone Minnesotan on the speechwriting team is Robert Burck, 28, who previously served on the staff of Rep. Bertram L. Podell, D-N.Y. Burck co-ordinates the administrative effort, making sure speech drafts reach Humphrey at the right place and at the right time.

"I know it sounds like a kiddie corps—except they are pretty good," an old friend of Humphrey's acknowledged privately. "I saw what they turned out last week on women's lib and it seemed to flow.

"I don't think they are any Richard Goodwins or Ted Sorensens, turning out stuff that anybody will chip in stone. But they are putting out competent and thoughtful speeches. And, between the two of them, Speigel and Epstein put out a hell of a lot of material."

Richard N. Goodwin, who wrote speeches for Presidents Kennedy and Johnson, was traveling in Brazil in mid-February and unavailable for comment on the extent of his current speechwriting activities. He is known, however, to be writing speeches for McCarthy. Goodwin was primarily responsible for Muskie's 1970 election eve televised response to President Nixon's remarks on law-and-order: the Goodwin draft helped catapult Muskie into an early front-running position for the Democratic Presidential nomination. Theodore C. Sorensen, now a partner in the New York law firm of Paul, Weiss, Rifkind, Wharton & Garrison, was at one time John F. Kennedy's chief speechwriter.

TECHNIQUE

"Humphrey is a unique man for a speechwriter to work for," his chief 1972 speechwriter said.

Spiegel added: "He is one of the few politicians in America today who doesn't need a speechwriter, because he's not helpless without a text. In fact, Humphrey is a totally oral man—the most totally oral man I've ever known—and there's no reason why he *should* have a speech text. He's also an oral editor: He will speak his revisions and not write them down as most people do. Invariably, he'll have someone take dictation. He can't work with a pencil over a text."

(On occasion, Humphrey will draft an important speech by dictating what he wants to say. The Humphrey Presidential announcement speech delivered in Philadelphia Jan. 10 was mainly drafted by Humphrey, with the aid of a stenographer.)

On average, Spiegel and Epstein provide Humphrey with one speech for each campaign day, although on a day with a heavy speaking schedule, the candidate may get two texts. They are distributed, usually in excerpt form, to the press; Humphrey, however, prefers to receive his speaking material on small note cards.

Speech themes are usually worked out a week or so in advance between Spiegel and Max M. Kampelman, a partner in the Washington law firm of Fried, Frank, Harris, Shriver & Kampelman.

Kampelman is the major figure outside the formal Humphrey campaign structure and the Senate office. His responsibilities are far wider than speech coordination; he is, for example, Humphrey's chief adviser on Middle East affairs.

Humphrey often confers with Kampelman on what themes should be stressed in his campaign speeches and it is Kampelman who frequently passes Humphrey's viewpoint on to Spiegel and, afterwards, edits his work. Neither Kampelman nor Spiegel regularly travels with Humphrey; for the most part, the three of them communicate by telephone.

REACTION

Spiegel said he does not mind if Humphrey discards a speech topic that has been prepared for him.

But he does resent the fact that, as he put it, "except for occasional dramatic statements, the (national) press isn't interested in covering Humphrey speeches."

"I'm talking about good solid stuff," Spiegel said. "Humphrey is talking a vital Populist theme in Florida and the press is just not picking it up. If I lived in California, I would have no way of knowing what Humphrey was saying in Florida."

Spiegel also said that Humphrey will readily discard a speech if he determines that the atmosphere in the hall is not conducive to his prepared material.

"A speechwriter working in Washington is unable to see if the dinner is too large and everybody is stuffed," he said.

Jackson

In 1968, when Humphrey was also seeking the Presidency, Ben J. Wattenberg, then on the Johnson White House staff, earned a reputation as one of Humphrey's most facile speechwriters.

Four years later, Wattenberg is working long hours as a top aide to Henry Jackson in Jackson's Presidential campaign. But now he is devoting only part of his time to preparing speech drafts.

"I occasionally do some stuff," Wattenberg said in an interview. "But I'm trying like hell to stay away from it because it's very time-consuming and because I'm doing other things: research, public relations, strategy work and some public speaking on my own.

"As in a lot of the campaigns I've been involved with, most of the speeches are joint participatory efforts. The man who makes the main input is Senator Jackson. He's too smart a guy to go off parrot-like and repeat what somebody else says."

Wattenberg, 38, is co-author with Richard M. Scammon of *The Real Majority* (Coward-McCann), which became the most important political handbook of 1970 because the authors were the first to define the many aspects of disruptive change in political terms as "the social issue."

WRITERS

Most of Jackson's Presidential campaign speech drafts are written by Tom Kahn, 33, a New Yorker on leave from the League for Industrial Democracy. Wattenberg described Kahn as "very bright, a brilliant writer." Kahn, Wattenberg said, has also compiled "one of the best personal civil rights' records of any guy I know."

Kahn, who is white, graduated from the predominately black Howard University in Washington. Since then, he has worked closely with Bayard Rustin, director of the A. Philip Randolph Institute. He was also an aide to the late Rev. Dr. Martin Luther King Jr. When King and Rustin planned the massive 1963 civil rights march on Washington, Kahn served as a key lieutenant in the organization and execution of the march.

Aside from Wattenberg and Kahn, Jackson campaign aides who participate actively in the speechdrafting effort include S. Sterling Munro Jr., the Senator's administrative assistant and a major campaign figure, and Grenville Garside, who is acting as campaign legal counsel and is also Jackson's top legislative assistant in the Senate.

Munro usually undertakes the final editing role while Garside, who is also a good writer, concentrates on research. The Jackson speechwriting task force also coordinates its efforts with those of Gerald Hoeck, the Jackson media consultant.

THE CANDIDATE

Jackson is not particularly good at reading prepared speeches before audiences.

"He does not read a text very well," Wattenberg acknowledged, "although he's very good on Q and A.

"As on any relatively good campaign staff, speeches are so important that everybody is involved in it one way or another. When an occasion demands a speech, we discuss it in advance with him and see what's what. We get all the inputs in it that we can.

"Then we'll do up a text to release to the press. But he [Jackson] will talk from notes. We stand by the text. But he really ends up winging it.

"It's awfully hard to go back and forth because he's in Florida or Wisconsin or someplace else and we're in Washington. So an awful lot of his most substantive stuff is right out of his own mouth."

COVERAGE

Wattenberg and other key members of the Jackson campaign staff are relatively pleased with the attention that the press has devoted to the Jackson Presidential drive in the Florida primary—particularly to his proposed constitutional amendment to bar the busing of schoolchildren from their neighborhoods to achieve racial balance in the school system.

As Wattenberg observed: "In Florida, we're doing right fine. Our ideas are getting out well. But, nationally, we're concerned. You end up thinking at times a little like [Vice President Spiro T.] Agnew as to how we're being covered.

"Some of the stuff that *The New York Times* is running about Jackson is just fantasyland. A recent piece that cites two right-of-center candidates— Henry Jackson and Sam Yorty—is just out of sight. It's like saying two left-of-center candidates are Ed Muskie and Gus Hall."

(Yorty is mayor of Los Angeles: Hall, a veteran leader of the U.S. Communist Party, was sentenced in 1949 to an eight-year prison term for advocating the violent overthrow of the U.S. government. He is the party's Presidential candidate this year.)

The Jackson campaign headquarters issues either a press release or a full speech text each day.

"Sometimes, the Senator will say, 'That's no good; that's not what we want to say,' " Wattenberg said.

"He's probably a more oral man than a writing editor, but he's both— especially when he's not pressed for time. He's a lawyer and he's very analytical. And he likes to get to the root of things. 'What are we really saying? How can we put this in a truly pungent way?' "

McGovern

By design, as much as by economic necessity, the McGovern speechwriting process is less elaborate than most. For one thing, the candidate is uneasy when delivering speeches written by others. For another, his chief assistants maintain the Senator is his own best speechwriter. Yet, he does rely on his staff for guidance and insight as he pursues his quest for the Democratic Presidential nomination.

SYSTEM

In an interview, McGovern said "there is not any pattern, there's no process" to his speechwriting apparatus. However, there is a basic understanding between him and his legislative assistant, John D. Holum, that speech drafts will be prepared whenever the candidate plans to deal with a specific issue. Most speeches, however, are delivered off-the-cuff, without a text. In those cases, "the text," Holum said, "is his own delivery."

Holum, a graduate of George Washington Law School, has been with McGovern since 1965. He served two years as publications director of the South Dakota Farmers Union.

With the exception of an economic task force, McGovern has no formal backup system for preparation of his speeches. "Committees," said Holum, "cannot write speeches."

Holum noted that he keeps track of the Senator's schedule on the campaign trail to "see what he needs a speech for. . . . If it is a specialized speech, I will write a draft or Gordon will write a draft." (Gordon L. Weil serves as McGovern's press secretary.)

McGovern has decreed that no speech draft should run more than five pages, at the outside, said Holum. "He tends to use the drafts as guidance . . . he'll extrapolate and extemporize."

Holum thinks that McGovern is "the best writer that ever worked for him. It's frustrating to see a speech that you worked on be improved upon, but he usually improves on it. If he has a weakness, it is that a sentence will sometimes become too long."

Ted Van Dyk also praised the candidate's style.

"He writes very well himself. Most politicians can't write at all," said Van Dyk.

McGovern, interviewed on a flight from Miami to Washington, said as much as 90 per cent of his campaign remarks are extemporaneous. "I've either spoken without a note or with nothing more than the key words on an envelope or the back of a piece of paper," he said.

On occasion, however, when he wants to "address a single theme in depth and I want to develop my position more clearly and perhaps with some fresh insights, I try to pick the person most competent in that area.

Then I will sit down with him and tell him as clearly as I can what I want to do and ask him to try a draft. Once it's completed, it comes right to me. If there's time, I try to show it to a couple of people. Then I do considerable revising myself. I may deliver it verbatim or put it in front of me and digress. I find that almost never can I take someone else's script and deliver it as written."

McGovern is suspicious of the perfectly prepared address. "While I admire a well-constructed speech, I always think it is written by some clever young speechwriter," he said.

ADVICE

Although McGovern trusts his own perceptions of developing issues, he also seeks counsel from Holum, who remains in Washington, and from Weil, who normally travels with him.

"I try to learn. I ask them a lot of questions," said McGovern. "I don't always know who they talk to."

McGovern recalled a discussion with Yancey F. Martin, a black special assistant, concerning the busing issue. Martin, a former head of the minorities division for the Democratic National Committee, recalled his childhood in the South. Martin told McGovern that black people have "been bused for 50 years. They bused me right by white schools to black schools."

"That's the kind of insight that hadn't occurred to me," said McGovern, who developed that thought in subsequent public addresses.

QUESTION AND ANSWER

McGovern, who believes that the old-style stand-up speech is a thing of the past, has been concentrating on audience participation whenever possible in the campaign.

He said he prefers question-and-answer sessions. "I'd never give a speech if it wasn't for the fact that speeches are required. I'd just say, 'Let's hear your questions.' "

He continued: "There are so many doubts on people's minds that it's important to get these questions out on the table. . . .

"I don't think the American voter is a very good listener any more. They have been subjected to so much radio and television. . . . Coming into its own is the question-and-answer kind of thing. I encourage people in the audience to offer advice, to get them talking ideas."

Holum said McGovern is at his best in the give-and-take sessions, without a prepared text. "The best kind of speech he gives is the response to a hard question," he said.

Lindsay

A sense of elitism binds the men around New York Mayor Lindsay. Rightly or wrongly, they feel that Lindsay's Presidential campaign possesses special qualities that set it apart from those of the other Democratic candidates.

SPEECH EDITOR

"After all, we've been running our own show for six years," said [Thomas B.] Morgan, the mayor's press secretary. "There's no issue that we haven't been up to our gut in during these years."

Morgan, 45, has been working for Lindsay since April 1969, having relinquished a successful writing career to join the mayor's staff. From 1953 to 1958, Morgan was a senior editor at *Look* magazine, which ceased publication last year. Morgan's specialty as a freelancer was political profiles. He has written four books.

Now, in private, Morgan refers to Lindsay as "the chief." Usually, he is at the mayor's side during a campaign trip. But, on Feb. 17, Lindsay was taking a brief rest in Nassau and Morgan, who had flown directly to New York from Florida, where Lindsay had been touring, was at his desk in City Hall.

For Morgan, who describes himself as Lindsay's chief speech editor, privacy does not come easily. Several aides work alongside him in the small office and, from time to time, reporters walk in unannounced. Five sculptured *Peanuts* cartoon characters form a plaque on Morgan's cluttered desk, with the inscription: "How Can We Lose When We're So Sincere?"

"We do an awful lot under enormous pressure," Morgan said, chain-smoking filtered cigarettes. "You work for six or seven days straight and then you disappear for a while. Our troops really pour it out."

TECHNIQUES

Lindsay's staff asserts that the mayor demands a high standard of professionalism in his speech texts, which are always distributed verbatim to the press, without an accompanying release. Accordingly, the Lindsay speech-writing team follows an elaborate, if informally managed, procedure in producing Lindsay texts for the Presidential campaign.

Briefings. Before Lindsay develops a public position for a major policy address, the mayor prefers to be briefed on all sides of the issue.

As Morgan described the process: "We invite a lot of people—insiders and outsiders. Each guy speaks up. We let them fight it out in front of the mayor. It helps shape his thinking if he knows the range of everybody else's thinking. He needs to know what the choice of evils are.

"That's how it is in real life. Say Consolidated Edison wants to put up a new power plant in Queens; if we say 'yes,' then you have a major new pollutant on your hands. But if we say 'no,' then the city soon runs short of power. It's this type of choice-of-evils question which faces the mayor, literally every day of his life. He's out on the firing line. That's a far different proposition than putting a bill into the Senate hopper."

The briefing session with Lindsay is customarily followed by a more nuts-and-bolts discussion with the mayor, in which the outline of a forth-coming speech is framed.

Taking part in the latter briefing are Morgan, Jay L. Kriegel, 31, the mayor's chief of staff, and one or another of the Lindsay speechwriters.

Currently, two men are bearing the brunt of drafting speeches for the Lindsay campaign:

• Ira S. Mothner, 39, who was named assistant to the mayor for research and policy studies in September 1971. Previously, Mothner was on the staff of *Look* for 14 years, serving for the last 10 as a senior editor.
• Gordon J. Davis, 30, who was named Feb. 13 as a special assistant to the mayor. Davis joined the Lindsay staff in 1968 and had served since 1970 as secretary to the mayor's cabinet. He is one of the few black speechwriters currently working on behalf of a Presidential candidate.

Drafts. "The first drafts come back usually within 48 hours, and Jay and I pull them apart," Morgan said. "If there's time, [Campaign Manager Richard R.] Aurelio will have a look at it.

"Once in a great while, a speech can go right through. But usually when it comes back to us there are problems and it must be ground up to a certain extent. It's a question of maintaining quality and meeting factual needs."

Mothner said: "The first draft goes back to Tom and Jay for the crude editing process. Tom tells us, 'Forget this, stress that.' The second draft is a very much cleaned-up version. After further editing, the mayor has to see that. As to who edits the second draft, that depends very much on who's there at the time.

"There are no formal meetings. We can't run this type of operation that way. Often, it's just a matter of who happens to be available. You cannot set up a production schedule for this as you would for a magazine because we never know when the mayor is going to be available. Also, we never know when issues are going to change or when schedules will be altered."

Morgan said the second draft of a Lindsay campaign speech comes back to him from the writer "in a day or so." That draft, Morgan noted, goes to the mayor, but only after yet another heavy editing session. "We do what we call a line-by-line," Morgan said.

Whenever Lindsay is out of the city, the speech draft is flown to him or, more often, sent via a telephone copying machine which first became available commercially last year. For an average Lindsay text of 2,000 to 2,500 words, the transmitting process takes about four minutes.

"The mayor sees the next-to-last draft," Morgan continued. "He takes a Flair pen to that and chops at it. He likes precision, a minimum of rhetoric and a maximum of substance."

RESOURCES

"Let's recognize that a speech is like a camel," Mothner said. (A camel, it has been said, is an animal that has been put together by a committee.) "No one man writes a Lindsay speech."

Morgan noted that the mayor's staff possesses "an enormous research capacity," which includes "volunteers from the universities and the foundation world," as well as New York City agencies. They compile a wide range of statistics—all of which are readily available to the Lindsay campaign organization.

Research Staff.   Before drafting a speech, Mothner or Davis will normally call upon the resources of the research staff attached to the Lindsay Presidential campaign headquarters on Madison Avenue.

"Local people are always sending us memos," Morgan said. "But it doesn't stop there. We sent Mothner to Wisconsin for four days to get some sense of issues in the state and to see what Lindsay's needs were going to be.

"The resource guys in the universities and foundations are always sending us texts, some of which are pretty good," Morgan said. (A speech on youth, written on a college campus, which had arrived that morning, lay, as yet unread, on his desk.)

Greenfield.   Some of Lindsay's best-written speeches are prepared by Jeff Greenfield, 29, an aide to David Garth, whose firm, Garth Associates Inc., is producing Lindsay's media campaign.

Greenfield, a 1967 graduate of Yale Law School, became Lindsay's chief speechwriter in October 1968 and served in that capacity longer than any other person before leaving last year. Previously, he was a legislative assistant to the late Sen. Robert Kennedy.

Lindsay and Greenfield remain close. In a brief telephone interview, Greenfield said that he is writing very few speeches for Lindsay's campaign, that task now having fallen mainly to Mothner. Recently, however, Greenfield drafted a speech that Lindsay delivered to a South Boston audience Feb. 10, dealing, in the main, with Northern Ireland.

Greenfield showed the Ulster speech to Lindsay while the mayor was riding to the airport to attend a meeting in Washington. The mayor indicated what changes he wanted made and that evening the final text was ready.

A few days later, Lindsay was reading these Kennedyesque words in South Boston: "We were told these Irishmen and women were breaking the law and threatening order—and for that offense, 13 men of Ireland will never walk again, never laugh, never raise a child or hear a song or love another human being."

UTILIZATION

While on the stump, Lindsay, on average, delivers two major policy speeches every three days. In late February, he stepped up his campaign schedule to four or five days a week.

If a speech is technical, Lindsay will usually read it word-for-word. On the other hand, for more polemical material, the mayor will often ad-lib his way along, a process that his aides describe as "working off the speech."

Morgan said: "When the mayor concludes his prepared remarks, he will sometimes lay down the text and say, 'Now let me tell you what this speech really means to me. . . .' "

Lindsay normally speaks for 20 to 25 minutes, which Kriegel and Morgan feel is about 10 to 15 minutes too long. They would like him to condense his remarks whenever he is in a political setting and devote more time to answering questions.

Press. The top Lindsay staff bitterly resents the kind of coverage—or, more properly speaking, non-coverage—that Lindsay's speeches have received in Florida, especially on national television.

Morgan cited as a glaring example Feb. 15, when Lindsay delivered two major speeches, on landlord-tenant relations and on crime. That day, the CBS *Evening News* featured a Lindsay walking tour of Miami Beach past the White House Hotel, which has many elderly residents.

The film depicted Lindsay being reviled by former New York City constituents, most of whom were identified as Jews.

"I think Lindsay has more of a problem with the press than the others," Morgan said. "First of all nobody is neutral about Lindsay. that kind of sets the stage. As far as the reporters are concerned, first they were writing the celebrity story and, after we did well in the delegate thing in Arizona, they began writing the reaction story. But at least they are treating him now as a viable candidate."

"We do a lot of stuff that never surfaces because he's treated as a celebrity," Mothner said. "It's unfair."

Expanding the Base. Nonetheless, the speechwriting effort plays an important role in the Lindsay campaign because Lindsay's interests were widely perceived before the campaign as being narrowly restricted to urban problems. Now the mayor feels the need to broaden his image and take on new issues.

"Let's face it," Mothner said. "We've always been damn good on urban issues. This is our *shtick*. This we do. But now the time has come to branch out—into the war, into environment, into a lot of other important things."

In branching out, the Lindsay staff denies that at the same time the mayor is seeking to become a media candidate—a charge that has been privately levelled against him by several of his Democratic opponents in the Florida Presidential primary.

"We have made only two events in all the time we've been in Florida," Morgan said. "One was to eat a tomato on a farm with migrant workers. The other was to go scuba diving in Biscayne Bay, which is polluted. In each case, we did so to dramatize a specific problem or situation. But if others are calling us a media candidate, we are willing to take that criticism."

ANALYSIS

So far, Lindsay has shown no signs of reducing his heavy speechmaking schedule in favor of media "events."

And, so far, Mothner and Davis have been drafting a steady round of Lindsay Presidential campaign speeches while remaining on the New York City payroll. Morgan said all the Presidential speechwriting occurs outside office hours.

Mothner composes his speech drafts in a dingy office in a run-down courthouse directly north of City Hall. The structure, built in the style of a Florentine palace, was erected by William M. ("Boss") Tweed, grand sachem of the Tammany Society, in the 1870s.

Occasionally, in the late evening, when Mothner and Davis are feeling the pressure of their work, they don formal top hats which hang on a peg by the door and dance around amid the peeling plaster.

"No one should be a speechwriter for more than a few years," Mothner said. "It's not good for the soul."

·B·

Financing a Nomination Campaign

Finance Structure and Strategy

BY XANDRA KAYDEN

Financial Determinants of Campaign Decisions

Much of the focus of campaign reform has been on the role of financial considerations in campaign decision-making. Some organizations integrated fund raising and spending with political activities, and some kept the two separate. Whether a campaign chose integration over separation depended on personal relations, fund-raising strategies, and the experience of the past. This was particularly true for the Ford primary campaign, which was haunted by the specter of Watergate, and felt that it could not afford the slightest confusion of Gerald Ford's activities, or those of his staff, in his role as president and his role as candidate. Once he had won the nomination, however, the President was somewhat less constrained. A major party nominee, even if he is an incumbent, has to campaign openly. And by then, of course, it was not necessary to raise much money because the general election was subsidized with public funds.

The Reagan campaign was integrated, more out of a lack of resources to afford separate personnel than as a matter of principle, but also because the major focus of its fund-raising strategy was direct mail appeals, which do not require separate staff at the policy level. It did require, however, a large clerical staff to open and record the small donations that are the bounty of direct mail campaigns. Late in the campaign, when Reagan began making television appeals, the staff was hopelessly inadequate to the

Excerpted from Xandra Kayden, *Report on Campaign Finance: Based on the Experience of the 1976 Presidential Campaigns* (Cambridge, Mass.: Institute of Politics, Harvard University, 1977), pp. 10–20. Reprinted by permission of the author, Xandra Kayden, Institute of Politics, Harvard University.

task; at such times the campaign got short term loans by weighing and sampling the contents of the mail bags the clerical staff could not handle.

Birch Bayh's campaign was perhaps the most integrated, largely because of a combination of personality, choice of tactics, and his relatively late entrance into the race. His campaign manager, James Friedman, had both political and financial campaign experience, which facilitated integration. Because of Bayh's late start, he had personally to engage in raising funds, making his campaign the only one that was forced to rely heavily on the candidate for such purposes during the primaries. According to Friedman, each day of the candidate's schedule had to include some fund-raising effort.

Fund-Raising Strategy

Most of the candidates began raising money before the new law went into effect. Henry Jackson began in July, 1974, and by the time the primaries began in February, 1976, had amassed several million dollars. While most campaign strategies relied upon early fund raising in order to free the candidate for political activity when the primary season really began in earnest, the major advantage of an early start in the 1976 election was, of course, the absence of $1,000 contribution limits, not imposed by law until January, 1975. Jackson, following the original Senate proposal, self-imposed a $3,000 limit ($6,000 per family), but the strategies of all campaigns reflected the belief that some limits would be imposed, and that the campaigns could not, therefore, politically afford an approach that did not at least reflect a concern for avoiding undue influence of large donors.

Fund-raising strategies included the following time-honored activities: direct mail campaigns, telephone banks, personal solicitations by the candidate and/or his staff, dinners, television appeals, and special events such as concerts and parties. The difference in 1976 was a vastly increased reliance on those activities that would reach more givers (particularly direct mail, television, and, in some cases, dinners), and less use of personal solicitation.

Contribution Limits

The new federal law imposes a limit of $1,000 on the amount that a donor can give to any one candidate, with an aggregate limit of $25,000 to all federal candidates in any calendar year. Certain groups can give up to $5,000. Donations of $100 and more must be reported to the Federal Election Commission (FEC) with the name, address, and occupation of the donor, and if the campaign is to receive matching funds, similar information about donations in lesser amounts must also be furnished. Gifts up to $250 from any individual donor can be matched.

In the past, it had not been inefficient for the candidate or his representative to spend an hour on the telephone raising $25,000 from one donor. In 1976, however, the $1,000 contribution ceiling made it twenty-five times more costly in time and energy to raise the same amount of money. For most of the conference participants,* this was the crux of the new campaign reform. The old boy network of large contributors became a relic of the past. They could no longer give in great sums and would no longer spend the time raising small amounts.

As one might expect from fund raisers, taking the large contributors out of politics received mixed reviews from the participants. Some felt strongly that a candidate learns a great deal by having to ask for money and from listening to the concerns and interests of those who can afford to give it. Such fund raising was viewed as providing a kind of accountability to one's donors that is more concrete than one's accountability to the voters.

On the other hand, others thought that asking for money is demeaning to the candidate, as well as to those who give it, if all parties are not sophisticated enough to know that it is a well-oiled process. A story was told about a candidate in an earlier campaign, whose fund raiser was on the phone with a large giver. The donor wanted to talk to the candidate. The fund raiser put the donor on "hold" while he briefed the candidate on the donor's family (his son's recent bar mitzvah, the engagement of his daughter, and so on). When the candidate got on the phone, he congratulated the man on the bar mitzvah and engagement, leading the donor to call the fund raiser later to marvel at the extraordinary memory and thoughtfulness of the candidate to have remembered family details at such a rushed time. Attention to such matters is typical of politics, but misleading unless seen in context.

Still others, of course, accepted the importance of precluding large donors in order to preclude undue influence.

Direct Mail Appeals

Because of the $1,000 ceiling on contributions, matching funds became critical to the strategy of every campaign, however opposed it might be ideologically to the idea of public financing. Although the Supreme Court has taken the position that campaigns have some option in this area, practice would suggest that campaigns do not, given the limited amount of

*Editor's note: Xandra Kayden's report came out of a conference she organized of campaign finance people—the "participants" referred to here.

time available for fund raising. Qualifying for matching funds, therefore, became preeminent in importance.

A major factor in the choice of fund-raising activities was determined by the administration of the campaign reform law. The Federal Election Commission would count toward matching entitlements all money raised by direct mail solicitation, but in the end discounted the market value of a concert or dinner from the price paid for the ticket. There was, therefore, a better return for the campaign organization in terms of its time and energy, if not money, to approach potential donors through the mail.

Direct mail solicitations are most effective when the appeal is made to special interest groups and to those at one end or the other of the ideological spectrum. Having to raise money by direct mail (or by television appeals which are based on identical strategies) caused at least one campaign to redirect its political strategy.

Several candidates tried to stay away from direct mail appeals because they thought they did not have constituencies who would be responsive, because they did not have effective lists of potential givers, or because they could not afford to finance the mailing. The first reason was true for Ford and Carter, both of whom ran more centrist campaigns hoping to appeal to traditional social values. In the end, Ford was forced to make direct mail appeals and raised more money by that means than any other.

All the participants regarded direct mail appeals as expensive and technologically difficult to mount and sustain. They thought it would not be worth the effort except for matching funds. Udall was the most successful in developing a list of 59,000 contributors and, by the end of the campaign, getting a 12 percent return from those on it. All of the candidates developed lists and made repeated use of them, going back again and again to those who had already given and asking for more. The Republicans' task was made easier by an agreement reached between Ford and Reagan to share the list maintained by the Republican National Committee.

Special Interest Appeals

Aside from the ideological appeals made most successfully perhaps by Reagan, Udall, and Church of the campaigns represented, there were two other effective fund-raising strategies: the appeal by Jackson to the Jewish community; and the almost ethnic appeal by Carter to Southerners in general and Georgians in particular.

Jackson was the only candidate able to tap into an already-organized special interest group, a strategy far more common in earlier years. Bayh tried to make a similar appeal to labor, but unions were not responsive. The political action committees, of which more is said below, were unsure of what they could do and fearful of overstepping the law. It is also probable that labor and similar groups did not perceive any clear reason for supporting one candidate over the others. Such groups often prefer to support an incumbent or a clear winner; the outcome in 1976 was too uncertain.

Geography

Geography played a major role in the fund-raising capability of the candidates. A good deal of the money comes from New York, Texas, and California. These three states accounted for 30 percent of Ford's total contributions. If a candidate has a strong geographic or organizational base of his own, however, as did Carter, that base can compensate for weaknesses in the traditional centers of political donations. Carter was sustained by Georgia, which provided 37 percent of his funds through March, 1976, and $270,000 in the period when matching grants could not be made by FEC (March to May, 1976), as a result of the Supreme Court's invalidation of the structure of the Commission. Jackson, too, was supported strongly by his home state of Washington. Both Reagan and Ford relied heavily on Republican money in California in the early stages of their campaigns.

Carter's Business a Potent Factor in Rise

BY NICHOLAS M. HORROCK

On the back cover of his autobiography, *Why Not The Best?*" Jimmy Carter lists his accomplishments as "former Governor of Georgia, farmer, engineer, naval officer, nuclear physicist, Christian, American."

He omitted businessman. Yet it is in the field of business, the management of a family-owned peanut warehousing and fertilizer operation, that Mr. Carter has achieved one of his major areas of success. It has also provided him with both the freedom to develop his political career and substantial amounts of cash at crucial moments in two races for the Governorship of Georgia.

Nicholas M. Horrock, "Carter's Business a Potent Factor in Rise," *The New York Times,* May 26, 1976, pp. 1 and 15. © 1976 by The New York Times Company. Reprinted by permission.

In the 23 years since Mr. Carter left the United States Navy to take over his father's business interests in Plains, Ga., the Carter warehouse has grown from a value of from $20,000 to $25,000, with a drought-year income in 1954 of $254, to an agribusiness that grossed nearly $2.5 million in sales in 1975 and is now estimated to be $1.6 million.

There is no comparison between the political impact of the wealth of the Kennedys or the Rockefellers and that of the Carter family, but the strong bonds between the Carter family members and their willingness to work together has made them a potent factor in Mr. Carter's rise to become front-runner for the Democratic Presidential nomination.

The Carter family holdings, in which Jimmy Carter has the principal interest, include the 3,100-acre Carter Farms Inc. and a family partnership that buys and sells peanuts, gins cotton and sells fertilizer and insecticides to farmers in the Plains area.

In 1974 Mr. Carter reported his personal worth at $588,628. In a recent interview Billy Carter, the candidate's younger brother, who operates the business, said that figures now being prepared for a new financial statement indicated that 1975 was the best year in the history of the warehouse business and that it would result in substantial increases in Jimmy Carter's income and worth.

Billy Carter said he expected the financial statement to show a "radical" increase in the worth of the business, which may put Jimmy Carter's personal worth close to $1 million. In December 1974, Mr. Carter issued a statement placing his net worth at $558,628.20.

Comparison with Others

That figure represents greater financial assets than those reported by President Ford and two of Mr. Carter's Democratic opponents, Senator Frank Church of Idaho and Representative Morris K. Udall of Arizona. But his 1974 holdings are far smaller than those of Ronald Reagan, the former Governor of California, who is challenging Mr. Ford for the Republican Presidential nomination.

Last week, at the request of *The New York Times*, Mr. Carter made available additional financial data: copies of his Federal and Georgia tax returns for the years 1970 through 1974. He is expected shortly to make known his 1975 tax returns.

Mr. Carter's income in the 1970–74 period ranged from a low in 1970 of $46,542 to a high in 1973 of $131,115. The fluctuation resulted largely from the varying profits of the family peanut warehouse in Plains. In 1973, for example, the warehouse earned some $220,000 of which Mr. Carter received about 60 percent.

Both President Ford and Mr. Reagan earn between $250,000 and

$300,000 a year. Mr. Church earns about $60,000 and Mr. Udall about $70,000, based on reports they have issued. Gov. Edmund G. Brown, Jr. of California, another Democratic Presidential candidate, has not issued a formal financial statement.

Figures Reviewed Twice

Mr. Carter's tax returns are prepared by the firm of Perry, Chambliss and Sutton in Americus, Ga., a respected, if small, organization of certified public accountants. The Times asked two C.P.A.'s, one in Atlanta and the other in Washington, to review the figures.

They declined to be identified for professional reasons but both said Mr. Carter's return was "not aggressive," with no apparent attempts to maximize his permissible tax writeoffs.

"Frankly, I think there are several more things he could have tried to avoid every possible tax," one of the accountants said.

In 1974, for instance, Mr. Carter paid $26,153 in Federal taxes on a gross income of $97,334, or just over 25 percent. The year before, Mr. Carter paid $51,836 on a gross income of $131,115 or about 39 percent.

A review of the returns shows that the Carters have not been very successful in their stock market investments.

Indeed, they once took a loss on a stock. They have made substantial charitable contributions, including large donations to their Baptist Church in Plains, and had relatively small medical costs over the last five years.

Among the Carters' current stock holdings are Coca-Cola, Rich's Department Store in Georgia and Advanced Investors.

Mr. Carter's charitable contributions totaled $2,397 in 1971 and $8,752 in 1974. The 1971 contributions included $1,995 to two Baptist churches and smaller amounts to Christmas Seals, Planned Parenthood, and the Naval Academy Alumni Association, among others. A much longer list of small donations was on the 1974 list.

Although Mr. Carter has said he would favor doing away with some tax deductions, such as interest payments, he has listed a variety of such deductions for several years.

Because of the close-knit relationship within the Carter family, it is hard to separate Jimmy Carter's wealth and fortunes from those of the family business.

From 1953, when he resigned from the Navy to take over the family interests until the late 1960's when he was deeply involved in his second campaign to become Governor of Georgia, Jimmy Carter was at the helm of the Carter enterprises.

Since 1969, the business has been supervised by Billy Carter, and it has continued to flourish.

Billy Carter attributed the most recent economic leap forward, from 1974 to 1975, in part to rising prices of fertilizer and in part to the first fruits of capital improvements—the installation of peanut-shelling equipment. The Carter warehouse is now able to buy peanuts from farmers, shell them and prepare them for market, rather than just to handle payments from transshipment on a commission basis.

The Carter warehouse is a partnership among the candidate, Billy Carter and their mother, Lillian Carter. Billy Carter said it had a replacement value of $1.6 million in buildings, stock and equipment.

The ownership of Carter Farms Inc. in Sumter and Webster Counties in southwest Georgia near Plains is shared by nine members of the Carter family, including the candidate's sister and two sons.

Seed Peanuts Raised

The centerpiece of Carter Farms is a Federal peanut allotment that permits it to plant and harvest 241 acres of peanuts each year. The Carters raise seed peanuts for sale to other farmers who grow peanuts for production.

Setting a value on land in rural areas is necessarily imprecise. However, Jimmy Carter values his share of the family holdings, some 2,083 acres, at $338,742. At this rate the entire 3,100 acres is worth over $500,000. Several family members own land in the area that is not part of Carter Farms.

By Georgia standards, the farm operation and the peanut business are medium-sized operations.

Several agricultural experts familiar with the area said that the farm and warehouse were probably worth between $2 million and $3 million.

The Carters built up their business, according to Thomas J. Chandler, who heads a peanut mill in nearby Americus, Ga., through "agressiveness." Until the Carters installed a peanut shelling machine they acted as agents for Mr. Chandler's operation, but now they are his competitors.

"I have known them 18 years and they are very reputable people," Mr. Chandler said in a telephone interview. "I'd say the key to their success was initiative. They've done better for their farmers and I can show you a lot of peanut businesses around here that have not improved, that are stagnant."

Business Aids Politics

In addition to being a profitable agribusiness, the Carter operation provided unusual advantages when Jimmy Carter decided to enter politics. When he first sought the governorship, unsuccessfully, in 1966, Mr. Carter told his close friend and political confidant, Charles Kirbo, an Atlanta lawyer, that he had amassed $80,000 from the business to use "if necessary."

Although Jimmy Carter was given little chance in the 1966 election, as the Democratic primary approached it appeared that he might win. Carter money—one former campaign aide estimated that it was as much as $65,000—was fed into the campaign, to buy last minute television and other advertising.

Mr. Carter lost in the primary but by only 20,000 votes and he established himself as a statewide candidate.

After the election his backers arranged a fund-raising dinner in Atlanta to pay some of the costs and Mr. Carter recovered a large part of his personal campaign investment.

"There's still $20,000 outstanding from that race," Billy Carter said with a grin, "and my accountant makes me carry it on the books as a bad debt."

Jimmy Carter also drew on money from the warehouse business at a crucial point in his successful gubernatorial race in 1970. Billy Carter estimated that the business provided $10,000 for Jimmy's campaign, mainly to pay for early advertising expenditures in the Democratic primary. Billy said that nearly all of this money had been paid back, from outside campaign contributions, after it became clear that his brother was going to win.

No Spending Controls

In 1966 and 1970 neither Georgia nor Federal law set any limits on the amount of money a candidate could spend on himself. Nor were there regulations on campaign loans from businesses or banks.

The family business has other political advantages. After his loss in 1966, with his younger brother on hand to take over and both of their wives involved in the business (both Rosalynn, Jimmy's wife, and Sybil, Billy's wife, have served as bookkeepers), Jimmy Carter was free to spend considerable time running for the 1970 gubernatorial nomination. Jimmy Carter once estimated that he made 1,800 speeches from 1966 through 1970.

Some of his political opponents do not disguise their envy. One Atlanta lawyer with political ambitions said in an interview: "I could have been Governor too if I could have up and left my law practice to gallivant around running for office."

In his autobiography, Jimmy Carter credits his younger brother for this. "Our friendship has grown steadily with the years," he wrote, "and I realize that his willingness to operate our farms and warehouses has made it possible for me to hold public office."

Carter Campaign Funds Raised by a Group of Georgia Lawyers

BY NICHOLAS M. HORROCK

A small group of influential Georgia lawyers who recognized Jimmy Carter's political potential 10 years ago have formed the core of his financial support ever since then.

The pattern took shape in Mr. Carter's two gubernatorial campaigns in 1966 and 1970, which became the organizational base for his present front-running effort for the 1976 Democratic Presidential nomination. Mr. Carter lost in the Democratic primary in 1966; four years later he was elected Governor of Georgia.

Interviews with persons familiar with Mr. Carter's political history produced the following major points on his campaign financing in 1966 and 1970:

• Mr. Carter's backers borrowed money from banks on their signatures to provide the "seed money," or early financing, of his 1966 and 1970 campaigns. The loans were usually repaid from later campaign contributions. At least two of Mr. Carter's key backers are in the banking business.

(In 1974, after changes in Federal and Georgia laws required the publication of names of political contributors, the present Governor, George Busbee, received widespread criticism because a group of bank officials had raised a $181,000 campaign fund for him by obtaining bank loans.)

• Mr. Carter lent money from his family business to his own campaigns in 1966 and 1970. He took a loss in 1966, but in 1970 he recovered all the money from contributions that came in after he won the Democratic primary and was virtually assured of victory in the general election.

• Mr. Carter collected money from political supporters on three occasions after he became Governor: First to "sell" his plan to reorganize state government to the public; later to supplement the salary of a state official, in order, he said, to attract the most qualified man for the job, and finally to seed his Presidential race.

• After it was clear, in the late summer of 1970, that Mr. Carter would be the winner of the gubernatorial election, he began to receive contributions from special interest groups and individuals. In a news conference reported by The Atlanta Constitution on Aug. 27, 1970, Mr. Carter was asked if he had received "large" contributions from corporations. Mr. Carter told the newsmen he had, but declined to state the amounts or the names of the contributors.

Nicholas M. Horrock, "Carter Campaign Funds Raised by a Group of Georgia Lawyers," *The New York Times*, May 27, 1976, p. 24. © 1976 by The New York Times Company. Reprinted by permission.

Under the Federal Corrupt Practices Act in effect at the time, it was illegal for corporations to contribute to the campaigns of persons running for Federal office, but the law did not mention recipients of such gifts.

Lawyers differ on whether the act, now superseded by the new Federal elections law, covered candidates for state, county and municipal races. In the recent prosecution of such violations by Federal authorities, none has been brought in connection with state and local campaigns.

Last March 18, Mr. Carter was asked about his 1970 contributions on NBC's "Tomorrow" television show. Mr. Carter said that "nobody ever made a report of contributors and we didn't maintain those records." He did say, however, "What we do have left of them will be made public."

In 1970 neither Georgia law nor Federal law required a candidate for state office to record financial contributions or to make them public.

This month, Jody Powell, Mr. Carter's principal press spokesman and Elizabeth Rainwater, another press spokesman, said that Carter workers and family members were hunting for the data.

David H. Gambrell, an Atlanta lawyer and one of Mr. Carter's key backers in 1970, said he had kept careful records of all contributions and expenditures that passed through the main Carter headquarters in Atlanta. He said he had turned these over to Mr. Carter after the election.

He also said that some contributions had been accepted and spent by local and county Carter organizations, and that no record would have been kept in the Atlanta office.

In addition to getting Mr. Gambrell's files, the 1970 Carter campaign set up a computerized list of supporters that became a nucleus for the lists that are now in use. Tom Lowndes, a Coca-Cola Company executive who worked on the project in 1970, said the list might give some indication of who gave money.

Richard Harden, an accountant who worked in the campaign, was quoted by the Capitol Hill News Service recently as saying: "The contributions were automated. They kept them on a computer, and there were monthly printouts of all the contributions."

Five men constituted the inner circle of support that made it possible for Mr. Carter to become governor.

The first is Charles Kirbo, an Atlanta lawyer who first met Mr. Carter in 1962, and is now regarded as one of his closest confidants. Mr. Kirbo is a senior partner of King & Spalding, a law firm here whose clients include the Coca-Cola Company and the Cox Broadcasting Corporation.

In an interview, Mr. Kirbo estimated that he contributed $2,000 to $3,000 to Mr. Carter in the two gubernatorial races. He also said he had raised money in Mr. Carter's behalf and had signed notes for loans, against uncollected contributions.

Philip Alston, who was first introduced to Mr. Carter in 1966, later became finance chairman of Mr. Carter's 1970 campaign. Mr. Alston is senior partner of Alston, Miller & Gaines, another Atlanta law firm whose clients include the Chrysler Corporation, the American Oil Company, Eastman Kodak and E. I. duPont de Nemours & Co.

$10,000 From Family

Mr. Alston said in an interview that in the two races he and his family might have contributed as much as $10,000 to Mr. Carter and that he had also raised contributions from friends and associates.

Mr. Gambrell, who also met Mr. Carter in the early 1960's was treasurer of the 1970 campaign. Mr. Gambrell and his father, E. Smythe Gambrell, are in separate, equally well-known Atlanta law firms. Smythe Gambrell, one of the early Carter backers, is a major stockholder in Eastern Airlines.

David Gambrell was appointed to the Senate seat of the late Richard Russell in 1971 by Governor Carter, whose political opponents charged that Mr. Gambrell's contributions to Mr. Carter "bought the seat."

Mr. Gambrell characterizes this attack as a "smear" and said that he and his father contributed a total of about $4,500 to the Carter campaign in 1970. He gave up his Senate seat in 1973 after losing the 1972 primary to Sam Nunn, who won the general election.

William Gunter, who in 1966 was a lawyer in Gainesville, Ga., in a firm that represented the Ralston Purina Company and Georgia poultry producers, is another major Carter supporter.

In 1972 Mr. Gunter was appointed to the Georgia Supreme Court by Mr. Carter. In an interview, he estimated that his personal contribution to Mr. Carter in the two political races totaled $2,500 to $3,000.

He said that he borrowed money for the 1966 campaign on his own signature but that the loan had been repaid from later contributions. "I would have had to stand for it had it not been paid," he said.

The fifth major backer is James B. Langford, a lawyer from Calhoun, Ga., whose firm represents major textile interests. Bert Lance, a principal with Mr. Langford in the ownership of the First National Bank of Calhoun, is another major supporter of Mr. Carter's. Mr. Lance was later appointed by Mr. Carter as director of the Georgia Department of Transportation.

Campaigns Not Expensive

Neither the 1966 campaign nor the one in 1970 was expensive, by either Georgia or national standards. In 1966, Mr. Carter's associates estimated the campaign cost at about $200,000 and said it had produced a deficit. Mr. Carter personally lost about $20,000 in his unsuccessful bid.

In 1970 the Carter campaign spent about $400,000 through the Democratic primary, which included a runoff, and about $100,000 in the general election, according to several associates.

In September 1970, when it became clear that Mr. Carter would be the next Governor, the so-called "smart money" began to pour in, these aides said, mainly from special interest groups and business executives who hoped to win favor with the new Governor. Although Mr. Carter's associates were willing to discuss their own contributions, they were unwilling to name other donors, on the ground that when these were given the contributor had a right to expect anonymity.

Mr. Gambrell said that he did not believe any one of these late contributions exceeded $10,000. Mr. Alston said he could recall one contribution of $7,500.

Mr. Gunter and several other Carter supporters said that even though Mr. Carter's campaign had accepted contributions from persons who did business with the state or "expected" something for their gifts, Mr. Carter had never satisfied these expectations or acted to "pay off political debts."

"In fact," Mr. Gunter said, "he did the opposite. He made several appointments of men who had supported Carl Sanders [Mr. Carter's principal rival] in the primary." Interviews with opponents of Mr. Carter in Georgia produced no concrete evidence that he took actions as Governor to favor any industry or special-interest group.

Among Mr. Carter's supporters was a colorful business man and pilot named H. Rabhan. Mr. Rabhan had interests in several nursing homes and was involved in speculative investments in Georgia and outside the state.

Free Airplane Rides

Early in the 1970 campaign Mr. Rabhan gave Mr. Carter free rides around the state in his private plane, which Mr. Rabhan piloted. These trips enabled Mr. Carter to enlarge his campaign schedule in Georgia. Mr. Gambrell said he believed that Mr. Rabhan's contribution had been limited to air flights, but Ray Abernathy, an advertising official who also worked on the campaign, said he believed Mr. Rabhan had made cash donations as well.

While Mr. Carter was Governor, Mr. Rabhan came under Federal investigation in connection with several cases, including one that involved Federal Housing Administration loans. Mr. Rabhan has reportedly left the country; numerous attempts to locate him were unsuccessful.

The Federal Bureau of Investigation is also known to have sought to interview Mr. Rabhan. According to Department of Justice sources, however, the investigation has never touched Mr. Carter or his staff.

After Mr. Carter became Governor he organized two collections of private funds, which his staff said were unconnected with his later Presidential race. He formed an ad hoc citizens group in support of his state reorganization plans that raised less than $10,000 to pay for advertising to gain public support for the plan.

Another private solicitation raised money to supplement the pay and allowances for the head of the prison system to attract a particular appointee from another state. Accounting on both projects was informal, according to several of Mr. Carter's associates.

Experts Say New Election Fund Law Saved Carter from a Blitz by Rivals

BY NICHOLAS M. HORROCK

Jimmy Carter has probably been the principal beneficiary of the new Federal legislation that controls the use of money in Presidential campaigns.

An examination of his 1976 effort shows that Mr. Carter has mounted an effective and imaginative drive for money that has provided his campaign with adequate, if not luxurious, financing.

Campaign financing experts and political aides inside and outside Mr. Carter's campaign agree that the new law, which limits both total spending and the size of individual contributions, protected Mr. Carter's early effort from a money blitz by Democrats with connections in traditional political-financing pools.

The new Federal election law thus sharply reduced the built-in advantage that might have gone to Senator Henry M. Jackson, Democrat of Washington, and that helped Representative Wilbur D. Mills, Democrat of Arkansas, in his Presidential effort in 1972.

Both these men embarked on Presidential campaigns as chairmen of powerful Congressional committees, offices that normally insure financial support from interest groups eager to gain favor on legislation. Such favor is useful even if the chairman being helped does not attain the White House.

Key Man in Campaign

Most sources in the political financing field attribute the success of the Carter financial effort to Morris Dees, an Alabama lawyer and former book publisher who raised millions by mail for Senator George McGovern in 1972.

Although Mr. Dees gained his national reputation raising money by mail, he centered Mr. Carter's effort on direct, personal solicitation by finance committees set up in various cities around the country. In an interview, Mr. Dees said that direct mail was less valuable to a "centrist" candidate such as Mr. Carter or in a campaign that lacked a single compelling issue such as the war in Vietnam.

Another asset has been Mr. Carter's personal habit of frugality and his background of running tight, low-budget campaigns, which have stretched his Presidential dollars further than those of several of his opponents.

The history of Mr. Carter's campaign financing falls in three stages. In late 1974, while still Governor of Georgia, Mr. Carter and his aides raised some $47,000 to be the "nest egg" of his Presidential campaign. It paid for the maintenance of early office space and a small staff.

In 1975, Carter supporters raised some $700,000 from January to November. The money, mainly from Georgia, paid for the nationwide campaigning Mr. Carter was undertaking at the time.

The Third Stage

Finally, Mr. Dees joined Mr. Carter in November 1975 after first being attracted to him in 1972, when he suggested Mr. Carter as a running mate for Senator McGovern. Several weeks after Mr. McGovern was defeated, Mr. Dees met with Mr. Carter in Atlanta and told him that if he ever ran for President, Mr. Dees would like to help him.

Mr. Dees said he had been unable to join Mr. Carter's campaign until last November because of several lawsuits he was trying and because he had promised to advise all Democrats on how to raise money by direct mail.

He said that aides to Senator Jackson and Gov. George C. Wallace had expressed an interest in the program. "I gave them the $2 short course in direct mail," he said.

By the time Mr. Dees joined Mr. Carter's campaign he had become convinced that direct mail solicitation would not be as successful in 1976 for Mr. Carter as it was in 1972 for Senator McGovern.

"Direct mail requires heavy front money," he said. "It costs 25 cents per letter and before the new law you could borrow this from major contributors. Now, however, you can't borrow more than a thousand dollars from any single person and the banks won't loan you that kind of money."

What Mr. Dees devised was a regional system of finance committees that would make direct, personal solicitations for money in their areas and that would be oriented to collecting money through "events."

$100 Cocktail Parties

The most successful events have been $100-a-person cocktail parties in which the guests meet the candidate. Breakfast sessions have also been productive.

Mr. Dees said that under the new restriction—no person may give more than $1,000 a candidate in a year—the campaign dinner has become a less valuable tool because the cost of arranging it often erodes the profits.

Before 1972, even though a dinner might have been priced at $100 a plate, many participants often gave more money, or the tickets were bought in blocks by large contributors.

Using lists of known Democratic contributors, the Carter campaign workers sent out carefully worded invitations to various functions around the country. For example, earlier this year several thousand New Yorkers received a richly appointed invitation to breakfast with Mr. Carter in the grand ballroom of the Plaza Hotel.

Among the hosts listed on the invitation were C. Douglas Dillon, Henry Luce 3d and Cyrus R. Vance. Mr. Dees said the breakfast had cost the Carter campaign $5,000 and "raised $75,000."

Mr. Dees said that the finance committee system was patterned on sales techniques often used by insurance companies. Like certain insurance salesmen, many finance committee members may be able to get money only from their friends. "Some people will get contributions from 15 friends and that's all they can raise," he said. At that point, he said, the finance committee must look for "new blood" and expand its circle of potential contributors.

$328,000 from Telethon

The campaign has used telethons and rock-band concerts, among other events, to raise money. Mr. Dees said that rock concerts were difficult because it is necessary to get a signed ticket or receipt from each person who attends to apply for Federal matching funds.

Telethons are more effective, he said. A telethon in Georgia, called "Spend Valentine's Day with Jimmy Carter (and some of his famous friends)" yielded the campaign $328,000.

The new election law has affected many of the fund-raising tactics in 1976. The Federal Government, for instance, will match only the first $250 contributed by each donor. So if a man wants to give $1,000 to the Carter campaign, the finance committee members urge that the donation be made in the names of the man and his wife, so that the Government will match $250 for each. (This technique is used in the campaigns of all contenders.)

Thus the total receipts to the Carter campaign would be $1,500 for a husband-wife contribution instead of $1,250 for the same gift if made by one individual.

Since Jan. 1, 1975, Mr. Carter has received $1,515,896.46 in matching funds from the Federal Election Committee.

In the Carter campaign, Mr. Dees has used direct mail mainly to solicit additional contributions from persons who had already given to Mr. Carter or had been identified as his supporters.

A personal letter sent out in December 1975, for instance, urged contributors to "double up" on the original donation. Mr. Dees said the mailing cost was $3,500 and the solicitation brought in about $225,000.

Fund-Raising Awareness

Mr. Dees said he had found Mr. Carter and his family more "oriented" to fund raising than other candidates and that Mr. Carter had been more willing than Senator McGovern to solicit funds personally. He said that the entire central group of Mr. Carter's campaign staff was alert to fund-raising possibilities.

There appears to be a basic theme of frugality in both Mr. Carter's private life and his earlier political campaigns. Money is carefully allocated by the Carter campaign treasurer, Robert J. Lipschutz, an Atlanta lawyer, and a committee of the key Carter aides. Mr. Lipschutz, Mr. Dees and several other senior campaign officials are volunteering their time. Expenses, particularly the use of the air travel card and telephone credit cards, are scrupulously monitored.

Even the highest paid staff members, W. Hamilton Jordan, the campaign manager, and Jody Powell, the press secretary, come at bargain rates. Mr. Jordan, for instance, earns less than $16,000 a year as Mr. Carter's campaign manager, while his counterpart in Senator Jackson's campaign was receiving $45,000.

Senator Jackson's press aide, Brian Corcoran, earned $34,000 a year, while Mr. Powell is paid slightly less than $17,000. Several adult professionals on Mr. Dees's finance staff are paid only $150 a week plus expenses.

As a result, the Carter campaign has faced no severe financial crisis.

Mr. Carter signed a note to continue salaries and costs at one point, and Mr. Lipschutz said there had been several instances in which he had to rush cashiers' checks to an airline before the planes would take off. But the Carter campaign has not suffered the difficulties faced, for instance, by Representative Morris K. Udall of Arizona.

Nevertheless, Mr. Dees and several others involved in political financing criticize the limits imposed by the new election law. Mr. Dees says it results in "running a Presidential race on a mayor's race budget."

But in overall terms, most veteran political financial experts agree Mr. Carter's candidacy could have been snuffed out had the new law not existed. They argue that its regulations are of enormous benefit to a new candidate who is largely unknown and who seeks general support without connections among major political finance sources.

Candidates Consult Master of Mail Fund-Raising
BY CHRISTOPHER LYDON

Democrats running for President make pilgrimages to Morris Dees's house these days much as they will later call on Mayor Richard J. Daley in Chicago or visit the big-state delegations at the 1976 convention.

For at a moment when political money is scarce, tightly regulated and still vaguely disreputable, Morris Seligman Dees Jr., is widely thought to be the man with a nearly miraculous remedy in direct-mail fund raising.

Mr. Dees himself is not so sure he has more miracles in store. His colleagues in the McGovern campaign of 1972 called him a "bona fide genius" for building up a computerized file of several hundred thousand small contributors and then milking that list inventively—some would say unmercifully—for all the money his candidate needed. At a postage and printing cost of roughly $3-million, Mr. Dees's intricate, persistent come-ons netted about $20-million for the McGovern campaign from almost 700,000 citizens—the record to date in popular political fund-raising.

Twenty-five miles up the road in Montgomery, Governor George C. Wallace seems well started on a comparable direct-mail triumph. With the

Christopher Lydon, "Candidates Consult Master of Mail Fund-Raising," *The New York Times,* January 24, 1975, p. 11. © 1975 by The New York Times Company. Reprinted by permission.

help of Richard A. Viguerie of Falls Church, Va., king of the right-wing (usually Republican) mailing lists, the undeclared Wallace campaign will have spent over $2-million on roughly 13 million "prospect letters" by the middle of this year to identify a core of 250,000 contributing supporters. And even if the Wallace campaign simply breaks even on that preliminary project, mail professionals say it will yield something better than money: a friendly base for re-solicitation.

The rest of the presidential field has little choice but to try the direct-mail approach because the new, $1,000-limit on contributions blocks their access to the larger donors of old. But will mail work for them?

The man the candidates ask is Mr. Dees, 38 years old, a gentleman farmer and civil rights lawyer who lives comfortably here off the mail-order fortune he amassed selling birthday cakes, cook books and encyclopedias in his twenties. In recent weeks, he has talked to a half-dozen Democrats, explaining the subtleties of his business, pointing them to mail-order houses, editing their letters and wondering out loud about the value of his advice.

"I think there are only two mail-donating segments of our society," he said, "the right-wing fringe and the left. The average American does not consider himself part of the political process other than going out to vote. The thing that concerns me this time is whether there's an issue to coalesce around—and a candidate that can arouse people."

Part of the fascination with Mr. Dees lies in the feeling he seems to inspire that he has tricks for overcoming any obstacle. And he is not so modest as to credit his 1972 success entirely to the antiwar fervor of Senator George McGovern's campaign. "It was marketing concepts that raised money for McGovern," he says.

Starting with the "good rich blue letterhead" over Senator McGovern's first plea for money, Mr. Dees's mailings were full of little stratagems especially in re-soliciting early donors.

Shortly before the Wisconsin primary in April, 1972, McGovern contributors got a letter that said, "I need your immediate help." On the eve of the Ohio primary, they were told in another letter: "The hour of decision is at hand . . . it is not easy for me to ask your help once more when I know you have already been so generous. But history has always been made not by the multitude but by the determined and courageous few." Supporters were urged to "add up all that you have sent me and rush me that same amount or more by return mail." That brought in $375,000.

A month later, just before the California primary, the same contributors were thanked and squeezed again, with the bait that Stewart Mott, the philanthropist, had promised to match each new contribution dollar for dollar. "Will you dig a little deeper as your investment in hope?" Senator McGovern signed off. That letter raised $600,000.

After Mr. McGovern was nominated the same contributors were enticed to give again by the promise of a sterling silver "F.M.B.M." pin (For McGovern Before Miami). Another mass mailing for a "McGovern for President Club" included a "sweepstakes" ticket for dinner at the McGovern White House—a fun-and-games postscript that Mr. Dees believes swelled response by 50 percent. Then came a series of mailgrams late in the campaign. "Tide turning," said one on Oct. 8, "urgently need funds for next TV talk."

Beyond copy-writing and timing, said Mr. Dees, the key test of the direct-mail art in the 1976 campaign will be the commercial lists that the candidates select. And in a campaign world now mostly open to public inspection, the testing and trading of various mailing lists is one of few technical secrets left.

Some politicians worry that special interests may reassert themselves in mail fund-raising as they customarily did through large contributions. Would a candidate be subtly encumbered in reaching a particularly rich response through a list of milk producers, for example, or from members of the National Rifle Association, or from lists of Bonds for Israel contributors?

Mr. Dees is not concerned about that. "Direct mail just doesn't work that way," he said, "because it's based on a very low percentage of return—usually between 1 and 3 per cent of the prospect list. If you sent a mail appeal to 250,000 doctors and got a 5 per cent response, that would be a miracle.

"I got involved in politics with McGovern because the work we do at the Southern Poverty Law Center [his working headquarters in Montgomery] was being totally frustrated by people Nixon appointed to the Supreme Court."

With the new crop of Presidential candidates, he said, "I've let it be known that my main interest is the judiciary. I want judges appointed who are sensitive to human rights, so we can continue the work we've been doing here all along."

Fund Raiser Becomes New Kind of Power Broker

The fund raiser Richard A. Viguerie is a new kind of power broker for the era of broad-based campaign finance and the small contributor. For a

"Fund Raiser Becomes New Kind of Power Broker," *The New York Times,* May 23, 1975, p. 16. © 1975 by The New York Times Company. Reprinted by permission.

number of conservative candidates he is already the indispensable man with the indispensable mailing lists. As such he may have as much control as any individual over the emergence of a new political party in the Presidential election of 1976.

The George C. Wallace campaign account is the biggest in a long series of Viguerie political ventures. It also represents a strategic leap for him and his company.

Mr. Viguerie, who was born in Houston 41 years ago, was introduced to the art of mail fund-raising when, as a law school dropout, he became executive secretary of the Young Americans for Freedom. In business on his own since 1965, his specialty until recently was conservative Republicanism.

'Cause Clients Listed'

He has had such "cause" clients as the Anti-Communist Book Club, the National Rifle Association's Legal Foundation and the Rev. Billy James Hargis' Christian Crusade, and such right-wing Republican candidates as Senator Strom Thurmond of South Carolina, Representative Philip Crane of Illinois and Max Rafferty, who ran for the Senate in California in 1966.

He mastered the tricks of the direct-mail trade, which is second only to television as an advertising medium. As a conservative specialist, he broke new ground in determining which rented lists responded to different kinds of rhetoric.

Most important, by contracting to keep his own copies of clients' contributors and by combing the public lists of campaign donors, he compiled what is now, at 1.5-million names, the largest file in the country on conservatives who respond to the mail.

But as Mr. Viguerie's list, his staff (now 250 employees) and his reputation grew, his disenchantment with the Republican party was becoming transmuted into an eager interest in the possibility of a third-party conservative movement.

Through six months of 1972, Mr. Viguerie recalls, he negotiated with the White House staff over a contract to raise money for President Nixon's re-election campaign. At the last minute, he says, he rejected the job "on principle," objecting to such unconservative departures as the Administration's wage and price control policy and détente with China and the Soviet Union.

Quotes His Wife

"But as my wife said at the time," Mr. Viguerie remembered in an interview, 'when the good lord closes a door, he opens a window.' It took me a few months to see what that window was," but eventually it appeared in the form of the Wallace campaign.

He views the emerging Wallace campaign—more outspokenly than Mr. Wallace or his aides do—as a short intermediate step toward a political marriage with Ronald Reagan, the former Republican Governor of California, and then to the birth of a new conservative party that could be a major force as soon as next year.

Mr. Viguerie can justly claim to have given the Wallace campaign the biggest and broadest finance operation in the field. He has helped to build a list of Wallace contributors, large and small, at least 10 times longer than Senator Henry M. Jackson's. The Senator is in second place.

Profit and Power

Mr. Viguerie, meanwhile, may have even more to show in profit and power from the Wallace mail campaign. The Wallace list is his list, yet it is only one strand in a widening web connecting the Viguerie company to right-of-center political money in the United States.

In the less than two years that he has been working on the Wallace campaign, Mr. Viguerie has revived The Right Report, a weekly newsletter, and started a slick-paper monthly conservative digest, which he boasts will have 100,000 subscribers by fall.

Mr. Viguerie is the director of fund-raising for three new political treasuries: the Conservative Campaign Committee, the Committee for the Survival of a Free Congress and the National Conservative Political Action Committee.

"It's my fervent hope." he said, "that George Wallace and Ronald Reagan will team up as the ticket of a new party next year."

"I don't know who should run for what," he added. "That's up to them."

PART III

Nomination Outcomes

The final outcome of each party's nomination contest is a convention majority which confirms a standard-bearer for the November general election. But along the way there are approximately fifty-five lesser outcomes in the states, the territories, and the District of Columbia. These subunits differ sharply among themselves in the composition of their Democratic and Republican parties. Moreover, the various delegate-selection devices which they impose on their parties make a major contribution to the selection process, so that the final state (or territorial) delegate distribution may sometimes owe as much to the formal institutional structure through which it was produced as to the basic character of the population from which it theoretically springs.

With fifty-five or so separate units, with five major delegate-selection devices, and with three major allocation rules, few simple generalizations can be made about delegate results. It is clear, however, that *turnout* in the various primaries and conventions has become a much more important matter than it was in the past. When most delegate-selection devices were party-oriented—like the party caucus, committee selection, and, to a lesser degree, the delegate primary—turnout was comparatively less important. Party leaders and public officials played the critical selection roles, and their ties to their own constituencies, leavened by their desire to rally behind a winner, largely determined the outcome.

But as the shift to participatory conventions and candidate primaries occurred, the question of who turns out at this early, low-participation stage became more important. The Democratic and Republican parties as represented in their primaries and conventions are evidently different from the Democratic and Republican parties as represented at the general elec-

179

tion. Moreover, that difference is not random; it is the better-educated and more highly motivated who appear at the earlier stage, although the degree to which this distorts the results can vary considerably. Moreover, the different delegate-selection devices themselves lead to varying levels and kinds of turnout, although the exact nature of these variations, too, is more debated than proved.

In Chapter 6 both William Cavala and James I. Lengle look at aspects of the California primary system. In "Changing the Rules Changes the Game," Cavala focuses on the preliminary caucuses of candidates' supporters, caucuses which in effect nominate the delegates who will later be elected if their candidate performs well in the primary. Lengle, on the other hand, uses "Demographic Representation in California's 1972 and 1968 Democratic Presidential Primaries" to investigate turnout and its impact on the actual election of these delegates. Both provide additional insights into caucuses and primaries generally. Lengle and Byron E. Shafer consider the real effect of allocation rules, as opposed to delegate-selection devices, in "Primary Rules, Political Power, and Social Change." Austin Ranney pulls both factors together and speculates on their relative influence, as well as on the influence of several other formal procedures, in "Participation in the 1976 Presidential Nominations."

As a group, these four pieces suggest the extent to which the candidates' attempts to influence delegate outcomes are constrained by other campaign requirements and by external forces over which *no* candidate can have much control. Cavala shows that while the McGovern campaign leadership was indeed concerned with assembling a delegate slate which could win the California primary, it was also forced to consider how the same slate would help motivate the activists upon whom the actual labor of the campaign depended. Lengle demonstrates some of the limits on all such maneuvers by pointing out that some candidates' voters are more easily brought out to the polls regardless of planning or organization. Lengle and Shafer show how the cumulation of a series of primary outcomes can begin to have effects which no one—not voters, not candidates, and not even the reformers who created the process—really intended. Ranney covers a larger number of lesser, but equally unintended consequences of primary election laws.

Much of what the general public comes to know about the nomination process necessarily arrives through the mass media—through news and features on developing events. The standard ways of covering these events, or any sort of press consensus about various facets of the campaign, can surely have an independent influence over the outcome. Most candidates—and probably all defeated candidates—believe that some aspects of the reporting on their personal story were inaccurate or positively malicious. Many analysts also find aspects of campaign coverage which seem to them perverse and pernicious. On the other hand, all campaigns are naturally diverse, sprawling, and multifaceted, and some of the criticism which newsmen receive for their coverage can be classed as the age-old response to the messenger who continually brings bad news.

Nevertheless, the structure of the campaign itself does limit the range of possible journalistic influence. For example, the particular content, or even the biases, of news coverage ordinarily have more impact at the nomination than at the election stage. By election time, voters' direct identifications with the two parties come strongly into play, and the field of contenders is usually pared to two, so that the electorate can more easily form independent judgments about leadership and personality. At the nomination stage, on the other hand, the party label provides few cues (that is, all Democrats are Democrats), many of the contenders are not initially well known, and the field may be confusingly large. Beyond such factors, and in some sense enveloping them all, is the level of public attention to news reports. The ability of the general public to escape contact with journalistic interpretations of events, and to filter and reinterpret them when contact is made, is increasingly challenged by the expanding presence of the media in our daily lives. Nevertheless, scholarly studies have been reliably "reassuring" when viewed as a measure of public resistance to reportorial bias.

In Chapter 7 the selection "On the Bus," from Timothy J. Crouse's book *The Boys on the Bus,* describes the daily fabric of news operations and the way it conditions campaign coverage. In " 'Winnowing'," from a collection of essays on the *Race for the Presidency,* Donald R. Matthews offers a more systematic look at the political functions which newsmen inevitably, inescapably, perform. The United Press International (UPI) blurb, "Reruns in Boot Hill," suggests the extent to which communications regulations—yet another aspect of the formal institutional environment for politics—can reach down and affect the political process. And Lanny J. Davis, who was youth coordinator in Edmund Muskie's ill-fated campaign for a presidential nomination, gives the archetypal also-ran's lament. "The Primaries: Which Winners Lost and Which Losers Won?" from his book *The Emerging Democratic Majority,* compares Davis's own interpretation of the 1972 nomination campaign with that of the press at large.

While each of these pieces is primarily about the news business and news coverage of nomination campaigns, each also contains some insights into the process being covered. Crouse, for example, portrays those characteristics of nomination campaigns which induce the press to concentrate on events that critics might call deviant or meaningless. Similarly, Matthews notes the way in which many newsmen try to come to grips with the more analytic roles that they are effectively forced to play. Davis echoes some of the selections in Chapters 5 and 6 of this reader when he talks about the impact of the rules governing delegate selection, and about the ways in which candidates organize to take advantage of those rules.

When all delegates have been selected, they gather at the national convention site for the purpose of balloting on a nominee. In the period since World War II, much of this activity has been pro forma. There have been few multiballot conventions, and fewer still where the ultimate result, however many ballots it requires, was ever seriously in doubt. In other words, the effective decision has usually been made at some point *during* the process of delegate selection, and that decision has merely been ratified at the convention itself. But this development, too, should not be overstated. The Republican Party in 1976 did produce a convention with some of the old-fashioned characteristics. And while the blocs with which various leaders bargained were perhaps smaller than they would have been in the past, many of the same considerations—the ideologies or pragmatic desires of the delegates, and the available rewards of the candidates—were very much in evidence.

The delegates themselves are never an exact microcosm of their electorate. While they may sometimes reflect that electorate's views accurately and at other times only distantly, they are always more highly educated and more politically interested. In the decade following World War II, Democratic and Republican delegates tended also to be far more sharply divided along ideological lines than the electorate as a whole, and Republican delegates tended to be considerably more conservative than that electorate. In the more recent past these patterns have become muddied. The possibility now exists that they have even become reversed—meaning that both parties' delegates are still more ideological than their voters, but that it is now the *Democratic* delegates who are far more *liberal* than the electorate as a whole.

In Chapter 8 Jules Witcover's "The Battle of Mississippi" from his book *Marathon: The Pursuit of the Presidency, 1972–1976,* reports on the struggle for the largest single bloc of uncommitted delegates at the 1976 Republican convention. James M. Naughton surveys their more scattered brethren in the other states in "Uncommitted Delegates: Real People." Warren Weaver, Jr., R. W. Apple, Jr., and *The New York Times* staff complete the story with accounts of the early Ford and Reagan victory claims ("Either Ford or Reagan Has It Sewed up, Maybe"), of the early indications that the Ford camp's claims were more accurate ("Ford is Backed on Early-Ballot Switches"), and of the last desperate opposition maneuvers as Reagan strategists tried to stem the Ford tide ("Reagan Men Seek Way to Deal Ford a Damaging Blow"). Herbert F. McClosky's piece, "Issue Conflict and Consensus among Party Leaders and Followers," is the classic analysis of the relationship between national convention delegates and their rank-and-file counterparts. It also reveals the more specific balance in both parties in the late 1950s. Jeane J. Kirkpatrick's "Representation in American National Conventions: The Case of 1972" brings the same analysis closer to the present and provides some additional comment about change in the interim.

CHAPTER 6

Delegate Selection: Primaries and Conventions

A. Rules and Results: Systems for Selecting Delegates

B. Rules and Results: Systems for Allocating Delegates

C. Caucuses, Primaries, Rules, and Turnout

·A·

Rules and Results:
Systems for Selecting Delegates

Changing the Rules Changes the Game: Party Reform and the 1972 California Delegation to the Democratic National Convention

BY WILLIAM CAVALA

During the 1968 Democratic National Convention at Chicago, while the attention of the press and public was focused on the chaos on the floor and in the streets, some institutional tinkering took place which, in retrospect, may well be the most significant action taken by that body. A minority of the Rules Committee of that convention had brought to the floor a series of proposals to "open up" the selection of delegates to future Democratic Conventions. These proposals, designed in part for the purely political purpose of dividing those delegates leaning toward the nomination of then Vice-President Hubert Humphrey, suggested sufficiently archaic delegate selection procedures in some states to provide a brief coalition for reform. Ultimately the full convention did pass a proposal which required that delegates to the 1972 and subsequent conventions be selected under a set of rules quite different from those operative to that point. Specifically, the following mandatory resolution was adopted:

> It is understood that a state Democratic Party, in selecting and certifying delegates to the National Convention, thereby undertakes to assure that

William Cavala, "Changing the Rule Changes the Game," *American Political Science Review*, Vol. 68, March 1974, pp. 27–42. Footnotes deleted. Reprinted by permission of The American Political Science Association.

such delegates have been selected through a process in which all Democratic voters have had full and timely opportunity to participate . . . [further] the convention shall require that: #1) The unit rules not be used in any states of the delegate selection process; and #2) All feasible efforts have been made to assure that delegates are selected through party primary, convention or committee procedure open to public participation within the calendar year of the National Convention.

This mandate, as interpreted and implemented by the Democratic National Committee's Commission on Delegate Selection and Party Reform, has had a major impact on what Polsby and Wildavsky have called the "strategic environment" of our political landscape.

All political strategies are worked out within a framework of circumstances which are in part subject to manipulation but to an even greater degree are "given." . . . Some of these circumstances are contingent and relate to the strategies being pursued by other active participants in the election process and to the resources at their command. Other circumstances are more stable and have to do with features of the American political system that have persisted over time.

This article is an effort to assess some of the effects on the strategic environment of the Democratic Party's new rules on the selection of delegates to the National Convention. The events described are limited to the experience of California, but it is assumed that some of the generalizations derived from that case will prove to have a more general applicability. The obvious difficulty with any effort of this type is to distinguish between those effects which are relatively stable and those primarily related to the specific configuration of events that occurred in 1972. If this problem can be surmounted, it should be possible not only to make some general statements about the impact of these changes on our national politics, but also, through an examination of the decision-making processes undergone by candidates and their campaign organizations faced with these new situations, to begin to understand the problems associated with transforming a set of ideas into a working reality.

New Rules

In 1972 California sent 271 delegates to the Democratic National Convention pledged to the winner of the June 6th primary. The sheer number of delegates, more than 17 per cent of those needed to nominate, along with the winner-take-all feature of the California primary, made it a strategically significant state for any serious candidate. The procedure for entering this primary remained unchanged from past years. Each candidate was required to file with the Secretary of State a slate of delegates pledged to the candidate and distributed by number equally among the state's 43 congressional districts. Then, within a specified period of time, each candidate had to file a minimum of 14,693 signatures of registered voters pledged to the support of his slate of delegates. Those slates which received the required number of valid signatures were then placed on the June ballot. The candidate whose slate won the highest number of votes in that election would receive the right to send all 271 of California's delegates to the National Convention.

The changes in party rules had no direct impact on the procedures described above. Rather the changes were reflected in the procedures for choosing the various slates of delegates themselves. Prior to 1972, delegates had been selected by an executive committee chosen by the candidate himself. The practice had been for this committee to ask a handful of their most prominent supporters in each district to recommend the delegates from that district. This practice traditionally resulted in delegations representative of the elite corps of the Democratic party: legislators, top party officials, and major contributors. In almost every case the criterion for choosing delegates was simply to select that individual who had shown through his past campaign record or other means that he would provide the greatest aid to the campaign in his district. Those responsible for selecting the delegates saw their role as primarily that of putting together a campaign team. Political criteria were virtually the only relevant ones involved in their decisions.

As one consequence of this method of selection, most women, minority group members, and young people were simply eliminated from serious consideration at the outset of the process. The vast majority of party officials, campaign chairmen, major contributors, and elected representatives were white, male, and more than 30 years old. In many cases to place a young person on a delegation might involve the loss of support from a prominent legislator or contributor who felt himself bypassed. There were few campaign committees willing to risk this type of loss for a symbolic gesture. It was against this system of selection and the types of delegates chosen under this system that the new rules were primarily directed.

In the Spring of 1971 the California Commission on Delegate Selection met to recommend changes in delegate selection procedures that would bring the state into compliance with the guidelines laid down by the National Reform Commission. The new rules adopted by the state party required that each candidate's campaign committee appoint a representative to a statewide steering committee from every congressional district. This person would be given the responsibility of locating and publicizing a meeting place for the delegate selection caucus for his candidate in that district. On February 12th, the day set by the new rules for the selection of delegates, the organization of every candidate would hold a public meeting open to every registered Democrat. The meetings would be held at the same time, but in a different location with the congressional district for each candidate. At that meeting any person could be nominated to fill one of the delegate slots allotted to that district (each district had between six and nine delegate slots, the number depending on whether or not the nominee of the party had carried that district in the 1968 general election). Each caucus would be permitted to nominate up to twice the number of allotted delegates and alternates for that district. Then, within 10 days, the steering committee representatives chosen by the campaign committee would meet to choose 88 per cent of the statewide slate which ultimately would run in the June primary pledged to their candidate.

The final slate of delegates and alternates chosen by the statewide steering committee had to be in compliance with the new guidelines that were designed to increase the numbers of some groups heretofore under-represented in the Democratic National Convention. While no specific numbers were laid down, it was obvious that black and brown Democrats would have to be represented in numbers no less than their proportion in the general population, that people 18–30 would have to be represented in numbers at least close to their strength in the state as a whole, and that the number of women would have to be dramatically increased over that of past years.

Old Players and the New Rules

In any assessment of the impact of the new delegate selection rules on the Democratic Party, it is important to remember that the implementation of those rules remained the responsibility of the party's elite. The party in California was reformed from above, not from below. Therefore it becomes important to try to understand how the leaders of the party perceived what was expected under the new rules, what they hoped to achieve, and how they set about trying to achieve those goals. Members of the California Reform Commission began their task with agreement on the premise that any slate of delegates had to be viewed first and foremost as a set of political resources. They saw in the new rules an opportunity to provide candidates with the ability to make a more effective use of the resources available to them.

The traditional method of selecting delegates, described earlier, had a series of important benefits, some of which will be described at a later point. The members of the California Reform Commission, however, were less concerned with such benefits than they were with the liabilities which had grown up around that system over the years. They saw in the changes of the rules a possible means of removing some of those liabilities. Specifically, they hoped to restore some of the discretion that had been chipped away from the candidate's executive committee by traditional practices.

Major contributors, for example, had originally been rewarded with a place on a candidate's delegation in return for their financial help in the primary campaign. But over the years, more and more of these contributors had come to view this reward as a right rather than as an earned privilege. More and more of them declined to contribute substantial amounts until the general election—and then only if they had received their reward in advance in the form of a convention seat. Similar situations prevailed in the case of elected officials. They expected a place on the delegation of the candidate they endorsed. While often the support of such an official meant little more than the use of his name, to refuse him his position could mean, because of his ties with local party activists, difficulties in mounting an effective campaign effort in his district.

The traditional system had evolved to the point where a great number of those selected as delegates felt that it was their right to be so selected. They felt little gratitude or obligation to the campaign organization. Moreover, because there were always more contributors and legislators than available positions on a delegation, many people who viewed those positions as their "right" had to be bypassed. Some of them were bound to become righteously resentful. Further, those people who had put in the long hard hours at the local headquarters simply had to resign themselves to the fact that there was virtually no chance of their being elevated to the status of delegate. The only real decision left to the campaign's slatemaking committee was that of determining whom they could least afford to offend.

The participants of the Reform Commission in California—many of whom had been involved in the slatemaking efforts of previous years—hoped that the combination of changes (the de facto quota requirements and the mandate to slatemakers that consideration must be given to nominees selected at district meetings) would restore some of the campaign advantages lost under the old system. It may appear odd that changes designed to limit the ability of the campaign's slatemaking committee to select whomever they wished were viewed by precisely those decision makers as the path toward greater flexibility. But as we have seen, the abstract freedom to choose under the old system meant in reality being forced to choose from a limited set of players. The new rules appeared to restrict the ability of the slatemakers to select exclusively from among that set.

Under these rules the slatemakers would operate in a situation similar to what Schelling has described as a "coercive deficiency." They would no longer have the authority necessary to comply with the demands placed on them by the traditional players. As Schelling notes, in such a situation the burden of avoiding mutual danger (in this case, loss of resources essential to the campaign) shifts to the other party. In our specific situation, this would mean that legislators or contributors could be refused a place on a delegation in a way which would make it less legitimate for them to hinder the campaign by withholding their resources. Thus by limiting the ability of the slatemakers to choose from the traditional group of politicos, the new rules were designed to give each candidate new opportunities to reward persons outside those more traditional categories.

The major expectation of the Reform Commission and of those involved in the actual slatemaking operation in 1972 and in the past was that the new rules would promote some of the lower echelon campaign people to positions on a delegation. The quota requirements were thought to be especially useful in this regard because the majority of those bypassed in previous years were women. In addition, the demands by liberal activists for greater representation on delegations was viewed as legitimate by most of these campaign professionals—a judgment that was motivated both by a concern for equity and by some hard pragmatic thinking. One of the primary purposes of those involved in the implementation of the new rules in California (as elsewhere) was to rekindle the enthusiasm of the party's liberal wing. The quotas and the caucus system seemed like a small price to pay at the time if the benefits included a party united behind its nominee in the fall.

Thus by the day of the delegate selection meetings, virtually all the important participants in every campaign were agreed that their delegations would look quite different in 1972. Few, however, expected that this difference might be counterproductive in their campaigns, because several safeguards were included in this process of reform. For example, the slatemaking committee that actually made the final selection of delegates was not required by the new rules to pick exclusively (or even at all) from the list of persons nominated in district meetings. Under the new rules, any actions by those district meetings were advisory in nature. Further, the quotas imposed by the new rules were thought to be neither rigid nor dramatically high: the relevant groups had to be represented only in "reasonable relationship to their numbers in the general population." In addition, considerable overlap in the various categories was both allowable and expected: many of the young would also be black and female, and so on. The new rules were not expected to eliminate the domination of white males over 30, but rather to chip away at that domination.

Finally, the new rules were seen to provide several advantages in the simple maneuvering room which they gave to the slatemakers because these persons were under no legal requirement to accept the recommendations of local district meetings (a fact that was not widely understood). The slatemakers fully expected to be able to use the general confusion about the new rules to turn aside a great number of the traditional requests for delegate slots. Those who continued to press for such slots could be told that it was politically necessary for them to stand for election at their own district meeting. If they still persisted in pressing for a slot after having been rejected by their local caucus, the slatemaker could either plead helplessness in the face of "the people's decision" or could override the decision of the caucus and place the person on the delegation in any case. If the latter course was taken, the slatemakers would appear in the role of benefactors. Under the old rules such appointments had become so traditional that exceptions required justification. But under the new rules it could reasonably be expected that any contributor appointed in such a fashion could legitimately be asked to go beyond his normal effort that year.

Clearly also, the need for more people from categories previously unrepresented on delegations was felt to provide the slatemakers with the opportunity to alter the status of a slot as a political reward. If all or most traditional political figures are not on a delegation, then being on a delegation is not necessarily a matter of distinction. Some argued this fact would help to minimize the number of competitive situations in which gaining the aid of one person by giving him a spot on the delegation meant losing the support of two others who felt slighted (and who might be individually less important but jointly more important to the campaign). With luck it was felt that traditional political figures could be convinced that they had lost little of value under the new rules, while those in the newly eligible categories could be convinced they had received a great honor.

Setting the Stage

While the foregoing discussion is a fair representation of the views of the great majority of California's campaign professionals, the decisions made by many of those same professionals at the time of the delegate selection meetings in 1972 produced outcomes quite different from those expected a year or so earlier. In order to understand what took place at those meetings we will have to try to understand the political situation of each campaign organization at the time the meetings were scheduled. For the way each campaign staff dealt with the changes in the delegate selection process was largely due to the strategic situation of the campaign staff at that time.

Decision making in a political campaign must be directed toward solving immediate needs and problems, partly because of the scarcity of resources. The number of emergencies that arise during the course of a long campaign is immense and often unforeseen. Limits on time and money make it impractical to plan alternative courses of action to meet circumstances which may never occur. Further, presidential primaries involve a number of different coalitions, each felt by the participants to be less than the minimum coalition needed to conduct a general election campaign against the other party. One of the jobs of a successful primary campaign staff thus involves assimilating the supporters of the losers into the camp of the winners. Ordinarily this means sharing decision-making responsibilities with those newly enlisted. This in turn implies that any long-range planning must be subject to constant review and change by the new participants if the sharing of authority is to be real. Finally, it is self-evident that a campaign which begins with little support will be forced to subordinate any long-range planning to the almost daily struggle for mere survival.

Thus, to understand what happened, it becomes important to understand the strategic situation of the various candidates in January, 1972—as that situation was perceived by the participants themselves. Such an understanding does not involve us in an analysis of the campaign strategies per se, for as we have seen, strategies tend to bloom late (if at all) in presidential primaries. Rather we must look to the relevant "scenarios" to see each campaign as it saw itself at the time. Political scenarios are chains of logical statements which purport to demonstrate the path to victory. They begin with a factual statement of the candidate's present situation. From this premise follows a series of conditional statements whose probability of coming true is directly dependent on the factual satisfaction of the previous conditions. Scenarios serve two major functions. One is to provide plausibility to a campaign, an argument that victory is possible even if unlikely. Although a surprisingly large number of the traditional political activists in California have expressed a willingness to support long-shot candidates, few have been willing to support a candidate they felt had no chance at all. A good scenario allows a campaigner to make a pragmatic argument for supporting even these long-shot candidates. In addition to being the equivalent of a series of predictions, a scenario becomes a set of campaign imperatives as well. The conditional statements amount to a series of goals for the campaign staff, the attainment of each making the next possible and so on. As such the scenario of a campaign serves as a rough substitute for strategy, helping to set priorities, allocate resources, and so on.

A "New" Politics?

To focus our discussion, we begin with an examination of the scenario of Senator George McGovern, the eventual winner of the California primary. McGovern's staff was initially in complete agreement with the general consensus of campaign professionals described earlier: that the new rules could be used to produce a more effective campaign. As we shall discover, however, the McGovern situation as perceived by his campaign people appeared to dictate a series of decisions which severely altered those expectations.

To most observers, George McGovern began 1972 in the weakest position of any major contender. His supporters and opponents alike agreed that his one chance in California's winner-take-all primary would be to become the only identified liberal candidate in a field that included Muskie, Wallace, Humphrey, and Jackson. In those circumstances, the minority of liberal Democrats in the state might provide McGovern with enough votes for a plurality victory. But such an outcome appeared unlikely at the beginning of the year. McGovern was faced with several liberal campaigns, each of which seemed to have some initial advantage: McCarthy began with greater strength in the polls; Lindsay had glamor, money, and a good press in California; and Chisholm appeared to be attracting support among both black and active women's groups. If the results in the early primaries proved to be inconclusive, then there was the strong possibility that all the liberal candidates would actively campaign in the California race. If that proved to be the case, it was widely assumed that Muskie would be an easy winner. But if a monopoly of the support and resources available to liberal candidates in California could be hoarded prior to that time, then it might be possible to pre-empt the state from the other liberals. This pre-emptive strategy, like all other strategies, would be useless if McGovern were out of the race after the Florida primary. But if both McGovern and Lindsay had shown enough strength to survive in the early going, then California's group of liberal activists would be forced to choose between them. The presumption of the McGovern group was that the campaign with the initial strength would get stronger as liberals rallied around the liberal candidate who appeared to have the best chance. If all went well, the scenario continued, the other liberal candidates would have to choose between entering the state (thereby dividing liberals and helping the centrist Muskie) or staying out, hoping that McGovern would win and that his liberal delegates would ultimately turn to one of them during a deadlocked convention.

This scenario suggested an early organizational effort in California. McGovern's strong liberal record, his interim candidacy in 1968, and his long opposition to American policies in Vietnam provided him with a small edge over the other liberal candidates—at least until such time as one or another of them demonstrated substantially greater appeal in the polls. In addition, McGovern was aided by seeming at the time to be the possible holding candidate for Senator Edward Kennedy; both because many politicos viewed his campaign as hopeless and because many former Kennedy campaign people were associated with his effort. This "stalking-horse" image made it possible for McGovern's people to attract the support of some traditional activists who hoped for a convention deadlock and an eventual Kennedy candidacy. An early organizational effort also seemed wise for purely defensive reasons. Senator Muskie's position at that point in time was strong enough to give credibility to the argument that his was the only real campaign of the year. It was hoped that, with the increased visibility that accompanies early organization, some rallying points could be established that would prevent a general stampede to Muskie.

Pursuing this strategy of early organization, the McGovern campaign staff had established by the beginning of 1972 at least the rudiments of an organization in every county in California. Their plan was to take the most effective advantage of the new rules from the perspective of four relatively distinct goals: (1) to obtain the largest attendance at their district meetings, thus obtaining greater publicity; (2) to have the most "democratic" delegation, in the sense that more of their delegates would actually be chosen from among those nominated in the district meetings than those of any other campaign; (3) to have the most "representative" delegation, in the sense that it would not only meet, but surpass, the quota recommendations set down by the State Commission on Delegate Selection; and, (4) to put together the best delegation possible from the standpoint of political effectiveness, the individuals best able to help Senator McGovern win the primary in California.

At the time these goals were formulated, none was felt to be incompatible with any other. The fact that the local committees had already been established and (in most cases) were functioning reasonably well supported the belief that enough publicity and personal contact could be generated to insure that large turnout which the state campaign staff had assured the press was an important indicator of "grass-root" strength. In addition, it was assumed that the individuals involved in the local organizations would be the largest and most cohesive voting bloc in any given caucus. If this crucial assumption proved to be correct, then all of the other goals laid out by the state campaign were easily reachable.

Members of the state campaign had been in contact with the executive committee of each local area in an effort to work out with them the rough outlines of a slate for each caucus. Districts which included large, politically cohesive black communities were told that blacks should be overrepresented on their slate of nominees (since they would be underrepresented in rural areas with small black populations). Local committees were asked to work for the election of several large contributors who lived in the district. In most cases, the names of specific individuals who would be supported by the local committee at the caucus were worked out well ahead of time. It was assumed that the result of this organizational activity would be that the local committee members would dominate the district meetings and, under the direction of the state campaign, "democratically" (by force of numbers) elect those individuals who met both the criteria of utility to the campaign and the quotas set down by the new rules.

The District Meetings

What actually took place at the district meetings was quite different from what had been planned. The efforts of the local committees had produced the large crowds required by the publicity strategy. But the other elements of that strategy—to produce by elections nominees that met both the McGovern Commission quotas and the politically qualified delegates needed to aid the campaign in California—was a failure.

There were several reasons for this failure. Of these reasons perhaps the most important was the impact of the appearance at the district meetings of many white liberal activists who had not been involved in the campaign effort up to that time. These activists had a quite different appraisal of the functions and purposes of the new rules, and this difference provoked a clash of viewpoints that drastically affected the ultimate outcomes at the district meetings. The campaign professionals, it should be recalled, saw the new rules primarily as a more effective means to the traditional goal of any political campaign: victory at the polls. The new categories which the rules mandated would allow the professionals more freedom to choose the best campaign personnel. The remedies which the new rules provided to placate liberals (both in terms of the quotas and the new opportunities for participation) were felt to be an effective means of preventing the defections of those activists in 1972. Little more was expected.

The liberal activists, however, were far less concerned with reform as a means to electoral victory. Suspicious of politics as an avenue of change, they had come not so much in order to participate in decisions believed by professionals to be in the campaign's interest as to judge the intent about application of the new rules. Only if they were satisfied that they were not being tricked into participation, being used to trick others into believing that something had changed, would they offer their conditional support. These activists focused on the fact that the convention would determine the nominee and platform of a major party. They were less interested in symbolic representation than in making it possible for a liberal candidate or a liberal platform to gain the legitimation that the Democratic Party's nomination was assumed to provide.

Partly as a consequence of this view, many of these activists expected persons selected as delegates to behave as "substantive" representatives, people who represented ideological perspectives or distinctive interest groups in the sense that they would "act for" those groups. In contrast to the campaign professionals who saw delegates as basically campaign personnel, the assembled activists viewed them as moral ambassadors, the equivalent of public officials. For them, political skills and resources thus became a minor consideration. The primary questions they asked were, "What do they believe?" and "Which group do they represent?" For the activists saw themselves in terms of groups to be represented by quotas of delegates of this type. Rather than acting primarily out of responsibility to the candidate or his campaign, most of this group saw themselves in a bargaining situation: they would support the candidate in return for representation on his delegation.

In virtually every district meeting this attitude led to a demand for a recess during which those assembled could break up into several sub-groups of women, blacks, chicanos, youth, and so on. Each of these sub-groups then met as a "caucus," formed a slate of two or three persons, and began a period of negotiation with other subgroups for reciprocal support. It is worthwhile noting that this procedure was encouraged not only by the representative goals of the Reform Commission but also by the organizational ideology of the liberal activists themselves. That is, the quota system established by the new rules appeared to legitimate the existing trend among liberal activists to claim representation for subgroups with theoretically distinct interests. Originally this argument provided a method for racial minority groups with low rates of active participation to legitimate their claim for greater representation in a group than the number of their activists would allow. The legitimacy of the subgroup's interest, the argument goes, is a question not to be determined by the number of people present and participating who share that interest. The success of this argument as a tactic—quite apart from its validity—has led to its adoption by other numerical minorities. The force of this argument, we should note, is that interests rather than people should be represented. This in turn implies both that those sharing the interest are best suited to determine who should speak for them and that it is not necessarily the case that a person who falls into a subgroup category will adequately represent the "interest" of that subgroup.

The planned strategy of the campaign staff, we should recall, dictated a cohesive voting bloc which would cut across ethnic, sex, and age lines, and which would be committed in advance to a politically as well as ethnically balanced slate. This plan failed for several reasons. First, most activists not previously involved in the campaign offered only conditional support. Evidence of planned slatemaking, although in accord with the letter of the new rules, was widely perceived as being of the species "old politics": a violation in spirit if not in fact. In those district meetings where the local campaign group made an effort to push through the prearranged slates, the noncampaign people quickly and unanimously closed ranks against this threat to popular sovereignty. In every case this coalition of opposition was so strong and so vehement that the local committee was forced to choose between two equally unpalatable choices: (1) to push ahead anyway, either losing all, or, if successful, running a strong risk of alienating a great deal of the potential support for its candidate within their district; (2) to seek accommodation. The local campaign people, the most pragmatic of those at the district meetings, quickly settled on the second course.

Further, to pursue the original strategy would have meant openly arguing against the legitimacy of selection by subgroups. This proved morally disturbing as well as politically difficult. Not only had subgroup representation acquired new legitimacy because of the imposed quotas, but also the notion of vote-trading among the various groups to produce a consensus seemed distinctly "democratic." The slates that resulted from these meetings had been arrived at only after a period of hours of rather intense politicking. Nerves had been frayed, tempers had flared as commitments were made and broken—to most of those assembled it was serious, hard work, not fun. Yet when the bargaining and voting were complete, each district had produced a slate which met not only the quota requirements but also a consensus satisfactory to most of the interests involved at the meeting. Representative goals had been achieved through democratic means.

But this strategy of subgroup representation produced consequences which left the state campaign staff far from satisfied. For one thing, many individuals with resources useful to the campaign, but without a "constituency" among the assembled activists at the congressional district caucuses, failed to achieve the necessary votes. The fact that the votes necessary for election by the assembly were obtainable in many cases only with a subgroup nomination means—in the case of women in particular—that many who fell into a quota category but were not perceived as "representing" that category's interest were eliminated. Many women who had been most active in the campaign, for example, were not ordinarily among the high finishers in the vote totals. Rather the various women's caucuses tended to nominate women whose reputation and concern were focused primarily on the issue of women's rights.

Additionally, the state campaign organization had asked the local committees in certain districts to make an effort at overrepresentation of some of the ethnic groups that formed a relatively large proportion of the population of that district. Rather than add one black delegate from each district (many of which had black populations considerably below 1 per cent), the campaign's theory was to select more black delegates from those areas that provided much of the black political leadership in the state. A district with a black congressman, assemblyman, mayor, and the vice-chairman of the state's Democratic party might have population figures which called for only two black delegates. Yet it was obviously more sensible to the campaign staff to choose more than required here in order to remove the pressure from those districts where the number of black residents was small or where the leadership was supporting some other candidate.

While this aspect of the strategy was successful, what the state staff had not anticipated was the possibility that districts with virtually no minority population would also nominate minority delegates. Yet in caucus after caucus that was precisely what happened. In the state's largest district meeting, for example, there were two persons of Spanish-speaking origin present out of a total of more than 900 activists. Those two individuals formed a "Chicano Caucus," ran as representatives of that "group," and were among the top seven vote-getters.

When the state campaign staff assembled later that evening to analyze the results of the delegate selection meetings, they were faced with a series of problems that offered no easy solutions. The procedure of subgroup nomination followed in almost every caucus had effectively isolated as a residual group the white males over 30 years of age. This group, although in some cases the largest single group at any caucus, was not provided for in the new quotas. Further, these people did not constitute a group in the sense of being bound together by any shared "interest." As a result, they did not constitute a voting bloc at any meeting. Those over-30 white males who were interested in running for delegate either made an unsuccessful effort to pursue traditional buttonholing strategies or in some cases simply decided not to run. Of the 105 delegates elected in district meetings in Northern California alone, only 8 per cent were in the over-30, white male category. The campaign staff had previously appointed ten white males as chairmen of some of the meetings and had made it clear that three additional men from this category would be appointed regardless of the caucus outcomes. But even with these appointments, the statewide composition of the slate that resulted from the delegate selection meetings was unbalanced, by any standard of "reasonable relationship to numbers in the general population":

51 per cent were women
40 per cent were under 30 years of age
21 per cent were black
20 per cent were Chicano, Indian, and Asian
19 per cent were white, male, and over 30.

The state campaign people, we should recall, were not forced by the new rules to accept these essentially advisory caucus results. Nor was that their initial inclination. Again, their hope had been that the new rules would provide them the freedom to select delegates who would come as close as possible—given the early date of the meetings—to involving the effective political leadership in each district. The McGovern district meetings were themselves unrepresentative of that leadership for the obvious reason that McGovern's appeal at that time was generally restricted to Democrats from the liberal side of the spectrum. Yet even the leaders of those liberal campaign people, labor organizers, and contributors who were committed to McGovern were generally bypassed by those at the district meetings. In fact, to agree to the results of the meetings would have meant accepting as delegates a large number of people who had never been involved in the McGovern campaign effort prior to that period.

To overrule the selections made in the district meetings would have created a different set of difficulties. The activists present at those meetings viewed themselves as constituting a sovereign body. They looked with disfavor on the notion that a few staff people could appoint persons not in attendance or without sufficient support at the meetings. Many communicated these sentiments vehemently to the campaign staff. The state campaign was thus put in such a position that not to accept the results of the meetings would have meant the subversion of "democracy." Worse still, it would have meant bypassing the democratic procedures of the caucuses in order to lower the number of women, young people, and minority representatives on the delegation.

As so often happens in political campaigns, the decision was made according to the rule which solves the most immediate needs and poses the fewest immediate problems. The immediate need dictated by the McGovern scenario was to establish the senator's campaign as the foremost liberal effort in the field. To violate the decisions of the district meetings in order to lower the number of minorities on the slate, the staff felt, would not have aided that cause. In addition, it was felt that those who had been excluded by the caucus process were those who, because of their own experience and attitudes, would be the most willing to accept the decision without withdrawing their support. Thus the final McGovern slate, later the California delegation to the Democratic National Convention, remained basically that chosen by the "people" in the meetings established by the new rules.

Evaluation

The foregoing description should make it obvious that the outcomes of the new delegate selection process were quite different from those expected. But did those outcomes follow from the changes in the rules, or did they grow out of the campaign's unique circumstances? There is no definitive answer to that question, but certain conclusions do appear clear. First, both the manner in which the delegates are chosen and the categories which must be represented under the new rules make it much more difficult to select delegates on the traditional basis of campaign criteria. In the past a delegate's ideological proclivities mattered very little; all that was asked was that he commit himself to the candidate's cause. Merit (at least in theory) was the criterion: persons were chosen because it was felt they were best able to help the campaign. These essentially technical standards are much less likely to be utilized in the district meetings established by the new rules, in part because most attendees share neither a belief in the value of the old standards nor the knowledge to apply them. Moreover, in the struggle for votes which dominates democratically organized meetings, the technical standards compete at a disadvantage with the more personal characteristics of the candidates. And, of course, the new criteria for increased representation would make the application of the old standards more difficult even if the caucus attendees were so inclined.

Second, the new rules produce a situation in which the delegates selected have a much less central relationship to the state and local campaign effort. In part this is because most delegates were chosen by other than campaign criteria. But it is also because the obligation of those chosen was to the people at their district meetings rather than to officials of the campaign list itself. Authority in a political campaign has traditionally been distributed in a hierarchical pattern. The candidates choose national leaders who choose state leaders who choose local leaders. Each group is responsible to those who appointed them. The new system of delegate selection breaks this pattern. Delegates are chosen by persons outside the campaign hierarchy and therefore are under no obligation to defer to the decisions of the campaign leadership or, indeed, to those of the candidate himself.

The establishment of quotas exacerbates the two previous consequences. The use of categories tends to legitimate the representation of "interests," which often produces criteria for delegation selection at odds with the traditional standards. Representatives of an "interest" chosen in caucus by others who share that interest, will be under no obligation to defer to the campaign leadership if they determine that exigencies require action to which the delegate is opposed. Finally, of course, the quotas make it more difficult to use political criteria in choosing delegates because most of those chosen under such standards are white, male, and over 30.

These general consequences proved to be particularly troublesome to McGovern's efforts after his California primary victory to broaden his base among the elite structure of the Democratic Party. In the past, the winner of California's primary balanced his delegation to the National Convention by adding representatives of the losing slates. This process often involved asking original members of the winner's delegation to resign. McGovern's delegates, however, were not selected by traditional political criteria and were less amenable to arguments which called for traditional political gestures. Because of the time and manner in which they were chosen, they were generally less willing to engage in practices which appeared to thwart the purposes of the new rules. Some were not inclined to trust anyone who had not been with McGovern in the beginning; others were opposed in principle to resignations and additions because they involved less representation for the categories that were victorious in February. Many were upset at the idea of rewarding those who had so recently been their enemies. For all these reasons—as well as the simple fact that each delegate wanted to be present at the triumph of his candidate—there were no resignations by McGovern delegates. In addition, however, of the 33 delegates chosen by the winning slate after the primary election, only 6 had been openly committed to another candidate. The rest had either remained neutral or joined the McGovern effort after the date of the district meetings.

The campaign strategists' inability to make any significant gesture to the representatives of the losers had several adverse consequences. Organized labor, for example, had virtually no representation on the final McGovern delegation. Only 15 per cent of California's incumbent Democratic officeholders were included on the delegation—and half of those had been chosen on the day of the district meetings. As a result, the resources of money, manpower, and public respectability ordinarily available to nominees from these groups came to McGovern late, only in part, and with little enthusiasm.

A final consequence of the new rules, damaging to the McGovern effort, but with possible long-term effects as well, involved the striking change in the public face of the Democratic delegation in 1972. Our National Conventions have served for more than 150 years as the arbitrators of that decision most crucial for our politics: Who is to be a legitimate and therefore a "real" candidate for the presidency? The nature and source of this authority to legitimate is something which we understand only poorly, but surely it has stemmed in part from the fact that in the past delegates were themselves persons of authority in their own locales—authority garnered by their ability to win elections and to elect others, the basic source of all legitimate authority in a democracy. The absence of most of these persons from the delegation in 1972 had consequences which are difficult to assess. What is clear is that many of the party's elite were unhappy with the final delegation—and felt less of an obligation to the nominee as a result. What remains to be discovered is the impact which this new face of the Democratic party will ultimately have on its voting affiliates. The categories prescribed by the new rules were intended to provide at least symbolic representation for several blocs of traditionally (or hopefully) Democratic voters. But in 1972, those rules and the dynamics of politics combined to produce a delegation which did not represent in either a symbolic or descriptive fashion the majority of those who have supported Democratic nominees in the past. If this fact proves to have the delegitimating effect which many in the party's elite structure fear, then the effect of the new rules may be to narrow rather than widen the party's ability to attract votes.

Conclusion

The purpose of this article has been to suggest that the new rules governing the selection of delegates to the Democratic National Convention have produced a series of major changes in the strategic environment within which presidential candidates compete for the Democratic nomination. An examination of the effect of these changes as they applied in the case of the California delegation to the National Convention provides support for the conclusion that the new rules did not aid, but in fact hindered the efforts of the eventual winner to mount an effective electoral campaign. While the major impact of these changes was related to the unique constellation of political events of 1972, the changes themselves could in all likelihood remain operative for the foreseeable future. Future candidates and the Democratic party as a whole will have to adapt as best they can to the new environment produced by reform.

Demographic Representation in California's 1972 and 1968 Democratic Presidential Primaries

BY JAMES I. LENGLE

Unrepresentativeness in Presidential Primaries

Almost 20 years ago, V. O. Key wrote:

> The effective primary constituency . . . may come to consist predominantly of the people of certain sections of a state, of persons of specified national origin or religious affiliation, of people especially responsive to certain styles of political leadership or shades of ideology, or of other groups markedly unrepresentative in one way or another of the party following.

To date, only Austin Ranney has addressed this warning at the presidential primary level. He discovered that those who voted in the 1968 New Hampshire and Wisconsin primaries were in several respects quite unrepresentative of those who did not. The voters were richer, better-educated, more interested in politics, and more likely to hold stronger opinions about the issues of the day. This paper is an attempt to retest Ranney's findings in a different state using a better data base and a more conventional operationalization of the concept of representation.

Excerpted from James I. Lengle, "Demographic Representation in California's 1972 and 1968 Democratic Presidential Primaries," paper presented at the Annual Meeting of the American Political Science Association, Chicago, Illinois, September 1976. Footnotes deleted. Reprinted by permission of The American Political Science Association.

The data are taken from Mervin Field's 1968 and 1972 postpresidential primary surveys of California's voting-age population. Field's data have three advantages over Ranney's. First, the surveys were conducted by the same organization asking identical questions of similarly derived samples over time. Thus, the presence, direction, and magnitude of demographic unrepresentativeness in two separate campaigns involving two different sets of candidates and issues can be empirically tested. Second, the data were collected in a state which, unlike New Hampshire and Wisconsin, possesses the demographic and ideological diversity that is characteristic of the Democratic party nationwide. Third, both California primaries had the major contenders on the ballot, were hotly contested and highly competitive, and were significant in determining who the Democratic presidential nominee would (i.e., McGovern in 1972) and would not be (i.e., McCarthy in 1968). Given this data and set of optimal political circumstances, the California primaries are more suitable case studies of the representative quality of Democratic presidential primaries. . . .

Demographic Representativeness

Measuring the demographic (un)representativeness of primary electorates is a simple procedure. First, measures of party membership and primary electorate are needed. In this paper, party membership is defined as *all Democratic party identifiers;* the primary electorate, as *all Democratic primary voters.*

Next, the demographic compositions of each are obtained. This step produces the percentage of the party membership and primary electorate that a particular social category (blacks, lower social class, college-educated) contributes.

Finally, a ratio is computed between the percentage of the Democratic primary electorate that a given demographic group composes and its percentage of the Democratic rank and file. These ratios reveal both the direction and degree of over and underrepresentation for various socioeconomic categories of Democrats. For example, Democrats with more than $20,000 annual income composed 10% of the entire California Democratic party membership in 1972. If they formed only 5% of the primary voters, they would be underrepresented by 50% and therefore receive a score of −50. If, on the other hand, they were 15% of the primary electorate, a score of +50 reflecting their overrepresentation would be assigned.

Table 1 presents the ratios of representation for various socioeconomic categories of Democrats. Positive signs indicate overrepresentation; negative signs, underrepresentation. The magnitude of over and underrepresentation per group is reflected in the ratio itself.

Table 1 · Demographic Representation in California's 1968 and 1972 Democratic Presidential Primaries

	REPRESENTATION IN 1972 PRIMARY			REPRESENTATION IN 1968 PRIMARY	
	Under	Over		Under	Over
Education:			*Education:*		
8th grade & under	-10		8th grade & under	-7	
9th-11th grade	-31		9th-11th grade	-11	
High school	-10		High school	-6	
1-3 college/bus./tech.		+4	1-2 college/bus./tech.		+17
College degree		+33	3-4 college*		+10
Advanced college degree		+50	Advanced college degree		+20
Income:			*Income:*		
Under $3,000	-18		Under $3,000	-25	
$3,000-$6,999	-11		$3,000-$6,999	-11	
$7,000-$9,999	-11		$7,000-$9,999	0	
$10,000-$14,999		+3	$10,000-$14,999		+17
$15,000-$19,999		+17	Over $15,000**		+18
Over $20,000		+30			
Social Class:			*Social Class:*		
Lower class	-25		Lower class	-29	
Lower middle	-15		Lower middle	-10	
Middle class		+2	Middle class		+5
Upper middle/upper		+20	Upper middle/upper		+8
Occupation:			*Occupation:*		
Laborers/Service	-11		Laborers/Service	-14	
Operatives/Semi-skilled	-25		Operatives/Semi-skilled	-8	
Craftsmen/Skilled/Foremen	-16		Craftsmen/Skilled/Foremen		+17
Clerical/Sales		+13	Clerical/Sales	0	
Professionals/Officials/Mgrs.		+10	Professionals/Officials/Mgrs.		+9
Race:			*Race:*		
White		+5	White		+1
Black	-17		Black	0	0
Asian/Spanish	-24		Asian/Spanish	-20	

*No separate college degree category used in 1968.
**Highest income category used in 1968.

Examining educational representation in 1972 quickly dispels any notions about demographically representative primary electorates. Democrats with an eighth-grade education or less, a ninth- to eleventh-grade education, and a high school degree were underrepresented in the primary electorate. Their respective scores of −10, −31, and −10 indicate that their percentage of the Democratic primary electorate was not commensurate with their percentage of the party's rank and file, but 10%, 31%, and 10% smaller.

In contrast, overrepresentation increased with education. Democrats with one to three years of college or business or technical training were slightly overrepresented (+4); Democrats with a college degree, even more so (+33); while Democrats with an advanced college degree were the most overrepresented contingent (+50). As these findings for education suggest, primaries are far from being a demographically representative collection of Democrats.

The 1968 primary was also skewed in the same direction. Although the magnitudes were smaller, less-educated Democrats were again underrepresented, while their better-educated counterparts were overrepresented. Thus in neither year is the educational composition of the party membership accurately reflected in the primary electorate.

Because of the magnitude of educational unrepresentativeness, and because education and income are interrelated, a similar pattern of unrepresentativeness should emerge for income. Table 1 confirms this expectation. In 1972, Democrats earning less than $3,000 were the most underrepresented group (−18), while Democrats earning $3,000–$6,999 and $7,000–$9,999 followed closely behind (−11, −11). On the other hand, all income categories over $10,000 were overrepresented, with the greatest disproportion occurring among Democrats earning over $20,000 (+30).

The 1968 primary electorate was a mirror image of 1972. Democrats earning under $3,000 and $3,000–$6,999 were underrepresented; Democrats earning $10,000–$14,999 and over $15,000 were overrepresented. Democrats with annual incomes between $7,000–$9,999 were perfectly represented since they composed equal proportions of the primary electorate and party rank and file.

Occupational unrepresentativeness coincided with my findings for education and income. In 1972, Democrats with blue collar occupations (laborers, service workers, semi-skilled, skilled, craftsmen, foremen) were underrepresented, and white collar Democrats (sales, clerical, officials, managers, professionals) were overrepresented. In 1968, a slight difference does appear. Craftsmen and foremen were overrepresented while Democrats with clerical and sales occupations were perfectly represented.

Since Field's measure of social class incorporates education, income, and occupation, as well as a subjective assessment by the interviewer, the findings for this variable are hardly surprising. In both 1968 and 1972, lower- and lower-middle-class Democrats were underrepresented; middle- and upper-middle/upper-class Democrats were overrepresented.

Comparing the racial composition of the primary electorate with the rank and file reveals an underrepresentation of racial minorities and overrepresentation of white Democrats. In 1972, black and Asian/Hispanic Democrats composed proportionately less of the primary electorate than they did of the party membership. This is reflected by their respective scores of −17 and −24. For white Democrats, the reverse was true. Their percentage of the primary voters exceeded their percentage of the party identifiers.

In 1968, white Democrats were again slightly overrepresented; Asian/Hispanic Democrats were underrepresented; black Democrats were perfectly represented.

The parallel between 1968 and 1972 becomes even more striking when you compare both years group for group. In 1968, ten groups of Democrats, *all lower SES,* were underrepresented. In 1972, the *same* ten groups were again underrepresented. In 1968, ten groups of Democrats, *all upper SES,* were overrepresented; in 1972, nine of the *same* ten groups were again overrepresented. As evidenced from the presence, direction, and magnitude of demographic unrepresentativeness in both primaries, political history, despite a different cast of characters, issues, and stimuli, *does* repeat itself.

. . . .

Although a necessary condition, variation in turnout is not sufficient to produce an unrepresentative primary electorate. A heterogeneous party is also needed. For example, primaries within a class-based party system would be troubled little by unrepresentativeness. If two or three parties existed in the United States, each with an *exclusive* base of support within one class, and closed primaries were conducted to choose the party's nominee, demographic unrepresentativeness would not surface—although these primaries might still be unrepresentative on other grounds. Turnout in primaries would still vary by party (i.e., the lowest turnout would occur in the party of the lower class; the highest turnout, in the upper-class party), but it would not vary significantly within each party. The Democratic party, however, is not exclusively lower-class, and the Republican party is not exclusively upper-class. As Fred Greenstein states, "Although each of the major parties tends to have somewhat different clientele of supporters among groups in society . . . neither has exclusive control of any group . . . and each party is sufficiently heterogeneous to receive some support from all groups." It is this combination of classless parties and class-related turnout that produces the particular direction and magnitude of unrepresentativeness found in Democratic primary electorates. A short analysis of these two conditions as they existed in 1972 and 1968 is presented below.

California Democratic Party Identification

Figure 1 presents California Democratic party identification in 1972 and 1968 by education, income, occupation, social class, and race. Overall, California Democrats remarkably resemble their national counterparts.

As the first and sixth graphs show, education and Democratic party affiliation were negatively related. In both years, Californians with an eighth-grade education or less, a ninth- to eleventh-grade education, and a high school education were more Democratic than the state as a whole, with the highest percentage of Democratic affiliation belonging to Californians with the least amount of formal education. Conversely, better-educated individuals were proportionately less Democratic, with the least support for the party coming from Californians with a college degree. They were 12% and 15% less Democratic than the state as a whole in 1972 and 1968, and 24% and 34% less Democratic than Californians with an eighth-grade education or less.

The remainder of the graphs in Figure 1 also show negative relationships between Democratic party identification and income, social class, and occupation. Disproportionate support in both years came from income groups below $10,000, blue collar workers, and the lower/lower-middle classes. Racial minorities (blacks, Asians, Hispanics) were also overwhelmingly Democratic.

For the moment, the direction and strength of these relationships are unimportant. More relevant to understanding the source of unrepresentativeness is the finding that support crosses all socio-economic categories. In 1972, for instance, Californians with a college degree were 24% less Democratic than Californians with an eighth-grade education. Nevertheless, two out of every five college-educated Californians were Democrats. To take another example, Californians earning over $20,000 were 21% less Democratic than Californians earning under $3,000, but 38% were still Democrats. Although Figure 1 clearly shows Democratic party identification centered among the lower classes, it is not exclusive, and it is this crosscutting support that sets the stage for the widespread unrepresentativeness in primary electorates.

Turnout in California's Democratic Presidential Primaries

The immediate explanation for recurring demographic unrepresentativeness is variation in turnout. If turnout were proportionally equal among all socio-economic groups of Democrats (e.g., 100%, 50%, or only 1%), the primary electorate would be an exact demographic replica of the party's rank and file. But turnout in general elections is socio-economic-related,

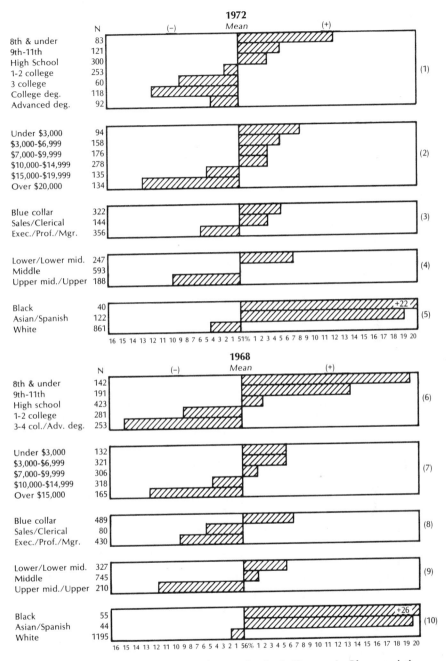

Figure 1 · Democratic Party Identification by Socio-Economic Characteristics

and there is no reason to suspect behavior in primaries to differ. Figure 2 presents 1972 and 1968 Democratic primary turnout by education, income, occupation, social class, and race.

Despite high turnouts in 1972 (66%) and 1968 (64%)—and high turnouts presumably repress this relationship—a relatively strong relationship still exists between education and turnout (graphs 1 and 6). Graph 1 shows that Democrats with an eighth-grade education or less, Democrats with a ninth- to eleventh-grade education, and Democrats with a high school diploma ranged from 18% to 6% *below* the state mean. In the same year, Democrats with at least some college experience or more ranged from 4% to 25% *above* the state average. Although the strength of the relationship is a bit weaker in 1968, the direction is identical (graph 6).

Comparing the differences between educational groups rather than their differences from the mean illustrates these variations more clearly. For example, 91% of all Democrats with an advanced college degree cast ballots in 1972, but only 53% of all Democrats with a high school education or less went to the polls—a difference of 38%. The turnouts for these same two groups in 1968 were 78% and 57%. Needless to say, these substantial variations produced the particular direction and magnitude of educational unrepresentativeness discovered in both primary electorates.

The direction and strength of the relationships between turnout and income for both years were also remarkably similar. Graphs 2 and 7 in Figure 2 show that turnout increased with income in both years. In 1972 (graph 2), turnout among Democrats with incomes below $10,000 fell short of the state average, with the lowest turnout registered by Democrats with incomes under $3,000 (55%, or 11% below the state mean). In contrast, all income groups above $10,000 exceeded the state mean, with the highest turnout found among Democrats with earnings in excess of $20,000 (82%, or 16% above the state mean). The difference between the lowest (under $3,000) and highest (over $20,000) income categories was 27%.

The figures for 1968 (graph 7) were almost identical. Compared to the statewide turnout of 64%, only 50% of all Democrats earning under $3,000 and 57% of all Democrats earning $3,000–$6,999 cast ballots for their favorite presidential contenders. In contrast, Democrats earning $10,000–$14,999 and over $15,000 surpassed the state average by 10% and 14%, and outvoted their low-income counterparts by 24% and 28%.

Examining Democratic turnout in 1972 and 1968 by occupation, social class, and race also reveals substantial variations. Democrats with executive/professional/managerial jobs outvoted blue collar Democrats by 16% in 1972 and 12% in 1968; upper-middle/upper-class Democrats outvoted lower-middle/lower-class Democrats by 20% in 1972 and 14% in 1968; white Democrats outvoted Democrats from racial minorities by 18% in 1972 and 6% in 1968. Consequently, equal representation of occupations, social classes, and race was also far from realized in both

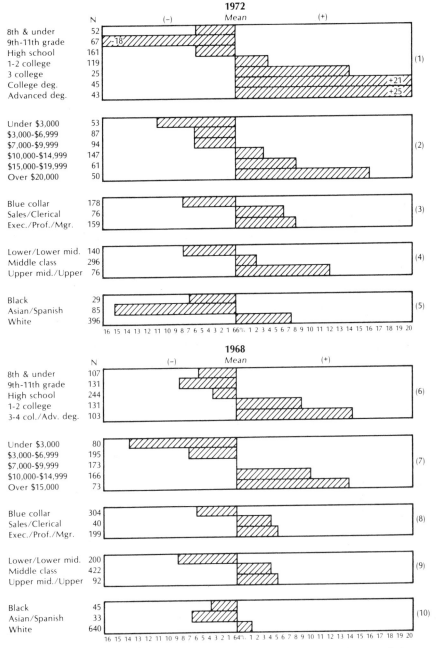

Figure 2 · Democratic Primary Turnout by Socio-Economic Characteristics

years. Without a doubt, the picture of primary electorates slowly emerging from the California experience confirms V. O. Key's twenty-year-old, untested suspicions.

Partisanship and Representation: Are Traditional Democrats Advantaged?

Theoretically, the ideal situation for any political party that relies upon rank-and-file control of the nomination process is 100% turnout. This guarantees the representation of all party members and the selection of the candidate who can garner the broadest first-choice support among all Democrats.

Given the reality of limited participation and no workable prescription for attaining the textbook ideal, presidential primaries could still be saved from unrepresentativeness by proportionally equal turnout. Under this condition, representation would at least be commensurate with strength inside the party. But as illustrated in the preceding section, turnout is strongly related to the socio-economic characteristics of Democrats.

While political theorists might be repelled by anything less than perfect demographic representation (resulting from either universal or proportionally equal turnout), practicing politicians might readily accept unrepresentativeness if it were strongly related to partisanship, i.e., if overrepresentation occurred among socio-economic groups disproportionately Democratic in party identification. The symbiotic relationship that exists between a party and its adherents would then be reinforced, since groups from whom the party receives disproportionate support, and to whom party policy is directed, would be exercising disproportionate influence in the nomination process. The end result would be a stronger, more responsive party. Thus, for a majority party, unrepresentativeness operating in a partisan direction might be preferable to perfect representation.

In order to determine if traditional Democratic party supporters are advantaged by unrepresentativeness, I have compared the partisanship of each demographic group (i.e., Democratic or Republican) to their degree of representation in primaries (i.e., over or underrepresented). The findings should be disconcerting to theorists and politicians alike.

Table 2 shows that those groups who have historically formed the nucleus of the Democratic party are underrepresented in their own party's most important decision-making process. In 1972, eleven of the thirteen socio-economic groups with disproportionately Democratic party identification were underrepresented in the primary. An identical analysis of 1968 provides additional evidence that this is the rule rather than the exception. Of the eight socio-economic groups underrepresented that year, all eight were predominantly Democratic in party affiliation.

Table 2 · Representation and Partisanship by Demographic Characteristics

1972 PRIMARY

	Under	Over	Democratic	Republican
Education:				
8th grade & under	X		X	
9th–11th grade	X		X	
High school	X		X	
1–3 college		X		X
College degree		X		X
Adv. col. degree		X		X
Income, $:				
Under 3,000	X		X	
3,000–6,999	X		X	
7,000–9,999	X		X	
10,000–14,999		X		X
15,000–19,999		X		X
Over 20,000		X		X
Social Class:				
Lower/Lower middle	X		X	
Middle class		X		X
Upper middle/Upper		X		X
Occupation:				
Blue collar	X		X	
Sales/Clerical		X	X	
Exec./Prof./Mgr.		X		X
Race:				
White		X		X
Black	X		X	
Oriental	X		X	
Other (Spanish)	X		X	

1968 PRIMARY

	Under	Over	Democratic	Republican
Education:				
8th grade & under	X		X	
9th–11th grade	X		X	
High school	X		X	
1–2 college		X		X
3–4 college		X		X
Adv. col. degree		X		X
Income, $:				
Under 3,000	X		X	
3,000–6,999	X		X	
7,000–9,999	—		X	
10,000–14,999		X		X
Over 15,000		X		X
Social Class:				
Lower/Lower middle	X		X	
Middle class		X	X	
Upper middle/Upper		X		X
Occupation:				
Blue collar	X		X	
Sales/Clerical	—		—	
Exec./Prof./Mgr.		X	X	
Race:				
White		X		X
Black	—		—	
Oriental	—		—	
Other (Spanish)	X		X	

As evidenced by both the 1972 and 1968 California experience, *the core of the Democratic party is composed of one well-defined segment of American society, but the party's nomination process, instead of rewarding this support, gives disproportionate influence to less Democratically partisan groups.*

Although these findings suffice to indict primaries, they constitute insufficient evidence for conviction. A strong argument could be made that demographic unrepresentativeness, its severity and pervasiveness notwithstanding, is irrelevant as long as ideology and candidate preferences are unrelated to, or independent of, the demographic characteristics of Democrats. For instance, if 30% of all lower-class Democrats, middle-class Democrats, and upper-class Democrats consider themselves strongly conservative, think crime and national defense are the most important problems facing the country, and choose Hubert Humphrey as their presidential nominee, and if the remaining 70% of each social class call themselves liberal, think pollution and conservation are the most pressing problems, and favor George McGovern as their presidential nominee, then variations in turnout and demographic unrepresentativeness are politically inconsequential because the primary electorate will still faithfully reflect the rank and file's 70–30 division over ideology, issues, and candidates. This empirical question merits further consideration and is addressed in the next two sections.

Because all the socio-economic variables examined in this paper are clearly correlated with education, and because of the strength of the relationship between education, turnout, and magnitude of unrepresentativeness in both years, and in order to simplify the data presentation but still illustrate the nature of my findings, I shall restrict my analysis to ideological and candidate differences among Democrats with varying levels of formal education.

"The Effective Primary Constituency may Come to Consist . . . of People Especially Responsive to Certain Shades of Ideology"

In this section I will examine the ideological perspectives of the California Democratic party membership to determine if overrepresented Democrats are ideologically similar to underrepresented Democrats. The data are presented in Table 3.

As the table shows, a significant ideological disparity exists among Democrats with varying educational backgrounds. While 76% of all Democrats with an eighth-grade education or less labeled themselves conservative and middle-of-the-road, only 17% of all Democrats with an advanced college degree adopted the same labels. In contrast, liberal self-

Table 3 · Ideological Self-Identification of Democrats by Education

	8th grade & under	9th–11th grade	High school	1–3 college	College degree	Advanced degree
Conservative[a]	31%	50%	46%	33%	26%	5%
Middle-of-the-Road	45%	22%	22%	15%	11%	12%
Liberal[b]	24%	28%	32%	53%	63%	83%
	100%	100%	100%	100%	100%	100%
N =	42	64	157	144	46	42

[a]Conservative combines "moderately conservative" and "strongly conservative."
[b]Liberal combines "moderately liberal" and "strongly liberal."

identification *dramatically* increases with the educational level of Democrats. Compared with only 24% of the Democrats with an eighth-grade education or less and 32% of the Democrats with a high school diploma, 63% of all college-educated Democrats and 83% of all Democrats with an advanced degree classified themselves as liberal.

Table 4 shows ideology and education similarly related in 1968. The most conservative and middle-of-the-road groups were Democrats with a high school education or less; the most liberal, Democrats with some college experience.

Thus, in both primaries, high turnout and overrepresentation occurred among overwhelmingly liberal groups, while conservative, middle-of-the-road leanings typified low-turnout, underrepresented groups.

In addition to uncovering direction, the analysis can be turned to determining whether strength of ideological conviction is related to the educational level of Democrats. These data are presented in Table 5.

As the top line indicates, strongly conservative self-identification is unrelated to education. Nearly identical proportions of Democrats with a high school education, college degree, and advanced college degree thought of themselves as strongly conservative.

The same cannot be said of strongly liberal convictions. Whereas only one of every fifty Democrats with an eighth-grade education or less adopted the strongly liberal label, two of every five Democrats with an advanced college degree identified themselves as strongly liberal. Thus, in addition to being more liberal than the rest of the party, high-turnout/overrepresented Democrats possess stronger liberal convictions.

Although intrinsically interesting, major ideological differences among groups within the party, even though associated with turnout variation and unrepresentativeness, may be politically insignificant. First, since ideology is subjectively rather than objectively measured, it may be meaningless, void of any coherent and consistent beliefs and attitudes. Second, the presence of ideological differences, even if rooted in cognitive issue posi-

Table 4 · Ideological Self-Identification of Democrats by Education—1968

	8th grade & under	9th–11th grade	High school	1–2 college	3–4 college	Advanced degree
Conservative	37%	33%	35%	27%	21%	10%
Middle-of-the-Road	38%	36%	34%	33%	22%	31%
Liberal	24%	31%	31%	40%	57%	59%
	*99%	100%	100%	100%	100%	100%
N =	86	106	226	122	68	29

*Due to rounding.

tions, does not necessarily mean Democrats choose their nominees accordingly. Voters may be unable to perceive issue or ideological differences among the candidates, or other factors, such as charisma, may override issue or ideological considerations.

"The Effective Primary Constituency may Come to Consist . . . of People Especially Responsive to Certain Styles of Political Leadership"

Since primaries place the candidate selection process into the hands of the rank and file, the important empirical question is whether candidate preferences are related to demographic characteristics. If not, the election outcome will be unaffected by either variations in turnout or demographic unrepresentativeness. On the other hand, if demographics and candidate preferences are related, the primary election will present a distorted picture of rank and file preferences.

Two measures were available to determine the candidate preferences of Democrats. The first alternative was to use the postprimary survey and to examine the candidate preferences of Democratic *voters*. Since candidate vote is the measure of preference, this offers no way, short of inference, to measure the preference of *nonvoters*. That is, if less-educated voters preferred one candidate over another, should the same candidate choice be attributed to less-educated nonvoters? This inference is probably quite reasonable, but there is still an absence of other corroborative evidence. The second alternative was to use a pre-election survey and to examine the candidate preferences of all Democratic identifiers. Since candidate preferences were asked of everyone, additional inferences would be unnecessary.

Fortunately, instead of having to choose and defend one approach, I could use both. As the reader will quickly discern from Figures 3, 4, and 5, both measures yielded identical findings.

The figures, standardized to the mean of zero to facilitate comparisons,

Table 5 · Strength of Ideological Conviction among Democrats
by Education—1972

	8th grade & under	9th–11th grade	High school	1–3 college	College degree	Advanced degree
Strongly conservative	2%	13%	6%	2%	4%	5%
Moderate[a]	95%	78%	85%	81%	78%	55%
Strongly liberal	2%	9%	9%	17%	17%	41%
	*99%	100%	100%	100%	*99%	*101%
N =	42	64	157	144	46	42

[a]Moderate combines "moderately liberal," "middle-of-the-road," and "moderately conservative" categories.
*Due to rounding.

show education related to the candidate preferences of the Democratic rank and file before the 1972 primary and related to the candidate choices of the 1972 and 1968 primary voters. Less-educated Democrats and Democratic voters disproportionately favored Humphrey in 1972 and Kennedy in 1968. In striking contrast, better-educated Democrats disproportionately preferred McGovern and McCarthy in those same years.

Note the similarity between Humphrey/Kennedy's major sources of support within the Democratic party (Figures 3, 4, and 5), the educational groups which were disproportionately Democratic in party affiliation (Figure 1), and the groups which were, due to low turnout (Figure 2), *underrepresented* in the primary electorate (Table 1). The inverse comparison can, of course, be made for McGovern's and McCarthy's sources of support.

These findings would seem to have serious ramifications for (democratic) political theorists and practicing (Democratic) politicians alike. Whereas *random* unrepresentativeness, either within a specific nomination campaign (i.e., overrepresentation of lower SES in one state and upper SES in another) or across several campaigns (i.e., overrepresentation one year, underrepresentation the next), might have no significant political impact, a *permanent* bias working to the advantage of the upper social and economic strata (and their issues and candidates) from the local to the national level, in primary after primary, year after year, could have serious consequences for the Democratic party. In the short run, utilizing a nomination process that gives disproportionate power to certain groups could affect the types of candidates chosen, types of issues stressed, and hence, the party's chances for success in a particular November general election. Ultimately, due to the perpetual and subtle conditioning of elites, masses, and issues, the structure and operation of both political parties could be substantially altered.

These broad assertions cannot be taken lightly. There is sufficient reason to suspect that demographic unrepresentativeness is not solely confined to one state (California) or one type of primary (presidential), but

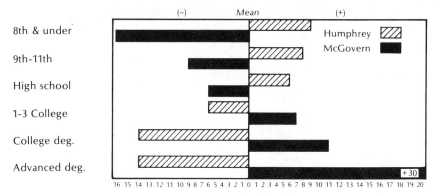

Figure 3 · Candidate Preferences of Democratic Party Identifiers by Education (1972 Pre-Election Survey)

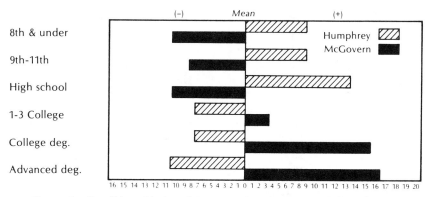

Figure 4 · Candidate Choice of Democratic Primary Voters by Education (1972 Post-Election Survey)

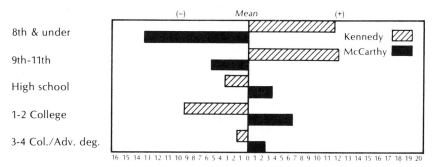

Figure 5 · Candidate Choice of Democratic Primary Voters by Education (1968 Post-Election Survey)

that its presence and particular direction exist in other states and in primaries for every office contested by Democrats. First, the socio-economic base of the California Democratic party (disproportionately but not exclusively lower SES) is typical of the Democratic party nationwide and within all large, urban, industrialized states. Second, every voting behavior study to date (including this one) has discovered turnout to be strongly related to socio-economic characteristics. Given these circumstances, one would be hard-pressed to argue that either the presence or direction of unrepresentativeness was unique to California or to presidential primaries.

One is on less firm ground when speaking about magnitude, for it may vary from state to state, year to year, and electoral office to electoral office. Additional empirical research in other states and other types of primaries is needed and will eventually confirm these differences. But for now, and in the absence of such research, one can reasonably infer that the magnitudes of demographic unrepresentativeness in the Democratic primary electorates of other states (and in the nation at large, given a national primary) are significantly *greater* than in California. Two facts form the basis for the inference. First, turnouts for California's Democratic presidential primaries are significantly higher than in any other state. For example, as noted in Figure 2, 66% of all California Democrats voted in 1972 and 64% voted in 1968. In comparison, turnouts for Pennsylvania's Democratic presidential primaries were 49% and 33%. Turnouts in New York, Oregon, and Rhode Island were even lower. Second, as turnout decreases, it decreases unevenly—faster among lower SES; slower among upper SES. Thus, with each percentage decrease in turnout, the magnitudes of under and overrepresentation increase at the demographic extremes (i.e., eighth-grade Democrats become more underrepresented; Democrats with a college degree, more overrepresented).

·B·

Rules and Results:
Systems for Allocating Delegates

Primary Rules, Political Power, and Social Change

BY JAMES I. LENGLE
& BYRON E. SHAFER

> *For want of a nail, the shoe was lost;*
> *For want of a shoe, the horse was lost;*
> *For want of a horse, the rider was lost;*
> *For want of a rider, the battle was lost;*
> *For want of a battle, the kingdom was lost;*
> *And all for the want of a horseshoe nail.*
>
> —MOTHER GOOSE

The Invisible Participant

The late 1960s and early 1970s were boom times for predictions about the future of American politics. Grand organizing concepts abounded—a "new ethical consciousness," an "emerging conservative majority," the "triumph of social engineering," a "revolt against the future," etc.—and each was asserted to be the trend which would sweep away institutional obstacles and human opponents, the "theme" which historians would use (50 to 100 years hence) to summarize our era.

Scholars who are more concerned with the mechanics of American politics were not often drawn into this argument, but many must have suspected that while history is often *written* in these terms, it seldom

James I. Lengle and Byron E. Shafer, "Primary Rules, Political Power, and Social Change," *American Political Science Review*, Vol. 70, March 1976, pp. 25–40. Footnotes deleted. Reprinted by permission of The American Political Science Association.

occurs that way. Instead, American political history wells up out of the situational calculations of candidates, activists, and voters. If any given tendency is to be judged, retrospectively, to have dominated the politics of our own era, it must reach that domination through the decisions which these actors make in order to influence public policy, and especially through the decisions which individual politicians make in order to gain and hold public office. If the rules of politics reliably cause the latter to seek votes in certain ways, to stress certain issues, and to address a certain clientele, those rules—far from being rolled over by the "current of history"—may be crucial in determining how that current will run.

The regulations governing presidential primaries are a shining example. These ground-rules—mandating either Winner-Take-All, Proportional, or Districted allocations of primary delegates—remain nearly invisible when compared with the groups, issues, and personalities that are the stuff of campaign coverage. Yet these inconspicuous channeling devices may ultimately affect the destinies not just of a few office-seekers but of entire political parties and major public issues as well. So far, only the Democrats have had enough contests in one year to support any sensible predictions, but that year makes it difficult to overrate the importance of primary rules. In 1972, a few simple alterations in these unseen "participants" could easily have produced a different Democratic nominee. (See the next section.) If 1972 is an adequate guide, altered primary regulations, over the medium run, could well determine which blocs will be influential within a party, thereby working fundamental (if unintended) change on that party. (See the third section.) Finally, in the long run, such ground-rules may even shape the grand conflicts of an epoch, indirectly but powerfully favoring some causes and not others.

In the last presidential nomination race, the beneficiary of the power hidden in the rules of the game was Senator George McGovern. Most primaries offered delegates by (Congressional) District, and Districted primaries maximized McGovern's strength. One simple shift, however, to generalized Winner-Take-All laws, would have *minimized* that strength, in the process guiding a healthy plurality of primary delegates (along with the nomination?) to Senator Hubert Humphrey. A second change, to Proportional regulations, would have undercut both McGovern and Humphrey, leaving only Governor George Wallace to derive electoral satisfaction from primary rules.

But beyond the fate of three particular politicians (none of whom may ever again seek the Oval Office) lies the fate of the social groups whose fortunes they hoped to advance, and whose backing they hoped to parlay into a presidency. The influence of these groups, too, was sharply affected in 1972 (and probably, for the foreseeable future) by the way primary rules modified the comparative power of different states within the national party. The old, eastern, industrial states, which had previously been essential to any Democratic nomination, shrank in importance. Two newly powerful blocs—one, of the persuasion known as "Southern Democratic," the other, Midwestern-Western (and presidentially Republican)—filled the vacuum, thanks to primary election laws which helped compensate for their smaller populations and which capitalized on their political homogeneity.

Nothing guarantees that the interplay among Democratic candidates, states' voters, and formal regulations in 1972 is essential to the prediction either of political trends in the late twentieth century or of what historians a half-century hence will say about them. Dramatic events (major wars or severe economic declines) may move the bulk of the general public so powerfully that no institutional arrangements can redirect the trend. But in the absence of such events, or if such events should occur but leave no enduring political legacy (i.e., until there is good reason to believe that the *pattern* of interaction between social forces and formal regulations which surfaced in 1972 will change), that interaction can be extrapolated to hint at the drift of American politics in the years to come.

The Primaries: Other Rules, Other Results

Political ground-rules are not always overlooked, underanalyzed, or passively lamented. Between 1968 and 1972, the Democrats' Commission on Party Structure and Delegate Selection reconsidered all of the party's internal regulations. The Commission deliberately instituted numerous changes in traditional party practice. It inadvertently created as many others, one of the most crucial being a vast increase in the percentage of delegates available in primaries.

The Commissioners did not want to multiply the number of primaries. Yet by issuing eighteen additional guidelines for delegate selection, they in effect announced eighteen new ways to unseat state delegations. Many state party leaders responded with what was apparently the surest method of avoiding this threat: They simply threw all aspiring delegates on the ballot. Thus states as diverse as Rhode Island, North Carolina, and New Mexico, which in 1968 had done their party business at state-level conventions, added primaries to the list for 1972.

The increase in the number of "effective" primaries was even greater, however, because (required) reforms upgraded previously less significant arenas into serious campaign sites. In fact, the biggest rise in the number of delegates along the primary route came not from new entries but from changes in old ones. In 1968, nearly half of all primaries had been "advisory," i.e., either voters could express a presidential preference but delegates would be chosen *independently* in party conventions, or, more commonly, a presidential preference could not be logically connected with the *separate* vote for delegates. By 1972, the linkage between candidate preference and delegate selection had been tightened so much that the free agents of past primaries—"favorite sons," "bosses," and "uncommitted" delegates—had almost disappeared.

The pattern of successes and failures in these primaries is already a historical footnote. The lightweights (Lindsay, Hartke, Yorty, Mills, etc.) and one ostensible heavy (Muskie) were squeezed out early. Three major factional leaders (McGovern, Humphrey, Wallace) then campaigned through the pre-California contests. With a victory in California, McGovern effectively smashed the last organized pre-Convention opposition, and moved "inexorably" (at least by hindsight) to the nomination.

What this familiar account omits is the tremendous impact of state primary *rules,* rather than state primary *voters,* on these candidates and their fortunes. While a first glance shows nearly as many recognizably different sets of rules as there were state primaries, all of these are in fact minor variations on three basic plans:

1. *Winner-Take-All.* The candidate with a *plurality in the total statewide vote acquires all that state's delegates,* regardless of the size of his vote or lead. Thus Rhode Island gave all 22 of its delegates to McGovern, whose 16,000 votes were twice Muskie's total, though still only 2 percent of the eligible electorate.

2. *Proportional.* Each candidate who tops a statewide vote threshold (usually expressed in percentage terms) gains a share of the delegation; *his percentage of the total vote cast for all candidates who pass the threshold determines the exact number.* Thus North Carolina used a 15 percent cut-off, which only two entrants (George Wallace and Terry Sanford) out of five met; Wallace, with 57 percent share of the two-man total, got 37 delegates, leaving Sanford with 27 (43 percent).

3. *Districted.* Delegates are apportioned to preestablished units (almost always congressional districts) on a fixed basis (past party vote, straight population, or half of each); the candidate with *the plurality in each district receives (all) its delegates.* Thus Florida put from 4 to 7 delegates, depending on prior Democratic vote, in each of 12 congressional districts. George Wallace carried 11 of these for 54 votes, and Hubert Humphrey picked off one for 7.

Individual states mixed or matched these three plans to suit local political needs. The desire to avoid credentials challenges, to preserve a strong state party organization, to enhance reformers' new-found clout, or just to get some sort of primary rules through a hostile (Republican) legislature were each major considerations in one or more states. Few, however, intended to favor one particular presidential aspirant. Fewer tried to guess how their regulations would affect the distribution of power within the "national party," which is, after all, a quadrennial fiction, not an ongoing body. None attempted to predict what their decisions would contribute to historians' judgments fifty or one hundred years later.

Table 1 · Pre-California Primaries

State	Date	Delegates
New Hampshire	March 7	18
Florida	March 14	81
Wisconsin	April 4	67
Pennsylvania	April 18	182
Massachusetts	April 18	102
Ohio	May 2	153
Indiana	May 2	76
Tennessee	May 4	49
North Carolina	May 6	64
Nebraska	May 9	24
West Virginia	May 9	35
Michigan	May 16	132
Maryland	May 16	53
Oregon	May 23	34
Rhode Island	May 23	22

But while purely local, tactical needs shaped most primary rules, this in itself promised only that any bias for or against a particular candidate or state would be accidental—not that it would be absent, nor that it would average out by convention time. In fact, a strong, consistent bias was operating. It escaped notice during the campaigns because any given primary could be conducted under only one set of rules. The final popular vote was filtered through a particular state's primary law, delegates were distributed among various contenders according to these results, and candidates and newsmen then rushed off to the next contest.

A lack of neutrality in the rules becomes very apparent, however, if *the final popular vote is used three different times to get three different delegate distributions for each state*—one Winner-Take-All, one Proportional, and one Districted. When the recorded vote is filtered through each of these three basic plans, the primaries can in effect be "rerun" to highlight the power inherent in their regulations.

Before the California result took the delegate hunt off the hustings and into the Credentials Committee, there were fifteen primaries which were entered by a major candidate (McGovern, Humphrey, or Wallace) and in which presidential preferences can be reliably attached to voters' choices (Table 1). When these fifteen are rerun on paper, they show the "invisible participant" hard at work.

Pennsylvania is the starkest example. Keystone voters thought most highly of Hubert Humphrey, who would have amassed the largest share of their delegates under *any* of the three basic plans (Table 2). But by leading the field under Districted rules, Humphrey garnered only half of what the same performance would have gotten him via Winner-Take-All—although

Table 2 · **Pennsylvania Results Change Radically Under Different Primary Rules**

	Winner-Take-All	Proportional	Districted
Humphrey	182	66	93
Wallace	—	40	16
Muskie	—	38	34
McGovern	—	38	39

this was still nearly half again as much as it would have given him under Proportional regulations. In fact, the *difference* (in delegates) between winning Pennsylvania through Winner-Take-All and winning Pennsylvania Proportionately is greater than the total number of delegates available in twelve out of the first fifteen primaries (see Table 1). On abstractly statistical grounds, then, Humphrey-for-President partisans might reasonably have cared more about primary law in Pennsylvania than about whether anyone at all voted for their man in, say, Massachusetts.

The runner-up in the Pennsylvania balloting, George Wallace, was also disadvantaged by the method for awarding delegates. His solid second would have gotten the Alabama governor the second greatest delegate total if his vote had been filtered through Proportional ground-rules. Under the actual Districting procedure, it made him a poor fourth in convention representatives—with the worst return per vote of any candidate entered. Clearly, without asking a single *voter* to change his mind, Pennsylvania state *legislators* could have juggled between one-sixth and two-thirds of the delegates going to their winner, while making either Wallace (Proportional), McGovern (Districted), or no one (Winner-Take-All) the "runner-up" (Table 2).

But if candidates can lose up to two-thirds of their delegate potential through the intervention of particular primary rules, they can also win those primaries in more than one way. Primary elections, of course, allow someone to amass the most delegates; this is the traditional notion of victory. Unlike the November election, however, they also allow contestants to "win" by attracting favorable notice through a "surprisingly strong" showing. Newsmen are the custodians of this second form of "victory," and a switch in the rules in Pennsylvania would undoubtedly have altered it as well.

Under existing Pennsylvania regulations (Table 2), there were two wins, one loss, and one draw in the media war. The "draw" went to Hubert Humphrey. By primary time, Humphrey was expected to win, but not romp. When he did just that, he picked up a sizable bloc of delegates, but only a ho-hum from the press. Gains with the latter were instead recorded by McGovern, who drew measurable support in a state that was

Table 3 · Other States Show the Same Strong Effect
of Primary Rules

Ohio		
Winner-Take-All	*Proportional*	*Districted*
Humphrey	153	78	96
McGovern	—	75	57

Indiana		
Winner-Take-All	*Proportional*	*Districted*
Humphrey	76	40	49
Wallace	—	36	27

widely thought to be "not his type" (while also piling up 102 delegates in Massachusetts that day); and by Wallace, who ignored Pennsylvania nearly completely but came in second anyway. Commentators pinned a "must-win" label on Edmund Muskie before the primary, and a "loss" on him after it. Muskie's camp concurred, and he deactivated his candidacy after the Pennsylvania votes were counted.

In a primary occurring as early as Pennsylvania's, media-pronounced victories can be worth every bit as much, in terms of future resources, as larger delegate collections. Such "victories" can in fact be crucial for renewing a potential nominee's reservoir of financial contributions, activists' energies, and popular support. By mid-April, no rules change short of vote fraud could have garnered favorable press reviews for the Muskie candidacy, but the other Pennsylvania press judgments ("wins" for McGovern and Wallace, with a "draw" for Humphrey) were really deduced as much from primary law as from the vote distribution. They would surely never have survived a Winner-Take-All primary, resulting in *182* delegates for Humphrey, and *0* for McGovern and Wallace together.

Pennsylvania was a particularly strong example of a relatively common, though not universal, phenomenon—the "intervention" of primary rules between the distribution of votes and the division of the delegation. In similar states, like Ohio and Indiana, similar percentages of delegates' allegiance derived from primary law rather than from voters' commands (Table 3). Thus a switch from Ohio's actual Districted system to Winner-Take-All would have altered the loyalties of close to forty percent of the state's convention representatives. A second move from Winner-Take-All to Proportional would have swung nearly fifty percent. An only slightly milder version of the same effect appeared in Indiana, where one-third and one-half of the delegates, respectively, would have shifted with these changes.

Table 4 · The Differential Impact of Rules of the Game Does *Not* Even Out in the Long Run

	Winner-Take-All	Proportional	Districted
Humphrey	446[a]	314	324
Wallace	379	350	367
McGovern	249	319	343
Muskie	18	82	52
Others	0	27	6

[a]Delegate totals for fifteen pre-California primaries.

Primary ground-rules might still be judged unimportant if the advantages which they concealed had eventually cancelled out. In theory, benefits might have gone randomly to candidates, with, for example, the Districted plan favoring McGovern in Ohio, Humphrey in Pennsylvania, Wallace in Indiana, etc. In fact, such averaging did *not* occur. When possible outcomes for the fifteen pre-California primaries are summed, alterations in "minor" rules lead to impressively different results (Table 4).

Under the existing welter of regulations, of course, George McGovern had become the "man to beat" by the June 6 California showdown. But if he had first faced fifteen Winner-Take-All primaries, he might well have loomed tiny as California approached. For given uniform Winner-Take-All ground-rules, Hubert Humphrey would have squeezed the most from the states with delegates on the ballot. He would have been pressed most closely by Governor Wallace, who would have been followed by a relatively distant Senator McGovern. Humphrey, who under the actual rules could never match McGovern's delegate collection, would have almost doubled his rival's total.

Unfortunately for Senator Humphrey, a majority of states actually adopted Districted primaries. If they *all* had, the Winner-Take-All leader (Humphrey) would have dropped from first to last, jettisoning a substantial share of his delegate potential in the process. The primary election crown would have passed to Governor Wallace, with about the same number of delegates under both plans. But the candidate for whom Districted rules would have been most congenial would have been Senator McGovern, who could have squeezed *half again as many* delegates out of a change from Winner-Take-All to Districting.

Governor George C. Wallace, alone among the three major factional leaders, could have looked with equanimity on any set of rules. Proportionality might have offered some added attractiveness, since it would have provided him with his largest lead, but Districting still would have made him the primary king, and Winner-Take-All regulations would have given him his greatest raw total of delegates. Proportional rules would also have pumped the maximum amount of "medicine" into the ailing candidacy of

Senator Edmund Muskie, although the extra (thirty to sixty) delegates would hardly have been enough to save the patient.

Since candidates and voters are not laboratory animals, the primaries must be rerun on paper, rather than in the voting booth. These "paper elections" are an excellent way to unmask the magnitude of the impact of different primary rules, but they are only a reasoned approximation to the (precise) number of delegates which particular candidates might have obtained if things had been different. If the rules had been changed, the strategic decisions of some participants would surely have changed, too, with some (changed) electoral outcomes. Yet only massive strategic shifts—the kind which are highly unlikely in the short run, where candidates are well known and citizens have reliable voting habits—could have altered the general thrust of each primary plan. Strategic shifts of a scope sufficient to keep the rules of the game from having *any* major impact on candidates' chances are, in practical terms, unimaginable. In short, in 1972, primary regulations were extremely important in determining who the nominee would be.

In fact, the ground-rules often did as much as the vote in establishing who "won," and by how much. Because they did, they give rise to a final, long chain of speculation: Changes in the rules would have significantly influenced the strength of early contestants, might well have altered (or neutralized) the result in the "key" California primary, could subsequently have led to a different (if unpredictable) nominee, and might ultimately have delivered "four less years"—in the same way that a single, unnoticed, fabled nail once toppled a kingdom.

Primary Rules and Political Power

Technical party regulations, no matter how great their power, are rarely debated during election campaigns, and 1972 was no exception. Once the presidential election was past, however, combat over party rules began again within the Democratic party. The site for the debate was the new Commission on Delegate Selection and Party Structure, and, while press attention was concentrated on the issue of representational quotas, primary ground-rules were also on the Commission's agenda.

On October 5, 1973, the Commissioners voted to outlaw Winner-Take-All regulations, and to limit states to a choice of Districting or Proportionality. The Winner-Take-All primary was killed off by a coalition of those who believed that the latter plans would increase the power of Democrats with the same policy preferences, those who felt that the latter plans were simply more "democratic," and those who were looking backward to the experience of one particular (1972) candidate or forward to the chances of a new (1976) one. Some combination of the same three criteria—the internal distribution of party power, conceptions of democracy, and candidate loyalties—will necessarily guide anyone else who passes judgment on the Commission's decision.

Diehard candidate loyalists, as always, have a very simple decision-rule at hand. Whichever primary system favored their man is equitable; all others are distortive. Thus Table 4 suggests that: (1) Devoted McGovernites may rest content with the actual mix, but could encourage the proliferation of Districted primaries; (2) Fervent Humphreyites should see justice solely in Winner-Take-All plans; (3) Rabid Wallaceites, alone among the partisans, might take the statesmanlike view. Proportionality may hold a special place in their hearts, but they could swallow Winner-Take-All or Districted regulations without difficulty.

Such hero worship is never very helpful in evaluating political arrangements, partly because it is far from objective, but mainly because heroes suffer political mortality while the rules which favored them live on. Reformers who want to avoid these selfish, personalized, and transitory standards can turn instead to "democratic theory," a realm untainted by past partisan attachments. For these rule-makers, party law should be deduced from general standards of democratic government and then extended to all facets of party activity, including primary elections.

Unfortunately, democratic theorists offer few consensual standards. Those who favor Proportionality claim the closest approximation to the actual vote, along with the greatest incentive for any and all hopefuls to enter the primaries—both clearly "democratic." Winner-Take-All advocates counter that by driving aspirants out of the race and by forcing voters toward compromise, they insure meaningful choices before the Convention and a chance of winning the election after it—both clearly "democratic." Lastly, Districting supporters hold out the "golden mean," promising some diversity in candidates but some hope that they will be forced to coalesce—and that is also "democratic."

Fortunately, there is a middle-ground between abstract theoretical guidelines and particularistic personal loyalties because all primary plans also advantage specific geographic areas; in other words, they give political power disproportionately to some states (and hence to some states' *residents*) and not to others. Since they do, primary rules can be used deliberately to alter the balance of power within a political party. In fact, regardless of whether reform commissioners consider the internal distribution of party power, their decisions *will* benefit either politically liberal or conservative areas, either electorally competitive or noncompetitive areas, and either reliably Democratic, waveringly Democratic, or regularly Republican areas.

The Democratic National Committee has always recognized this impact of the rules on constituents' fortunes when it allocates Convention delegates to the states. At this (earliest) stage of the delegate selection process, the D.N.C. engages in some deliberate manipulation of party blocs, through an allocation formula which rewards both sheer (Electoral College) size and past Democratic support. The party-voting criterion, by inflating states which normally go Democratic, is an attempt to guarantee that individuals who are most typical of the Democratic vote will have the most weight within the party. The size criterion, by rewarding states which have most to offer in the Electoral College, is an attempt to guarantee that the nominee will be a winner. Inadvertently, it also increases the likelihood that he will be devoted to the social-welfare policies and coalition-of-minorities politics which traditionally characterize the national Democratic party, and which find special favor in the big, urban, industrialized, working-class, ethnic- and racial-minority-oriented states.

As long as top state party officials could select and direct their delegations, a state's power at the Convention faithfully reflected the size and Democratic-vote criteria. The bigger the state, the more claim it could have on potential nominees. The more reliably Democratic the state, the more muscle it could throw behind its choice. Thus the dozen largest states were more important than all their brethren combined. And thus, for states of similar population, a look at the last presidential vote would predict comparative importance at the next convention.

The proliferation of (reformed) primaries since 1968 has changed all this. The first allocation of delegates no longer insures the internal party power of large and/or reliably Democratic states if their delegates end up on the ballot. To be sure, there are primary plans which maintain the original advantages bestowed by the Democratic National Committee, there are also systems which neutralize these advantages, and there are even arrangements which reverse them. In 1972, primary regulations had a strong, unintended impact on which states were vital to candidates' fortunes: They magnified the influence of Democrats in areas which are likely to go Republican in most general elections or which, while remaining Democratic for most lower offices, are apt to desert the party at presidential election time.

If all states had implemented Winner-Take-All primaries in 1972, this redistribution of state party power would not have occurred. A state's "political value"—the delegate *margin* obtained by the candidate who finished first in its primary—would have corresponded exactly with the size of delegation authorized by national party rules (Figure 1). The key battlefields would have been generally northeastern, urban, industrial, minority-oriented, populous, and two-party competitive in November, while the lesser ones would have been southern and western, more rural, agricultural, homogeneous, sparsely populated, and politically one-party.

Candidates would have been forced to attend to the former states, on pain of losing any chance at nomination. Campaigners would have been particularly drawn to states like Pennsylvania and Ohio, which are not just

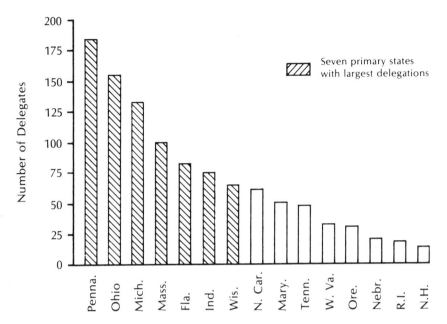

Figure 1 · Winner-Take-All[a] Rules Maintain Original Delegate Advantages

[a]Bars represent the state's "political value," i.e., the delegate *margin* obtained by the candidate who finished first in that primary. Under Winner-Take-All rules, the "political value" is the same as the size of the state's delegation; under other rules, it may not be (see Figures 2 & 3). The seven primary states with the largest delegations have the striped bars in Figures 1, 2, & 3; the eight primary states with the smallest delegations have the plain bars.

competitive at the general election, but are highly competitive within the state Democratic party itself. Narrow victories there (and victories would predictably be narrow) could swing a huge phalanx of delegates. Consequently, such states would have a maximum opportunity to extract policy promises from candidates. Pennsylvania, for example, offers multiple bases of support for presidential aspirants: the coal regions, inner-city Philadelphia or Pittsburgh, wealthy suburbs, extensive farm belts, etc. The man who could best appeal to a plurality of these Pennsylvanians would receive a net gain of 182 delegates; the man who attracted New Hampshiremen, by contrast, would inherit one-tenth of that. In fact, placing first in Pennsylvania would have been worth as much as a comparable performance in all six of the smallest primary states *combined* (New Hampshire, Rhode Island, Nebraska, Oregon, West Virginia, and Tennessee).

The position of the largest states would begin to erode seriously if all primaries were instead run Proportionately. Where a Winner-Take-All plan favors states with the greatest *total number* of delegates, and in effect offers a bonus to those which are internally competitive, a Proportional arrangement favors those which can generate the greatest *vote difference*— an extra reward for the noncompetitive (Figure 2). As a result, the more

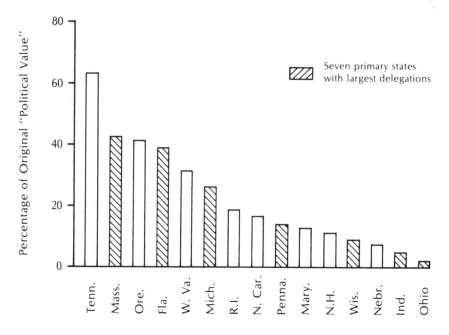

Figure 2 · Proportional Rules[a] Erode Original Delegate Advantages

[a]Bars represent the share of the state's *political value* (under Winner-Take-All rules) which it can retain under Proportionality.

politically homogeneous of the middle-sized states would increase their ability to command candidates' attention and to wield power within the party, at the expense of the more politically diverse among the big states.

Tennessee, in 1972, was the outstanding example of the way that Proportionality would confer benefits on such middle-sized, noncompetitive states. Given Proportional rules, George Wallace's Tennessee landslide (75 percent of the ballots cast) would have been worth as large a lead in delegates (an edge of 31) as Hubert Humphrey's much narrower victory in Pennsylvania (a margin of 26). Tennesseans would have generated the same delegate margin for their favorite as Pennsylvanians did for theirs— even though the latter were entitled to four times as many convention votes. Politicians would have had to learn to calculate accordingly: The magnitude of a potential winner's lead, not the size of the states he could win, would become the key to nomination hopes.

The benefits which Proportionality could have brought to Tennessee would have been felt as severe costs in, for example, Ohio, where a net gain of *three* delegates would have been skimpy spoils for the victor (Figure 2). A three-delegate *lead* in Ohio would not be trivial in the winner's quest for a convention majority, since it still represents a large *total* of delegates. (See Table 3.) But it would not be too much consolation either, since at least one other candidate (and possibly more) would be gaining only three fewer convention votes.

Because it has a substantial delegation in total size, Ohio would not be crossed off the itineraries of presidential aspirants; they would still be well advised to rally their partisans there. But if they had the capacity to attract Tennesseans as well, they should certainly transfer more of their time and, presumably, policy promises to the Volunteer state. Even if they could not do so—and not everyone can roll up three-quarters of the vote in Tennessee—they would still be facing a changed environment within the party. Where Winner-Take-All rules once made Ohio (153 delegates) more than three times as large as Tennessee (49), Proportionality would now reverse the situation (+3 versus +31). In tactical terms, a candidate who finished first in Ohio and a poor third in Tennessee could, historically, have thumbed his nose at a competitor who finished first in Tennessee but third in Ohio; he would, after all, have beaten the latter by better than 3-to-1. In the post-Winner-Take-All era, however, the Ohio winner would have to stifle his contempt, since a Tennessee victor could often eclipse him in the delegate race.

Tennessee and Ohio were, of course, extreme cases. In general, Proportional plans would subtract unevenly from the edge of the big states, since these states are not necessarily more internally competitive than their medium-sized or tiny counterparts. Residents of Michigan or Massachusetts, for example, voted as lopsidedly in their primaries as anyone. The big states which *are* competitive would shrink in importance, relative to both noncompetitive big states and noncompetitive smaller ones. Their slack would be taken up by the more one-sided among the middle-sized. Few of the states in this size range could derive as dramatic gains as Tennessee, although the fact that these states are predominantly southern might have substantial policy implications for the party as a whole (see last section). The smallest states (New Hampshire, Rhode Island, Nebraska) would derive much less of an advantage, since a huge *percentage* victory in any of them still represents a comparatively small *number* of delegates (e.g., nine in Rhode Island). Under Proportionality, then, big, competitive states decline in importance; middle-sized, noncompetitive states rise, and small states stay at the bottom of the heap.

The latter could be rescued from this position by a broad-scale implementation of Districted primaries. If all primaries had been Districted—as most were—the net benefits coming with a first-place finish would have been almost unrelated to size of delegation, and hence to Winner-Take-All margins (Figure 3). Where a Winner-Take-All victory in Pennsylvania would have been equivalent to victories in all *six* of the smallest states, any *two* of these states could have offered about the same delegate margin as the Keystone state under Districted regulations, and North Carolina and Tennessee could have matched its political value by themselves. In the battle for power within the Democratic party, it would have been North Carolina over Pennsylvania, Tennessee over Ohio, Nebraska over Indiana, and Oregon over Wisconsin.

The shift from universal Winner-Take-All to universal Districted plans sharply alters the tactical environment on the way to the convention. The largest states suffer a tremendous diminution in political influence because they contain pockets of strength for any number of candidates. The smaller states will never face this problem: each of the six primary states with the fewest delegates could have given exactly the same share of those delegates—100 percent—to its favorite under either Winner-Take-All or Districted rules (Figure 3). Where once a candidate could only hope to gain the nomination if he had substantial muscle in the eastern industrial states, the change to Districted primaries should make it every bit as feasible to pursue a "southern" or "western" strategy. A presidential contender can now secure a decent minority of districts in the biggest states and then aim for all the districts in either those states which are normally Republican in the November election (mainly western or midwestern) or those states which are of the hybrid persuasion known as "Southern-Democratic."

Selection of delegates by District is, in fact, an excellent example of the way that one set of rules (those governing primaries) can nullify the effects of another (those governing apportionment of delegates to the states). A Winner-Take-All system supports the original apportionment formula, giving extra power to large and/or reliably Democratic states (Figure 1, where the striped bars precede the plain ones). Proportionality operates to neutralize the formula (Figure 2, where the striped and plain bars are mixed randomly). Districting works to *reverse* it (Figure 3, where the plain bars precede the striped ones).

Each primary plan, by the way it parcels out delegates, favors a particular blend of delegation size and internal competition. Consequently, each plan leads to a different distribution of power within the party. A Winner-Take-All system fragments *no* delegations, thereby making the larger and more competitive states more powerful. A Proportional system, on the other hand, fragments *all* delegations, making the larger and less competitive states more powerful. A Districted system takes the final step by fragmenting the delegations of the big states but not those of their less populous counterparts—in effect maximizing the power of the smaller and less competitive states. The widespread adoption of Districted primaries after 1968, or the prohibition of Winner-Take-All primaries after 1972, were not, then, just inconsequential decisions to hand out delegates via a certain mechanism. They were indirect, apparently accidental, but far-reaching choices about the types of candidate who would bear the party's standard, the types of voter who would have the power to choose those standard-bearers, and the types of issue with which both groups would try

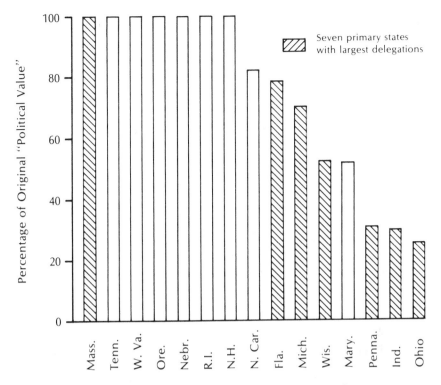

Figure 3 · Districted Rules[a] Destroy Original Delegate Advantages

[a]Bars represent the share of a state's *political value* (under Winner-Take-All rules) which it can retain under Districting.

to shape history. They were, in short, a decision on how to (re)construct the Democratic party.

Primary Rules, Political Power, and Social Change

Primary rules necessarily change the balance of power within a party. In any single campaign, that altered balance can elicit moderate tactical adjustments; it cannot remake political personalities. A presidential aspirant is, after all, a man with a past. In his political career, he will have accumulated friends and enemies, and have arrived at stands on most major questions of the day. If his following is mainly urban, not farm-belt, Democrats, he cannot practically desert Ohio for Nebraska (although he *can* shift barnstorming time). If he has built a name in civil liberties, he cannot court street-crime victims by urging unlimited detention of suspects (although he *can* switch positions on other, less publicized controversies). Even if he can discover ways to remodel himself to benefit from changed conditions, he may not make the effort. If attaining the presidency had required Senator McGovern to accept the war in Vietnam, Senator Humphrey to back away from universal medical insurance, or Governor Wallace to forsake the neighborhood school, the presidential contest would have had three fewer entrants.

But if primary regulations do change the balance of power within a political party, they do so regardless of the ability or desire of any particular contender to adapt. Any given man may move only slightly in response to an altered political environment, but the types of contestants, of issues, and of electoral strategies which characterize politics will shift more markedly. If candidates must attract newly powerful areas in order to campaign realistically for the nomination, candidates will appear who can attract those areas. If a certain set of issues is important there, champions will arise who have those issues as their major claim to fame. Over the course of several elections, the men who seek the nomination, the voters they must appease to get it, and the policies they use to do so will, together, constitute a recognizably different era in American politics.

A theoretical outline of what would happen *if* a new political environment were produced by primary rules is not, of course, a description of that new environment; it is not evidence that the new "era" will continue beyond the election in which it was first detected; it is not a set of logical deductions about what the new situation implies for (future) national politics. The previous section of this paper is an attempt to meet the first of these objectives, and it contains an implicit argument about the second: If "size" and "degree of internal competitiveness" are in fact the key links between primary rules and a state's influence within the Democratic party, then the new political environment should endure. This is not to say, on the one hand, that charismatic leaders or dramatic events (sufficient to overwhelm any rule-related effect) cannot appear, nor, on the other hand, that party officials might not reverse themselves and restore the pre-reform regulations. But by assuming the absence of both of these situations, it should be possible to meet the final objective—and to produce some deductions about the policy outcomes of a new and different balance of power within the national Democratic party.

The inadvertently retailored Democratic party toward which Districted primaries contribute features two groups of states on the rise and one in decline. The biggest losers are the northeastern industrial states (plus, in the future, California?), which have always been the mainstay of the Democratic party, and which remain essential for the election of a Democratic president. These are the states which epitomize the old coalition-of-minorities politics, and which are the heart of support for "social-welfare" programs (e.g., aid to education, plentiful jobs and guaranteed employment, Social Security, Medicare and universal health insurance). Their residents have been opposed to the more radical "social engineering" approach to policy making (busing, job quotas, etc.), but that opposition has not (in most cases) induced them to react against progressive legislation in the social-welfare mode.

Under Winner-Take-All rules in the primaries and then in the Electoral College, the ten largest of these states can nominate a Democrat and elect him. Obviously, primary rules which shift control over the nominee to areas favoring social engineering, or areas desiring a reaction against it (see below), risk cracking the Democratic coalition in the large states. Because the latter are usually highly competitive in November, substantial cracks in the coalition are likely to drive them into the Republican column, and that, in turn, should be enough to decide most presidential elections. The party power of the large, politically heterogeneous states is thus intimately tied to a style of politics, a wide-ranging set of policies, and a strategy for winning elections.

Recent alterations in primary law reduce that power, and increase the party role of two (mutually hostile) groups of smaller, more politically homogeneous states—each with its own preferred course for the Democratic party. First are the Midwestern and Western states, which can deliver well over three-quarters of their delegates to the same man without any need for a Winner-Take-All provision. Unlike the Northeastern states, where policy preferences, party politics, and general election strategy form an internally consistent package, these (Midwestern-Western) areas present a contradiction: While most are presidentially Republican across the state as a whole, and while as a group they provide the bedrock of which senatorial and congressional conservatism is founded, their *Democratic delegates* often support candidates who are markedly more liberal than the bulk of the party. These delegates were the essential base for a liberal-left challenge to Northeastern candidates and social-welfare policies even before the reform of the delegate selection process, and that tendency was exaggerated afterwards.

Increased power for the plains and mountain states, then, promises a double result: First, greater convention support for social engineering policies, and second, sharply curtailed electoral prospects for the nominee. More influence for Midwestern-Western areas means greater irritation for the other (Southern-Border) areas which primary rules have revitalized, making it even more likely that the Democrats will not carry the latter (see below). A larger role for the plains-mountain states is at the very least an additional problem for electoral politics in the big states, since the policy concerns of (delegates from) the former are unlike those of the industrial core of the party's voters. Finally, and ironically, greater party power for these areas will probably not make it more likely that any more of them will go Democratic in November. Even if it were possible to "trade" the Midwest and West for the Northeast, the deal would be a bad one in numerical terms, but in reality the question is unlikely to arise: The plains-mountain states are still solidly Republican presidentially, and greater delegate power at the Democratic Convention will do little to overcome that.

The Southern and Border states make up the second group for which Districted (and even Proportional) regulations are a major boon. Like their Midwestern-Western counterparts, all of the states below the Mason-Dixon line can deliver more than three-quarters of their delegates to one man, in the absence of any aid from Winner-Take-All provisions. Compared with the plains-mountain states, however, these areas have historically been more conservative before the nomination and more Democratic at election time. They remain more conservative in convention, but the situation at the presidential level has changed over the past decade: Southern-Border electorates have increasingly been attracted by generalized attacks on social change and, when Democratic nominees have failed to endorse such attacks, have subsequently crossed over to the Republicans. A combination of historical ties plus social-welfare programs (a presumed "need" in the lowest-income section of the country) has kept them from doing the same thing at the senatorial and congressional levels, although their legislators have been restless on social-welfare matters and have defected to the Republicans on many others. Whether the same combination can be used to allay the general Southern suspicion that the national Democratic party has been captured by social engineers, and thus to bring the presidential vote back into line with the vote at lower levels, is an open question. Whether future Democratic national conventions will make the effort is equally open.

New patterns of convention decision making do seem very likely to follow the new party power configuration, and such decisions will, in turn, be critical in determining what the party stands for, and how much of that can be implemented. These new patterns may, again, be accelerated or delayed by the American economic or international situation. They may even be interrupted entirely by the appearance of charismatic figures or unforeseen events. Barring such developments, however, the power distribution created by primary rules does provide a basis for speculation on the direction in which future conventions will take the party, and on its subsequent fate. At the very least, the combination of more potent Midwestern-Western (left) and Southern-Border (right) wings should decrease the probability of Democratic presidential election victories, although the amount of the decline is, as yet, unclear. More imaginative political analysts can certainly find more extreme scenarios: The new political environment, for example, could permanently detach a huge minority of all Democrats from their (former) party and convert them into registered Republicans.

Of the three basic primary plans, Districting promises the most sharply divided conventions and the most severe problems in postconvention electioneering. Under this plan, the more radical candidates on both ends of the party's ideological spectrum will have a maximum number of delegates. Aspirants at the center will, conversely, be at their weakest, leaving the convention with a dilemma. It can appease the delegates on the left, settling on a contender who favors social engineering policies, and who will drive off more conservative Democrats in November. Or, it can placate the delegates on the right, settling on a candidate whose electability is purchased through a closer resemblance to the Republican standard-bearer, a much closer resemblance than pre-reform Democratic nominees needed or wanted.

Under Districting, the bargaining capacity of the big industrial states is reduced severely, to the point where their old-line party "regulars" may well be unable to insist on the usual moderate-liberal candidate with a social-welfare program. Instead, they will have to join either a left-leaning or a right-leaning coalition. Because the regulars are (so far, at least) unwilling to move toward the Republicans on basic economic issues or on civil rights and liberties, conventions will in all likelihood compromise to the left. But since Districting also increases the influence of the party's more conservative members, providing them with recognized leaders in the process, a left-leaning compromise at the convention is very likely to shove them into the Republican column in November. If the same rules which strengthen the Midwestern-Western bloc and its sympathizers did not also magnify the power of the Southern-Border alliance and its affiliates, conservative Democrats might be swept along at the general election. But because the rules do empower both extremes, they inevitably foster short-run defection.

Prognosticators who are willing to drive this argument to a further conclusion might well argue that the problem of desertion by a sharply defined (and large) body of registered Democrats will not be a long-lasting one. No major group is likely to work hard year in and year out to influence the nomination of one party, and then just as regularly be forced to flee to the opposition on election day. If subsequent Democratic conventions persist in deferring to their Midwestern-Western wing, with the nomination and/or with major policy concessions, the problem of debilitating dissension within the party could ease: The South, the Border states, and a significant share of the Northern working class could simply leave permanently. Defections by Democrats would decline sharply, as the most likely deserters became Republicans. Harmony and consistency would be restored—within the new *minority* party. A minimum of political difficulty would then surround the selection of a left-liberal contender who could present a far-reaching program of social engineering, and public policy debate would center on these new issues. The costs of restructuring the American policy agenda in this way might well, however, include: First, the loss of social-welfare program expansion, and second, a continual rejection by a majority of the American people of both the policies and the candidate of the (new, minority) Democrats.

If Districted rules remained in effect, but if a greater share of party leaders began to agree that left-leaning coalitions were electorally risky, conventions might compromise toward their Southern-Border wing instead. This might, in turn, permit retention of both reformed regulations and hopes for victory. A right-leaning compromise would generate some desertions by left-wing Democrats, but these would be limited by the fact that there is nowhere (at least at present) for dissident leftists to go. Such desertions as did occur would, in any case, be politically less costly than conservative defections, since they would not be gains for the Republican candidate. The (newly conservatized) Democratic party could retain a mild social-welfare orientation, while retrenching on civil rights and civil liberties, but it could probably put this program forward only after remarkably acrimonious conventions.

Even if one were programmatically undismayed by these developments, however, Southern-oriented compromises at the convention might still have some serious tactical drawbacks. If the Democratic party leans toward its right, its nominee and his policies would be less clearly distinguishable from those of the Republicans. In one sense, this makes it unnecessary for conservative Democrats to jump the fence. But in a second sense, it makes defection less costly. If a convention is characterized by virulent protests on the part of Midwestern-Western delegates and their sympathizers, and if it does not both squelch these firmly *and* produce the vigorous advances in bread-and-butter economic matters which would attract lower-income conservatives, many Democrats might decide to desert anyhow.

Proportional regulations could rearrange the same dilemmas, reducing the chance that the party will be captured by a minority on its left, but maintaining the risk of substantial defections to the right. By restoring the bargaining power of the big industrial states, Proportionality would make traditional Democratic presidential politics (the "moderate-liberal with a social-welfare program" approach) at least more practical. By cancelling the advantages which Districting (and only Districting) offers to left-liberals, Proportionality ought to give them the sole option of joining a moderate-liberal coalition at the convention or of forcing the moderates to turn to the conservatives for support. By removing left-liberalism as a realistic "threat," Proportionality should, finally, lessen conservative Democrats' incentive to desert.

But the same tactical problems which a right-leaning coalition presented under Districted rules would probably be only very partially solved by Proportionality. Attempts to contain potential right-wing defections by broadening the nominating coalition to include (many) Southern-Border delegates should, indeed, be more common under Proportional rules than under Districting. Resulting coalitions would have familiar policy consequences—a diminished social-welfare program, plus retrenchment on civil rights and liberties. They would generate a familiar political irony—a mild shift toward conservatism, propelled by reforms which ostensibly were designed to make the party more change-oriented. And, ultimately, they would face a familiar tactical problem—some defections on the left, coupled with the (more serious) possibility that a narrowed gap between Democrats and Republicans would facilitate crossovers, rather than eliminate them. This latter problem might be exacerbated by Proportional rules' generosity to the type of splinter movements which cannot hope to secure a nomination, but which can generate extremist delegates and which may guarantee a high enough level of dissension at the convention to reliably infuriate conservatives. A plan which maximizes the number of Southern-oriented delegates can hardly make their displeasure less evident to those who follow the convention. By the same token, it can hardly make the Democratic right-wing less able to organize a party bolt at election time.

Each primary plan, then—like all of the laws that regulate politics—is itself "political" because it distributes power in one way rather than in others. Each different power distribution, in turn, leads directly to a different set of strategies for winning elections and a different policy agenda. Thus each basic plan can be judged not only for its theoretical structure or through the particular men it favors in any one year, but by the social interests it rewards and by the kind of politics and policies this should create. In these latter terms, the contribution of primary rules reform is toward the emergence of a more conservative era in American politics.

In the longest run, an era of consolidation and order, rather than experimentation, may be in the wind *regardless* of any party's regulations. It may be that the American people are tired of governmental intervention in the market system of delivering health care and other services, tired of a standard of living for the poorest elements of society which is artificially augmented, and tired of aggressive assertions of civil liberties. There must be many, however, who think that it would be more than a shame if history recorded that after 1968 the American people grew tired of all these things—when what really happened was that the Democratic party changed its delegate selection rules.

·C·

Caucuses, Primaries, Rules, and Turnout

Participation in American Presidential Nominations
BY AUSTIN RANNEY

Participation in the 1976 Presidential Nominations

PARTICIPATION IN PRECINCT CAUCUSES

The main thrust of the 1969 McGovern-Fraser rules and their 1973 revision by the Mikulski commission was to open up participation in party affairs to all Democrats who wanted to participate and to strip the party regulars of any special advantage they might previously have enjoyed. In 1976 by far the most common form of participation was voting in primaries, which were held in thirty of the fifty-one states (including the District of Columbia). Accordingly, most of this paper focuses on voting in the primaries. But we should not overlook the fact that twenty-one states, with a combined voting-age population of 33,389,000 (22.2 percent of the national voting-age population) chose their national convention delegates by processes that began with caucuses of (self-designated) party members in the precincts and ended with state conventions selecting delegates to the national convention.

To keep a check on how many people participated in this manner, *Congressional Quarterly* collected reports from Democratic state party organizations (no data for the Republicans were gathered) estimating the numbers of people who participated in the first-round precinct caucuses. These reports are, at best, only approximations, for they depend upon the

Excerpted from Austin Ranney, *Participation in American Presidential Nominations, 1976* (Washington: American Enterprise Institute, 1977), pp. 15–37. Most footnotes deleted.

Table 1 · Estimated Participation in Democratic First-Level Precinct Caucuses for National Delegate Selection, Nonprimary States, 1976

STATE	ESTIMATED VOTING-AGE POPULATION	ATTENDANCE AT PRECINCT CAUCUSES	
		Estimated number of persons	*Percent of voting-age population*
Alaska	231,000	1,000	0.4
Arizona	1,555,000	26,700	1.7
Colorado	1,773,000	30,000	1.7
Connecticut	2,211,000	106,600	4.8
Hawaii	600,000	3,000	0.5
Iowa	2,010,000	45,000	2.2
Kansas	1,610,000	N.A.	—
Louisiana	2,532,000	120,000	4.7
Maine	741,000	6,500	0.9
Minnesota	2,721,000	58,000	2.1
Mississippi	1,544,000	60,000	3.9
Missouri	3,348,000	20,000	0.6
New Mexico	771,000	10,000	1.3
North Dakota	432,000	3,000	0.7
Oklahoma	1,937,000	65,000	3.3
South Carolina	1,933,000	63,000	3.2
Utah	783,000	16,300	2.1
Vermont	327,000	2,500	0.8
Virginia	3,528,000	20,000	0.6
Washington	2,536,000	60,000	2.4
Wyoming	266,000	600	0.2

Source: Voting-age population for the states is taken from Bureau of the Census, *Population Estimates and Projections*, Series P-25, no. 626, issued May 1976. Attendance at the Democratic precinct caucuses is taken from estimates given to *Congressional Quarterly* by Democratic state chairmen and reported in various issues of *Congressional Quarterly Weekly Report* from January 24, 1976, to May 15, 1976.

diligence and accuracy of local as well as state party officials, and there is reason to believe that some inflated the numbers to make their organizations look good. Nevertheless, their reports are the best data we have or are likely to get. And, as summarized in Table 1, they show how much less participation there was in the participatory caucuses than in the primaries.

The mean proportion of the voting-age population attending the caucuses in the twenty-one states was 1.9 percent, while the mean proportion of the voting-age population voting in Democratic primaries in the closed-primary states (the best direct comparison we can make with the caucus states) was 18.6 percent—nearly ten times higher. Or again, the highest caucus turnout, according to *Congressional Quarterly*, came in Connecticut, where the 106,000 persons reported as attending constituted about 19 percent of the state's registered Democrats. By contrast, in California, the state with the highest turnout of registered voters in the primary elections, . . . 71.7 percent of the registered Democrats voted in their primary.

In short, no matter how much more open and participatory the local caucuses of 1976 may have been than those in any previous year, they attracted far less actual participation than the direct primaries.

MEASURES OF VOTING TURNOUT IN PRIMARIES

Political scientists have long been concerned with measuring levels of popular participation in political affairs, and a number of typologies of participation have been developed. For most people the sole form of political participation is voting in official elections, including primary elections. Hence political scientists have made more studies of voting and nonvoting elections than of any other form of participation.

In the course of these studies three main measures of the degree of participation, or voting turnout, have been developed:

(1) Based on voting-age population (VAP). Most studies of voting turnout use a simple measure:

$$\text{voting turnout} = \frac{\text{number of votes cast}}{\text{voting-age population}}$$

This measure has a number of advantages, which do much to account for its widespread use. First, the data are easily obtained. Official election returns for both primary and general elections for President, governor, U.S. senator, and U.S. representative, have been collected, verified, and published in a series of authoritative volumes edited by Richard Scammon. The denominator for the formula has been provided since 1960 by estimates of the number of persons in each state who achieved the minimum voting age or more by the first day of November, issued periodically by the Bureau of the Census.

Not only does this measure permit the use of the most easily obtained information, but also it allows analysts to include in the calculations the two states, Ohio and Wisconsin, which do not require or maintain any statewide summary of the number of registered voters.

However, the measure also has several disadvantages. In particular, the VAP base exaggerates the potential electorate and therefore makes turnout figures lower than they should be. The Bureau of the Census includes all persons of voting age, including a number who are legally ineligible to vote—aliens, inmates of penal institutions, ex-convicts, and others. The measure also makes no allowance for the considerable variations in difficulty in the registration laws of the various states and their impact on differences in voting turnout. Accordingly, some scholars prefer a second measure.

(2) Based on registered voters (RV). This measure, too, has a simple formula:

$$\text{voting turnout} = \frac{\text{number of votes cast in a given election}}{\text{number of registered voters eligible for that election}}$$

The RV measure has several advantages. The denominator is the true *legal* potential electorate; hence it provides a more accurate picture than the VAP measure of how many of the people who could have voted actually did. By largely eliminating the problems caused by variations in registration laws, it provides a much truer comparison with turnout rates in European nations. In addition, studies of turnout in primary elections, such as this one, are enabled (at least in all states with party registration) to focus on each party's primary and see if there are significant differences between the parties.

. . . .

In what follows, accordingly, I shall use the RV base as the denominator for the measure of turnout, except in a few instances in which the VAP base will be noted as more useful.

TURNOUT RATES IN THE 1976 PRESIDENTIAL PRIMARIES

Thirty states held presidential primaries in 1976. Our purposes, however, require that four of them be omitted from the analysis. In New York no statewide data were assembled or are now available for the number of persons who cast votes for national convention delegates in the state's complicated primary. In the District of Columbia, only the Democrats held a presidential primary, so the turnout was misleadingly low compared with that in the other states, all of which held primaries for both parties. Neither Ohio nor Wisconsin kept statewide figures on the number of registered voters. These four states will be ignored in this discussion.

The remaining twenty-six states . . . had a mean turnout rate of 42.9 percent on the RV basis and 27.6 percent on the VAP basis. We should also note, however, that there was a considerable variation among the turnout rates of the various states. On the RV basis, the range was from California's high of 74.1 percent to Rhode Island's low of 14.5 percent, with a mean of 42.9 and a standard deviation of 13.94. These interstate variations constitute the principal phenomena we are trying to explain.

It is interesting to note that in 1972 twelve of these states also held formally contested presidential primaries (that is, more than one candidate was on the ballot for each party in each of the twelve states in both 1972 and 1976). The mean RV turnout for these states in 1972 was 46.7 percent. This was nearly four percentage points *higher* than in the same states in 1976 despite the fact that the 1972 Republican contests were token fights only while both parties' primaries were hotly contested in 1976.

One other comparison with earlier years may be of interest. In an article published in 1972, I reported on turnout in all competitive presidential primaries from 1948 through 1968, using the VAP measure and defining a competitive primary as one in which (a) two or more candidates or candidate-pledged slates appeared on each party's ballot, (b) at least one major national contender appeared on each party's ballot, and (c) in neither party did the winning candidate or slate get more than 80 percent of the votes. Only eleven primaries satisfied these criteria in the 1948–68 period (all of them falling in either 1952 or 1968), and their mean voting turnout was 39 percent.

Using the same criteria, no 1972 primaries qualified as competitive; but in 1976 no less than twenty-two of the twenty-eight states (including Ohio and Wisconsin for this analysis) met the standards. For those states the mean turnout, using the comparable VAP base, was 28 percent—a drop of eleven percentage points from the figure for the 1948–68 period.

Accordingly, while in 1976 the nation had far more presidential primaries—and far more closely contested ones—than ever before, there was a sharp drop-off in turnout. That drop, moreover, was larger than the much-discussed drop-off in turnout in presidential general elections. The highest VAP turnout in general elections in the 1948–68 period was 62.8 percent in 1960, which fell to 53.4 percent in the 1976 general election. This drop of 9.4 percentage points, considerable though it is, is still lower than the eleven-point drop in turnout in competitive presidential primaries in the same period.

THE TWO PARTIES COMPARED

As noted earlier, fifteen of the thirty state primary laws restricted voting to preregistered party members. For reasons already stated, we must exclude two of these, the District of Columbia and New York, from our analysis. The turnout of RVs for both parties in each of the remaining thirteen states is shown in Table 2. Table 2 shows that the mean turnouts for both parties were almost identical—50.3 percent for the Democrats, and 50.6 percent for the Republicans.

As is usually the case, however, these mean turnouts conceal substantial variations in turnout within each of the parties and substantial disparities between the parties. For instance, the Democrats' greatest turnout margin over the Republicans was in Massachusetts (57.3 percent to 42.0 percent), where Reagan did not campaign and where the Democrats had a close fight, with Jackson edging Udall, Wallace, and Carter. The other big Democratic margin was in Pennsylvania (49.4 percent to 35.9 percent) where Ford was the only candidate on the Republican ballot and where

Table 2 · Turnout of Registered Voters, by Party, in Closed-Primary States, 1976

STATE	DEMOCRATS			REPUBLICANS		
	Number regis-tered	*Votes cast in primary*	*Percent of RVs voting*	*Number regis-tered*	*Votes cast in primary*	*Percent of RVs voting*
California	4,701,736	3,373,732	71.7	3,000,152	2,336,121	77.9
Florida	2,380,954	1,300,330	54.6	1,000,796	609,819	60.9
Kentucky	1,077,360	306,006	28.4	468,555	133,528	28.5
Maryland	1,240,042	591,746	47.7	439,084	165,971	37.8
Massachusetts	1,305,863	747,634	57.3	460,949	193,411	42.0
Nebraska	358,702	181,910	50.7	377,865	213,480	56.5
Nevada	125,705	75,242	59.9	72,368	47,749	66.0
New Hampshire	142,665	75,638	53.0	177,215	111,674	63.0
North Carolina	1,708,048	604,832	35.4	557,000	193,727	34.8
Oregon	714,917	432,632	60.5	462,992	297,535	64.3
Pennsylvania	2,801,649	1,385,042	49.4	2,221,629	796,660	35.9
South Dakota	177,459	58,671	33.1	189,397	84,077	44.4
West Virginia	705,062	372,577	52.8	337,440	155,692	46.1
Mean turnout			50.3			50.6

Source: The data on registration and votes in the 1976 primaries were compiled by the Congressional Research Service of the Library of Congress and were furnished to the author by the courtesy of Carol F. Casey. The data on estimated voting-age population are from Bureau of the Census, *Current Population Reports*, Series P-25, no. 626, issued May 1976.

the Democratic race was billed by the news media as Jackson's last stand against Carter (indeed, Jackson did drop out after losing this race to Carter). The Republicans' biggest turnout edges over the Democrats came in South Dakota (44.9 percent to 33.1 percent) and New Hampshire (63.0 percent to 53.0 percent); both states had close Ford-Reagan contests, but the Democrats had hot contests as well. Thus, it seems that closeness of competition is not the sole cause of high primary turnouts. We shall return to this point later.

PRIMARY-GENERAL ELECTION DIFFERENTIALS IN 1976

One of the most persistent features of American elections is the fact that turnout in primary elections is almost invariably much lower than that in the ensuing general elections for the same offices. For example, my data show that the mean VAP turnout in primary elections for governor in the period 1962–72 was 29.8 percent compared to a mean turnout of 52.5 in the ensuing general elections; for U.S. senators the mean turnout in primary elections was 24.5 percent compared with a mean turnout in the general elections of 51.0 percent.

The 1972 study mentioned earlier showed that the seventy-two presidential primaries between 1948 and 1968 produced a mean VAP turnout

Table 3 · VAP Turnouts in Primary and General Elections in Competitive
Primary States, 1976

STATE	EST. VAP, NOVEMBER 1976	PRIMARY ELECTION		GENERAL ELECTION		DIFFERENCE BETWEEN PRIMARY AND GENERAL ELECTION TURNOUTS
		Total votes cast	Turn-out, in per-cent	Total votes cast	Turn-out, in per-cent	
Alabama	2,501,000	665,855	26.6	1,139,897	45.6	−19.0
Arkansas	1,503,000	534,341	35.5	762,622	50.7	−15.2
California	15,294,000	5,709,853	37.3	7,456,917	49.3	−12.0
Florida	6,326,000	1,910,149	30.2	2,936,679	46.4	−16.2
Idaho	567,000	164,960	29.1	330,550	58.3	−29.2
Illinois	7,718,000	2,087,807	27.0	4,562,865	59.1	−32.1
Indiana	3,640,000	1,245,715	34.2	2,175,780	59.8	−25.6
Kentucky	2,374,000	439,534	18.5	1,140,377	48.0	−29.5
Maryland	2,863,000	757,717	26.5	1,384,598	48.4	−21.9
Massachusetts	4,173,000	941,950	22.6	2,453,359	58.8	−36.2
Michigan	6,268,000	1,771,480	28.3	3,579,255	57.1	−28.8
Montana	518,000	196,620	37.9	316,852	61.2	−23.3
Nebraska	1,080,000	395,390	36.6	579,888	53.7	−17.1
Nevada	424,000	122,991	29.0	193,014	45.5	−16.5
New Hampshire	574,000	187,312	32.6	333,090	58.0	−25.4
North Carolina	3,847,000	798,559	20.7	1,662,078	43.2	−22.5
Ohio	7,459,000	2,083,207	27.9	3,992,495	53.5	−25.6
Oregon	1,653,000	730,167	44.2	969,948	58.7	−14.5
Rhode Island	648,000	74,700	11.5	389,129	60.0	−48.5
South Dakota	469,000	142,748	30.4	297,772	63.5	−33.1
Tennessee	2,958,000	574,359	19.4	1,455,478	49.2	−29.8
Texas	8,503,000	1,979,001	23.3	3,917,065	46.1	−22.8
Vermont	327,000	72,270	22.1	176,862	54.1	−32.0
Wisconsin	3,211,000	1,333,373	41.5	2,040,095	63.5	−22.0
Mean turnout			28.9		53.3	−24.4

Source: Data on voting-age population and votes cast in the primaries are from the source cited in Table 2.
Votes cast in the 1976 general election are taken from the final summary in *Congressional Quarterly Weekly Report*, November 6, 1976, p. 3118.

of 27 percent compared with a mean VAP turnout of 62 percent in the
ensuing general elections—an increase of thirty-five percentage points from
the primary to the general election. For the eleven competitive primaries,
the mean VAP turnout was 39 percent and the mean VAP turnout in the
ensuing general elections was 69 percent—an increase of thirty points from
primary to general elections.

In 1976, as we have seen, twenty-two of twenty-six states . . . satisfied
the criteria for having competitive presidential primaries. Their VAP turnouts in the primaries and general election are shown in Table 3. The
figures in Table 3 show that the mean VAP turnout in the 1976 competitive primaries was 28.9 percent, while the mean VAP turnout in those

states in the general election was 53.3 percent. Thus both the primary and general-election turnout figures were substantially lower in 1976 than in the 1948–68 period, while the increase from the primary to the general election also fell to 24.4 percentage points. Even so, the established turnout rule continues to hold: turnout in primary elections is generally about half as large as turnout in the ensuing general elections for the same offices.

The figures in Table 3 also show some striking variations in primary-general turnout increase from one state to another. The increase varies from a low of 12 points for California to a high of 48.5 points for Rhode Island. Indeed, knowing a state's turnout in its competitive presidential primary is not a very good basis for predicting its turnout in the ensuing general election: the correlation (r_s) between the states' rankings on primary turnouts and their rankings on general-election turnouts was only .39.

So, while turnout in presidential general elections may be a respectable stream (if not a mighty river), turnout in presidential primaries is a small brook, and in local participatory caucuses it is, as Table 1 shows, a tiny trickle. These disparities among the sizes of the various nominating and electing electorates raise grave questions about the representativeness of the nominators and the likelihood that they will choose the kinds of candidates that are most appealing to the voters. But those are questions that must be answered in other studies.

Correlates of Turnout in Presidential Primaries, 1976

REGISTRATION LAWS

Three recent studies have shown that variations in the states' registration laws explain a good deal of the variance in their voting turnout in presidential *general* elections. It therefore seems appropriate to begin by asking whether registration laws do not also explain much of the variance in VAP turnout in presidential primary elections.

To approach that question, I scored each of the twenty-eight primary states we have been considering according to how many of the five provisions its registration laws have that Rosenstone and Wolfinger regard as the greatest inhibitions against voting in presidential general elections.[1] I

[1]Information about the registration laws as of 1972 was taken from Rosenstone and Wolfinger, "Effect of Registration Laws," Table 4, pp. 14–15. The main restrictive measures are: registration closed 21 days or more before the election; voting rolls purged every three years or less; registration offices not open in the evening or on Saturdays; registration only at the city level, not at the precinct level; and no absentee registration allowing for registration of the sick, disabled, and absent.

found that the four states with only one restrictive law had a mean turnout in their presidential primaries of 29.8 percent, and the nine states with two restrictive laws had a mean turnout of 25.5 percent—so far, according to expectations. But the seven states with three restrictive laws had a mean turnout of 33.5 percent, the highest of all; the seven states with four restrictive laws had a mean turnout of 29.8 percent, the same as the states with only one such law; and Kentucky, the only state with all five restrictive laws, had a turnout of 18.5 percent.

It seems, then, that registration laws do not explain as much about turnout in primary elections as they do about turnout in general elections. This finding should not surprise us unduly, in the light of the fact, noted above, that the correlation (r_s) between the states' VAP turnouts in the 1976 presidential primaries and in the general election was only .39.

Holding the registration factor constant by using the RV base, the figures . . . show that in the twenty-six states on which we have voting *and* registration data, by the time of the 1976 primaries a grand total of 57,709,858 persons had overcome whatever barriers their states' registration laws posed and were eligible to vote in the primaries. Yet only 25,508,673 of these persons actually voted. The mean turnout for the twenty-six states was 42.9 percent of RVs and 28.2 percent of VAP. But the individual state figures . . . show that there were wide variations among the states, and we need to look at a number of correlates to seek explanations for these variations.

PRIMARY LAWS

In the course of the general drive in recent years for more participation in presidential nominations, a number of states have amended their presidential primary laws or written new ones incorporating various features that are expected to increase the ease and meaningfulness of voting and therefore the size of turnout. We will examine four of these provisions.

(1) Binding presidential-preference polls. Many law-makers have felt that voters are more likely to vote in primaries if the ballot gives them an opportunity to express their preference for a national presidential candidate directly—rather than indirectly, by voting for a candidate for convention delegate who has expressed a preference for that national candidate. Presidential preference polls have been established for this purpose, and only two of our twenty-six states (Alabama and Texas) have no such poll. Their mean RV turnout was 37.0 percent, compared with a mean turnout of 43.4 percent for the twenty-four states that held preference polls.

But there are preference polls and preference polls. For example, in seven of the states with preference polls (Illinois, Nebraska, New Hampshire, New Jersey, Pennsylvania, Vermont, and West Virginia) the poll is not binding upon the delegates, but is only advisory—a "beauty contest," some journalists call it. In these states the mean turnout was 41.0 percent.

In three states (Georgia, Maryland, and Montana) the preference poll's results are binding on the delegates of one party but not the other; their mean turnout was 42.0 percent.

The remaining fourteen states adopted what is presumably the participatory deal: the results of the preference polls are binding on all the delegates of both parties. These states had a mean turnout of 44.9 percent. In short, though the differences in mean turnouts among these groups of states were small, they did proceed in a linear fashion: the more closely the presidential preference poll approached the ideal of binding the delegates, the higher—by a small margin—was the turnout.

(2) Proportionality. The Democratic party's post-1972 Commission on Delegate Selection and Party Structure, or Mikulski commission, adopted several rules intended to improve the states' presidential primary laws. One of the most radical changes from the past was decreed by Rule 11, which required that each state's delegates be allocated in proportion to the popular votes cast for presidential aspirants:

> At all stages of the delegate selection process, delegations shall be allocated in a fashion that fairly reflects the expressed preference of the primary voters . . . except that preferences securing less than 15 percent of the votes cast for the delegation need not be awarded any delegates.

However, in a later ruling the Democratic National Committee allowed an exception to this requirement: the committee held that if a state so desires, it can adopt a winner-take-all system for delegates selected at the congressional district level—a system that soon came to be labeled the loophole primary, since it was presumably a way of escaping from the full rigors of strict proportionality.

Perhaps the main argument in favor of proportionality was that of justice—justice to the candidates in that they would get the full benefit of their popular support, and justice to the voters in that the vote of each would count in selecting some delegates and few voters' votes would be wasted (by being cast for candidates who received no delegates). But a strong secondary argument was that voters would be more inclined to vote in a primary where their votes would not be wasted than in a winner-take-all statewide primary or even in a loophole primary with a winner-take-all system at the congressional-district level.

This latter argument receives little support from the actual turnout figures. Of our twenty-six states, twelve required proportionality for both parties, and they had a mean turnout of 42.6 percent. Ten had loophole primaries for both parties, and their mean turnout was 40.9 percent. Four states required proportionality for the Democrats but not for the Republicans; their mean turnout was 47.9 percent, but that figure was heavily influenced by the inclusion of California, which, with 74.1 percent, had the highest RV turnout of all the states. If we omit California, the mean turnout of the three other states in this group was 39.2 percent. It seems, then, that there was only a small relationship between the extent of proportionality and primary turnout.

(3) Blanket ballot versus volunteer ballot.   A paper by William D. Morris and Otto A. Davis reported that in pre-1976 presidential primaries turnout was increased by the use of the Oregon-style "blanket ballot." This is a system in which state officials determine who are each party's serious presidential contenders and put them on the preference poll ballot without any action by the contenders. Indeed, persons placed on the ballot in this manner can have their names removed only by filing affidavits that they are not candidates for the presidency (an action that, among other things, makes them ineligible for federal campaign funds).

As we have already seen, two of our twenty-six states did not have a presidential preference poll of any kind. Of the remaining twenty-four, fourteen used the blanket ballot, and they had a mean RV turnout of 44.5 percent. The other ten used the "volunteer ballot" system, in which contenders have their names placed on the preference poll only if they or their supporters petition to do so. If they take no initiative, the contender's name will not be on the ballot. These ten states had a mean turnout of 41.8 percent. The turnout differences are small, but they do correspond with the Morris-Davis finding, so the blanket ballot may indeed have some small relationship with increased turnout.

(4) Closed versus crossover primaries.   The Mikulski commission's Rule 2-A required that "State Parties must take all feasible steps to restrict participation in the delegate selection process to Democratic voters only." The object, of course, was to prevent Republicans from participating in the selection of Democratic presidential nominees. But, as we noted earlier, the various state primary laws have provided two very different ways of accomplishing this objective. One is the closed primary, in which the voter must register his party preference well in advance of primary day to be eligible to vote in the primary of the party he prefers. The other is the crossover primary, in which the voter can choose on primary day to vote in whatever party's primary he wishes.

It is often argued that the crossover primary encourages greater participation, since the voter is freer to vote in the party contest that interests him most at the time of voting and does not restrict him to a party choice made weeks or months earlier. This seems plausible enough, but the data show just the opposite—and by one of the widest margins encountered in this entire study. The closed-primary states had a mean turnout of 50.9 percent, while the crossover states had a mean turnout of only 34.9 percent.

This difference is so large and so contrary to the expectations of advocates of crossover primaries that it seems reasonable to ask whether it is a truly independent relationship or merely a reflection of other factors. I sought to answer this question by controlling for the only other two factors that produce comparably large differences in turnout—educational level of the states' populations and levels of primary-campaign spending. The results are summarized in Table 4.

The figures in Table 4 show clearly that controlling for education or campaign spending does not weaken the differences in turnout between closed and crossover primaries at all. Within each of the four groups of states—higher education, lower education, higher campaign spending, lower campaign spending—the closed-primary states had substantially higher mean levels of turnout than the crossover states. *Why* this should be so is an intriguing question far too complicated to be considered here; but the fact that it *is* so might well give those who write the states' primary laws something to think about.

To summarize: the data presented above make it clear that variations in the primary rules did affect turnout somewhat. The states with presidential preference polls had a somewhat higher mean turnout than those with none; those with binding preference polls had a slightly higher mean turnout than those with nonbinding polls; those with some proportionality had a slightly higher mean turnout than those with loophole primaries; and those with blanket ballots had slightly higher mean turnout than those with volunteer ballots. All these differences were modest, and in the direction of the participatory reformers' expectations. But by far the greatest difference was in the *opposite* direction: the states with closed primaries had a substantially higher mean turnout than the states with crossover primaries. So the rules made some difference but hardly *the* difference. We turn now to other correlates.

DATES OF THE PRIMARIES

A number of commentators have remarked on the special importance of the early primaries. The candidates who do well in these races are soon established by the news media as the front runners.[2] This happy status enables them to attract still more attention from the media, elevate their standing in the public opinion polls, raise more money, and generally enjoy the advantage of "momentum," which is so important in the early going. This is why New Hampshire, despite the mere handful of convention delegates it elects (less than 1 percent of all delegates) and despite the

[2]Doing well usually means winning more votes than expected by the news media, not necessarily winning more votes than the other candidates.

Table 4 · Primary Voting Turnout Related to Openness of Primary, by
Educational Level and by Campaign Spending

EDUCATIONAL LEVEL

STATES WITH ABOVE MEDIAN PROPORTIONS OF POPULATION WITH MORE THAN 8 YEARS' EDUCATION				STATES WITH BELOW MEDIAN PROPORTIONS OF POPULATION WITH MORE THAN 8 YEARS' EDUCATION			
Closed primaries		Crossover primaries		Closed primaries		Crossover primaries	
CA	74.1	ID	36.0	KY	28.4	AL	37.1
FL	56.5	IN	42.8	NC	35.2	AR	55.6
MA	53.3	MI	38.7	PA	43.5	GA	33.0
MD	45.1	MT	47.8	SD	38.9	IL	36.3
NE	53.7	VT	27.1	WV	50.7	NJ	17.2
NH	58.6					RI	14.5
NV	62.1					TN	30.2
OR	62.0					TX	36.9
Mean:	58.2%	Mean:	38.5%	Mean:	39.3%	Mean:	32.6%

CAMPAIGN SPENDING

STATES WITH ABOVE MEDIAN PRIMARY-CAMPAIGN SPENDING				STATES WITH BELOW MEDIAN PRIMARY-CAMPAIGN SPENDING			
Closed primaries		Crossover primaries		Closed primaries		Crossover primaries	
CA	74.1	IL	36.3	KY	28.4	AL	37.1
FL	56.5	IN	42.8	PA	43.5	AR	55.6
MA	53.3	TN	30.2	SD	38.9	GA	33.0
MD	45.1	TX	36.9	WV	50.7	ID	36.0
NE	53.7					MI	38.7
NH	58.6					MT	47.8
NV	62.1					NJ	17.2
NC	35.2					RI	14.5
OR	62.0					VT	27.1
Mean:	55.6%	Mean:	36.5%	Mean:	40.4%	Mean:	34.1%

Source: Author's calculations. Data on educational level obtained from Bureau of the Census, *Statistical Abstract of the United States, 1974.* Data on campaign spending are set forth in a memorandum, dated October 19, 1976, to the Federal Election Commission from staffer Robert Pease. I was furnished a copy through the courtesy of Dr. Herbert Alexander, director of the Citizens Research Foundation. For source of turnout data, see Table 2.

unrepresentativeness of its population, is important: for a generation it has been the first state to hold a primary in each presidential year.

Accordingly, it seems reasonable to hypothesize that the greater importance of the early primaries will be reflected in higher turnouts. The 1976 data, however, do not confirm this view: the correlation (r_s) between the earliness of primary dates and turnouts is only .16. . . . The highest turnout in 1976 came in the California primary, which was held on June 8, the *last* date on which primaries were held. The second and third highest turnouts came in Nevada and Oregon, both of which were held on May 25, the third date from the last.

It could be argued, of course, that the Democratic contest was effectively over after Carter's elimination of Jackson in the Pennsylvania primary of April 27, and this explains why turnouts in the later Democratic primaries declined. Perhaps so—but the Republican experience does not support this explanation. The contest between Ford and Reagan stayed hot right up to the very end, indeed, to the convention itself. Yet when we look at the Republican turnout in the thirteen closed-primary states, the correlation between earliness of the primary date and turnout is −.13. Accordingly, whatever the importance of the earlier primaries for momentum, it is not reflected in significantly higher turnouts.

CAMPAIGN SPENDING

The prime objective of a political campaign is to stimulate a candidate's potential voters sufficiently that they will go to the polls on election day and vote for him. In recent years many campaigns, and certainly those for the primary and general elections for the presidency, have come to be managed by highly paid professionals—campaign consultants, public relations experts, advertising and media specialists, pollsters, fund-raisers, and the like. The new professionalism presumably makes for more effective campaigns, and one might reasonably hypothesize a strong relationship between variations in the money spent in the 1976 presidential primary campaigns and variations in the size of the voting turnouts.

At the time of writing the best data available on campaign spending in the primaries were figures from the Federal Election Commission on the total amount spent in each state by the three leading candidates, Jimmy Carter, Gerald Ford, and Ronald Reagan. Since the candidates were permitted by law to spend larger amounts in larger states, the absolute spending figures are misleading, and we need a standardized measure of campaign spending for purposes of comparing one state with another. Accordingly, in each state I have taken the candidates' reported total actual expenditures as a percentage of their legal limit. Consider Florida, for example:

Candidate	Legal Limit	Actual Expenditures	Percent of Legal Limit
Carter	1,050,851	498,458	47.4
Ford	1,050,851	844,215	80.3
Reagan	1,050,851	790,979	75.3
Total	3,152,553	2,133,652	67.7

Using the total percentage—the actual expenditures of all three candidates as a percentage of their combined legal limit—as the measure of campaign spending in each state's primary, for all twenty-six states the correlation (r_s) between campaign spending and primary turnout of registered voters was .40—one of the strongest relationships we have encountered in this analysis.

It could be argued, however, that the independent variable is misleading because it includes expenditures by Carter but not by any of the other Democratic candidates. To test this objection, I took the data for Ford and Reagan in the thirteen closed-primary states and correlated it with the turnout of registered Republican voters in those states. The correlation (r_s) was .42, only two points higher than that for both parties combined. It therefore appears that campaign spending is one of the factors most strongly associated with primary turnout.

CLOSENESS OF THE CONTESTS

It seems reasonable to expect a strong relationship between the perceived closeness of the contests in the 1976 presidential primaries and the size of the turnouts. It would seem that the closer the voters expect the contest to be, the more they will feel that their votes will significantly affect the outcome; and the more they expect their votes to "count for something," the more likely they are to vote.

Testing this hypothesis would be easier if we had survey data for each of the twenty-six states showing directly how close the voters expected their state's primary would be. Since we do not, we have to get at the voters' expectations indirectly by looking at the actual closeness of the contest when the votes were cast. For this purpose I have borrowed the index of competition developed by William Morris and Otto Davis for their analysis of turnout in presidential primaries. The formula for any given party's primary in a state is:

$$\frac{\text{percent of the leading candidate}}{\text{difference between the percents of the two top candidates}}$$

(1) The two parties combined. Since most of the 1976 primaries were close contests for both parties, for each state I first calculated an index of competition for each of the parties and then averaged the two figures for an overall index of competition for the state. This procedure yielded a wide variety of scores, ranging from a high of 7339 for Michigan to a low of 0065 for New Jersey. Contrary to expectations, however, the correlation between the closeness of the contest and turnout of registered voters was only .09.

(2) The two parties considered separately. Looking at the two parties separately in the thirteen closed-primary states did not materially strengthen the correlation. For the Democrats the correlation was only .02. To illus-

trate its components: California, which had the highest Democratic turnout of all, 74.1 percent, had a competition index of only 0153 (Brown swept the field against all comers). On the other hand, Nebraska, with the highest competition index, 4311, had a turnout of only 50.7 percent, which ranked it ninth out of the thirteen states.

The Republicans had an overall correlation of −.04. California Republicans also had the highest turnout, 77.9 percent, but Reagan's sweep produced a competition index of only 0289. Meanwhile, the Republican primary with the highest index of competition, New Hampshire with 3529, produced a turnout of 63.0 percent, and Kentucky, with the second highest index of competition, 1273, had the lowest turnout, 28.5 percent. In 1976, then, there was no significant relationship in either party between the closeness of the presidential primary and the proportion of registered voters who voted in that primary.

DEMOGRAPHIC CHARACTERISTICS OF THE STATES

There is little of interest to report concerning the relationships between the demographic characteristics of the states and their turnouts in presidential primaries. The only correlations of any significance were those that turn up in all studies of turnout in all kinds of elections. They show strong relationships between high educational levels and high voting turnouts. In this study the correlation between primary turnout and percent of population with thirteen or more years of education was .39, and that between turnout and percent of population with eight years or less of education was −.51. The other demographic factors yielded no significant correlations. For example, the correlation between primary turnout and percent of population living in urban areas was .14, and that between turnout and per capita personal income was .22. So, however powerful the demographic characteristics of states may be in explaining their turnouts in general elections, only the education variable explains much of the variance in turnout in primary elections.

Conclusion

Early in this study I noted that advocates of the two different ways of increasing popular participation in presidential nominations have both won notable victories since 1968. One group has demanded that the state and local party caucuses and conventions involved in the presidential nominating process be opened up to full participation by all local activists whose enthusiasm for a candidate or a cause makes them want to participate. Most of their demands have been written into the Democratic party's rules and, to a lesser extent, into the Republican party's as well. The result in 1976 was that an estimated 700,000 activists participated in the Democrats' caucuses in the twenty-one nonprimary states. These 700,000 constituted only 2 percent of the voting-age population in those states, but it was undoubtedly a higher proportion than had ever attended caucuses before.

The other groups are not impressed by these figures. They have sought to encourage participation by millions of ordinary voters rather than thousands of activists, and their main device has been the presidential primary. Their greatest success to date came in 1976, when twenty-nine states and the District of Columbia held presidential primaries, with the result that over two-thirds of the delegates to both parties' conventions were either chosen or bound by primaries. In 1976 over 29 million people voted in the primaries. They constituted about 20 percent of the voting-age population. This was not only a higher proportion than had ever participated before, but ten times more people than took part in the participatory caucuses.

The question now becomes: where do we go from here? It seems to me there are four main possibilities:

1. We can have a moratorium on reforming the nominating process and work with the one we have—much as our forebears did from 1832 to 1904 and from 1920 to 1968.
2. We can undo some of the recent reforms, perhaps by persuading some states to repeal their presidential primaries (as New Mexico did after 1972) and/or by persuading the parties, particularly the Democrats, to revise their delegate selection rules to give a greater voice to party regulars.
3. We can make the process even more participatory by encouraging more states to enact presidential primaries.
4. We can take the final step on the participatory road by having Congress enact some form of a national presidential primary.

Whatever may be the relative desirability of these alternatives, the third and fourth seem to be the waves of the future. Accordingly, this paper, by setting forth the nature and correlates of turnout in the 1976 presidential primaries, has sought to provide some data and other considerations that might help us estimate the consequences of certain rules changes for turnouts in future primaries. On the basis of the preceding analysis, I believe we can make at least the following educated guesses:

First, if we have more state primaries or adopt a national primary, the overall voting turnout at the primaries will certainly be larger in absolute numbers than it was in 1976. As a *proportion* of all potential voters, however, it will be not much more than half of the turnout in the ensuing general elections.

Second, if we confine ourselves to manipulating the rules internal to the primaries themselves, moving from crossover to closed primaries will stimulate turnout by 10 percent or more.

Third, if we also change the laws regulating the environment in which primaries operate, then the adoption of universal registration and a raise in or abolition of the limits on campaign spending will help boost turnout as well.

No matter how many rules we change, however, turnouts in presidential primaries will always be substantially smaller than those in presidential general elections. Whether nominations made by these special primary electorates will achieve the goals claimed for them of more representative conventions, more legitimate nominations, and greater general popular support for our political system is still an open question. All we can say on the basis of what we have learned about 1976 is that they have not yet done so.

CHAPTER 7

Interpreting
the Campaign

A. The Press and the Process

B. Press Accounts and Candidate Fortunes

The Press and the Process

On the Bus

BY TIMOTHY J. CROUSE

June 1—five days before the California primary. A grey dawn was fighting its way through the orange curtains in the Wilshire Hyatt House Hotel in Los Angeles, where George McGovern was encamped wtih his wife, his staff, and the press assigned to cover his snowballing campaign.

While reporters still snored like Hessians in a hundred beds throughout the hotel, the McGovern munchkins were at work, plying the halls, slipping the long legal-sized handouts through the cracks under the door of each room. According to one of these handouts, the Baptist Ministers' Union of Oakland had decided after "prayerful and careful deliberation" to endorse Senator McGovern. And there was a detailed profile of Alameda County (". . . agricultural products include sweet corn, cucumbers, and lettuce"), across which the press would be dragged today—or was it tomorrow? Finally, there was the mimeographed schedule, the orders of the day.

At 6:45 the phone on the bed table rang, and a sweet, chipper voice announced: "Good Morning, Mr. Crouse. It's six forty-five. The press bus leaves in forty-five minutes from the front of the hotel." She was up there in Room 819, the Press Suite, calling up the dozens of names on the press manifest, awaking the agents of every great newspaper, wire service and network not only of America but of the world. In response to her calls, she was getting a shocking series of startled grunts, snarls and obscenities.

The media heavies were rolling over, stumbling to the bathroom, and tripping over the handouts. Stooping to pick up the schedule, they read: *"8:00–8:15, Arrive Roger Young Center, Breakfast with Ministers."* Suddenly, desperately, they thought: "Maybe I can pick McGovern up in Burbank at nine fifty-five and sleep for another hour." Then, probably at almost the same instant, several score minds flashed the same guilty thought: "But maybe he will get shot at the ministers' breakfast," and then each mind branched off into its own private nightmare recollections of the correspondent who was taking a piss at Laurel when they shot Wallace, of the ABC cameraman who couldn't get his Bolex to start as Bremer emptied his revolver. A hundred hands groped for the toothbrush.

It was lonely on these early mornings and often excruciatingly painful to tear oneself away from a brief, sodden spell of sleep. More painful for some than others. The press was consuming two hundred dollars a night worth of free cheap booze up there in the Press Suite, and some were consuming the lion's share. Last night it had taken six reporters to subdue a prominent radio correspondent who kept upsetting the portable bar, knocking bottles and ice on the floor. The radioman had the resiliency of a Rasputin—each time he was put to bed, he would reappear to cause yet more bedlam.

And yet, at 7:15 Rasputin was there for the baggage call, milling in the hall outside the Press Suite with fifty-odd reporters. The first glance at all these fellow sufferers was deeply reassuring—they all felt the same pressures you felt, their problems were your problems. Together, they seemed to have the cohesiveness of an ant colony, but when you examined the scene more closely, each reporter appeared to be jitterbugging around in quest of the answer that would quell some private anxiety.

They were three deep at the main table in the Press Suite, badgering the McGovern people for a variety of assurances. "Will I have a room in San Francisco tonight?" "Are you sure I'm booked on the whistle-stop train?" "Have you seen my partner?"

The feverish atmosphere was halfway between a high school bus trip to Washington and a gambler's jet junket to Las Vegas, where small-time Mafiosi were lured into betting away their restaurants. There was giddy camaraderie mixed with fear and low-grade hysteria. To file a story late, or to make one glaring factual error, was to chance losing everything— one's job, one's expense account, one's drinking buddies, one's mad-dash existence, and the Methedrine buzz that comes from knowing stories that the public would not know for hours and secrets that the public would never know. Therefore reporters channeled their gambling instincts into late-night poker games and private bets on the outcome of the elections. When it came to writing a story, they were as cautious as diamond-cutters.

It being Thursday, many reporters were knotting their stomachs over their Sunday pieces, which had to be filed that afternoon at the latest. They were inhaling their cigarettes with more of a vengeance, and patting themselves more distractedly to make sure they had their pens and notebooks. In the hall, a Secret Service agent was dispensing press tags for the baggage, along with string and scissors to attach them. From time to time, in the best Baden-Powell tradition, he courteously stepped forward to assist a drink-palsied journalist in the process of threading a tag.

The reporters often consulted their watches or asked for the time of departure. Among this crew, there was one great phobia—the fear of getting left behind. Fresh troops had arrived today from the Humphrey Bus, which was the Russian Front of the California primary, and they had come bearing tales of horror. The Humphrey Bus had left half the press corps at the Biltmore Hotel on Tuesday night; in Santa Barbara, the bus had deserted Richard Bergholz of the Los Angeles *Times,* and it had twice stranded George Shelton, the UPI man.

"Jesus, am I glad I'm off the Humphrey Bus," said one reporter, as he siphoned some coffee out of the McGovern samovar and helped himself to a McGovern sweet roll. "Shelton asked Humphrey's press officer, Hackel, if there was time to file. Hackel said, 'Sure, the candidate's gonna mingle and shake some hands.' Well, old Hubie couldn't find but six hands to shake, so they got in the bus and took off and left the poor bastard in a phone booth right in the middle of Watts."

To the men whom duty had called to slog along at the side of the Hump, the switch to the McGovern Bus brought miraculous relief. "You gotta go see the Hump's pressroom, just to see what disaster looks like," a reporter urged me. The Humphrey pressroom, a bunker-like affair in the bowels of the Beverly Hilton, contained three tables covered with white tablecloths, no typewriters, no chairs, no bar, no food, one phone (with outside lines available only to registered guests), and no reporters. The McGovern press suite, on the other hand, contained twelve typewriters, eight phones, a Xerox Telecopier, a free bar, free cigarettes, free munchies, and a skeleton crew of three staffers. It was not only Rumor Central, but also a miniature road version of Thomas Cook and Son. As the new arrivals to the McGovern Bus quickly found out, the McGovern staff ran the kind of guided tour that people pay great sums of money to get carted around on. They booked reservations on planes, trains and hotels; gave and received messages; and handled Secret Service accreditation with a fierce, Teutonic efficiency. And handed out reams of free information. On any given day, the table in the middle of the Press Suite was laden with at least a dozen fat piles of handouts, and the door was papered with pool reports.

. . . .

Around 8:15 A.M. on June 1 the buses rolled past the stucco housefronts of lower-middle-class Los Angeles and pulled up in front of a plain brick building that looked like a school. The press trooped down a little alley and into the back of the Grand Ballroom of the Roger Young Center. The scene resembled Bingo Night in a South Dakota parish hall—hundreds of middle-aged people sitting at long rectangular tables. They were watching George McGovern, who was speaking from the stage. The press, at the back of the room, started filling up on free Danish pastry, orange juice and coffee. Automatically, they pulled out their notebooks and wrote something down, even though McGovern was saying nothing new. They leaned sloppily against the wall or slumped in folding chairs.

McGovern ended his speech and the Secret Service men began to wedge him through the crush of ministers and old ladies who wanted to shake his hand. By the time he had made it to the little alley which was the only route of escape from the building, three cameras had set up an ambush. This was the only "photo opportunity," as it is called, that the TV people would have all morning. Except in dire emergencies, all TV film has to be taken before noon, so that it can be processed and transmitted to New York. Consequently, the TV people are the only reporters who are not asleep on their feet in the morning. Few TV correspondents ever join the wee-hour poker games or drinking. Connie Chung, the pretty Chinese CBS correspondent, occupied the room next to mine at the Hyatt House and she was always back by midnight, reciting a final sixty-second radio spot into her Sony or absorbing one last press release before getting a good night's sleep. So here she was this morning, bright and alert, sticking a mike into McGovern's face and asking him something about black ministers. The print reporters stood around and watched, just in case McGovern should say something interesting. Finally McGovern excused himself and everybody ran for the bus.

8:20–8:50 A.M.	*En Route/Motorcade*
8:50–9:30 A.M.	*Taping—"Newsmakers"* *CBS-TV 6121 Sunset Boulevard,* *Hollywood*
9:30–9:55 A.M.	*En Route/Motorcade*
9:55–10:30 A.M.	*Taping—"News Conference"* *NBC-TV 3000 West Alameda Ave.,* *Burbank*
10:30–10:50 A.M.	*Press filing*
10:50–Noon	*En Route/Motorcade*
Noon–1:00 P.M.	*Senior Citizens Lunch and Rally* *Bixby Park—Band Shell* *Long Beach*
1:00–1:15 P.M.	*Press filing*

The reporters began to wake up as they walked into the chilly Studio 22 at CBS. There was a bank of telephones, hastily hooked up on a large worktable in the middle of the studio, and six or seven reporters made credit card calls to bureau chiefs and home offices. Dick Stout of *Newsweek* found out he had to file a long story and couldn't go to San Francisco later in the day. Steve Gerstel phoned in his day's schedule to UPI. Connie Chung dictated a few salient quotes from McGovern's breakfast speech to CBS Radio.

A loudspeaker announced that the interview was about to begin, so the reporters sat down on the folding chairs that were clustered around a monitor. They didn't like having to get their news secondhand from TV, but they did enjoy being able to talk back to McGovern without his hearing them. As the program started, several reporters turned on cassette recorders. A local newscaster led off by accusing McGovern of using a slick media campaign.

"Well, I think the documentary on my life is very well done," McGovern answered ingenuously. The press roared wtih laughter. Suddenly the screen of the monitor went blank—the video tape had broken. The press started to grumble.

"Are they gonna change that first question and make it a toughie?" asked Martin Nolan, the Boston *Globe*'s national political reporter. "If not, I'm gonna wait on the bus." Nolan, a witty man in his middle thirties, had the unshaven, slack-jawed, nuts-to-you-too look of a bartender in a sailors' café. He grew up in Dorchester, a poor section of Boston, and he asked his first tough political question at the age of twelve. "Sister, how do you *know* Dean Acheson's a Communist?" he had challenged a reactionary nun in his parochial school, and the reprimand he received hadn't daunted him from asking wiseacre questions ever since.

The video tape was repaired and the program began again. The interviewer asked McGovern the same first question, but Nolan stayed anyway. Like the others, Nolan had sat through hundreds of press conferences holding in an irrepressible desire to heckle. Now was the big chance and everyone took it.

"Who are your heroes?" the newscaster asked McGovern.

"General Patton!" shouted Jim Naughton of the *Times*.

"Thomas Jefferson and Abraham Lincoln," said McGovern.

"What do you think of the death penalty?" asked the newscaster.

"I'm against the death penalty." There was a long pause. "That is my judgment," McGovern said, and lapsed into a heavy, terminal silence. The press laughed at McGovern's discomfiture.

By the time the interview was over, the press was in a good mood. As they filed back onto the buses, the normal configurations began to form: wire-service reporters and TV cameramen in the front, where they could get out fast; small-town daily and big-city daily reporters in the middle seats, hard at work; McGovern staffers in the rear seats, going over plans and chatting. Dick Stout and Jim Naughton held their tape recorders to their ears, like transistor junkies, and culled the best quotes from the TV interview to write in their notebooks. Lou Dombrowski of the Chicago *Tribune*, who looked like a hulking Maf padrone, typed his Sunday story on the portable Olympia in his lap. The reporters working for morning newspapers would have to begin to write soon, and they were looking over the handouts and their notes for something to write about.

So it went. They went on to another interview in another chilly studio, at NBC. This time the reporters sat in the same studio as McGovern and the interviewer, so there was no laughter, only silent note-taking. After the interview there were phones and typewriters in another room, courtesy of the network. Only a few men used them. Then to Bixby Park for a dull speech to old people and a McGovern-provided box lunch of tiny, rubbery chicken parts. Another filing facility, this one in a dank little dressing room in back of the Bixby Park band shell. While McGovern droned on about senior citizens, about fifteen reporters used the bank of twelve phones that the McGovern press people had ordered Pacific Telephone to install.

At every stop there was a phone bank, but the reporters never rushed for the phones and fought over them as they do in the movies. Most of them worked for morning papers and didn't have to worry about dictating their stories over the phone until around 6 P.M. (Eastern Standard Time). Earlier in the day they just called their editors to map out a story, or called a source to check a fact, or sometimes they called in part of a story, with the first paragraph (the "lead") to follow at the last moment. There was only one type of reporter who dashed for the phones at almost every stop and called in bulletins about almost everything that happened on the schedule. That was the wire-service reporter.

If you live in New York or Los Angeles, you have probably never heard of Walter Mears and Carl Leubsdorf, who were covering McGovern for the Associated Press, or Steve Gerstel, who covered him for the United Press International. But if your home is Sheboygan or Aspen, and you read the local papers, they are probably the only political journalists you know. There are about 1,700 newspapers in the U.S., and every one of them has an AP machine or UPI machine or both whirling and clattering and ringing in some corner of the city room, coughing up stories all through the day. Most of these papers do not have their own political reporters, and they depend on the wire-service men for all of their national political coverage. Even at newspapers that have large political staffs, the wire-service story almost always arrives first.

So the wire services are influential beyond calculation. Even at the best newspapers, the editor always gauges his own reporters' stories against the expectations that the wire stories have aroused. The only trouble is that the wire stories are usually bland, dry, and overly cautious. There is an inverse proportion between the number of persons a reporter reaches and the amount he can say. The larger the audience, the more inoffensive and inconclusive the article must be. Many of the wire men are repositories of information they can never convey. Pye Chamberlyne, a young UPI radio reporter with an untamable wiry moustache, emerged over drinks as an expert on the Dark Side of Congress. He could tell you about a prominent

Senator's battle to overcome his addiction to speed, or about Humphrey's habit of popping twenty-five One-A-Day Vitamins with a shot of bourbon when he needed some fast energy. But Pye couldn't tell his audience.

In 1972, the Dean of the political wire-service reporters was Walter Mears of the AP, a youngish man with sharp pale green eyes who smoked cigarillos and had a nervous habit of picking his teeth with a matchbook cover. With his clean-cut brown hair and his conservative sports clothes he could pass for a successful golf pro, or maybe a baseball player. He started his career with the AP in 1955 covering auto accidents in Boston, and he worked his way up the hard way, by getting his stories in fast and his facts straight every time. He didn't go in for the New Journalism. "The problem with a lot of the new guys is they don't get the formula stuff drilled into them," he told me as he scanned the morning paper in Miami Beach. "I'm an old fart. If you don't learn how to write an eight-car fatal on Route 128, you're gonna be in big trouble."

About ten years ago, Mears' house in Washington burned down. His wife and children died in the fire. As therapy, Mears began to put in slavish eighteen-hour days for the AP. In a job where sheer industry counts above all else, Mears worked harder than any other two reporters, and he got to the top.

"At what he does, Mears is the best in the goddam world," said a colleague who writes very non-AP features. "He can get out a coherent story with the right point on top in a minute and thirty seconds, left-handed. It's like a parlor trick, but that's what he wants to do and he does it. In the end, Walter Mears can only be tested on one thing, and that is whether he has the right lead. He almost always does. He watches some goddam event for a half hour and he understands the most important thing that happened—that happened in public, I mean. He's just like a TV camera, he doesn't see things any special way. But he's probably one of the most influential political reporters in the world, just because his stuff reaches more people than anyone else's."

Mears' way with a lead made him a leader of the pack. Covering the second California debate between McGovern and Humphrey on May 30, Mears worked with about thirty other reporters in a large, warehouse-like press room that NBC had furnished with tables, typewriters, paper and phones. The debate was broadcast live from an adjacent studio, where most of the press watched it. For the reporters who didn't have to file immediately, it was something of a social event. But Mears sat tensely in the front of the press room, puffing at a Tiparillo and staring up at a gigantic monitor like a man waiting for a horse race to begin. As soon as the program started, he began typing like a madman, "taking transcript" in shorthand form and inserting descriptive phrases every four or five lines: HUMPHREY STARTED IN A LOW KEY, or MCGOV LOOKS A BIT STRAINED.

The entire room was erupting with clattering typewriters, but Mears stood out as the resident dervish. His cigar slowed him down, so he threw it away. It was hot, but he had no time to take off his blue jacket. After the first three minutes, he turned to the phone at his elbow and called the AP bureau in L.A. "He's phoning in a lead based on the first statements so they can send out a bulletin," explained Carl Leubsdorf, the No. 2 AP man, who was sitting behind Mears and taking back-up notes. After a minute on the phone Mears went back to typing and didn't stop for a solid hour. At the end of the debate he jumped up, picked up the phone, looked hard at Leubsdorf, and mumbled, "How can they stop? They didn't come to a lead yet."

Two other reporters, one from New York, another from Chicago, headed toward Mears shouting, "Lead? Lead?" Marty Nolan came at him from another direction. "Walter, Walter, what's our lead?" he said.

Mears was wildly scanning his transcript. "I did a Wallace lead the first time," he said. (McGovern and Humphrey had agreed near the start of the show that neither of them would accept George Wallace as a Vice President.) "I'll have to do it again." There were solid, technical reasons for Mears' computer-speed decision to go with the Wallace lead: it meant he could get both Humphrey and McGovern into the first paragraph, both stating a position that they hadn't flatly declared before then. But nobody asked for explanations.

"Yeah," said Nolan, turning back to his Royal. "Wallace. I guess that's it."

Meanwhile, in an adjacent building, *The New York Times* team had been working around a long oak desk in an NBC conference room. The *Times* had an editor from the Washington Bureau, Robert Phelps, and three rotating reporters watching the debate in the conference room and writing the story; a secretary phoned it in from an office down the hall. The *Times* team filed a lead saying that Humphrey had apologized for having called McGovern a "fool" earlier in the campaign. Soon after they filed the story, an editor phoned from New York. The AP had gone with a Wallace lead, he said. Why hadn't they?

Marty Nolan eventually decided against the Wallace lead, but NBC and CBS went with it on their news shows. So did many of the men in the room. They wanted to avoid "call-backs"—phone calls from their editors asking them why they had deviated from the AP or UPI. If the editors were going to run a story that differed from the story in the nation's 1,700 other newspapers, they wanted a good reason for it. Most reporters dreaded call-backs. Thus the pack followed the wire-service men whenever possible. Nobody made a secret of running with the wires; it was an accepted practice. At an event later in the campaign, a New York *Daily News* reporter looked over the shoulder of Norm Kempster, a UPI man, and read his copy.

"Stick with that lead, Norm," said the man from the *News*. "You'll save us a lot of trouble."

"Don't worry," said Norm. "I don't think you'll have any trouble from mine."

2:00–2:45 P.M.	*Fullerton Junior College*
	321 East Chapman, Fullerton
2:45–3:00 P.M.	*Press filing*
3:00–3:30 P.M.	*En Route/Motorcade*
3:30–3:40 P.M.	*Load Aircraft*
3:40 P.M.	*Depart Orange County Community Airport*
4:45 P.M.	*Arrive Oakland, California*
5:00–5:40 P.M.	*En Route/Motorcade*
5:40–6:45 P.M.	*Private dinner*
6:45–7:30 P.M.	*Rest—San Francisco Hilton*
7:30–8:30 P.M.	*En Route/Motorcade*
8:30–9:15 P.M.	*McGovern for President Rally*
	St. James Park, San Jose
9:15–10:00 P.M.	*En Route/Motorcade*
10:00–10:45 P.M.	*Private meeting*
10:45–11:15 P.M.	*En Route/Motorcade*
11:15 P.M.	*Arrive San Francisco Hilton*

At Bixby Park, Walter Cronkite showed up and rode on the press bus to Fullerton Junior College. Most of the reporters were quite dazzled and wanted to know why Cronkite was around. "He wants to be one of the guys and to get a feel for something outside Moscow," Connie Chung explained. Fred Dutton, Gary Hart and Bill Dougherty of the McGovern staff had joined the bus too. They were singing football songs and hymns in the back seats. In fact, things were getting chummy as hell. Shirley MacLaine was sitting in Marty Nolan's lap. Gary Hart was cracking up with the men from *The New York Times* and *Newsweek*. Bill Dougherty was chatting with David Schoumacher of CBS.

"I'd like to lock up the candidate," Dougherty confided.

"Like to take the vote right now, huh?" said Schoumacher.

Fullerton Junior College looked like a large complex of parking garages. The sweltering gym was packed with kids who treated McGovern as if he were Bobby Kennedy. The cameramen surrounded McGovern as he fought his way to the platform and the kids tried to push through the cameramen. The heat and commotion energized reporters as they squatted around the platform. When McGovern began to speak, they made frantic notes, although he said nothing new. Gradually they wound down.

"If there is one lesson it is . . ." said McGovern.

Carl Leubsdorf put up his finger. "I know what it is," he said to Elizabeth Drew of PBS. "Never again."

"It is that never again . . ." said George.

By the end of the speech no one was taking notes. As deadlines began to loom for the big-city daily reporters, the early afternoon euphoria began to give way to grumpy sobriety. Walter Cronkite went back to Los Angeles because his back was bothering him and he needed to rest. The rest of the press flew to Oakland.

The schedule began to go to hell. Instead of going to San Francisco, the bus took the press to an airport hotel called the Oakland Inn, where McGovern was going to have a hastily scheduled press conference with some black ministers. The press went to a small function room in the motel that had phony wood paneling on the walls and gold vinyl chairs. While reporters began to munch at the Danish lying on a small table at the rear, or worked at the five typewriters on a large table pushed up against a side wall, the cameramen set up in the front. Soon there was an outcry from the print press. "Do *you* want to go to a press conference where we stand behind the cameras?" James Doyle of the Washington *Star* asked Adam Clymer of the Baltimore *Sun*.

Doyle found Kirby Jones, McGovern's press secretary, and chewed him out. Jones made some excuses.

"Yeah," said Doyle, "but you're *never* organized at these press conferences."

Jones shrugged and walked away.

The press had to sit behind the cameras for the press conference, which was short and dull. As the reporters were getting up to stretch, Kirby Jones and Gordon Weil, another McGovern aide, began to pass the word that the Field Poll results were out: McGovern was twenty points ahead.

It was the only hard news of the day. Harry Kelly of Hearst, Steve Gerstel of UPI, and James Doyle all headed for the typewriters and began to hunt-and-peck. Pye Chamberlyne, Curt Wilkie, and about twenty other reporters headed for the four pay phones in the hall outside the function room. People were getting testy. Carl Leubsdorf of the AP leaned over Jim Doyle's shoulder, took a good look at Doyle's lead and then asked, "Hey, can I see?"

Doyle looked up and registered what was happening. "Jesus, no!" he exploded. "Fuck you! Get outa here!"

A few moments later Steve Gerstel sauntered over to Doyle and said, "Let me see your lead, Jim."

"You might as well," Doyle said unhappily. "The AP just catched it."

Leubsdorf walked by again on his way to the phones and patted Doyle on the back. "I like it," he said, and chuckled.

A hour went by, and everybody got a chance to file on the Field Poll. The scene began to look like a bad cocktail party. Haynes Johnson of the Washington *Post*, Elizabeth Drew of PBS, and Jules Witcover of the Los Angeles *Times* were doing Humphrey imitations. Kirby Jones was trying to get nine people to go in the helicopter to San Jose as "pool" reporters—

that is, to write a report for all the reporters who could not fit in the chopper. The San Jose rally promised to be McGovern's major lunge for the Bobby Kennedy Chicano constituency, but no one wanted to go. San Francisco lay ahead, and it was a great restaurant town. Finally Jim Naughton, Marty Nolan, and a couple of camera crews signed up.

At 7:00, Kirby Jones announced another press conference—McGovern would read a statement on Nixon's Moscow trip. At 7:30, Jones announced that *he* would read the statement. There was a general groan. Kirby launched into a predictable text. "Stop the presses," said Haynes Johnson, shutting his notebook.

The campaign day was drawing to a dreary close. Had all the events taken place in a single room, the reporters would have been climbing the walls with boredom by mid-afternoon. It was the bus rides and plane flights, the sense that a small army was being efficiently deployed, that had given the day its pace, variety, and excitement. Yet the reporters seldom wrote about this traveling around, which was so important in forming their gut feelings about the campaign. The day had yielded its one easy story: McGovern was leading Humphrey by twenty points in the Field Poll. This statistic sounded somehow *right* to the reporters, for it jibed with their half-digested notion that the McGovern campaign was a juggernaut about to flatten Hubert Humphrey. And where had this notion come from? "They partly got it from the slickness of the McGovern press operation," said a reporter who was covering Humphrey in California. "When a reporter got to his room at night his bag was there. When he called the pressroom, he didn't get a yo-yo saying there was nobody there. He got handouts telling him where the candidate was going to be the next morning and who he could interview at 2 A.M. if he needed to get a fast quote. And so pretty soon the reporter started saying to himself, half-consciously, 'If the press operation is this good, they must have a helluva voter registration operation!' The press didn't create the McGovern juggernaut, but they sure as hell *helped* create it."

On June 1, a normal campaign day, the reporters had gained no fresh insights into George McGovern; they had not gone out of their way to look for any. They had not tried to find out whether the large sums of money that were suddenly pouring into the campaign coffers had changed the candidate; or whether the prospect of the nomination, now so close at hand, was tempting him to bend on some of his more controversial stands; whether, as some of his detractors charged, he had a ruthless streak to match Bobby Kennedy's. "We spent tons of ink on that guy," one of the reporters later lamented, "and I'd be willing to bet that on the night he got the nomination we hadn't told anybody in the United States who the hell we were talking about, what kind of man he was."

"Winnowing": The News Media and the 1976 Presidential Nominations

BY DONALD R. MATTHEWS

The news media have become a part of national political campaigns. Contemporary television is obtrusive. Campaigns have had to adjust to the needs of the medium. National political campaigns have become little more than a series of performances calculated to attract the attention of television news cameras and their audiences. But the change in the political role of news gathering organizations can not be ascribed solely to this new technology. The long-run decline in the effectiveness of party organization, combined with recent efforts to "democratize" nominating procedures, have also fueled this development. No longer do party officials and associated elites meet in nominating conventions to choose a presidential candidate from among their own numbers. Today rank and file voters are directly and indirectly involved in the choice. Party officials have lost most of their control over nominations and self-starting presidential aspirants contest in open arenas for control over national convention delegates and their votes. The news media are the main way the actors in this dispersed and prolonged drama communicate with one another and with those who prefer to stand aside and watch. A struggle over the content of political news has become the core of presidential nominating politics.

None of these generalizations are likely to surprise the readers of this book. But the new political role of the news media raises problems for journalists and politicians—and those of us who spend our time studying them—for which we have no adequate answers. *How does the enhanced importance of newspeople and news organizations—their values, organizational needs and technologies—affect presidential nominations? Specifically, how and how much did the media affect the nominations of Jimmy Carter and Gerald Ford in 1976?*

Donald R. Matthews, " 'Winnowing': The News Media and the 1976 Presidential Nominations," from James D. Barber, ed., *Race for the Presidency* (Englewood Cliffs, N.J.: Prentice-Hall, Inc., 1978) pp. 55–66. Charts deleted. © 1978, by the American Assembly, Columbia University. Reprinted by permission of Prentice-Hall, Inc., Englewood Cliffs, New Jersey.

Some Preliminary Distinctions

Most discussions of the political effects of the news media are overly simple, either too benign or too lurid. The news media are depicted either as all powerful political forces or as neutral observers merely reflecting reality. It does not help much to say that neither of these views is entirely correct nor entirely wrong. The news media are very powerful but there are limits on (and other contenders for) this power. If the news media really dominated our political life as some allege, Jimmy Carter would not be President of the United States today. Nor, in all probability, would Gerald Ford or Richard Nixon or Lyndon Johnson or Harry Truman or Franklin Roosevelt have been President in the past. Thus while the news media inevitably shape "reality," this distortion need not invariably favor the media's preferences between political parties, candidates, or policies.

If we are to make any headway in this inquiry we must begin by drawing a few clarifying distinctions. First of all, we must distinguish between *causes* and *covariation*. Winning candidates for presidential nominations, for example, attract more space on the nation's front pages than losing ones—but is this *cause* (the greater exposure results in victory) or *covariation* (winners are more newsworthy than losers and would win anyway)? The effects of the media may be either *manifest* or *latent*. If the news media had self-consciously and intentionally set out to "sell" Jimmy Carter to the American people as President, their success would have been a manifest effect. This was clearly not the case. But the news media, in their pursuit of large audiences and "good reporting" may have depicted the events of 1976 so as to lead to Carter's nomination—a latent effect. A third and final distinction may also help: media effects can be felt on either the *process* or the *outcome* of presidential nominations. It is rather easy to demonstrate how the news media affect the strategies, behaviors, and style of presidential nominating contests, that is, the process of collective choice. But the more important question is outcomes—what kind of persons are chosen as presidential nominees? This chapter tries to look at the results of news media coverage (cause-effect relationships), whether they are intended or not (manifest or latent), on who wins (outcomes).

This concern directs our attention primarily toward the early stages of the nominating process. Causes must precede effects. And the early stages of the nominating process are so unstructured and ambiguous that the press then enjoys maximum discretion in defining the situation. "I can't wait until next January," one of the nation's leading political journalists said in late 1975, "then I'll *know* what I should be writing about." Paradoxically, the media's greatest opportunities to affect outcomes are when most of the audience are paying the least attention.

This by no means implies that the media play no significant role in presidential nominations. Rather it means that those newspeople who report upon the early stages of presidential nominating politics (reporters specializing in national politics) and the news organizations who employ them (a half dozen elite newspapers, the news magazines, the wire services and newspaper editors, and the broadcasting networks) have most of whatever independent media power there is.

The Lessons of '72

Presidential nominations occur at four-year intervals. Their predictability allows ambitious politicians to begin their assaults on the Presidency years ahead of time. They occur frequently enough that one round of presidential nominating politics provides the foundation for the next four years of maneuvering, and the participants in the current round of presidential nominations—candidates, managers, activists, the press—draw "lessons" from four years before.

But the cycle is slow. Few people are personally active in more than a handful of presidential nominations. Generalizations about how they work are based on very small "Ns." And so much can change in four years that conventional wisdom can be outdated even before it is applied.

Nonetheless, the "lessons" of 1972 were pretty clear to the political specialists in the news media, and these "lessons" had some effects in 1976.

DON'T PREDICT THE WRONG WINNER AGAIN

In 1971 and 1972, political pundits nearly to a man had predicted that Senator Ed Muskie of Maine would be the Democratic nominee. His campaign's collapse after a lackluster showing in the early primaries was a source of considerable embarrassment to the political reporters whose stories had informally "elected" him. They were to be extra careful not to make the same mistake again four years later. Besides, our reporter-informants told us in 1975, political reporting placed much too much emphasis on winning and losing anyway. 1976 seemed to be the year to rise above the imagery of the sports page and to write and talk about more important things.

DON'T COUNT ANYBODY OUT

In 1972 the news organizations had ruled Senator George McGovern out of contention before the primaries.

Most of the reporting on the preprimary stage of presidential nominating contests is done by reporters based in Washington, D.C. And they "knew" firsthand that McGovern was a run-of-the-mill Senator who inexplicably wanted to become President. Despite McGovern's appeal to anti-war protesters on college campuses and in middle-class suburbs, the Senator from South Dakota scarcely surfaced in national opinion polls. He seemed to have no chance to develop the stature or attract the resources necessary for a nationwide campaign. Hence, he was dismissed as a "lightweight."

The mistake in 1972 had been to overlook the possibility that McGovern could convert vehement opposition to the Vietnam War into enough money and an amateur campaign organization which could win low-turn-out political contests such as presidential primaries and precinct caucuses. McGovern's miraculous string of primary victories and subsequent nomination was explained primarily by time-specific factors—the Vietnam War and the organizational savvy of McGovern and his youthful aides. The latter explanation became less plausible after McGovern's heroically inept general election campaign. But the winding down of the war in Southeast Asia seemed to make a McGovern-style victory by a long-shot candidate unlikely in 1976—there was no other issue capable of mobilizing amateur campaigners on the horizon. Nonetheless, the news media were still reluctant to eliminate entirely *any* possible winners in 1976, including a number of possibilities who neither campaigned nor admitted they were candidates.

DON'T LET "THEM" CONTROL THE NEWS

Every modern day campaign for high political office is (among other things) a struggle for control over the content of the news. Campaigners try to get the press and broadcast media to carry their campaign appeals to supporters; the news media try to carry interesting and accurate and useful political information to their audience. Neither side can achieve its goals without the cooperation of the other. Yet there is much manipulation and conflict, and the news organizations do not always prevail. The "news" which the media carry is not always to their own liking.

In the 1972 general election campaign, for example, President Richard Nixon had escaped close press scrutiny simply by not campaigning. Press attention had focused by default upon the inept McGovern. The Watergate break-in occurred during the campaign; still, Nixon won reelection in a landslide. There was a self-conscious concern in 1976 that an incumbent President not be allowed to use the White House to dominate the news in this fashion again.

But the problem is broader than how to cover an incumbent President running for reelection. Campaign reporting traditionally consists of reporters following individual candidates around the country, reporting on where the candidates went, what they said, how the audience reacted, and the like. The ease with which national political campaigns can coopt or otherwise manipulate a traveling pack of reporters was irreverently described by Timothy Crouse in his *The Boys on the Bus* based on the 1972 campaign. While the tone of the book was unappreciated by many of its subjects, most political reporters seemed to agree with its basic thesis. The "lesson" was clear enough—the news media must not allow themselves to be captured and exploited by the candidates this time.

BEYOND THE HORSE RACE

The deep thinkers among the press corps and broadcast networks—urged on by their academic friends and critics—set out in 1976 to do a better job covering political issues and presidential character and qualifications than they had four years before. Four years before, a massively flawed President had been reelected by a landslide: how could and should the news organizations do a better job in assessing and depicting the character and qualifications of the contenders? The treatment of "issues" in 1972 was unsatisfactory as well. Nixon managed to avoid talking about them; McGovern did talk. But the media had not paid much attention to McGovern's policy statements until the California primary—when it turned out that some of what McGovern had been saying made little sense. By then McGovern's nomination was virtually assured: would it have been if Democratic primary voters had known more about McGovern's issue positions earlier in the game? No one will ever know. But a better job on "issues" was in most reporters' minds as the 1976 round of presidential nominating politics began.

THE "LESSONS" IN 1976

So many things about presidential politics had changed by 1976 that some of the lessons of 1972 quickly proved irrelevant.

The trauma of Watergate had resulted in a new President with no previous national campaign experience pitted against one of the nation's most formidable and experienced campaigners—concern over an incumbent bias in the news seemed a lot less appropriate with Gerald Ford in residence at 1600 Pennsylvania Avenue. The worry over premature predictions eroded as the number of Democratic contenders grew to more than a dozen; somehow that number had to be reduced quickly if the news media were to do a halfway decent job of reporting on the Democrats. (The sagging economy and hence tighter budgets and shrinking news holes made the problem worse.) Then, too, the formal rules of the game had changed a lot since 1972. The number of presidential primaries had increased from twenty-three to thirty—at which 73 percent of Democratic convention delegates and 68 percent of the Republicans were to be popularly elected. The Democrats had banned "winner-take-all" primaries, and required candidates for convention seats to reveal their presidential preferences. And the nominating campaigns were to be partially funded by tax dollars for the first time; along with the federal dollars came strict limitations on expenditures and elaborate reporting procedures.

All these changes over four years meant that the game was to be significantly different in 1976. How it was to differ and who would benefit from the changes was not clear.

Predicting Outcomes

The "people who brought you Ed Muskie as President" were wary of predictions in 1976. But this conflicted sharply with the need to do something about the extraordinarily large list of Democratic contenders (and possible contenders). Somehow they needed to be sorted out in order to write interesting and dramatic stories. One basis of classification was expected performance—"serious candidates" versus "lightweights." Other classification schemes were used as well—especially "liberal-conservative" and "insider-outsider" distinctions—but predicted performance was by far the most important of these criteria since early predictions can become self-fulfilling prophecies. "Serious" candidates receive more press attention than "lightweights"; this publicity can lead to improved name recognition, higher poll standings, and the availability of more resources, which in turn leads to still more favorable predictions of performance.

Even when they prove to be grossly wrong, the press' early predictions can have major consequences. The history of both parties' nominations in 1976 illustrates this latter point.

THE "BROKERED CONVENTION" SCENARIO

During 1974 and 1975 few political reporters believed that *any* of the growing list of active Democratic candidates could win the nomination in 1976. The polls showed Senator Edward Kennedy, Senator Hubert Humphrey, and Governor George Wallace to be the most popular leaders in the party. Senator Kennedy had withdrawn from consideration and Humphrey had sworn not to campaign for the nomination. If taken literally—and as time passed, more and more people did—that left Governor Wallace the only Democratic possibility with a sizable national following. And Wallace, despite serious questions about his health, was actively raising money and developing a grass roots organization in anticipation of what was expected to be an aggressive campaign.

But, virtually all reporters were convinced that Wallace would not win. Rather it seemed probable that he would go into the convention with about a third of the delegates. The dozen or more other candidates would divide up the remaining delegates so that no one could attract the 50 percent-plus-one votes needed to win, and the convention would deadlock.

Table 1 · Direct Reference to Candidate Nomination by Process in the Washington Post and New York Times in 1975

Candidate Nominated & Process	Jan.–April	May–Aug.	Sept.–Dec.	All Year
Humphrey drafted	4	9	29	42
Kennedy drafted	9	9	6	24
Muskie drafted	2	3	2	7
Other nonactive candidates drafted	0	2	6	8
Brokered outcome; no candidate named	2	8	6	16
Wallace nominated	2	3	1	6
Other active candidates nominated	1	5	12	18

Ultimately the party would be forced to turn to an established leader not actively seeking the nomination—probably Hubert Humphrey. The overwhelming play which this scenario received in 1975 in the *Washington Post* and *New York Times* can be seen in Table 1.

This scenario had many advantages for the media, especially during the early stages of the nominating process. It made sense out of a complex situation without declaring any active candidate the front runner. It did not eliminate anyone—except Wallace, and it actually overestimated the Alabama Governor's strength. For while Wallace had more money and better organization than ever before, the fire was gone, a casualty of an assassin's bullet and the cooling of racial conflict. This overestimation of Wallace, of course, resulted in Carter receiving more credit than he deserved for his narrow victory over Wallace in Florida.

Interestingly, the brokered convention scenario persisted even after it became apparent that George Wallace was a great deal weaker than he seemed in 1974 and 1975 and despite Senator Humphrey's refusal actively to campaign in the primaries. The Humphrey noncandidacy was kept very much alive by the CBS–*New York Times* postelection surveys and other polls which showed that Humphrey would have done well if he had been on the ballot in the early primaries:

1. Humphrey would have received 24 percent of the vote in Massachusetts if he had been on the ballot. Jackson received only 23 percent without that competition. (*New York Times,* March 4, 1976.)
2. "The *Times*-CBS Poll showed that almost one-third of Florida Democrats would have voted for Humphrey had he been on the ballot." (*New York Times,* March 10, 1976.)
3. "About 40 percent of those who voted [in Illinois] for all Democratic candidates except Mr. Wallace said they would have voted for Senator Hubert H. Humphrey of Minnesota had his name been on the preferential ballot. Had

he campaigned here, the figure might have been larger." (*New York Times*, March 17, 1976.)

This process of making Humphrey the beneficiary of primaries in which he did not run gradually altered the brokered convention scenario into a stop-Carter-with-Humphrey story as the ex-Georgia Governor pulled away from all the other active contenders.

THE "FORD CAN'T BE SERIOUS" SCENARIO

Several misjudgments in the coverage of the preprimary stage of the Republican contest seem to have had important effects on the ultimate renomination of President Ford.

Ironically, one such error was a widespread and systematic underestimation of Ford as a campaigner. Partly this resulted from Gerald Ford's pre–White House reputation in the Washington community as a clean cut, reliable boob. Brilliant, witty, clever, quotable he was not—as House Minority Leader or as President. His early efforts at organizing a national campaign looked amateurish to experienced observers. "Any President with Ron Nessen as his press secretary and Bo Callaway as his campaign manager can't be serious about running for reelection." Rumors about Mrs. Ford's health added to widespread speculation that the President might not run for reelection at all.

All this led to Ford entering the primary season with very little expected from him. Ford's narrow "victory" over Governor Ronald Reagan in New Hampshire would have been interpreted as a defeat if almost any other President had been involved. Reagan attracted a larger share of the New Hampshire voters than McCarthy in 1968 or McGovern in 1972 and yet, unlike them, was *not* declared a "winner."

The media coverage of the Republican contest tended to assume that the early primaries would be crucial, as they proved to be for the Democrats. Yet Ford's early victories did not lead to the irresistible momentum that Carter's early wins did, despite the news media's best efforts. The main reason for this probably was the important differences in the situation within the two parties in 1976. On the Democratic side there were many candidates—in this kind of situation people choose among candidates on the basis of personal preferences *plus* estimates of their probable chances of victory. It makes little sense to most people to back a first choice if he has no chance of winning. Jimmy Carter was not the first choice of many people outside his home state of Georgia, but as the prospects of his success increased (and of other candidates diminished) his following multiplied very rapidly as the persons for whom he was a second or third choice abandoned their fading first preference candidates to join his bandwagon. But the Republican contest was a two-way race. In such a situation reasonable people support their first choices without regard to who will win or lose, and the early leader's margin is not magnified by the same kind of bandwagon effects which prevail in multiple candidate situations.

Declaring Winners and Losers

Who wins—or loses—a presidential primary is frequently unclear. Getting the most votes or electing the most pledged delegates are not automatically interpreted as "victories." And it is possible in some states for a candidate to get the most votes without winning the most delegates, or vice versa. More often than not, winning a presidential primary means doing better than expected; losing means disappointing expectations. The media find a winner in these curious contests by arriving at a rough consensus on how candidates should do and then measuring the vote and delegate outcomes by this rubbery yardstick. This "numbers game" is a big part of primary election reporting—how many votes and/or delegates must candidate "X" win before he can be said to have "won" (or "lost")? Without such "analysis" the raw facts and figures of presidential primaries would be virtually meaningless to most Americans.

SETTING EXPECTATIONS

But how are these expectations arrived at? What kinds of evidence are used? Obviously the candidates have an interest in keeping expectations about their performance low enough to make it possible to exceed them while not discouraging their own following. But "winners" must succeed in doing this in a competitive situation in which others are following the same strategy. Reporters are not usually misled by all this preelection day gloom. But they must look beyond the campaigns to local political experts and other reporters for help in setting these expectations.

The *bases* upon which expectations of performance are set can be several. In 1976 few of the active campaigners had run for the nomination before, hence *historical experience* was not widely used as the basis of expectations. The most important exception was George Wallace's strong showing in Florida in 1972, which contributed to excessively high expectations four years later under quite different circumstances. These changed conditions—Wallace's health, the lack of a busing issue, the existence of a "respectable" southerner on the ballot in 1976—were all discussed in the preprimary and postprimary analyses. But Wallace's 42 percent vote in 1972 still remained the standard by which his 1976 performance was judged. *Preprimary polls* seemed to have affected expectations on many occasions—Ford's showing in New Hampshire and Florida, Reagan's in North Carolina were viewed as "victories" partly because they did better on election day than in the polls. *Geographical propinquity* is frequently used as a basis for setting expectations. Candidates are not only expected to run strongly in their own states but also in states nearby (e.g., Bentzen in Oklahoma, Brown in Nevada, Udall in Wisconsin, etc.). Finally, *cost-benefit calculations* are often utilized—how well a candidate does considering his investment of time, energy, money in the state. This approach is mostly used to explain away relatively poor showings in gaining votes and delegates, but occasionally is used to discount an arithmetic victory (e.g., Jackson's in New York). Obviously which of these bases are used to judge the performance of which candidates can make a difference.

THE GREAT NEW HAMPSHIRE OVERKILL

The interest of news organizations in predicting outcomes—preferably earlier than the competition—leads to a special interest in the first formal steps in the presidential nominating process early in the presidential year. Political reporters who were having trouble getting their work printed in 1975 ("Only my mother can find my stories back among the shipping news") suddenly start to get some stories on the front page. The number of reporters assigned to political stories increases. Television camera crews show up at more and more occasions. There is a brief surge of media attention focused heavily on one of the nation's smallest and least typical states, New Hampshire (Table 2).

Presidential primaries are made to order for television news. They are predictable and hence relatively easy to cover on camera. They combine human interest, conflict, drama, and uncertainty. New Hampshire's small size, nearness to the metropolitan centers of the East Coast, and New England landscape and culture make it an especially attractive subject for national television. The fact that it is also the first presidential primary makes it nearly irresistible. In 1976 the three national television networks presented 100 stories on the New Hampshire primary or exactly 2.63 stories per delegate selected there! None of the other early primaries received half as much attention from television. While the print media did not overdo New Hampshire as extravagantly as NBC, CBS, and ABC, they were not too far behind in the great New Hampshire overkill of 1976.

The consequences of the media infatuation with the New Hampshire primary are obvious—"winners" of that contest receive far more favorable publicity and a far greater boost toward the Presidency than the "winners" of other primaries. A week after New Hampshire, for example, Senator Jackson won the Massachusetts primary by a very solid margin. While this clear victory temporarily improved his perceived chances for the Presidency, it did not generate the kind of momentum in subsequent primary states that a New Hampshire triumph usually does.

New Hampshire overkill favored Carter and Ford in 1976. It is unlikely that either could have won their party's nomination without it.

Table 2 · Number of Television Network News Stories
on Early Primaries, 1976*

Primary State	Date	Number of Stories	Number of Delegates	Number of Stories per Delegate
New Hampshire	Feb. 24	100	38	2.63
Massachusetts	Mar. 2	52	147	.35
Vermont	Mar. 2	6	30	.20
Florida	Mar. 9	50	147	.34
Illinois	Mar. 15	38	270	.15
North Carolina	Mar. 23	19	115	.17
New York	Apr. 6	30	428	.07
Wisconsin	Apr. 6	42	113	.37

Source: Michael J. Robinson, "Television News and the Presidential Nominating Process: The Case of Spring," unpublished manuscript, 1976.

*Note: All three networks' nightly news stories combined, weekdays only.

Carter's entire strategy was based on keeping expectations (read: media expectations) low while winning the Iowa caucuses in January, the New Hampshire primary in February, and Florida primary in March. He had been quietly cultivating these three states for several years. His carefully nurtured strength in these states, combined with the fact that he was little known anywhere else (except, of course, in his home state of Georgia) gave his early victories a shock value that made them especially newsworthy to a novelty-prone press. A few national political reporters, most particularly R. W. Apple, Jr. of the *New York Times,* revealed Carter's strategy and growing strength in late 1975, and this resulted in his being cast in the unexpected role of front runner in the New Hampshire Democratic primary. But he managed to edge Morris Udall by 4,300 votes and to be declared the victor nonetheless.

Press Accounts and Candidate Fortunes

Reruns in Boot Hill

WASHINGTON (UPI) — Television stations that broadcast old Ronald Reagan movies will be liable for equal time demands by other Republican presidential candidates, a Federal Communications Commission spokesman said today. The same would apply to the Death Valley Days television series on which Reagan served as narrator, he said.

The Primaries: Which Winners Lost and Which Losers Won?

BY LANNY J. DAVIS

By April 3, the eve of the Wisconsin primary—the decisive confrontation between Muskie and McGovern, with the leadership of the liberal–New Politics wing of the Democratic Party at stake—Senator Muskie was riding high indeed.

He had beaten McGovern five out of five times during the past six weeks—in Iowa, neighbor to McGovern's South Dakota, even though McGovern's highly motivated constituency of New Politics activists had turned out for the local party caucuses in large numbers during a heavy blizzard; in Arizona, where McGovern couldn't even beat John Lindsay, who had been a Democrat for only a few weeks; in New Hampshire, where Muskie's nine-percentage-point margin would be considered under most circumstances a very good showing; in Florida, where, once again, McGovern couldn't even better Lindsay; and, most important, head-to-head in Illinois, where Muskie overwhelmed McGovern, winning sixty-two delegates to McGovern's fifteen—even though McGovern, who was well organized and had waged an active campaign throughout the state, had predicted he would win twice as many delegates.

With four victories out of five over all competition (five out of five over George McGovern), and continued evidence of the broadest appeal across all factions of the Democratic Party, Muskie on the eve of the Wisconsin primary was steamrollering toward the nomination precisely as expected. George McGovern's campaign was demoralized, still confined essentially to the narrow base of New Politics purists with which he had begun the year before.

Right?

Wrong. The reality was that Ed Muskie came into the Wisconsin primary as a loser, on his way down. George McGovern came in as a winner, with the air of inevitability around him.

How was reality turned on its head? And what could Muskie have done to prevent it? . . .

Through the course of 1971, Muskie was exposed to a political cross fire between New Politics purists, whose support George McGovern had actively sought, and the more conservative party-regular elements, on whom Hubert Humphrey based his campaign. As long as McGovern and Humphrey could run viable campaigns, and with George Wallace winning support in Catholic, working-class neighborhoods where Muskie had expected to do well, Muskie's candidacy was doomed in a primary in which all the candidates ran at the same time. In comparison to these men, Muskie had no hard constituency he could call his own.

Party primaries often draw voters who want to express a particular grievance—to "send them a message," as George Wallace put it—rather than to judge who would make the best candidate against the opposition or, for that matter, who would make the best president. In 1956, for example, Estes Kefauver, a "message" candidate, consistently defeated Adlai Stevenson in the primaries. The party leaders, who still controlled a majority of the delegates, acknowledged Kefauver's showing by nominating him for vice president. But they still believed Stevenson had a broader appeal within the Democratic Party. Had that system prevailed in 1972, Ed Muskie, who remained the first or second choice of a substantial majority of Democrats, would probably have been nominated.

As it happened, just at a time when the "message" phenomenon was at an unprecedented high—in the form of the McGovern candidacy on the left and the Wallace candidacy on the right—the Democrats' nominating system—more precisely, the winner-take-all primary, exaggerated the political impact of "message" voters.

Under such a system in a multicandidate primary, a candidate with a small minority of the vote could win 90 or 100 percent of the delegates, while candidates with sizable minority votes of their own would be denied fair proportional representation.

In the past, the public and the press could look to the polls of party leaders and the results of a few key head-to-head primary contests to indicate the relative strengths of the candidates. But in 1972, with the "message" vote phenomenon, the new delegate selection procedures, and numerous winner-take-all, multicandidate primaries, the press was forced to interpret the results of a large variety of state contests.

Understandably, the press reverted to the past "keys" to political analysis—for example, headlining the winner, in absolute numbers, of a multicandidate primary, with little attention to his breadth of support among all factions of the party. Also understandably, the press drew upon Muskie's front-runner and McGovern's underdog status in the national opinion polls through much of 1971 to apply a double standard in assessing the results of the state contests. This led, for example, to the projection of Muskie's 47 percent victory in New Hampshire as insignificant but his weak showing in Florida as significant, whereas McGovern's disastrous showing in Illinois was projected as insignificant but his 30 percent showing in Wisconsin was depicted as impressive.

This is not to say that Muskie was in any way the victim of a press vendetta. Actually Muskie received more than his share of favorable press treatment between 1968 and 1972, and much of the negative publicity he received in 1972 was a result of the legitimate spotlighting of his weaknesses as a candidate.

Nor can the press be blamed for its failure to reassess old definitions and to grasp the full implications of the intermeshing of new political forces and new political procedures in the Democratic Party in 1972. Most of the presidential candidates were in the same boat, not least of all, Senator Muskie himself.

Arizona: The Advantages of Being a Minority

There couldn't be a better example of a system designed to maximize the impact of minority constituencies than the primary system employed by Arizona in 1972.

Arizona held its primary—the second contest of the year—on January 29. Senator Muskie had accumulated the endorsements of all the state's major Democratic Party officials, past and present, including former Governor Sam Goddard and the widely respected congressman from Tucson,

Morris Udall. The press understandably regarded such endorsements as evidence of political strength (though their real value in voter turnout proved minimal). Muskie was seen as an easy victor in Arizona. *Newsweek,* for example, projected Muskie as the winner of *all twenty-five* delegates.

However, what much of the press never understood was that the Arizona system had been specifically designed to make it impossible for any one candidate to sweep all the delegates. In fact, under the Arizona system, even a 50 percent delegate win for one candidate would be an unusual show of strength.

Here's the way the Arizona system worked: A statewide primary for the state's three hundred thousand registered Democrats elected five hundred delegates to a statewide convention. The state convention would subsequently select Arizona's twenty-five delegates to a national convention. A voter had the right to cast the number of votes equal to the number of state convention delegates running from a particular senatorial district (the state was divided into thirty senatorial districts). The voter could allocate those votes any way he wished. For example, if a senatorial district, based on the size of its Democratic Party registrations, was entitled to elect twenty delegates to the state convention, a voter in that district could cast twenty different votes for twenty different candidates, or twenty votes all for one candidate, or ten votes for one candidate and ten votes for another. This "cumulative voting" has frequently been employed to protect the power of minority stockholders in a corporation.

Under cumulative voting systems, if every voter cast each of his votes for the same number of different candidates, then the one-man, one-vote principle remains unaffected. But as soon as anyone cumulates his votes to a greater degree than others, the one-man, one-vote principle is distorted and a minority can assume power disproportionate to their actual numbers.

Suppose, for example, in that twenty-delegate senatorial district cited above, candidate A runs twenty delegate-candidates (the delegates would be identified as "committed to candidate A") and candidate B runs ten. Suppose candidate A gets nineteen of his supporters to go to the polls, and they vote for each of his twenty delegate-candidates. Each receives nineteen votes. However, candidate B, who is not as popular as candidate A, can convince only ten of his voters to come to the polls. But he instructs those ten voters to cumulate their twenty votes for his delegates and for no others. His ten delegates will receive twenty votes each. Thus, although, in real voter turnout, candidate A beat candidate B by nearly two to one, candidate B's delegate candidates all ran ahead of candidate A's. In other words, while candidate B actually only got 34 percent of the vote, he was able to capture 50 percent of the delegates.

It would be instructive to relate how one young political organizer working for John Lindsay took advantage of this system in the best tradition of the New Politics mixture of brainpower, manpower, and sheer gallpower.

Arthur Kaminsky was a graduate of the Al Lowenstein school of the New Politics. He grew up in Nassau County, Long Island, and worked in Lowenstein's successful congressional campaign in 1968. After graduating from Cornell University in 1968 and Yale Law School in 1971, Kaminsky worked for Lowenstein during the latter's tenure as chairman of the Americans for Democratic Action; it was Kaminsky who coordinated all of Lowenstein's Dump Nixon rallies around the country during 1971.

Kaminsky was sent into Arizona by the Lindsay forces in early January. He quickly understood the advantages the cumulative voting system offered a candidate who needed only a strong showing—not necessarily a win—to give his campaign a lift. His most important decision involved a realistic goal of national convention delegates Lindsay could win and running the smallest number of state convention delegates necessary to meet that goal. He set his goal at five delegates, representing 20 percent of Arizona's twenty-five National Convention delegates, and ninety to a hundred of the five hundred state convention delegates.

"A lot of people in the press simply didn't understand that it was impossible to win more than 50 or 60 percent of the delegates under this system, especially given the fact that the McGovern people were going to single-shot [cumulate] their votes just like us," Kaminsky recalled. "The press' expectations about Muskie's sweeping the primary simply meant they didn't understand the system."

As it happened the Muskie people also appeared to have little grasp of the realities of the system. Kaminsky recalls being utterly incredulous when he learned that the Muskie campaign people were going to run a full slate of delegates—in fact, Muskie's organization had initially filed 587 delegate candidates for only 500 places. Muskie's people had the usual problem of being too top-heavy with party officials who insisted on running as delegates. But Kaminsky dismisses that excuse out of hand, with the impatience of a hard-boiled party professional who knows how to use political muscle when it's necessary. "We had over 240 Lindsay delegates who filed initially, and we just twisted arms until we had the number down to 185, below the total of McGovern's organization" (which filed only 192 delegate candidates).

Next Kaminsky determined how many "single-shot" voters (voters who would agree to cast all their ballots for one Lindsay delegate-candidate) would be necessary to guarantee the election of a Lindsay state convention delegate. Kaminsky turned to Chuck Perry, one of the many young New Politics activists Kaminsky had recruited on short notice to work in the Arizona campaign. Perry, twenty-seven years old, a shrewd political organizer who had formerly worked at the Democratic National Committee, used a rented electronic calculator to calculate what he called a "universal single-shot number"—the number of "single-shot" voters necessary to elect at least one state convention delegate. The "universal single-shot number" would vary proportionally according to the vote turnout, that is, the higher the turnout, the higher the number of "single shots" necessary to assure the election of a state convention delegate. Assuming a turnout of about 10 percent, Perry calculated a "universal single-shot number" of thirty. All of Lindsay's delegate-candidates would win if each of them could find thirty friends who would agree to "single-shot" all their votes.

Among the delegates Kaminsky recruited were the police chief of a small mining town in Southwest Arizona and the student-body presidents of all three state universities and three other junior colleges. "A lot of people forget," Kaminsky observed some months later, "that student-body presidents usually have the best political organization around on campus, and sometimes off campus as well."

In addition, Kaminsky ran as delegate-candidates fourteen members of the Phoenix Chicano organization named Nosotros. This organization had previously been committed to Muskie's candidacy. By the time Kaminsky arrived in Arizona, the Nosotros leaders had become so irritated at the failure of the Muskie managers to give them much attention, especially financial, that Kaminsky was able to take full advantage of the situation. He made the same pitch to the Chicanos as he had to the Muskie-leaning student-body presidents: "Muskie has too many heavies in his campaign who are going to have the first shot at going to the national convention. You guys are going to get shafted by Muskie. If you endorse Lindsay, we'll guarantee you financial help and a slot as a delegate or alternate to the national convention."

Central to Kaminsky's system was an election-day operation efficient enough to keep track of how many votes were being cast for Lindsay delegates throughout the day and disciplined enough to control specific votes at any particular time. Once the totals for a particular candidate reached Chuck Perry's "universal single-shot number," thus ensuring his election, Kaminsky's poll captains would inform subsequent voters to switch their votes to another Lindsay delegate who needed help. Kaminsky printed a set of three-by-five cards instructing voters how they should allocate their votes. Another set of cards had blank spaces to permit Kaminsky and his staff to write in different vote allocation numbers as the day progressed. A table in front of each polling place was manned by Lindsay workers with a sign: "All Lindsay voters report here for instructions before voting."

Kaminsky also distributed to each of the thirty senatorial district coordinators an election-day staff sheet, listing the job responsibilities which had to be filled for the election day operation. These included the "single-shot scribe," responsible for keeping track of the turnout of "single-shot" voters; the "voter adviser," who would "cordially explain how we would like voters to distribute votes"; and a "guide-card noodge," who would hand out the three-by-five-card instructions and, where possible, direct "strays (Lindsay voters who happened to show up at the polls but weren't on anyone's single-shot list) to voter adviser for instruction." An added instruction to the "guide-card noodge" advised, "At all times be as inoffensive as possible."

One of Kaminsky's more creative young staff people, Curt Mead, installed telephones at all of his polling places to keep a running tally of how the votes were coming in and to permit him to make sudden switches in vote allocations. In one instance, when a polling official refused to permit Mead to set up his telephone and table at the polling place, Mead had a telephone installed in a tree. One Lindsay staffer picked up students from Arizona State in buses well supplied with beer and marijuana. Meanwhile, out in the barren wilds of southwest Arizona, another Kaminsky-recruited activist, Mitch Goldman, visited every bar and ranch in sight. It was a tough assignment for a young Jewish boy from Long Island, but somehow Goldman managed to plead, cajole, and bully leading local Democrats and civic leaders to support Lindsay.

The results of the primary more than vindicated Kaminsky's skillful combination of old politics muscle and grease and New Politics activism and creativity. One good example of the operation of the cumulative voting system was senatorial district 23, a wealthy residential area in downtown Phoenix which had thirteen state convention delegates up for election. Muskie ran thirteen candidates, Lindsay and McGovern nine delegates each. One of Muskie's delegates, a candidate for Congress, spent a considerable amount of money on his delegate campaign. He came in first by three times as many votes as he needed; this overkill was a serious hindrance to Muskie, because it deprived other Muskie delegates of votes they needed. The results dramatically show the effects of cumulative voting. Overall (votes cast), Muskie came in first by a large margin, winning 7559 cumulative votes to 4314 for the "uncommitteds," 3883 for McGovern and running last was Lindsay, with 3796 cumulative votes. Yet out of the thirteen state convention delegates in that district, Muskie won only five, Lindsay came in *second* with four, and McGovern won three (the uncommitteds won only a single delegate).

In addition to Kaminsky's organizational techniques, his use of money and media was also important to Lindsay's strong showing in Arizona. Kaminsky spent abour $4400 on billboards throughout Phoenix and Tucson, giving Lindsay, for a modest sum of money, instant visibility and the appearance of an extensive, highly financed political operation. Kaminsky spent about $12,000 on TV and radio ads, which he described as "frosting on the cake." Despite charges by embittered Muskie and McGovern staffers about Lindsay's having spent as much as $50,000 to $75,000 in Arizona, in fact that total was about $20,000 to $25,000, and, as Kaminsky put it, "If all our single-shot voters had showed up, we could have done without most of the media and still done just as well."

The final delegate vote totals statewide gave Muskie 188 delegates (out of 489 candidates); Lindsay, 120 (out of 185); and McGovern, 102 (out of 192). On a proportional basis, Muskie ultimately received nine delegates (out of 25) to the national convention; Lindsay won six (one more than Kaminsky's initial goal); and McGovern, following the same limited strategy as Lindsay, won five delegates.

The McGovern showing in Arizona struck some as disappointing, since it was assumed that McGovern should have beaten at least Lindsay. Actually, McGovern's totals should have been an impressive signal of the kind of grass-roots organization which he and his staff could put together with minimal resources and maximum political handicaps. With Rick Stearns in charge, the Arizona McGovernites, quietly and almost invisibly—without media or billboards, without the high-powered endorsements of the Muskie campaign and the computerized complexity of the Kaminsky operation—held their loyalists together, analyzed the workings of the cumulative voting system accurately, concentrated their votes on each other, and somehow managed to elect five delegates, all, according to Stearns, with a budget of less than $5000.

As in the Iowa caucuses the week before, the results in Arizona bore out the disadvantages of entering the primary season as a front-runner. Expectations that the front-runner will do well lead to expectations by the press that he *must* do well. If he then does less well than predicted, that is news: the front-runner might be slipping. Once a campaign is depicted in the press as "slipping," the description can become a self-fulfilling prophecy, for at a time when presidential campaigns require huge sums of money to remain viable, any reversal in momentum can be fatal.

After the Arizona primary, the press emphasized that Muskie's showing was "disappointing." Some of the political press, such as R. W. Apple of *The New York Times,* misleadingly referred to a combined "44 percent" delegate total for Lindsay and McGovern as evidence of a "potent" bloc of liberal-New Politics Democrats in the Arizona Democratic Party. In the first place, only 15 percent of all registered Arizona Democrats voted.

In addition, subsequent opinion surveys by Harris and Yankelovich indicated that most Lindsay voters preferred Muskie over McGovern.

Given all of Muskie's organizational mistakes, Muskie's showing—winning nearly 40 percent of the delegates—was, as Kaminsky himself pointed out, "quite extraordinary."

. . . .

Florida: Who Lost Worse?

Prior to New Hampshire, Ed Muskie had two major advantages: the national polls showed him to be the front-runner, so he had the air of a winner about him; and the public impression of him remained that of the quiet-spoken, calm, stable man from Maine whose demeanor and style reminded people of Abraham Lincoln.

The newspaper headlines which resulted from the New Hampshire primary destroyed the first advantage, and the Manchester *Union Leader* "crying" incident destroyed the second.

During the week before the New Hampshire primary, Florida newspapers headlined that Muskie was "slipping" and his campaign "deteriorating." Over and over again, headlines bannered Muskie's "sobbing breakdown" and his "emotional display" in front of the *Union Leader*. The day after the New Hampshire primary—March 8—the Florida newspapers described Muskie's 47 percent vote as a severe setback to his campaign.

The quickness of the fall was dizzying for Muskie and his organization. Just two weeks before, Muskie had appeared to be the party's inevitable nominee. Almost overnight, everything seemed to be falling apart. "You had this oppressive sensation of being in the middle of a slide, and you couldn't get out of it," recalls Keith Haller, a Muskie national staff political organizer who was in Florida during the primary. "Once the press gets negative, the people you canvass get negative, then the staff gets negative, then you feel it sagging all around you, and you begin to feel utterly helpless to do anything about it."

The New Hampshire publicity only added to Muskie's formidable problems in Florida. Underlying all of them was the cross-fire phenomenon. George Wallace, running hard on the busing issue, was clearly far out in front. Senator Henry Jackson of Washington picked up strength by attacking Muskie not only on his pro-busing stand but, in the central Florida area, where the aerospace industry is strong, for his announced opposition to the space shuttle.

Meanwhile, the liberal–New Politics forces, largely centered around the Miami area in the south and the Gainesville (University of Florida) area in the north, continued to attack Muskie from the left. At an appearance at the University of Florida in Gainesville, Muskie was cross-examined by a small group of McGovern supporters for close to an hour on his positions on amnesty, abortion, and marijuana.

Muskie's positions on the issues may have been sharply defined—to his detriment—as far as the conservatives in Florida were concerned. But, for the large number of middle-of-the-road, less issue-oriented voters in Florida, Muskie's inability during 1971 to develop a personal identity associated with some important issue proved to be very damaging.

The beneficiary of that fudgy Muskie image was Hubert Humphrey. Ironically, Humphrey's position on the issues was far less defined than Muskie's. He seemed to be both for and against busing, depending on which audience he was talking to. He was in favor of the space shuttle, but he was in favor of "reordering our priorities." However, where Humphrey stood on the issues was less important than the intense loyalty felt toward him among his constituents—blacks, Jews, senior citizens, and labor. All of these groups—especially the first three—were concentrated in significant numbers in many of Florida's cities, especially Miami, Tampa, St. Petersburg, and Jacksonville. As soon as Humphrey declared his candidacy, these middle-of-the-road voters were in his corner, blocked off from Muskie.

Meanwhile, John Lindsay was waging what his strategists thought was a classic New Politics campaign—combining hard, tough stands on the issues with a sophisticated blitz of television and radio spots which sold Lindsay's shirt-sleeved, blond-haired charisma. The Lindsay Florida managers kept leaking stories to the press that Lindsay would "surprise" everyone, that he was "moving fast and might even win it all." In mid-January *The New York Times* ran a news analysis which concluded that Lindsay was the man to watch in Florida.

The Lindsay Florida campaign was a classic case of the "advance man" mentality which afflicted all of us in the New Politics more than we cared to admit. Two key Lindsay aides, Jeff Greenfield and Jerry Bruno, had coauthored a book entitled *The Advance Man* and had written a last chapter entitled "Lindsay Will Beat Nixon in 1972." The theory was that Lindsay's charisma would carry him over the top. "The press sees crowds . . . [and] the crowds sense that they're part of something exciting and important," Greenfield and Bruno wrote. "And that's what goes on the TV and in the press while the intellectuals debate the last sentence on the first page of the speech. But the average voter, he sees excitement and enthusiasm, and *that's* what he wants to be part of."

Lindsay's campaign, both in Florida and later on in Wisconsin, showed that most voters needed more than that to be won over. Lindsay had two major political problems in Florida which neither he nor his advisers understood until the end of his campaign. First, people thought his probusing stand was not only wrong but hypocritical. "It burns me up to see that man come down to Florida and tell me to bus my kids while he's put his own kids in private schools back in New York," one lady from the Miami area told me in late January, echoing a comment I must have heard fifteen or twenty times. One also heard repeated references to the effect that "Lindsay can't even run New York City. How's he going to run the country?"

Meanwhile, George McGovern had told the press that he didn't consider Florida important, thereby wisely discounting from the beginning the effects of a poor showing. He spent one or two campaign days in the state in the week before the primary, but concentrated his energies in Illinois and Wisconsin. The McGovern organization in Florida, meanwhile, was frantically organizing the small bloc of liberal activists who, they hoped, would at least be large enough to come in ahead of John Lindsay.

The final results on March 14 had Muskie running a weak fourth, with 9 percent—behind Wallace's 42 percent, Humphrey's 18, and Senator Henry Jackson, who ran strongly in military and aerospace areas, coming in third with 13 percent. Lindsay's weak fifth-place showing—at 7 percent—was at least larger than McGovern's sixth-place showing of less than 6 percent.

Understandably the press zeroed in on Muskie as the big loser, and totally ignored McGovern. And why not? Muskie's people had been projecting Florida as an easy win through 1971. After Wallace came in, they increased their efforts and talked about a strong second-place finish. When the returns were in, the press reported Muskie's "lack of political appeal," and more and more journalists projected his imminent demise.

The day after the Florida primary, *The New York Times* published a poll taken by Daniel Yankelovich Associates as voters were leaving the election booths throughout the state. Each voter was asked to vote for president in a series of contests between Richard Nixon and each of the Democratic candidates. The results should have stunned the news media: *The only candidate who beat Richard Nixon in the poll was Ed Muskie!* The meaning was clear: In a multicandidate primary, where voters could "message" vote their personal preferences, Muskie ran poorly; but when it came time to vote for president, Muskie had far more support against Richard Nixon among the supporters of the other candidates than anyone else.

Muskie's speech denouncing the Wallace victory on the evening of the Florida primary added a third negative impression of him in the mind of the general public: not only was he overly emotional and a loser, he was also an overly emotional sore loser. Before Muskie went down to face the television cameras, one of his top aides, Mark Shields, urged him to be magnanimous and to focus everyone's attention on the Illinois primary the following week. As Muskie recalls it, as he walked up to the microphone he still didn't know what he was going to say. But, the more he spoke, the angrier he seemed to get. "What disturbs me," he said, "is that Wallace's victory reveals to a greater extent than I had imagined that some of the worst instincts of which human beings are capable have too strong an influence on our elections."

It was not only a petulant remark; it was an arrogant one—for it said that 42 percent of the people who had voted in the Democratic primary had done so for racist reasons. And it totally misread the deeper issues of alienation and voter frustration with establishment politics which gave Wallace an appeal far beyond the racial issue.

In retrospect, Muskie regretted the speech. "It probably was too harsh an attack," he said glumly some time later. "It presented too one-sided a characterization of the Wallace campaign. His campaign in Florida had a broader ideological base than just the race question. He was talking about the tax issue, the responsiveness-of-government issue, as well as the busing issue."

Interestingly, Muskie's explanation of why he made the speech was strikingly similar to the one offered concerning the *Union Leader* incident: his sensitivity to assertions by New Politics liberals and the press that he lacked passion, that he was unwilling to "break a lance" on an issue.

Illinois and Wisconsin: From One-on-one to the Cross Fire

By March 15, the day after the Florida primary, Muskie headed for the March 21 Illinois primary, a totally debilitated candidate. His campaign seemed to be falling apart, with squabbling among his top political staff, money running out, and a stream of negative commentary about him in the national and local press. To add to the atmosphere of deterioration and disarray, Berl Bernhard, the campaign manager, announced the day after the Florida primary that the staff would be going off the payroll indefinitely.

A comparison between Muskie's showing in the March 21 Illinois primary and in the April 4 Wisconsin primary, and the contrasting treatment accorded by the news media to these two primaries, holds the key to an understanding of why Muskie lost the nomination in 1972.

In the Illinois primary, Muskie defeated George McGovern overwhelmingly, winning 62 delegates to McGovern's 15, despite the fact that McGovern had predicted he would win at least 30 delegates. Two weeks later, in Wisconsin, Muskie came in a weak fourth, winning just nine percent of the vote.

The same Muskie ran in both primaries. The difference was that in Illinois Muskie was running against only one candidate, while in Wisconsin, he was in the political cross fire of a multicandidate winner-take-all primary.

Of course, all of the mistakes which Muskie and his political organization had made in the course of the campaign contributed to his early downfall—his lack of identity or association with an issue or set of issues; the overemphasis on political endorsements and a top-heavy Washington national staff at the expense of grass-roots state organizations; his failure to be more selective about which states should be emphasized; and, especially, the decision to go in front of the *Union Leader* and the anti-Wallace speech after the Florida primary. But these mistakes hurt his candidacy in Illinois just as they did in Wisconsin.

First, a few words about the Illinois system for selecting national convention delegates. Here, delegates ran in each congressional district directly in an open primary. Their names—and the names of the candidates they supported—were listed directly on the ballot (or they were listed as "uncommitted," if that was the case). The top vote-getters were elected, up to the number of delegates to which that district was entitled. There was also a statewide nonbinding presidential "preference" primary in which voters could cast their ballots directly for a presidential candidate. There is simply no justification for this dual system of electing delegates directly plus a nonbinding preferential contest, for it permits one candidate to run in the congressional districts and not in the preference contest. This is actually what happened in Illinois. McGovern, not wanting to split up the liberal vote with Eugene McCarthy, who was committed to run on the preference line, had at least an implicit agreement with McCarthy: McGovern ran delegates in the congressional districts and McCarthy ran only in the preference contest, supporting McGovern's delegates.

I arrived in Illinois about four weeks before the primary to coordinate Muskie's campaign for the 21st Congressional District. At that point, Muskie had absolutely no local political organization. Few people knew where he stood on any issue, and after the *Union Leader* incident, the voters we canvassed asked, "How come he cried like that up there in New Hampshire?"

Meanwhile, McGovern had had a functioning grass-roots organization for at least six months and had completed a full canvass of Democratic voters in Champaign-Urbana, the largest city in the district, with twice as many Democratic votes as any other city.

In Illinois, however, Humphrey, Jackson, Wallace and Lindsay voters were supporting Muskie over McGovern. We had no trouble building a political organization for Muskie in a very short time. A week after we arrived in Champaign-Urbana, we had published full-page advertisements in the Champaign and Bloomington newspapers of a "Citizens Committee" for Muskie which included representatives of every major interest group in the district: students, party regulars, reformers, farmers, businessmen, lawyers, organized labor. A week later we sent out a personal letter from Muskie to all registered Democrats in the district asking them to vote for all six of his delegates.

In Champaign, the Democratic Party was split, with a "reform" organization in power that had defeated the party regulars the previous year. At meetings of both the reform organization and the regulars, I found considerable support for the Muskie campaign. Meanwhile, the McGovern organization was totally confined to the academic-student constituencies surrounding the University of Illinois and Illinois State University. The McGovern organizer in Champaign rarely even showed up at the meetings of the party regulars or of local farm groups.

In Decatur, the third largest city of the district, with a large population of blue-collar workers and no major college or university, the McGovern campaign had almost no organization at all. After a few days of negotiations, the Decatur Democratic organization agreed to support four Muskie delegates out of a total of six running in the district. This meant that the party precinct workers would distribute sample ballots with four Muskie delegates marked off as endorsed by the organization. The other two delegates supported by the Decatur regulars were two uncommitted labor leaders who leaned to Humphrey. We agreed not to open a separate campaign headquarters in Decatur and, while we insisted on the right to do a mailing pushing all six Muskie delegates, we agreed not to "oppose" the two uncommitted candidates in speeches and campaign literature.

The McGovern Illinois campaign manager had predicted that their only safe district was this particular congressional district—the 21st—on the assumption that the heavy student population at the University of Illinois and Illinois State would turn out heavily for McGovern and put his six delegates over. The McGovern campaign had registered more than 3500 students at the University of Illinois alone and, as it happened, turned out almost all of them to vote for McGovern in margins as high as ten to one.

Despite that vote margin, the Muskie campaign organization did make an extensive effort on the campuses to challenge McGovern's student support. We spoke in classes, at fraternities, and at sororities, wrote articles for the campus newspaper, debated leaders of the McGovern organization on all-night student radio programs. And for the first time since I had been in the Muskie campaign, we put out anti-McGovern literature, citing McGovern's past votes in favor of the war (the Gulf of Tonkin resolution and war appropriations) and asking whether McGovern had the right to say he was "right from the start."

The McGovern organizers were livid at the literature. When McGovern appeared at the University of Illinois a few days before the primary, he also denounced any criticisms of his record on the war and went on to assert that Muskie's foreign-policy views were indistinguishable from those of the then hawkish Senator Jackson.

McGovern denounced Muskie throughout Illinois for failing to meet the quotas on young people, women, and minorities which, he said, were required by the Reform Commission. McGovern never reminded people about the footnote which he himself had inserted in the Reform Commission report forswearing the imposition of quotas. Nor did he point out that in Illinois the candidate has no control over the makeup of the individual congressional district delegation.

The returns on election night in Illinois's 21st C.D. showed McGovern with a 3000 to 4000 vote margin in Champaign County—a direct result of the heavy student vote from the University of Illinois. But Muskie delegates carried the other five counties of the district—including McClean, which included Bloomington, the site of Illinois State University (Muskie ran even with McGovern among the students at Illinois State, who were largely from blue-collar and farming families). When I went to bed on election night, I assumed that McGovern had won all six delegates in the district. I couldn't conceive that Muskie would be able to make up the margin he had lost to McGovern in Champaign County. The next morning at six o'clock, I got a call from the local McGovern campaign director. "I still can't believe it, but Muskie's won two delegates and he's not far from winning four."

In fact, the two Muskie delegates who ran seventh and eighth—just out of the money—were fewer than 500 and 1000 votes, respectively, behind the last two elected McGovern delegates. And, as it turned out, if the Decatur Democratic organization hadn't spread its votes for six delegates among eight candidates (the six Muskie delegates plus the two uncommitteds), Muskie would probably have won all six delegates handily.

Throughout the rest of Illinois, Muskie's delegates swept McGovern slates by wide margins, with the same phenomenon repeating itself: McGovern won the hard core of New Politics activists and liberal intellectuals, and Muskie picked up all the rest of the Democratic vote. Although McGovern hadn't run in the separate preference primary—a direct vote for president that had no legally binding effect on the delegates—Eugene McCarthy had. There was almost a direct one-to-one correlation between people who voted for McGovern delegates and people who voted for McCarthy over Muskie, as can be seen by comparing McGovern's local delegate totals to McCarthy's popular vote totals in the same district. Muskie's margin over McCarthy—65 to 35—probably represented a relatively accurate breakdown of a Muskie-McGovern popular vote contest, had it taken place.

Despite this impressive win by Muskie in the Illinois primary, much of the news media gave it scant attention in the next day's newspapers. In fact, the Illinois primary was the great nonevent of the 1972 campaign. One explanation once again relates to the expectations associated with a front-runner. It was widely assumed that Muskie would have no trouble beating McGovern in Illinois. This sentiment was apparently shared by McGovern's staffers. Frank Mankiewicz began to suspect Illinois would be a disaster and, a few days before the primary, made excessively pessimistic predictions and dismissed the importance of the primary. Given these expectations, Muskie's victory could hardly have been treated as important news.

Another explanation for the downplaying of the Illinois results was that, as in Arizona, much of the press simply didn't understand the new realities and procedures within the Democratic Party. Most reporters viewed the Illinois primary as a contest between Muskie and McCarthy;

and, of course, McCarthy couldn't be taken seriously. There were two serious fallacies in that analysis. First, as indicated above, there was just about a one-to-one correlation between McCarthy's preference votes and McGovern's delegate votes; second, there was in fact little distinction, as a test of political strength, between delegate contests, where the delegates are clearly labeled on the ballots as committed to their respective candidates, and the Wisconsin type of primary, where voters vote for the candidates directly. Moreover, few in the press seemed to appreciate fully that the McGovern organization had conducted an active, energetic grass-roots effort and that McGovern had spent at least as much—and probably more—campaign time in Illinois as Muskie. Yet, he could do no better than to win fifteen delegates.

A crucial misconception of the news media which hurt Muskie more than the other candidates was that, somehow, a multicandidate primary was a better test of strength than a one-on-one contest. Thus, a lot of reporters dismissed Illinois because the other candidates, like Humphrey and Wallace, weren't competing. In fact, a head-to-head contest gives a clear indication of the relative strength of each candidate across a broad cross section of the party and hence, a much better indication about relative political strength in the general election. In that sense, one could argue that the news media should have focused on Illinois as a crucial contest between McGovern and Muskie, with the leadership of the liberal wing of the party at stake.

CHAPTER 8

At the Convention

A. Bargaining at National Party Conventions

B. The Delegates and the Character of Convention Representation

·A·

Bargaining at National Party Conventions

The Battle of Mississippi

BY JULES WITCOVER

For the last ten years, when anybody in the Republican Party wanted anything done in Mississippi, there was one man and one man only to go to: Clarke Reed, the forty-eight-year-old state party chairman. Tall and wiry, with square, clean-cut features topped by an impressive silver-white mane that belied his otherwise youthful appearance, Reed was right out of some Hollywood casting director's dream of the political operator. He was slick and so fast-talking as to be almost incomprehensible. On top of that he was a whisperer; he liked to pull people aside and exchange confidences mouth-to-ear. He was Byzantine in style, and consumed with the intricacies of politics. He was consumed also, to his ultimate misfortune, with a desire to be always on the winning side, to hold on to power and influence—which after ten years had extended far beyond Mississippi in Republican ranks. He was chairman of the Southern Republican State Chairmen's Association and as such the Dixie GOP's leading *apparatchik* in the pulling-and-hauling to get a better deal for the South during the Nixon and Ford administrations. And a better deal to Clarke Reed got down primarily to having the feds get off the South's back—whether in the field of civil rights or education or any number of social-welfare impositions dictated from Washington.

At the White House, during the Nixon years particularly, it was customary in any major political decision affecting the Deep South to "clear it with Clarke," or at least to touch base with him. When you said "Clarke" you didn't have to provide any further identification; it was a sign of Reed's eminence that must have been particularly pleasing. But as the

Jules Witcover, *Marathon: The Pursuit of the Presidency, 1972–1976* (New York: Viking Press, 1977), pp. 471–483. Footnotes deleted. Copyright © 1977 by Jules Witcover. Reprinted by permission of Viking Penguin Inc.

presidential election year opened in 1976, the assumption at the White House and in Republican circles generally was that Clarke Reed would be with Ronald Reagan and so, undoubtedly, would the Mississippi delegation. The Ford people did not have to know that he had been one of the earliest proponents of a Reagan candidacy back in the spring of 1975, when the nucleus of the embryo Reagan staff met in Los Angeles to lay the groundwork; they, and the world, knew enough about his ideology to guess he would be a Reagan man. He was and always had been a True Believer in conservative positions, foreign and domestic, and he liked to think and say that he acted out of ideological conviction. But the truth was that Clarke Reed's strongest ideological conviction was that the causes in which he believed were best served if he ran with a winner, if he could retain power.

Another motivation, however, beat strongly in Clarke Reed's breast. That was an instinct for self-preservation. After the 1975 gubernatorial election, in which the Republican candidate, Gil Carmichael, ran an unexpectedly strong race and emerged as a new power in the state party, people said Clarke's days were numbered as Mississippi's unchallenged Republican boss. And when he suddenly disclosed that he would not seek another term as state chairman but would only stay on as Mississippi's member of the Republican National Committee, some speculated that he was merely facing the inevitable. Reed himself insisted he could have been reelected chairman unopposed, but that he had had enough. At any rate, Charles Pickering, a young state senator with his eye on the governorship, was elected Reed's successor. It was agreed that Pickering would not take over until after the national convention, where Reed would have his last hurrah.

The state convention was held unusually early, in April, to take advantage, Reed said later, of the enthusiasm brought to the party by Carmichael's close race. He wanted, he said, to enlist much of the new talent that had been recruited during that campaign. No thought at all was given to the question of whether those who wanted to be delegates to the national convention were for Ford or Reagan. And in that nonchalance lay the roots of all the turmoil that was to follow.

The new recruits tended on the whole to be younger and more moderate than the old group headed by Reed, and at the state convention many of them were elected as alternates, which in Mississippi was almost as good as being a principal delegate. The state convention continued a long-time policy whereby each of its thirty delegates and thirty alternates would have one-half a vote on issues before the delegation, with the unit rule—the majority getting all thirty votes—applying unless specifically rescinded by a majority vote of the sixty. So although no candidate preference was asked or stated at the time, the climate for the later blossoming of Ford support within this supposedly solid, conservative delegation was enhanced by the procedure that gave the more moderate alternates a vote.

In planning the state convention, Reed explained later, it was decided that party service would be rewarded and candidate preference at the national convention "would not be as important, because the nomination would be settled by the time we got there." If the Ford-Reagan competition were not decided in the primaries by April, everybody thought, it would be soon thereafter, and so Mississippi would have no real choice in determining the party standard-bearer anyway. With this prospect in mind, it was agreed also that the delegation would go to Kansas City uncommitted. There, the unit rule would be observed, casting Mississippi's thirty votes for whichever candidate had eliminated the other in the primaries. "The argument of who anybody was for really never came up because under the unit rule, we always felt we'd come out reflecting the state position," Reed said. To keep peace, individuals favoring the President were placed on the delegation with known Reagan backers, who were in the clear majority.

Reagan's campaign in Mississippi, led rather casually at the beginning by Billy Mounger, an ace fund-raiser for the party, went along, Reed said, on the theory, "Don't worry about Mississippi, it's a Deep South state." David Keene, Reagan's Southern coordinator, said later, however, that while it was true his side was not concerned about Mississippi in the early stages, the reason was that Reed had pledged his own support and guaranteed the state would be with Reagan if he were at all in contention at the national convention. Keene had been recruited by John Sears at least in part because he was an old and good friend of Reed's. "I think one of the reasons John wanted me at the outset," Keene said, "was because he figured I could probably handle Clarke a little better than some people. Clarke committed to me early, but that was an easy commitment for him to make: he thought at the time that it was going to be over quickly one way or the other, and so did we. He said, 'I'll deliver Mississippi to you unless it's a joke, unless you've completely lost it by then.' I said, 'Look, I won't ask you then, but if I ask you, you've got to deliver.' He said, 'Fine.' "

Keene, as a one-time aide to Vice President Spiro Agnew and Senator James Buckley of New York, was one of the most effective young operatives in the conservative wing of the Republican Party. He had dealt closely with Reed for six or eight years and he knew his man. He knew that the idea of Reed as some latter-day Machiavelli was off-target, in fact exactly contrary to reality. "Clarke is not an evil guy," Keene said later. "He's weak. He's a guy whose reputation was made in part out of whole cloth. He's brighter than most of the people on the national committee; he's good copy, so the press like him; he's good at maneuvering to some extent, although not as good as he thinks he is. But his reputation was made fighting Nelson Rockefeller and Jacob Javits, and that doesn't take any courage, not if you're from Mississippi. You're rather expected to do that. He hadn't been in many battles where it was really tough. He had this feeling always that he should never lose, that you should never get into a thing where you're really tested because you might come out on the wrong side. So he took this assumption that this was going to be an easy one, because it was going to be over one way or the other. And when it came time to put together the delegation, he thought it didn't really matter. If it was going to be over, there wasn't going to be any trouble delivering it to whoever the winner was. And therefore they could remain neutral, and Clarke would get all the credit one way, or get the credit the other way for not coming out, and deliver his thirty votes to the guy who won. The worst thing that happened to Clarke Reed in his entire career was the fact that it wasn't over early. Because he then discovered that he put his delegation together in the sloppiest manner imaginable, that he had trouble on both sides, that he couldn't deliver it—at least to the extent that he thought he could. That was not a result of deviousness. That was a result of weakness, and a result of trying to please everybody."

Patching together a mixed delegation was a typical hedge for Reed, who felt he could always control it for Reagan by using the unit rule. "I kept badgering him, 'You know, Clarke, you'd better be sure of these people,'" Keene said. "And he'd say, 'Oh, don't worry about it.' Well, he eventually had as much to worry about as we did."

In the interest of having all segments of the state party leadership represented, the delegation that everyone assumed was for Reagan included Carmichael, who was very pro-Ford, and Douglas Shanks, a twenty-nine-year-old Jackson city commissioner, who was head of what passed for a Ford campaign in the state. It turned out to be, in due time, like boarding a couple of vampires at a blood bank. Carmichael and Shanks together would eventually start preying on the other members of the delegation in Ford's behalf, in direct challenge to Reed's leadership, and with telling effect.

Reed insisted later that from the time of the state convention at which he constructed this Trojan Horse delegation until late June or early July, there really was no Reagan organization in Mississippi. He said he warned the Reagan people in Washington and in the state that "this thing may get a little tight." But the Reagan camp denied that he had ever done so.

Meanwhile Shanks and Carmichael were having troubles of their own persuading the President Ford Committee in Washington that there was any constructive business to be done in Mississippi. Reagan had upset the President in North Carolina and was running his string of victories through Texas, Alabama, and Georgia, and the Ford strategists were wondering whether they were wasting time and money trying to win more delegates in the South. It was decided, in fact, to cut back the Southern field operations (run under the direction of Governor Holshouser of North Carolina), and in late May the Ford committee turned to that old Dixie political warhorse, Harry Dent, to be a kind of one-man overseer in the South.

Back in the lucrative practice of law in Columbia, South Carolina, after his somewhat frustrating years as Nixon's political adviser in the White House, Dent resisted for a time but finally acceded. He was in the soup politically, anyway, having bucked the efforts of his own governor, James Edwards, to engineer a solid Reagan slate, and getting himself elected as an uncommitted delegate. His efforts for Ford really began one day after the closing down of the Ford field office, when he received a phone call that in a sense was the first, unheard shot in the 1976 battle of Mississippi.

Dent's caller was John Davis, a twenty-nine-year-old Ole Miss graduate who had worked in Carmichael's campaign and had just been laid off with the closing of the Ford Southern field office. Dent had asked that Davis be assigned to him but the Washington office said the campaign couldn't afford him. "Harry," Davis said, "I want to see this campaign through. I can go get a job but I'd rather do this. If you'll just feed me, I'll help you."

Dent, his hands more than full with his law practice and already working every night and weekend for Ford, readily agreed. "I took him into my home," Dent recounted, "and he just lived with me. He went to work with me every day and I set him up in my law office. He went everywhere with my family, just like another son."

And that was how Dent got onto the opportunity in Mississippi. "Harry," young Davis told him, "there's gold to be mined in Mississippi." Davis was aware of the inclinations of Carmichael and Shanks, and of the vulnerability of the delegation as constituted under Reed's misguided plan for party unity. Shanks was beginning to suggest that he for one would not go along with the unit rule, a position that provided the first crack in what had been expected to be unanimity for Reagan among Mississippi's thirty delegates. With the thirty delegates and thirty alternates each having one-half a vote on issues before the delegation, it would take a vote of 31–29 to break the unit rule. Shanks could be the tip of an iceberg that could sink Reagan's campaign.

Dent, who had been through all the civil-rights wars with Reed and had observed that since his own departure from the White House Reed had not gotten quite the same kid-glove treatment, knew how to approach him. He called his old friend and told him, half-joking, that he had wisely "put himself in the catbird seat." "I told him, 'Clarke, you're gonna be the kingmaker of this convention.'" Ford had taken a beating all over the South, except in Florida, and the die was cast for Reagan except among pockets of uncommitted delegates, the largest of which was in Mississippi. It was a golden opportunity for Clarke Reed to come to the rescue of the President, and put the South back into the front ranks of influence in the White House.

Dent was a great needler, and an entertaining storyteller and mimic. At an outing in mid-June held for the Southern state party chairmen by Governor Holshouser at Atlantic Beach, North Carolina, he started working on Reed openly, half-kidding him about being "kingmaker" in front of the other state chairmen, most of whom had backed Ford and lost in their states.

"Now, Clarke," he would say in soothing, fatherly tones, "I want to tell you the updated version of the parable of the talents. Now, just imagine. After Ford's won this nomination, and we're sitting around the big table carving up the pie. There's Rosey Rosenbaum sitting up there at the head of the table, where he belongs. Boy, he's really been delivering, and holding every time he delivers. And the President's gonna turn to Rosey and say, 'Well done, thy good and faithful servant. Thou hast five talents and thou has increased them five-fold. Therefore, thou hast twenty-five votes at this table.'

"And, Clarke, then he's gonna look down and he's gonna see me sitting at the other end, at the foot of the table. And he's gonna say, 'Well done, thy good and faithful servant Harry Dent. Thou wast entrusted with one talent and thou increased it onefold. Therefore, thou hast two votes at the table.'

"So there we are. Old Rosey Rosenbaum, the new king of the Republican Party. The new Northeastern strategy is gonna be put into effect. There's gonna be ol' Harry. Strom Thurmond [supporting Reagan] isn't gonna be there. Clarke Reed ain't gonna be there.

"But, Clarke, baby, you got thirty pieces of silver you can walk in there and throw on that table. Those thirty pieces of silver, in a timely fashion, would cover those twenty-five talents that Rosey had on the table. Then I could just see you coming in there, and the President could say, 'Well done, thy good and faithful servant Clarke.' And he could put you at the head of the table and put Rosey at the foot of the table. The Southern Strategy would prevail again. Long live the king!"

Reed protested that he didn't want to be a kingmaker, but he was listening. Dent started calling him "the reluctant kingmaker" in the presence of the other state chairmen and even sometimes before Dave Keene, who was keeping the heat on Reed from the other side. But it was Dent who had Reed's ear constantly. "I tried to explain to him this would be great for Mississippi, this would be great for the South; that the South had short-changed the President in those primaries and state conventions, and the Clarke would not only be the kingmaker for Ford but the savior of the South and the Southern Strategy."

Luckily for Dent, also present at the Holshouser outing were the two heavies of the Ford campaign, Dick Cheney and Stu Spencer. Dent had known Cheney at the White House and took the opportunity to inform him at length about the possibilities for Ford in Mississippi. As an old White House political hand, Dent knew where the power lay. Up to now, according to Dent later, the PFC had been cool to spending much time or money on Mississippi, finding it hard to believe anything constructive could be achieved there, and generally brushing aside the efforts of Carmichael and Shanks. But Dent successfully got Cheney's ear, even flying back to Washington with him after the weekend to press his case.

Shortly thereafter, John Davis went by the White House to see Dr. Richard Brannon, formerly Dent's minister. Brannon had been taken on, Dent said, as "Mr. Southern Comfort" with Elliot Richardson at HEW, "to hold the South's hand while they desegregated the schools," and later was transferred to the White House. Davis showed Brannon a list of potential Ford delegates and alternates in Mississippi. Brannon was so impressed that he took him immediately to see Cheney, and one of his assistants, Jim Field. Cheney was interested, but the PFC continued to object, partly because Dent, Davis, and Carmichael were working with Cheney at the White House. A jurisdictional tug-of-war ensued.

Finally Rogers Morton at the PFC phoned Dent. "Look," he said firmly, according to Dent, "play this game right. Quit dealing with the White House. We're the ones responsible for Mississippi."

To which Dent replied: "If Cheney calls me, as long as the White House calls me, I'm gonna talk to them."

Dent told Cheney about all of this, and Cheney in turn advised Morton that he was taking a special interest in Mississippi. The Cheney-Dent conversations continued.

Meanwhile Dent and Davis were working the state through Carmichael and Shanks. As it became clearer and clearer that Ford would be crowding the 1130-delegate mark, they began agitating in mid-July for a big push to rally Ford support and possibly steal the state's 30 delegates out from under Reagan—and Reed. "We had goose egg in our column on Mississippi," Dent said, talking of the delegate count. "We'd been just sitting there all this time, just shy of enough votes for the newspapers and wire services to say Ford was over the top. It was all part of the psychological warfare thing, and Reagan had these thirty votes listed in his column. What I was trying to do was take the thirty out of the Reagan column and put them in the Ford column, which would mean a change of sixty votes. Whenever that was accomplished, it was going to be the end of Ronald Reagan. We were going to give them to the President and suggest he walk out to the Rose Garden and say 'There it is.' "

The key to engineering this big switch, as Harry Dent believed all along, was "the reluctant kingmaker"—Clarke Reed. Dent continued working on him, enlisting even the President himself to try to shake him loose. One day in July, during a Republican party meeting, Reed and Charles Pickering, as the incoming state chairman, were among a group of party functionaries invited to a White House reception—a happenstance that Dent, the old White House operator, seized with alacrity. Knowing

Reed's insecurity, Dent engaged him in conversation while awaiting the President's arrival, and meanwhile Cheney took Pickering into the Oval Office for a forty-five-minute conversation with Ford. "When it came time for the President to come in," Dent recalled later, "who comes walking in with him but Charles Pickering! He was about ten feet high. This was his first treatment like this.

"Well, Clarke's sitting in the big room there, and he sees Charles Pickering walk in. So, in the course of the reception, I grab Dick Cheney and I tell him, 'Now we take Clarke in.' And Cheney said, 'Okay.' The President was plugged in by Cheney and me. He knew what we were doing. So Cheney says, 'As soon as this is over, the President and I will be sitting in the Oval Office. You bring Clarke.' Well, Jim Field escorted us from the Lincoln Room, and Clarke says, 'Where we going, cat?' and I said, 'Oh, come on, cat, you gonna get the biggest stroking job you ever seen in your life. We're gonna *make* you the kingmaker whether you want to be or not.' Well, we take him in there, and we have an hour with him—the President, Dick and me."

Dent made all the arguments again for joining Ford, including of course the talents story. And the President, knowing Reed's feelings about ideological purity, assured him he would pick as a running mate somebody philosophically in tune with himself.

Even after this presidential massage, though, Reed was hanging back. Dent stepped up the good-natured—but purposeful—ribbing. "The train's pulling out," he would say to Reed in front of his colleagues.

"Don't give me that," Reed would answer, "that's not gonna work."

Dent kept telling him anyway. But he was not eternally patient. "Doug Shanks kept saying to me, 'Man, you're never gonna get through to Pickering and Clarke. They're both committed.'" So Dent finally told Cheney that he was worn out cajoling Reed, listening to his gripes about the voting-rights act and such. "I'm going to the delegates and alternates now," he said, "and when I do, it's gonna make Clarke mad. But if we keep sticking with Clarke and Pickering, in the end we're probably gonna end up with nothing."

Cheney was close to being convinced now that Mississippi could be fertile ground for Ford. Nose-counting in the delegation by Dent, Davis, Carmichael, and Shanks indicated that with Reagan's prospects for the nomination cloudy at best, there were more than twenty half-votes for Ford already of the thirty-one half-votes needed to gain control. But in light of the PFC's reluctance, something more was needed to trigger the kind of White House offensive they believed was required, and warranted. Dent pleaded that an energetic drive for Mississippi, if nothing else, made tactical sense. "If we don't do anything else but tie the Reagan forces down in Mississippi, in a place they've already got," Dent told Cheney, "then we will have accomplished a tremendous amount."

To strengthen Cheney's hand, and to persuade PFC, Dent, Carmichael, and the others hit on a scheme that would also pressure the Mississippi delegates and alternates to climb aboard Ford's bandwagon. Without informing Reed, the four Ford men began calling delegates and alternates, with Carmichael telling them he had nearly enough votes to swing the delegation for Ford. Carmichael's pitch went like this: "I've got thirty votes committed to the President, and we just need yours to put him over. Yours will be the thirty-first. You can give the President the nomination." He then would ask the individual to send a telegram to the White House inviting the President to Mississippi, to prove that the Ford strength was there. The effort was surprisingly successful; Dent said later they had commitments from twenty-seven delegates or alternates and were pushing hard for the other four needed when Clarke Reed got wind of the maneuver.

"He went through the ceiling," Dent said later. "And so did Pickering, because we were going around them to their troops, and they wanted to be the brokers. They got on the phone and they stopped it."

Reed was, indeed, livid. "By God, Carmichael was not telling the truth [on having thirty half-votes]. But he had in the low twenties, and that scared the fool out of me." So Reed called Billy Mounger, the head of Reagan's delegation in the state, and told him, " 'Look, this guy's conning everybody.' But Billy told me, 'Well, I got a tennis tournament this week.' So help me." Reed as delegation and state chairman was trying to stay neutral, but he was so outraged by Carmichael's telephone calls, and so frustrated by Mounger's tennis tournament, that he moved in. This effort by Reed to save the situation for Reagan was largely overlooked in the vitriol heaped upon him later. Together with Pickering, Reed called a meeting of the full delegation, at which he planned to confront the Carmichael gambit and remind the delegation of its vow to go to Kansas City uncommitted. He obviously hoped for a strong reaction against Carmichael's audacious move.

But there was some question later about Reed's motivation: Was it essentially an effort to save the delegation for Reagan? Or was it a reflexive reaction to a challenge against his already waning power in the state and party delegation? Some, including Keene, professed to have seen signs for weeks that Reed himself had been influenced by the over-all race after the primaries and final state conventions. "He began to hedge," Keene recalled. "I never counted more than twenty-five [full] votes [for Reagan], because I knew Doug Shanks and Gil Carmichael were going to break, and probably a couple of others were going to go with them, even under the unit rule. But I didn't realize that we had real trouble until Clarke started to waver personally. He concluded after the primaries that we weren't going to win. And at that point he couldn't go to Ford. He's a man of his word; he hates to give his word, but he isn't gonna just flat-out lie to you, or break it. So he began looking for a way out. And in the absence of that, he began giving out stories like, 'Yeah, most of our guys are for Reagan, but Reagan can't win,' which was hurting us not so much in the South but everywhere else. People began telling us, 'You can't even hold your own people.' "

And indeed this kind of slippage was causing great troubles in Reagan's campaign outside of Mississippi, and forcing the master strategist John Sears to cast about for a stopper. For the time being, though, whatever his motivation, Reed was undeniably helping Reagan's cause by blowing the whistle on the Carmichael telegram scheme.

As soon as Reed scheduled the delegation meeting, Dent asked for a chance to address the group. Reed readily agreed. Dent urged Cheney to come, too, so as to provide the strongest possible evidence of President Ford's own interest, and to do some person-to-person persuading. According to Dent, the PFC balked at even this show of White House clout, for fear that the delegation might in some way rebuff Ford—a risk to be avoided in the continuing psychological warfare. But Dent prevailed on Cheney and, together with Field, he flew to Jackson on Sunday afternoon, July 25, for the delegation meeting at the Ramada Inn, just minutes from the airport.

By now news stories had appeared about Carmichael's bold move to steal the delegation out from under Reagan, and television and newspaper reporters from around the country converged on the motel. Everybody knew that if Mississippi cracked for Ford, Reagan's candidacy would be finished. The Mississippi delegates and alternates, obscure folks leading normal lives, were besieged for interviews, which many of them granted on the run between being buttonholed by leaders of the Ford and Reagan campaigns. Into this maelstrom on Sunday afternoon came Clarke Reed, on a short flight from his home in Greenville. He was milling around the crowded lobby when Keene came up and said he had to talk to him privately. Reed figured Keene just wanted to bolster him in his determination not to let Carmichael get away with his ploy, or perhaps to go over the latest delegate count. But he figured wrong. The two went into Reed's room down the hall on the first floor, talked for a while, and then hurried out to attend the start of the meeting. Neither said anything to anybody about their talk, nor did they indicate that anything notable had been discussed.

At the delegation caucus, Dent, Cheney, and Keene all were allowed to make pitches for their candidates. First came Dent—Dr. Harold Hill incarnate. He told the assembled how "Mississippi is in the catbird seat" and Clarke had done a great job putting it there, but they ought to use the power now. He told them it was "the Battle of Mississippi" and he buttered them up some more in his inimitable style: "Now my good friend Clarke is probably a little peeved with us because we've been down here trying to lobby you good folks. But I told Clarke that you can't dress sixty beautiful women up in bikinis and put them on Broadway, and not expect Gerald Ford and Ronald Reagan to turn their heads and look at 'em. . . . Friends, we looking at you. My goodness, you're in the catbird seat if I've ever seen it. You know it took the whole South to do that in '68 in the convention. Now it's coming down to just Mississippi. Mississippi's got a chance to strike a real blow for the South." And he repeated his updated version of the parable of talents. "It's a question," he said, "of whether Clarke's gonna be the kingmaker or Rosey Rosenbaum's gonna be the kingmaker. That is, New York, or Mississippi. Don't let us down, friends. I'm not talking about Ford. I'm talking about the South. I'm in this thing because I'm for the South, and I feel what's good for the South is good for the country and good for the Republican Party. You know, we're all worried whether it's going to be a Northeastern strategy or a Southern strategy; it's gonna be a national strategy, and we better make sure it is. We haven't put anything on the table down here [for Ford] except Florida."

Cheney then took over, trying to reassure the delegation that Ford wasn't writing off the South. He answered some questions, then gave way to Keene, who reviewed the situation, unusually quickly it seemed, and also fielded some questions.

Neither side at this point thought it had the thirty-one votes needed to break the delegation's agreement to go to Kansas City uncommitted, or to put it on record for Ford or Reagan. And so the meeting adjourned with a decision only to remain uncommitted—a victory for Reed in that it nipped Carmichael's effort in the bud.

The delegation did, however, invite President Ford to Jackson to address it the next Friday, an invitation that would bring to a head the internal Ford campaign debate as to how aggressively Mississippi should be pursued. Cheney would say only that the trip was under serious consideration, and that tentative plans were being laid for Ford to come. That night, after talking to small groups of delegates, Cheney dined with Dent and some Ford delegates at LeFleurs, which passes for a good restaurant in Jackson. Reed and some Reagan people were dining there also, and after dinner Reed joined a table of reporters. He seemed unusually defensive and several times made the point that although he liked Reagan he had never been committed to him publicly. As he was holding forth, Dent came over too, and gave us yet another rendition of the parable of the talents. Reed smiled, but did not seem overly amused.

Later that evening, Cheney got together with Dent, Reed, and Pickering and sat around, talking and drinking, until nearly two o'clock. Reed said nothing special to influence him, but Cheney went to bed satisfied that it was politically safe to bring the President to the state later in the week. "I did not want to run the President into Mississippi and have the delegation caucus go for Reagan," Cheney said later—recalling that Ford the previous month had gone into Missouri blind and gotten burned. "It was clear that however you counted it, it was deadlocked, and there was not going to be a decision before Kansas City, and on that basis it made sense for the President to go in."

Uncommitted Delegates: Real People

BY JAMES M. NAUGHTON

John Sellie conducted a poll in a booth at the North Dakota State Fair. Sherry Martschink asked her South Carolina dentist, who happens to be the Governor. Thomas Bruinooge consulted luncheonette waitresses, bank tellers and clients of his New Jersey law firm. All to no avail.

They are three of the diminishing band of Republican National Convention delegates who can't decide. Despite much unsolicited advice, the blandishments of powerful politicians and the steady inquiries of reporters, they still are agonizing—with about five dozen other delegates—about the choice between Gerald R. Ford and Ronald Reagan to be their party's Presidential nominee.

The closest nominating contest in Republican Party history may be on the edge, at least, of an outcome. A possible switch from the Reagan to the Ford camp by the Mississippi delegation or some other bloc could confirm the President's claim to a convention majority and settle the score before delegates like Mary Masterson in Wyoming figure out what to do. "My husband says, 'Mary, you've got to make up your mind,'" she said recently, imitating his exasperation with a laugh before adding: "I'm in no hurry."

But Mr. Ford and Mr. Reagan are. They clawed, feinted and orated their separate ways through 30 primaries and 20 state conventions to find 97 percent of the 2,259 delegates committed but the nomination dependent on the remaining 3 percent.

So a President and a former California governor, acting like rival vacuum cleaner peddlers in hot pursuit of the company-prize trip to Bermuda, began sticking their feet in the delegates' doors. The wonder is any of the delegates still has some resistance.

James M. Naughton, "Uncommitted Delegates: Real People," *The New York Times*, July 25, 1976, Section IV, p. 2. © 1976 by The New York Times Company. Reprinted by permission.

There are several kinds of uncommitted Republicans. There are barterers, canny politicians in search of a legal hustle. Some Wyoming uncommitteds advertised that their votes would depend on Mr. Ford's signature on a mineral leasing bill affecting the state. He vetoed it, and a few of the delegates drifted to Mr. Reagan. The leader of six Long Island neutrals won a 10-minute audience to remind the President of the importance of Federal dollars to a big sewer project there. He sympathized, and, without any quid pro quo, the six Long Islanders fell in line behind Mr. Ford last week.

There are also pragmatists, holdout delegates trying to get a fix on which candidate is likely to win before moving to claim credit for deciding the contest. The seemingly gathering momentum of the Ford candidacy impressed Hawaiian delegates who had ducked into an impartial posture after watching the President take some pastings in primaries last May; 15 of the 19 Hawaiians affirmed their support of Mr. Ford on Friday, putting him over the top by his own delegate tally. Now Mr. Ford's agents are trying for a convincing lead by working on a turbulent Mississippi delegation that originally was in the Reagan camp.

There were, at least for a while, some individual thrill seekers too. Uncommitted Republicans became overnight celebrities in their home towns as they were courted—with long telephone chats, with private breakfasts and with invitations to sup at the White House with a queen or chancellor—by two of America's political potentates. It was heady stuff, but, as Mary Masterson remarked, "It's not fun any more."

She and most of the other still-unpledged delegates are of the last, most tortured type, those who Tom Bruinooge believes are suffering a "crisis of conscience." Mostly novices at national conventions, they are genuinely awed by their obligation to party constituents and country. They talk incessantly of "electability," a word that sometimes trips their tongues, and cannot decide if Mr. Ford or Mr. Reagan would have a better chance to save the White House from what they regard as the dread Democrats.

Sherry Martschink is willing to risk the disaffection of her family's former oral surgeon, James B. Edwards, who stopped practicing when he was elected Governor of South Carolina two years ago and who is an ardent Reagan man. "He told me if I didn't vote for Reagan he'd quit pulling my teeth and start knocking them out," Mrs. Martschink said. "But he was only kidding."

Kidding or not, it was but one of the tugs in opposing directions that have got the Martschinks and Sellies and Mastersons and Bruinooges reeling. Mrs. Martschink dined with King Juan Carlos of Spain at the White House last month, got a phone call from the President 10 days ago, and another from Mr. Reagan last Tuesday. She questioned both candidates about electoral strategy, possible running mates, anti-Washington attitudes, Watergate and electability. "Both of them impressed me," she said, torn by the choice.

"The Republicans this year have two such fine men," echoed an indecisive Mrs. Masterson. Mr. Bruinooge breakfasted with Mr. Reagan in New Jersey and met with Mr. Ford in Washington within a few days. He found the Californian "more electric" but was impressed with the competitiveness of the chief executive. "An athlete, he was running, running hard," Mr. Bruinooge said.

Mr. Bruinooge wants to make "an educated decision." So he sent out 600 postcards asking for the advice of Bergen County Republicans. He questioned everyone he encountered: busboys, cab drivers, law partners, neighbors. But the answers were not uniform, and he waits, resenting suggestions by Mr. Ford's aides that his timing is crucial to the candidate. "I'm not concerned with timing," he told one of them, "I'm concerned with my conscience."

So is John Sellie. He stood at the Republican Party booth at the fairgrounds in Minot, soliciting advice and discovering "every other person is on the other side." Some delegates may waver, shift and tack as opportunity directs, but the North Dakota farmer wants to be sure his decision is firm. "Either one of them could stub a toe between now and the convention," he said. "Once you commit you're locked in."

Although they may wind up locking themselves in too late to make any difference, the conscience-stricken uncommitteds don't seem to mind. Several say that they may hold off until they arrive in Kansas City next month. "You kind of wonder," said Mr. Bruinooge, "why we have a convention if we have to decide before it begins. Why convene at all?"

Either Ford or Reagan Has It Sewed Up, Maybe

The candidates for the Republican Presidential nomination, Gerald Ford and Ronald Reagan, have together produced a mathematical impossibility: Both contenders now claim more than a majority of the delegates to the nominating convention. By the unofficial estimate of The New York Times, neither man has a majority, although President Ford is close to one.

The conflicting totals put forward by the Republican rivals illustrate the difficulty of counting delegates with precision. Although some delegates to the convention are bound by state law or party rules to vote for

"Either Ford or Reagan Has It Sewed Up, Maybe," *The New York Times, July 25, 1976, Section IV, p. 2.* © *1976 by The New York Times Company. Reprinted by permission.*

one candidate or the other, more than half are free to change their minds until a ballot is taken, even though they may be nominally committed.

Throughout last week Mr. Ford and Mr. Reagan claimed to have acquired new delegates, each contender hoping to convince the uncommitted and the wavering that they were about to miss a bandwagon, albeit a slow-moving one. Mr. Ford's efforts were rewarded by a commitment on Friday from the previously unpledged Hawaii delegation; the Mississippi delegation was also said to be considering a switch from the Reagan to the Ford camp.

By the end of the week, Mr. Ford said that he had acquired 1,135, five more than the majority needed for nomination; Mr. Reagan laid claim to 1,140. The New York Times tally showed 1,124 for the President and 1,063 for the former California governor with 72 uncommitted.

In the contest for delegates, Mr. Ford has the advantage of his tenancy of the White House. He met with several state delegations there last week in an effort to make converts.

Mr. Ford also took steps last week to try to defuse what is likely to be a loaded political issue for him: He dropped his opposition to creating a special prosecutor to investigate crimes by high Government officials. Apparently concerned that opposing a reform inspired by Watergate might add weight to the issue already raised by the Democrats, Mr. Ford said he would agree to a permanent prosecutor, appointed by the President. The Senate, which had proposed temporary, court-appointed prosecutors, accepted that modification and passed the bill. It now goes to the House, where its chances are uncertain.

Ford is Backed on Early-Ballot Switches

BY WARREN WEAVER JR.

Supporters of President Ford won an easy preliminary victory today by persuading a Republican committee to adopt a new party rule barring early ballot switches from one candidate to another by delegates bound by state law.

Warren Weaver, Jr., "Ford is Backed on Early-Ballot Switches," *The New York Times,* August 11, 1976, p. 14. © 1976 by The New York Times Company. Reprinted by permission.

Affected by the rule, if it is adopted by the convention that opens here next Monday, will be 938 delegates from 19 states, 367 of them now required to vote for Mr. Ford and 571 for his rival for the Presidential nomination, Ronald Reagan, the former California Governor.

Unless the convention formally decides to enforce the state election laws binding these men and women, some Ford strategists fear that the President will lose some delegates to Mr. Reagan or that these "soft" supporters may abstain.

This could deny Mr. Ford a first-ballot majority and thus delay the final decision on the nomination until virtually all delegates are automatically released from legal requirements to support any candidate.

Under the rule approved today, if one or more delegates bound to a candidate abstained, the secretary would record their votes as cast for that candidate anyway.

Another Vote Tomorrow

The full Republican National Committee is expected to adopt the proposed rule change here tomorrow. That group, like the rules unit that voted today, is heavily dominated by backers of President Ford.

But this action is all preliminary. Beginning on Saturday, the same loyalty issue will be taken up again by the Rules Committee of the convention, a different 105-member group that includes many more Reagan supporters than the committee that acted today. A convention floor fight on the question next week is all but certain.

Attempting unsuccessfully to block the proposed rule, two Reagan attorneys maintained that, under the present status of the law, no state law or court can compel a convention delegate to cast his vote for any particular candidate—and they obviously prefer to keep it that way.

"Let the individual delegates be arbiters of their own consciences," Loren A. Smith, general counsel of Citizens for Reagan, declared. "Let's trust the delegates to make these decisions."

Roger Allan Moore, special counsel for the Reagan committee, suggested that the rule would deprive individual convention delegates of constitutional freedoms of speech and franchise, which he said could not be done without a legal hearing to determine "whether the convention has properly construed and applied state law—all in the middle of a roll-call."

But these legal arguments had little effect on the pro-Ford committee. After nearly two hours of discussion, A. Lynn Lowe of Arkansas formally introduced the proposed rule to hold the 938 delegates in line and it was approved by a voice vote with only a half dozen "no's" audible among the 54 members.

Actually, the rule would have the effect of freezing the vote of one additional delegate, Robert G. Shaw of North Carolina. Under a proportional state law, he has been sent to Kansas City as officially uncommitted because more than 3,000 primary voters voted that way instead of for President Ford or Mr. Reagan.

Mr. Shaw told the committee today he would vote "uncommitted" on the first ballot, reflecting the will of his constituency, whether the new rule was in effect or not.

Robert P. Visser, general counsel of the President Ford Committee, maintained that it would be "relatively simple" for the permanent chairman of the convention to determine during the early Presidential roll-calls whether votes from 19 jurisdictions in question were being cast in accordance with the results of their primaries and the applicable state laws.

The jurisdictions involved are Arkansas, California, the District of Columbia, Florida, Georgia, Indiana, Kentucky, Maryland, Massachusetts, Michigan, Nebraska, Nevada, New Hampshire, North Carolina, Oregon, South Dakota, Tennessee, Texas and Wisconsin.

President Ford picked up another vote on the convention Rules Committee that will re-examine this sensitive issue beginning on Saturday. With one committed committee member from Virginia announcing for the President today, the committee lined up as 54 votes for Mr. Ford, 45 for Mr. Reagan, one uncommitted but leaning to Mr. Ford, four uncommitted and one vacancy.

The committee vote on a given procedural issue that did not appear to affect the Presidential competition directly could obviously be very close.

Reagan Men Seek Way to Deal Ford a Damaging Blow

BY R. W. APPLE JR.

Ronald Reagan's managers probed today for weaknesses in the defenses of President Ford, searching for some way to inflict an early and psychologically damaging defeat on the incumbent.

"What we intend to do this week is raise a number of matters without committing ourselves to all-out battles on any of them," said John P.

R.W. Apple, Jr., "Reagan Men Seek Way to Deal Ford a Damaging Blow," *The New York Times,* August 11, 1976, p. 1. © 1976 by The New York Times Company. Reprinted by permission.

Sears, the California conservative's chief strategist. "By this weekend, it will be clear to everybody which are the best ones to pursue."

Although Mr. Sears continued to insist that Mr. Reagan had "at worst a 50–50 chance" to be nominated at the Republican National Convention here next week, another senior aide to the former Governor said, "We started out as a long shot, and we still are—maybe 30–70."

Given that situation, the Reagan managers are prepared to improvise a floor fight on whatever procedural question promises to lure some of the President's delegates or to create sufficient passions to cloud the outcome.

Some of the Possibilities

These possibilities came up in preliminary committee meetings yesterday and today:

- An attempt to push through the Rules Committee, which meets Saturday, an amendment requiring all Presidential candidates to name their Vice-Presidential choices in advance, and if that fails, an attempt to push it through on the floor.
- An attempt, either in the Rules Committee or on the convention floor, to defeat the so-called "justice" rule, which would prevent delegates legally bound to support one candidate from voting for another or from abstaining.
- An attempt to stage a major floor fight on one or more platform planks, most likely the one on abortion.

In an effort to counter the Reagan moves, aides to the President let it be known in Washington that he would consult the former California Governor and other opponents before making his selection of a running mate next week.

Here in Kansas City, Ford partisans belittled their rivals' activity.

"This is nothing more than a thrashing about by the Reagan forces in an attempt to establish a beachhead," said Richard M. Rosenbaum, the New York State Republican chairman, at a briefing tonight. "It isn't going to work."

Mr. Ford continued to hold a clear but indecisive lead in the race for the Republican Presidential nomination.

He gained three delegates during the day in *The New York Times*'s national tabulation. The switches put Mr. Ford at 1,113 votes, 17 short of the 1,130 needed for nomination, and Mr. Reagan at 1,034. The remaining 112 delegates are uncommitted.

Paul Stolfo of Philadelphia was one of the President's new supporters. He had reportedly been told by the party leaders that his plane fare to Kansas City would not be paid unless he endorsed Mr. Ford before he left Pennsylvania.

John J. Biondolillo of Staten Island, listed as uncommitted, was scratched from the New York delegation because of an attack of hepatitis. He was replaced by an alternate, Nano Tufaro, a supporter of President Ford.

Virginia Lampe of Arlington, Va., the other delegate who switched, said that Mr. Reagan's selection of Senator Richard S. Schweiker of Pennsylvania as a prospective running mate had been the prime factor in her decision.

"I am very disappointed with Governor Reagan on Senator Schweicker," she said. "The Governor and his advisers failed to understand what the American people will accept in the name of expediency."

Mrs. Lampe's decision gave the President another vote on the potentially pivotal Rules Committee. According to the Times' count, he now controls only 54 of 105 votes, a highly fragile majority.

The Reagan camp believes that it can command a majority—or, at the worst, a very large minority—on the Rules Committee. And the spokesman for the President Ford Committee, Peter Kaye, conceded today that Mr. Reagan would have something like 10 to 25 votes more on procedural questions on the floor than he would have on the roll-call for a Presidential nominee.

Thus, the Reaganites' problem is to find a way to convert their strength on the committees and on procedural votes into votes on the nominating roll-call.

That goal lies behind Mr. Sears's proposal on the Vice-Presidency. He said in an interview today that he was convinced that if Mr. Ford were forced to make an early choice, he would lose some of the delegates that now supported him.

The Ford camp apparently believes it unlikely that Mr. Reagan will tie his fate directly to the proposal.

"A lot of Reagan people on the floor will vote against this thing," said Richard L. Herman, an Omaha trucking executive who serves on Mr. Ford's six-man strategy board, "because it would obviously exclude their man from the second spot on a Ford ticket. Some of them want to keep that option available."

A more direct approach for the Reagan forces would be the defeat of the "justice rule," which would at least theoretically free the pro-Reagan delegates in such states as North Carolina, Kentucky and Florida, now bound by state law, to vote in accordance with their preferences.

The Rules Committee of the Republican National Committee approved the "justice rule" on an overwhelming voice vote today, after Loren A. Smith, general counsel of Citizens for Reagan, described it as a "Catch 22" proposal. The entire national committee is expected to approve it tomorrow.

But both of those committees are overwhelmingly pro-Ford, unlike the rules committee of the national convention.

The situation on the platform is much cloudier.

Having obtained a copy of the draft platform and read it overnight, Reagan agents said today that it was in "horrible" condition, containing nothing about abortion and only the vaguest language dealing with gun control. They also described it as a "rewrite" of parts of President Ford's most recent State of the Union message, which they considered highly unacceptable.

On the one hand, they said, they are still hopeful of writing a unity platform with the cooperation of key Ford supporters on the Platform Committee.

On the other, they said, they are ready, either for substantive or tactical reasons, to force protracted fights over key planks if they cannot gain sufficient ground. Mr. Sears said, for example, "If these people seriously oppose any plank on abortion, sure we'll go to the floor."

Whatever the final tactical decision, the Reagan forces were clearly relying on a bruising contest.

"This is an emotional business," said Lyn Nofziger, Mr. Reagan's convention director. "There are a number of ways to awaken the delegates' emotions. You can give them dinner at the White House, or promise them a sewer plant, or you can give them something to fight for."

The Delegates and the Character of Convention Representation

Issue Conflict and Consensus among Party Leaders and Followers

BY HERBERT McCLOSKY, PAUL J. HOFFMANN, & ROSEMARY O'HARA

American political parties are often regarded as "brokerage" organizations, weak in principle, devoid of ideology, and inclined to differ chiefly over unimportant questions. In contrast to the "ideological" parties of Europe—which supposedly appeal to their followers through sharply defined, coherent, and logically related doctrines—the American parties are thought to fit their convictions to the changing demands of the political contest. According to this view, each set of American party leaders is satisfied to play Tweedledee to the other's Tweedledum.

I. Pressures toward Uniformity and Cleavage

Although these "conclusions" are mainly derived from *a priori* analysis or from casual observations of "anecdotal" data (little systematic effort having been made so far to verify or refute them), they are often taken as

Excepted from Herbert McClosky, Paul J. Hoffmann, and Rosemary O'Hara, "Issue Conflict and Consensus Among Party Leaders and Followers," *American Political Science Review,* Vol. 54, June 1960, pp. 406–427. Footnotes deleted. Reprinted by permission of The American Political Science Association.

confirmed—largely, one imagines, because they are compatible with certain conspicuous features of American politics. Among these features is the entrenchment of a two-party system which, by affording both parties a genuine opportunity to win elections, tempts them to appeal to as many diverse elements in the electorate as are needed to put together a majority. Since both parties want to attract support from the centrist and moderate segments of the electorate, their views on basic issues will, it is thought, tend to converge. Like giant business enterprises competing for the same market, they will be led to offer commodities that are in many respects identical. It is one thing for a small party in a multi-party system to preserve its ideological purity, quite another for a mass party in a two-party system to do so. The one has little hope of becoming a majority, and can most easily survive by remaining identified with the narrow audience from which it draws its chief supporters; the other can succeed only by accommodating the conflicting claims of many diverse groups—only, in short, by blunting ideological distinctions.

Constraints against enlarging intellectual differences also spring from the loosely confederated nature of the American party system, and from each national party's need to adjust its policies to the competing interests of the locality, the state, and the nation. Many party units are more concerned with local than with national elections, and prefer not to be handicapped by clear-cut national programs. Every ambitious politician, moreover, hopes to achieve a *modus vivendi* tailored to the particular and often idiosyncratic complex of forces prevailing in his constituency, an objective rarely compatible with doctrinal purity. Often, too, local politics are largely non-partisan or are partisan in ways that scarcely affect the great national issues around which ideologies might be expected to form. The development and enforcement of a sharply delineated ideology is also hindered by the absence in either party of a firmly established, authoritative, and continuing organizational center empowered to decide questions of doctrine and discipline. Party affiliation is loosely defined, responsibility is weak or non-existent, and organs for indoctrinating or communicating with party members are at best rudimentary.

Cultural and historical differences may also contribute to the weaker ideological emphasis among American, as compared with European, parties. Many of the great historical cleavages that have divided European nations for centuries—monarchism *vs.* republicanism; clericalism *vs.* anti-clericalism; democracy *vs.* autocracy, etc.—have never taken root in this country. Apart from the slavery (and subsequently the race) issue, the United States has not experienced the intense class or caste conflict often found abroad, and contests of the capitalism *vs.* socialism variety have never achieved an important role in American politics. In addition, never having known a titled nobility, we have largely been freed from the conflicts found elsewhere between the classes of inherited and acquired privilege.

Consider, too, the progress made in the United States toward neutralizing the forces which ordinarily lead to sharp social, and hence intellectual and political, differentiation. The class and status structure of American society has attained a rate of mobility equalling or exceeding that of any other long established society. Popular education, and other facilities for the creation of common attitudes, have been developed on a scale unequalled elsewhere. Improvements in transportation and communication, and rapid shifts in population and industry have weakened even sectionalism as a source of political cleavage. Rural-urban differences continue to exist, of course, but they too have been diminishing in force and have become less salient for American politics than the differences prevailing, for example, between a French peasant proprietor and a Parisian *boulevardier*. In short, a great many Americans have been subjected in their public lives to identical stimuli—a condition unlikely to generate strong, competing ideologies.

The research reported here was designed not to refute these observations but to test the accuracy of the claim that they are sufficient to prevent differences in outlook from taking root in the American party system. We believed that the homogenizing tendencies referred to are strongly offset by contrary influences, and that voters are preponderantly led to support the party whose opinions they share. We further thought that the competition for office, though giving rise to similarities between the parties, also impels them to diverge from each other in order to sharpen their respective appeals. For this and other reasons, we expected to find that the leaders of the two parties, instead of ignoring differences alleged to exist within the electorate, would differ on issues more sharply than their followers would. We believed further that even in a brokerage system the parties would serve as independent reference groups, developing norms, values, and self-images to which their supporters could readily respond. Their influence, we felt, would frequently exceed that of ethnic, occupational, residential and other reference groups. In sum, we proceeded on the belief that the parties are not simply spokesmen for other interest groups, but are in their own right agencies for formulating, transmitting, and anchoring political opinions, that they attract adherents who in general share those opinions, and that through a feedback process of mutual reinforcement between the organization and its typical supporters, the parties develop integrated and stable political tendencies. Other hypotheses will be specified as we present and analyze our findings.

II. Procedures

The questions considered in this paper were part of a large field study made in 1957–1958 on the nature, sources, and correlates of political affiliation, activity, and belief in the American party system (hereafter referred to as the PAB study). Pilot studies on Minnesota samples had led us to suspect that many "settled" notions about party affiliation and belief in America would not stand up under careful empirical scrutiny; further, we felt that little progress would be made in the exploration of this subject until a comprehensive portrait of party membership in America had been drawn. Accordingly, a nationwide study was launched to acquire a detailed description of party leaders and supporters, gathering data on their backgrounds, political experiences, personality characteristics, values, motivations, social and political attitudes, outlooks on key issues, and related matters.

For our samples of party "leaders" we turned to the Democratic and Republican national conventions, largely because they are the leading and most representative of the party organs, their delegates coming from every part of the United States and from every level of party and government activity. Our samples ranged from governors, senators, and national committeemen at the one end to precinct workers and local officials at the other. In the absence of comprehensive information about the characteristics of the party élites in America, no one can say how closely the convention delegates mirror the total party leadership. We felt it fair to assume, nevertheless, that the delegates represented as faithful a cross section of American party leadership as could be had without an extraordinary expenditure of money and labor. Using convention delegates as our universe of leaders also held some obvious advantages for research, since the composition of this universe (by name, address, party, state, sex, place of residence, and party or public office) can usually be ascertained from the convention calls. Of the 6,848 delegates and alternates available to be sampled, 3,193 actually participated; 3,020 (1,788 Democrats and 1,232 Republicans) completed and returned questionnaires that were usable in all respects. The proportion of returns was roughly equivalent for both sets of party leaders.

The rank and file sample, which we wanted both for its intrinsic value and for its utility as a control group, was obtained by special arrangement with the American Institute of Public Opinion. In January 1958, Gallup interviewers personally distributed our questionnaire to 2,917 adult voters in two successive national cross-section surveys. Some 1,610 questionnaires were filled out and returned, of which 1,484 were completely usable. This sample closely matched the national population on such characteristics as sex, age, region, size of city, and party affiliation, and, though it somewhat oversampled the upper educational levels, we considered it sufficiently large and representative for most of our purposes. Of the 1,484 respondents, 821 were Democratic supporters (629 "pure" Democrats, plus 192 whom we classified as "independent" Democrats) and 623 were Republican supporters (479 "pure" Republicans, plus 144 "independent"

Table I · Average Differences in the Ratio-of-Support Scores among Party Leaders and Followers for Five Categories of Issues

Category of Issues	Dem. Leaders vs. Repub. Leaders	Dem. Followers vs. Repub. Followers	Dem. Leaders vs. Dem. Followers	Repub. Leaders vs. Repub. Followers	Dem. Leaders vs. Repub. Followers	Repub. Leaders vs. Dem. Followers
a. Public Ownership of Resources	.28	.04	.06	.18	.10	.22
b. Government Regulation of the Economy	.22	.06	.08	.10	.12	.16
c. Equalitarianism, Human Welfare	.22	.05	.08	.21	.06	.25
d. Tax Policy	.20	.06	.06	.20	.04	.26
e. Foreign Policy	.16	.02	.05	.08	.07	.10
Average Differences in Ratio Scores for all Categories	.21	.04	.07	.15	.08	.20

Sample Sizes: Democratic Leaders, 1,788; Republican Leaders, 1,232; Democratic Followers, 821; Republican Followers, 623.

Republicans). Forty respondents could not be identified as adherents of either party.

. . . .

III. Findings: Comparisons between Leaders

No more conclusive findings emerge from our study of party issues than those growing out of the comparisons between the two sets of party leaders. Despite the brokerage tendency of the American parties, their active members are obviously separated by large and important differences. The differences, moreover, conform with the popular image in which the Democratic party is seen as the more "progressive" or "radical," the Republican as the more "moderate" or "conservative" of the two. In addition, the disagreements are remarkably consistent, a function not of chance but of systematic points of view, whereby the responses to any one of the issues could reasonably have been predicted from knowledge of the responses to the other issues.

Examination of Tables II-a–e and III shows that the leaders differ significantly on 23 of the 24 issues listed and that they are separated on 15 of these issues by .18 or more ratio points—in short, by differences that are in absolute magnitude very large. The two samples are furthest apart in their attitudes toward public ownership and are especially divided on the question of government ownership of natural resources, the Democrats strongly favoring it, the Republicans just as strongly wanting it cut back. The difference of .39 in the ratio scores is the largest for any of the issues tested. In percentages, the differences are 58 per cent (D) vs. 13 per cent (R) in favor of increasing support, and 19 per cent (D) vs. 52 per cent (R) in favor of decreasing support. Both parties preponderantly support public control and development of atomic energy, but the Democrats do so more uniformly.

V. O. Key, among others, has observed that the Republican party is especially responsive to the "financial and manufacturing community," reflecting the view that government should intervene as little as possible to burden or restrain prevailing business interests. The validity of this observation is evident throughout all our data, and is most clearly seen in the responses to the issues listed under Government Regulation of the Economy, Equalitarianism and Human Welfare, Tax Policy. Democratic leaders are far more eager than Republican leaders to strengthen enforcement of anti-monopoly laws and to increase regulation of public utilities and business. Indeed, the solidarity of Republican opposition to the regulation of business is rather overwhelming: 84 per cent want to decrease such regulation and fewer than .01 per cent say they want to increase it. Although the Democrats, on balance, also feel that government controls on business

Table II-a · Comparison of Party Leaders and Followers on "Public Ownership" Issues, by Percentages and Ratios of Support

ISSUES	LEADERS		FOLLOWERS	
	Dem. N = 1,788	*Repub.* N = 1,232	*Dem.* N = 821	*Repub.* N = 623
		(*%s down*)		
Public Ownership of Natural Resources				
% favoring: Increase	57.5	12.9	35.3	31.1
Decrease	18.6	51.9	15.0	19.9
Same, n.c.*	23.8	35.2	49.7	49.0
Support Ratio	.69	.30	.60	.56
Public Control of Atomic Energy				
% favoring: Increase	73.2	45.0	64.2	59.4
Decrease	7.2	15.3	7.1	10.0
Same, n.c.	19.6	39.7	28.7	30.6
Support Ratio	.83	.65	.79	.75
Mean Support Ratios for the Public Ownership Category	.76	.48	.70	.66

*n.c. = no code.

should not be expanded further, the differences between the two samples on this issue are nevertheless substantial.

The two sets of leaders are also far apart on the farm issue, the Democrats preferring slightly to increase farm supports, the Republicans wanting strongly to reduce them. The Republican ratio score of .20 on this issue is among the lowest in the entire set of scores. The magnitude of these scores somewhat surprised us, for while opposition to agricultural subsidies is consistent with Republican dislike for state intervention, we had expected the leaders to conform more closely to the familiar image of the Republican as the more "rural" of the two parties. It appears, however, that the party's connection with business is far more compelling than its association with agriculture. The Republican desire to reduce government expenditures and to promote independence from "government hand-outs" prevails on the farm question as it does on other issues, while the Democratic preference for a more regulated economy in which government intervenes to reduce economic risk and to stabilize prosperity is equally evident on the other side. Party attitudes on this issue appear to be determined as much by ideological tendencies as by deliberate calculation of the political advantages to be gained by favoring or opposing subsidies to farmers. Comparison of our findings with Turner's earlier data on farm votes in Congress suggests, in addition, that the sharp party difference on the farm issue is neither a recent development nor a mere product of the personal philosophy of the present Secretary of Agriculture.

Having implied that agricultural policies partly result from principle, we must note that on three other issues in this category (trade unions, credit, and tariffs), principle seems to be overweighed by old-fashioned economic considerations. In spite of their distaste for government interference in economic affairs, the Republicans almost unanimously favor greater regulation of trade unions and they are more strongly disposed than the Democrats toward government intervention to restrict credit and to raise tariffs. Of course, party cleavages over the credit and tariff issues have a long history, which may by now have endowed them with ideological force beyond immediate economic considerations. The preponderant Democratic preference for greater regulation of trade unions is doubtless a response to recent "exposures" of corrupt labor practices, though it may also signify that the party's perspective toward the trade unions is shifting somewhat.

The closer Republican identification with business, free enterprise, and economic conservatism in general, and the friendlier Democratic attitude toward labor and toward government regulation of the economy, are easily observed in the data from other parts of our questionnaire. Republican leaders score very much higher than Democratic leaders on, for example, such scales as economic conservatism, independence of govern-

Table II-b · Comparison of Party Leaders and Followers on "Government Regulation of the Economy" Issues, by Percentages and Ratios of Support

	LEADERS		FOLLOWERS	
ISSUES	Dem. N = 1,788	Repub. N = 1,232	Dem. N = 821	Repub. N = 623
	(%s down)			
Level of Farm Price Supports				
% favoring: Increase	43.4	6.7	39.0	23.0
Decrease	28.1	67.4	27.6	40.3
Same, n.c.	28.5	25.8	33.4	36.7
Support Ratio	.58	.20	.56	.41
Government Regulation of Business				
% favoring: Increase	20.2	0.6	18.6	7.4
Decrease	38.5	84.1	33.4	46.2
Same, n.c.	41.3	15.3	48.0	46.4
Support Ratio	.41	.08	.43	.31
Regulation of Public Utilities				
% favoring: Increase	59.0	17.9	39.3	26.0
Decrease	6.4	17.6	11.1	12.0
Same, n.c.	34.6	64.5	49.6	62.0
Support Ratio	.76	.50	.64	.57
Enforcement of Anti-Monopoly Laws				
% favoring: Increase	78.0	44.9	53.2	51.0
Decrease	2.9	9.0	7.9	6.6
Same, n.c.	19.1	46.1	38.9	42.4
Support Ratio	.88	.68	.73	.72

Regulation of Trade Unions				
% favoring: Increase	59.3	86.4	46.6	57.8
Decrease	12.4	4.5	8.9	10.6
Same, n.c.	28.3	9.2	44.5	31.6
Support Ratio	.73	.91	.69	.74
Level of Tariffs				
% favoring: Increase	13.0	19.2	16.6	15.2
Decrease	43.0	26.3	25.3	21.3
Same, n.c.	43.9	54.5	58.1	63.4
Support Ratio	.35	.46	.46	.47
Restrictions on Credit				
% favoring: Increase	24.8	20.6	26.1	25.7
Decrease	39.3	20.6	22.2	23.8
Same, n.c.	35.9	58.8	51.8	50.5
Support Ratio	.43	.50	.52	.51
Mean Support Ratios for "Government Regulation of the Economy" Category	.59	.48	.58	.53

ment, and business attitudes. On a question asking respondents to indicate the groups from which they would be most and least likely to take advice, 41 per cent of the Democratic leaders but only 3.8 per cent of the Republican leaders list trade unions as groups from which they would seek advice. Trade unions are scored in the "least likely" category by 25 per cent of the Democrats and 63 per cent of the Republicans. Similarly, more than 94 per cent of the Republican leaders, but 56 per cent of the Democratic leaders, name trade unions as groups that have "too much power." These differences, it should be noted, cannot be accounted for by reference to the greater number of trade union members among the Democratic party leadership, for in the 1956 conventions only 14 per cent of the Democrats belonged to trade unions, and while an even smaller percentage (4 per cent) of the Republicans were trade unionists, this disparity is hardly great enough to explain the large differences in outlook. The key to the explanation has to be sought in the symbolic and reference group identifications of the two parties, and in their underlying values.

Nowhere do we see this more clearly than in the responses to the Equalitarian and Human Welfare issues. The mean difference in the ratio scores for the category as a whole is .22, a very large difference and one that results from differences in the expected direction on all six issues that make up the category. On four of these issues—federal aid to education, slum clearance and public housing, social security, and minimum wages—the leaders of the two parties are widely separated, the differences in their ratio scores ranging from .36 to .21. The percentages showing the proportions who favor increased support for these issues are even more striking. In every instance the Democratic percentages are considerably higher: 66 *vs.* 22 per cent (education); 78 *vs.* 40 per cent (slum clearance and housing); 60 *vs.* 23 per cent (social security); and 50 *vs.* 16 per cent (minimum wages). The Democratic leaders also are better disposed than the Republican leaders toward immigration: twice as many of them (36 per cent *vs.* 18 per cent) favor a change in policy to permit more immigrants to enter. The over-all inclination of both party élites, however, is to accept the present levels of immigration, the Democratic ratio score falling slightly above, and the Republican slightly below, the mid-point.

More surprising are the differences on the segregation issue, for, despite strong Southern influence, the Democratic leaders express significantly more support for enforcing integration than the Republicans do. Moreover, the difference between the two parties rises from .12 for the national samples as a whole to a difference of .18 when the southern leaders are excluded. In his study of Congress, Turner found that the Republicans gave more support to Negro rights than the Democrats did. The reversal of this finding in our data does not necessarily mean that a change has occurred since Turner made his study, but only that the votes of the congressional parties do not always reflect the private feelings of the national party leadership. Then, too, Southern influence is disproportionately stronger in the Democratic congressional party than in the national Democratic organization as a whole, and disproportionately weaker in the Republican congressional party than in the Republican organization as a whole.

Examination of the actual magnitude of the ratio scores in this category reveals that the Republicans want not so much to abrogate existing social welfare or equalitarian measures as to keep them from being broadened. The Democrats, by comparison, are shown to be the party of social equality and reform, more willing than their opponents to employ legislation for the benefit of the underprivileged. Support for these inferences and for the greater liberalism of the Democrats can be found elsewhere in our data as well. Analysis of the scale results show Republican leaders scoring higher than Democratic leaders on such measures as chauvinism, élitism, conservatism, and right-wing values, and lower on tolerance, procedural rights, and faith in democracy. No differences worth noting, however, were found for ethnocentrism, faith in freedom, or the California F scale. The Democrats had a slightly higher average score on the left-wing scale, but the number of leaders in either party who scored high on this measure was fairly small.

The self-images and reference group identifications of the two parties also should be noted in this connection. For example, many more Democratic than Republican leaders call themselves liberal and state that they would be most likely to take advice from liberal reform organizations, the Farmers' Union, and (as we have seen) from the trade unions; only a small number consider themselves conservative or would seek advice from conservative reform organizations, the National Association of Manufacturers, or the Farm Bureau Federation. The Republicans have in almost all instances the reverse identifications: only a handful regard themselves as liberal or would seek counsel from liberal organizations, while more than 42 per cent call themselves conservative and would look to the NAM or to conservative reform organizations for advice. Almost two-thirds of the Republicans (compared with 29 per cent of the Democrats) regard the Chamber of Commerce as an important source of advice. Businessmen are listed as having "too much power" by 42 per cent of the Democrats but by only 9 per cent of the Republicans. The Democrats are also significantly more inclined than the Republicans to consider Catholics, Jews, and the foreign born as having "too little power." While self-descriptions and reference group identifications often correspond poorly with actual beliefs—among the general population they scarcely correspond at all, in fact—we are dealing, in the case of the leaders, with a politically informed and highly articulate set of people who have little difficulty connecting the beliefs they hold and the groups that promote or obstruct those beliefs.

Table II-c · Comparison of Party Leaders and Followers on "Equalitarian and Human Welfare" Issues, by Percentages and Ratios of Support

ISSUES	LEADERS		FOLLOWERS	
	Dem. N = 1,788	Repub. N = 1,232	Dem. N = 821	Repub. N = 623
		(%s down)		
Federal Aid to Education				
% favoring: Increase	66.2	22.3	74.9	64.8
Decrease	13.4	43.2	5.6	8.3
Same, n.c.	20.4	34.5	19.5	26.8
Support Ratio	.76	.40	.85	.78
Slum Clearance and Public Housing				
% favoring: Increase	78.4	40.1	79.5	72.5
Decrease	5.6	21.6	5.8	7.9
Same, n.c.	16.0	38.3	14.6	19.6
Support Ratio	.86	.59	.87	.82
Social Security Benefits				
% favoring: Increase	60.0	22.5	69.4	57.0
Decrease	3.9	13.1	3.0	3.8
Same, n.c.	36.1	64.4	27.5	39.2
Support Ratio	.78	.55	.83	.77
Minimum Wages				
% favoring: Increase	50.0	15.5	59.0	43.5
Decrease	4.7	12.5	2.9	5.0
Same, n.c.	45.2	72.0	38.1	51.5
Support Ratio	.73	.52	.78	.69

Enforcement of Integration				
% favoring: Increase	43.8	25.5	41.9	40.8
Decrease	26.6	31.7	27.4	23.6
Same, n.c.	29.5	42.8	30.7	35.6
Support Ratio	.59	.47	.57	.59
Immigration into United States				
% favoring: Increase	36.1	18.4	10.4	8.0
Decrease	27.0	29.9	52.0	44.6
Same, n.c.	36.9	51.7	37.6	47.4
Support Ratio	.54	.44	.29	.32
Mean Support Ratios for "Equalitarian and Human Welfare" Category	.71	.50	.70	.66

Table II-d · Comparison of Party Leaders and Followers on "Tax Policy" Issues, by Percentages and Ratios of Support

ISSUES	LEADERS		FOLLOWERS	
	Dem. N = 1,788	*Repub.* N = 1,232	*Dem.* N = 821	*Repub.* N = 623
	(*%s down*)			
Corporate Income Tax				
% favoring: Increase	32.3	4.0	32.0	23.3
Decrease	23.3	61.5	20.5	25.7
Same, n.c.	44.4	34.5	47.5	51.0
Support Ratio	.54	.21	.56	.49
Tax on Large Incomes				
% favoring: Increase	27.0	5.4	46.6	34.7
Decrease	23.1	56.9	13.8	21.7
Same, n.c.	49.9	37.7	39.6	43.6
Support Ratio	.52	.24	.66	.56
Tax on Business				
% favoring: Increase	12.6	1.0	24.6	15.9
Decrease	38.3	71.1	24.1	32.6
Same, n.c.	49.1	27.8	51.3	51.5
Support Ratio	.37	.15	.50	.42

Tax on Middle Incomes				
% favoring: Increase	2.7	0.8	4.5	3.0
Decrease	50.2	63.9	49.3	44.3
Same, n.c.	47.1	35.3	46.2	52.6
Support Ratio	.26	.18	.28	.29
Tax on Small Incomes				
% favoring: Increase	1.4	2.9	1.6	2.1
Decrease	79.2	65.0	77.5	69.6
Same, n.c.	19.4	32.1	20.9	28.3
Support Ratio	.11	.19	.12	.16
Mean Support Ratios for "Tax Policy" Category	.36	.19	.42	.38

Our fourth category, Tax Policy, divides the parties almost as severely as do the other categories. The mean difference for the category as a whole is .20, and it would doubtless have been larger but for the universal unpopularity of proposals to increase taxes on small and middle income groups. Table II-d shows that the differences between the parties on the tax issues follow the patterns previously observed and that tax policy is for the Democrats a device for redistributing income and promoting social equality. Neither party, however, is keen about raising taxes for *any* group: even the Democrats have little enthusiasm for new taxes on upper income groups or on business and corporate enterprises. The Republican leaders are overwhelmingly opposed to increased taxes for *any* group, rich *or* poor. This can be seen in their low ratio scores on the tax issues, which range from only .15 to .24. But while they are far more eager than the Democratic leaders to cut taxes on corporate and private wealth, they are less willing to reduce taxes on the lower income groups. These differences, it should be remarked, are not primarily a function of differences in the income of the two samples. Although there are more people with high incomes among the Republican leaders, the disproportion between the two samples is not nearly great enough to account for the dissimilarities in their tax views.

Of the five categories considered, Foreign Policy shows the smallest average difference, but even on these issues the divergence between Democratic and Republican leader attitudes is significant. Except for defense spending the Democrats turn out to be more internationalist than the Republicans, as evidenced in their greater commitment to the United Nations and to American participation in international military alliances like NATO. Twice as many Democrats as Republicans want the United States to rely more heavily upon such organizations, while many more Republicans want to reduce our international involvements. Both parties are predominantly in favor of cutting back foreign aid—a somewhat surprising finding in light of Democratic public pronouncements on this subject—but more Republicans feel strongly on the subject. Our data thus furnish little support for the claim that the parties hold the same views on foreign policy or that their seeming differences are merely a response to the demands of political competition.

Nevertheless, it would be incorrect to conclude that one party believes in internationalism and the other in isolationism. The differences are far too small to warrant any such inference. Traces of isolationism, to be sure, remain stronger in the Republican party than in the Democratic party—an observation buttressed by the finding that twice as many Republicans as Democrats score high on the isolationism scale. The pattern of Republican responses on both the issue and scale items signifies, however, that the leaders of that party generally accept the degree of "internationalism" now in effect, but shrink from extending it further. Consider too, the similarities in the leaders' scores on defense spending, for despite their greater

Table II-e · Comparison of Party Leaders and Followers on "Foreign Policy" Issues, by Percentages and Ratios of Support

ISSUES	LEADERS		FOLLOWERS	
	Dem. N = 1,788	Repub. N = 1,232	Dem. N = 821	Repub. N = 623
	(%s down)			
Reliance on the United Nations				
% favoring: Increase	48.9	24.4	34.7	33.4
Decrease	17.6	34.8	17.3	19.3
Same, n.c.	33.5	40.7	48.0	47.3
Support Ratio	.66	.45	.59	.57
American Participation in Military Alliances				
% favoring: Increase	41.5	22.7	39.1	32.3
Decrease	17.6	25.7	14.0	15.4
Same, n.c.	40.9	51.6	46.9	52.3
Support Ratio	.62	.48	.62	.58
Foreign Aid				
% favoring: Increase	17.8	7.6	10.1	10.1
Decrease	51.0	61.7	58.6	57.3
Same, n.c.	31.1	30.7	31.3	32.6
Support Ratio	.33	.23	.26	.26
Defense Spending*				
% favoring: Increase	20.7	13.6	50.5	45.7
Decrease	34.4	33.6	16.4	15.4
Same, n.c.	44.8	52.8	33.0	38.8
Support Ratio	.43	.40	.67	.65
Mean Support Ratios for "Foreign Policy" Category (excl. Defense Spending)	.54	.39	.49	.47

*See footnote on p. 338.

leaning toward isolationism, the Republicans are no more inclined than the Democrats to leave the country defenseless.*

In treating issues in the Elmira election study of 1948, Berelson, Lazarsfeld, and McPhee found it helpful to distinguish between "style" and "position" issues. "Style" issues principally yield symbolic, psychological, or subjective gratifications, and have relatively intangible consequences; "position" issues reflect direct, personal and material interests, and have more objective consequences. According to the Elmira report, "position" issues (or what politicians might call "bread and butter" issues) divide voters more sharply than style issues. Most of the issues tested in the present study would have to be classified as "position" issues, but five of them—United Nations, international alliances, foreign aid, immigration, and segregation—could be classified as style issues. Four others—natural resources, atomic energy, education, and slum clearance—contain both symbolic and material elements and can best be described as "mixed."

Although the classification is crude, the findings it yields are generally consistent with the claims of the Elmira study. On the fourteen position issues—taxes, trade unions, tariffs, minimum wages, farm prices, social security, credit restrictions, and the regulation of business, public utilities and monopolies—Democratic and Republican leaders show an average ratio score difference of .21. On the style issues the two parties differ by .13—a significantly smaller difference. Largest of all, however, are the differences for the "mixed" issues, which average more than .30. This result should occasion little surprise, for when ideology and interest are *both* at work, partisanship is likely to be intensified. Several considerations could account for the superiority of position over style issues as causes of political cleavage: they are "bread and butter" issues, and are thus more often subject to pressure by organized interest groups; they have immediate and tangible consequences, which may lead politicians to pay greater attention to them than they do to issues whose payoff is more uncertain; and, finally, they are not so likely to be part of the common core of values upon which the community structure rests.

Comparison of the magnitude of the differences between groups can be seen in Table III, where we have ranked the issues, high to low, according to the size of the difference between the groups being compared. By presenting a rank-order of differences for the two leader groups, for the two follower groups, and for the leaders and followers of each party, this table makes it possible to observe not only which issues most and least divide the several party groups, but whether they divide the leaders and followers in the same way.

Notice that the issues commonly thought to be most divisive do not

---

*The issue of defense spending has been kept separate from the other foreign policy issues because the magnitude of the scores for some of the leaders and all of the followers were obviously inflated by the launching of Sputnik I in November 1957.

always evoke the greatest cleavage between the parties. Immigration, tariffs, civil rights, monopoly control, and credit regulation fall toward the lower end of the rank order, while farm supports, federal aid to education, slum clearance, social security, minimum wages, public housing, and issues dealing with the regulation and taxation of business fall toward the upper end. Though by no means uniformly, the older, more traditional issues appear to have been superseded as sources of controversy by issues that have come into prominence chiefly during the New Deal and Fair Deal.

IV. Comparisons between Followers

So far we have addressed ourselves to the differences between Democratic and Republican *leaders*. In each of the tables presented, however, data are included from which the two sets of party *followers* may also be compared.

The observation most clearly warranted from these data is that the rank and file members of the two parties are far less divided than their leaders. Not only do they diverge significantly on fewer issues—seven as compared with 23 for the leader samples—but the magnitudes of the differences in their ratio scores are substantially smaller for every one of the 24 issues. No difference is larger than .14, and on the majority of the issues the disparity is smaller than .05. Insofar as they differ at all, however, the followers tend to divide in a pattern similar to that shown by the leaders, the correlation between their rank orders being .72. All the issues on which the followers significantly disagree are of the "bread and butter" variety, the more symbolic issues being so remotely experienced and so vaguely grasped that rank and file voters are often unable to identify them with either party. Policies affecting farm prices, business regulation, taxes, or minimum wages, by contrast, are quickly felt by the groups to whom they are addressed and are therefore more capable of arousing partisan identifications. It should also be noted that while the average differences are small for all five categories, they are smallest of all for foreign policy— the most removed and least well understood group of issues in the entire array.

Democratic and Republican followers were also compared on a number of scales and reference group questions. The results, while generally consistent with the differences between the leaders, show the followers to be far more united than their leaders on these measures as well. Even on business attitudes, independence of government, and economic conservatism, the differences are small and barely significant. No differences were found on such scales as tolerance, faith in democracy, procedural rights, conservatism-liberalism (classical), the California F scale and isolationism. The average Democrat is slightly more willing than the average Republican

Table III · Rank Order of Differences in the Support-Ratio Scores of Party Leaders and Followers

DIFF. BETWEEN RATIO SCORES**	DEM. VS. REPUB. LEADERS Issues	DEM. VS. REPUB. FOLLOWERS Issues	DIFF. BETWEEN RATIO SCORES	DEM. LEADERS VS. FOLLOWERS Issues	DIFF. BETWEEN RATIO SCORES	REPUB. LEADERS VS. FOLLOWERS Issues	DIFF. BETWEEN RATIO SCORES
+.39	1. Natural Resources	Farm Supports	+.14	Immigration	+.25	Fed. Aid to Edu.	−.39
+.38	2. Farm Supports	Gov't. Reg. of Business	+.12	Anti-Monopoly	+.15	Taxes-Large Income	−.32
+.37	3. Fed. Aid. to Edu.	Taxes-Large Income	+.10	Taxes-Large Income	−.15	Taxes-Corp.	−.28
+.33	4. Taxes-Corp.	Minimum Wages	+.09	Taxes-Business	−.13	Taxes-Business	−.27
+.33	5. Reg.-Business	Taxes-Business	+.09	Reg. Pub. Util.	+.12	Natural Resouces	−.23
+.28	6. Taxes-Large Inc.	Reg. Pub. Util.	+.07	Tariffs	−.11	Pub. Housing	−.23
+.27	7. Pub. Housing	Taxes-Corp.	+.07	Restrict. Credit	−.09	Reg. Business	−.22
+.26	8. Reg. Pub. Util.	Social Security	+.07	Natural Resources	+.09	Social Security	−.22
+.23	9. Social Security	Fed. Aid to Edu.	+.06	Fed. Aid to Edu.	−.08	Farm Supports	−.22
+.22	10. Taxes-Business	Reg. Trade Unions	+.05	Foreign Aid	−.05	Minimum Wages	−.18
+.21	11. Minimum Wages	Natural Resources	+.05	Reliance on U.N.	+.05	Reg. Trade Unions	+.17
+.21	12. Reliance on U.N.	Public Housing	+.05	Minimum Wages	+.05	Immigration	+.13
+.20	13. Anti-Monopoly	Taxes-Small Income	−.04	Social Security	−.04	Reliance on U.N.	−.12
+.18	14. Atomic Energy Control	American Participation, NATO	+.04	Reg.Trade Unions		Enforce Integration	−.12

#	Issue	Value	Issue	Value	Issue	Value	Issue	Value
15.	Reg. Trade Unions	−.18	Atomic Energy Control	+.04	Atomic Energy Control	+.04	Taxes-Middle Income	−.11
16.	American Participation, NATO	+.13	Immigration	−.03	Farm Supports	−.03	Atomic Energy Control	−.10
17.	Enforce Integration	+.12	Defense Spending	−.02	Reg. Business	+.02	American Participation, NATO	−.10
18.	Tariffs	−.11	Taxes-Middle Income	+.02	Enforce Integration	−.02	Reg. Public Utilities	−.07
19.	Foreign Aid	+.10	Reliance on U.N.	+.02	Taxes-Middle Income	+.02	Anti-Monopoly	−.04
20.	Increase Immigration	+.10	Tariffs	−.01	Taxes-Corporation	−.01	Foreign Aid	−.03
21.	Taxes-Small Income	−.08	Enforce Integration	−.01	Taxes-Small Income	−.01	Taxes-Small Income	+.03
22.	Taxes-Middle Income	+.08	Restriction Credit	+.01	American Participation, NATO	+.01	Reriction Credit	−.01
23.	Restriction Credit	−.07	Foreign Aid	−.01	Public Housing	−.01	Tariffs	−.01
24.	Defense Spending	+.03	Anti-Monopoly	.00	Defense Spending	***	Defense Spending	**

Ns. Democratic Leaders: 1,788; Republican Leaders: 1,232; Democratic Followers: 821; Republican Followers: 623.

*The plus sign means that the first group listed in the heading is more favorable to the issue named than the second group; the minus sign means that the second group is the more favorable.

**Size of difference required for differences to be significant at .01 level: Democratic Leaders vs. Republican—.048; Democratic Followers vs. Republican Followers—.063; Republican Leaders vs. Democratic Followers—.054; Democratic Leaders vs. Democratic Followers—.068; Republican Leaders vs. Republican Followers—.063.

***Leaders and Followers cannot be compared on defense spending, for reasons given in footnote to Table II-e.

to label himself a liberal or to seek advice from liberal organizations; the contrary is true when it comes to adopting conservative identifications. Only in the differential trust they express toward business and labor are the two sets of followers widely separated.

These findings give little support to the claim that the "natural divisions" of the electorate are being smothered by party leaders. Not only do the leaders disagree more sharply than their respective followers, but the level of consensus among the electorate (with or without regard to party) is fairly high. Inspection of the "increase" and "decrease" percentage scores (Tables II-a–e) shows that substantial differences of opinion exist among the electorate on only five of the 24 issues (credit restrictions, farm supports, segregation, and corporate and business taxes). Of course, voters may divide more sharply on issues at election time, since campaigns intensify party feeling and may also intensify opinions on issues. Available data from election studies allow no unequivocal conclusion on this point, but even the party-linked differences found among voters during elections may largely be echoes of the opinions announced by the candidates—transient sentiments developed for the occasion and quickly forgotten.

V. Leader Conflict and Follower Consensus: Explanations

Considering the nature of the differences between the leader and follower samples, the interesting question is not why the parties fail to represent the "natural division" in the electorate (for that question rests on an unwarranted assumption) but why the party élites disagree at all, and why they divide so much more sharply than their followers?

Despite the great pressures toward uniformity we have noted in American society, many forces also divide the population culturally, economically, and politically. The United States is, after all, a miscellany of ethnic and religious strains set down in a geographically large and diverse country. Many of these groups brought old conflicts and ideologies with them, and some have tried to act out in the new world the hopes and frustrations nurtured in the old. Then, too, despite rapid social mobility, social classes have by no means been eliminated. No special political insight is needed to perceive that the two parties characteristically draw from different strata of the society, the Republicans from the managerial, proprietary, and to some extent professional classes, the Democrats from labor, minorities, low income groups, and a large proportion of the intellectuals. Partly because the leaders of the two parties tend to overrespond to the modal values of the groups with which they are principally identified, they gradually grow further apart on the key questions which separate their respective supporters. The Republican emphasis on business ideology is both a cause and a consequence of its managerial and proprietary support; the greater Democratic emphasis on social justice, and on economic and social levelling, is both the occasion and the product of the support the party enjoys among intellectuals and the lower strata. These interrelationships are strengthened, moreover, by the tendency for a party's dominant supporters to gain a disproportionate number of positions in its leadership ranks.

The differences which typically separate Democratic from Republican leaders seem also to reflect a deep-seated ideological cleavage often found among Western parties. One side of this cleavage is marked by a strong belief in the power of collective action to promote social justice, equality, humanitarianism, and economic planning, while preserving freedom; the other is distinguished by faith in the wisdom of the natural competitive process and the supreme virtue of individualism, "character," self-reliance, frugality, and independence from government. To this cleavage is added another frequent source of political division, namely, a difference in attitude toward change between "radicals" and "moderates," between those who prefer to move quickly or slowly, to reform or to conserve. These differences in social philosophy and posture do not always coincide with the divisions in the social structure, and their elements do not, in all contexts, combine in the same way. But, however crudely, the American parties do tend to embody these competing points of view and to serve as reference groups for those who hold them.

Party cleavage in America was no doubt intensified by the advent of the New Deal, and by its immense electoral and intellectual success. Not only did it weld into a firm alliance the diverse forces that were to be crucial to all subsequent Democratic majorities, but it also made explicit the doctrines of the "welfare state" with which the party was henceforth to be inseparably identified. Because of the novelty of its program and its apparently radical threat to the familiar patterns of American political and economic life, it probably deepened the fervor of its Republican adversaries and drove into the opposition the staunchest defenders of business ideology. The conflict was further sharpened by the decline of left-wing politics after the war, and by the transfer of loyalties of former and potential radicals to the Democratic party. Once launched, the cleavage has been sustained by the tendency for each party to attract into its active ranks a disproportionate number of voters who recognize and share its point of view.

Why, however, are the leaders so much more sharply divided than their followers? The reasons are not hard to understand and are consistent with several of the hypotheses that underlay the present study.

(1) Consider, to begin with, that the leaders come from the more articulate segments of society and, on the average, are politically more aware

than their followers and far better informed about issues. For them, political issues and opinions are the everyday currency of party competition, not esoteric matters that surpass understanding. With their greater awareness and responsibility, and their greater need to defend their party's stands, they have more interest in developing a consistent set of attitudes—perhaps even an ideology. The followers of each party, often ignorant of the issues and their consequences, find it difficult to distinguish their beliefs from those of the opposition and have little reason to be concerned with the consistency of their attitudes. Furthermore, the American parties make only a feeble effort to educate the rank and file politically, and since no central source exists for the authoritative pronouncement of party policy, the followers often do not know what their leaders believe or on what issues the parties chiefly divide. In short, if we mean by ideology a coherent body of informed social doctrine, it is possessed mainly by the articulate leadership, rarely by the masses.

(2) Differences in the degree of partisan involvement parallel the differences in knowledge and have similar consequences. The leaders, of course, have more party spirit than the followers and, as the election studies make plain, the stronger the partisanship, the larger the differences on issues. The leaders are more highly motivated not only to belong to a party appropriate to their beliefs, but to accept its doctrines and to learn how it differs from the opposition party. Since politics is more salient for leaders than for followers, they develop a greater stake in the outcome of the political contest and are more eager to discover the intellectual grounds by which they hope to make victory possible. Through a process of circular reinforcement, those for whom politics is most important are likely to become the most zealous participants, succeeding to the posts that deal in the formation of opinion. Ideology serves the instrumental purpose, in addition, of justifying the heavy investment that party leaders make in political activity. While politics offers many rewards, it also makes great demands on the time, money, and energies of its practitioners—sacrifices which they can more easily justify if they believe they are serving worthwhile social goals. The followers, in contrast, are intellectually far less involved, have less personal stake in the outcome of the competition, have little need to be concerned with the "correctness" of their views on public questions, and have even less reason to learn in precisely what ways their opinions differ from their opponents'. Hence, the party élites recruit members from a population stratified in some measure by ideology, while the rank and file renews itself by more random recruitment and is thus more likely to mirror the opinions of a cross section of the population.

(3) Part of the explanation for the greater consensus among followers than leaders resides in the nature and size of the two types of groups. Whereas

the leader groups are comparatively small and selective, each of the follower groups numbers in the millions and, by its very size and unwieldiness, is predisposed to duplicate the characteristics of the population as a whole. Even if the Republicans draw disproportionately from the business-managerial classes and the Democrats from the trade union movement, neither interest group has enough influence to shape distinctively the aggregate opinions of so large a mass of supporters. Size also affects the nature and frequency of interaction within the two types of groups. Because they comprise a smaller, more selectively chosen, organized, and articulate élite, the leaders are apt to associate with people of their own political persuasion more frequently and consistently than the followers do. They are not only less cross-pressured than the rank and file but they are also subjected to strong party group efforts to induce them to conform. Because their political values are continually renewed through frequent communication with people of like opinions, and because they acquire intense reference group identifications, they develop an extraordinary ability to resist the force of the opposition's arguments. While the followers, too, are thrown together and shielded to some extent, they are likely to mingle more freely with people of hostile political persuasions, to receive fewer partisan communications, and to hold views that are only intermittently and inconsistently reinforced. Since, by comparison with the leaders, they possess little interest in or information about politics, they can more easily embrace "deviant" attitudes without discomfort and without challenge from their associates. Nor are they likely to be strongly rewarded for troubling to have "correct" opinions. The followers, in short, are less often and less effectively indoctrinated than their leaders. The group processes described here would function even more powerfully in small, sectarian, tightly organized parties of the European type, but they are also present in the American party system, where they yield similar though less potent consequences.

(4) Political competition itself operates to divide the leaders more than the followers. If the parties are impelled to present a common face to the electorate, they are also strongly influenced to distinguish themselves from each other. For one thing, they have a more heightened sense of the "national interest" than the followers do, even if they do not all conceive it in the same way. For another, they hope to improve their chances at the polls by offering the electorate a recognizable and attractive commodity. In addition, they seek emotional gratification in the heightened sense of brotherhood brought on by the struggle against an "out-group" whose claim to office seems always, somehow, to border upon usurpation. As with many ingroup-outgroup distinctions, the participants search for moral grounds to justify their antagonisms toward each other, and ideologies help to furnish such grounds. Among the followers, on the other hand, these needs exist, if at all, in much weaker form.

Leaders versus Followers

In comparing each party élite with its own followers we were mainly interested in seeing how closely each body of supporters shared the point of view of its leaders, in order to test the hypothesis that party affiliation, even for the rank and file, is a function of ideological agreement. In predicting that the parties would tend to attract supporters who share their beliefs, we expected, of course, to find exceptions. We knew that many voters pay little attention to the ideological aspects of politics and that, in Gabriel Almond's phrase, a party's more "esoteric doctrines" are not always known to its followers. Nevertheless we were not prepared for the findings turned up by this phase of the inquiry, for the differences between leaders and followers—among the Republicans at least—are beyond anything we had expected. Indeed, the conclusion is inescapable that the views of the Republican rank and file are, on the whole, much closer to those of the Democratic leaders than to those of the Republican leaders. Although conflicts in outlook also exist between Democratic leaders and followers, they are less frequent or severe.

If we turn once again to the table of rank order differences, we see that the Democratic followers differ significantly from their leaders on twelve of the 23 issues, and that the average difference in the ratio scores of the two samples is .07. Democratic leaders and Republican followers differ significantly on only eleven of the 23 issues, with an average difference between them of only .08. Notice, by contrast, that Republican leaders and followers diverge significantly on 18 of the 23 issues, and show an average difference of .16. To complete the comparison, the Republican leaders and Democratic followers were in disagreement on 19 of the 23 issues, their average difference being .20. As these comparisons make plain, there is substantial consensus on national issues between Democratic leaders and Democratic and Republican followers, while the Republican leaders are separated not only from the Democrats but from their own rank and file members as well.

Examination of the Democratic scores shows the leaders to be slightly more "progressive" than their followers on most of the issues on which differences appear. The leaders are, for example, more favorable to public ownership of natural resources, to regulation of monopolies and public utilities, to a reduction of tariffs, and to a liberalized credit policy. They are more internationalist on the foreign aid and United Nations issues and substantially more sympathetic to the maintenance and expansion of immigration. The results showing the relative radicalism of the two samples are not unequivocal, however, for on several issues—federal aid to education, minimum wages, and taxes on business enterprise and large incomes—the followers take the more radical view. Nor are the differences significant on such issues as atomic energy, slum clearance, segregation, farm price supports, government control of business and trade unions, and taxes on middle and small income groups. In general, the followers turn out more radical chiefly on a few of the bread and butter issues—a reflection, no doubt, of their lower socio-economic status. When we control for occupation, the differences between Democratic leaders and followers on these issues largely disappear.

Consideration of the scores of Republican leaders and followers shows not only that they are widely separated in their outlooks but also that the leaders are uniformly more conservative than their followers. Only on the immigration issue is this trend reversed. The followers hold the more "radical" ideas on the two public ownership issues, on five of the six equalitarian and human welfare issues, on four of the seven regulation-of-the-economy issues, and on four of the five tax policy issues. They are also willing to place more reliance upon the U.N. and upon international military alliances. Observe that the largest differences occur on those issues which have most sharply separated New Deal–Fair Deal spokesmen from the hard core of the Republican opposition—federal aid to education, redistribution of wealth through taxes on business, corporations and the wealthy, public ownership of natural resources, public housing, regulation of business, social security, farm price supports, minimum wages, and trade union regulations.

In short, whereas Republican leaders hold to the tenets of business ideology and remain faithful to the spirit and intellectual mood of leaders like Robert A. Taft, the rank and file Republican supporters have embraced, along with their Democratic brethren, the regulatory and social reform measures of the Roosevelt and Truman administrations. This inference receives further support from the scores on our Party Ideology scale where, on a variety of attitudes and values which characteristically distinguish the leaders of the two parties, the Republican followers fall closer to the Democratic than to the Republican side of the continuum. Thus, in addition to being the preferred party of the more numerous classes, the Democrats also enjoy the advantages over their opponents of holding views that are more widely shared throughout the country.

Assuming the findings are valid, we were obviously wrong to expect that party differentiation among followers would depend heavily upon ideological considerations. Evidently, party attachment is so much a function of other factors (*e.g.,* class and primary group memberships, religious affiliation, place of residence, mass media, etc.) that many voters can maintain their party loyalties comfortably even while holding views that contradict the beliefs of their own leaders.

Still, we are not entitled to conclude that issue outlook has no effect on the party affiliation of ordinary members. It is conceivable, for example, that the Republican party has come to be the minority party partly because the opinions of its spokesmen are uncongenial to a majority of the voters.

We have no way of knowing from our data—collected at only a single point in time—how many "normally" Republican voters, if any, have defected to the Democrats or fled into independency because they disapprove of Republican beliefs. At the present stage of the analysis, we have no grounds for going beyond the proposition that political affiliation without conformity on issues is possible on a wide scale. In future analyses we shall attempt to learn more about the nature of the relationship between belief and party affiliation by stratifying voters according to the frequency with which they conform to the beliefs of their party leaders. We hope, in this way, to discover whether those who conform least are also less firm in their party loyalties.

VII. The Homogeneity of Support for Leaders and Followers

So far we have only considered conflict and agreement *between* groups. We should now turn to the question of consensus *within* groups. To what extent is each of our samples united on fundamental issues?

In order to assess homogeneity of opinion within party groups, standard deviation scores were computed on each issue for each of the four samples. The higher the standard deviation, of course, the greater the disagreement. The range of possible sigma scores is from 0 (signifying that every member of the sample has selected the same response) to .500 (signifying that all responses are equally divided between the "increase" and "decrease" alternatives). If we assume that the three alternative responses had been randomly (and therefore equally) selected, the standard deviations for the four samples would fall by chance alone around .410. Scores at or above this level may be taken to denote extreme dispersion among the members of a sample while scores in the neighborhood of .300 or below suggest that unanimity within the sample is fairly high. By these somewhat arbitrary criteria we can observe immediately (Table IV) that consensus within groups is greater on most issues than we would expect by chance alone, but that it is extremely high in only a few instances. Although the Republican leaders appear on the average to be the most united and the Democratic leaders the least united of the four groups, the difference between their homogeneity scores (.340 vs. .310) is too small to be taken as conclusive. The grounds are somewhat better for rejecting the belief that leaders are more homogeneous in their outlooks than their followers, since the hypothesis holds only for one party and not for the other.

While generalizations about the relative unity of the four samples seem risky, we can speak more confidently about the rank order of agreement *within* samples. In Table IV we have ranked the issues according to the degree of consensus exhibited toward them by the members of each of the four party groups. There we see that the leaders of the Republican party are most united on the issues that stem from its connections with business—government regulation of business, taxes (especially on business), regulation of trade unions, and minimum wages. The Democratic leaders are most united on those issues which bear upon the support the party receives from the lower and middle income groups—taxes on small and middle incomes, anti-monopoly, slum clearance, social security, and minimum wages. The Republican leaders divide most severely on federal aid to education, slum clearance, U.N. support, segregation, and public control of atomic energy and natural resources; the Democratic leaders are most divided on farm prices, segregation, credit restrictions, immigration, and the natural resources issue. Among the followers the patterns of unity and division are very similar, as attested by the high correlation of .83 between the rank orders of their homogeneity scores. Both Republican and Democratic followers exhibit great cohesion, for example, on taxes on small and middle incomes, social security, slum clearance, and minimum wages. Both divide rather sharply on segregation, farm price supports, defense spending, U.N. support, and taxes on large incomes. The two sets of followers, in short, are alike not only in their opinions on issues but in the degree of unanimity they exhibit toward them.

Inspection of the homogeneity data furnishes additional evidence on the between-group comparisons made earlier. Whereas Democratic and Republican followers divide on issues in approximately the same way, the two sets of leaders differ from each other in this respect also (the correlation between their rank orders on homogeneity is only .28). Democratic leaders and followers tend to unite or divide on the same issues for the most part (r equals .77), but Republican leaders and followers are not parallel in this respect either (r equals .30). The pattern of homogeneity and dispersion among Republican followers is, in fact, much closer to that of the Democratic leaders (r equals .75).

In computing scores for homogeneity we were in part concerned to test the belief that political parties develop greatest internal solidarity on those questions which most separate them from their opponents. According to this hypothesis, external controversy has the effect of uniting the members further by confronting them with a common danger. Whether or not this hypothesis would be borne out in a study of small, sectarian parties we cannot say, but it receives no support from the present study of the American mass parties. Comparisons of the rank order data in Tables III and IV show that there is no consistent connection between inter-party conflict and intra-party cohesion. The correlations between the rank orders of difference and the rank orders of homogeneity are in every case insignificant.

Table IV · Consensus within Party Groups: Rank Order of Homogeneity of Support on Twenty-Four Issues

AVERAGE RANK ORDER*	ISSUE	DEMOCRATIC LEADERS		REPUBLICAN LEADERS		DEMOCRATIC FOLLOWERS		REPUBLICAN FOLLOWERS	
		Rank Order	Sigma	Rank Order	Sigma	Rank Order	Sigma	Rank Order	Sigma
1	Tax on Small Incomes	1	.220	6	.270	1	.224	1	.250
2	Tax on Middle Incomes	3	.276	4	.248	6	.292	2	.278
3	Social Security Benefits	5	.282	8	.296	2	.266	3	.286
4	Minimum Wages	6	.292	5	.268	4	.276	4	.294
5	Enforcement of Anti-Monopoly	2	.246	13	.321	8	.324	7	.314
6	Regulation of Public Utilities	8	.307	10	.300	10	.336	5.5	.310
7	Slum Clearance	4	.276	23	.386	3	.274	5.5	.310
8	Regulation of Trade Unions	12	.356	3	.240	9	.331	15	.345
9	Government Regulation of Business	17	.376	1	.192	20	.363	8	.315
10	Tax on Business	9	.338	2	.236	19	.362	16	.348
11	Level of Tariffs	10	.350	16	.344	11	.338	9	.316
12	Public Control of Atomic Energy	7	.302	20	.362	7	.312	13	.340
13	Federal Aid to Education	13	.360	24	.394	5	.283	11	.322
14	Foreign Aid	19	.383	12	.317	12.5	.340	12	.340
15	Tax on Large Incomes	11	.356	9	.298	17	.358	22	.379
16	American Participation in Military Alliances, NATO	14	.370	18	.351	14	.350	14	.344
17	Immigration into U.S.	21	.399	17	.345	12.5	.340	10	.318
18	Corporate Income Tax	16	.375	7	.284	21	.371	17	.361
19	Restrictions on Credit	22	.400	14	.324	16	.358	18	.362
20	Defense Spending	15	.371	15	.334	22	.380	21	.366
21	Public Ownership of Natural Resources	20	.393	19	.354	15	.352	19	.362
22	Reliance on U.N.	18	.380	22	.384	18	.359	20	.365
23	Level of Farm Supports	24	.421	11	.306	23	.414	23	.397
24	Enforce Integration	23	.416	21	.382	24	.418	24	.399

*The range of sigma scores is from .192 to .421, out of a possible range of .000 (most united) to .500 (least united). Hence, the lower the rank order the greater the unity on the issue named.

Summary and Conclusions

The research described in this paper—an outgrowth of a nationwide inquiry into the nature and sources of political affiliation, activity, and belief—was principally designed to test a number of hypotheses about the relation of ideology to party membership. Responses from large samples of Democratic and Republican leaders and followers were compared on twenty-four key issues and on a number of attitude questions and scales. Statistical operations were carried out to assess conflict and consensus among party groups and to estimate the size and significance of differences. From the data yielded by this inquiry, the following inferences seem most warranted:

(1) Although it has received wide currency, especially among Europeans, the belief that the two American parties are identical in principle and doctrine has little foundation in fact. Examination of the opinions of Democratic and Republican leaders shows them to be distinct communities of co-believers who diverge sharply on many important issues. Their disagreements, furthermore, conform to an image familiar to many observers and are generally consistent with differences turned up by studies of Congressional roll calls. The unpopularity of many of the positions held by Republican leaders suggests also that the parties submit to the demands of their constituents less slavishly than is commonly supposed.

(2) Republican and Democratic leaders stand furthest apart on the issues that grow out of their group identification and support—out of the managerial, proprietary, and high-status connections of the one, and the labor, minority, low-status, and intellectual connections of the other. The opinions of each party élite are linked less by chance than by membership in a common ideological domain. Democratic leaders typically display the stronger urge to elevate the lowborn, the uneducated, the deprived minorities, and the poor in general; they are also more disposed to employ the nation's collective power to advance humanitarian and social welfare goals (*e.g.,* social security, immigration, racial integration, a higher minimum wage, and public education). They are more critical of wealth and big business and more eager to bring them under regulation. Theirs is the greater faith in the wisdom of using legislation for redistributing the national product and for furnishing social services on a wide scale. Of the two groups of leaders, the Democrats are the more "progressively" oriented toward social reform and experimentation. The Republican leaders, while not uniformly differentiated from their opponents, subscribe in greater measure to the symbols and practices of individualism, *laissez-faire,* and national independence. They prefer to overcome humanity's misfortunes by relying upon personal effort, private incentives, frugality,

hard work, responsibility, self-denial (for both men and government), and the strengthening rather than the diminution of the economic and status distinctions that are the "natural" rewards of the differences in human character and fortunes. Were it not for the hackneyed nature of the designation and the danger of forcing traits into a mold they fit only imperfectly, we might be tempted to describe the Republicans as the chief upholders of what Max Weber has called the "Protestant Ethic." Not that the Democrats are insensible to the "virtues" of the Protestant-capitalistic ethos, but they embrace them less firmly or uniformly. The differences between the two élites have probably been intensified by the rise of the New Deal and by the shift of former radicals into the Democratic party following the decline of socialist and other left-wing movements during and after the war.

(3) Whereas the leaders of the two parties diverge strongly, their followers differ only moderately in their attitudes toward issues. The hypothesis that party beliefs unite adherents and bring them into the party ranks may hold for the more active members of a mass party but not for its rank and file supporters. Republican followers, in fact, disagree far more with their own leaders than with the leaders of the Democratic party. Little support was found for the belief that deep cleavages exist among the electorate but are ignored by the leaders. One might indeed more accurately assert the contrary, to wit: that the natural cleavages between the leaders are largely ignored by the voters. However, we cannot presently conclude that ideology exerts no influence over the habits of party support, for the followers do differ significantly and in the predicted directions on some issues. Furthermore, we do not know how many followers may previously have been led by doctrinal considerations to shift their party allegiances.

(4) Except for their desire to ingratiate themselves with as many voters as possible, the leaders of the two parties have more reason than their followers to hold sharply opposing views on the important political questions of the day. Compared with the great mass of supporters, they are articulate, informed, highly partisan, and involved; they comprise a smaller and more tightly knit group which is closer to the wellsprings of party opinion, more accessible for indoctrination, more easily rewarded or punished for conformity or deviation, and far more affected, politically and psychologically, by engagement in the party struggle for office. If the leaders of the two parties are not always candid about their disagreements, the reason may well be that they sense the great measure of consensus to be found among the electorate.

(5) Finding that party leaders hold contrary beliefs does not prove that they act upon those beliefs or that the two parties are, in practice, gov-

erned by different outlooks. In a subsequent paper we shall consider these questions more directly by comparing platform and other official party pronouncements with the private opinions revealed in this study. Until further inquiries are conducted, however, it seems reasonable to assume that the views held privately by party leaders can never be entirely suppressed but are bound to crop out in hundreds of large and small ways—in campaign speeches, discussions at party meetings, private communications to friends and sympathizers, statements to the press by party officials and candidates, legislative debates, and public discussions on innumerable national, state, and local questions. If, in other words, the opinions of party leaders are as we have described them, there is every chance that they are expressed and acted upon to some extent. Whether this makes our parties "ideological" depends, of course, on how narrowly we define that term. Some may prefer to reserve that designation for parties that are more obviously preoccupied with doctrine, more intent upon the achievement of a systematic political program, and more willing to enforce a common set of beliefs upon their members and spokesmen.

(6) The parties are internally united on some issues, divided on others. In general, Republican leaders achieve greatest homogeneity on issues that grow out of their party's identification with business, Democratic leaders on issues that reflect their connection with liberal and lower-income groups. We find no support for the hypothesis that the parties achieve greatest internal consensus on the issues which principally divide them from their opponents.

In a sequel to this paper we shall offer data on the demographic correlates of issue support, which show that most of the differences presented here exist independently of factors like education, occupation, age, religion, and sectionalism. Controlling for these influences furnishes much additional information and many new insights but does not upset our present conclusions in any important respect. Thus, the parties must be considered not merely as spokesmen for other interest groups but as reference groups in their own right, helping to formulate, to sustain, and to speak for a recognizable point of view.

Representation in American National Conventions: The Case of 1972

BY JEANE J. KIRKPATRICK

Representing Opinions

If the representation of opinions lies at the heart of the representative process, then the question of whether the two conventions represented the political views and values of the rank and file lies at the heart of an inquiry into the representativeness of the conventions. A pioneering inquiry into this question was undertaken by Herbert McClosky nearly two decades ago.

It seems desirable to reaffirm that representation and representatives are not identical: that having representative opinions does not insure that a body will actually make decisions reflecting those opinions any more than its having unrepresentative opinions will necessarily mean that the opinions of constituents will be ignored. But in social science as in life we deal in probabilities not certainties, and probably the relationship between representativeness and the representation of opinion is closer than insistence on the distinction might suggest. It is more probable that an assembly, a majority of whose members share the general views and values of the community, will represent those views and values in their decisions than will an assembly, a majority of whose members do not share them. If the national conventions are supposed to represent the rank and file of their parties, then the correspondence or non-correspondence of the opinions of representatives and represented matters, and matters a good deal.

Such correspondence or non-correspondence will not tell us whether the political system is democratic, since an autocrat may share the opinions of the masses, reflect them in his policies and still remain an autocrat;

Excerpted from Jeane J. Kirkpatrick, "Representation in American National Conventions: The Case of 1972," *British Journal of Political Science*, Vol. 5, No. 3 (1975), pp. 265–322. Footnotes deleted. Copyright © 1975 Cambridge University Press. Reprinted by permission of Cambridge University Press.

or whether the elite's policy decisions will or will not reflect shared opinions in any specific instance, since decision-makers who share mass opinions may decide that some overriding concern makes it undesirable to translate those opinions into policy, just as an elite not sharing mass opinion may decide to enact policies reflecting that opinion either from hope of re-election or out of a sense of obligation; or whether decisions based on shared opinions will be wise, just or liberal, because the masses may acquiesce in foolish, oppressive and discriminatory policies. But the extent of correspondence does tell us whether the system of representation is working in such a way that it offers citizens the opportunity of supporting leaders who share their views and values and of opposing those who do not.

The correspondence—or rather the non-correspondence—of Democratic elite and mass opinion about who the party's candidate should be is readily established. While the McGovern Commission affirmed a 'special concern' with the fair representation of all Democratic presidential preferences, Ranney has pointed out that 'Nearly two-thirds of the convention's delegates were chosen or bound by presidential primaries but 57 per cent of its first-ballot votes and the nomination went to a candidate who won only 27 per cent of the popular vote cast in the primaries and who had only 30 per cent of the first choice preferences in Gallup's last pre-convention poll of Democrats.'

But presidential preference is only one aspect of opinion, albeit an important one. A political party concerned with representation presumably desires that its convention will also be representative of the views and values of its rank and file on other matters.

Representing Opinions on Issues

No one doubts that issues played an unusually large role in the politics of the early 'seventies. The conflicts of the 'sixties injected into the political arena divisive questions of national policy and identity, many of which were caught up in the contest for the Democratic nomination and in the subsequent general election. The importance of ideology in the presidential race enhances the importance of the political opinions of the two conventions. Identical measures of mass and elite opinion are not available for all important policy questions and for all relevant groups; but the range of issues, groups and personalities on which there are identical data is large enough to determine the extent to which the opinions of delegates to the two conventions were representative of Republican and Democratic party identifiers and also of all voters and independents.

Voters and Presidential Elites: Opinions Compared in Five Policy Areas

A comparison of the political attitudes of voters and presidential elites documents the estrangement of the Democratic presidential elite (defined here as all delegates to the convention)—and especially of the dominant McGovern elite—from the views and values of the majority of Americans. It documents, too, that in 1972 formal rules and political outcomes combined to produce a Democratic convention which, although it may up to a point have resembled the 'face of America,' did not at all 'think, feel, reason and act' like America.

Everyday observation and previous research would not lead us to expect that leaders—even elected leaders—would reflect exactly the political opinions of the electorate. McClosky, Stouffer and others have documented the tendency of political leaders to be more involved, informed and effective, if liberal, to be more liberal, if conservative, to be more conservative. But the discontinuities in mass and elite opinion are not usually very large in democratic systems, because the voters tend to choose leaders who share their basic views and commitments and to reject those who do not, and because an awareness of this fact normally keeps the parties responsive to the electorate's views and values.

In 1972, however, the difference between the Democratic party's elite and mass so far exceeded the norm that, on a range of issues central to the politics of that year, the Democratic elite and rank and file were found on opposite sides and the Republican elite held views that were more representative of the views and values of rank-and-file Democrats than were the views of Democratic delegates.

The question of the 'representativeness' of the 1972 Democratic convention is controversial as well as important. It seems desirable therefore to provide full data on the opinions of both delegates and rank and file and comparisons based on 'difference scores' which summarize the extent of correspondence and non-correspondence between elite and rank-and-file opinions. Furthermore, because aggregation of interests and opinions may or may not take place in political conventions and is least likely to occur when, as in 1972, ideological differences among factions are large and one faction has all the votes it needs to win, it seems desirable to provide data on the relations of various portions of the Democratic elite to the Democratic rank and file. Aggregate statistics on Democratic delegates not only conceal intra-elite differences, they also obscure the extent of the differences between 1972's dominant Democratic elite and the party's rank and file because they average the views of McGovern delegates, who were ideologically homogenous and in control of the convention, of Wallace delegates, who were also ideologically homogenous but without influence, and of other delegate groups, who although they were less homogenous, also were without influence. The delegate averages describe an aggregate which did not exist in the real world. In considering the relations between Democratic mass and presidential elite, we must therefore look at the opinions of the various candidate-support groups as well as of the convention as a whole.

WELFARE POLICY

Sometime during the late 'sixties welfare policy collided with the achievement ethic, and the resulting sparks produced political fireworks. Once basic beliefs about the value of work and the distribution of rewards became entangled with questions about how, when and under what circumstances government should expend public funds to support the needy, the welfare-policy debate took on new intensity and importance. Almost everyone had an opinion. A majority of the Democratic and the Republican rank and files and the Republican elite all gave priority to the obligation to work; a majority of the Democratic presidential elite gave priority to abolishing poverty. Analysis of the structure of elite opinion on this issue (1) reveals that the views of all Democratic candidate-support groups except Wallace's were substantially different from those of Democratic party identifiers (and of their own candidates' rank-and-file supporters), (2) confirms the existence of an especially large gap between the opinions of the McGovern elite and the party rank and file and (3) reveals that the Republican elite's views were closer to those of the Democratic rank and file than were those of any Democratic candidate-support group. Difference scores (which range from 0 to 200) summarize these distances: the difference between Democratic delegates and the Democratic rank and file on this issue is 76; that between Republican delegates and the Democratic rank and file is only 19. (That between the Republican elite and Republican identifiers is zero.) The difference between McGovern delegates and Democratic identifiers was therefore substantially larger than that between rank-and-file Democratic identifiers and all Democratic delegates. Among Democratic candidate-support groups, only Wallace supporters contained a majority, 95 per cent, who emphasized the obligation to work. Wallace delegates were more nearly unanimous than rank-and-file Democrats in their emphasis on the obligation to work, but they, at least, were on the same side as the voters.

BUSING

In 1972 controversy about government action in the field of race relations was focused on the desirability (and constitutionality) of busing schoolchildren across district lines in order to achieve 'racial balance' within the schools of some area. Busing had little salience nationally but did have

Table 1 · Welfare Policy: Rank-and-File Identifiers and Elite Compared (Per Cent)

	DEMOCRATS						REPUBLICANS	
	Identifiers n = 1,040	All delegates n = 2,532	McGovern delegates n = 1,281	HHH delegates n = 411	Muskie delegates n = 277	Wallace delegates n = 145	Identifiers n = 604	All delegates n = 1,070
Abolish poverty								
1	12	28	38	15	19	0	8	3
2	6 } 22	17 } 57	24 } 75	6 } 33	17 } 46	2 } 2	2 } 13	2 } 10
3	4	12	13	12	10	0	3	5
4	9	15	12	21	21	3	8	15
5	7	6	4	11	10	9	6	13
6	12 } 69	7 } 28	3 } 12	12 } 45	12 } 33	8 } 95	13 } 79	22 } 75
Obligation to work 7	50	15	5	22	11	78	60	40

Sources: Data on rank-and-file identifiers (voters) were taken from the Pre-Convention Study. Delegate groups' *n*s are weighted. Face-to-face interviews were conducted with 985 Democratic and 351 Republican delegates. Weighted *n*s (developed by the Center for Political Research, University of Michigan) were employed for the analysis. Candidate-support groups are defined by responses to the question 'Which of your party's candidates for president did you personally prefer?' *Question:* 'Some people believe that all able-bodied welfare recipients should be compelled to work. Others believe that the most important consideration is that no American family should live in poverty whether they work or not. Suppose the people who stress the obligation to work are at one end of this scale, at point number 7, and the people who stress that no one should live in poverty are at the other end, at point number 1: where would you place yourself?' N.B. Percentages do not necessarily add to 100 per cent due to rounding off.

Table 2 · Busing Policy: Rank-and-File Identifiers and Elite Compared (Per Cent)

	DEMOCRATS						REPUBLICANS	
	Identifiers $n = 1,275$	All delegates $n = 1,492$	McGovern delegates $n = 846$	HHH delegates $n = 184$	Muskie delegates $n = 131$	Wallace delegates $n = 62$	Identifiers $n = 867$	All delegates $n = 796$
Bus to integrate								
1	8	34	45	14	17	3	2	2
2	4 } 15	20 } 66	29 } 87	11 } 38	12 } 41	0 } 3	1 } 5	2 } 8
3	3	12	13	13	12	2	2	4
4	6	9	7	12	19	2	4	8
5	4	4	2	10	8	2	4	7
6	7 } 82	4 } 25	2 } 7	8 } 51	9 } 41	2 } 96	8 } 93	13 } 84
Keep children in neighborhood schools 7	71	17	3	33	24	92	81	64

Sources: Data on rank-and-file identifiers (voters) were taken from the 1972 Pre-Election (Post-Convention) Study. Data on delegates are from mail questionnaires. These are raw *ns*. *Question:* 'There is much discussion about the best way to deal with racial problems. Some people think achieving racial integration of schools is so important that it justifies busing children to schools out of their own neighborhoods. Others think letting children go to their neighborhood schools is so important that they oppose busing. Where would you place yourself on the following scale ranging from agreement with busing to achieve integration (point 1) to agreement with keeping children in neighborhood schools (point 7)?' N.B. Percentages do not necessarily add to 100 per cent due to rounding off.

intense importance in some states, for example, in Michigan and Maryland, where court decisions requiring busing had angered many. All candidates were forced to take positions on busing during the course of the campaign.

Comparison of rank-and-file Democratic identifiers with the party's elite once again reveals large differences. On busing as on welfare policy, all Democratic candidate-support groups except Wallace's were more 'liberal' than the Democratic rank and file—and, our data show, more liberal even than their own supporters among the rank and file. Again the largest gap is between the Democratic rank and file and delegates supporting George McGovern. While 71 per cent of Democratic voters took the strongest possible anti-busing position, only 3 per cent of McGovern delegates took this position. Again the Republican presidential elite closely reflected the opinions of both the Republican and the Democratic rank and file. Again, too, Wallace delegates were more unanimous in their support of the anti-busing position than were the voters of either party or Republican delegates; but they were on the same side of the issue as both Republican and Democratic voters, while a majority of McGovern delegates were on the other side.

Difference scores sum up these comparative gaps. The distance between Democratic elite and rank and file was 108 as compared with 9 between Democratic voters and the Republican elite. The difference separating McGovern supporters from Democratic voters was still larger, 147, as compared with 26 for Wallace. The distance between the views of Republican voters and the Republican elite was, again, negligible.

CRIME

The 'law and order' issue has its origins in the rising crime rates, urban violence, civil disobedience and popular anxieties of the late 1960s; but by 1972 broader attitudes toward obedience to the law, the coercive power of government, the legitimacy of the social order, race, poverty, social causation and the morality of law-breakers had become entangled in the issue. As in the case of welfare policy and busing, a question developed by the Center for Political Studies was used to probe attitudes toward 'getting tough' *vs.* protecting the rights of the accused. Responses to this question revealed yet another large disagreement between Democratic voters and elite. About half of Democratic voters gave priority to stopping crime; but 78 per cent of the Democratic delegates gave priority to protecting the rights of the accused. Here, too, the distance between Democratic rank-and-file and elite views was large (79) and that between rank-and-file and McGovernite views larger still (107). Once again, the views of the Republican delegates were more representative of both the Republican and the Democratic rank and file.

Table 3 · Get Tough vs. Protect the Accused: Rank-and-File Identifiers and Elite Compared (Per Cent)

	DEMOCRATS						REPUBLICANS	
	Identifiers n = 1,013	All delegates n = 1,493	McGovern delegates n = 850	HHH delegates n = 183	Muskie delegates n = 128	Wallace delegates n = 62	Identifiers n = 590	All delegates n = 769
Protect the accused								
1	19	53	67	32	33	11	15	9
2	10	18	22	13	20	0	8	5
3	7	7	6	13	6	0	5	7
(1–3)	36	78	95	58	59	11	28	21
4	14	9	4	17	23	10	17	23
5	10	5	1	12	9	16	13	20
6	11	3	0	5	6	13	15	19
Stop crime regardless of rights of accused 7	29	5	1	10	4	50	28	17
(5–7)	50	13	2	27	19	79	56	56

Sources: Data on rank-and-file identifiers (voters) were taken from the Pre-Convention Study. The ns for delegates are unweighted raw ns because data are from the mail questionnaires. Question: 'Some people are primarily concerned with doing everything possible to protect the legal rights of those accused of committing crimes. Others feel that it is more important to stop criminal activity even at the risk of reducing the rights of the accused. Suppose that those who stress protecting rights of the accused are at one end of this scale—at point number 1, and those who stress stopping crime even at the risk of reducing the rights of the accused are at the other end—at point number 7, where would you place yourself?' This question was included in the CPS Post-Election Study. The Democratic electorate split as follows: 1=14%; 2=7%; 3=7%; 4=19%; 5=17%; 6=15%; 7=21%. The Republican electorate split as follows: 1=23%; 2=10%; 3=9%; 4=19%; 5=12%; 6=10%; 7=19%. N.B. Percentages do not necessarily add to 100 per cent due to rounding off.

FOREIGN POLICY: SUPPORT FOR SOUTHEAST ASIA

In 1972 American involvement in Southeast Asia continued to have large importance for voters, though less than for party elites. Disagreement about U.S. policy continued to divide the rank and file and the elites of both parties, and to divide the Democratic rank and file from its elite. The questions used to measure attitudes in this area concerned the amount and kind of aid that should be provided to Southeast Asia. Only McGovern delegates were relatively united on this question: 57 per cent were opposed to any aid whatsoever, as compared to 23 per cent of voters. On balance approximately 40 per cent of Democratic voters were more negative than positive toward aid for Southeast Asia, as compared to 75 per cent of Democratic delegates. Sixty per cent of voters were on balance favorable to some aid for the area, as compared to 16 per cent of Democratic delegates. On this question, too, the views of the Republican elite were similar to those of both the Democratic and the Republican rank and file.

INFLATION

At last on inflation—a New Deal–Fair Deal–Great Society issue which involves the use of government power to solve economic problems—we find substantial agreement between Democratic voters and Democratic delegates. It was, of course, just such issues that created the Roosevelt coalition, bringing together white southerners and northern industrial workers. Even in 1972, on this issue Wallace and McGovern delegates and their rank-and-file supporters were to be found on the same side. But the Republicans were also on this side. This is the only issue tested on which a majority of all candidate-support groups were in rough agreement. The broad consensus on the desirability of using government to solve the problem of inflation testifies to the withering away of *laissez-faire* economics and perhaps also to the fading importance of this issue in distinguishing between the parties. Republican delegates were less overwhelmingly in favor of government activity to halt inflation than were Democrats or rank-and-file Republicans; but 63 per cent were on the same side as all of three-fourths of Democratic voters, the Democratic elite and the Republican rank and file. On this issue, the opinions of the Democratic elite were more representative of the Democratic rank and file than were those of the Republican elite. Furthermore, the views of the Democratic elite were closer to the views of Republican voters than were those of the Republican elite.

Groups

Politics is conducted by collectivities. Activities are undertaken and demands are made in the name of groups which become 'we' and 'they' in the

Table 4 · Inflation Policy: Rank-and-File Identifiers and Elite Compared (Per Cent)

	DEMOCRATS						REPUBLICANS	
	Identifiers n = 608	All delegates n = 1,449	McGovern delegates n = 824	HHH delegates n = 183	Muskie delegates n = 126	Wallace delegates n = 55	Identifiers n = 394	All delegates n = 759
Government action against inflation								
1	52	43	46	37	37	46	39	23
2	13 } 78	28 } 87	34 } 93	22 } 81	21 } 82	7 } 60	16 } 74	18 } 63
3	13	16	13	22	24	7	19	22
4	14	9	6	12	15	20	21	24
5	3	2	2	2	2	0	3	7
6	2 } 9	1 } 4	1 } 3	2 } 7	1 } 4	6 } 21	1 } 6	5 } 14
No government action against inflation 7	4	1	0	3	1	15	2	2

Sources: Data on rank-and-file identifiers (voters) were taken from the 1972 CPS Pre-Election Study. Delegates' *n*s are unweighted. *Question*: 'There is a great deal of talk these days about rising prices and the cost of living in general. Some feel that the problem of inflation is temporary and that no government action is necessary. Others say the government must do everything possible to combat the problem of inflation immediately or it will get worse. Where would you place yourself on this scale, ranging from agreement with total government action against inflation to agreement with no government action against inflation?' N.B. Percentages do not necessarily add to 100 per cent due to rounding off.

competition for power and other goods. Ideologies emphasize groups (the proletariat, imperialists, the Ibo, Communists, liberals, conservatives, hawks, doves, Europeans, the enemies of Allah) and groups serve for many as the principal guideposts by which they locate themselves and others in the political arena. There is no more effective way of locating respondents in a political universe than by reference to their orientations toward groups.

'Feeling thermometers' were used to elicit voter and delegate attitudes toward groups which played a role—as contenders and as symbols—in the politics of 1972. The results are consistent with the patterns revealed in our analysis of issue positions. With regard to the most controversial groups, the sympathies of Democratic voters differed substantially from those of the Democratic elite, and the Republican leaders shared more orientations with Democratic voters than did the Democratic leaders. Political demonstrators, civil rights leaders, black militants, welfare recipients and the military fall into this category. The feelings of McGovern delegates toward these groups were the most remote from the feelings of Democratic voters.

Democratic delegates' orientations were, however, closer to their own rank and file on two of the symbols of 'New Deal' politics—trade unions and business interests—and also on 'liberals,' a general ideological category on which Democrats have a more favorable opinion than Republicans. Democrats were also closer to one another in their feelings about 'politicians' (though the most important fact about attitudes toward politicians is that the voters of both parties were much more negative about politicians than were the elites of both).

Democratic Schisms Explored

It is widely known that the new issues—war, race, law and order—divided the electorate in ways different from the old issues growing out of the New Deal and the rise of the welfare state. But the extent to which the new issues divided normally Democratic voters from the Democratic elite is less well known. The fact that the Democratic rank and file and the party's elite remained united on inflation, union leaders and business interests reflects the persistence of the 'New Deal consensus' on these questions; but the sharp divisions between elite and rank and file on the 'new' cultural and social issues provides evidence of how those issues cut across the old alignments.

The fact that a general consensus on economic policy survived among Democrats in the year of the party's landslide defeat indicates either that the consensus was no longer perceived as having much relevance to interparty conflict because the Republicans had joined the Democrats on these issues, or that the electorate perceived economic issues as being less impor-

Table 5 · Attitudes toward Political Demonstrators: Rank-and-File Identifiers and Elite Compared (Per Cent)

		DEMOCRATS						REPUBLICANS	
		Identifiers $n=1,058$	All delegates $n=2,582$	McGovern delegates $n=1,311$	HHH delegates $n=428$	Muskie delegates $n=283$	Wallace delegates $n=148$	Identifiers $n=619$	All delegates $n=1,036$
Unfavorable	0	35	7	1	9	6	40	40	24
	10	12	3	1	7	5	11	11	12
	20	8	3	1	4	3	9	10	16
	30	6	4	2	7	8	6	9	10
	40	6	5	3	11	5	3	6	10
	(total)	67	22	8	38	27	69	76	72
Neutral	50	18	19	16	16	31	20	16	14
	60	4	12	14	12	9	0	3	5
	70	4	13	18	13	9	0	2	4
	80	3	14	18	11	14	5	1	3
	90	1	10	15	4	5	0	1	2
Favorable	100	2	10	13	6	5	6	1	0
	(total 60–100)	14	59	78	46	42	11	8	14

Sources: Data on rank-and-file identifiers (voters) were taken from the Pre-Convention Study. Delegate *n*s are weighted. *Question:* 'This is called a "feeling thermometer," and we would like to use it to measure your feelings toward various groups. If you don't feel particularly warm or cold toward a group, then you would score yourself at the 50° mark. If you have a warm feeling toward a group, you would give it a score somewhere between 50° and 100°. On the other hand, if you don't feel very favorably toward a group, then you would place it somewhere between 0° and 50°. How would you rate overall impressions of political demonstrators?' N.B. Percentages do not necessarily add to 100 per cent due to rounding off.

Table 6 · Attitudes toward Welfare Recipients: Rank-and-File Identifiers and Elite Compared (Per Cent)

	DEMOCRATS						REPUBLICANS	
	Identifiers n=1,058	All delegates n=2,533	McGovern delegates n=1,297	HHH delegates n=420	Muskie delegates n=279	Wallace delegates n=129	Identifiers n=619	All delegates n=1,003
Unfavorable 0	10	2	0	2	0	26	11	4
10	5	1	0	1	0	12	7	5
20	8 (43)	1 (11)	1 (5)	1 (11)	2 (20)	13 (63)	11 (53)	5 (43)
30	10	3	1	3	9	7	12	11
40	10	4	3	4	9	5	12	18
Neutral 50	30	31	32	27	27	24	29	32
60	8	10	11	13	13	0	6	7
70	7	14	15	16	11	2	4	8
80	4 (26)	15 (58)	16 (64)	16 (63)	15 (53)	5 (14)	2 (17)	7 (25)
90	3	10	11	11	10	2	2	2
Favorable 100	4	9	11	7	4	5	3	1

Sources: Data on rank-and-file identifiers (voters) were taken from the Pre-Convention Study. Since data on delegates were drawn from the interviews, all *n*s were weighted.
Question: "This is called a "feeling thermometer" and we would like to use it to measure your feelings toward various groups. If you don't feel particularly warm or cold toward a group, then you would score yourself at the 50° mark. If you have a warm feeling toward a group, you would give it a score somewhere between 50° and 100°. On the other hand, if you don't feel very favorably toward a group, then you would place is somewhere between 0° and 50°. How would you rate your overall impressions of welfare recipients?" N.B. Percentages do not necessarily add to 100 per cent due to rounding off.

tant to them in 1972 than the 'new issues,' or alternatively that economic issues had such low salience for the dominant Democratic elite in 1972 that voters never fully grasped the persistence of differences in orientation between the parties. Probably all three factors were involved.

The power of welfare-state issues to move diverse masses of people was reflected in Democratic victories from 1932 to 1968. But because the new issues link basic values, authority and policy, they, too, have the capacity to move masses. The massive defeat of George McGovern and the attitudes of defecting Democrats testified to the importance of these cross-cutting issues. Not everyone has views about the public ownership of communications or about whether new concessions should be made in the SALT talks, but almost everyone has views about obedience to the law and punishment for disobedience, the relation of work to rewards, about the nation's armed forces, about parents' roles in the bringing up of children. While questions about how government should be conducted are not necessarily perceived as involving the self, cultural prescriptions concerning work, authority, 'just deserts' and race become part of the definition of the self. This intimate relation of culture to self gives to cultural politics its capacity to involve mass publics. It explains why student riots, remote from the experience of most citizens, nevertheless capture the attention of millions who remain unconcerned about large but impersonal questions of public policy. It also explains why political conflict concerning cultural matters is often so intense—as in religious, linguistic and tribal wars.

Issues become important in politics because of their perceived relation to political contests and because of their bearing on individuals' core values and commitments. Identifying these values and commitments is difficult. However, on all the indicators available—presence of an opinion, intensity of opinion, issues important in determining vote, salience of issues, factor analysis of issues and inter-item correlations—the issues on which the Democratic elite and the Democratic rank and file disagreed were undoubtedly important in 1972.

The new issues pitted the traditional culture against the values and perspectives of the political counter-culture. The counter-culture was broader than its political manifestations; it included new attitudes toward work, sex, drugs, crime, language, dress, hair styles, childrearing, music, science, reason, discipline, spontaneity and many other matters, some of which had little relevance for politics. By no means all the exponents of the 'new politics' embraced the life styles and social doctrines of the counter-culture; but the two were connected by bonds of mutual tolerance, by a shared antagonism toward traditional symbols, values and practices and by the conviction that many of society's institutional practices were no longer legitimate.

All of the political issues that sharply distinguished Democratic mass from Democratic elite involved the clash of old and new political cultures.

Table 7 · Attitudes toward the Military: Rank-and-File Identifiers and Elite Compared (Per Cent)

		DEMOCRATS						REPUBLICANS	
		Identifiers n=1,058	All delegates n=2,619	McGovern delegates n=1,330	HHH delegates n=427	Muskie delegates n=283	Wallace delegates n=148	Identifiers n=619	All delegates n=1,068
Unfavorable	0	4	4	7	1	4	0	1	0
	10	2	8	14	1	4	2	2	0
	20	1 (16)	7 (43)	12 (66)	1 (15)	3 (32)	0 (4)	2 (12)	1 (4)
	30	5	11	16	4	4	2	3	1
	40	4	13	17	8	17	0	4	2
Neutral	50	16	14	16	14	15	11	18	12
	60	8	7	6	5	14	3	7	10
	70	12	10	7	16	6	10	15	18
	80	13 (67)	9 (42)	2 (20)	21 (71)	9 (53)	21 (85)	16 (71)	24 (84)
	90	13	7	3	14	9	17	12	17
Favorable	100	21	9	2	15	15	34	21	15

Sources: Data on rank-and-file identifiers (voters) were taken from the Pre-Convention Study. Delegate groups' ns are weighted. Question: 'This is called a "feeling thermometer" and we would like to use it to measure your feelings toward various groups. If you don't feel particularly warm or cold toward a group, then you would score yourself at the 50° mark. If you have a warm feeling toward a group, you would give it a score somewhere between 50° and 100°. On the other hand, if you don't feel very favorably toward a group, then you would place it somewhere between 0° and 50°. How would you rate your overall impressions of the military?' N.B. Percentages do not necessarily add to 100 per cent due to rounding off.

Table 8 · Attitudes toward the Police: Rank-and-File Identifiers and Elite Compared (Per Cent)

	DEMOCRATS						REPUBLICANS	
	Identifiers n=1,058	All delegates n=2,616	McGovern delegates n=1,327	HHH delegates n=432	Muskie delegates n=283	Wallace delegates n=148	Identifiers n=619	All delegates n=1,070
Unfavorable								
0	1	1	1	1	0	0	0	0
10	1	1	1	1	0	0	0	0
20	1 {7}	2 {13}	3 {18}	0 {6}	1 {5}	0 {2}	1 {5}	0 {2}
30	2	3	5	0	1	0	2	1
40	2	6	8	4	3	2	2	1
Neutral								
50	11	17	24	9	10	12	9	5
60	9	11	14	6	12	0	7	7
70	13	13	16	12	9	4	12	11
80	16 {81}	19 {71}	17 {59}	27 {87}	17 {86}	12 {87}	19 {84}	16 {94}
90	16	15	8	25	27	16	19	32
Favorable 100	27	13	4	17	21	55	27	28

Sources: The data on rank-and-file identifiers (voters) were taken from the Pre-Convention Study. Delegate groups' *n*s are weighted. *Question:* "This is called a "feeling thermometer" and we would like to use it to measure your feelings toward various groups. If you don't feel particularly warm or cold toward a group, then you would score yourself at the 50° mark. If you have a warm feeling toward a group, you would give it a score somewhere between 50° and 100°. On the other hand, if you don't feel very favorably toward a group, then you would place it somewhere between 0° and 50°. How would you rate your overall impressions of the police?' N.B. Percentages do not necessarily add to 100 per cent due to rounding off.

Welfare policy had become caught up with conflicting views about the achievement ethic, about whether work was an obligation, whether deprivation of income was an appropriate response to those who chose to be idle. Law enforcement policy had obvious relevance to questions about the legitimacy of the social order and the moral status of the coercion used to defend that order. Foreign policy became enmeshed in cultural conflict not only because of the affinity between the counter-culture and the anti-war movement but also because the two opposing sides held conflicting views about citizenship and the nation. Racial policy was also entangled in the clash of cultures, because traditional America took white supremacy for granted, because equality is a basic value of the society, because political protest, civil disobedience and urban riots were associated with the movement for racial equality, because busing mixes cultures, deprives parents of traditional prerogatives and challenges accepted notions about government's appropriate functions. Attitudes on each of these issues suggest the existence of an entire syndrome. Lack of agreement between Democratic elite and mass about these public policy issues signaled the likelihood of lack of agreement also on broader cultural perspectives and commitments.

Because George McGovern was the standard bearer for the new politics as well as for the Democratic party, his association with the 'new' issues was especially strong, and the differences between the beliefs, sympathies and preferences of McGovern delegates and of rank-and-file Democratic identifiers were especially large. On all of the issues on which rank-and-file Democrats were closer to Republican than to Democratic delegates, a still wider gap separated them from the McGovern delegates. On busing, for example, the margin of difference between all Democratic identifiers and all delegates was 108; but the difference between Democratic identifiers and McGovern delegates was 147. The difference between the rank and file's and McGovern delegates' rating of political demonstrators soared to 123, as compared to a 90 margin of difference for all delegates. On work and welfare policy, the difference between Democratic voters and all delegates was 76, but between Democratic identifiers and McGovern delegates it was 110. On crime, the margin of difference between voters and McGovern delegates was 107, as compared to 79 for all Democratic delegates. On the military, the margin of difference rose from 52 for all Democratic delegates to 97 for McGovern delegates. The pattern is clear and consistent: McGovern delegates were peculiarly 'unrepresentative' of the views and values of the party's rank and file.

It can be seen from Table 9 that on all but two of the groups asked about—union leaders and politicians—McGovern delegates were less representative of the views of the Democratic rank and file than were delegates to the Republican convention, and also that they had fewer views in common with rank-and-file Democrats than did the delegates supporting all of the other candidates, including George Wallace. On only three issues

Table 9 · Differences between Democratic Rank-and-File Identifiers and Selected Groups of Convention Delegates

	McGovern delegates	Humphrey delegates	Wallace delegates	Muskie delegates	Republican delegates	Democratic delegates
Welfare	110	35	46	60	19	76
Busing*	147	54	26	67	9	108
Crime	107	45	54	54	21	79
Civil rights leaders	94	59	74	69	4	67
Welfare recipients	76	69	32	50	1	64
Political demonstrators	123	61	5	68	5	90
Police	33	7	11	7	18	16
Military	97	5	30	30	29	52
Blacks	34	45	6	37	26	34
Conservatives	89	42	66	48	41	64
Liberals	75	24	99	37	73	46
Union leaders	10	43	52	21	52	15
Politicians	55	76	16	66	75	57
Inflation*	21	5	30	9	20	14
Abortion*	89	43	2	67	50	68
Laying off women first*	54	32	4	38	18	42
Women's liberation†	61	32	55	21	57	25
Business interests†	57	2	2	15	45	35
Black militants†	93	26	15	32	9	61
Vietnam	109	29	14	62	34	79
Ideological self-classification†	83	40	80	54	59	59
Mean differences	77.0	36.9	34.2	43.5	31.6	54.9

*These data on rank-and-file identifiers—used to compute differences—were taken from the CPS Pre-Election (Post-Convention) Study.
†These data on rank-and-file identifiers—used to compute differences—were taken from the CPS 1972 Post-Election Study.
The remaining data on rank-and-file identifiers were taken from the Pre-Convention Study.
N.B. The difference scores above were computed from preponderance scores carried to the first decimal place.

or groups—union leaders, liberals and inflation—were the views of McGovern delegates closer to those of the Democratic rank and file than were the views of Wallace delegates. Delegates supporting the two 'moderate' candidates included more persons with views resembling those of the Democratic rank and file. But, as we have already noted, on questions of welfare policy, busing, crime, political demonstrators, civil rights leaders, etc., no candidate-support group at the Democratic convention represented the views and values of the Democratic rank and file as closely as did the Republican delegates. The McGovern, Humphrey and Muskie groups all had views that were too 'liberal' on most issues; the Wallace delegates were, as a group, too 'conservative.' Among Democrats, the Humphrey group most closely approximated the views of Democratic voters on welfare policy, crime, civil rights leaders, the military, conservatives and liberals, inflation and ideological self-classification; the Muskie group was closest to the Democratic rank and file on women's liberation. Humphrey's and Muskie's delegates tied as closest on police. Wallace's delegates most closely approximated Democratic rank-and-file views on busing, welfare recipients, political demonstrators, blacks, politicians, abortion, black militants, Vietnam and job policies for women. Humphrey and Wallace were equally close in attitudes to business interests. The McGovern delegates' orientations were closest to those of the Democratic rank and file on only a single issue or group: union leaders.

Although the views of the Republican mass and the Republican elite in general corresponded closely, on some issues and groups the Republican delegates were actually closer to Democratic than to Republican party identifiers: busing, civil rights leaders, blacks, welfare recipients, political demonstrators, job policies for women and politicians. On each of these issues and groups Republican delegates were more sympathetic to the group involved than were the Republican rank and file. Democratic identifiers were somewhat less unfriendly to these groups than were ordinary Republicans, but they were far less sympathetic than the Democratic elite. Their views therefore meshed nicely with those of the Republican delegates. On a number of subjects—including liberals, Vietnam, the military, women's liberation and politicians—the position of the Republican elite was substantially more 'conservative' than the position of the Republican rank and file; the elite's position was slightly more 'conservative' on inflation, police, business interests, crime, union leaders and ideological self-classification. The two Republican groups were in virtually complete agreement on welfare policy. Differences between Republican elite and rank and file were not large and were generally consistent with previous findings. The Republican elite's distance from Democratic as well as from Republican voters was undoubtedly small enough to permit them to compete for Democratic votes.

The relative proximity of the Democratic rank and file and the Repub-

Table 10 · Least Differences of Democratic Rank-and-File Identifiers from Various Delegate Groups on Selected Issues

	McGovern delegates	Humphrey delegates	Muskie delegates	Wallace delegates	Republican delegates	Democratic delegates
Welfare					x	
Busing*					x	
Crime					x	
Civil rights leaders					x	
Welfare recipients					x	
Political demonstrators				x		
Police		x	x			
Military		x				
Blacks				x		
Conservatives					x	
Liberals		x				
Union leaders	x					
Politicians				x		
Inflation*		x				
Abortion*				x		
Laying off women first*				x		
Business interests†		x		x		
Black militants†					x	
Women's liberation†			x			
Vietnam				x		
Ideological self-classification†		x				

*Data on rank-and-file identifiers used to compute least differences on these issues were taken from the 1972 CPS Pre-Election (Post-Convention) Study.

†Data on rank-and-file identifiers used to compute least differences on these issues were taken from the 1972 CPS Post-Election Study.

The remainder of the data on rank-and-file identifiers were taken from the Pre-Convention Study.

N.B. The difference scores above were computed from preponderance scores carried to the first decimal place.

Table 11 · Differences on Selected Issues: Democratic and Republican Rank-and-File Identifiers and Party Elites Compared

	Republican/Democratic voters	Republican/Democratic elite
Welfare	18	95
Busing*	21	117
Crime	14	100
Civil rights leaders	28	71
Welfare recipients	19	65
Political demonstrators	16	95
Police	5	34
Military	8	81
Blacks	17	8
Conservatives	42	105
Liberals	39	119
Politicians	7	18
Union leaders	41	67
Inflation*	1	34
Abortion*	10	18
Laying off women first*	14	24
Women's liberation†	22	82
Business interests†	34	80
Black militants†	18	70
Vietnam	1	113
Ideological self-classification†	52	118
Mean differences	20	72

*The data on rank-and-file identifiers for these issue-questions were taken from the 1972 CPS Pre-Election (Post-Convention) Study.
†The data on rank-and-file identifiers for these issue-questions were taken from the 1972 CPS Post-Election Study.
All other data on rank-and-file identifiers were taken from the Pre-Convention Study.
N.B. The difference scores above were computed from preponderance scores carried to the first decimal place.

lican elite does not indicate that no differences existed between the two mass parties. On the contrary, attitudinal differences between the voters of the two parties were consistent enough to confirm once more that there exist reliable, if not large, differences in orientation and emphasis between them. Democratic identifiers were more likely to take up the 'liberal' position on welfare policy, busing and crime; they felt somewhat more sympathetic than did Republican identifiers toward civil rights leaders, welfare recipients, political demonstrators, liberals, union leaders and blacks, somewhat less sympathetic toward the police and the military and much less sympathetic toward conservatives. The mean difference between Democratic and Republican identifiers on busing, welfare and crime is 17, or slightly more than that which separates Republican voters and delegates. More significant for our purposes is that the same issues and symbols which separated the Democratic from the Republican rank and file still further separated Democratic voters from their own party's elite.

In 1956 McClosky concluded that 'there is a substantial consensus on national issues between Democratic leaders and Democratic and Republican followers, while the Republican leaders are separated not only from the Democrats but from their own rank-and-file members as well. By 1972 the position of Republicans and Democratic elites had been reversed and it was the Democratic presidential elite that was 'odd man out.' The Republican presidential elite more faithfully mirrored the views and values of its own party identifiers and of voters generally than did the Democratic elite, which failed to reflect the views either of ordinary Democrats or of voters generally. But perhaps the Democrats reflected the views of the 'new constituencies'—the women, blacks, and youth who were numerous in the Democratic convention and important in the electorate.

PART IV

The General Election

The practical framework for the general election—both its institutional arrangements and political structure, on the one hand, and the resulting strategies and tactics, on the other—is longer established, more stable, and hence better understood than the corresponding framework for the nomination stage. Despite frequent moves for reform, the basic device by which presidential elections are conducted, the Electoral College, remains unchanged, and it has clear and well-understood effects on the campaign itself. In fact, among institutional rules and procedures for the general election, only finance regulations have undergone significant changes in the period since World War II. With the introduction of full public financing for presidential election campaigns, however, these changes are indeed substantial enough to qualify as a major alteration in nearly everyone's election analyses—including the candidates'.

The two-party system also provides certain extralegal, but still very consistent and strong, constraints on behavior in the election period. In general the system encourages each party to find a nominee who is sufficiently different from his opponent to argue that he offers clear policy advantages, without being *so* different that he risks surrendering the allegiance of large segments of the general public. Unlike Electoral College arrangements or campaign finance laws, this constraint is informal, so that national party conventions are free to ignore it if they wish. Nonetheless, a party which fails to heed this particular informal requirement is very likely to pay the highest short-run price: the loss of a presidential election.

The bases for major-party support among the general public, and thus for a possible majority in November, are also well established. Although they have been shifting slowly in the postwar period, they do not demand major strategic adjustments between any one election and the next. That is to say, the social categories and regions which reliably support the Republican candidate, and those which do the same for the Democrat, are fairly well known. Candidates accordingly know which groups they must mobilize and retain and which others they must detach from their opponent's coalition in order to hope for victory in November. Over time the Democratic coalition has been expanding relative to its Republican counterpart, but because the fastest-growing group has been those who consider themselves "independents," this drift has not created foregone conclusions at the polls.

The means by which these voters make up their minds are also fairly well understood, or at least fairly well classified. In the entire postwar period, the most powerful factor in predicting how an individual will vote has been party identification, although voters' orientations toward particular political issues or toward the personality and style of the candidates have not been unimportant. In summary, then, candidates have had to plan their strategies within three sets of parameters: a generally stable institutional context; a stable (though certainly not fixed) societal backdrop; and a partially manipulable cluster of three elements—partisan attachment, candidate personality, and policy positions.

In Chapter 9 Alexander M. Bickel examines the most basic institutional underpinning for the general election in "The Electoral College," from his book *Reform and Continuity*. He describes the dominant characteristics of this institutional mechanism and the way in which they shape the campaign patterns and policy promises of major-party nominees. Bickel also touches on the effect on campaign patterns of the leading proposed reform of the Electoral College, namely, direct election of the President. To the impact of the Electoral College as a campaign channeling device, Anthony Downs then adds the constraints provided by a two-party system. In "The Statics and Dynamics of Party Ideologies" from his longer work on *An Economic Theory of Democracy*, Downs provides both a model for the normal behavior which a two-party system should produce over time *and* a framework for explaining the result when one or the other of the parties decides to deviate from such behavior.

James L. Sundquist's piece, "The Realignment of the 1930s" from his book *Dynamics of the Party System*, begins to add the societal, as opposed to institutional, constraints on general election politics. Sundquist focuses on the basic partisan loyalties which continue down through the present and which explain American voting behavior in the absence of substantial unsettling elements. Robert Axelrod also looks at this basic (re)alignment and traces it through the last three elections. His article "Where the Votes Come From: An Analysis of Electoral Coalitions" and its subsequent updates chart the additions, subtractions, and revaluations of the voting trends along the way.

The mechanics of conducting campaigns under these constraints have also been fairly well studied, at least by comparison with the nomination process. Organizationally, a candidate's personal following, his party's regular machinery, and a range of outside, independent groups must all be blended to produce a campaign. Over time the weighting of these elements within such campaigns has probably changed, with more emphasis on the independent bodies and less on the party, but the dilemmas in meshing such mutually suspicious operations remain much the same. Financially the change has been sharper. Finances for a general election campaign have probably always been less of a problem than those for a nomination, unless the nominee looked like a certain loser, but now, with public financing and expenditure limitations, money raising has given way to internal allocation decisions as the crux of financial planning.

Despite all this, there remains a place for strategic decisions. Candidates still weigh the relative emphasis to be placed upon issues generally, and the choice of particular issues or themes for central display. They still consider different ways to present themselves, as well as possible alternative uses for their own campaign time and energy. And they still adopt differing degrees and forms of identification with their political parties. In addition, each candidate comes to the contest with his personal strong and weak points, which he must attempt either to exploit or to neutralize. Ultimately his maneuvers may or may not affect the outcome of the general election, but they spring from those elements which are under direct control of the nominee, and he always tries to manipulate them for whatever they may be worth.

In Chapter 10 John H. Kessel's "Strategy for November," from the larger collection *Choosing the President,* reviews the general election battle plans of major-party nominees from 1964 through 1972. W. Hamilton Jordan in "Blueprint/Carter," and Congressman Richard B. Cheney in "The 1976 Presidential Debates: A Republican Perspective," add the 1976 strategies to Kessel's earlier review. Kessel's examination of the Republican strategy of 1964 and the Democratic counterpart of 1972 also gives concrete meaning to Downs's more abstract argument about the inevitable result when one or the other party deviates from normal party positions (Chapter 9). Jordan reveals his precise planning for use of the candidate's *time,* and that of his potential Vice President and their wives as well. Finally, Cheney puts special emphasis on the preparation for, and use of, the head-to-head confrontations between the two candidates which led the Ford campaign staff in 1976 to reconsider the role of issues, the style of personal presentation, and so on.

The short Xandra Kayden selection on financial decisions, "The General Election," outlines a few such decisions and hints at the character of the larger political environment which has been created by the arrival of full public financing. For example, what would once have been choices about fund *raising* have primarily become arguments about fund *allocation*. Kayden also hints that public financing may have ended the traditional notion of a "campaign"—with local headquarters, buttons and bumper stickers, and get-out-the-vote drives. David S. Broder closes with "Political Reporters in Presidential Politics" from the book *Inside the System*. In this piece he talks about the various roles which newsmen play in a general election campaign. The same general picture of a reporter's daily life emerges in both the Broder essay and the Crouse excerpt (Chapter 7). Crouse, however, emphasizes the social and even physical organization of the news business. Broder dwells on the place of that business in the larger political system.

After all these grand strategic (and lesser tactical) maneuvers have contributed what they can, general election outcomes fall roughly into three categories: those which affirm the common understanding about the balance of political forces in American society, those which lead to a temporary deviation from the expected pattern, and those (the least common) which show that the basic balance itself has altered. In the period after World War II there have been an impressive number of deviations—elections in which the Republican Party secured the Presidency—but there has been nothing to indicate that the underlying pattern has been more permanently disturbed by these results.

In Chapter 11 Angus Campbell contributes the principal overview, "A Classification of Presidential Elections," which spells out the internal characteristics of the three major types of outcomes. In "Continuity and Change in American Politics: Parties and Issues in the 1968 Election," Philip E. Converse and his associates analyze one of Campbell's "deviating elections" in detail. They look not only at the role of personalities, issues, and party identifications in that year, but also at the special nature of the most successful third-party presidential bid of the postwar period—the Wallace (American Independent) campaign of 1968. Finally, although an extrapolation of these interpretations suggests that 1980 should bring a comfortable reelection for incumbent President Jimmy Carter, Richard M. Scammon and Ben J. Wattenberg attempt to provide grounds for a more ambiguous prediction in "Jimmy Carter's Problem." And Normal Siegel closes with a very peculiar way to predict which analysis will be correct.

CHAPTER 9

The Framework for Election

A. Institutional Constraints: Electoral Rules and Party Systems

B. Societal Constraints: Public Loyalties and Partisan Support

·A·

Institutional Constraints:
Electoral Rules and Systems

The Electoral College
BY ALEXANDER M. BICKEL

The "Humpty Dumpty electoral college," as one of its critics has called it, is another old institution put to interesting new uses. Now the chief target of reformers,[1] the electoral college was unquestionably intended to serve ends we no longer care to serve, and which it no longer serves. Only in form does it remain what it was invented to be.[2] Pursuant to Article II of the Constitution and the Twelfth Amendment, it still consists of as many electors for each state as the state has senators and representatives; and the electors still convene quadrennially in their states to elect a president and a vice-president of the United States. But although it was probably intended to act independently in performing its function, the electoral college has hardly ever done so, certainly not in modern times. Electors compete for the office in a popular election in each state, but with very infrequent exceptions, which have never proved significant, they do so in complete anonymity, being pledged as a body to presidential and vice-presidential candidates for whom, if they win by a majority or plurality, they cast their state's total electoral vote.

[1]See, e.g., N. R. Peirce, The People's President (New York: Simon and Schuster, 1968); J. D Feerick, "The Electoral College—Why It Ought To Be Abolished," 37 Fordham Law Review I (1968); W. T. Gossett, "Direct Popular Election of the President," 56 American Bar Association Journal 225 (1970).

[2]See L. Wilmerding, Jr., The Electoral College (New Brunswick: Rutgers University Press, 1958), pp. 3–67.

Excerpted from Alexander M. Bickel, Reform and Continuity (New York: Harper Colophon Books, 1971), pp. 4–36. Reprinted by permission of Mrs. Josephine Ann Bickel.

The Great Divide and Urban and Minority Power

These features of the system, unforeseen and unintended by its originators, and dependent on custom, not on the Constitution, have bred in modern times the disproportionate influence in presidential elections of the large, populous, heterogeneous states, and more particularly, of ethnic and racial minorities or other interest groups in these states. Given vigorous party competition, which is the prevailing condition in the big states, cohesive groups, voting substantially en bloc, are capable of determining the result. A portion of the popular vote in the smaller, relatively more homogeneous states is, very often, simply wasted. Politicians and political scientists have at any rate long assumed that the presidency is won or lost in the large industrial states, where one or another group can make all the difference. In theory, pluralities in these states could elect a president who had a smaller total national popular vote than his runner-up in the electoral college. It hardly mattered that nothing of the sort has happened in this century and that it is extremely unlikely to happen. No one was altogether sure that the theory was valid, but the assumption that it was governed the strategy of presidential campaigns, and the theory was thus self-validating. It determined the allocation of influence in presidential politics.

Formally, to be sure, the assignment to each state of as many electoral votes as that state has congressmen and senators malapportions the electoral college in favor of the small states, since each state has two senators regardless of its size, and gets one congressman even if it is a good bit smaller than any single congressional district in a larger state. If each state's electoral vote were divided—precisely or roughly—in proportion to the popular vote cast for each candidate in each state, the malapportionment would become quite real, and might have considerable effect. But the practice for nearly a century and a half has been to cast the electoral vote of each state by the unit rule—winner-take-all. It is under these conditions that the malapportionment in favor of the small states becomes for the most part only apparent, not in practice real. The consequence of the unit rule is that even a small popular majority or plurality in a state gains for a candidate that state's entire electoral vote. This means, in turn, that to carry New York, or Illinois, or California, or Texas by 50,000, or even 5,000, popular votes is to win a much larger number of electoral votes than could be gained by getting great popular majorities in any number of smaller states.

Recently John F. Banzhaf, III, has demonstrated all this mathematically, or at least so expressed it. Using a computer, Mr. Banzhaf has analyzed the various possible arrangements of electoral votes, and the circumstances in which any given state could change the result of an election. He has also calculated the chances of a voter affecting the outcome in his state and the chances that the outcome of a national election would then itself be altered. He has thus arrived at an estimate of the voting power—not unnaturally—as "simply the ability to affect decisions through the process of voting." And his conclusion is that voters in "states like New York and California have over two and one half times as much chance to affect the election of the President as residents of some of the smaller states." Pennsylvania, Ohio, Michigan, and even a lesser industrial state like Massachusetts, are also in advantageous positions. The reason is that while a voter in a large state has a diminished chance of influencing the result in his state, because there are, of course, more people voting, he potentially influences a larger number of electoral votes, and so despite the apparent dilution of his vote, he actually exercises much greater control over the outcome of the national election. This power he derives directly from the electoral college system.[3]

So what we have assumed to be true is true. And we can establish mathematically why modern presidents have been particularly sensitive to urban and minority interests—modern presidents of both parties, this is to say, have been more responsive to urban interests than have other factions in their parties. And only men who can be so responsive are generally nominated and elected. Senator Barry Goldwater in 1964 was an exception; he was nominated. Richard Nixon in 1968 demonstrated in some measure that other strategies are possible. He demonstrated also how risky they are, and why, therefore, they are uncommon, even though he did not by any means entirely abandon the conventional strategy. If both he and Hubert Humphrey made some unfamiliar sounds, that was because of the particular urban mood of the day. But neither man's campaign was ultimately geared to the Mountain States or to the South, and Mr. Nixon's presidency is not so geared. If there was and if there is a southern strategy, its premise is that policies which will carry the South have appeal also to groups that can be decisive in several of the industrial states.

In modern times and in most of our politics, urban interests in the big states have contended against interests that have a more rural, nativist, and Protestant orientation. The latter interests have tended to dominate Congress, the former the presidency. Urban/rural, pluralist/homogeneous—this has been the great divide in American politics. No party is permanently entrenched on either side of the divide. The task of the presidential candidate, Republican or Democratic, has been to bridge it from either side. The electoral college does not guarantee the presidency to a Democrat or to a liberal. The system does require both parties to at least make inroads in the urban and minority vote in order to win. It thus opens up for cohesive groups of liberal orientation in large industrial states a possibility of influence that they would not otherwise have, even though it holds out no guarantee that the influence will always be effective.

[3]See J. F. Banzhaf, III, "One Man, 3.312 Votes: A Mathematical Analysis of the Electoral College," 13 *Villanova Law Review* 303 (1968).

Each of our major parties is, in consequence, as James M. Burns has reminded us, two allied parties—a congressional party, rural and small-town moderate to conservative in orientation, and a presidential party, which is substantially more urban-liberal. (How often has it been true that the Republicans have lost Congress to the Democrats, and the urban liberals have lost the Democrats to Congress!) No doubt, the urban electorate is not always progressive, humane, and large-minded, and the more homogeneous rural and small-town electorate sometimes is. The drift of attitudes among big-city voters is nothing to be proud of just now, nor was it in the early 1950s. Groups other than those that have been dominant in the past generation may seize the balance of power in the large industrial states, use it to other ends, and orient the presidency in a different direction than that to which we have become accustomed. The electoral college would give them full opportunity to do so. On the other hand, the Progressive Movement of a half-century ago had deep roots in the rural West and Midwest. Still, the urban and the rural-small-town outlooks and interests do generally differ. And so long as that remains true, the former should exert particular influence through the presidency because the latter are likely to prevail in Congress.

The difference in interest and outlook may not always obtain. The demography of the United States and its politics will not necessarily abide unaltered, world without end. The country, we are told, is increasingly urban (or at any rate, suburban and metropolitan), and TV and other media are leveling cultural and other distinctions. But urban is a term that can cover many ways of life, and the ethnic and racial composition—and traditions and attitudes—of an urbanized Nebraska or Georgia are still not quite those of New York, Chicago, Cleveland, and the like. If there are major changes in the offing, they are not here yet, and their nature is not readily predicted. And when they come, will they not be digestible by the present system, as the great changes of the past have been? The expectation that the present system will satisfactorily accommodate demographic changes is at least as plausible as the surmise that we now know how to alter the system so that it will suit us in circumstances only dimly foreseen.

The big states would undoubtedly matter in any scheme that took account of the popular vote in whatever fashion, directly or with qualifications. But the electoral college system as it has evolved gives the big states an additional edge. That is its critical attribute. On balance, therefore, the system imposes a disadvantage on the smaller states, especially those that are relatively homogeneous and nearly one-party. Yet it also has its attractions for them.

There is first of all a symbolic value in play for the small states, since the electoral college, on its face, confirms the federal structure, and in some measure the equality, as in the Senate, of all states, large and small. Secondly, combinations remain conceivable which would make the malapportionment in favor of the smaller states very real. Circumstances are imaginable in which tiny shifts of popular votes in a group of small states, combined with equally minor shifts in at least one big state, could swing the election, regardless of the total national popular vote. In 1960, small shifts of popular votes, totalling no more than some 11,000, in New Mexico, Hawaii, and Nevada, as well as in Illinois and Missouri, could have put Mr. Nixon in office.

The possibility of such a decisive role falling to a group of small states is highly remote. Actually, it is narrow margins of the popular vote in the big states that have sometimes been decisive, and in any event, this much greater likelihood exerts its powerful influence on the nominating process, and on the strategy of presidential campaigns. But those who have the interests of small states at heart may take comfort in the other possibility, however remote; they may think it worthwhile to retain the present system because the apparent but usually ineffective malapportionment in favor of the small states may at some point actually work out that way. This is a remote expectation, but it is not an irrational one, and those who entertain it are entitled to it. It does not alter the common reality, and should not control the judgment of representatives of the big states.

. . . .

The question about the electoral college, then, should not be whether it is inevitably and purely majoritarian. It is not, although it is very considerably more so than our other national institutions. The question should be whether or not the electoral college tends to enhance minorities' rule; whether it tends to include or exclude various groups from influence in the institution of the presidency, and whether if it assigns somewhat disproportionate influence to some groups, they are the ones which are relatively shortchanged in Congress, so that the total effect is the achievement of a balance of influence? Practical men interested in perfecting the American democracy should disenthrall themselves from the romance of pure majoritarianism. That romance leads them to diminish the influence of the urban voter in the election of presidents, which is not a democratic result—not as the concept of democracy has been understood and applied in our tradition, or as it could conceivably be applied to the structure of our national government in the conditions of our vast and varied country.

The Statics and Dynamics of Party Ideologies

BY ANTHONY DOWNS

INTRODUCTION

If political ideologies are truly means to the end of obtaining votes, and if we know something about the distribution of voters' preferences, we can make specific predictions about how ideologies change in content as parties maneuver to gain power. Or, conversely, we can state the conditions under which ideologies come to resemble each other, diverge from each other, or remain in some fixed relationship.

OBJECTIVES

In this chapter we attempt to prove the following propositions:

1. A two-party democracy cannot provide stable and effective government unless there is a large measure of ideological consensus among its citizens.
2. Parties in a two-party system deliberately change their platforms so that they resemble one another; whereas parties in a multiparty system try to remain as ideologically distinct from each other as possible.
3. If the distribution of ideologies in a society's citizenry remains constant, its political system will move toward a position of equilibrium in which the number of parties and their ideological positions are stable over time.
4. New parties can be most successfully launched immediately after some significant change in the distribution of ideological views among eligible voters.
5. In a two-party system, it is rational for each party to encourage voters to be irrational by making its platform vague and ambiguous.

I. The Spatial Analogy and Its Early Use

To carry out this analysis, we borrow and elaborate upon an apparatus invented by Harold Hotelling. It first appeared in a famous article on spatial competition published in 1929, and was later refined by Arthur

Smithies. Our version of Hotelling's spatial market consists of a linear scale running from zero to 100 in the usual left-to-right fashion. To make this politically meaningful, we assume that political preferences can be ordered from left to right in a manner agreed upon by all voters. They need not agree on which point they personally prefer, only on the ordering of parties from one extreme to the other.

In addition, we assume that every voter's preferences are single-peaked and slope downward monotonically on either side of the peak (unless his peak lies at one extreme on the scale). For example, if a voter likes position 35 best, we can immediately deduce that he prefers 30 to 25 and 40 to 45. He always prefers some point X to another point Y if X is closer to 35 than Y and both are on the same side of 35. The slope downward from the apex need not be identical on both sides, but we do presume no sharp asymmetry exists.

These assumptions can perhaps be made more plausible if we reduce all political questions to their bearing upon one crucial issue: how much government intervention in the economy should there be? If we assume that the left end of the scale represents full government control, and the right end means a completely free market, we can rank parties by their views on this issue in a way that might be nearly universally recognized as accurate. In order to coördinate this left-right orientation with our numerical scale, we will arbitrarily assume that the number denoting any party's position indicates the percentage of the economy it wants left in private hands (excluding those minimal state operations which even the most Hayekian economists favor). Thus the extreme left position is zero, and the extreme right is 100. Admittedly, this apparatus is unrealistic for the following two reasons: (1) actually each party is leftish on some issues and rightish on others, and (2) the parties designated as right wing extremists in the real world are for fascist control of the economy rather than free markets. However, we will ignore these limitations temporarily and see what conclusions of interest we can draw from this spatial analogy.

Both Hotelling and Smithies have already applied their versions of this model to politics. Hotelling assumed that people were evenly spaced along the straight-line scale, and reasoned that competition in a two-party system would cause each party to move towards its opponent ideologically. Such convergence would occur because each party knows that extremists at its end of the scale prefer it to the opposition, since it is necessarily closer to them than the opposition party is. Therefore the best way for it to gain more support is to move toward the other extreme, so as to get more voters outside of it—i.e., to come between them and its opponent. As the two parties move closer together, they become more moderate and less extreme in policy in an effort to win the crucial middle-of-the-road voters, i.e., those whose views place them between the two parties. This center area becomes smaller as both parties strive to capture moderate voters;

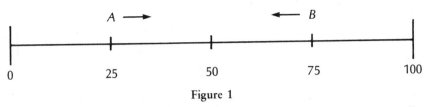

Figure 1

Notes for Figures 1–4: Horizontal scale represents political orientation. Vertical scale represents number of citizens.

finally the two parties become nearly identical in platforms and actions. For example, if there is one voter at every point on the scale, and parties A and B start at points 25 and 75 respectively, they will move towards each other and meet at 50, assuming they move at the same speed (Fig. 1). Like the two grocery stores in Hotelling's famous example, they will converge on the same location until practically all voters are indifferent between them.

Smithies improved this model by introducing elastic demand at each point on the scale. Thus as the grocery stores moved away from the extremes, they lost customers there because of the increased cost of transportation; this checked them from coming together at the center. In our model, this is analogous to political extremists becoming disgusted at the identity of the parties, and refusing to vote for either if they become too much alike. At exactly what point this leakage checks the convergence of A and B depends upon how many extremists each loses by moving towards the center compared with how many moderates it gains thereby.

II. The Effects of Various Distributions of Voters

A. IN TWO-PARTY SYSTEMS

An important addition we can make to this model is a variable distribution of voters along the scale. Instead of assuming there is one voter at each point on the scale, let us assume there are 100,000 voters whose preferences cause them to be normally distributed with a mean of 50 (Fig. 2). Again, if we place parties A and B initially at 25 and 75, they will converge rapidly upon the center. The possible loss of extremists will not deter their movement toward each other, because there are so few voters to be lost at the margins compared with the number to be gained in the middle. However, if we alter the distribution to that shown in Figure 3, the two parties will not move away from their initial positions at 25 and 75 at all; if they did, they would lose far more voters at the extremes than they could possibly gain in the center. Therefore a two-party system need not lead to the convergence on moderation that Hotelling and Smithies predicted. If voters' preferences are

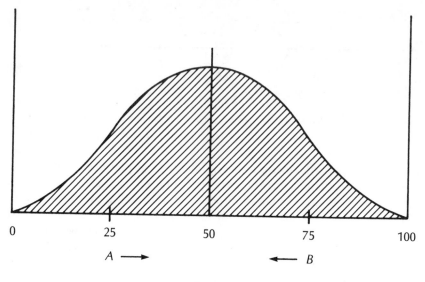

Figure 2

distributed so that voters are massed bimodally near the extremes, the parties will remain poles apart in ideology.

The possibility that parties will be kept from converging ideologically in a two-party system depends upon the refusal of extremist voters to support either party if both become alike—not identical, but merely similar. In a certain world—where information is complete and costless, there is no future-oriented voting, and the act of voting uses up no scarce resources—such abstention by extremists would be irrational. As long as there is even the most infinitesimal difference between A and B, extremist voters would be forced to vote for the one closest to them, no matter how distasteful its policies seemed in comparison with those of their ideal government. It is always rational *ex definitione* to select a greater good before a lesser, or a lesser evil before a greater; consequently abstention would be irrational because it increases the chances of the worse party for victory.

Even in a certain world, however, abstention is rational for extremist voters who are future oriented. They are willing to let the worse party win today in order to keep the better party from moving towards the center, so that in future elections it will be closer to them. Then when it does win, its victory is more valuable in their eyes. Abstention thus becomes a threat to use against the party nearest one's own extreme position so as to keep it away from the center.

Uncertainty increases the possibility that rational extremist voters will abstain if the party nearest them moves toward its opponent, even if it does not become ideologically identical with the latter. When information is limited and costly, it is difficult to detect infinitesimal differences between

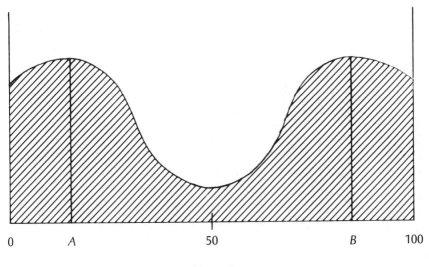

0   *A*   50   *B*   100

Figure 3

parties. Perhaps even relatively significant differences will pass unnoticed by the radical whose own views are so immoderate that all moderates look alike. This means that the differential threshold of such extremists is likely to be very high—they will regard all small differences between moderate parties as irrelevant to their voting decision, i.e., as unreal distinctions.

Having established the rationality of abstention by extremist voters, let us again consider a bimodal distribution of voters with modes near each extreme (Fig. 3). In a two-party system, whichever party wins will attempt to implement policies radically opposed to the other party's ideology, since the two are at opposite extremes. This means that government policy will be highly unstable, and that democracy is likely to produce chaos. Unfortunately, the growth of balancing center parties is unlikely. Any party which forms in the center will eventually move toward one extreme or the other to increase its votes, since there are so few moderate voters. Furthermore, any center party could govern only in coalition with one of the extremist parties, which would alienate the other, and thus not eliminate the basic problem. In such a situation, unless voters can somehow be moved to the center of the scale to eliminate their polar split, democratic government is not going to function at all well. In fact, no government can operate so as to please most of the people; hence this situation may lead to revolution.

The political cycle typical of revolutions can be viewed as a series of movements of men along the political scale. Preliminary to the upheaval, the once centralized distribution begins to polarize into two extremes as the incumbents increasingly antagonize those who feel themselves oppressed. When the distribution has become so split that one extreme is imposing by force policies abhorred by the other extreme, open warfare

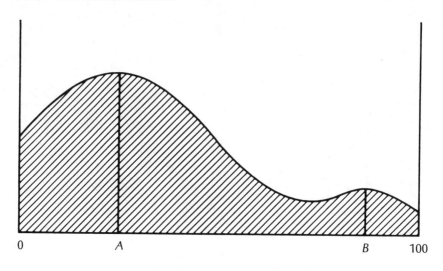

Figure 4

breaks out, and a clique of underdogs seizes power. This radical switch from one extreme to the other is partly responsible for the reign of terror which marks most revolutions; the new governors want to eliminate their predecessors, who have bitterly opposed them. Finally violence exhausts itself, a new consensus is reached on the principles of the revolution, and the distribution becomes centralized again—often under a new dictatorship as rigid as the old, but not faced with a polarized distribution of opinions.

Under more normal circumstances, in countries where there are two opposite social classes and no sizeable middle class, the numerical distribution is more likely to be skewed to the left, with a small mode at the right extreme (Fig. 4). The large mode at the left represents the lower or working class; on the right is the upper class. Here democracy, if effective, will bring about the installation of a leftish government because of the numerical preponderance of the lower classes. Fear of this result is precisely what caused many European aristocrats to fight the introduction of universal suffrage. Of course, our schema oversimplifies the situation considerably. On our political scale, every voter has equal weight with every other, whereas in fact the unequal distribution of income allows a numerically small group to control political power quite disproportionate to its size . . .

In spite of this oversimplification, it is clear that the numerical distribution of voters along the political scale determines to a great extent what kind of democracy will develop. For example, a distribution like that of Figure 2 encourages a two-party system with both parties located near the center in relatively moderate positions. This type of government is likely to have stable policies, and whichever party is in power, its policies will not be far from the views of the vast majority of people.

Societal Constraints: Public Loyalties and Partisan Support

The Realignment of the 1930s
BY JAMES L. SUNDQUIST

After 1932: The Democrats Commit Themselves

Barring a sudden, miraculous recovery from the depression, only one thing could possibly have saved Herbert Hoover in 1932—a division of the opposition between the Democratic party and a more radical third-party movement along the lines of 1924. But this time the potential organizers of a third party had no available leader of stature to make the try. Norris and Pinchot were too old, Bob La Follette, Jr., too young, other insurgent senators either too individualistic or too committed to party regularity. More important still, the Democratic party, again in contrast to 1924, appeared headed toward progressive leadership, for Governor Franklin D. Roosevelt of New York was its front runner for the presidential nomination.

A CAUTIOUS CAMPAIGN

Roosevelt did not enter the presidential race as a crusading progressive of the La Follette stamp. He had a head start for the nomination by virtue of his 1928 victory as governor of the largest state (while Smith was losing) and his reelection by a whopping 725,000 majority in 1930. He had had national exposure as the party's vice-presidential candidate in 1920 and as the man who nominated Smith in 1924 and again in 1928. He had maintained his political contacts across the country through incessant letter-

Excepted from James L. Sundquist, *Dynamics of the Party System* (Washington: The Brookings Institution, 1973), pp. 190–214. Some footnotes deleted. Copyright © 1973 by the Brookings Institution, and reprinted by their permission.

writing, and his personal charm had registered. With all these advantages his strategy was to proceed cautiously and avoid mistakes. So his positions on some of the major issues of the day—the tariff, for instance, the World Court, and even Prohibition repeal—were disappointingly ambiguous to many would-be supporters. He even agreed with Hoover that relief should be a state and local responsibility.

Roosevelt could afford to be cautious because his standing as a progressive was secure. He was an old Wilsonian. He had consistently maintained in his correspondence that the Democratic party should commit itself to progressive, though not radical, principles. As governor, he had supported public development of St. Lawrence River power, which endeared him to progressives everywhere, and he had made a positive record on conservation and on labor and welfare legislation. He was one of only three or four governors (others were Pinchot of Pennsylvania and Philip F. La Follette of Wisconsin, both Republicans) who had initiated significant programs of state aid for relief. He had endorsed the principle of unemployment insurance. Progressives were prominent in his state administration—Frances Perkins, Harry Hopkins, Leland Olds. As early as June 1930, Senator Burton K. Wheeler of Montana, the Democratic insurgent leader who had been La Follette's running mate in 1924, had come out for Roosevelt for President. "You more nearly typify the progressive thought of the Nation than anyone else," he told Roosevelt.[1]

As the campaign progressed, Roosevelt struck a progressive tone, even if he did not offer much in the way of a program. In April came his Forgotten Man speech—"These unhappy times call for . . . plans that . . . build from the bottom up and not from the top down, that put their faith once more in the forgotten man at the bottom of the economic pyramid." The following month, at Oglethorpe University in Georgia, he called for a "more equitable distribution of the national income" and expressed in purest form the activist temper: "Take a method and try it; if it fails, admit it frankly, and try another. But above all, try something." To some editors, this was "radicalism," and the idea that the country should "gamble its way out of the depression" was dangerous.[2]

Roosevelt's principal rival for the nomination, Al Smith, drew the ideological issue from the conservative side. Seizing on the Forgotten Man speech, he swore to "fight to the end any candidate who persists in any demagogic appeal to the masses of the working people of the country to destroy themselves by setting class against class and rich against poor."[3] But Roosevelt entered the convention with a majority of pledged votes and

---

[1]Arthur M. Schlesinger, Jr., *Crisis of the Old Order 1919–1933* (Houghton Mifflin, 1957), pp. 277–78, 389–93.

[2]Quoted from newspaper comment on the Oglethorpe speech, by *Literary Digest* (June 4, 1932), pp. 3–4.

[3]*Literary Digest* (April 23, 1932), p. 11.

got the necessary two-thirds on the fourth ballot. The progressives once again had captured the Democratic party.

Paul Douglas, among others, continued to advocate a new party. Despite Roosevelt's "many progressive tendencies and a certain feeling for the underdog," he argued, the "Democratic party will remain the Democratic party under his administration"[4] But the response was negligible, and Douglas and many of his fellow members of the League for Independent Political Action finally voted for Socialist Norman Thomas. Others gave up their independence to throw in their lot with Roosevelt.

It probably did not matter what kind of campaign Roosevelt conducted, cautious or otherwise. When unemployment stands at 24 percent, as it did in 1932, an incumbent President is not reelected. The Democrats' share of the popular vote rose from 34 percent in 1920, 29 in 1924, and 41 in 1928 to 57 percent in the landslide of 1932. Almost one-third of the Republican strength of 1928 was lost to Roosevelt or to minor-party candidates.

But one landslide is not a party realignment. A realignment requires that the switching voters remain switched. In this case they would have to become more than just Hoover haters or Roosevelt supporters; they would have to come to think of themselves as Democrats.

The Democratic party was still an unknown quantity, however, in regard to the issues that had caused the massive crossing of the party line. It would have to prove, in office, that its philosophy and program were an improvement over those of Herbert Hoover. And it would have to find a way to absorb the newcomers into its institutional structure in order to retain them.

AN ACTIVIST ADMINISTRATION

As it was in the character of Herbert Hoover to lead the Republican party to the conservative pole on the issues of the depression, so it was in the personality and temperament of Franklin Roosevelt to cast his party in the role of activism. Yet while the distinctive quality of Rooseveltian leadership had much to do with the form and timing of the realignment that followed, he still seems to have been more instrument than author. At a time of suffering beyond all precedent, the policies of the government could not have remained forever frozen. An activist government would have been installed somehow; if not through Roosevelt, then through someone else; if not through the Democratic party, then through some other party; if not in 1932, then assuredly in 1936. And realignment would have come about in any case. The key variable in the 1930s was not leadership but the overwhelming intrinsic power of the Great Depression as a realigning issue.

[4]Paul H. Douglas, *The Coming of a New Party* (Whittlesey House, 1932), pp. 168–69.

If Roosevelt had not been on the scene as a declared activist, it still seems scarcely conceivable that the Democrats in 1932 would have joined the GOP and nominated another states' rights conservative. The candidacy of Governor Albert C. Ritchie of Maryland, who represented that point of view, never got off the ground. John Garner or Al Smith, one of whom might have been nominated if there had been no Roosevelt, would in all probability have campaigned for and accepted the nomination as a committed activist. Or someone else would have emerged. But if by any chance the Democratic party had halted the leftward movement that was so apparent in the Congress in 1932 and chosen instead to share the conservative side of the political spectrum with Hoover, then the insurgents of both parties would have had to unite behind someone—Wheeler or La Follette or Borah or someone less conspicuous—who would have caught the spirit of the times. The forces of protest were too powerful to be denied political expression in one of the major parties of the two-party system. If they had not captured one of the existing parties, as the forces of protest did in 1896, they would have formed their own, as in 1854. And in that case, if the new party did not at once appear as one of the two major parties, the strength of the issue would have carried it forward until it did attain that status. Realignment would have been different in form but not in essence.

As it happened, the forces demanding change captured the Democratic party. And even after Roosevelt's election, they, more than he, controlled the direction of the party and the government. If Roosevelt led his party and the people, he was also led by them. That the Congress during the Hundred Days passed major bills that had not even been printed suggests not only the depth of the crisis but Congress's reading of the depth of the President's support. And Congress was more than a "rubber stamp"; it too was responding to pressure from the country. Some major enactments of the New Deal were of congressional origin—including the National Labor Relations Act and public housing—and other measures credited to Roosevelt were spurred by pressure from the Hill. "In these early years," says Arthur M. Schlesinger, Jr., "Congress was as often to the left of Roosevelt as to the right."[5]

Mass organizations that were rising at the activist pole kept Roosevelt constantly reminded that, if the Democratic party flagged in its pursuit of reform, it could be superseded as the party of protest by a coalescence of formidable forces. The Reverend Charles E. Coughlin, a parish priest of Royal Oak, Michigan, had a radio audience of ten million people a week and was organizing a political movement called the National Union for Social Justice. Dr. Francis E. Townsend of Long Beach, California, author of a radical pension plan, was printing 200,000 copies of his weekly newspaper and forming "Townsend Clubs" across the country, which

[5]*The Coming of the New Deal* (Houghton Mifflin, 1958), pp. 554–55.

were potential components of a party organization. Senator Huey P. Long of Louisiana was planning a Share Our Wealth party for 1936 which, according to a poll commissioned by Democratic Chairman James A. Farley, would receive from three to six million votes. Milo Reno and his National Farmers' Holiday Association—a militant midwestern farm organization—were planning to support a third-party movement. The Democratic party in several states was far to the left of Roosevelt: in California, where Upton Sinclair ran for governor in 1934 on his End Poverty in California plan; in Washington State, where the Washington Commonwealth Federation captured control of the party. The Farmer-Labor governor of Minnesota, Floyd B. Olson, was a radical with a national following. The La Follettes in Wisconsin seceded from the GOP and formed a Progressive party that swept the state in 1934. The League for Independent Political Action became the Farmer-Labor Political Federation with a demand for "a new social order." While the programs of these organizations and leaders differed in scope and content, they tended in the same direction: a planned economy, public ownership of some or all basic industries, "production for use instead of for profit," redistribution of wealth and income. The radical threat had at least some effect on Roosevelt's decisions as he reinvigorated the New Deal, after a period of pause and uncertainty, in 1935. He cited Long's Share Our Wealth proposals and spoke of "stealing Long's thunder" when he proposed his own share-the-wealth tax plan: a federal inheritance tax, higher personal income taxes in the top brackets, a graduated corporation income tax.

With these and other measures, Roosevelt maintained a pace of reform fast enough to keep the forces of the left from converging. Olson and the La Follettes remained loyal. Long's assassination in September 1935 removed the only other leader who might have seriously challenged Roosevelt. Coughlin, Townsend, and Gerald L. K. Smith finally formed a Union party in 1936 with Representative William Lemke, North Dakota Republican and Nonpartisan Leaguer, as its candidate. But Lemke polled fewer than 900,000 votes, a showing no better than that of Norman Thomas four years before.

Meanwhile the Republican party remained immobile at the conservative pole. As the government finally changed direction, under Roosevelt, Hoover continued to be the best-publicized spokesman both for the conservative ideologues and for the GOP. In his plea for vindication he denounced the New Deal and all its works in terms that grew harsher year by year: "a muddle of unco-ordinated reckless adventures in government," "the color of despotism ... the color of Fascism ... the color of Socialism," "flagrant flouting of the Constitution," "the era of the Great Fear," "dipped from cauldrons of European Fascism or Socialism," "the philosophy of collectivism and ... greed for power," "repudiation of obligations ... violation of trust," "the gospel of class hatred preached from the

White House," "a revolutionary design to replace the American system with despotism," "the poisoning of Americanism."[6] Republican congressional minorities had gone along with some of the New Deal reforms, such as social security and the National Labor Relations Act, but they had gone down fighting against others—the farm bills, the reciprocal trade agreements act, the Tennessee Valley Authority, the public utilities holding company act. In 1936, Governor Alfred M. Landon as the Republican presidential candidate began his campaign attacking only New Deal extravagance and maladministration but ended sounding not much different from Hoover. The Republican National Committee talked of Stalin and Kerensky and Earl Browder and joined with organized business and the Hearst newspapers in a concerted effort to equate social security with European totalitarian ideas.

All this was a matter of compulsion as well as choice. If the country's activists were enraged by the fact of human suffering, its conservatives were no less incensed by the nature of the remedies proposed. To the conservatives, the New Deal genuinely threatened the very basis of the country's free economic system and political tradition. They too constituted a polar force that had to have political expression, and in the Republican party they found their instrument. A new generation of Republican moderates was to emerge later, but in the early New Deal years the militant conservatives had no difficulty retaining control of the national Republican party and stamping it with their philosophy.

By 1936, then, the polarization of the country was reflected in the polarization of the major parties. The election of that year, in which Roosevelt achieved his most stunning victory, therefore marked the climax of the realignment.

Substance of the Realignment

The realignment of the 1930s took the form shown in Figure 1. It followed the pattern of . . . realignment through the two existing major parties.

The millions of voters who switched from the Republican to the Democratic party, shown as block B_1 in the diagram, made the latter the country's clear majority party for the first time in eighty years. In the eight years from 1928 to 1936, the Democratic presidential vote rose from 15.0 to 27.8 million, while the Republican vote fell from 21.4 to 16.7 million. Some of that swing appears as a deviation that was corrected in 1938 and 1940, when the Republicans snapped back. But the GOP has never recovered the majority position it lost in the realignment of the 1930s.

[6]Various addresses, November 1935 to June 1936; Herbert Hoover, *Addresses upon the American Road, 1933–38* (Scribner's, 1938), pp. 76, 88, 101, 105, 132, 175–78.

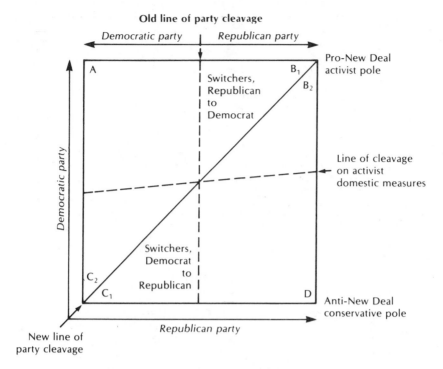

Figure 1 · The Realignment of the 1930s[a]

[a]This figure is schematic rather than quantitatively precise. The size of the compartments does not measure the proportion of the electorate contained in each.

URBAN, WORKING CLASS, AND ETHNIC SWITCHERS

The millions who switched parties between 1928 and 1936, and stayed switched, can be identified most readily by place of residence. They were concentrated in the industrial cities of the North. Franklin Roosevelt and the issues of the Great Depression completed what Alfred E. Smith and the issue of Prohibition had begun—the transformation of the northern urban centers into the network of Democratic bastions they have since remained. In cities that historically had been preponderantly Democratic, like New York, the Republican party ceased to be a competitive force. Cities that had been converted to Democracy in the Smith campaign, like Boston, were confirmed in their new allegiance. And cities that had resisted the Smith appeal responded to Roosevelt and were transformed.

Figure 2 shows the distinctly different voting behavior of three types of communities in the North. The top line shows the trend in the Democratic share of the presidential vote for a composite of the five northern counties of over 100,000 population with the highest proportion of Catholics and foreign born. These are the cities that were swept up in the

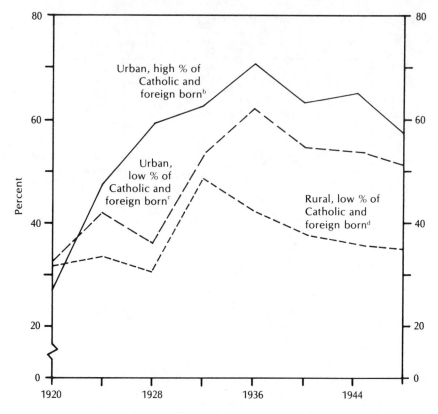

**Figure 2 · Democratic Percentage of the Presidential Vote
in Selected Counties, 1920–48[a]**

Sources: U.S. Bureau of the Census, *Fifteenth Census of the United States:1930,* Vol. 3, Pts. 1 and 2; *Religious Bodies: 1936,* Vol. 1, summary and detailed tables.

[a]The percentages shown for 1924 are of the combined Democratic-Progressive vote.

[b]Composite of the five counties of over 100,000 population in the North and West with the highest proportion of Catholics and foreign born (as of 1930). They are Suffolk (Boston); Wayne (Detroit); Passaic, N.J.; Bronx, N.Y.; New York, N.Y.

[c]Composite of the five counties of over 100,000 population in the North and West with the lowest proportion of Catholics and foreign born (as of 1930). They are Marion (Indianapolis); Franklin (Columbus); Summit (Akron); King (Seattle); Hennepin (Minneapolis).

[d]Composite of thirty rural counties (ten contiguous counties each from New York, Michigan, and Illinois) that lost population from 1900 to 1930 and had a low proportion of Catholics and foreign born. In New York the counties are: Chenango, Columbia, Delaware, Greene, Madison, Oswego, Otsego, Rensselaer, Schoharie, Ulster. In Michigan: Barry, Branch, Clinton, Hillsdale, Huton, Mecosta, Montcalm, Sanilac, Tuscola, Van Buren. In Illinois: Brown, Cass, Greene, Hancock, McDonough, Mason, Menard, Morgan, Pike, Warren.

"Al Smith revolution." With the combined La Follette–Davis vote of 1924 taken as the base, the Democrats showed an eleven-point gain in 1928. While that party enjoyed further gains in the next two presidential elections, most of its permanent increment in strength had come by 1928. The second line is a composite of the five urban counties of over 100,000 population at the other end of the scale of Catholic and foreign-born proportions. These communities the Al Smith revolution passed by, but they were caught up in the New Deal sweeps of 1932 and 1936. Although, as would be expected from their population composition, they are among the more Republican of urban counties, they still registered consistent Democratic majorities in the postrealignment period. Both groups of urban counties stabilized at a Democratic strength in 1948 ten points above the La Follette–Davis 1924 base. The rural North, on the other hand, experienced no such conversion. Thirty counties in three states selected as representative of rural, old-stock, Protestant America (shown in the bottom line) registered only a two-point Democratic gain over that time span. There the Democratic vote of 1932 turned out to be largely a deviation, and most of the Democratic gains of the depression years were lost by 1944.

Within the cities, the Republicans-turned-Democrats were predominantly of the working class. Polling evidence confirms what the behavior of the parties and the politicians suggests: the party system that emerged from the revolution of the 1930s reflected a pronounced class cleavage. Businessmen and professional men were preponderantly Republican; the working class predominantly Democratic. Following is a breakdown of responses (by percent) given early in 1940 to the question, "In politics, do you consider yourself a Democrat, Independent, Socialist, or Republican?"[7]

	REPUBLICAN	DEMOCRAT	INDEPENDENT	OTHER
Total sample	38	42	19	1
Professional	44	29	25	2
Business	48	29	22	1
White-collar workers	36	40	22	2
Skilled workers	36	44	19	1
Semiskilled workers	33	47	18	2
Unskilled workers	27	55	16	2

And to another question, "Which party would you like to see win the Presidential election in 1940?" the breakdown of responses for each party (by percent) was:

[7]*Public Opinion Quarterly*, Vol. 4 (1940), pp. 340–41, summarizing American Institute of Public Opinion (Gallup) polls.

	DEMOCRAT	REPUBLICAN
Upper income	36	64
Middle income	51	49
Lower income	69	31
Labor union members	66	34

Since polling only began in the 1930s, comparative data are not available for the pre–New Deal period. The party system undoubtedly reflected some degree of class bias before the realignment, but there can be little doubt that it was accentuated by the event. It was in the New Deal era that tight bonds were formed between organized labor and the Democratic party, that ties equally close if less formal and overt were formed between business organizations and the GOP, and that partisan politics for the first time since 1896 sharply accented class issues. An activist-conservative line of cleavage and a class-based rationale for the party system are two ways of describing the same structure, for it was the lower economic classes who wanted to use the powers of government for the relief of economic hardship and the reform of the economic system in their interests. The party conflict thus reflected at the same time a policy disagreement as to the role of government and a struggle between broad class and interest groups for the control of government.

Burnham and others have cited the *Literary Digest* polls to confirm not only that the realignment of the 1930s had a class basis but also that it took place after 1932 rather than before or during that year's election. The 1932 *Digest* poll accurately predicted the outcome of that year's election in spite of the pronounced bias of the sample in favor of upper-income groups. It missed Roosevelt's percentage of the popular vote by only three points, predicting 56 percent instead of the 59 percent he actually received. The 1932 Democratic majority must therefore have been relatively uniform among all groups in the population. But when the *Digest* used the same sampling technique in 1936, it miscalculated by eighteen points. It predicted 42 percent of the popular vote for Roosevelt; he received 60. This large discrepancy could only be accounted for by the underrepresentation of the lower-income groups in the sample, and their conversion to the Democrats in markedly disproportionate numbers must therefore have occurred after 1932.[8]

The polls have also consistently shown Democratic support to be far higher among Catholics, Jews, and blacks than among white Protestants,

[8]Walter Dean Burnham, *Critical Elections and the Mainsprings of American Politics* (Norton, 1970), p. 56. For comments on the unrepresentativeness of the *Digest* sample, see George Gallup, *A Guide to Public Opinion Polls* (Princeton University Press, 1940), pp. 73–75, quoted in Julian L. Simon, *Basic Research Methods in Social Science: The Art of Empirical Investigation* (Random House, 1969), pp. 114–15. The sample was taken largely from telephone books and lists of automobile owners and so was heavily concentrated in the upper half of the income scale.

and while this disparity dates to 1928 in the case of the Catholics and perhaps the Jews, it was solidified by the realignment of the 1930s, as Figure 1 indicates. Perhaps the most careful study of the realignment of individual ethnic groups was done by John Myers Allswang, covering nine groups in Chicago during the period when the city was converted from a normally Republican one (it reelected its Republican mayor in 1927) to one so solidly Democratic that the Republican party could not offer a serious challenge. Of Allswang's nine groups, only the Czechs and the Lithuanians gave a majority to the Democratic candidate for senator in 1924. In the 1928 presidential contest, five other groups swung over to Democratic majorities—the Poles (71 percent), Italians (63 percent), Jews (60 percent), Germans (58 percent), and Yugoslavs (54 percent). By that time, the Czech Democratic majority had risen to 73 percent and the Lithuanian to 77 percent. In 1932, a Protestant ethnic group, the Swedes, went Democratic by a bare majority of 51 percent. Finally in 1934, the ninth group, the blacks, left the party of Lincoln on their way to becoming the most solid of all the Democratic ethnic groups.[9] In that year they unseated Republican Congressman Oscar De Priest, the first black ever sent to the House of Representatives from a northern constituency and still the last black Republican to be sent there from any district.

EVIDENCE FROM PARTY REGISTRATION FIGURES

In addition to the data from public opinion polls, another source of quantitative data on party attachment is available in the twentieth century to supplement election returns, which are the only source of such data for the nineteenth. This new set of indicators consists of figures on voter registration (or enrollment) by parties, a requirement that was introduced in some states when direct primaries were instituted, beginning in the Progressive Era.

　Registration is a positive act by a voter to identify with a party as such, as distinct from giving his support to the party's candidate in a particular election. For purposes of analyzing party alignment, therefore, registration data have the great advantage of ignoring the deviant voting behavior that so frequently confuses the interpretation of election returns: a deviant, by definition, does not change his party affiliation. On the other hand, registration data have their own weaknesses. Since registration is a public act, it is subject to coercive influences. In any local jurisdiction, the majority party will always be overregistered. Some voters who oppose that party in November in the secrecy of the voting booth may register with it because it

[9]John Myers Allswang, "The Political Behavior of Chicago's Ethnic Groups, 1918–1932 (Ph.D. dissertation, University of Pittsburgh, 1967), esp. table, pp. 39–40. The Irish, who were not among the ethnic groups whose political behavior was studied, were, as elsewhere, traditionally Democratic.

holds the more significant primaries. Or they may find it prudent to affiliate publicly with the party that controls local patronage as well as the police, the courts, and property tax assessment.[10] And since registration requires a deliberate overt act, registration shifts lag behind permanent shifts in voting behavior. Registrars are also slow in purging the voting lists of persons who have died or moved away.

Party registration data, moreover, are not universally available. In some states, voters are not required to register by party. In still other states, the figures are not centrally compiled and published. But for five states—New York, Pennsylvania, West Virginia, Oregon, and California—continuous series of party registration figures by counties have been published since the 1920s.

Registration trends in selected areas in the five states are presented in Figures 3, 4, 5, 6, and 7. They show how sharp and decisive was the break with the past in some areas and how limited it was in others. They also give evidence of the timing of the realignment where it appeared.

Party enrollment trends in New York State (Figure 3) show a massive realignment in New York City and in Albany County, beginning from a Democratic low point in 1920 and reaching its climax in the 1930s, but no comparable trend in other places. Not only the rural areas but also some major industrial cities were bypassed in the New Deal realignment. In upstate New York as a whole the 1930s appear as a period not of realignment but of deviation. Political lines in Onondaga County (Syracuse), which Franklin Roosevelt could never carry, remained untouched by the New Deal era. Even Erie County (Buffalo) resembled the rural upstate more than it did New York City: Democratic strength stabilized at a level somewhat higher than in the 1920s, but the shift was limited. The new Democrats were primarily in the city of Buffalo, which elected a Democratic mayor in 1933. The rural areas of the county remained as Republican as the rest of upstate New York.

Figure 4, which presents the registration trends for six West Virginia counties, portrays again the sharp realignment of the 1930s—especially between 1932 and 1934—and a picture of relative stability since. The upheaval was greatest in the southern coalfields. (Logan and McDowell counties) and in Ohio County (Wheeling, steel). In McDowell County, the Democratic percentage rose from 29.5 to 58 percent in a single two-year period following the election in 1932 of the first Democratic governor in a dozen years (along with Franklin Roosevelt). In the coal counties, the Republican party continued the struggle for a time after the Democrats had attained a clear preponderance, then gradually disappeared. The ur-

---

[10]In one county in New York State, the local political folklore held that a change in enrollment meant an automatic $500 increase or decrease in the assessed value of a homeowner's real estate, depending on the direction of the change.

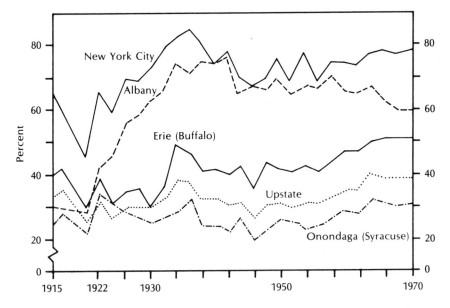

Figure 3 · Democratic Percentage of Two-Party Enrollment in New York, Selected Areas, 1915–70[a]

Source: *Manual for the Use of the Legislature of the State of New York,* various years.
[a]Plotted biennially for even years, except 1915 is included and data for 1918 are not available.

ban counties of Kanawha (Charleston) and Wood (Parkersburg) underwent a more limited realignment in the 1930s and have shown remarkable stability since. Preston County, which is agricultural, shows the typically lower Democratic strength of rural areas but reflects greater gains for the party than were recorded in the typical rural county of New York. Unlike the New York counties, the West Virginia localities in no case experienced a peaking of Democratic strength in the 1930s followed by a sustained decline. The shift of voters in the registration books was sudden, decisive, and permanent.

Registration figures for Pennsylvania (Figure 5) show some of the most revolutionary changes of all. In the metropolis of Allegheny County (Pittsburgh), the proportion of Democratic voters rose between 1930 and 1938 from 7 percent to 58 percent—a shift equivalent to more than half the county's voters. Rises nearly as steep were recorded in other coal and steel counties, including Westmoreland and Lackawanna. In these areas, the shifts took place mainly between 1932 and 1936, and they were sustained. By contrast, the Pennsylvania Dutch county of York, which was predominantly Democratic before the realignment, experienced no appreciable Democratic gain.

The political shifts in six of Oregon's major counties, shown in Figure

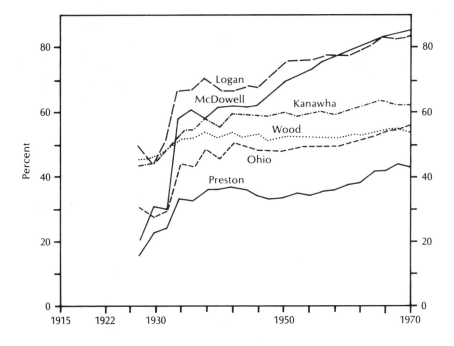

Figure 4 · Democratic Percentage of Two-Party Registration in West Virginia, Selected Counties, 1928–70[a]

Source: *West Virginia Blue Books,* various years.
[a]Plotted biennially.

6, reveal a remarkable uniformity, unlike the divergent patterns of the East—a testament, probably, to the absence of disciplined party organizations in the West and also of sharp urban-rural and ethnic cleavages. In every county, Democratic registration declined slightly in the 1920s from the levels of the Wilson period, remained fairly stable until 1930, climbed steeply until 1938 or 1940, and stabilized at the new heights. A similar pattern is shown for California counties in Figure 7.

COUNTERMOVEMENT TO THE REPUBLICANS

In the cities, the early years of the realignment of the 1930s saw an almost entirely one-way movement. As the Democratic party gained its massive infusion of working-class Republicans who were ready for radicalism, it lost few of its own previous adherents who were not. In 1934, Al Smith, John W. Davis, and other eminent leaders of the pre–New Deal Democratic party organized the American Liberty League as a vehicle for anti–New Deal Democrats, but it never developed mass support and collapsed a few years later. Nevertheless, the net shift of voters to the Democratic side

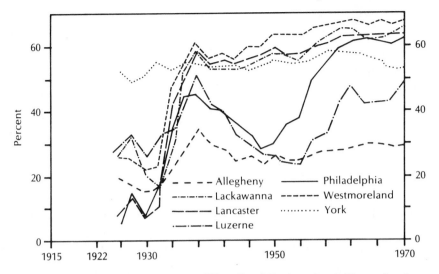

Figure 5 · Democratic Percentage of Two-Party Registration in Pennsylvania, Selected Counties, 1926–71[a]

Source: *The Pennsylvania Manual,* various years.
[a]Plotted biennially, except 1971 instead of 1970 data were used.

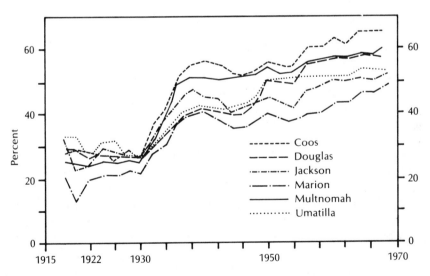

Figure 6 · Democratic Percentage of Two-Party Registration in Oregon, Selected Counties, 1918–68.[a]

Source: *Oregon Blue Books,* various years.
[a]Plotted biennially.

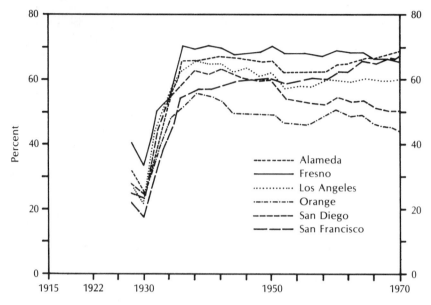

Figure 7 · Democratic Percentage of Two-Party Registration in California, Selected Counties, 1928-70[a]

Sources: For 1928–62, Eugene C. Lee, *California Votes 1928–1960,* with 1962 supplement (University of California, Berkeley, Institute of Governmental Studies, 1961, 1963); for 1964 and later, *A Review and Analysis of Registration and Voting* (California legislature handbook).
[a]Plotted biennially.

undoubtedly concealed some countermovement of conservatives. If leaders like Smith, who after all had been the archetypal urban Democrat, found the New Deal philosophically intolerable, he could not have been alone.

In traditional rural areas of native white Protestant Democratic strength, a measurable countermovement occurred. Particularly in Ohio, Indiana, and Illinois, Democratic losses among conservative rural voters were sufficient to substantially offset the party's gains in the cities. These were traditional Democrats, most of them living in communities founded by settlers from the South who had brought their Democratic politics with them. The communities had been steadfast through the Civil War, when many were Copperhead in sentiment, and through all the years thereafter until, having attained prosperity along with their neighbors of Yankee stock, they found they could not take "the spending, farm, and civil rights policies of the New Deal."[11] They were probably influenced too by the Democratic party's becoming, after 1928, even more markedly the party of the big cities, the Catholics, and the foreign born. Fenton finds a comparable pro-Republican

[11]John H. Fenton, *Midwest Politics* (Holt, Rinehart and Winston, 1966), p. 145. Fenton identifies the areas of the three states where the defections took place and analyzes the reasons on pp. 145–46, 162–63, 182–83, 215–18.

reaction to the New Deal in the Bourbon rural areas of the border states, such as Maryland's traditionally Democratic Eastern Shore, and in areas of subsistence agriculture like south central Kentucky.[12]

That traditionally Democratic York County, Pennsylvania, showed no gain in its Democratic registration majority between 1932 and 1938 (Figure 5) could be accounted for in one of two ways: either all of its Republican industrial workers defied the national surge toward the Democrats or those who followed the trend were offset by an equal number number of conservative Democrats—probably rural residents—who left their party when it was transformed. Since the former is hardly conceivable, the latter must be the case. A town-by-town examination of York County records would in all probability reveal what Fenton's county-by-county studies of the Midwest revealed—a two-way flow of voters across the party lines.

To be an integral part of the realignment of the 1930s, however, the countermovement did not have to take place immediately. In 1938, the Republicans began a comeback. That year they nearly doubled their strength in the House of Representatives, gained seven Senate seats, and recaptured the governorships of fourteen states, including the industrial strongholds of Massachusetts, Connecticut, Pennsylvania, Ohio, and Michigan. Most of the gains can undoubtedly be explained by the normal cycle of politics: the independent voters were by now rebelling against Democratic excesses and swinging to a Republican party that in many states had acquired new progressive leadership, and deviant Republicans, having chastised their party sufficiently, were returning home. But it may well be that a considerable part of the resurgence of the Republicans beginning in the late 1930s was due to a delayed flow of conservative Democrats into the GOP. In other words, the traditional Democrats who shared Al Smith's antipathy toward the New Deal did not leave in significant numbers when he did, but they began to do so not long thereafter.

DEMOCRATIC BOURBONISM DIES IN THE NORTH

When the Democratic party made its abrupt swing to the activist end of the political spectrum, during the first Roosevelt administration, it left

[12]John H. Fenton, *Politics in the Border States: A Study of the Patterns of Political Organization and Political Change Common to the Border States—Maryland, West Virginia, Kentucky and Missouri* (Hauser Press, 1957), pp. 75–78, 117–21, 162–63, 198–99. In addition, communities settled by Germans, particularly German Catholics, who had initially affiliated with the Democratic party because of the nativist tendency of the GOP made the transition to the Republican party. But it is not clear how many were alienated by the economics of the New Deal and how many realigned because of two "Democratic" wars against Germany. William H. Flanigan and Nancy H. Zingale observe that, in Minnesota, a significant proportion of traditionally Democratic rural voters, mainly in German communities, crossed to the Republican side in the 1930s. "Measurement of Electoral Stability and Change, 1832 to 1968" (paper delivered to the annual meeting of the American Political Science Association, September 1971; processed), p. 20.

stranded not only its national leadership of the 1920s—Smith, Davis, Raskob, and their associates—but a host of conservative Democrats in elected office. By James T. Patterson's calculations, eastern and midwestern Democrats in the Senate were actually more conservative during the 1933–39 period than their southern Democratic colleagues. The House also had a substantial conservative contingent of Democrats from the East and the Midwest.[13] At least two leading Democratic governors, Ritchie of Maryland and Joseph B. Ely of Massachusetts, were also vigorously opposed to FDR's New Deal.

The political base of the northern Bourbon Democrats was eroded not just by the leftward movement of the electorate as a whole and the conversion to the Democrats of action-minded Republicans, but also by the movement of a portion of the remaining conservative Democrats into Republican ranks. So the conservative strain in the Democratic party died quickly as the realignment of the 1930s took effect. (Where the realignment was delayed, of course, the conservative Democrats could hold their political support.)

A few of the anti–New Deal Democrats were unseated by pro–New Deal Democratic challengers; John J. O'Connor of New York City, the House Rules Committee chairman, was the sole victim of Roosevelt's 1938 "purge," but in 1940 three of the most antiadministration Democratic senators—Rush D. Holt of West Virginia, Edward R. Burke of Nebraska, and William H. King of Utah—were deposed by the Democrats of their respective states. As other conservative Democrats retired, died, or were defeated by Republicans, they were not replaced by men of the same views. Men as conservative as Senators Peter G. Gerry of Rhode Island (who opposed Roosevelt on 68 percent of the roll calls selected by Patterson), Royal S. Copeland of New York (50 percent), Francis T. Maloney of Connecticut (37 percent), or David I. Walsh and Marcus A. Coolidge of Massachusetts (29 percent each) no longer rose to leadership in the Democratic party of those states. As the generation of Democratic anti–New Dealers passed without replacement, the Democratic party of the industrial North found itself with an extraordinarily high degree of philosophical and ideological unity—for an American party.

The new Democratic party—the New Deal Democratic party—was issue-oriented, working-class-based, even more urban-centered than before, activist, radical, and wholly devoted to Rooseveltian leadership.

[13]James T. Patterson, *Congressional Conservatism and the New Deal: The Growth of the Conservative Coalition in Congress, 1933–39* (University of Kentucky Press, 1967), pp. 339–52. Defining as "conservative" Democrats the senators who opposed Roosevelt on at least 12 percent of key roll calls in the 1933–39 period and House members who opposed him on at least 25 percent, Patterson lists thirty-five senators and seventy-seven House members. These included half the eastern and midwestern Democratic senators and only 46 percent of the southern Democratic senators, 11 and 14 percent of eastern and midwestern House Democrats, respectively, and 32 percent of those from the South.

Within the party, new groups—Italians, Jews, Poles, and all the other new ethnic groups of European origin, blacks, and working-class Democrats of older Anglo-Saxon and German stock—began to contest the entrenched Irish for a share of party leadership and recognition. Organized labor, particularly the industrial unions that formed the Congress of Industrial Organizations (CIO) in 1936, became a virtual party adjunct, and labor wrote its legislative program into Democratic platforms. Its leaders won a role—often a veto—in candidate selection and occasionally accepted nomination themselves.

Evolution of the New Deal Party System

In some communities, the movement of voters to Smith and Roosevelt at the presidential level was translated at once into Democratic voting for other offices, and the realignment was complete by 1936. Chicago and Pittsburgh are examples. But in other communities, the realignment set in motion in the critical presidential elections was completed only later— sometimes much later—at the state and local levels.

This introduced a new phenomenon into American politics. In the nineteenth century, a man who was a Whig, a Democrat, or a Republican in presidential politics belonged automatically to the same party in state and local politics, and vice versa. Tickets were split occasionally, especially in times of third-party turmoil, but not consistently, election after election, in the same direction.[14] In the four decades since 1932, however, a persistent pattern of divergence between voting behavior in presidential elections and behavior in state and local elections has appeared in many states.

In the South, tens of thousands of voters have regularly supported Republicans for president but Democrats for every other office. In the North, particularly during the early decades of the New Deal party system, the same phenomenon of divergence found its expression in the "Roosevelt Republicans" who supported FDR and the New Deal but maintained their Republican identification and voting habits (or, in Wisconsin and Minnesota, third-party identification and voting) in state and local elections.

Divergence between national and state-local political behavior is inherently unstable. A voter who identifies with one party nationally and another locally enters into such a contradiction with reluctance in the first place; once in it, he normally feels some degree of pressure to resolve it. This is evidenced by the steady if slow decline in the degree of divergence

[14]One reason for the limited ticket-splitting in the nineteenth century was the use of party-printed, rather than government-printed, ballots. The party ballot listed only the party's nominees. The modern secret ballot, which lists the nominees of all parties and is a true "multiple-choice instrument," was introduced in most states in the 1890s. Jerrold G. Rusk, "The Effect of the Australian Ballot Reform on Split Ticket Voting: 1876–1908," *American Political Science Review*, Vol. 64 (1970), pp. 1220–21.

since the phenomenon first appeared in the 1930s. In other words, one of the striking trends of the decades since has been that of *convergence*—the conformity of state and local with national patterns.

A voter can resolve divergence by returning to his original party at the national level, but this is contingent on events that remove the reasons for his original disaffection. Or he can resolve it by changing parties locally, which may also be contingent on changes in the local party structure that will make his new party acceptable to him. The voter who resolves his conflict by returning to his original loyalty at the national level has simply deviated; the voter who resolves it by changing his party identification at state and local levels to accord with his new national loyalty has realigned. The realignment cannot be considered to have occurred until the reidentification is completed, for until that time the possibility exists that the conflict may be resolved the other way and the voter may turn out to have been only a deviant. As long as the conflict is unresolved—and that may last many years, even a lifetime—the realignment is only in process. It has not yet happened.

Unlike the major realignments of the nineteenth century, then, the realignment of the 1930s has been drawn out over an extraordinarily long period. Some voters were realigned in 1928, in the Smith campaign. Others were realigned in the early years of the Great Depression. But others shifted their party attachments at that time only at the national level, and the realignment has been completed gradually, as voters singly and in groups brought their state-local political attachments into line with those they had established at the national level.

Where the Votes Come From: An Analysis of Electoral Coalitions, 1952–1968
BY ROBERT AXELROD

Where do the Democrats get their votes from? Where do the Republicans get *their* votes from? Because of the great interest of scholars, politicians, and the public in the changing shape of electoral politics in America, these

Robert Axelrod, "Where the Votes Come From: An Analysis of Electoral Coalitions 1952–1968," *American Political Science Review*, Vol. 66, March 1972, pp. 11–20. Footnotes deleted. Reprinted by permission of The American Political Science Association.

questions have been asked over and over. V. O. Key has argued that one party or the other usually dominates American politics for decades by putting together a stable winning coalition and that since the Depression the dominant party has been the Democrats. He has, however, also pointed to the existence of slow but steady secular trends in electoral coalitions. In 1968 the rise of a third party challenge and the election of a Republican President led to numerous reassessments of the future of the party coalitions. Kevin Phillips's assertion of *The Emerging Republican Majority* is perhaps the best known of these recent prognostications, but a critical review by Nelson Polsby has already undermined much of Phillips's argument. The Republican Ripon Society has given a liberal interpretation of the *Lessons of Victory*, while the less partisan interpretation of Scammon and Wattenberg has emphasized the size of the middle groups in American politics. The long term cyclical pattern in American electoral politics has been reported by Sellers, and Burnham and Converse *et al.* have done excellent studies of some of the factors in recent presidential elections. Yet a number of basic questions about the sources of partisan support remain.

Surprisingly enough, even professional politicians have only a rough and ready idea of how their own national coalitions are formed. For example, many do not know whether Blacks contribute more or less than union members to the vote totals of the Democratic party. As another example, we may ask whether the common wisdom is really correct that the Republicans do worse than the Democrats among the young and the poor. Questions such as these require measurement of groups and their voting behavior. Measuring where the parties have been and where they are now is the first step toward a sophisticated analysis of where they are going.

This paper has two purposes. The first is analytic—to specify the components of a group's contribution to a party's electoral coalition. The second is empirical—to measure the actual magnitudes of the contributions that have been made by selected groups in each of the last five presidential elections.

The Meaning of a Contribution to a Coalition

What does it mean to ask how large a contribution a group makes to the electoral total of a party? Clearly, a large group can contribute more votes to a party than can a small group. It is also true that a group with a high turnout can contribute more votes than a slightly larger group with a lower turnout. And yet it is also true that a relatively small group with a poor turnout can contribute votes to a party quite out of proportion to its size if the group loyally gives overwhelming support to that party. Thus measurement of the contribution of a group to a party's total vote must depend on three factors: the size of the group, its turnout, and its loyalty to the given party.

Each of these three components of a group's contribution is important. Much confusion arises in political discussions about how the parties build their coalitions because no one of these components tells the whole story. Only when all three components are taken into account can the actual contribution of a group be fully determined.

The coalition literature from game theory is of little help here because of its assumption that groups are unified actors. Each group is assumed to be able to turn out all of its members and deliver them with complete loyalty to the coalition of its choice. While this assumption is suitable for certain legislative bodies, it is a gross distortion when applied to a mass electorate whose turnout and loyalty are always less than complete.

Fortunately, the three components of size, turnout, and loyalty can be fitted together in a rather simple way to determine a group's contribution to a party's vote total. The formula is:

$$\text{Contribution} = \frac{(\text{Size}) \times (\text{Turnout}) \times (\text{Loyalty})}{(\text{National Turnout}) \times (\text{National Loyalty})}$$

This formula says that if you multiply the size, turnout, and loyalty of a given group, and divide the result by the product of the national turnout and national loyalty, you get the magnitude of the contribution of that group to the electoral coalition of the party. The *size* of a group is the proportion of all adults of voting age who are members of that group. The *turnout* of a group is the proportion that voted in a given election. The *loyalty* of a group to a certain party is simply the proportion of the votes of that group which are cast for that party. The *national turnout* is the proportion of all adults who vote, and *national loyalty* is the proportion of all votes that go to the given party. Finally, the *contribution* of a group to the electoral coalition of a party equals the proportion of all the party's votes that come from members of that group.

$$\frac{(\text{size})\,(\text{turnout})\,(\text{loyalty})}{(\text{natl. turnout})\,(\text{natl. loyalty})} = \frac{\left(\dfrac{\text{no. in group}}{\text{no. in nation}}\right)\left(\dfrac{\text{voters in group}}{\text{number in group}}\right)\left(\dfrac{\text{voters for party in group}}{\text{voters in group}}\right)}{\left(\dfrac{\text{voters in nation}}{\text{number in nation}}\right)\left(\dfrac{\text{voters for party}}{\text{voters in nation}}\right)}$$

$$= \frac{\text{voters for party in group}}{\text{voters for party}}$$

$$= \text{contribution}$$

The value of this formula is that it specifies how the three components can be combined to form the total contribution of a given group. It allows us to study contributions of a group over time, to determine how the contribution is attained in terms of the separate components, and to compare the contribution of one group to that of another.

Since any combination of groups may be chosen for analysis, the groups will typically overlap. A comparison can still be made between the overlapping groups in terms of their separate contributions, size, turnout, and loyalty, but these factors cannot be added together directly. For example, in 1968 the poor (i.e., families with incomes less than $3000 per year) contributed 12 per cent of the Democratic votes, while the Blacks contributed 19 per cent. The contribution of the group consisting of those who are poor or Black (or both) can be determined by adding the separate contributions and subtracting the contribution of the overlapping group, namely the poor Blacks. Since the poor Blacks contributed 5 per cent of the Democratic votes, the contribution of those who were poor or Black (or both) was 12% + 19% − 5% = 26%. A similar procedure applies to measuring the *size* of the group which is the union of two overlapping groups.

The procedure for handling overlaps readily generalizes to any group describable in terms of more than two component groups. This means that the contribution and size of any group can be analyzed if the relevant information is available about the component groups and their intersections. While this type of information is difficult to get from aggregate data, it is readily available from survey data. Thus, the poor, the Blacks, the poor Blacks and those who are poor or Black can all be analyzed if desired. This paper will fully report a selected set of overlapping groups and note a few of the interesting properties of their intersections and unions.

It should be clear that the term "contribution" as it is being used in this study refers to the proportion of a party's total votes that is provided by a given group. It does not tell how the votes were gathered or even whether the group membership provides a reference point for its members. For example, it does not measure a group's contribution in terms of money, policy, or organizational strength. It simply counts what ultimately matters in elections, namely votes.

The Coalition Members

Since the New Deal there has been a generally accepted answer to the question of where the Democrats get their votes. The answer is that the Democrats are a coalition of diverse overlapping minorities: the poor, Blacks, union members, Catholics and Jews, Southerners, and city dwellers. In the last few years it has been suggested that, at least for presidential elections, the Southerners may have left the Democratic coalition while the young people have entered it.

The Republicans are a different matter. It is possible to think of the Republicans also as a coalition of minorities such as the rich and the people of Anglo-Saxon descent. But the Republican party itself tries to avoid this sort of formulation in favor of the view that Republicans appeal to the nonminorities, while the Democrats appeal to the minorities. In these terms, the Republicans can be thought of as a coalition of the non-poor, Whites, nonunion families, Protestants, Northerners, and those outside the central cities.

The Republican groups are larger in size than the corresponding Democratic groups, and they generally have a higher turnout, but size and turnout are only two of the components of a group's contribution to a party's coalition. The Democrats' relative advantage is in the third component, namely partisan support, because the pro-Democratic minorities generally give a higher percentage of their votes to the Democrats than the corresponding nonminorities give to the Republicans.

To measure the magnitude of the three components and the total contribution of each group to its party's electoral coalition, a combination of survey data and election returns can be used. The election returns show the total national loyalty each party received, and they can also be used in conjunction with census data to estimate the national turnout. A survey based upon a carefully drawn national sample can be used to measure the components for each of the separate groups. Fortunately, the Survey Research Center of the University of Michigan has conducted such a national survey for every presidential election since 1952, so comparable data for the last five presidential elections are now available. Income, race, union membership, religion, and place of residence, being relatively objective criteria, present few of the problems associated with measuring attitudes. There are still problems in determining how a person actually voted, even if the person is reinterviewed after the election as these respondents were. Some of them evidently reported that they had voted when in fact they did not, and a small percentage reported that they voted for the winner when they actually voted for the loser. The raw survey data have been adjusted with the use of national election data to compensate for these two types of error. The numbers will still contain some random sampling error, but most of them are probably within three or four per cent of their true value.

THE DEMOCRATS

Table 1 gives the data for the Democratic coalition in terms of the selected groups. Along the top of the table is written the formula for a group's contribution to a party, and within each block of the table are listed the different groups by year. Directly under the block for loyalty is a block which shows how a group's loyalty differs from the national loyalty.

(1) The Poor. The poor are defined to be those with an annual family income less than $3000. Column 1 of Table 1 shows that the contribution

Table 1 · The Democratic Coalition, 1952–1968

PERCENTAGE CONTRIBUTION = (SIZE × TURNOUT × LOYALTY) ÷ (NT×NL)

Year	PERCENTAGE CONTRIBUTION						(SIZE						× TURNOUT						× LOYALTY)						÷ (NT×NL)	
	P	B	U	C	S	CC	P	B	U	C	S	CC	P	B	U	C	S	CC	P	B	U	C	S	CC	NT	NL
1952	28	7	38	41	20	21	36	10	27	26	28	16	46	23	66	76	35	68	47	83	59	57	55	51	63	44.4
1956	19	5	36	38	23	19	25	9	26	25	29	14	40	23	64	72	39	63	47	68	55	53	52	55	60	42.0
1960	16	7	31	47	27	19	23	10	25	25	34	13	46	31	60	74	50	74	48	72	66	82	52	65	64	49.7
1964	15	12	32	36	21	15	19	11	23	26	28	12	45	42	69	72	49	65	69	99	80	75	58	74	63	61.1
1968	12	19	28	40	24	14	16	11	24	26	31	10	44	51	61	68	53	63	44	92	51	61	39	58	62	42.7
COLUMN	1	2	3	4	5	6	7	8	9	10	11	12	13	14	15	16	17	18	19	20	21	22	23	24	25	26

P poor (income under $3,000/yr.)
B Black (and other nonwhite)
U union member (or union member in family)
C Catholic (and other non-Protestant)
S South (including border states)
CC central cities (of 12 largest metroplitan areas)
NT national turnout
NL national loyalty to Democrats

Percentage Deviation in Loyalty to Democrats

Year	P	B	U	C	S	CC
1952	+2	+38	+14	+12	+10	+ 6
1956	+5	+26	+13	+11	+10	+13
1960	-2	+22	+16	+32	+ 2	+15
1964	+8	+38	+19	+14	- 3	+13
1968	+1	+49	+ 8	+18	- 4	+15
COLUMN	27	28	29	30	31	32

of the poor to the Democratic coalition has fallen dramatically: from 28 per cent of Democratic votes in 1952 to only 12 per cent in 1968. The main reason their contribution has fallen is that their size has shrunk over these years, from 36 per cent of the total adult population to 16 per cent (Column 7). This decrease in the "poor" is partly due to the fact that $3000 per year is a more restrictive definition for the 1960's than it is for the 1950's because of inflation. Much of the decrease, however, is due to gains in real income. Since their turnout has been steady but low at about 45 per cent (Column 13) and their loyalty (Column 19) has been about 45 per cent Democratic (except in 1964), the decrease in the contribution of the poor to the Democrats is due almost solely to the dwindling size of this group.

The curious fact about the voting pattern of the poor is that, contrary to popular belief, they are not distinctly loyal to the Democrats. Column 19 shows that only in 1964 did they give the Democrats a majority of their votes, and Column 27 shows that to within a few percentage points, their vote generally divides the same as does the entire nation's vote. In brief, the poor are *not* part of the Democratic coalition. The working class may be loyal, but the poor are not.

(2) The Blacks.   The Blacks are another story altogether. Their contribution has grown substantially from 5–7 per cent in 1952–1960 to 12 per cent in 1964 and 19 per cent in 1968 (Column 2). This increase in their contribution to the total Democratic vote is not due to an increase in the number of the Blacks, since their size has been almost constant at about 10 per cent of the population throughout this period (Column 8). It is their turnout that has increased dramatically, nearly doubling between 1952 and 1968. The biggest jumps came in 1960 and 1964 as Blacks began to exercise their franchise in greater numbers, not only in the South but throughout the nation. The Blacks have always been very loyal to the Democrats (Column 20), especially in relation to voting patterns of other groups (Column 28). Curiously enough, this overwhelming loyalty of the Blacks was present in 1952, but not in Stevenson's second effort or in Kennedy's campaign. It returned to and exceeded its previous high level in the campaigns of Johnson and Humphrey. Only in 1968, however, did high loyalty and moderately good turnout combine to produce a Black contribution to the Democrats that was strikingly larger than their population percentage. Of course, the low national loyalty to the Democrats in 1968 also helped account for the high percentage of all Democratic votes that were contributed by Blacks in that year.

(3) The Unions.   Union members and their families provide yet a different story. They contributed more than a third of all Democratic votes in the 1950's but in the 1960's their contribution fell slightly to a still very

respectable figure of 28 per cent (Column 3). This large contribution arises because about a quarter of all adults are in union families (Column 9), they have a turnout close to the national average (Column 15 versus Column 25), and they consistently vote more Democratic than the nation as a whole (Column 29). The gradual decline of the union contribution to the Democratic party is due to a slight decline in their relative size (Column 9) and a large drop in their loyalty in 1968 (Column 21).

A comparison of the Black contribution and the union contribution is revealing, provided one bears in mind that people in both groups vote the way they do for many reasons other than their race and union membership. In 1960 the union voters contributed more than four times as many votes to the Democrats as the Blacks did, but by 1968 the unions contributed only one and a half times as many votes as the Blacks (Column 3 versus Column 2). So until recently the voters from union families made a much, much larger contribution than the Blacks, and they still make a significantly greater contribution.

(4) The Catholics.   The Catholics have formed a large and reliable segment of the Democratic coalition. They have always provided more than a third of the Democratic votes (Column 4), even though they are only a quarter of the population (Column 10). Part of the reason is their exceptionally high turnout (Column 16). The other part of the reason is their steadfast loyalty (Column 22) which has always been more than 10 per cent greater than that of the population as a whole (Column 30). Included in the Democratic coalition with the Catholics are the Jews, whose numbers are small, but whose turnout and loyalty have consistently been very high.

Of course a special year for the Catholics was 1960, when John Kennedy was the Democratic nominee. In that year the Catholics gave more than four-fifths of their vote to the Democrats (Column 22), thereby providing nearly half of all the votes the Democrats got in 1960 (Column 4).

(5) The Southerners.   The South, including the border states, offers something of a surprise. Voters from this region have provided roughly one-fourth of all Democratic votes (Column 5). The size of the group has held steady (Column 11), while the turnout has increased since 1956 (Column 17), partly because of the increased turnout of the Blacks in the South. The surprise is that overall, Southerners have not been exceptionally loyal to the Democrats since 1956 (Column 23). In the Eisenhower elections they split their vote down the middle, and since then have voted within a few percentage points of the national Democratic average (Column 31).

It appears from these figures that the South is moving away from the Democrats. The Southerners were about 10 per cent more pro-Democratic than the nation as a whole in the 1952 and 1956 elections, but only 2 per cent more in 1960; in 1964 and 1968 they voted 3 per cent and 4 per cent *less* Democratic than the country as a whole did (Column 31). This trend has occurred despite the countertrend of Black Southerners, who are very loyal Democrats, to increase their turnout in those same years. The Democratic loss is not necessarily the Republican gain, for in 1968 a third of the White Southern votes went to Wallace (not shown in the table), accounting for slightly more than half of all Wallace's votes.

(6) The Central Cities.   Only about 10 per cent of the nation's population now lives in the central cities of the dozen largest metropolitan areas, a figure that has been falling slowly since 1952 (Column 12). Central city dwellers used to have a slightly better than average turnout (Column 18), and since 1956 they have been 13 per cent to 15 per cent more Democratic than the nation as a whole (Column 32). These trends make the central cities an important but slowly decreasing part of the Democratic coalition, having provided about 20 per cent of the Democratic votes in the 1950's and about 15 per cent of the Democratic votes in the last two elections (Column 6).

A person may, of course, belong to more than one of these overlapping groups. For this reason the contributions and sizes of the groups listed on Table 1 can add up to more than 100 per cent. Some of the Democratic groups overlap more or less than would be expected from their sizes alone. Thus, for instance, the Blacks constitute a higher proportion of the population of the South than of the North, while on the other hand, the Blacks represent a lower proportion of Catholics than they do of Protestants. Typically, the overlap of two given Democratic groups has a higher loyalty than the average of the loyalties of the two given groups. For example, in 1968, Catholic union members had a loyalty of 65 per cent which is actually greater than the loyalty of either the Catholics (61 per cent) or the union members (51 per cent).

Some people belong to none of the six overlapping groups listed on Table 1. Actually about one-fifth to one-fourth of the adult population is neither poor, Black, unionized, Catholic, Southern, nor in central cities. This residual group tends to vote Republican, as would be expected, and in fact votes about 20 per cent more Republican than the nation as a whole.

One could go on almost indefinitely examining the partisan support provided by people with different attributes. But one additional group merits particular attention: that is the young. Those between 21 and 29 years of age are about 18 per cent of the voting age population, yet they provide only about 14 per cent of all Democratic votes. There are two reasons for this curious fact. First, the young have a turnout record about 15 per cent below the national average. Second, the young are simply not loyal to the Democrats. In fact, in four of the last five presidential elections the young have given the Democrats the same proportion of their vote (within 3 per cent) as has the whole country. In 1968 the young, with their weak party loyalties, were slightly pro-Wallace compared to the nation as a whole. So like the poor, the young have not been part of the loyal Democratic coalition. Now that the 18 to 21 year olds have been enfranchised, the size of the under-30 group will increase. Their turnout is likely to remain below average, but it is uncertain whether their pattern of not being loyal to either major party will continue.

THE REPUBLICANS

The Republican coalition can be thought of as consisting of the ovelapping majorities that are the precise complements of the minorities that describe the Democratic coalition. This makes the Republican coalition a combination of the nonpoor, Whites, nonunion families, Protestants, Northerners, and those outside the central cities. Virtually everyone is in at least one of these overlapping groups, and most people are in four or five of them.

Most of the facts about how these groups contribute to the Republican party follow directly from what has already been said about how their complements contribute to the Democratic party. For example, the fact that the poor are no more loyal to the Democrats than is the nation as a whole implies that the nonpoor cannot be especially loyal to the Republicans. Because of these relationships we can discuss only a few of the more salient facts and let Table 2 tell the rest of the story of how the Republican coalition is put together.

(1) The Nonpoor. Those with incomes greater than $3000 have contributed an increasing proportion of all Republican votes since 1952 (Table 2, Column 1), mainly because more and more people have crossed this line over the years (Column 7). But as was just pointed out, the nonpoor do not deviate much from the national average in their loyalty to the Republicans (Column 27).

(2) The Whites. Virtually all Republican votes come from Whites (Column 2). Even in 1960 when a quarter of the Black vote went to Nixon, 97 per cent of Nixon's votes came from Whites, while in 1968, 99 per cent of Nixon's votes came from Whites. Whites are about 90 per cent of the population (Column 8) and they vote 1 per cent to 3 per cent more Republican than the nation as a whole (Column 28). This is just the obverse of the statement that the Blacks, who are about 10 per cent of the population, vote heavily Democratic.

(3) The Nonunion Families. Nonunion families have voted 5 per cent or 6 per cent more Republican than the nation as a whole from 1952 to 1964

Table 2 · The Republican Coalition, 1952–1968

Year	PERCENTAGE CONTRIBUTION =						(SIZE						× TURNOUT ×						LOYALTY)						÷ (NT × NL)	
	NP	W	NU	P	N	NCC	NP	W	NU	P	N	NCC	NP	W	NU	P	N	NCC	NP	W	NU	P	N	NCC	NT	NL
1952	75	99	79	75	87	84	64	90	73	74	72	84	72	67	61	58	73	61	56	57	61	61	57	57	63	55.1
1956	84	98	78	75	84	89	75	91	74	75	71	86	67	64	58	56	69	60	59	59	63	62	60	60	60	57.4
1960	83	97	84	90	75	90	77	90	75	75	66	87	70	68	65	61	71	63	50	51	55	63	50	52	64	49.5
1964	89	100	87	80	76	91	81	89	77	74	72	88	67	66	61	60	68	63	40	42	45	44	38	40	63	38.5
1968	90	99	81	80	80	92	84	89	76	74	69	90	65	63	62	60	66	62	44	47	46	49	47	45	62	43.4
COLUMN	1	2	3	4	5	6	7	8	9	10	11	12	13	14	15	16	17	18	19	20	21	22	23	24	25	26

NP nonpoor (income over $3,000/yr.)
W White
NU nonunion
P Protestant
N Northern (excluding border states)
NCC not in central cities of 12 largest metropolitan areas
NT national turnout
NL national loyalty to Republicans

Percentage Deviation in Loyalty to Republicans

Year	NP	W	NU	P	N	NCC
1952	+1	+2	+6	+6	+6	+2
1956	+1	+1	+5	+4	+2	+2
1960	0	+1	+5	+13	0	+2
1964	+1	+3	+6	+5	-1	+1
1968	0	+3	+2	+5	+3	+1
COLUMN	27	28	29	30	31	32

(Column 29). This figure takes on real importance when combined with the fact that three-quarters of all adults are in families without a union member (Column 9).

(4) The Protestants. The Protestants are also about three-quarters of the population (Column 10), and have usually voted about 5 per cent more Republican than the nation as a whole (Column 30). The special year, of course, was 1960 when a Catholic candidate opposed a Protestant for President and 90 per cent of the Republican votes came from Protestants (Column 4).

(5) The Northerners. The Northerners have an unusually high turnout (Column 17), relative to the turnout in the South. When it comes to loyalty, however, the Northerners have never been more than 3 per cent pro-Republican in these five presidential elections, and twice have not been pro-Republican at all (Column 31).

(6) Outside the Central Cities. Those living outside the central cities of the twelve largest metropolitian areas have slowly increased from about 85 per cent of the total population in the 1950's to 90 per cent in 1968 (Column 12). Their turnout, however, is only about average and their loyalty is only slightly more Republican than the nation as a whole (Column 32), partly because they are so close to equaling the whole nation.

The Party Coalitions

The most obvious fact about American party coalitions is that they are very loose. They are loose first in the sense that most group loyalties are not total. Except for Blacks, none of the twelve groups that have been examined in the tables ever gave more than 80 per cent of their votes to one party. Second, the coalitions are loose in the sense that group loyalties are not constant from one election to the next. Fianlly, when a group's loyalty shifts it is as likely to shift in response to a national trend as it is for reasons specific to the group. Indeed, again with the exception of Blacks, each of the groups usually divided their votes no more than 15 per cent differently than did the nation as a whole.

The data from Table 1 and Table 2 do not point to an election in these years which suddenly shifted the nature of the coalitions and then set the pattern for the elections to follow. In Key's terms, none of these elections is an obvious choice for a critical election, although there have been secular realignments. These gradual shifts have been in different factors for different groups: loyalty of the South, size of the poor and central cities dwellers, and both turnout and loyalty of the Blacks. There have also been dramatic short-term shifts, for instance by the Catholics.

Table 3 · Percentage of Party Identification, 1952–68

	PARTY		
YEAR	*Democrat*	Independent	*Republican*
1952	47	22	27
1956	44	24	29
1960	46	23	27
1964	51	23	24
1968	44	29	25

(Note: Several per cent "apolitical" and "don't know" in each year are not shown).

The data on party identification provide another point of view about what has been happening to the party system. In each year the respondents were asked, "Generally speaking, do you usually think of yourself as a Republican, a Democrat, an Independent, or what?" The results in Table 3 show that the party identification has remained almost stable since 1952. Neither major party has gained strength, and the Democrats still have a considerable edge over the Republicans. A new factor in 1968 was an increase in the number of Independents to 29 per cent of the national sample. This increase is not due solely to the appeal of George Wallace, because fully 28 per cent of those who did not vote for Wallace thought of themselves as Independents in 1968.

The third-party coalition put together by Wallace can be measured just as the coalitions of the other two parties have been. In 1968 Wallace received 14 per cent of the national vote. The only one of the twelve groups that gave him a great deal more than this was the South (including the border states) which had a loyalty to Wallace of 28 per cent. The Catholics gave Wallace only 9 per cent of their vote, the central city dwellers 8 per cent, and the non-Whites a mere 1 per cent. The other categories did not have much of a net impact. The poor gave him 16 per cent of their vote, compared to 13 per cent from the nonpoor; the union families gave him 15 per cent, compared to 13 per cent from the nonunion families; and the young gave him 18 per cent, compared to the 13 per cent from those 30 and older.

All in all, there have been and still are significant differences in the electoral coalitions of the two major parties, despite Wallace's claim that there isn't a dime's worth of difference in what they stand for. Race, union membership, religion, and place of residence still matter. The Democrats usually get major contributions of votes from the Blacks, the union members, the Catholics, and those in central cities. The Republicans usually have slightly greater appeal for the Whites, the nonunion families, the Protestants, and those outside the central cities. The poor and the young, however, divided their votes just about the same way as did the nation as a whole and were not really part of any party's electoral coalition.

Some Strategic Considerations

There is little a party can do to increase the size of a demographic group, but there is much it can do to try to increase its turnout and loyalty. A major consideration for a party in deciding whether to appeal to a given group is what might be called the group's "elasticity of response." The question is not whether a group will be receptive to an appeal, but whether a greater or lesser appeal will make much difference in the behavior of the members of the group. From a strategic point of view, the problem is to use scarce resources in the best way, presumably to maximize the chances of victory. If a group has a nearly constant response, independent of the intensiveness of the appeal to it, there is little sense in devoting many resources to that group. But if a group's response is sensitive to the magnitude of the efforts to appeal to it, then a party would do well to devote scarce resources to increase this appeal.

A good example of how a group can respond to a particular appeal is provided by the Catholics. In 1960, the Democrats nominated a Catholic for President, and the proportion of the Catholic vote that went to the Democrats went up almost 30 per cent from 53 per cent in the previous election to 82 per cent. In the same four year period the nation as a whole increased its loyalty to the Democrats by only 8 per cent. Thus the Catholics' response to the appeal of a Catholic candidate was highly elastic. Unfortunately for the Democrats, it was also elastic in the other direction as well. In the next two presidential elections, when Protestants were again nominated, the deviation in loyalty of the Catholics to the Democrats fell back almost to its previous levels (Table 1, Column 3).

Another approach is for a party to direct some of its resources to increase the turnout of a group, through such means as a registration drive. If loyalty is to be increased, voters must be converted from another party, but if turnout is to be increased, they need only be mobilized. The mobilization strategy has the disadvantage that a newly mobilized voter who votes for the party is only half as valuable as a voter who is newly converted from the other party of a two-party system. The mobilization strategy has the further disadvantage that the newly mobilized voter may not vote for the intended party. Mobilization is sometimes relatively inexpensive, however, and it can often be accomplished without antagonizing other groups in the coalition. The ideal opportunity for a mobilization strategy by a party arises when a group has high loyalty combined with low turnout. Such has been the case with the Blacks, and the Democrats have acted accordingly. If there is new evidence that the young will depart from their previous pattern of behavior and start to be loyal to a given party, that party would be wise to use a mobilization strategy aimed at the young.

The expression of a group's contribution in terms of its size, turnout, and loyalty can be used to analyze hypothetical strategic choices involving any division of the population. The first step is to notice that the contribution of any group plus the contribution of its complementary group is always one. Using the definition of contribution, this gives

$$\frac{s_g t_g l_g}{t_n l_n} + \frac{s_c t_c l_c}{t_n l_n} = 1.00$$

where s, t, and l are size, turnout and loyalty respectively and the subscripts g, c, and n signify the group, its complement, and the nation. The national turnout can be expressed as a function of the size and turnout of the group and its complement,

$$t_n = s_g t_g + s_c t_c,$$

and the size of the complement can be expressed in terms of the size of the group itself,

$$s_c = 1 - s_g.$$

Substituting the last two equations into the first one, and solving for the national loyalty gives what might be called the strategic equation,

$$l_n = \frac{s_g t_g l_g + (1 - s_g) t_c l_c}{s_g t_g + (1 - s_g) t_c}.$$

The strategic equation has six variables. A typical application would assume that the values of several of them are known from previous measurements or extrapolations, and would ask what would be the effect of varying one or two of the remaining variables. For example, if one knew the size, turnout, and loyalty of a group he could determine what levels of turnout and loyalty would have to be achieved from the people *outside* the group in order to get a given percentage of the national vote.

As a concrete example, consider as a single group the people that Scammon and Wattenberg emphasize, the "unyoung, unpoor and unblack." Using 1968 SRC data and the previous definitions, the size of this group is 62 per cent and its turnout is 70 per cent, while the turnout of all the others is 50 per cent. Substituting these values in the strategic equation and solving for l_c gives

$$l_c = .3281_n - .2281_g.$$

Thus if a party could count on 55 per cent of the vote of the "unyoung, unpoor and unblack," it would still need at least 39 per cent of the other voters to win a majority in a two party race. In a three party race in which it could count on 50 per cent of the "unyoung, unpoor and unblack," it would still need 34 per cent of the other voters to get 45 per cent of the national vote.

Other problems can also be analyzed with the strategic equation. If an appeal to a group increases its loyalty by a given amount, how much can the loyalty of the other voters decrease before the break-even point is reached? If the turnout of a given group is increased by a given amount, how much does this increase a party's percentage of the national vote? Finally, a generalized form of the strategic equation can be used to analyze similar questions involving the partitioning of the population into more than two nonoverlapping groups.

This paper has described how the contributions that different groups make to a party's total strength can be specified. It has also shown how these contributions can be broken down into their three components—size, turnout, and loyalty. Through the examples of selected groups, the actual magnitude of these contributions and their components for each of the last five presidential elections have been presented and discussed with the hope that measuring these previous coalitions can be helpful in the task of understanding what may come next. I leave that greater task to others, whether they be scholars, politicians, or voters.

Letter to the Editor, June 1974
BY ROBERT AXELROD

Since the publication of my article on "Where the Votes Come From: An Analysis of Electoral Coalitions, 1952–1968" I have been asked a number of times what a parallel analysis of the 1972 presidential election would reveal. Few people are in a position readily to generate the required statistics for themselves because an iterative procedure is necessary to correct for overreporting of voting and especially overreporting of voting for the winner. So for those who wish to gloat or mourn over the landslide of Richard Nixon over George McGovern, here are the figures. The figures are presented with the data from the original article so that all six presidential elections since 1952 can be readily compared. The coalitions are described in terms of the three components of a group's contribution to a party, namely the size of the group, its turnout, and its loyalty to the given party. The *contribution* of a group to the electoral coalition of a party is the proportion of all the party's votes that come from members of that group. The *loyalty* of a group to a certain party is simply the proportion of the votes of that group which are cast for that party.

Robert Axelrod, Letter to the Editor, *American Political Science Review*, Vol. 68, June 1974, pp. 717–720. Footnotes deleted. Reprinted by permission of The American Political Science Association.

Before looking at the coalitions themselves there are two well-known facts about the 1972 election that bear repeating. The first is that it really *was* a landslide, with the Democrats getting only 37.5 per cent of the votes to the Republicans' 60.7 per cent. The second basic fact is that the turnout was the lowest in at least twenty years, with only 56 per cent of the adults of voting age actually voting.

More interesting than these overall facts is what happened to the "traditional" coalitions of the two major parties. Let us consider the Democrats first (Table 1). The Democrats are often thought of as a coalition of diverse overlapping minorities: the poor, Blacks, union families, Catholics and Jews, Southerners, and city dwellers. In 1972 this combination suffered serious defections. The Blacks and central cities remained highly loyal in both absolute and relative terms (col. 20, 24, 28, and 32). In contrast, although the poor, the unions, and the Catholics were each six to eight points more loyal to the Democrats than the nation as a whole (col. 27, 29, and 30), all three of these groups gave less than half of their votes to the Democrats (col. 19, 21, and 22). The South was not even relatively pro-Democratic in 1972 (col. 23 and 31). Looking at it another way, the contribution of the Blacks has continued to grow until in 1972 they accounted for 22 per cent of all Democratic votes (col. 2). Nevertheless, both the union and the Catholic contributions to the Democrats (col. 3 and 4) were substantially larger than the Black contribution due to the much larger size of these two groups (col. 9 and 10).

The Republicans did well among all six of their traditional coalition groups with 60 per cent or more of the vote of the nonpoor, the Whites, the nonunions, the Protestants, the Northerners, and those outside the central cities (Table 2, col. 19–24). But even more impressive is that the Republicans received a majority of the votes from the complements of four of these groups, namely the poor, the unions, the Catholics, and the Southerners, as we have seen in examining the traditional Democratic supporting groups.

The young, who were previously not part of anyone's coalition, made a large contribution to the Democratic coalition in 1972. In each previous election since 1952 people under thirty years of age accounted for only 13 per cent to 15 per cent of the Democratic votes, but in 1972 they accounted for fully 32 per cent of the Democratic votes. There are three reasons for this dramatic increase. First, their size went up from 18 per cent to 28 per cent of the adults of voting age principally due to the lowering of the voting age, but also due to the baby boom. Second, their turnout went up relative to the nation as a whole from 15 per cent below average to 9 per cent below average. Third, their loyalty which had never been more than 3 per cent pro-Democratic since 1952 went up in 1972 to 12 per cent pro-Democratic.

The future of the electoral coalitions cannot be predicted with cer-

Table 1 · The Democratic Coalition, 1952–1972

Year	PERCENTAGE CONTRIBUTION (=)						SIZE (×)						TURNOUT (×)						LOYALTY						÷ (NT×NL)	
	P	B	U	C	S	CC	P	B	U	C	S	CC	P	B	U	C	S	CC	P	B	U	C	S	CC	NT	NL
1952	28	7	38	41	20	21	36	10	27	26	28	16	46	23	66	76	35	68	47	83	59	57	55	51	63	44.4
1956	19	5	36	38	23	19	25	9	26	25	29	14	40	23	64	72	39	63	47	68	55	53	52	55	60	42.0
1960	16	7	31	47	27	19	23	10	25	25	34	13	46	31	60	74	50	74	48	72	66	82	52	65	64	49.7
1964	15	12	32	36	21	15	19	11	23	26	28	12	45	42	69	72	49	65	69	99	80	75	58	74	63	61.1
1968	12	19	28	40	24	14	16	11	24	26	31	10	44	51	61	68	53	63	44	92	51	61	39	58	62	42.7
1972	10	22	32	34	25	14	12	11	25	25	34	8	37	47	58	65	44	60	45	86	45	43	36	61	56	37.5
COLUMN	1	2	3	4	5	6	7	8	9	10	11	12	13	14	15	16	17	18	19	20	21	22	23	24	25	26

P poor (income under $3,000/yr.)
B Black (and other nonwhite)
U union member (or union member in family)
C Catholic (and other non-Protestant)
S South (including border states)
CC central cities (of 12 largest metropolitan areas)
NT national turnout
NL national loyalty to Democrats

Percentage Deviation in Loyalty to Democrats

Year	P	B	U	C	S	CC
1952	+2	+38	+14	+12	+10	+6
1956	+5	+26	+13	+11	+10	+13
1960	-2	+22	+16	+32	+2	+15
1964	+8	+38	+19	+14	-3	+13
1968	+1	+49	+8	+18	-4	+15
1972	+8	+49	+8	+6	-2	+24
COLUMN	27	28	29	30	31	32

Table 2 · The Republican Coalition, 1952–1972

Year	PERCENTAGE CONTRIBUTION						=	(SIZE						×	TURNOUT						×	LOYALTY)						÷	(NT×NL)	
	NP	W	NU	P	N	NCC		NP	W	NU	P	N	NCC		NP	W	NU	P	N	NCC		NP	W	NU	P	N	NCC		NT	NL
1952	75	99	79	75	87	84		64	90	73	74	72	84		72	67	61	58	73	61		56	57	61	61	57	57		63	55.1
1956	84	98	78	75	84	89		75	91	74	75	71	86		67	64	58	56	69	60		59	59	63	62	60	60		60	57.4
1960	83	97	84	90	75	90		77	90	75	75	66	87		70	68	65	61	71	63		50	51	55	63	50	52		64	49.5
1964	89	100	87	80	76	91		81	89	77	74	72	88		67	66	61	60	68	63		40	42	45	44	38	40		63	38.5
1968	90	99	81	80	80	92		84	89	76	74	69	90		65	63	62	60	66	62		44	47	46	49	47	45		62	43.4
1972	93	98	77	74	73	95		88	89	75	75	66	92		58	57	55	52	62	55		61	66	63	64	60	63		56	60.7
COLUMN	1	2	3	4	5	6		7	8	9	10	11	12		13	14	15	16	17	18		19	20	21	22	23	24		25	26

Percentage Deviation in Loyalty to Republicans

Year	NP	W	NU	P	N	NCC
1952	+1	+2	+6	+6	+6	+2
1956	+1	+1	+5	+4	+2	+2
1960	0	+1	+5	+13	0	+2
1964	+1	+3	+6	+5	-1	+1
1968	0	+3	+2	+5	+3	+1
1972	+1	+5	+3	+3	-1	+2
COLUMN	27	28	29	30	31	32

NP nonpoor (income over $3,000/yr.)
W White
NU nonunion
P Protestant
N Northern (excluding border states)
NCC not in central cities of 12 largest metropolitan areas
NT national turnout
NL national loyalty to Republicans

tainty, but several important shifts which have taken place in recent years can now be seen more clearly. The members of union families used to be 13 per cent to 19 per cent pro-Democratic but since 1968 they have been only 8 per cent pro-Democratic (Table 1, col. 29). The South, which used to be 10 per cent pro-Democratic, has continued the pattern started in 1960 of voting within a few percentage points of the nation as a whole (Table 1, col. 31). To offset these losses the Democrats can at least be pleased that the young in 1972 have finally made a large contribution to their electoral coalition.

Letter to the Editor, June 1978
BY ROBERT AXELROD

Analyses of the contributions of particular groups to a party's electoral coalition have long been a mainstay of both scholarship and strategy. In recent years, this kind of calculation has also become a vehicle for the assertion of claims of political merit. Black leaders who remind Carter of the contribution of black voters to his victory are the latest of these claimants.

Having published an analysis of electoral coalitions for each presidential election from 1952 to 1972, I am pleased to be able to provide an update for the 1976 election. Few people are in a position to generate the required statistics from survey data readily because an iterative procedure is necessary to correct for overreporting of the turnout.

The figures are presented with the data from the earlier studies so that all seven presidential elections since 1952 can be compared. The coalitions are described in terms of the three components of a group's contribution to a party, namely the size of the group, its turnout, and its loyalty to the given party. The *contribution* of a group to the electoral coalition of a party is the proportion of all the party's votes that come from members of that group. The *loyalty* of a group to a certain party is simply the proportion of the votes of that group which are cast for that party.

Two well-known facts about the 1976 election are worth elaborating before we look at the coalitions themselves. The first is that the election was close. Only 2.1 percent of the popular vote separated Carter from Ford. This is quite a contrast from only four years before when Nixon's

Robert Axelrod, Letter to the Editor, "1976 Update," *American Political Science Review,* Vol. 72, June 1978, pp. 622–624. Footnotes deleted. Reprinted by permission of The American Political Science Association.

Table 1 · The Democratic Coalition, 1952–1976

Year	PERCENTAGE CONTRIBUTION =						(SIZE					×	TURNOUT				×	LOYALTY)					÷ (NT×NL)	
	P	B	U	C	S	CC	P	B	U	C	S	CC	P	B	U	C	S	CC	P	B	U	C	S	CC	NT	NL
1952	28	7	38	41	20	21	36	10	27	26	28	16	46	23	66	76	35	68	47	83	59	57	55	51	63	44.4
1956	19	5	36	38	23	19	25	9	26	25	29	14	40	23	64	72	39	63	47	68	55	53	52	55	60	42.0
1960	16	7	31	47	27	19	23	10	25	25	34	13	46	31	60	74	50	74	48	72	66	82	52	65	64	49.7
1964	15	12	32	36	21	15	19	11	23	26	28	12	45	42	69	72	49	65	69	99	80	75	58	74	63	61.1
1968	12	19	28	40	24	14	16	11	24	26	31	10	44	51	61	68	53	63	44	92	51	61	39	58	62	42.7
1972	10	22	32	43	25	14	12	11	25	31	34	8	37	47	58	65	44	60	45	86	45	45	36	61	56	37.5
1976	7	16	33	35	36	11	9	11	23	30	32	8	32	44	62	55	57	58	67	88	63	57	53	61	54	50.1
COLUMN	1	2	3	4	5	6	7	8	9	10	11	12	13	14	15	16	17	18	19	20	21	22	23	24	25	26

P   poor (income under $3,000/yr.)
B   Black (and other nonwhite)
U   union member (or union member in family)
C   Catholic (and other non-Protestant)
S   South (including border states)
CC central cities (of 12 largest metropolitan areas)
NT national turnout
NL national loyalty to Democrats

Percentage Deviation in
Loyalty to Democrats

Year	P	B	U	C	S	CC
1952	+2	+38	+14	+12	+10	+ 6
1956	+5	+26	+13	+11	+10	+13
1960	-2	+22	+16	+32	+ 2	+15
1964	+8	+38	+19	+14	- 3	+13
1968	+1	+49	+ 8	+18	- 4	+15
1972	+8	+49	+ 8	+ 8	- 2	+24
1976	+17	+38	+13	+ 7	+ 3	+10
COLUMN	27	28	29	30	31	32

Table 2 · The Republican Coalition, 1952–1976

Year	PERCENTAGE CONTRIBUTION						= (SIZE)						× TURNOUT						× LOYALTY						÷ (NT × NL)	
	NP	W	NU	P	N	NCC	NP	W	NU	P	N	NCC	NP	W	NU	P	N	NCC	NP	W	NU	P	N	NCC	NT	NL
1952	75	99	79	75	87	84	64	90	73	74	72	84	72	67	61	58	73	61	56	57	61	61	57	57	63	55.1
1956	84	98	78	75	84	89	75	91	74	75	71	86	67	64	58	56	69	60	59	59	63	62	60	60	60	57.4
1960	83	97	84	90	75	90	77	90	75	75	66	87	70	68	65	61	71	63	50	51	55	63	50	52	64	49.5
1964	89	100	87	80	76	91	81	89	77	74	72	88	67	66	61	60	68	63	40	42	45	44	38	40	63	38.5
1968	90	99	81	80	80	92	84	89	76	74	69	90	65	63	62	60	66	62	44	47	46	49	47	45	62	43.4
1972	93	98	77	70	73	95	88	89	75	69	66	92	58	57	55	53	62	55	61	66	63	65	60	63	56	60.7
1976	97	99	80	76	67	98	71	89	77	70	68	92	56	56	52	54	53	54	49	52	52	53	49	49	54	48.0
COLUMN	1	2	3	4	5	6	7	8	9	10	11	12	13	14	15	16	17	18	19	20	21	22	23	24	25	26

Percentage Deviation in Loyalty to Republicans

Year	NP	W	NU	P	N	NCC
1952	+1	+2	+6	+6	+6	+2
1956	+1	+1	+5	+4	+2	+2
1960	0	+1	+5	+13	0	+2
1964	+1	+3	+6	+5	−1	+1
1968	0	+3	+2	+5	+3	+1
1972	+1	+5	+3	+4	−1	+2
1976	+1	+5	+4	+5	+1	+1
COLUMN	27	28	29	30	31	32

NP   nonpoor (income over $3,000/yr.)
W   White
NU   nonunion
P   Protestant
N   Northern (excluding border states)
NCC   not in central cities of 12 largest metropolitan areas
NT   national turnout
NL   national loyalty to Republicans

lead over McGovern was 23.2 percent. The second basic fact is that the turnout was very low: only 54 percent of the voting-age population voted, the lowest turnout in the seven elections analyzed. Especially significant in this regard is that only 41 percent of those under thirty voted.

For the Democrats, the New Deal coalition made a comeback in 1976. For the first time since the Johnson landslide of 1964, the Democrats got a majority of the votes from each of the six diverse minorities which make up their traditional coalition: the poor, blacks, union families, Catholics, southerners, and city dwellers (Table 1, cols. 19–24). The blacks have continued their pattern of very high loyalty, in this year giving 88 percent of their vote to the Democrats (col. 20), but with a turnout of only 44 percent (col. 14). Thus with 11 percent of the population (col. 8), they contributed 16 percent of Carter's vote (col. 2). Union families and Catholics (and other non-Protestants) provide an interesting contrast to the blacks. Both of these groups provided more than twice as many votes to the Democrats as did the blacks. They voted 13 and 7 percent respectively more Democratic than the nation as a whole (col. 29 and 30), they had comparatively good turnout (col. 15 and 16), and most importantly they were more than twice as numerous as the blacks to begin with (col. 9 and 10). Finally, there is the South, including the border states. Surprisingly, the South gave only 53 percent of its votes to Carter (col. 23). This can be understood as the combination of the trend since 1960 whereby the South is moving away from its loyalty to the Democrats (col. 31), and the immediate appeal of a Democratic candidate from the South.

The Republicans have experienced a dramatic comedown since 1972, when they attracted 60 percent or more among all six of their traditional coalition groups: the nonpoor, whites, nonunion families, Protestants, northerners, and those living outside the central cities (Table 2, col. 19–24). In 1976 they got no more than 53 percent from any of these groups, and failed to get even a majority of the loyalty of the nonpoor, northerners, and noncity dwellers (col. 19, 23, and 24).

One lesson from the 1976 election is that even when the Democrats can put together all of the elements of their traditional coalition, the election can be very close. The experience of the Democrats after running a Catholic candidate in 1960 shows that the gains in Catholic deviation in loyalty may not be lasting (Table 1, col. 30). The same may apply in the South after Carter. If the Democrats lose the South again, or if they lose the enthusiasm of the blacks or the loyalty of any of their other traditional groups, they will be in trouble. This could easily happen despite their large and steady lead in party identification.

CHAPTER 10

The Presidential Election Campaign

A. The Nature of Election Campaigns

B. Strategies and Tactics: Issues, Themes, and Images

C. Press Coverage and Interpretation

·A·

The Nature of Election Campaigns

Strategy for November
BY JOHN H. KESSEL

Campaign Experience

THE "NORMAL" COALITIONS

The groups in the normal party coalitions have been familiar since the days of Franklin Roosevelt. The Democratic party has been assembled over time as a coalition of minorities. The first two groups were the South and the West, the agrarian supporters of William Jennings Bryan. Another group of urban voters had grown in power, finally winning control of the nomination of Al Smith in 1928. In the 1930s organized labor became important as well, and in the same decade most blacks moved from the party of Lincoln to the party of Roosevelt. Democratic tickets typically had a presidential candidate acceptable to the urban-labor-black wing of the party, and a vice-presidential candidate from somewhere in the South or West: Franklin Roosevelt and John Nance Garner, Adlai Stevenson and John Sparkman, John Kennedy and Lyndon Johnson. The Republicans, the erstwhile majority party, were split between moderates and conservatives. The former group had been more successful in nomination politics; the latter was much stronger on Capitol Hill. The Republicans engaged in ticket-balancing, too (witness Thomas Dewey and John Bricker in 1944), but the balance of power between moderates and conservatives was much more important. In the last of four consecutive nomination contests between New York-based and Ohio-based coalitions, Dwight Eisenhower

John H. Kessel, "Strategy for November," from James D. Barber, ed., *Choosing the President* (Englewood Cliffs, N.J.: Prentice-Hall, Inc., 1974), pp. 97–119. © 1974 by the American Assembly, Columbia University. Reprinted by permission of Prentice-Hall, Inc., Englewood Cliffs, New Jersey.

had 595 votes and Robert Taft had 500 votes before vote switches gave the general the 1952 nomination. At this point (and in this specific context) the moderates were successful, but the crucial fact was that the two wings were of approximately equal size. Both had the potential of leading the party.

STRAIN IN THE FABRIC: THE REPUBLICANS IN 1964

By 1964, the conservatives had grown in power to the point where they could nominate their own candidate, Barry Goldwater. To understand this campaign, it is useful to distinguish among types of conservatives. Four groups could be discerned in the Goldwater coalition. First were the conservative ideologues who had long felt that contests with the Democrats should be fought in terms of liberty vs. socialism, and who favored a much less active role for the government in the management of the economy. Second was a group of foreign policy hard-liners who saw a bipolar world in which there was a total struggle between the free world and the Communists, us against them. The third group was made up of southerners who saw a chance to build a Republican party based on states' rights, and who felt their cause would be advanced by opposition to federal power on many issues, including civil rights. After Goldwater's nomination, these groups were joined by a fourth, the organizational loyalists whose Republican credentials were so impeccable that the Goldwaterites had no doubt about them, and whose party loyalty was so strong that they never had any doubts about supporting the Republican nominee. There was a fair amount of attitudinal overlap between the conservative ideologues and the foreign policy hard-liners (although the government should not simultaneously cut taxes and buy expensive weapons systems), but there was less agreement between these groups and the organizational loyalists or the southerners. The former were less ideological; the latter preferred a more strident conservatism which they thought would help build a party organization in the South. Tensions between these groups were to affect strategy throughout the campaign.

The first phase of the campaign was an attempt, in which the organizational loyalists played a key role, to reunite the moderates and the Goldwaterites. These two factions never had understood one another very well, and relations had been further strained by the Goldwater references to extremism and moderation. . . .* Richard Nixon sent a letter to the senator:

> I believe it would be helpful to clear the air once and for all . . . and I would appreciate it . . . if you would send me . . . further comments . . . with regard to the intended meaning of these two sentences.

Editors' note: This was the famous line at the end of Goldwater's speech accepting the Republican nomination, wherein he had asserted: "Extremism in the defense of liberty is not vice! Moderation in the pursuit of justice is not virtue."

The Goldwater reply came immediately:

> If I were to paraphrase the two sentences in the context in which I uttered
> them I would do it by saying that whole-hearted devotion to liberty is
> unassailable and that half-hearted devotion to justice is indefensible.

Further intergroup diplomacy led to a meeting hosted by Dwight Eisenhower at Hershey, Pennsylvania, in mid-August. All Republican governors
and gubernatorial candidates were invited, and there was some frank discussion between Senator Goldwater and these moderate leaders. Any hope
of bringing an important group of moderates into the Goldwater coalition,
though, ended with the senator's first answer at a subsequent press conference when he denied any intent to be conciliatory.

The second phase of Goldwater strategy came with the formal opening
of the campaign in early September. The goal then was to win the West
and the Midwest, to add these regions to the South, which was assumed to
be in favor of Goldwater. The emphasis was to be conservative, and the
technique was to give major speeches which would illustrate what the
senator meant by his broader themes: a resolute foreign policy with an
emphasis on military preparedness and a domestic conservatism stressing
free enterprise and law-and-order. Several such speeches were given, one in
Los Angeles on programmed tax cuts, another in Chicago criticizing the
Supreme Court for infidelity to the principle of limited government, one in
Montgomery, Alabama, calling for revenue-sharing with the states, and
one in Fargo, North Dakota, advocating reduction of farm supports. The
strategists assumed that President Johnson would reply, and that a princi-
pled discussion about issues would be joined.

By late September, three things were evident. President Johnson was
not going to reply in kind; the existing strategy was not improving Senator
Goldwater's standing with the voters; two issues—control of nuclear arms
and social security—were in fact doing a good deal of harm to the senator.
Each group had its own prescription. Each preferred a new strategy that
would shift the emphasis in *its* own direction. Faced with agreement that
the strategy needed to be changed, and disagreement as to what the new
emphasis should be, the core group decided to respond to the two issues
seen as being harmful. So for about two weeks, Republican leaders explained that Senator Goldwater's position on the authority of field commanders (as NATO) did not differ from the practice of the Eisenhower,
Kennedy, or Johnson administrations, and that the senator had voted several times to increase social security benefits.

The results of this defensive strategy were the same: no change in the
survey results and criticism from supporters that Senator Goldwater was
conducting an ineffective campaign. Hence, on October 11 the strategy
committee shifted again, this time to approve "Operation Home Stretch," a
plan drafted by Public Relations Director Lou Guylay. The point was to

develop an override strategy, to shift attention away from Johnson's strengths by developing new issues. This fourth plan called for contrasting the moral decay of the Johnson administration (to be tied to rising crime at home and a weakening American posture abroad) with Senator Goldwater's "Hope for a New America." This strategy was given an unexpected boost with the announcement of the arrest of a Johnson aide on a morals charge, but the same fate that smiled briefly on this plan quickly frowned. Within 48 hours, Khrushchev was deposed as the Soviet leader, Harold Wilson led the Labour party to an unexpected victory in Great Britain, and China exploded her first atomic "device." The net of all this was to shift public attention right back to foreign affairs, an area in which voters deemed President Johnson more competent than Senator Goldwater.

By late October, it was clear to the candidate and core group that Goldwater was not going to win. The reaction to this was a final strategy, a reassertion of the correctness of Goldwater beliefs (in *his* heart, the senator knew he was right) and an appeal to the faithful to stay in line so the conservative cause would not be damaged by too overwhelming a defeat. In New York, on Monday, the senator asked plaintively, "I can't help wondering... if you think I don't *know* what views would be the most popular." And on Saturday night, he appeared on a platform in Columbia, South Carolina, with a number of prominent southern Democrats, and spoke on a television network confined to the old Confederacy. This was not a case of a general southern strategy (which most observers quite incorrectly alleged had been going on throughout the campaign). Rather, it was end-of-the-campaign fighting for votes which a few weeks earlier had been taken for granted.

THE EXPANDING UMBRELLA: THE DEMOCRATS IN 1964

The Goldwater nomination gave President Johnson considerable flexibility in choosing his strategy. He had been developing a unity appeal since he had entered the White House. He spoke, for example, on the idea of a "Great Society" at the University of Michigan and the need for a "broad national consensus" at the University of Texas on two successive weeks in late May. This strategy was well designed to hold together a coalition of minorities, and the Goldwater nomination gave President Johnson the opportunity to appeal to an even larger set of political groups. The result was the Johnson coalition: moderate Republicans added to the southern-western-urban-labor-black base. Four of the five "normal" Democratic groups were certain to vote for Johnson in 1964; only the loyalty of the South was endangered by the Goldwater nomination. Hence, there were three aspects to the Johnson strategy: a "normal" campaign to remind labor, blacks, urbanites, and westerners that they had been well served by Democratic administrations, a defensive campaign to protect southern support from Republican incursions, and an offensive campaign to convince moderate Republicans that their views lay closer to the Johnson coalition than the Goldwater coalition.

The appeal to normal Democratic groups combined personal empathy, recitation of Democratic accomplishments, and promises in principle to pursue new goals. In Miami Beach, Johnson told machinists that workers' earnings had risen eight times as much since 1961 as they had in a comparable Eisenhower period. In Denver, he promised to put education at the top of America's agenda. In Portland, Oregon, he ticked off a five-point program for a "new conservation." Blacks needed little encouragement since they were convinced that Senator Goldwater had the support of known racists in community after community. But these appeals to labor, urbanites, westerners, and blacks were easy. How often does a presidential candidate get a chance to win votes by promising not to eliminate social security or by reminding voters that his opponent has said it would be well to saw off the eastern seaboard and let it float out to sea?

The southern strategy followed by the Johnson coalition was more interesting. There were four parts to this amalgam. The first was a mobilization of newly registered black voters who were numerous enough to provide the winning margin in many southern states. Second was a reminder of traditional Democratic loyalties, and of the Johnsons' own southern origins. For example, in North Carolina, Mrs. Johnson said that her main reason for coming "was to say to you that to this Democratic candidate, and his wife, the South is a respected, valued, and beloved part of the country." A third element was organizational: local Democrats who had been complaisant in the face of Republican presidential voting were reminded that they were now facing the prospect of Republican candidates for congressman, state senator, and sheriff. The final, and most important, part of the campaign was an economic appeal. When President Johnson met the "Lady Bird Special" campaign train in New Orleans, he quoted an unidentified southern senator:

> I would like to go back there and make them one more Democratic speech. I just feel like I've got one more in me. Poor old state, they haven't heard a Democratic speech in thirty years. All they ever hear is Negro, Negro, Negro! The kind of speech they should have been hearing is about the economy and what a great future we could have in the South if we just met our economic problems, if we just took a look at the resources of the South and developed them.

The South had made considerable economic progress since the Democrats had become the majority party in the 1930s, and President Johnson hoped to remind southerners that they had more to gain by staying with the Democrats than by responding to Senator Goldwater's conservative appeals.

The theme of the campaign for Republican votes was set by Hubert Humphrey in his vice-presidential acceptance speech: Barry Goldwater was not a typical Republican.

> Yes, yes my fellow Americans, it is a fact that the temporary Republican spokesman is not in the mainstream of his party, in fact he has not even touched the shore. . . . I say to those responsible and forward-looking Republicans—and there are thousands of them—we welcome you to the banner of Lyndon B. Johnson. . . .

The President picked up this theme in many of his speeches. In Harrisburg, Pennsylvania, at a Democratic fund-raising dinner, he went out of his way to praise both President Eisenhower and Governor Scranton. Campaigning in Indiana, he acknowledged that Hoosiers had often supported GOP candidates, but declared, "I'm not sure whether there is a real Republican candidate this time." In Rockford, Illinois, four days before the election, Lyndon Johnson pointed out:

> I have always been the kind of Democrat who could work together with my fellow Americans of the party of Lincoln and McKinley, Herbert Hoover and Dwight Eisenhower, Robert Taft, Arthur Vandenberg, and Everett Dirksen.

It had been some time since a Democratic presidential candidate had spoken kindly about William McKinley and Herbert Hoover just before an election, but 1964 gave President Johnson unusual freedom to maneuver. He was not completely free of intraparty criticism, but he was able to make his appeals to Republicans, carry out his defense of Democratic support in the South, and conduct his "normal" campaign for other groups without being subject to the kinds of pressures that would force him to switch from one set of campaign plans to another.

1968 AND THE POSSIBILITY OF A REPUBLICAN VICTORY

If 1964 was a year when an abnormally large coalition could be put together in behalf of a Democratic candidate, 1968 was not. With George Wallace joining those other figures—Theodore Roosevelt in 1912, Robert LaFollette in 1924, and Strom Thurmond in 1948—who had led dissatisfied groups into third-party efforts, it was possible for a normal Republican coalition to win. But for Richard Nixon to hold the coalition together, very delicate balancing was necessary. Mr. Nixon had to remain sufficiently progressive to keep moderate Republicans from supporting Hubert Humphrey if Nixon was to carry enough large states to win. He also had to convince conservatives that he was the authentic antiliberal candidate, that a vote for George Wallace would only be a wasted vote. Doing either of these things by itself would be relatively easy; doing them both at the same time required real political skill. This meant that exactly the right thing had to be said. Richard Nixon had to give voice to attitudes that would be acceptable to all his followers.

This task was begun at the convention in two ways. One was to obtain an acceptable Vietnam plank in the platform by negotiations between Nixon leaders, Rockefeller leaders, and the Platform Committee. The resulting statement began by advocating what later came to be called "Vietnamization."

> We pledge to adopt a strategy relevant to the real problems of the war, concentrating on the security of the population, on developing a greater sense of nationhood, and on strengthening the local forces. It will be a strategy permitting a progressive de-Americanization of the war, both military and civilian.

Then followed words appealing to hawks:

> We will see to it that our gallant American servicemen are fully supported with the highest quality equipment, and will avoid actions that unnecessarily jeopardize their lives.

And to doves:

> We will pursue a course that will enable and induce the South Vietnamese to assume greater responsibility. . . . We will sincerely and vigorously pursue peace negotiations as long as they offer any reasonable prospect for a just peace.

The other important question was the selection of a vice-presidential candidate. Here the party was blessed with a surfeit of possibilities: Nelson Rockefeller, Charles Percy, Mark Hatfield, Dan Evans among the moderates, John Tower or Howard Baker among the conservatives. But to pick a strong moderate would have produced consternation among the conservatives and to pick a strong conservative would have had a like effect with the moderates. So: "Dick gave us a list. Everybody on the list was unsatisfactory, but Agnew was the *least* unsatisfactory," as a conservative leader allegedly put it. The statement could just as easily have come from a moderate. Neither group was happy with the Agnew nomination, but neither was moved to rebellion. Given a need to hold an unstable coalition together, a vice-presidential candidate whose name was not a household word was a positive virtue.

The Nixon statements on issues during the campaign were similarly calculated to avoid giving offense. On Vietnam:

> We need new leadership that will not only end the war in Vietnam but keep the nation out of other wars for eight years.

On crime:

> I say that when crime has been going up nine times as fast as population, when 43 percent of the people living in American cities are afraid to go out after dark, I say we need a complete housecleaning.

And on welfare:

> Instead of more millions on welfare rolls, let's have more millions on the payrolls.

Richard Nixon did develop an interesting technique of giving more detailed statements on radio, using a low-visibility medium to reach the smaller audience seriously interested in issues. Here he discussed, for example, black capitalism, the alienation of Americans from the governmental process, and the Presidency as a moral and political office. The applause points quoted above, though, were the verbal equivalent of all the balloons released at televised rallies. They took up time with little danger of alienating any support, yet they *sounded* definite.

Mr. Nixon followed a very cautious course throughout September. In spite of a huge lead in the polls (43 percent to 31 percent in the Gallup Poll of September 10), he did not think the election was locked up by any means. He avoided debates, which would have posed high risk to his coalition. By early October, Governor Wallace was still gaining and Vice-President Humphrey was not. Consequently, he moved against the Alabamian. In a speech to a blue-collar audience in Flint, Michigan, on October 8, Nixon addressed three questions to his listeners:

> Do you just want to make a point or do you want to make a change? Do you want to get something off your chest, or do you want to get something done? Do you want to get a moment's satisfaction, or do you want to get four years of action?

He continued with direct attacks on Wallace and LeMay:

> We cannot threaten to run a presidential car over our people and expect peace in our cities. We cannot put an irresponsible finger on the nuclear trigger and expect to avert the horror of a nuclear war.

The timing of this attack was related to an estimate that Wallace had probably peaked; Nixon's hope was that his move would help reverse this tide and that Wallace strength could be confined to the Deep South. This was what happened. In later October, Wallace faded while Humphrey began to gain rapidly in the large states.

In the face of the threat from the Vice-President, Nixon stepped up attacks on him. Earlier, when Hubert Humphrey had made a speech in Salt Lake City advocating a change in our Vietnamese policy, Nixon charged that what Humphrey brought to foreign policy was "the fastest, loosest tongue in American politics." Now Mr. Humphrey was said to be "the most expensive senator in American history." Further, the Vice-President was accused of taking a "lackadaisical, do-nothing approach to public order." By the end of the campaign (October 30), the race was so close that there was a real chance the election might be thrown into the House of Representatives. At this point, Nixon invited Humphrey to join him in a pledge to support the winner of the popular vote. "I do not fear the voice of the people," Nixon said. "Does Hubert Humphrey?"

THE WALLACE BID FOR NORTHERN SUPPORT

George Wallace's basic problem was that he lacked the support needed to be a viable national candidate. Although the ablest third-party candidate since 1924, he was supported primarily by a single group, southern Democrats. He needed to attract another group, northern blue-collar workers. The governor had to persuade those who were *talking* Wallace to *vote* Wallace, and to do this without losing his base of Dixiecrat support. Therefore Governor Wallace aimed his appeal at "the honest working man," those of average income and education who felt threatened by a rising crime rate, rapid changes in race relations, rising taxes, and a complex world beyond their control. The items Wallace attacked—bureaucrats, briefcases, guidelines— symbolized both federal power and a complex modern society.

Governor Wallace did not have any trouble as long as he stayed with the well-tried applause points in his speeches.

> Turn absolute control of the public schools back to the people of [whatever state he was speaking in].
>
> We're going to see the end of those bureaucrats in Washington who send us guidelines telling us when we can go to sleep at night and when we can get up in the morning.
>
> Militant revolutionary anarchism and communism are the cause of the breakdown of law and order.
>
> You'd better be thankful for the police and firemen, 'cause if it wasn't for them you couldn't walk the streets. The wife of a workingman can't go to the supermarket without the fear of being assaulted.

Wallace certainly did not hurt himself by defining his enemies as "militant revolutionary anarchists" and "Communists" and numbering "police," "firemen," "workingmen," and "wives" among his friends. Nor did he have much exceptionable in his more serious speeches. For example, he delivered an address on foreign policy to the National Press Club that could have been given by almost any American leader since World War II.

Governor Wallace did begin to run into real trouble in early October. He had probably reached his maximum strength by that time, and it was then that he finally selected a vice-presidential candidate, General Curtis LeMay. In the Pittsburgh press conference announcing this choice, the following exchange took place:

Question: If you found it necessary to end the war, you would use nuclear weapons, wouldn't you? *LeMay:* If I found it necessary, I would use anything we could dream up—anything we could dream up—including nuclear weapons, if it was necessary.

Governor Wallace fairly sped to the microphone.

All General LeMay has said—and I know you fellows better than he does because I've had to deal with you—he said that if the security of our country depended on the use of any weapon in the future he would use it. But he said he prefers not to use any sort of weapon. He prefers to negotiate. I believe that we must defend our country, but I've always said we can win and defend in Vietnam without the use of nuclear weapons. But General LeMay hasn't said anything about the use of nuclear weapons.

Of course, General LeMay had said enough about nuclear weapons to produce a good many headlines. The general was promptly sent to Vietnam on an inspection tour, but the damage had been done.

Wallace strength faded perceptibly after this point. The LeMay remark was by no means the only cause. As we have already seen, Richard Nixon had attacked him. And labor unions, to whose ability to lead their own members the Wallace candidacy was a threat, had mounted a massive anti-Wallace, pro-Humphrey campaign. They gave wide circulation, for example, to a letter from an Alabama worker detailing unpleasant working conditions in the governor's home state. When national surveys showed that Wallace's support was falling, he attacked the polls as a conspiracy. All of this added up. By the day before the election, he was fighting to retain what had once been ceded to him by campaigning in front of the Georgia Statehouse in the company of Governor Lester Maddox.

THE TRUNCATED COALITION OF HUBERT HUMPHREY

Hubert Humphrey came away from the Chicago convention in serious trouble. He had selected a vice-presidential candidate who would bring strength to the ticket. But with Wallace playing Pied Piper to the southern Democrats, Humphrey had to make do with a truncated Democratic coalition of westerners, urbanites, labor, and blacks. Worse still, the trauma of the convention had created animosities among these groups. Not only was there a prolonged debate over the character of the Vietnam platform plank, but the specter of Chicago police in conflict with young demonstrators disturbed collegians and blacks who thought too much force was being used, *and* union members and urbanites who thought too little force was being used. Moreover, since the convention was not held until the end of August, there were only two months to put the pieces back together.

During September, Vice-President Humphrey worked very hard. He tried talking to the groups in his coalition, concentrating on the issues that would unify them: medicare, the creation of a Department of Housing and Urban Development, the Job Corps, education, Food for Peace, the Peace Corps, disarmament and arms control, and civil rights. But for whatever reason, nothing happened. By the end of September, it seemed that Humphrey's chances depended on some break of which he could take advantage: such as a decision by Hanoi that it would prefer to deal with Johnson rather than waiting for Nixon, a Johnson decision to stop bombing, or a Nixon decision to engage in debates or battle Humphrey on the issues. Instead, the Vice-President made his own break. On September 30, after having the vice-presidential seal removed from the rostrum, he made a speech suggesting the policy a Humphrey administration would follow in Vietnam:

> As President, I would stop the bombing of the North as an acceptable risk for peace because I believe it could lead to success in the negotiations. . . . In weighing that risk . . . I would place key importance on evidence . . . of Communist willingness to restore the demilitarized zone between North and South Vietnam. . . . Secondly, I would take the risk that the South Vietnamese would meet the obligations that they say they are now ready to assume in their own self-defense.

In this speech, Hubert Humphrey departed from the policy then being followed by the Johnson administration. This did not end all criticism; the Johnsonites were furious. But it did create an environment that made it a little easier for the groups in the Democratic coalition to work together.

Shortly thereafter, some state-by-state polls showed the Vice-President to be in better shape than the national polls. Humphrey was beating Nixon in Minnesota and Massachusetts, and held a slight edge in Michigan, Missouri, New York, Connecticut, New Jersey, Pennsylvania, and Texas. To the Humphreyites, this suggested a geographical emphasis to the campaign. Mr. Humphrey could win by carrying these larger states by narrow margins even though Richard Nixon was likely to carry smaller states by very large margins. The results of these surveys were quickly communicated to Democratic leaders who had been hitherto inactive and to potential donors. The effort and cash flow thus stimulated helped galvanize the truncated Democratic coalition.

The campaign strategy which had hitherto unified these groups, especially urbanites, union members, and blacks important in the large industrial states, was pressed into service once again. Hubert Humphrey listed Democratic accomplishments: social security, medicare, eight years of prosperity. At one point he asked:

> Imagine what it'll be like if the unemployment rate is up to 7 percent. Who's to be unemployed? Which worker is to be laid off? Which family is to be without a check?

Memories of the depression of the thirties were further stirred by a Democratic pamphlet that urged young people to ask their fathers what things were like during the depression if they could not remember themselves. On civil rights, the Vice-President argued that he was in the best position to assure racial harmony after the election as he was the only candidate who was trusted by both whites and blacks. But at the same time, he made it clear that he was not threatening the jobs held by white workers.

> I know what the opposition puts out to the blue-collar white worker. He says, "Watch out for that Humphrey. He is going to get a black man a job, and that means your job." I said, now listen here. I am for jobs. I am for an expanded economy in this country. I am for decent jobs and I am for jobs and I don't care whether the worker is black, white, green, or purple; fat, thin, tall, or short. I am for jobs.

Nixon attacked Hubert Humphrey more sharply as the campaign grew close; Humphrey returned the favor. (In both cases, there was more to this than personal animosity. One way to hold disparate groups together is to remind them of their common dislike for the opposition leader.) Mr. Nixon was characterized as "Richard the Chicken-Hearted." "You want me to tell the truth about this fellow Nixon?" asked Humphrey. "It won't take much time because there isn't much truth." At the same time, campaign chairman Lawrence O'Brien, respected by Democratic groups because of his role in the successful campaigns of 1960 and 1964, was privately telling members of the Democratic coalition they could win, and publicly charging a Nixon–Wallace deal. As we know, all of this *almost* worked. The election was extremely close. It had taken at least a month after Chicago to create the conditions in which Democratic groups could work together. But since the truncated Democratic coalition was about the same size as the normal Republican coalition, and since Democratic leaders were able to use themes which were familiar to Democratic ears from many previous campaigns, the month of October was almost all the time they needed.

REMNANT POLITICS: THE DEMOCRATS IN 1972

George McGovern could have campaigned until November, 1973, and it would not have made any difference in the outcome of that contest. Consider what the McGovern nomination meant to the groups in the normal Democratic coalition. So far as the South was concerned, the situation was best summed up by the comment that McGovern could not carry the South with Robert E. Lee as his running mate and Bear Bryant as his campaign manager. As an authentic inheritor of William Jennings Bryan's moral righteousness, Senator McGovern might have had appeal to westerners. But with major battles seen to be coming in New Jersey, Pennsylvania, Ohio, Michigan, and Illinois, the West was scheduled for relatively little attention in the McGovern campaign. There was some labor support; a National Labor Committee for the Election of McGovern–Shriver was headed by Joseph D. Keenan of the Electrical Workers and Joseph A. Beirne of the Communication Workers. Still, workingmen were not enchanted by McGovern positions on the war and amnesty, nor by his seeming intent to raise welfare payments to a level above what they were earning through their own hard work. Considering this, and the highly advertised neutrality of George Meany, labor support for McGovern was about half of what a Democratic candidate could normally expect. As for the urban vote, the effect of the McGovern nomination was well assessed by Rev. Andrew Greeley of the National Opinion Research Center:

> Everybody is noticing the ethnic these days. And it's too late for McGovern. The good Senator has a Catholic problem. The McGovern problem with the Catholic vote starts back in Miami Beach when ethnics, along with other parts of the old Democratic coalition, were clearly excluded, written off, and told we don't need you any more. That's why they are gone this year—that and the McGovern inclination to radicals and hippies and his peculiar behavior since the nomination. The ethnics are just turned off. And they aren't the only ones. You throw out Dick Daley and you throw out a lot of the country. They are gone for 1972. Oh, but they will be back.

Vito Marzullo, Democratic leader in Chicago's Twenty-fifth Ward, put it more bluntly:

> I been here since 1920. For all that time now I been seeing these do-gooder boobs come and go, and I'm still here. They come up overnight and think they're going to take over the machine. . . . Me and my official family don't believe in the McGovern policies. Those kooks couldn't even be elected street cleaners in Chicago.

Of all the major groups in the normal Democratic coalition, only the blacks were not disenchanted.

The coalition that had dominated American politics since the days of Franklin Roosevelt had been split asunder. And mind-boggling though it be, this was an intentional act. George McGovern had explained his plans to reporter Tom Wicker in 1969:

> I've made up my mind. I'm going all the way. I'm going to run for President and the coalition I'm going to put together is going to be built around the poor and the minorities and the young people and the anti-war movement.

Consequently, the McGovern coalition that could be assembled after Miami Beach was made up of young militants, blacks, some labor, and organizational loyalists who stood ready to support any Democratic candidate.

The McGovern plan had called for a "left-centrist" strategy: co-opt the left in order to win the nomination, and then reunite with the Democratic center in order to win the election. The latter part of this plan proved difficult to execute. It might have begun with the selection of a vice-presidential nominee and a national chairman who had good ties to non-McGovern groups in the normal Democratic coalition. Indeed, an immediate postconvention headline read "Eagleton to Woo Labor and Daley." But any centrist strategy based on Senator Eagleton became moot after his departure from the ticket, and his resignation less than a week after George McGovern had said he was "1,000 percent for Tom Eagleton" did not help form a favorable image for the still not well-known South Dakotan. Incumbent National Chairman Lawrence O'Brien had good ties to many groups in the Democratic party, but it turned out that Senator McGovern had promised the national chairmanship to Jean Westwood and to Pierre Salinger as well. So Ms. Westwood became Democratic national chairman, Mr. O'Brien became "national campaign chairman," and Mr. Salinger went off to Paris to contact some North Vietnamese (only to be *again* disavowed by Senator McGovern when he returned). Senator McGovern then tried personal appeals himself in visits to the LBJ Ranch, to Mayor Daley in Chicago, and to Hilton Head, South Carolina, where southern governors were meeting on Labor Day weekend. All for naught. September opened with less chance of bringing other groups into the McGovern coalition than had been the case in July.

As active campaigning began, McGovern was still being urged to concentrate on recapturing lost Democratic votes. But the corruption of those in power was a theme that suited the senator's moral posture, and one that appealed to the nonestablishment groups in the McGovern coalition. As his jet flew from campaign event to campaign event, he was denouncing Watergate, denouncing the war in Vietnam, denouncing special interest groups, and, above all, denouncing Richard Nixon. In Cleveland, he said:

> We didn't have the security chief of our campaign indicted for burglary. We didn't have our campaign manager resigning under strange circumstances.

Speaking to a western conference on water and power on September 25, he declared:

> In growing numbers, the people of this country have become as fed up as I am with the war in Vietnam and the special-interest government here at home. . . . Under the administration of Richard Nixon, the banks, the conglomerate giants, the oil and utility corporations and their coal subsidiaries have received the tender loving care of our government. . . . You have to go back to the time of Warren G. Harding to find an administration so beholden and dominated by big business as the one we have today.

In Pittsburgh, he told a ghetto audience:

> Here in the Hill district, countless children are deprived of a decent chance in life almost before they can walk. But Richard Nixon has vetoed aid to education, day care centers, and health care assistance. Do you want four more years of that? . . . Why aren't there better schools here? Because your money has been used to blow up schools in Vietnam. Because every bomb that is dropped and every bullet that is fired in Southeast Asia has an echo that is heard in the Hill district. We have paid for the devastation of another land with the devastation, not just of our conscience, but of our country.

The senator's moralizing continued to build as he campaigned, and reached a crescendo at the end of September.

With no visible progress, groups in the McGovern coalition were becoming anxious. Campaign director Gary Hart described the mood at that point: "[T]here was nothing tangible, nothing concrete, nothing to show movement and progress. At the headquarters, the staff grasped at straws for encouragement . . . longing for some proof that victory lay ahead." Shortly after this another shift in strategy became manifest. The negative tone that had been building during September was muted. Emphasis was now to be placed on a series of major television addresses. The first of these came on October 10, the anniversary of a 1968 Nixon statement that "those who have had a chance for four years and could not produce peace should not be given another chance." Senator McGovern presented his own "public plan," and pointed out hopefully:

> This is what I would do to bring America home from a hated war, and it is a program that will work. The people of France were once trapped in a war in Vietnam—even as we are. But in 1954, they chose a new President [sic], Pierre Mendes-France, whose highest commitment was to achieve peace in Indochina. His program was very similar to mine. And within just five weeks, the war was over. Within just three months, every last French prisoner had been returned.

This address, together with a policy statement on "The Imperatives of Environmental Restoration" released the same week, represented the most positive stance the senator took throughout the campaign.

Two more television addresses followed, but the October television strategy had no more effect on the polls than the "media events" and moralizing rhetoric of September. A twenty-point margin remained between Senator McGovern and President Nixon, and the experienced politicians in the McGovern camp knew that time was now too short for the senator to win. The result was a final change of strategy in the last week. Those who had been urging more negative television spots had their way, and the senator's own comments revealed more animosity than at any other time in the campaign. For example he ruled out any postelection effort at unity with Nixon because:

He's conducted an evil administration. . . . The use of sabotage and espionage and wiretapping, I think those are evil and dangerous practices. I think the exploiting of racial fears is a evil practice. I think the aerial bombardment of Southeast Asia by Richard Nixon is the most evil thing ever done by any American President.

And in comments on the Saturday before the election, Senator McGovern seemed as upset with the voters he had failed to convince as he was with the President:

It's all right for the people to be fooled once as they were in 1968. If they do it again, if they let this man lead them down the false hope of peace in 1972, then, the people have nobody to blame but themselves. So I make that warning just as clear and sharply as I can here this morning. Don't be fooled by an American President who time after time has put the survival of General Thieu ahead of peace, ahead of the release of our prisoners and ahead of the survival of our young men who are still tied down in this war. I'm going to give one more warning. If Mr. Nixon is elected on Tuesday, we may very well have four more years of war in Southeast Asia. Our prisoners will sit in their cells for another four years. Don't let this man trick you into believing that he stands for peace when he's a man who makes war.

For Senator McGovern, as for Senator Goldwater before him, the general election campaign had been a frustrating experience. Both had begun with the hope of raising fundamental questions about the course of public policy; both had shifted from one strategy to another in the hope of finding success; both had ended their campaigns in an almost completely negative posture.

NIXON TRIUMPHANT: THE REPUBLICANS IN 1972

If George McGovern was perplexed about the reaction of the electorate, Richard Nixon was not. He was confident of his plan for peace in Vietnam, and while final agreement was elusive, he could point out that 90 percent of American troops had been brought home, casualties had been cut by 98 percent, and America's ground combat role had been ended. His generally admired foreign policy included detente with Russia and China along with maintenance of a strong American defense posture. Domestically, President Nixon well understood that the Republicans were vulnerable as long as they remained the minority party, and many of his policies appealed to groups that had been part of the normal Democratic coalition. He had been photographed receiving a hard-hat in his office, and his April, 1972, declaration, "I am irrevocably committed to these propositions: America needs her nonpublic schools; that those nonpublic schools need help; that therefore we must and will find ways to provide that help," did not hurt his standing with Catholics. The McGovern nomination thus provided a real chance for Richard Nixon to continue his courtship of the South and to add urban and labor groups to the normal Republican coalition. The result was what Richard Nixon referred to as the "New Majority."

Southerners had been swelling the ranks of conservative Republicans for some years, and in 1972 the process was facilitated by a sizable Democrats for Nixon organization. Texan John Connally was the head of this group, and a dinner at the Connally ranch was part of the September campaign. Earlier in the day, the President had stopped at a small Texas high school because, he told the diners, students from that high school had earned their way to Washington in the spring of 1971, and he had spoken to them in the Rose Garden.

> As I came back into the White House that day, one of the members of my staff said, "Isn't it a shame that those poor kids had to work all year in order to make that trip?" . . . and my answer was "Not at all." Because they told us something about the spirit of America. They didn't want something for nothing, and that is the kind of spirit we need in America if we are going to meet the challenges that America faces today.

This tale was quintessential Nixon. He was speaking to an elite audience whose leadership was necessary to create the sinews of organization, but the story praised an important population grouping, spoke positively about the country, and exalted the hard work which he thought important to his own success.

In shaping an appeal to labor, Republican leaders arranged that 1972 would be the first year for some time that a Republican platform did not carry a right-to-work plank which labor leaders found so distasteful. While some labor spokesmen were making their unhappiness with McGovern positions known, workers were also reading that George Meany and Richard Nixon had been golfing together. And of the hundreds of So-and-So for Nixon groups organized, one of the few for whom a White House reception was arranged was "Young Labor for Nixon." The President told them that he had been forced to make some difficult decisions while in office relating to American defense, and that he had always found his staunchest support came from the working men and women of America.

The President did not spend much time in campaigning during September and early October, and his choices of location and audience revealed his desire to add urban voters to the 1972 Nixon coalition. He turned up in Wilkes-Barre, Pennsylvania, to express sympathy to flood victims (and stopped his car to be photographed with a bride and groom), appeared at the Statue of Liberty to celebrate this sight seen by so many immigrants, came to an Italian picnic in suburban Maryland, and took a ride on San Francisco's new Bay Area Rapid Transit. Mr. Nixon spoke of many things, but part of his remarks to a Columbus Day dinner provide a good example of the themes of this bit of 1972 strategy:

Italian immigrants came to this country by the hundreds of thousands, and then by the millions. They came not asking for something, asking only for the opportunity to work. They have worked and they have built. . . . Those of Italian background bring with them a very deep religious faith. . . . The moments that have perhaps touched me most . . . have been those when . . . new citizens have . . . said, "I am so proud to be an American citizen."

Whereas Senator McGovern raised questions about the propriety of American actions, the Nixon strategy was to speak positively about groups of Americans and the country itself.

Mr. Nixon did not neglect the values that held the normal Republican coalition together, nor did he spend all of his time at rallies or other public gatherings. As in 1968, he delivered a series of radio addresses aimed at those who were sufficiently interested in issues to follow them on a low-salience communication medium. In an address on October 21, for example, he identified himself with a series of individualist values:

The new American majority believes that each person should have more of the say in how he lives his own life . . . in taking better care of those who truly cannot care for themselves . . . in taking whatever action is needed to hold down the cost of living . . . and in a national defense second to none. . . . These are not the beliefs of a selfish people. On the contrary, they are the beliefs of a generous and self-reliant people, a people of intellect and character, whose values deserve respect in every segment of our population.

President Nixon did not begin full-time campaigning until shortly before the election itself. Crisscrossing the country by jet, he ended with a giant rally at Ontario, California. The President reviewed the themes of the campaign: peace that will last . . . the trip to Peking and the trip to Moscow . . . negotiations to limit arms . . . full prosperity without war . . . fighting the rise in crime . . . an equal chance for every American. And then:

Tonight, as I speak to you in Ontario, I think you should know that this . . . is the last time I will speak to a rally as a candidate in my whole life, and I want to say to all of you here who worked on this, and to all of you who took the time to come, thank you very much for making it probably the best rally we have ever had.

A Few Conclusions

COALITION CONSTRAINTS

There have been a number of generalizations about campaign strategy implicit in this recapitulation of particular campaigns. As noted at the outset of the chapter, coalition dynamics lead a candidate to appeal to voters in a manner acceptable to the groups already supporting him. Thus we saw Barry Goldwater promising to reduce government expenditures, Lyndon Johnson defending southern support by stressing Democratic loyalties and economic progress, Richard Nixon picking a 1968 vice-presidential candidate who was not unacceptable to either moderates or conservatives, George Wallace seeking blue-collar support outside the South, Hubert Humphrey relying on traditional New Deal–Fair Deal appeals, George McGovern denouncing corruption, and Richard Nixon celebrating the importance of hard work in the American Way of Life.

But even more important—at least a stronger test of this interpretation of campaign strategy—is what has *not* happened. There were many other strategies that could have been employed. Barry Goldwater and George McGovern could have moderated their springtime appeals, and made real efforts to follow paths trod by more traditional leaders of their parties, but this would have cost Goldwater support of conservative ideologues and would have disappointed the young militants supporting McGovern. Senator Goldwater could have, in fact, pursued a vigorous southern strategy, and Senator McGovern could have become more shrill in his denunciations of corruption. Either strategy would have made it difficult to retain the support of their organizational loyalists. President Johnson or President Nixon could have attacked the opposition party quite openly by telling voters: "For years, we've been telling you that the Republicans/ Democrats were hidebound reactionaries/wild radicals, and you wouldn't believe us. Now you have proof! They've nominated Barry Goldwater/ George McGovern!" Such an appeal might well have had a long-term payoff by causing members of the opposition party to think about the appropriateness of their loyalty, but in 1964, this would have hampered Lyndon Johnson's appeal to moderate Republicans, and in 1972, it would have slowed Richard Nixon's program to get urban Democrats to cast Republican votes. In 1968, Richard Nixon could have told the electorate that better relations with China were needed, and Hubert Humphrey could have admitted that the glut of social legislation passed by the Eighty-ninth Congress meant that there were few resources available for new social programs. Neutral observers were making both points. But many conservatives were dismayed when Richard Nixon went to Peking, and frank talk about the fiscal consequences of Great Society programs was not what the urban/labor/black wing of the Democratic party wanted to hear. Many more examples of plausible strategies that would have been consistent with some campaign goal or a fair reading of the evolution of public policy could be inferred. But the central point is that none of these strategies were used. They were avoided, I would suggest, simply because they would have given offense to some group in the candidate's coalition, and were therefore unavailable.

DISTINCTIONS

The selection of a campaign strategy, however, cannot be explained simply on the basis of avoiding appeals that would give offense to members of your own coalition. There is an election to be won, and voters must be reached. To do this, one must bear some important distinctions in mind. The first distinguishes *the activist* from *the nonactivist*. The activist, who almost by definition has a high interest in politics, will likely have been following the nomination contest for some time. He knows what issues separate the contenders, and how he feels about them. Furthermore, he will have a fairly well-developed set of attitudes concerning the opposition candidate. Given all this, the activist is likely to have made at least a tentative voting decision by convention time. The nonactivist, on the other hand, may know that nominees are being chosen primarily because some of his favorite television programs have been pre-empted for reports on the primary campaigns or for the convention itself. And the policy preferences of the nonactivists may be quite different. Any number of studies have shown that Republican activists are likely to be more conservative than many other Republican voters, and the McGovern nomination, at least, was more acceptable to Democratic activists than to nonactivists. So, ways may have to be found to appeal to nonactivists who want the party to move in a different direction. Even if the policy preferences of the activists and nonactivists correspond, there is still a difference in the sophistication of appeals directed to activists and nonactivists. The activists must be appealed to, but not in such a way as to alienate the passive, unattentive mass of voters attuned to simplistic appeals—and vice versa.

A second distinction is that between *partisans* and *independents*. This is akin to the party identification scale, a five-magnitude version of which would read: strong partisan, weak partisan, independent, weak opponent, strong opponent. From the viewpoint of the strategists, independents and opponents are treated the same way for different reasons. The independent is uninterested in partisan appeals, and unlikely to be attracted by them. The opponent would resent partisan appeals, and would be likely to return to his own partisan camp if the fact of his leaving his normal partisan home became more salient than policy or candidate-oriented reasons for doing so. These are strong reasons for avoiding a partisan appeal. But if a candidate does so, he may have difficulty with his own partisans who *want* to hear an appeal on these grounds. If the candidate is a member of the majority party, strategists may feel there is more payoff to a partisan appeal than avoiding one. And if he is a member of a minority party, advisors may feel that a favorable year is the time to hold the party's banner high in the hope of increasing their ranks. In either case this is another dilemma facing the strategists.

In the real world of politics, the most fundamental distinction is *us vs.*

them, the groups belonging to the coalition vs. everybody else. This distinction does not coincide with the two previous distinctions. Those referred to differences within the electorate to whom the appeals were being directed. The "us" in this case refers to the relatively small groups of partisan activists who have supported the aspirant through his struggle for the nomination, and, usually with a slight augmentation from other party loyalists, constitute his firmest support in the general election campaign. This coalition distinguishes itself not only from the coalition supporting the opposing candidate, but also from other groups within the same party. When coalition members speak in public about fellow partisans who supported other aspirants in the spring, they say, "Of course, we expect all loyal Republicans/Democrats to support the senator." In private, they may express more reservations. Fellow partisans who are not close to the candidate say, "You bet we're working for him! You know who they're going to blame if he doesn't win." With this as a motivation, the extra effort they would put forth for *their* preferred candidate may not be forthcoming. In short, in-group/out-group distinctions are to be found in political campaigns as in all areas of life.

The reason this distinction is the most fundamental is that it affects the candidate most directly. Whatever the exact nature of the core group with whom the candidate holds his strategy discussions, it is likely to include some leaders of each group in the coalition. Their interpretation of the political situation is the last to reach the candidate before he makes up his mind, and the interpretation presented to the candidate depends on the information each person has received from his own trusted informants. Further, these relationships of trust and confidence have been developed during the preceeding months as the members of the core group demonstrated the competence that led the candidate to come to rely on their judgment. Consequently, the candidate is led to adopt a strategy satisfactory to all groups in the coalition for two reasons. First, he wants to retain the loyalty of the inner group and, by extension, the groups they represent. Second, the coalition itself constitutes a communication network that may or may not tell the candidate what the real political situation is, but certainly does lead him to adopt strategies acceptable to coalition members.

CAMPAIGN A TEST FOR OFFICE

What does all of this mean to the candidate? It means he is not a free agent who can choose among strategies at will. It further implies that he is subject to a good many tensions. The course of action that is acceptable to one group in his coalition is opposed by another. The detailed discussion of policy nuances appreciated by the activist will bore the nonactivist, and the simplistic appeal that attracts the apathetic voter may seem unworthy to the attentive elite. The ringing call for partisan support will not produce independent votes, and the less passionate analysis directed to independents may lose the faithful worker who began ringing doorbells in February. The interplay of all these tensions lends dynamism to the campaign, and presents a different challenge to the candidate. He must make his way carefully lest he forfeit vital support, yet at the same time convey those qualities of confidence that win the trust of the people. This is a somewhat different kind of task than those to be confronted in the Oval Office. If elected, mastering the intricacies of international involvement and economic management will take the place of seeking votes. But a President also has to make difficult choices in the face of conflicting evidence. In both settings, leadership requires one to seek some complex goals while maintaining the support of one's coalition. The ability to do this in an electoral setting is no guarantee that the candidate will become an able chief executive, but there are enough similarities for the campaign to serve as one important test.

·B·

Strategies and Tactics: Issues, Themes, and Images

Blueprint/Carter

BY W. HAMILTON JORDAN

Jimmy Carter's strategy for the fall campaign was shaped through the months of summer. It was detailed in two memos written by Hamilton Jordan. The first was handed to the candidate in June, well before the Democratic convention. The second was handed him in early August, addressed to both Carter and Walter Mondale.

I. Confidential Memorandum for Jimmy Carter

YOUR IMAGE WITH THE AMERICAN PEOPLE

Once a political image is fully developed, it is not easily changed or even modified. To create an impression on the American electorate, you have to penetrate the reluctant consciousness of a people who are alienated from their government and its leaders. Only by bombarding them with impressions over an extended period of time is an image created. But just as you lack control over the image that is created (Jimmy Carter is "fuzzy" on the issues), you have even greater difficulty changing those initial impressions in specific ways or refining them.

Because your rise politically this year has been so rapid and dramatic, I do not believe that your image is fully developed or has much depth. I believe that there is still time for wrong impressions to be corrected and certain strengths to be magnified. . . .

It is important that we carefully consider the image you project during the summer months.

OVEREXPOSED

I started worrying back in March that you were being overexposed. There were very few Tuesday nights and Wednesday mornings that you were not on television and all over the newspapers winning another primary. Toward the end of the primaries, I believe that some people just started to get tired of you and all of the "original" candidates and for that reason turned to "new faces" like Church and Brown.

As compared to Gerald Ford, you are still a "new face" and an "outsider." And I know nothing that will do more to fully restore these qualities to your image than for you to spend a lot of time at home with your family and friends while maintaining a low political profile. At the same time, it is likely that Ford and Reagan will occupy centerstage fighting for delegates and the nomination.

ELECTORAL COLLEGE PROJECTIONS

Needed to Be Elected President: 270 Electoral Votes

   I. Southern States Carter Is Likely to Carry:

	1. Alabama	9
	2. Arkansas	6
	3. Georgia	12
	4. Kentucky	9
	5. Louisiana	10
	6. Mississippi	7
	7. North Carolina	13
	8. South Carolina	8
	9. Tennessee	10
	10. Virginia	12
		96

   II. Southern States Likely to Be Heavily Contested:

	11. Texas	26
	12. Florida	17
		43

   III. Important Border States Which Can Be Carried:

	13. Maryland	10
	14. Missouri	12
		22

   IV. States of High Democratic Perfomance/Likely to Vote Democratic:

	15. Massachusetts	14
	16. Wisconsin	11
	17. Minnesota	10
	18. District of Columbia	3
		38

V. *Critical Large/Industrial States:*

19.	California	45
20.	New York	41
21.	Pennsylvania	27
22.	Illinois	26
23.	Ohio	25
24.	Michigan	21
25.	New Jersey	17
26.	Indiana	13
		215

ELECTORAL VOTE ANALYSIS

(1) Presume that Jimmy Carter is able and likely to win the electoral votes from the states in categories I, II, III, and IV.

I.	Southern/Likely to Carry	96
II.	Southern/Contested	43
III.	Important Border States	22
IV.	Probable Democratic States	38
		199

These electoral votes (199) represent 74% of the electoral votes that Carter will need to win the Presidency. Of the states included in this analysis, those in categories II and III are most likely to be seriously challenged by the Republican nominee. The states included in categories II and III—Texas, Florida, Missouri, and Maryland—are states that we can win. If you assumed that we would lose these four states, we would still have 134 electoral votes from the Southern states we are likely to carry and the probable Democratic states. Those 134 electoral votes would represent 49% of the votes needed to win the Presidency.

(2) Presume then that Carter is able to win the electoral votes of the states in categories I, II, III, and IV giving him a base of 199 electoral votes on which to build. Consider the various options available to achieve the necessary votes to win a majority of the Electoral College.

Review the states in V—described as "Critical Large/Industrial States":

California	45
New York	41
Pennsylvania	27
Illinois	26
Ohio	25
Michigan	21
New Jersey	17
Indiana	13
	215

Presuming then that Carter carries states in I, II, III and IV, he will need 71 electoral votes to achieve a majority in the Electoral College. From the states above, he could get the 71 votes needed from any of the following combinations:

1. *Carry New York and California*

New York	41
California	45
	86

2. *Carry New York or California and One of the Three Large Industrial States*

New York	41	
Pennsylvania	27	
	68	(Technically, 3 votes short)
New York	41	
Illinois	26	
	67	(Technically, 4 votes short)
New York	41	
Ohio	25	
	66	(Technically, 5 votes short)
California	45	
Pennsylvania	27	
	72	
California	45	
Ohio	25	
	70	(Technically, 1 vote short)
California	45	
Michigan	21	
	66	(Technically, 5 votes short)

3. *Lose New York and California, but Carry 3 or 4 Other Large States*

Pennsylvania	27
Illinois	26
Ohio	25
Michigan	21

3 of the above 4 = 71 plus electoral votes

STRATEGIC CONCLUSIONS

The conclusions that can be drawn from these . . . analyses are quite simple:

1. The Southern states provide us a base of support that cannot be taken for granted or jeopardized.
2. The Republicans cannot win if they write off the South. Consequently, we

have to assume that they will challenge us in the South. I believe that they will challenge us in those larger Southern and Border states that they view as contestable—Texas, Florida, Maryland, and Missouri.

3. I believe that we can win each of those four states that are likely to be contested.

4. A Southern or Western running mate might be selected by the Republican nominee to assist them in their challenge to us in the South.

5. Based on the analysis of Democratic potential in each state, we should not publicly concede a single state to the Republicans. This should be our public posture which will result in their having to worry and spend time and resources defending states that are likely to vote Republican.

6. If Ford is the nominee, you will have the same advantage over him that you had over many of your primary opponents—full time to devote to the campaign. This should result in our being able to spend some time campaigning in states that they will either write off or ignore because of size or lack of comparable time to spend campaigning.

7. We obviously can and must do well in the large industrial states.

8. Although the Southern states provide us with a rich base of support, it would be a mistake to appear to be overly dependent on the South for victory in November. It would be harmful nationally if we were perceived as having a "Southern strategy." The strength of the South in the Electoral College is quite obvious to the media. But to the extent that regional bias exists in this country—and it does—there would be a negative reaction to a candidacy that was perceived as being a captive of the Southern states and/or people. Sad but true. Southern regional pride can be used to great advantage without unnecessarily alienating potential anti-Southern voters.

THE GENERAL ELECTION CAMPAIGN

Preface. For the first time in recent history of American politics, the Democratic Party will have the opportunity to conduct a well coordinated and integrated national campaign that mutually benefits the national ticket, Congressional and gubernatorial candidates, legislative and local candidates. The reason is that the party's nominees will receive Federal monies and will not be competing with state and local candidates for the same dollars. To the contrary, the Presidential and Vice-Presidential nominees will be able to help them raise monies for use in their own campaign. This lack of competition for the same dollars coupled with the ability of the nominees to raise monies for Democratic candidates should give the national ticket and party the leverage it will need to insure an integrated national and state effort. . . .

It is my strong recommendation that Bob Lipshutz continue as Treasurer of the campaign. The Budget Director will report to him and Bob will maintain control over all expenditures, accounting and Federal reports. I do not know any person in the campaign who has made a greater contribution to our success than Bob Lipshutz. I do not know where we would be today without him.

II. Personal and Confidential

To: Jimmy Carter
       Walter Mondale
From: Hamilton Jordan

You will find in the following pages an analysis of our present political posture and some strategic premises for the general election campaign.

Also, a formula which attempts to provide us a framework for the allocation of our major resources.

We will begin soon to make commitments in terms of the schedule, media and organization. Your comments, criticisms and suggestions are needed.

INTRODUCTION

As we look ahead to the general election, it is important that we establish a framework and mechanism for the allocation of our resources.

We had three long years to prepare and execute a strategy for winning the Democratic nomination. Our public campaign lasted two years. Our finances were limited only by our own ability to raise funds. We spent two hundred and fifty days on the road in 1975 and another one hundred and twenty-five in 1976. Most of this time was well spent—some was wasted. But, there was always enough time to make adjustments.

Yet, in the general election we are dealing with limited and finite resources.

We will have—at most—forty-five (45) campaign days between Labor Day and Election Day.

We will have $21.8 million to spend.

When that time is gone and that money is spent, there will be no more.

Consequently, it is important that we develop a realistic and precise framework for allocating these finite resources that takes into account the major political considerations and our own strategy while providing us with an appropriate amount of flexibility.

STRATEGIC PREMISES FOR THE GENERAL ELECTION

Before presenting the formula for the allocation of resources, it is necessary first to understand the strategic premises on which this formula was constructed.

These premises are basic to our total strategy. To the extent that there is a strong objection to the premises stated here, it should be presented and resolved so that the formula can be adjusted.

They are:

1. *Our clear and single goal must be to simply win 270 electoral votes.* We cannot afford initially to become so enamoured with our own survey results and the prospects of a landslide that we lose sight of the 270 electoral votes we will need. To expand our limited resources trying to win 400 electoral votes, we could very easily fall short of the 270 we need to win the election.

2. *We should spend a small amount of time early in the campaign challenging Ford in states that are traditionally Republican states in a Presidential election.* Ford lacks a base of support—there is not a region of the country nor a political grouping of states that he can count on in November. Consequently, he lacks the mathematical base on which to build a majority of the electoral votes. Without a base, he lacks a strategy. By making a trip early in the campaign into several traditionally Republican states, I believe that we can effectively put Ford on the defensive, making him spend time and money in states he should carry. Perhaps more importantly, we can prevent the Republicans from ever developing a clear strategy for winning.

3. *The Southern and Border states are our base of support that cannot be taken for granted or jeopardized—the only way we can lose in November is to have this base fragmented.* We need to spend early time campaigning in the South and several key Border states. If our solid lead here holds, we can probably cut back on time here in October and simply "show the flag" regularly.

4. *We must resist tremendous pressures and always retain a high degree of flexibility in the allocation of our resources and the objectives of our strategy.* We must never forget that in 1968 in six weeks Hubert Humphrey closed twenty points on Richard Nixon and almost won the Presidency. We will probably not know until mid-October if the election is going to be close or if there is potential for a big victory. Either way, flexibility is critical and necessary and will be maintained at all costs.

5. *Jimmy Carter and Walter Mondale will play to their strengths.* As he heads the ticket, it obviously will be necessary for Carter to campaign in all areas of the country. However, Carter obviously will have to play the lead role in protecting our base in the South. Mondale should work areas of the country where he is stronger than Carter and work with certain groups and elements of the party that he has a special relationship with—liberals, labor unions, members of Congress, etc.

6. *If by mid-October we have a commanding lead and have the flexibility previously advocated, the goals and objectives of the campaign can*

be appropriately broadened. If our projected lead in the Electoral College is commanding and our survey results solid in mid-October, we can begin to spend an appropriate amount of time and resources trying to win the mandate we will need to bring real and meaningful change to this country.

EXPLANATION OF FORMULA FACTORS

The formula which is described and presented in the following pages takes into account three basic factors:

- •the *size* of a state
- •the *Democratic potential* of a state
- •the *need* we have to mount an effective campaign

Size. As the objective is to win a majority of the votes in the Electoral College (270), it follows that the major consideration in allocating the campaign's resources is the relative size of each state. I have made the judgment in assigning numerical values to each factor that the size of the state is as important as the *Democratic potential* and *need* combined. Consequently, fifty percent (50%) of the points allocated in the formula are based on the relative size of each state. Using the total number of votes in the Electoral College as a mathematical base (538), I have assigned a single point in value (1) for each electoral vote a state has.

Democratic Potential. We must, of necessity, focus our resources first on those states that have the greatest Democratic potential and are most likely to vote Democratic if worked effectively. For that reason, twenty-five percent (25%) of the points assigned (280) are allocated based on the relative Democratic potential of each state.

Need. "Need" is best described as our judgment as to the relative amount of time, resources and energies that we should invest in a particular state. This is the most arbitrary of the factors considered and a rationalization is presented later in this section for the numerical values assigned each state. Factors considered in establishing the relative need are:

- •survey information from Pat Caddell
- •strategic premises of the general election
- •whether or not we campaigned in the state in the primaries
- •how well or poorly we did in the state in the primaries
- •other information which is presented

Approximately twenty-five percent (25%) of the points assigned (265) are assigned based on the relative need of the states.

Summary.

$$\frac{\text{Size} + \text{Democratic Potential} + \text{Need} = \text{Total Points}}{50\% + \qquad 25\% \qquad + 25\% = \quad 100\%}$$

OR

$$\frac{538 \text{ pts.} + 280 \text{ pts.} + 265 \text{ pts} = 1083 \text{ pts.}}{}$$

[Jordan then presented thirty-one pages of separate, detailed formulas allotting points to each state for size, Democratic potential, and need. He measured Democratic potential by assigning what he called "indicator" points for the number of elected Democratic members of Congress and state officials. He reduced the "need" to campaign in each state to numerical terms by dividing the states into four groups: states in Group A each received 9.8 points; Group B, 6.2; Group C, 3.5; Group D, 2.0. Then he put all of these totals into his original formula to determine the "percent of effort" the Carter campaign needed to devote to each state.

[Next, Jordan arbitrarily assigned a numerical value to indicate what one day of campaigning by each of the Carter-Mondale celebrities would be worth. Jimmy Carter topped the list with a 7. Walter Mondale was worth a 5, Rosalynn Carter 4, Joan Mondale 3, Jack and Judy Carter 2, Chip and Caron Carter 2, Jeff and Annette Carter 2.

[Jordan multiplied these figures by the number of days each person would be out on the campaign, and wound up with what he called "total scheduling points." And he multiplied the total scheduling points for the campaign by the "percent of effort" that had already been calculated for each state, and wound up with a precise number of points for each state.

[It was then up to the schedulers to determine just how to apportion the time of the various campaigners to equal the total points allotted to each state.]

SUMMARY

As a result of this exercise, we can determine how much time should be spent in a particular state. For example, the state of Oregon earned 16 scheduling points. This might result in the following trips to that state:

1. Jimmy Carter spends ½ day there	3.5 points
2. Walter Mondale spends 1 day there	5.0 points
3. Joan Mondale spends ½ day there	1.5 points
4. Rosalynn Carter spends 1 day there	4.0 points
5. Jack and Judy spend 1 day there	2.0 points
	16.0 points

These five trips—spread over an eight-week period—would give the ticket good exposure in the state of Oregon.

The 1976 Presidential Debates: A Republican Perspective

BY RICHARD B. CHENEY

The concept of debates between President Ford and Governor Carter was an integral part of the Ford general election campaign strategy in 1976. The decision to challenge Governor Carter to debate was based on the unique set of circumstances the Ford campaign faced in the summer of 1976 and on the experiences of the candidate and campaign staff in the contest for the Republican presidential nomination.

The Campaign for the Republican Nomination

At the beginning of 1976, President Ford began his campaign for reelection in an unusual situation for an incumbent. As a result of his having come to power under the Twenty-fifth Amendment, his name had never appeared on a ballot outside the Fifth Congressional District of Michigan. Since no national Ford organization was in place from a prior campaign, one had to be built, especially in key primary states.

Though the economy was improving, the nation was still experiencing the residue of high unemployment and high inflation after having weathered the worst recession in decades. The economic situation, the legacy of Watergate, and the Nixon pardon had served to erode the President's standing with the public. His approval rating, as measured by Gallup, had fallen sharply from August of 1974 to below 40 percent in the spring of 1975. It rose above 50 percent briefly at the time of the Mayaguez incident in the summer of that year but remained well under 50 percent throughout the rest of 1975.

In November, one year before the election, former Governor Ronald Reagan had announced that he would be a candidate for the Republican nomination for president; as events would later demonstrate, he was a formidable opponent. A nationwide poll conducted by NBC News in early December had shown that Governor Reagan held a four percentage point lead over President Ford among Republicans. Ford's private polls were producing similar results.

Richard B. Cheney, "The 1976 Presidential Debates: A Republican Perspective," in Austin Ranney, ed., *The Past and Future of Presidential Debates* (Washington: American Enterprise Institute, 1979), pp. 107–130. Footnotes deleted. Copyright 1979 American Enterprise Institute.

Thus, as the election year opened, we on Ford's campaign staff felt we had no choice but to campaign aggressively in each of the major early primaries. We simply did not have the option of staying in the White House through the primary season as previous presidents had done when seeking reelection. The necessity of campaigning actively in the spring had a direct bearing on the later decision to issue the debate challenge in the fall contest with Governor Carter.

The Primaries

In spite of the narrow victory in New Hampshire, the Ford campaign went on to win primaries by comfortable margins in Massachusetts, Florida, and Illinois. By the time of the North Carolina primary in late March, there was considerable speculation that Governor Reagan would be forced to drop out before long, and that the Republican contest would be wrapped up within a matter of weeks.

North Carolina, however, proved to be a major stumbling block for the Ford campaign. Governor Reagan's surprising victory there gave new life to his efforts and ensured that the second wave of primaries, beginning with Texas on May 1, would be hotly contested. After winning all 100 delegates in Texas, the governor went on to impressive wins in Alabama, Georgia, Indiana, and Nebraska in the next ten days. By the middle of May it was clear that the struggle for the Republican nomination would not be finally resolved until August at the Kansas City convention.

After the final primaries in California, New Jersey, and Ohio on June 8, the remainder of the summer was devoted to wooing small groups of delegates, either in Washington, D.C., or during visits to key convention states such as Missouri, Connecticut, and Mississippi. The bulk of our resources had to be devoted to the continuing contest for the nomination because of our inability to lay to rest the Reagan challenge.

One of the products of having to campaign from January through August was that the President came to be publicly perceived more as a candidate than as President. Although his active campaigning was instrumental in winning important primaries in New Hampshire, Florida, Michigan, and Ohio and in carrying important convention states such as Mississippi, the nationwide impact was negative. Instead of presidential travel to Peking and Moscow, we found it essential to arrange candidate appearances in Peoria and Miami. Instead of spending the summer as a secure incumbent watching the Democrats struggle, we found it necessary to do battle for the Republican nomination while Governor Carter sat in Plains planning his fall campaign.

In presenting this review, I do not want to imply any criticism of Governor Reagan or his campaign. While the GOP contest was obviously an important factor in setting the stage for the fall contest, the problems we encountered were due to the fact that we failed to win decisively early on. I believe it can be persuasively argued that, without a contest of some kind in our own party, the Ford campaign organization would have been in much worse shape than it was by Labor Day. We learned a great deal about our operations and capabilities as a result of having to surmount the governor's nearly successful drive for the nomination.

The Democrats

In late April and early May President Ford was still winning head-to-head trial heats with potential Democratic opponents in the polls. By early June, when it became obvious that Governor Carter would be the Democratic nominee, things changed rapidly. With the collapse of all Democratic opposition to Carter immediately after the final round of primaries, we suddenly found ourselves in the position of the underdog. By the time of the Democratic convention in July, polls by both Gallup and Harris showed Governor Carter with a lead exceeding thirty percentage points.

The governor looked like a winner. He had designed and carried out a masterful campaign. Beginning as relatively unknown, he had defeated all his competitors for the Democratic nomination by mid-June, some two months before there would be a definite answer to the question of who would run on the Republican ticket. By midsummer, neither Ford nor Reagan appeared to have any serious prospect of overtaking Carter by November.

Planning the Fall Campaign

Some planning for the general election contest as well as for the preconvention period had been undertaken by the Ford organization in late 1975, but focused efforts to design the fall campaign plan did not really begin until June, at the conclusion of the California and Ohio primaries. Planning was delayed by the need to devote time and energy to the hunt for Ford delegates, and we were hampered by the legal requirement that money raised for the primaries could not be spent for general election purposes and by our efforts to ensure that White House personnel were not misused for campaign purposes. When planning did begin in June and July, most of the work was done by a small group of campaign and White House officials working evenings and weekends.

The draft plan was presented to the President some two weeks before the Kansas City convention. Changes were made at his discretion over the next few weeks, but many decisions were postponed until the President met with his aides and advisors in Vail during the week immediately following the convention.

The Debate Option

The possibility of challenging Governor Carter to a series of debates was first raised in mid-June in a memo prepared by Foster Channock and Mike Duval of the White House staff. The memo urged consideration of the debate option as part of a "no campaign" campaign strategy. The basic idea was that continuing to pursue the aggressive style of traditional campaigning that had been necessary in the spring would guarantee our defeat in November. As part of a package of proposals prepared after discussions with our pollster, Bob Teeter of Market Opinion Research, debates were suggested as a means of deemphasizing traditional campaigning, maximizing the advantages of incumbency, and forcing Governor Carter to deal substantively with issues. Specifically, Channock and Duval recommended that Carter be challenged to a series of four debates on domestic affairs, the economy, national defense, and foreign policy. Although not all the recommendations in this memo were adopted, they were based on an underlying set of considerations that shaped our overall strategy.

The debate option was discussed with the President and became an integral part of the final draft of the campaign plan. The President gave instructions to keep the possibility of debates as secret as possible to preserve the element of surprise. He wanted to include the challenge to debate in his acceptance speech in Kansas City in August. To avoid any leaks, it was not mentioned in any draft of the speech. A few hours before the speech was delivered, the President himself inserted the challenge to Jimmy Carter to debate in the fall campaign.

The Ford Strategy

As serious planning efforts began in July, the outlook for the fall was fairly bleak. Our campaign strategy had to begin with a realistic appraisal of the situation. Even though the very large gap between the two candidates was expected to close somewhat once the Republican contest was resolved, we still were faced with a unique situation for an incumbent president.

No president had ever overcome the obstacles to reelection that we expected to face after the convention. President Truman's great victory over Dewey in 1948 was often suggested as a historical precedent for coming from behind. But on close analysis, the 1948 experience offered little solace. President Truman had been only eleven points behind Dewey in the polls in the summer of 1948. We expected to be some twenty points behind at the close of our convention, and the lateness of the convention meant we would have only seventy-three days in which to overtake our opponent.

Furthermore, several constraints could not be altered no matter which strategy we pursued, and they would make our task even more difficult.

1. We were the minority party. Among voters, the Democrats outnumbered Republicans more than two to one (43 percent to 21 percent). Truman's success in 1948 had been possible in part because he was building on the base of the majority party.
2. Under the new campaign laws and given the necessity of accepting federal funding, our campaign expenditures would be matched dollar for dollar by the Carter campaign. We would not be able to spend more than our opponent.
3. The GOP convention was late. The party would be divided after the struggle for the nomination, and we would have little time to devote to binding up the wounds.
4. Unlike previous incumbents, we could not campaign by wooing various voter blocs with promises of massive new government programs. Budget dollars were not available to fund extensive new spending programs, and broken promises of previous candidates had undermined the utility of such an approach. Most important, the President's philosophy and record of asking the public to make short-term sacrifices in return for long-term gains (energy proposals, legislative vetoes, and economic policies) ruled out such a strategy. Changing our philosophy in midstream would have been bad policy and would have led to widespread criticism.

Our goal had to be to win enough popular votes to carry enough states to obtain the required 270 electoral votes. To reach that objective, we would have to close a twenty-point gap in seventy-three days, while working from the base of a minority party and spending the same amount of money as our opponent.

The Carter Lead

Although the Carter lead appeared formidable in July, we were convinced that it would decrease significantly as we drew closer to Labor Day. We believed that much of his support was very soft and based primarily on his media image as a "winner." Governor Carter had risen from relative obscurity almost overnight and was suddenly a major national figure by virtue of his victories in the primaries. After the Democratic convention, we believed his popularity would decline without more "victories" to sustain it. His image as a winner would fade as his primary successes receded into the past and other aspects of his candidacy came to the fore.

A careful analysis of the results of the Democratic primaries indicated that he had not been as formidable as his presence at the top of the Democratic ticket implied. Governor Carter had never received more that 54 percent of the vote in a contested primary. He had never won in a two-man, head-to-head race. Finally, he had been defeated in eight out of the last eleven contested primaries.

Thus, we anticipated that his rapid rise in the polls might well be followed by a fairly rapid decline, and that he would prove more vulnerable than most people expected in a head-to-head contest with President Ford. We believed that the governor's support was susceptible of erosion once the public came to know him better. The outlook was therefore not totally pessimistic. We believed that with the right strategy and a few breaks we could win on November 2.

Campaign Style

In spite of our optimism that the Carter lead would diminish substantially by Labor Day, we obviously still faced a difficult problem. We were so far behind that we had to conduct a very aggressive come-from-behind campaign to have any prospect of winning. Ford was not in a position to spend September and October in the White House ignoring his opponent, as had some of his predecessors. At the same time, we had ample evidence that aggressive campaigning in the past had harmed the President's standing in the eyes of the public. Survey research undertaken in the summer of 1976 had picked up disturbing, but not surprising, evidence that a portion of the public increasingly perceived the President as too political. He was criticized by some for spending too much time on politics and not enough time on the people's business. We also believed that declines in the President's popularity during his two years in office had coincided with, and to some extent been caused by, periods of active partisan campaigning.

The Ford presidency had enjoyed a very brief honeymoon during August of 1974, which came to an end with the issuance of the Nixon pardon in early September. During October and early November, after having been in office only two months, the President had undertaken a heavy schedule of campaign appearances on behalf of Republican House and Senate candidates in the 1974 elections. In July of 1975, after having been in office less than a year, it was announced formally that the President would be a candidate for reelection. The announcement was made early because of the need to build an organization and start fund-raising efforts and because we wanted to comply fully with the requirements of the campaign spending and reporting laws.

During the fall of that same year, we undertook a heavy schedule of appearances at state GOP fund-raisers. The party was in considerable disarray after the 1974 elections. Many state organizations had extensive debts, and the President's activities were instrumental in paying off those debts and raising party funds for the upcoming 1976 elections. We also knew that there would be little time to devote to such activities during the presidential election campaign itself. Finally, as mentioned above, extensive media coverage of the President's active campaign for the nomination had a negative effect nationwide and lessened the value of his number one asset—incumbency.

The problem was starkly portrayed on the cover of a weekly newsmagazine prior to the Republican convention. The cover gave equal billing to pictures of three candidates for the presidency—Governor Carter, Governor Reagan, and President Ford. In part because of extensive campaigning, the President had come to be perceived by many voters as just another candidate, rather than as President.

These conclusions played an important role in shaping the strategy for the fall campaign. One objective was to reemphasize the fact that our candidate was the incumbent. At the same time, we had to devise an approach that was aggressive without projecting the image of the President as just another candidate. Part of the answer was provided by the debates.

Public Perceptions of the Candidates

As part of the planning process, the campaign staff spent a good deal of time analyzing the strengths and weaknesses of Governor Carter as perceived by the public. In citing his positive personal traits, those interviewed described the governor as a winner, a man with strong spiritual and moral values, an honest man of character, truly concerned about government efficiency, and dedicated to making government work better. On the negative side, he was perceived as somewhat arrogant and lacking in humility; a man who tried to be all things to all men; a man about whom very little was known; a man who was fuzzy on the issues and lacked the experience to be president.

With respect to his philosophy or general position on the issues, Governor Carter had indeed succeeded in being all things to all men. When asked to locate themselves and Governor Carter on a seven-point scale ranging from "extremely liberal" to "extremely conservative," respondents tended to place the governor very close to the point they chose for themselves. Thus, Republicans tended to identify the governor as somewhat conservative, ticket-splitters moved him closer to the middle of the spectrum, and Democrats perceived him as slightly liberal. They all saw significant similarities between their own views and their perceptions of Governor Carter's views.

A separate analysis, done by Market Opinion Research, reinforced this belief that a large number of voters perceived Jimmy Carter's views much as they perceived their own. Bob Teeter and his staff developed a perceptual map that graphically demonstrated the problem. The methodology permitted voters to locate on two dimensions their own philosophical attitudes on a variety of domestic and foreign policy issues, and also to indicate on the same dimensions the voters' perception of the views of the candidates. The results indicated clearly that Governor Carter occupied a position somewhat unique among major national political figures in the summer of 1976. The voters perceived him as having views much closer to their own than had President Ford or any other national political leader.

The governor had successfully avoided getting pinned down on many issues during the primaries. To the extent that he had taken positions, we believed he had done so with a certain amount of regional selectivity, and they had not been fully communicated to those who could be expected to disagree with him. Furthermore, we believed that the public's perception of the governor's position was based in part on the fact that he was very new to the national scene.

By contrast, we believed that the President's positions on major issues were better known. After two years in office, over fifty vetoes of legislation, and numerous proposals on everything from abortion and busing to taxes, we felt that any negative impact from the President's taking a firm position had already occurred, that the public had already discounted any significant differences they felt on specific concerns. This is not to say that all potential voters had a solid understanding of the administration's policies in every area. As in all campaigns, a large portion of the electorate either did not know what the President had done on a particular problem or incorrectly identified his position. But we did believe that when an issue had direct relevance for a particular group, the President's views were much better known in most cases than were Governor Carter's views. We did not expect any significant decline in our standing in the polls as a result of restating positions already articulated in the past.

We did not overestimate the role issues had played or would play in the campaign. With few exceptions, they had been relatively insignificant during the primaries, and the Ford campaign plan clearly indicated that issues, in and of themselves, were unlikely to have a significant impact on the outcome of the election. But they were felt to be significant in terms of how the candidates dealt with them—that is, they were useful tools for displaying those personal characteristics, or lack thereof, that might qualify a man to be president. At the same time, it was hoped that trying to force a greater focus on issues during the fall would benefit the Ford candidacy. As long as the public perceived Governor Carter as holding views very close to their own, our prospects of winning in November were slim indeed. If, on the other hand, we were successful in forcing greater specificity in his positions and communicating those views to those who disagreed with them, we would have a chance to peel off key voter groups in important states. One of our key objectives came to be changing the public's perceptions of Jimmy Carter.

These considerations supported the decision to challenge the governor to a series of debates. Debates offered the opportunity to encourage greater specificity on issues and provided maximum potential impact through instantaneous communication to millions of voters via television. If Governor Carter failed to be more specific, he would run the risk of increasing the number of people who perceived him as fuzzy and indecisive. We did not believe his "trust me" approach would be very effective in a debate setting when he was asked for specific views on major national issues.

Television

Throughout our deliberations, we were well aware of the enormous importance of television. Given the size of Governor Carter's lead, we would have to change the voting intentions of literally millions of Americans by election day. No matter how extensively the President campaigned, it would have been impossible to reach enough people in person to achieve the desired result. Therefore, we operated on the assumption that personal appearances were useful only to the extent that they received extensive favorable coverage on the evening news. Whatever strategy we adopted had to take into account the reality that any activity which did not receive extensive television coverage was likely to be wasted activity.

Although television was the only vehicle which offered the potential of reaching sufficient voters to turn the situation around by election day, in past elections the networks had not devoted much time to communicating the candidates' positions on the issues. The final draft of the campaign plan cited the work of Patterson and McClure on the 1972 campaign. Their content analysis of the network evening news for the seven-week period from September 18 through November 6, 1972, demonstrated that all three networks had devoted considerably more attention to campaign activities such as rallies and motorcades than they had to issues:

	ABC	CBS	NBC
Total coverage for all issues (minutes)	35	46	26
Average coverage for each issue (seconds)	80	105	60
Total for campaign activities (minutes)	141	122	130

Patterson and McClure also indicated that there was much more issue content in 1972 in the paid political advertising of the two candidates than on the evening news. This does not necessarily mean the networks had chosen to ignore issues. It could simply be a reflection of the way the 1972 campaign was conducted by the candidates. Regardless of the reason, the findings had significance for our planning efforts.

Although we had to rely on television to convey our message, we also recognized that little would be communicated about the policy views of the two candidates if we pursued a conventional campaign strategy. If we gave them rallies and motorcades, that would be the message conveyed to the public. The traditional campaign hoopla was not ignored—we undertook our fair share of riverboat rides, train trips, and balloon drops. But our objective of encouraging a greater focus on Governor Carter's policy views could not be achieved with a conventional approach.

A series of televised debates offered an opportunity to reach the maximum number of voters in a setting designed to focus attention on substantive issues. We did not expect to change the nature of the campaign in seventy-three days, nor did we believe that issues would replace the importance of the personal attributes and characteristics of the candidates. Indeed, we wanted to emphasize the President's personal strengths as well as what research told us were Carter's weaknesses. We also believed that by showing our opponent and the President responding to specific questions about their views on substantive issues, the debates would play to our strengths and to Governor Carter's weaknesses and might convince a number of voters that they disagreed with him in certain areas, something they did not believe in July.

The Arguments for and against Debates

As we developed the campaign strategy, we were very much aware that arguments could be mustered against the idea of debates. The traditional wisdom was that an incumbent president did not debate his challenger, but then this was not a traditional incumbency. The concern that debates would place President Ford and the governor on an equal plane in the eyes of the public was of little consequence. Frankly, we would have been delighted in July to have been perceived on "equal" terms.

While it was true that televised debates would give Governor Carter extensive exposure to the public, just as it would President Ford, we believed this would serve to decrease his lead in the campaign. On the basis of our analysis of his strength in the polls, the softness of his support, and his ability to seem all things to all people, we wanted the governor to have such exposure; it was thought necessary if we were to win.

We also considered the experience of Kennedy and Nixon in the 1960 debates. To the extent that physical and stylistic factors were important in public perceptions of who would "win" or "lose" the debates, we believed our candidate would come off very well. The President's physical size and presence presented none of the negatively perceived personal characteristics which had supposedly caused Nixon to lose the first debate to Kennedy in 1960.

Substantively, the President was well equipped to enter the debates. From his service on the Hill and his two years as President he possessed a wealth of information about the functions of government. He had spent his entire professional career wrestling with the kinds of issues that were bound to come up in the course of the debates. In the past he had done very well in similar formats. In January of that year, the President had given the annual briefing on the federal budget, thus becoming the first President in nearly thirty years to do so. A format which let him respond to questions had always been more effective for him than a formal set speech.

In addition to the arguments cited above for deciding to debate, there were the President's own strong feelings on the subject. During his congressional career, he had frequently participated in debates in his reelection campaigns. The President had a strong personal desire to take on his opponent, and the whole concept of debates appealed to his competitive instincts.

The Strategy

By the time of the Kansas City convention, the broad outlines of the general election strategy had been determined, although much of the detail was left to be worked out at Vail after the convention.

The central element in the strategy was to hold active travel to a minimum until late in the campaign. When we did travel, the events would be designed to achieve maximum television impact. The centerpiece of the last ten days of campaigning, eventually developed by Bob Teeter and John Deardorff, were the half-hour specials broadcast on statewide television hook-ups in the large target states. We produced the shows ourselves, using video tape footage of the President and members of the first family campaigning in the state, and discussions between the President and Joe Garagiola of the issue in the campaign—the "Joe and Jerry Show."

When the President was in Washington we conducted what came to be known as the Rose Garden campaign. We expected our opponent to travel extensively throughout the fall, and we were confident that the news media, particularly the television networks, would cover all those events. Since the networks' measure of fairness consisted of giving both candidates equal time, whatever the President did during the day at the White House would also receive coverage on the evening news. We could therefore convey our message to the electorate, emphasizing that the President was the incumbent, and avoiding the pitfalls of too much campaign travel too soon.

To change the public's perception of Governor Carter, we relied heavily on our advertising program designed and produced by Doug Bailey and John Deardorff. The advertising campaign itself made a major contribution to our success in closing the gap during the fall and deserves far more extensive treatment than I can give it here.

The debates would give Governor Carter's policy views the exposure they had previously lacked and would perhaps help persuade several million Americans that he disagreed with them on several issues. More important, the debate challenge satisfied the need to mount an aggressive, come-from-behind campaign and provided a justification for staying off the campaign trail as much as possible. Our unconventional circumstances called for an unconventional response. We had few alternatives.

As we departed Kansas City for Vail, we felt we had achieved everything that could reasonably be expected, given the circumstances. The Reagan challenge was finally ended. We had maintained an effective, if sometimes tenuous, control of the convention, and the intraparty wounds created by the long preconvention struggle appeared to be healing rapidly. The President's acceptance address to the convention and the nation had clearly been one of the finest of his career. The debate challenge had achieved its desired result. In the opening round of the fall campaign, we had captured the initiative and gone on the offensive. The President had come out swinging, and the Carter campaign was forced to react to us in spite of their substantial lead and status as the challenger. This in turn provided time for a much needed rest and for completing detailed arrangements for the general election contest.

Preparation for the Debates

The negotiations establishing the ground rules for the debates were somewhat protracted, but once the challenge had been issued and accepted, there was never any question about going ahead with them. Our negotiating posture was based on the assumption that the more exposure provided the candidates, the better. We asked for lengthy sessions on specified subjects with follow-up questions from the panel. In return for agreement on these items, we agreed to specify no subject matter for the final debate and to take up foreign and defense matters in the second debate rather than in the first as we had originally suggested.

During the weeks preceding the first debate in Philadelphia on September 23, the President and part of the staff devoted considerable time to preparing for the event. We obtained film of the Kennedy-Nixon debates of 1960 and reviewed them with a special focus on the supposedly decisive first debate. We also viewed video tapes of appearances by Governor Carter in debates and on talk shows during the primaries.

Extensive briefing books were prepared, including material on the policy positions of both the administration and the governor. Some of the most useful information concerned Mr. Carter's record as governor of Georgia. Much of this material was used during the first debate and later included in our advertising. We also developed questions that we expected would be asked and reviewed the published works of the panelists to ascertain their areas of expertise and interest.

We conducted several dry runs, with the President taking questions from staff people on the subjects we expected to come up in the first debate. Our preparations were as complete and comprehensive as we could make them. We did not spend as much time preparing for the second and third debates, because theere was less time to do so and we did not feel it was necessary to repeat all the activities undertaken before the first debate.

Measuring the Impact of the Debates

The Ford campaign used two research methods to measure the impact of the debates. During the actual course of the debates, we collected data from an instant response analysis of a panel of registered voters. The panels consisted of approximately fifty voters from the Spokane, Washington, area. Each of the respondents had declared themselves to be undecided when asked about their voting intention prior to viewing the debate, although some of them were classified as "leaning" toward Ford or Carter. Our assumption was that the debates would have little effect on voters firmly committed to one or the other of the candidates. The composition of the panels was designed to give us as much information as possible about the reactions of voters who had not yet made up their minds.

Each member of the panel was equipped with a dial mechanism labeled from zero to one hundred. Zero indicated that the respondent was feeling much closer to Governor Carter and one hundred indicated that they were feeling much closer to President Ford. A value of fifty was an indication that the panelist was not leaning toward either man. Members of the panel were instructed before the debate to set their dial at a value that described their attitude as being closer to Ford, closer to Carter, or in the middle. The panelists were to move the dial toward zero in response to positive feelings about Governor Carter and toward one hundred for positive feelings about President Ford.

The dial mechanisms were tied in with a computer, and throughout the broadcast the responses were summed continuously and a means calculated for the entire group as well as for two subgroups: those who at the beginning of the broadcast had been identified as leaning toward the governor or toward the President. Finally, these continuous average scores were superimposed on a video tape of the debate for later viewing and analysis. This system provided useful information on the reaction of a group of uncommitted voters to the arguments and presentations of the two candidates. It was helpful in shaping our approach to later debates and enabled us to highlight those issues on which the President scored most heavily against the governor, and vice versa.

Our second research effort involved nationwide telephone surveys conducted as part of the ongoing research program for the campaign. These surveys were not limited to measuring reactions to the debates, although questions were included that produced data on the impact of the debates. Prior to the first debate, between September 10 and September 14, Market Opinion Research (MOR) conducted a nationwide telephone survey of a sample of 1,500 registered voters. Beginning on the evening of September 23, as the first debate ended, 758 of these individuals were reinterviewed. In both predebate and postdebate interviews, data were collected on the voters' perceptions of the issue positions of the candidates as well as on their personal attributes and abilities to deal with various problems, such as unemployment and inflation.

Immediately after the second debate, MOR conducted another nationwide telephone survey of approximately 500 registered voters. We did not do a predebate study in conjunction with the second debate. By the time of the third debate, we did not conduct any additional national surveys. Such a survey would have had no real value from the standpoint of making decisions about the conduct of the campaign during the few days remaining before the election, and all our resources were by then committed to tracking developments in the target states.

We of course followed the results of the postdebate polls conducted by the Associated Press and the Roper organization, but for our purposes they provided little useful information. Responses to the simple question of who won or lost a particular debate did not, in my opinion, shed much light on the impact of the debates on the voting intentions of those who had not yet made up their minds. Their greatest significance, perhaps, lay in the convenient tool they gave the press and public to "judge" the debates and draw some conclusions about them. We had to deal with the results of those surveys because they tended to shape press reaction and commentary after a debate. But they had little relevance for assessing the progress of the campaign especially when the two organizations produced conflicting conclusions about which candidate had "won," as occurred after the final debate.

The First Debate

The research undertaken in conjunction with the first debate indicated that we had made significant progress in several areas. The analysis of the instant responses of the Spokane panel showed the President had done very well overall, and the national pre- and postdebate surveys provided evidence that the public's information about the candidates' positions had increased and their perceptions of the personal attributes of the President had been strengthened.

According to the results of the panel study, the President had scored very well whenever he talked about taxes. On four separate occasions during the ninety-minute debate, he had raised the issue in some form, each time generating a very positive reaction on the part of the respondents. The President also scored very high when he talked about crime and when he criticized Carter's record during his term as governor of Georgia and his spending proposals. Governor Carter had been most successful on the subjects of the bureaucratic mess in Washington, the energy crisis, and the need for tax reform.

The results also indicated the importance of giving full and complete answers to each question. The instant response analysis clearly demonstrated that the President had the greatest impact on those leaning toward Carter when he took the time to explain his position on an issue and his reasons for holding that view. A fairly lengthy answer moved the "Carter leaners" a significant distance toward a pro-Ford response, but brief answers did not provide sufficient explanations to overcome their bias. At the same time, the scores for the subgroup composed of "Ford leaners" did not drop off even during a lengthy response. As a result, we altered our original belief that short, punchy answers were sometimes desirable and sought to emphasize lengthier answers in later debates.

The data generated in the pre- and postdebate telephone surveys provided solid support for the proposition that those interviewed had obtained considerable information on the issue positions of the candidates. The predebate interviews had asked about abortion, busing, welfare spending, national health insurance, the legalization of marijuana, and defense spending, but these issues were not included in the postdebate survey because they were not discussed during the first debate. On three issues, we obtained both pre- and postdebate measures of the amount of information the viewers possessed about the candidates' positions: amnesty for Vietnam-era draft resisters, the use of public funds to guarantee jobs, and the alternative of stimulating the development of jobs in the private sector. After the debate there was a significant shift from the predebate responses of "don't know" to "it depends" to identification of Ford's or Carter's stand on each issue.

On the question of amnesty, the number of voters correctly identifying President Ford's position (against) increased from 40 to 60 percent between the predebate and postdebate surveys, and the "don't know" category declined from 29 to 13 percent. In the predebate survey, 53 percent indicated Governor Carter was in favor of an amnesty program; after the debates, this had increased to 70 percent, and the "don't know" category declined from 33 to 16 percent.

On the question of using federal funds to guarantee jobs, there was similar movement. Those citing President Ford as being opposed to such guarantees rose from 35 to 58 percent; the "don't know" category declined from 43 to 22 percent. The number citing Governor Carter as being in favor of federal guarantees increased from 44 to 71 percent, and the "don't know" category declined from 45 to 22 percent.

Changes in the amount of information the public possessed about the candidates' position on the question of stimulating jobs in the private sector were not as pronounced but were still significant. Before the debate, 46 percent believed President Ford supported this proposition, 8 percent said he was against it, 43 percent said they did not know what he thought. After the debate, 63 percent said the President was for the concept, 16 percent against, and 21 percent said they did not know. Those citing Governor Carter as being in favor of stimulating jobs in the private sector increased from 39 to 45 percent, those saying he opposed the idea increased from 12 to 27 percent, and the "don't knows" declined from 46 to 28 percent.

The postdebate survey also indicated we had improved the respondents' perceptions of President Ford's leadership qualities and his ability to deal with specific problems. During the interviews, registered voters had been asked to identify which of the candidates they most trusted to make the right decision, which was most effective in dealing with tough problems, and which demonstrated the most concern for the average citizen. On the question of trust, President Ford had the edge before the debate (45 percent to 36 percent for Carter). After the debate, the President had increased his lead somewhat to 48 percent with only 35 percent citing Governor Carter as being more trustworthy. Before the debate, both candidates had been viewed as being equally effective in dealing with tough problems—39 percent for each. After the debate, President Ford had a slight advantage: 44 percent viewed him as more effective, compared with 41 percent for Governor Carter. On concern for the average citizen, Governor Carter clearly had the edge (Carter 46 percent and Ford 28 percent) in the predebate survey and maintained it in the postdebate survey (48 to 31 percent).

The voters were also asked to indicate their perception of the relative capabilities of the two candidates to deal with problems such as inflation, unemployment, holding down taxes, reducing crime, running the federal government, handling foreign affairs, and maintaining a strong national defense. On all seven items, perceptions of President Ford improved between the predebate and postdebate surveys from two to nine percentage points. For Governor Carter, the maximum gain had been two percentage points and in one instance he suffered a decline of six points.

On five of the seven issues, President Ford had the advantage going into the debate. Governor Carter had a clear advantage on the issue of reducing unemployment, and there was no significant difference on the seventh issue, combating crime. The debates did not reverse any of these advantages, but the number of voters citing President Ford as being more capable of handling these problems increased, and the percentage taking a "don't know" or middle ground position had declined from two to five percentage points on each item.

Obviously, some caution is in order in interpreting these results. A definitive judgment about the impact of the debates would require a far more rigorous analysis than is possible here or can be supported by the data we collected during the 1976 campaign. Our predebate and postdebate surveys did not permit us to separate out the influence of other factors, and many other developments over the ten-day period separating the surveys could have accounted for some of the changes observed. For example, even though foreign policy and defense were not discussed during the debates, we observed changes in the voters' perceptions of the candidates' ability to handle these issues. The administration's diplomatic efforts in southern Africa could have had an impact, or changes in the President's perceived ability to deal with domestic issues could have rubbed off on public perceptions of his ability to function in the area of foreign policy. In addition, Governor Carter had been actively campaigning around the country, and President Ford had appeared repeatedly in the Rose Garden to comment on issues and developments in the campaign.

Our research effort was not designed to generate a rigorous and definitive judgment of the relative impact of the debates on the public. The intent was to measure progress toward our goal of winning on November 2 and to gather information that would be useful in running the campaign and implementing the campaign strategy. Data focusing on the debates were useful in highlighting which aspects to emphasize in the future and in making relatively minor adjustments in our approach. But at that point, late September, the strategy was set and could not be changed significantly. The only data of any relevance were those that might affect how we implemented that strategy.

On the basis of the information available, we judged the first debate a success. We believed the President had scored well on a number of key points, that we had enhanced the voters' understanding of the candidates' issue positions, strengthened the President's image as a leader, and gained ground on the question of his ability to deal with difficult problems. It was clear we had reached a large portion of the electorate. According to our surveys, some 89 percent of all registered voters had seen or heard the first debate.

The Second Debate

A good deal has been written about the impact or lack of impact of the second Ford-Carter debate on the outcome of the 1976 election. Most attention has focused on the President's misstatement concerning the degree of Soviet influence in Eastern Europe. My own view is that it was not as decisive as some have suggested.

There is no question that the second debate was less successful from our standpoint than the first had been. In my opinion, however, its impact was more significant on the press than on the public at large. This in turn had an impact on the public after the fact and became a problem which had to be dealt with. But I do not believe the Eastern European statement determined the outcome of the election.

I viewed the second debate on a television set in the President's holding room backstage at the theater in San Francisco. My initial reaction, before seeing any results from our research, was that the President had done well on substance. I was aware that his response to the question on the Soviet role in Eastern Europe had not been accurate, but I also knew what he meant and hoped that the public would also. I felt Governor Carter had improved his style and the way he handled himself since the first debate. But I also believed that substantively he had made a weak showing. Admittedly, I was not then, and may not be now, totally objective about the relative ability of the two men to conduct U.S. foreign policy.

My view at the time was based on a feeling that the President had been very effective in discussing U.S.-Soviet relations, SALT, the defense budget, China, and our arms policy in the Middle East. Governor Carter, on the other hand, had been vague when asked which elements of U.S. foreign policy he disagreed with. I did not believe his comments had demonstrated any deep understanding of the problems the United States faced in the world. When he had scored rhetorically, I felt his comments had focused on the form rather than the substance of national security concerns.

The seriousness of the problem was brought home by the press corps shortly after the second debate ended. As we had done after the first debate, Brent Scowcroft, the President's national security advisor, Stu Spencer of the campaign committee, and I met with the press to respond to their questions. We knew we had a problem when the first question put to us was, "Are there Soviet troops in Poland?"

As mentioned previously, the research efforts for the second debate were less extensive than for the first. We did not do a predebate survey, but we conducted an instant response analysis in Spokane and a nation-wide telephone survey of some 500 registered voters that began immediately after the debate on the West Coast and continued through the next evening.

The Spokane panel analysis, when compared with the results for the first debate, showed generally lower (that is, more pro-Carter) scores for the second debate. Part of this may have been due to the predebate inclinations of the respondents. They had set their dials at a value reflecting how close they felt to either of the candidates before the debate began, and the average score was some five points below that for the first debate.

Nonetheless, it was clear that the governor had scored better than in the first debate. The President had scored well at the outset on the question of Communist involvement in the Italian government and again toward the close in discussing the Mayaguez incident and the Arab boycott. In the central portion of the debate, the President's remarks on negotiations with the Soviets, his opposition to selling arms to the Chinese, and his comments about Korea had generated positive responses. Governor Carter, however, had generated more positive responses in his criticisms of secret diplomacy and arms sales to Iran, in his call for fireside chats to discuss foreign policy, and on his comments about nuclear proliferation, the Arab boycott, and the Panama Canal.

The panel study showed virtually no immediate impact with respect to the President's comments on Eastern Europe. Average scores during the debate swung from a low of 29 (pro-Carter) to a high of 64 (pro-Ford). During the exchange on Eastern Europe between Max Frankel and the President, the average score held fairly stable between 44 and 48. It was clear the comments failed to generate any positive response, but neither was there any immediate negative reaction.

The nationwide postdebate survey also indicated a delayed reaction to this portion of the debates. At the time, we had immediate access only to the raw data collected in the interviews. On October 6, the night of the debate, 101 interviews were conducted on the West Coast. Because of the lateness of the hour in the East, however, interviewing there took place the following day between 9:00 A.M. and midnight (EST), when 397 respondents were questioned. Care had to be exercised in evaluating the data over time, because we did not have matched national samples. But there were substantial shifts in voter perceptions between Wednesday night and Thursday night, even allowing for the built-in bias of having all of the interviews on the first night conducted in the West.

The first wave of interviews showed that President Ford was perceived as having done the better job in the debate by a margin of nine percentage points. The interviews taken the next night showed a drastic reversal, and Governor Carter had taken a substantial lead on this item. Throughout the twenty-four-hour period there was a decline in pro-Ford responses and a corresponding increase in pro-Carter responses. Morrison's paper, mentioned above, corrects for the built-in bias of using only results taken from subgroups of the total sample and validates the basic conclusion of serious erosion over time.

Respondents were also asked to specify what they felt each candidate had done well and not done well during the debates. On Wednesday evening, immediately after the debate, not a single respondent mentioned President Ford's comments on Eastern Europe. Yet by the next evening, 20 percent of the 121 interviews conducted after 5:00 P.M. mentioned this statement as one of the things he had not done well. In my mind, the data indicate that for much of the viewing public, the misstatement about the status of Eastern Europe was not a significant item until it received extensive comment and coverage in the press after the debate. Regardless of whether the public perceived it as a problem immediately or only after being told it was by the media, we still faced the task of clarifying the situation over the next several days.

The second debate obviously was not a plus for the Ford campaign. It created difficulties in several areas. The debate and the commentary afterward generated a negative reaction from the public. It cost us time as the issue ran its course and placed us on the defensive for the next several days as we clarified the President's position. Furthermore, the intense focus on Eastern Europe meant that little or no attention was paid to what I felt were substantive weaknesses in the Carter presentation—specifically his denial of ever having advocated a $15 billion cut in the defense budget, and his charge that the Ford administration had been responsible for overthrowing a democratically elected government in Chile. (The Chilean coup had occurred during the Nixon years.) Finally, I did not believe the governor had demonstrated any broad understanding of U.S. foreign policy. But all of this proved to be of little consequence as we tried to cope with reaction to the statement on Eastern Europe.

Another problem that affected our campaign during the same period was the publicity given the investigation by the Watergate special prosecutor into allegations that President Ford had misused campaign funds while he was a member of Congress. We were able to correct the difficulties stemming from the second debate by making clear the President's views on Eastern Europe and meeting with political leaders of the relevant ethnic groups. But there was absolutely nothing we could do to alleviate the impact of extensive coverage of the special prosecutor's activities. We were confident that we would ultimately obtain a clean bill of health when the prosecutor found there was no substance to the charges, but we had no way of knowing when that would be. All we could do was to deny the allegations, but such statements are hardly designed to win over voters in the midst of a come-from-behind presidential campaign especially in light of the track record for previous White House denials of allegations being investigated by the special prosecutor. For the Ford campaign, the latter problem was more serious and difficult to cope with than was the controversy over the second debate.

The Third Debate

As we prepared for the final debate October 22 in Williamsburg, circumstances improved considerably for the Ford campaign. The special prosecutor had closed his investigation, the flap over Eastern Europe faded, and the polls showed continued erosion in Governor Carter's lead. In the major target states, our polls showed us moving to within striking distance.

The third debate took on less significance for us than the first two. We had less time to prepare, and by then debates between the candidates had become somewhat routine, not only for the public but also for the campaigners. The debate itself turned out to be routine, generating no real surprises for either side. Our own research activities were shifted to tracking developments in the handful of big states which we felt would determine the outcome of the election.

Our primary focus during the last ten days of the campaign moved away from the debates and onto our advertising campaign and a heavy schedule of travel in the large electoral vote states. One of our more successful efforts was the television shows we produced ourselves in six of those states. They permitted us to reach the maximum number of people at a very low cost. To the extent we were able to close in on Carter in those final days, I believe these activities were more significant than the third and final debate.

Conclusion

A year after the election, with the benefit of hindsight, I still believe the decision to include the debate option in our 1976 campaign strategy was the right one. Given the circumstances we faced in the summer before the convention and the size of our opponent's lead, we had few alternatives. The debate challenge satisfied our need to mount an aggressive campaign without having to spend all our time on the road throughout the months of September and October.

Beyond the dynamics of the campaign itself, I believe it is very difficult to separate out the debates from other activities and determine exactly their impact on the election day result. It seems clear that the debate challenge gave the Ford campaign the initiative at the close of the Kansas City convention and that the first debate was a major plus for the President. The second debate clearly went to Carter in the public mind and threw the Ford organization off stride for several days. There appears to be a consensus that the third debate was somewhat anticlimatic and did not have much impact one way or the other.

I believe the evidence supports the contention that the debates did increase public awareness about the positions of the candidates on issues, although some of that would certainly have occurred without the debates. It would be a mistake, however, to conclude that this was their only impact. Although we did not collect much information on this point, it seems clear that the voters also judged the candidates in the debates on general perceptions of their personal qualities and competence.

While the debates did provide a means by which candidates could communicate directly with the voters via television, the role of the news media was substantial in interpreting the events after the fact. After both the first and second debates, we believed the press commentary served to magnify the actual outcome and to shape voter sentiment even though the voters had seen the event themselves.

In the end, we were unable to overcome the Carter lead, and from that perspective our strategy was unsuccessful. But in the light of our July deficit of more than 30 percent, we felt we had run a successful campaign. I believe the debates were an important part of that success and would recommend them again under similar circumstances.

The General Election

BY XANDRA KAYDEN

The increase in primaries put a severe strain on the ability of candidates to make rational decisions about how and where to put their resources. But as one participant* noted, "The primaries are manageable because they are finite and you can plan ahead. But in the general election, only the media is manageable. You have to put together 50 state organizations and a party. You don't want a lot of grass roots to deal with. There are organizational constraints to deal with, not financial ones. You can't continually control the grass roots."

---

*Editors' note: Xandra Kayden's report came out of a conference she organized of campaign finance people—the "participants" referred to here.

Xandra Kayden, *Report on Campaign Finance: Based on the Experience of the 1976 Presidential Campaigns* (Cambridge, Mass.: Institute of Politics, Harvard University, 1977), pp. 55–57. Reprinted by permission of the author, Xandra Kayden, Institute of Politics, Harvard University.

Neither Ford nor Carter actually ran in all of the 50 states. As one of the Ford people put it, "It was something like a few hard primaries. We didn't spend in Georgia. The only difference is that they all fall due the same day. Eight states determined both our political and our financial strategy." As in the primaries, the campaigns watched each other and sometimes made choices to do things because the opposition was doing it. The Ford media people kept an eye, for instance, on where and when the Carter people bought time on television.

Because both candidates accepted public financing in the general election they were freed from some of the financial constraints and activities in the primaries. But both candidates were constrained in their ability to plan for the general by the legal separation between the primaries and general: money raised in the former could not be used in the latter. And that extended to plans, objects bought for the primary (such as office furniture), a Ford film, etc.

The timing of the national conventions had an effect on how soon each campaign organization could begin planning for the general election. The Democratic convention in July enabled Carter to begin laying the groundwork for his campaign several weeks before Ford. There was time to work out a budget with the state people and to make them adhere to it. There was time for feedback both ways. They worked on a cash basis, using a draft system for the states which was cleared through Atlanta. Local organizations had to use drafts to buy anything. There was a fixed maximum. They could spend as they wanted, as long as they stayed within the agreed-upon guidelines. In all, Carter spent $3 million on his field organization, including what was considered a miniscule $300,000 for California and New York. To the Carter people, there was not enough money for visibility at the field level.

Ford did not run in many more states than did Carter. Priorities were established according to votes and the electoral college. Their strategy called for the carrying of at least 4 to 6 to 8 electorally important states: California, Illinois, Michigan, New Jersey, New York, Ohio, Pennsylvania, or Texas. Even one of these states, such as Ohio, combined with smaller states like Wisconsin, Louisiana, or Mississippi, would have been sufficient. Most of their money went into those states, especially after a national poll following the second debate. Because of the lateness of the Republican convention, the Ford campaign was unable to make television commercials until very late. Producing the paid media took time, and the campaign representatives felt they did not have enough exposure with them.

·C·

Press Coverage and Interpretation

Political Reporters in Presidential Politics

BY DAVID S. BRODER

It is nine o'clock in the morning—almost any morning of the Presidential campaign—and one of the great unpublicized rituals of American political journalism is about to begin.

The reporters, sleepy-eyed, file aboard the chartered 727 jet, many of them reaching for Bloody Marys to steady their nerves, then slump into their seats to grab some extra sleep while the candidate and his entourage are transported westward across the country to begin another day's stumping.

There is silence aboard the plane, except for the click-clack of a single typewriter in the staff section up front, where one of the candidate's speechwriters is putting the finishing touches on the advance text for tonight's speech. He is working under pressure, with his portable typewriter in his lap, because he knows that, when breakfasts and naps have been concluded, the reporters will be demanding the speech that should furnish the lead for their stories for the next morning's papers.

As the speechwriter finishes each page of the text, it is taken from his typewriter and handed to a staff secretary, who cuts a mimeograph stencil. A few more minutes, and one hundred copies have been run off on the airborne mimeograph machine, and shortly thereafter the whole speech has been distributed to the reporters.

Now their sloth disappears, as they quickly read through the offering.

Excerpted from David S. Broder, "Political Reporters in Presidential Politics," in Charles Peters and Timothy J. Adams, eds., *Inside the System: A Washington Monthly Reader* (New York: Praeger Publishers, 1970), pp. 20–37. Footnotes deleted. Copyright © 1970 by The Washington Monthly Company. Reprinted by permission of Holt, Rinehart and Winston and The Washington Monthly Company.

"Where's the lead?" someone asks. "Bottom of page six!" shouts a wire-service man, who took a course in speedreading. Everyone underlines the designated passage.

In a trice, the click-clack of the speechwriter's portable has been replaced by the amplified chatter of a hundred typewriters, as every reporter on the plane struggles to rephrase the speechwriter's prose in a fashion that will meet the demands of his own journal. By the time the plane lands, one hundred versions of The Speech will be in the hands of the Western Union man aboard. He will, if he is forehanded, have a dozen teletype operators at the airport, ready to punch tapes that will carry the stories into the newsrooms and wire-service headquarters, and thence to the presses, where millions of copies of the papers will be printed.

As often as I have seen and participated in this ritual of campaign journalism, the artificiality of the process never ceases to amaze me.

If the speech is, let us say, prepared for delivery at an evening rally in Los Angeles, the stories in the Eastern morning papers will be on the newsstands long before the event itself takes place. Indeed, the candidate may not—if he is as harassed as candidates often are—even have seen the speech on which the stories have been based; he may not deliver it when the time arrives; but he will, as his press secretary assures the reporters, stand behind every word of the prepared text.

There is an element of essential phoniness to the whole procedure: all parties agree to delude the reader into thinking he has read something the candidate has said and to conceal from him the reality that nothing has happened more significant than the passage of words from typewriter to mimeograph machine to typewriter to printing press. From beginning to end, the process has a life of its own, unrelated to reality, as the word moves from the speechwriter's typewriter to the newspaper headlines almost untouched by human minds.

Yet, ironically, it is when he is performing this almost imbecile function of digesting and regurgitating someone else's thoughts that the political writer or campaign reporter is in his least controversial role. Almost anything else he attempts—and he does attempt other roles—will land him in some sort of difficulty.

. . . .

The classic plea for the reporter to act as a neutral observer was given by Richard Nixon in his famous "last press conference" after his 1962 campaign for governor of California. Employing that delicacy of phrase for which he was noted, Nixon said he recognized the right of newspapers, "if they're against the candidate, to give him the shaft," but asked plaintively if they could not "put one lonely reporter on the campaign who will report what the candidate says now and then."

. . . .

Selectivity is the essence of all contemporary journalism. And selectivity implies criteria. Criteria depend on value judgments, which is a fancy term for opinions, preconceptions, and prejudices. There is no neutral journalism.

Now, it happens that a great deal of a political reporter's time is spent in doing what Nixon recommended: summarizing the candidate's own statements. The anecdote at the beginning of this article gave only a slightly exaggerated picture of a typical campaign day. Obviously, the stories filed from the campaign plane contain more than just excerpts from an undelivered speech. But it is a rare day in the campaign that the candidate's words do not comprise a substantial portion of the story.

Even here, however, we find that the values or prejudices of the reporters play a part. Reporters are—or at least fancy themselves—literary fellows. They pride themselves on their "feel for words." Thus, literary values, graceful phrases, balanced sentences have an importance to reporters that is hardly reflective of the value the general public attaches to eloquence. A candidate like John F. Kennedy, whose writers can turn a phrase, will enjoy an advantage over those like Humphrey and Goldwater, whose writers are pedestrian. There is very little justice in this, but a wise politician recognizes the premium on literary values and seeks to equip himself accordingly. Nixon, for example, reaped great publicity mileage from the series of radio speeches he gave in the 1968 campaign—not because very many people heard them on the radio, but because the quality of the writing that went into them—much of it by Raymond K. Price, Jr., former editorial page editor of the late, lamented *New York Herald Tribune*—was so extraordinarily high that papers like the *New York Times* and the *Washington Post* were often urged by the reporters covering Nixon to print full texts or extended excerpts of these addresses.

So, the reporter's first role is that of a summarizer of the candidate's positions. As we have seen, his own prejudices—or at least his literary tastes—enter into this role, even though, of all his functions, it is probably the least controversial.

In a sense, I have leaped ahead of my own story in talking of this role. Serious attention to the man's words implies that he is worth paying attention to. And who decides that? The political reporters do—in their second role, that of talent scouts.

At any given time in this country, there are several hundred persons who are potential candidates for nomination as President or Vice President. They are senators, representatives, governors, Administration officials, mayors, military men, scientists, businessmen, educators, astronauts, and other assorted celebrities. Who is it that winnows this field down to manageable size? The press—and particularly that small segment of the press called the national political reporters.

Russell Baker has given us the concept of The Great Mentioner, that mysterious Someone whose existence is implied when we read that so-and-so "is being mentioned for President or Vice President." He works in clandestine ways. The Great Mentioner mentioned George Romney as a possibility before Romney made his first race for governor of Michigan. The Great Mentioner has mentioned Mark Hatfield for Vice President every four years since Hatfield turned thirty, and he never seems discouraged by Hatfield's failure to win the job. On the other hand, The Great Mentioner never mentioned Edmund S. Muskie for anything until just a few days before he was actually nominated for Vice President. Just why The Great Mentioner mentions some names and not others is very puzzling. It has something to do with personality, but more, probably, to do with the black arts of public relations.

The function the political reporters perform in their role as talent scouts is one that most people would regard as a positive service. After all, the individual citizen can hardly be expected to discover for himself all the able people who feel a calling to public service. The reporter's job makes him a constant traveler in the political community; he is uniquely well positioned to detect the early intimations of greatness, to discover these statesmen in embryo and bring their rare qualities to the attention of a wider public.

But, alas, it is not quite that simple—or noncontroversial. In his function as a talent scout, the political reporter not only puts some men forward; he also rather ruthlessly bars the door to advancement for other men. Martin F. Nolan of the *Boston Globe* has compared the national political reporters to a band of traveling drama critics, covering the new political acts at their out-of-town openings in Sacramento or Lansing or Harrisburg. Their reports, like those in *Variety,* are frequently make-or-break. "No talent," they will say of one man, and his name is forgotten. "Promising," they'll say of another, and he is booked into the Gridiron Dinner or "Meet the Press." It's a formidable power, and one that the screening committee of reporters is thoroughly conscious of possessing.

It is important at this point to say something about the members of this screening committee. Obviously I am not the one to describe their shortcomings, since as a member of the group I probably have more than my own share of the characteristic failings, but I think I can give some description of the fraternity.

The group is small. It probably includes a couple of dozen members, representing news organizations with a commitment to coverage of national politics year in and year out, in dull seasons as well as exciting times. Those organizations would include the three news magazines, the two wire services, the three radio-television networks, and the *New York Times,* the *Washington Post,* the Washington *Evening Star,* the *Los Angeles Times,* the *Christian Science Monitor,* the *Baltimore Sun,* the Knight newspapers, the Field papers, and the Gannett, Newhouse, Scripps-

Howard, and Hearst chains. The political reporters of these organizations, plus a few syndicated columnists who cover politics along with other subjects, comprise the screening committee.

Not only is the group small, but its characteristics make it a highly atypical group of Americans. Its members are all Easterners, by residence if not by birth. They are all college graduates. Despite the low-paying reputation of newspapers, they all enjoy incomes well over the national median. Not one of them is black. More of them vote Democratic, and fewer of them regularly attend church, I would guess, than in a random sample of the population. None is under thirty, and few, except for the columnists, are over forty-five. I am deliberately not commenting on their social, political, or ethical views, but I think I have said enough to indicate that they—or we, I should say—represent a narrow and rather peculiar slice of this society.

Nonetheless, the fact is that the reporters do function as a screening committee for aspirants to national office. (Other reporters do the same thing at state and local levels.) And whether their standards are good or bad, whether they are characteristic or eccentric so far as the society is concerned, they make their standards stick.

Thus, the same George Romney who was touted as a Presidential possibility before he ever ran for governor was discarded as a Presidential possibility (by the press) before he ever got around to declaring his candidacy in late 1967. "I was the victim of the Teddy White syndrome," Romney has said, referring to the influence the author of *The Making of the President* books has had in impelling reporters to start covering Presidential possibilities long before they formally enter the race. There's not much doubt in my mind that Romney is right—he was the victim of serious, sustained scrutiny at a point when he was not prepared for that kind of critical cross-examination. Whether the reporters performed a national service or caused a great wrong in eliminating Romney as a contender is an arguable proposition. What is not debatable is that the reporters have this power and regularly exercise it.

Closely related to the function of talent scout is the political reporter's third role, that of race caller or handicapper. He is supposed to tell his public, every day, how the Presidential (or gubernatorial or senatorial) sweepstakes stand.

Here is a point where serious problems enter. Much of the reading and viewing public really doesn't care much about what happened yesterday in politics or in the campaign. Still less are these readers enamored of weighty analyses of why something happened. What they want to know is: What's going to happen tomorrow? Who's going to win or lose? And if the reporter has even a vestige of conscience, he knows that this is the one question he can never answer with confidence.

Yet much of political journalism is an artful effort to disguise prediction as reporting. Look at the use of public-opinion polls by newspapers. A public-opinion poll, when properly conducted and presented, is a perfectly legitimate tool for measuring opinion at a point in the past, i.e., the period of several days when the questions were actually being asked. But if the significance of the poll were accepted in those limited terms, few newspapers would give polls the prominence they now accord them. There is, let's face it, almost nothing as insignificant as a measure of how people would have decided last May a question that we know will not come to them for decision until November. Newspapers print and give prominence to the polls because they know their readers will take the poll to be exactly what it is not—a predictive device for guessing how the actual vote will come out.

A lot of political reporting is in the newspapers under exactly the same false pretenses, i.e., the assumption that a description of the standing in the race in May has some relevance to the actual order of finish in November. Indeed, we have now so far advanced this pseudo science of political handicapping that all of us, myself included, write two or three *years* in advance of a Presidential election that so-and-so is the front-runner.

And what is the basis on which the political reporter makes these judgments? What are the landmarks we rely on in calling the race?

There are four types of evidence that go into the reporters' judgments, and I will list them in descending order of reliability.

First, there are the nationally known public-opinion polls—Gallup and Harris—that give periodic reports on the standing of the Presidential contenders. These polls are not without their problems, but they do offer the journalist a relatively standardized set of measurements, made by reputable practitioners whose methods of operation are open to scrutiny and whose full results are disclosed.

Far more often, the reporter bases his judgment, in part, on a private poll someone has given him. These may or may not be as carefully prepared as the Gallup and Harris polls, but they are much less reliable from the reporter's point of view. Rarely is he informed how the poll was made; rarely does he see the full results. Typically, a private poll on the standing of the Presidential (or other) race in some state is "leaked" to him by an interested party—often the candidate who is favored by the poll or one of his managers. If the reporter is properly skeptical, he will let his readers know that his information is secondhand and tainted by the possible bias of his source. But, however he qualifies it, his reporting of the poll lends it an air of authority.

There are literally dozens of examples of inaccurate private polls distorting the journalist's and the public's judgment of a political race. Do such misjudgments have an effect on the outcome? Obviously, in many cases they do. The candidate reported trailing in these polls has a substantially harder time raising money, building an organization, or attracting publicity than the presumed front-runner.

To guard against the multiple distortions implicit in the "leaked poll" procedure, the reporter has two other sources of information. Unfortunately, these two sources are even flimsier, in most cases, as a basis for handicapping the race.

He can consult the judgment of so-called informed politicians. Typically, a reporter making a political survey of a state will begin by asking, say, the Democratic chairman, what he thinks of the situation—"I mean *really,* not for attribution, I want to know what you really think." The chairman hems and haws for a few minutes and finally allows as how his candidate just might win by 10,000 votes if he gets all the breaks the rest of the way. The reporter thanks him, phones his Republican counterpart, and goes through the same procedure with him, eliciting the view that, if they can manage to keep the candidate's alcoholic wife from making too many more public appearances, he ought to win by 40,000 votes.

Now, the scientific method, journalistic style, comes into play. The Democratic chairman has—sort of—claimed victory for his man by 10,000 votes. The Republican chairman has—with a shade more confidence—claimed victory for his man by 40,000 votes. The reporter cogitates and composes the following sentence: "While informed observers do not discount the possibility of a Democratic upset, the betting favors Republican candidate so-and-so to carry the state, perhaps by less than 40,000 votes."

That description is something of a caricature, I confess. The reporter will talk to more than two people, and he will weigh the words of each source according to his own past experience with the quality of the man's judgments. He will attempt to find some witnesses with no particular ax to grind. But, in the end, he will attempt to construct some kind of consensus of informed judgment. Almost every one of the news organizations I listed earlier goes through this kind of process for its pre-election surveys, contacting party officials, informed citizens, and newspapermen in all fifty states in order to make an "educated guess" in advance on the election results.

The enterprise of this kind that I happened to be involved in during the fall of 1968 was notably successful. Not only did we hit very close to Nixon's actual electoral vote, but we were equally on target in our estimates of changes in Congress and the governorships. But using exactly the same methodology in 1966, we managed to be off by a factor of 100 per cent on the size of the Republican gain in the House. We said twenty-four seats; they gained forty-seven. What I would like to know, and what no one has told me, is how we could be so smart one year and so dumb the other, when the procedure was exactly the same?

Many veteran newsmen would say that all this is stuff and nonsense. They scorn the polls, published or private; they have only minimum trust in the judgment of politicians. What they rely on is their own "feel" of the situation.

Reporters of this school are easy to identify in the campaign. They are the ones who stand on their chairs to stare intently at the faces in the crowd when the candidate makes his entrance. I have never known what they see in those faces, just as I have never known how the emotions in a crowd at a political rally give you any clue to the likely voting behavior of the city or state in which the rally is taking place. I have yet to see the first bit of evidence establishing a positive correlation between the size of the crowd a candidate draws in a city and the number of votes he later receives there. But, like everyone else, I count the crowds and measure their reaction as "friendly" or "cool." Just because an old method has no validity is no reason to get rid of it.

The reporter as summarizer, as talent scout, and as handicapper has his problems, but he is behaving in a role that recognizably has some relation to the demands of his newspaper and, presumably, his readers.

In his fourth role, however, the political reporter tends to carve out for himself a function just a bit more glorious than any that his employer or his readers ever envisaged for him. He becomes, in his own eyes, the Public Defender.

Reporters—unless they are highly opinionated columnists to begin with—really don't start the campaign with this role in mind. They couldn't care less who wins, they assure each other. There are no heroes or bad guys in the political drama they see, just mortals struggling with terribly complex problems.

But for months on end, they are locked up covering one of these mortals, engaged in an endless discussion of his personality, his mentality, his strategy, and his tactics. They become, in short, monomaniacs on the subject of the man they are covering. And eventually some of them, at least, will discover that The Candidate Is Trying to Pull Something We Don't Like. The candidate and his men are artful manipulators, propagandists, slick Madison Avenue operators. The reporter is the truth seeker. And he resolves, "I'm not going to let him [the candidate] get away with it. He's duping the poor voter and it's up to me to see that the poor little sap isn't conned by This Slicker."

Now, in any setting less irrational than a campaign plane, the reporter would probably recognize that the charge of "duping the voter" really involves no more than the customary trimming of issues to suit the public mood. The companion charge—that the candidate is "deliberately obscuring his stand"—rarely indicates more than bafflement by the candidate on how to solve such essentially insoluble problems as the rise in crime or the decline in the dollar.

But no matter. A wave of moral outrage sweeps over the reporters. It is expressed in the declaration, "We're not going to let him get away with this." Demands are sounded for press conferences. Questions are plotted that will cut off every avenue of escape or evasion for the candidate. The trap is carefully set, and, unless he is very wary, the candidate sooner or later walks into it.

Now, the serious point I would make about this mode of behavior is that once the reporter appoints himself Public Defender he abandons almost all pretense of being anything less than an arbiter of the outcome of the election. There is no consistency and no predictability as to when or whether he will adopt the role of Public Defender. Usually, he is provoked into it by the candidate's repeated use of an argument that is offensive to the reporter's own prejudices. Nixon, for example, "got away with" his law-and-order argument all through the 1968 campaign, even though many of the reporters thought there was an element of demagoguery in it. What finally provoked the reporters covering Nixon to play Public Defender was a day in late October when the candidate delivered a dozen whistle-stop speeches in Ohio (six times the usual number for a single day) and managed at each successive stop to give a more lurid description of the dangers that stalked the city streets under the unconcerned Democrats. That night, for the first time, a wave of we-can't-let-him-get-away-with-it talk swept the Nixon press corps, and the toughest stories of the campaign went whizzing out over the wires.

Nixon averted further press criticism by softening his tone on that issue in succeeding days, a response that was in itself a measure of the power of the press when it goes on the warpath.

But it doesn't always go on the warpath. Often, it is strangely passive. In 1960, for example, when John F. Kennedy promised day after day to get the country moving again, no petitions were passed in the press car demanding that he spell out how. When he spoke of a missile gap, no proof of evidence was demanded. When he spoke of America's falling prestige, no one pressed him on the definition and relevance of "prestige."

By contrast, Humphrey in 1968 was hounded at almost every press conference to spell out his differences with the Johnson Administration on Vietnam policy. First Romney and then Nixon were pressed unceasingly to specify their program for ending the war. Innumerable other examples could be cited. The point is simply that with some candidates and on some issues—but not others—the press will "bore in." And in choosing when to push and when not, we are responding almost exclusively to our own values and prejudices and opinions.

Fifth and finally, I am constrained to report that from time to time the political reporter will so far forget himself that he becomes a volunteer, unpaid assistant campaign manager for the candidate he is covering.

This is the opposite of the Public Defender syndrome and is, in every respect, more obnoxious. When he is playing Public Defender, the reporter at least is living up to the stereotype of the hard-nosed, independent, aggressive newshound—even though his motives may have precious little to do with the pursuit of news.

But when he appoints himself Assistant Campaign Manager, he becomes a fawning lackey of the candidate, waiting on him with bits of advice, reveling in the supposed intimacy of his relationship. He takes to defending the candidate in the press bus and may even go so far as to remonstrate with his colleagues who are writing "unfriendly" pieces about his new hero. He is a sad spectacle, but there is no blinking the fact that, on every campaign I have seen, one or more of our colleagues have strayed from the paths of righteous skepticism and become avowed, active promoters of the candidacy of the man they are covering.

There is a subtle revenge, however, for the candidate who allows this to happen. Invariably, the advice that newspapermen give candidates is the worst claptrap imaginable. I could cite examples, but I will not. I have probably said enough already to be expelled from the press bus for life.

CHAPTER 11

The Outcome of Elections

· A ·

The Different Kinds of Election Outcomes

A Classification of the Presidential Elections

BY ANGUS CAMPBELL

In some way each election is unique. New candidates, contemporary issues, the changing tides of domestic and international affairs—all these contribute to its individuality. Election rules do not differ significantly from year to year, but each election has its own characteristics, and to the voter who focuses on detail rather than generality each election seems like a new experience. We must assume, however, that with all their idiosyncrasies, elections do have common attributes and that these may be used to develop a descriptive model of all presidential elections. We propose to draw on the theory of the flow of the vote . . . as a basis for a classification of presidential elections.

Our basic assumption is that the standing commitments of the electorate define the "normal" division of the vote, and that fluctuations from this normal vote result from short-term forces which become important in specific elections. Depending on whether the movement of the vote results in the election of the candidate of the majority or the minority party, and on whether this movement is associated with a basic shift in long-term partisan attachments, each elections can be classified as maintaining, deviating, or realigning. We will draw on the four elections for which we have survey data to illustrate these classifications and will refer, but less confidently, to earlier elections in American history for further documentation.

Maintaining Elections

In a maintaining election the pattern of partisan attachments prevailing in the preceding period persists, and the majority party wins the Presidency. If the short-term forces are weak, the total turnout will be relatively low, and the partisan division of the vote will approximate the normal vote. If the short-term forces are strong, the turnout will be high, and the vote will typically swing away from the normal level to the advantage of one or the other candidate. If the short-term forces are advantageous to the majority party, its candidate will receive a higher than normal proportion of the vote. If they are disadvantageous, he will receive less of the vote than normal but may still win the election.

Most presidential elections during the last hundred years have been maintaining elections. If we assume that during the period immediately following the Civil War the majority of the electorate was Republican in its partisan sympathies, that this majority declined to something near an even balance during the 1876–1892 period and was revitalized in 1896, we may conclude that the numerous Republican victories down through the 1920's fall in this category. More recently, the later Roosevelt elections maintained a Democratic majority which had been established in the New Deal elections of the early thirties. Of the elections within the scope of our research program, two may be classified as maintaining. The elections of 1948 and 1960 differed greatly in important respects, but they both returned the candidate of the majority party to the White House.

THE 1948 ELECTION

The most striking feature of the presidential election in 1948 was the extraordinarily low turnout, only 51.5 per cent of the total citizenry. This was the smallest presidential vote since the establishment of the two-party system except for the two elections immediately following the advent of women's suffrage. It was obviously a year in which the electorate was not greatly moved by the circumstances, issues, or personalities of the movement . . . Mr. Truman was elected with slightly less than half the popular vote. Mr. Dewey received 45 per cent of the vote, and the remaining portion was divided between Thurmond (States' Rights Democrats) and Wallace (Progressives.)

Our understanding of the nature of the presidential elections leads us to expect that the vote in an election with an abnormally low turnout will demonstrate the following characteristics:

1. The dropout of voters will be sharpest among those members of the electorate who are least strongly party-identified, that is, the Independents and weak identifiers. The strong identifiers will be sustained by the high level of political involvement associated with their party identification.

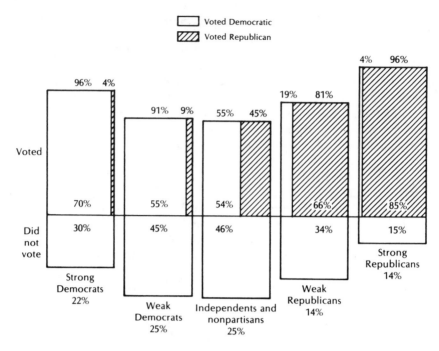

Figure 1 · The Vote of Partisan Groups in 1948.

(The data in this figure are based on recalled 1948 votes given by the respondents of the Survey Research Center's 1952 election study. Votes for Wallace and Thurmond are grouped with Democratic votes.)

2. Among the strong party identifiers defections to the opposite party, resulting primarily from idiosyncratic influences, will be few in number and will balance between the two parties. The absence of short-term forces, which produces the low turnout, also removes the stimulus to defection from accustomed party loyalties.

3. Among the weak party identifiers there will also be idiosyncratic defections, more numerous than among strong identifiers but balanced between the two parties.

4. Those Independents who vote will divide their vote equally between the competing parties.

5. The partisan division of the total vote will approximate the "normal vote" determined by the standing strength of the competing parties at the time.

We see in Figure 1 the extent to which our data regarding the vote in 1948 conformed to these expectations. Unfortunately we did not measure party identification in our 1948 survey, and we must draw on data from our 1952 survey to construct this figure. We asked the respondents in our 1952 survey to recall their vote in 1948, and we can combine this statement with their party identification as stated in 1952. When this is done we find that our expectations are generally supported, the deviations apparently being related to the inadequacies of our reports based on memory. The configuration of turnout is as anticipated, and the sharpness of the drop in turnout of the weakly identified groups is especially impressive when compared with the slope of turnout in the higher turnout elections which followed 1948. The strong identifiers did indeed adhere to their parties, although it is noteworthy that the 4 per cent of defections on both sides is perceptibly higher than we find among strong Republican partisans in the Eisenhower elections when the short-term advantages of the Republican Party eliminated even the infrequent idiosyncratic defections. Defections were more numerous among the weak identifiers, as predicted, although much less frequent than in the elections which followed. The balance of these defections was not as close as expected, there being a larger proportion of weak Republicans reporting voting Democratic than weak Democrats reporting voting Republican. The Independent voters split their votes in about an even division, with a slight inclination toward the Democratic candidate. Both of these minor discrepancies appear to reflect the Democratic bias in the recall of the 1948 vote by respondents who were questioned in 1952.

Although it would appear from Figure 1 that the Democratic vote in 1948 exceeded normal expectations, this is entirely a function of the overstatement of the Democratic vote by our 1952 respondents. If we consider the actual election statistics and assume that those voters who supported Thurmond or Wallace were largely Democrats, we find that the combination of their votes and those for Mr. Truman approximates the proportion of the total vote which we take to represent the "normal" Democratic strength. The minority party was not able to swing the Independent vote or capture any advantage from defecting voters in 1948, and the majority party was maintained in power.

THE 1960 ELECTION

The Democratic Party was still the majority party in 1960, and it elected its presidential candidate. The election was thus also a maintaining election, although it differed substantially from the election of 1948. The characteristics of this election are discussed in detail in the ensuing chapter; we need only note two distinguishing attributes, the high turnout and the great discrepancy between the vote of the Democratic candidate and the vote for the congressional candidates who ran with him. It is obvious from these characteristics of the vote that short-term forces played a much stronger role in 1960 than they had in 1948. The general level of voter stimulation was high, as demonstrated by expressions of interest in our interviews as well as by the election statistics. The partisan direction of these forces is indicated by the fact that Mr. Kennedy failed by several percentage points to achieve the normal expectation of a Democratic presidential candidate.

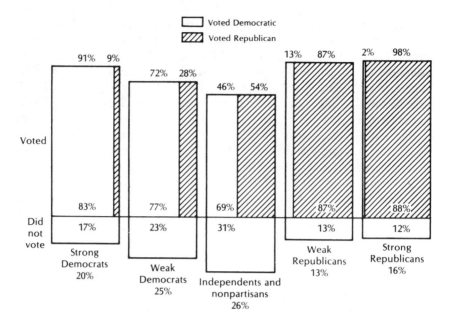

Figure 2 · The Vote of Partisan Groups in 1960.

When we compare Figure 2, showing the voting record of the partisan groups in 1960, with Figure 1, in which comparable data from 1948 are presented, we see first, the source of the substantial increase in turnout, and second, the location of the swing away from the normal vote toward the Republican candidate. It is clear that although all the party identification groups increased their turnout from the abnormally low levels of 1948, the increment was proportionately smallest in the strongly partisan groups and greatest in those groups with the weakest party commitment. It is also apparent that it was the weakly identified Democrats who are most susceptible to the impact of short-term forces in 1960. The Independent vote was split about equally between the two candidates. The total movement away from the normal vote was not large (as we shall see, the movement in 1952 was much larger), but it very nearly cost the Democratic Party the Presidency.

Deviating Elections

In a deviating election the basic division of party loyalties is not seriously disturbed, but the influence of short-term forces on the vote is such that it brings about the defeat of the majority party. After the specific circumstances that deflected the vote from what we would expect on the basis of party disappear from the scene, the political balance returns to a level which more closely reflects the underlying division of partisan attachments. A deviating election is thus a temporary reversal which occurs during a period when one or the other party holds a clear advantage in the long-term preferences of the electorate.

The election of Woodrow Wilson in 1916 is an obvious example of a deviating election. There seems little doubt that during the period of the Wilson elections the electorate was predominantly Republican. Wilson attained the White House in 1912 with a minority (42 per cent) of the total vote, as Roosevelt and Taft split the Republican Party. His incumbency and the public emotion aroused by the darkening shadow of the First World War apparently provided the additional votes he needed in 1916 to reach the narrow plurality that he achieved over his Republican opponent. According to V. O. Key, the Democratic gains of 1916 were due principally to "a short-term desertion of the Republican Party by classes of British origin and orientation." The temporary character of the Democratic victory began to become apparent in the 1918 elections when the Republican Party won control of both the Senate and the House of Representatives. In 1920 and the two following elections, the minority status of the Democratic Party was again convincingly demonstrated.

A similar situation occurred forty years later when, during a period of Democratic ascendancy, the Republican Party nominated General Dwight D. Eisenhower as its presidential candidate. These two elections fell within the coverage of our research program, and we can consider them in the light of our extensive survey data.

THE 1952 ELECTION

In November 1952, 62.7 per cent of the adult citizenry went to the polls, an increase of some 27 per cent over the total turnout four years earlier. They made the event further memorable by overturning a Democratic Administration which had been in office for twenty years, the longest unbroken period of party supremacy since the Republican Administrations of Lincoln and his successors. Mr. Eisenhower received over 55 per cent of the popular vote, and the Republican Party won both houses of Congress. This dramatic increase in turnout and the shift in the vote are illustrated in Figure 3.

The essential fact which emerges from Figure 3 is that in 1952 the number of people in the electorate who identified themselves as Democrats outnumbered those who called themselves Republicans by a ratio of three to two, and that the Eisenhower majority was assembled within this distribution without basically changing it. The impact of the combination of political forces which were important in 1952 was felt throughout the spectrum of party identification. Normal Republicans held solidly to their

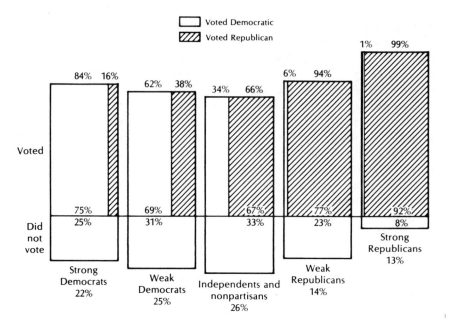

Figure 3 · The Vote of Partisan Groups in 1952.

party with only minor defections, even among those who called themselves "weak Republicans." A clear majority of the Independent voters supported Mr. Eisenhower, and serious inroads were made among those groups who ordinarily voted Democratic. The political circumstances of the moment were very unfavorable to the Democratic Party and resulted in its defeat, but they did not alter the underlying majority which it held in the standing partisan commitments of the electorate.

The Republican victory in 1952 was accomplished by a temporary movement of normal Democrats and nonpartisans toward the Republican candidate. The extent to which this was a movement toward the candidate and not toward the party is dramatically demonstrated by the high rate of ticket-splitting reported by these voters. Three out of five of those Democrats and Independents who voted for Mr. Eisenhower in 1952 were not willing to support the rest of the Republican slate. Subsequent events, beginning with the 1954 election when the Democratic Party again took both houses of Congress, made it clear that the election of 1952 deviated from normal expectations during a period of Democratic majority.

THE 1956 ELECTION

Mr. Eisenhower was re-elected to the Presidency in 1956 with a slightly higher majority (57 per cent) than he had received four years earlier. The

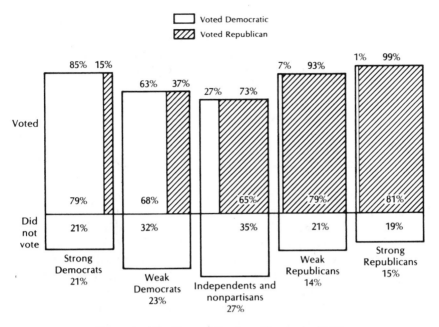

Figure 4 · The Vote of Partisan Groups in 1956.

distribution of party identification was almost precisely the same as it had been in 1952, and the contribution of the various party groups to Mr. Eisenhower's total vote closely resembled that of the previous election. This small increment in his support appeared to come largely from those voters who had no consistent partisan identification. (See Figure 4). The separation which the voters made between Mr. Eisenhower and the Republican ticket was clearly demonstrated as the Democratic candidates won both houses of Congress, the first time since 1848 that a split of this kind had occurred. This was accomplished by an even larger proportion of ticket-splitting by Democrats and Independents than was observed in 1952. Three out of four of these people who voted for Mr. Eisenhower rejected the party whose ticket he headed.

This increasing discrepancy between the vote for Mr. Eisenhower and the vote for his fellow candidates foreshadowed the failure of the Republican Party to bring about a basic shift of party loyalties during the Eisenhower years. The congressional elections of 1958, in which the Democratic Party won 58 per cent of the popular vote, made the Republican weakness apparent. As the Eisenhower period drew to a close, it became clear that Mr. Eisenhower had attracted a tremendous personal following in his two elections, but his administration had not produced a significant realignment in the distribution of partisan attachments. The Democratic Party remained the majority party and in 1960, when the Eisenhower appeal was no longer a factor, it was re-instated in power.

The two Eisenhower elections were deviating elections; our survey data from 1952 and 1956 may provide a key to an understanding of the other elections of this type that have occurred in American history. The most striking fact about the flow of the vote in the 1952 election (and again in 1956) was the universality with which the various segments of the electorate moved toward the Republican candidate. It was not a situation in which some groups became more Republican than they had been in 1948 but were offset by other groups moving in the other direction. There was virtually no occupational, religious, regional, or other subdivision of the electorate which did not vote more strongly Republican in 1952 than it had in 1948.

The second impressive fact about these two elections was the relative insignificance of policy issues in the minds of the voters. There were no great questions of policy which the public saw as dividing the two parties. In 1952 the voters were thinking about the "mess in Washington," the stalemate in Korea, and General Eisenhower's heroic image. In 1956 they were no longer concerned with the Truman Administration or the Korean situation, but they were even more devoted to Mr. Eisenhower than they had been in 1952. It would appear that the flow of the vote from the Democratic majorities of the previous twenty years to the Republican victories in the 1950's was a response to short-term forces which had little policy content and did not set interest group against interest group, class against class, or region against region.

It is our belief that it is this absence of great ideological issues which provides the basic quality of these deviating elections. Professor Charles Sellers concludes from his application of these concepts to the full range of presidential elections since 1789 that the "essential ingredient" of such elections is the presence of a "popular hero" candidate. He points out that all the presidential elections displaying some aspects of temporary surge featured a military hero, Eisenhower, Harrison, Washington, Grant, Taylor, and Jackson. The fact that so many of these elections have been dominated by persons of military background dramatizes their lack of ideological content. If Mr. Eisenhower may be taken as an example, the public image of these gentlemen has little to do with great issues of public policy. With certain notable exceptions, which we will consider shortly, the dramatic swings of turnout and partisanship during the last hundred years do not give the impression of an aroused electorate taking sides in a great debate on national policy. On the contrary, these swings in the vote appear to grow out of some immediate circumstance which is exploited by a candidate blessed with unusual personal appeal. Public interest in these events and persons is translated into political action, with a movement toward the party which happens to be in a position to profit from the situation. The movement is unidirectional because the circumstances which produce it are not seen as favorable by one section of the electorate and unfavorable by another. They tend rather to create a generally positive or negative attitude throughout the electorate, resulting in the almost universal type of shift which we observed in 1952. The movement is temporary because the circumstances and personalities with which it is associated pass from the scene without having introduced a new dimension of party position around which the electorate might become realigned.

Realigning Elections

Key has pointed out that there is a third type of election, characterized by the appearance of "a more or less durable realignment" of party loyalties. In such a realigning election, popular feeling associated with politics is sufficiently intense that the basic partisan commitments of a portion of the electorate change, and a new party balance is created. Such shifts are infrequent. As Key observes, every election has the effect of creating lasting party loyalties in some individual voters, but it is "not often that the number so affected is so great as to create a sharp realignment."

Realigning elections have historically been associated with great national crises. The emergence of the Republican Party and its subsequent domination of national politics were the direct outgrowth of the great debate over slavery and the ultimate issue of secession. The election of 1896 divided the country again as the East and Midwest overcame the Populist challenge of the South and West. According to Key, "The Democratic defeat was so demoralizing and so thorough that the party made little headway in regrouping its forces until 1916." It might be argued that the Democratic Party did not in fact hold a clear majority of the electorate at the time of the Cleveland elections, but the election statistics make it clear that whatever hold it did have on the voters was greatly weakened after 1896.

The most dramatic reversal of party alignments in this century was associated with the Great Depression of the 1930's. The economic disaster which befell the nation during the Hoover Administration so discredited the Republican Party that it fell from its impressive majorities of the 1920's to a series of defeats, which in 1936 reached overwhelming dimensions. These defeats were more than temporary departures from a continuing division of underlying party strength. There is little doubt that large numbers of people who had been voting Republican or had previously not voted at all, especially among the younger age groups and those social and economic classes hardest hit by the Depression, were converted to the Democratic Party during this period. The program of welfare legislation of the New Deal and the extraordinary personality of its major exponent, Franklin D. Roosevelt, brought about a profound realignment of party strength which has endured in large part up to the present time.

Key has pointed out that the shift toward the Democratic Party which occurred in the early 1930's was anticipated in the New England area in the 1928 election. It is difficult to ascertain whether the changes in these successive election years were actually part of the same movement. Since the shifts in New England were highly correlated with the proportions of Catholic voters in the communities studied, it would not be unreasonable to attribute them to the presence of Governor Alfred E. Smith at the head of the Democratic ticket in 1928. Had the Depression not intervened, the New England vote might have returned to its pre-1928 levels in the 1932 election. It may be recalled, however, that the Smith candidacy had not only a religious aspect but a class quality as well. It may well be that New England voters, having moved into the Democratic ranks in 1928 for reasons having to do with both religious and economic considerations, found it easy to remain there in 1932 when economic questions became compellingly important.

It is worth noting that the nationwide shift toward the Democratic Party during the 1930's was not fully accomplished in a single election. Although Mr. Roosevelt's margin of victory in 1932 was large (59 per cent of the two-party vote), it was not until 1936 that the Democratic wave reached its peak. The long-entrenched Republican sympathies of the electorate may not have given way easily in the early years of the Depression. Had not Mr. Roosevelt and his New Deal won the confidence of many of these people during his first administration—or even his second—there might have been a return to earlier party lines similar to that which occurred in 1920. From this point of view we may do well to speak of a realigning electoral era rather than a realigning election.

The total redistribution of party attachments in such an era does not necessarily result from a unilateral movement toward the advantaged party. The far-reaching impact of the crises which produce these alignments is likely to produce movements in both directions as individual voters find their new positions in the party conflict. It is also likely to increase the political polarization of important segments of the electorate, usually along sectional or class lines. We know that this happened during the 1930's as the Depression and the New Deal moved working-class people and certain minority groups toward a closer identification with the Democratic Party and middle-class people toward the Republican Party. Which party gains more from this sort of reshuffling depends on the relative size of the groups affected and the solidarity with which their membership moves.

The fact that the different regional and class divisions of the electorate become associated with the competing parties helps the shifting of loyalties develop into a lasting realignment. When an entire group polarizes around a new political standard, the pressures associated with group membership tend to hold the individual members to the group norm. Attitudes having the strength of group support are likely to be more stable than those which are merely individual. The development of the Solid South after the period of Reconstruction, when the expression of Republican sympathies became tantamount to sectional treason, is an illuminating case in point.

We may note finally that in contrast to those elections in which deviations from the normal vote were only temporary, the realigning elections have not been dominated by presidential candidates who came into office on a wave of great personal popularity. It is significant that neither Lincoln, McKinley, nor F. D. Roosevelt was a military figure, and none of them possessed any extraordinary personal appeal at the time he first took office. The quality which did distinguish the elections in which they came to power was the presence of a great national crisis, leading to a conflict regarding governmental policies and the association of the two major parties with relatively clearly contrasting programs for its solution. In some degree national politics during these realigning periods took on an ideological character. The flow of the vote was not a temporary reaction to a heroic figure or a passing embarrassment of the party in power; it reflected a reorientation of basic party attachments brought about during critical periods in the nation's history.

Conclusion

The ultimate significance of an election victory or defeat is often difficult to assess at the time. The immediate implications for the contending candidates are apparent, but the fuller meaning of the vote may not become clear until the succeeding elections have given a perspective within which it may be judged. The basic element in the long-term trend of the vote is the underlying division of party loyalties. If a substantial majority of the electorate are held by long-established commitments to one or another of the competing parties, the vote will oscillate from election to election around this party balance. If the circumstances in a particular election excite the electorate sufficiently, the oscillation may be large enough to dislodge the majority party temporarily from power. If the circumstances are so drastic as to force a new orientation of party positions, a period of realignment of partisan attachments may be induced, and a new balance of party strength created.

·B·

Results and Post Mortems

Continuity and Change in American Politics: Parties and Issues in the 1968 Election

BY PHILIP E. CONVERSE, WARREN E. MILLER, JERROLD G. RUSK, & ARTHUR C. WOLFE

Without much question, the third-party movement of George C. Wallace constituted the most unusual feature of the 1968 presidential election. While this movement failed by a substantial margin in its audacious attempt to throw the presidential contest into the House of Representatives, in any other terms it was a striking success. It represented the first noteworthy intrusion on a two-party election in twenty years. The Wallace ticket drew a larger proportion of the popular vote than any third presidential slate since 1924, and a greater proportion of electoral votes than any such movement for more than a century, back to the curiously divided election of 1860. Indeed, the spectre of an electoral college stalemate loomed sufficiently large that serious efforts at reform have since taken root.

At the same time, the Wallace candidacy was but one more dramatic addition to an unusually crowded rostrum of contenders, who throughout the spring season of primary elections were entering and leaving the lists under circumstances that ranged from the comic through the astonishing to the starkly tragic. Six months before the nominating conventions, Lyn-

Philip E. Converse, Warren E. Miller, Jerrold G. Rusk and Arthur C. Wolfe, "Continuity and Change in American Politics: Parties and Issues in the 1968 Election," *American Political Science Review*, Vol. 63, December 1969, pp. 1083–1105. Most footnotes deleted. Reprinted by permission of The American Political Science Association.

don Johnson and Richard Nixon had been the expected 1968 protagonists, with some greater degree of uncertainty, as usual, within the ranks of the party out of power. The nominating process for the Republicans followed the most-probable script rather closely, with the only excitement being provided by the spectacle of Governors Romney and Rockefeller proceeding as through revolving doors in an ineffectual set of moves aimed at providing a Republican alternative to the Nixon candidacy. Where things were supposed to be most routine on the Democratic side, however, surprises were legion, including the early enthusiasm for Eugene McCarthy, President Johnson's shocking announcement that he would not run, the assassination of Robert Kennedy in the flush of his first electoral successes, and the dark turmoil in and around the Chicago nominating convention, with new figures like Senators George McGovern and Edward Kennedy coming into focus as challengers to the heir apparent, Vice President Hubert Humphrey.

No recent presidential election has had such a lengthy cast of central characters, nor one that was kept for so long in flux. And under such circumstances, there is an inevitable proliferation of "what ifs?" What if Lyndon Johnson had decided to run again? What if Robert Kennedy had not been shot? What if George Wallace had been dissuaded from running, or had remained simply a regional states-rights candidate? What if Eugene McCarthy had accepted party discipline and closed ranks with Humphrey at the Chicago convention? What if Hubert Humphrey had handled the interaction with Mayor Daley and the Chicago demonstrators differently?

Strictly speaking, of course, there is no sure answer to questions of this type. If the attempt on Kennedy's life had failed, for example, an enormous complex of parameters and event sequences would have been different over the course of the campaign. One can never be entirely confident about what would have happened without the opportunity to live that particular sequence out in all its complexity. Nonetheless, given sufficient information as to the state of mind of the electorate during the period in question, plausible reconstructions can be developed which do not even assume that all other things remained constant, but only that they remained *sufficiently* constant that other processess might stay within predictable bounds. And answers of this sort, if not sacrosanct, carry substantial satisfaction.

One of our purposes in this paper will be to address some of these questions, as illuminated by preliminary analyses from the sixth national presidential election survey, carried out by the Survey Research Center of the University of Michigan. An effort to develop answers gives a vehicle for what is frankly descriptive coverage of the 1968 election as seen by the electorate. At the same time, we would hope not to miss along the way some of the more theoretical insights which the peculiar circumstances of the 1968 election help to reveal. In particular, we shall pay close attention to the Wallace campaign, and to the more generic lessons that may be drawn from this example of interplay between a pair of traditional parties, potent new issues, and a protest movement.

I. The Setting of the Election

The simplest expectation for the 1968 election, and one held widely until March of that year, was that President Johnson would exercise his option to run for a second full term, and that with the advantages of incumbency and the support of the majority party in the land, he would stand a very good chance of winning, although with a margin visibly reduced from his landslide victory over Barry Goldwater in 1964.

We will probably never know what role public opinion may have actually played in his decision to retire. But there is ample evidence that the mood of the electorate had become increasingly surly toward his administration in the months preceding his announcement. When queried in September and October of 1968, barely 40% of the electorate thought that he had handled his job well, the rest adjudging the performance to have been fair to poor. A majority of Democratic and Independent voters, asked if they would have favored President Johnson as the Democratic nominee had he decided to run, said they would not have. Affective ratings elicited just after the election for all the prominent political figures of the campaign showed Johnson trailing Robert Kennedy in average popularity by a wide margin, and lagging somewhat behind Humphrey and Muskie as well, among other Democrats (see Table 2). Given the normal head-start that a sitting president usually enjoys in such assays of opinion, Johnson completed his term amid a public bad humor matched only in recent elections by the cloud under which Harry Truman retired from the presidency in 1952. It is correspondingly dubious that Lyndon Johnson could have avoided the embarrassment of defeat had he set his sails for another term.

Indeed, the pattern of concerns exercising the voters and turnover in the players on the presidential stage combined to produce a shift in popular preferences between 1964 and 1968 which was truly massive. It is likely that the proportion of voters casting presidential ballots for the same party in these two successive elections was lower than at any time in recent American history. Among whites who voted in both elections, a full third switched their party. Almost one Goldwater voter out of every five turned either to Humphrey or to Wallace four year later (dividing almost 3 to 1 for Wallace over Humphrey); at the same time, three in every ten white Johnson voters switched to Nixon or Wallace, with Nixon the favorite by a 4-to-1 ratio. A full 40% of Nixon's votes came from citizens who had supported Lyndon Johnson in 1964! Much of this flood, of course, came from Republicans who were returning home after their desertions from Goldwater.

Nevertheless, Democrats and Independents who had voted for Johnson and then turned to Nixon four years later made up nearly half of *all* the remaining vote switches, more than matching the combined flow of Johnson and Goldwater voters who supported Wallace, and almost equalling the total Wallace vote. The Johnson-Nixon switchers easily outweighed the flow away from Goldwater to Humphrey and Wallace, and the Republican presidential vote rose from 39% to 43% in 1968 as a consequence. At the same time, the loss of more than a quarter of the total Johnson vote to Wallace and Nixon was scarcely offset by the trickle of votes from Goldwater to Humphrey, and the Democratic proportion of the vote across the land dropped a shattering 19 percentage points from more than 61 percent to less than 43 percent.

Such a massive drain from the Democratic ranks establishes a broader parallel with 1952, for in both cases an electorate professing to be of Democratic allegiance by a considerable majority, had arrived at a sufficient accumulation of grievances with a Democratic administration as to wish it out of office, thereby producing what we have labelled elsewhere a "deviating election." Indeed, the frantic motion of the electorate in its presidential votes between 1964 and 1968 may be ironically juxtaposed against the serene stability of party identifications in the country, for the overall proportions of self-proclaimed Democrats, Independents and Republicans have scarcely changed over the past twenty years, much less in the past four. Of course this juxtaposition calls into question the predictive value of party identification, relative to other kinds of determinants of the vote, and we shall undertake a more intensive discussion of this matter presently. For now, however, let us simply point out that while the inert distribution of party loyalties cannot by definition explain the complex flows of the presidential vote between 1964 and 1968, it was handsomely reflected in the 1968 congressional elections, as it has been in virtually all of the biennial congressional contests of the current era. Despite widespread dissatisfaction with Democratic performance, the Republican proportion of seats in the House rose only a minute 1 percent, from 43 in 1966 to 44 percent on the strength of the Nixon victory. Even at more local levels, the continuing dominance of Democratic partisanship across the nation is documented by the results of thousands of races for state legislative seats. Prior to the election, Democrats controlled 57.7 percent of all legislative seats. After the election, which saw contests for some or all seats in 43 states, Democratic control had dropped from 4,269 seats (or 57.7%) to 4,250 seats (57.5%).

In view of such continued stability of partisanship, it is clear we must turn elsewhere to account for the remarkable changes in voting at the presidential level between 1964 and 1968. The classic assumption is, of course, that such change must spring from some flux in "short-term forces"—the impact of the most salient current issues, and the way in which these issues interlock with the leadership options, or the cast of potential presidential figures in the specific year of 1968. These terms obviously best define the setting of the 1968 election.

When asked on the eve of the presidential election to identify the most important problem facing the government in Washington, over 40% of the electorate cited the war in Vietnam. The salience of this issue provided another striking parallel with 1952. In both presidential elections, widespread public discouragement with the progress of a "bleeding war" in the Far East, seen as initiated by a Democratic administration, was a major source of indignation.

But the Vietnam issue did not, of course, stand alone. Offering vivid testimony to another bitter current of controversy was a simple, though little-noted, pattern in the popular presidential vote itself: while some 97% of black voters in the nation cast their ballots for Hubert Humphrey, less than 35% of white voters did so. Thus the presidential vote must have been as sharply polarized along racial lines as at any time during American history. One major irony surrounding this cleavage was the fact that it was the comfortable white majority that was agitating to overturn control of the White House, while the aggrieved black minority was casting its vote as one in an effort to preserve the partisan status quo.

Indeed, this irony is compounded when the role of the Vietnam issue is jointly taken into account. We have indicated above that the public was deeply impatient with the Johnson administration, in part because of the handling of the war. Blacks stood out as the major demographic grouping most exercised about the entanglement in Vietnam. They were more likely than whites to opine that the government should never have undertaken the military commitment there. They also were more likely to feel that American troops should be brought home immediately, a position not generally associated with the Johnson administration. Nonetheless, as Table 2 (below) will document, Negro enthusiasm not only for Hubert Humphrey but for Lyndon Johnson as well remained high to the very end. It seems quite evident that when black citizens were making decisions about their vote, Vietnam attitudes paled into relative insignificance by contrast with attitudes toward progress on civil rights within the country; and that where such progress was concerned, the Johnson-Humphrey administration was seen as much more friendly than the other 1968 alternatives.

Because of the near-unanimity of the black vote, many of our analyses below have been focussed on differences within the white vote taken alone. At the same time, this treatment must not be allowed to obscure in any way the deep imprint of racial cleavage on the election outcome. The additional "between-race" variance in the vote, concealed when data are presented only for whites, remains extreme, and is a faithful reflection of the crescendo to which civil rights tumult had risen over the four preceding years. It should be kept in mind.

To say that Vietnam and civil rights were dominant issues for the public in 1968 is not equivalent, however, to saying that voter positions on these issues can account for the large-scale voting change we have observed for whites between 1964 and 1968. As the comparisons provided by Table 1 suggest, changes in public thinking about strategic alternatives in Vietnam or civil rights outcomes over this period were rather limited. Where Vietnam was concerned, opinion was somewhat more crystallized in 1968 than in 1964 but there had been no sweeping shift of sentiment from hawk to dove in mass feeling. On civil rights, the drift of white opinion had been if anything toward a more liberal stance, and hence can hardly explain a vote which seemed to vibrate with "blacklash." Thus public positioning on these two central issues taken alone seems no more capable of illuminating vote change from 1964 to 1968 than the inert partisan identifications.

What *had* changed, of course, was the public view of the success of Administration performance in these areas. As we have discussed elsewhere, throughout the 1950's citizens who felt the Republicans were better at keeping the country out of war outnumbered those who had more confidence in Democrats by a consistently wide margin, much as the Democratic Party tended to be seen as better at keeping the country out of economic depression. In 1964, however, the pleas of Barry Goldwater for an escalation of the Vietnam War in order to produce a military victory served to frighten the public, and rapidly reversed the standing perception: by the time of the November election more people felt the Democrats were better able to avert a large war. But this novel perception was transient. President Johnson himself saw fit to authorize an escalation of bombing in Vietnam almost immediately after the 1964 election. By the time of the 1966 congressional election, the balance in popular assessments had already shifted back to the point where a slight majority chose the Republicans as more adept in avoiding war. By 1968, exasperation at the handling of the war had increased sufficiently that among people who felt there was a difference in the capacity of the two parties to avoid a larger war, the Republicans were favored once again by a margin of two to one.

To the bungled war in Vietnam, the white majority could readily add a sense of frustration at a racial confrontation that had taken on increasingly ugly dimensions between 1964 and 1968. Although national opinion had evolved in a direction somewhat more favorable to desegregation, largely through the swelling proportions of college-educated young, some persistently grim facts had been underscored by the Kerner Commission report in the spring of the year: forbidding proportions of the white citizenry outside of the South as well as within it had little enthusiasm for the redress of Negro grievances to begin with. And even among whites with some genuine sympathy for the plight of blacks, the spectacle of city centers aflame had scarcely contributed to a sense of confidence in the Administration handling of the problem.

Table 1 · Comparison of Attitudes on Current Vietnam Policy and Racial
Desegregation, 1964 and 1968, for Whites Only

"Which of the following do you think we should do *now* in Vietnam?"
  1. Pull out of Vietnam entirely.
  2. Keep our soldiers in Vietnam but try to end the fighting.
  3. Take a stronger stand even if it means invading North Vietnam.

	PULL OUT	STATUS QUO	STRONGER STAND	DON'T KNOW, OTHER	TOTAL
		Northern Democrats			
1964	8%	25	29	38	100%
1968	20%	39	35	6	100%
		Northern Republicans			
1964	8%	19	38	35	100%
1968	20%	39	36	5	100%
		Southern Democrats			
1964	8%	25	28	39	100%
1968	17%	36	38	9	100%
		Southern Republicans			
1964	10%	18	42	30	100%
1968	15%	29	48	8	100%

"What about you? Are you in favor of desegregation, strict segregation, or something in between?" (This was the fourth question in a series asking about others' attitudes toward racial desegregation.)

	DESEGREGATION	MIXED FEELINGS	STRICT SEGREGATION	OTHER	TOTAL
		Northern Democrats			
1964	31%	50	17	2	100%
1968	38%	45	14	3	100%
		Northern Republicans			
1964	32%	51	13	4	100%
1968	35%	50	10	5	100%
		Southern Democrats			
1964	12%	35	52	1	100%
1968	18%	45	30	7	100%
		Southern Republicans			
1964	15%	44	40	1	100%
1968	15%	60	20	5	100%

From Vietnam and the racial crisis a corollary discontent crystallized that might be treated as a third towering issue of the 1968 campaign, or as nothing more than a restatement of the other two issues. This was the cry for "law and order" and against "crime in the streets." While Goldwater had talked in these terms somewhat in 1964, events had conspired to raise their salience very considerably for the public by 1968. For some, these slogans may have had no connotations involving either the black race or Vietnam, signifying instead a concern over rising crime rates and the alleged "coddling" of criminal offenders by the courts. More commonly by 1968, however, the connection was very close: there were rallying cries for more severe police suppression of black rioting in the urban ghettos, and of public political dissent of the type represented by the Vietnam peace demonstrations at Chicago during the Democratic convention.

In view of these latter connotations, it is not surprising that people responsive to the "law and order" theme tended, like George Wallace, to be upset at the same time by civil rights gains and the lack of a more aggressive policy in Vietnam. Therefore it might seem redundant to treat "law and order" as a third major issue in its own right. Nevertheless, we have found it important to do so, even where the "order" being imposed is on black militants or peace demonstrators, for the simple reason that many members of the electorate reacted as though the control of dissent was quite an independent issue. This becomes very clear where support for blacks and opposition to the war are accompanied with a strong revulsion against street protest and other forms of active dissent. And this combination occurs more frequently than an academic audience may believe.

One would expect, for example, to find support for peace demonstrations among the set of people in the sample who said (a) that we made a mistake in getting involved in the Vietnam War; and (b) that the preferable course of action at the moment would be to "pull out" of that country entirely. Such expectations are clearly fulfilled among the numerous blacks matching these specifications. Among whites, however, the picture is different. First, a smaller proportion of whites—about one in six or seven—expressed this combination of feelings about Vietnam. Among those who expressed such feelings it remains true that there is relatively less disfavor vented about some of the active forms of peace dissent that had become customary by 1968. What is striking, however, is the absolute division of evaluative attitudes toward peace dissenters among those who were themselves relative "doves," and this is probably the more politically significant fact as well. Asked to rate "Vietnam war protestors" on the same kind of scale as used in Table 2, for example, a clear majority of these whites who themselves were opposed to the Administration's Vietnam policy located their reactions on the negative side of the scale, and nearly one-quarter (23%) placed them at the point of most extreme hostility.

Even more telling, perhaps, are the attitudes of these same whites toward the peace demonstrations surrounding the Democratic convention at Chicago, for in this case the protestors were given undeniably sympathetic coverage by the television networks. Keeping in mind that we are dealing here with only those whites who took clear "dove" positions on Vietnam policy, it is noteworthy indeed that almost 70% of those giving an opinion rejected the suggestion that "too much force" was used by Chicago police against the peace demonstrators, and the *modal* opinion (almost 40%) was that "not enough force" had been used to suppress the demonstration.

It should be abundantly clear from this description that the white minority who by the autumn of 1968 felt our intervention in Vietnam was a mistake and was opting for a withdrawal of troops turns out to fit the campus image of peace sentiment rather poorly. Such a disjuncture between stereotypes developed from the mass media and cross-section survey data are not at all uncommon. However, as certain other aspects of the election may be quite unintelligible unless this fact has been absorbed by the reader, it is worth underscoring here. This is not to say that the more familiar Vietnam dissent cannot be detected in a national sample. Among whites resenting Vietnam and wishing to get out, for example, a unique and telltale bulge of 12% gave ratings of the most extreme sympathy to the stimulus "Vietnam war protestors." Now this fragment of the electorate shows all of the characteristics expected of McCarthy workers or the New Left: its members are very young, are disproportionately college-educated, Jewish, and metropolitan in background, and register extreme sympathy with civil rights and the Chicago convention demonstrations. The problem is that this group represents such a small component (one-eighth) of the 1968 dove sentiment on Vietnam being singled out here that its attitudes on other issues are very nearly obscured by rather different viewpoints held by the other 88% of the dove contingent. On the larger national scene, in turn, those who opposed Vietnam policy and were sympathetic to Vietnam war protestors make up less than 3% of the electorate—even if we add comparable blacks to the group—and law and order were not unpopular with the 97 percent.

In the broad American public, then, there was a widespread sense of breakdown in authority and discipline that fed as readily on militant political dissent as on race riots and more conventional crime. This disenchantment registered even among citizens who apparently were sympathetic to the goals of the dissent on pure policy grounds, and everywhere added to a sense of cumulative grievance with the party in possession of the White House. Thus the "law and order" phrase, ambiguous though it might be, had considerable resonance among the voters, and deserves to be catalogued along with Vietnam and the racial crisis among major issue influences on the election.

While the 1968 situation bore a number of resemblances to the basic ingredients and outcome of the 1952 election, the analogy is far from perfect. In 1952, the public turned out to vote in proportions that were quite unusual for the immediate period, a phenomenon generally taken to reflect the intensity of frustrations over the trends of government. It is easy to argue that aggravations were fully as intense in 1968 as they had been in 1952, and more intense than for any of the elections in between. Yet the proportion turning out to vote in 1968 fell off somewhat from its 1964 level.

Of course any equation between indignation and turning out to vote does presuppose the offering of satisfactory alternatives, and there was somewhat greater talk than usual in 1968 that the candidate options in November were inadequate. Certainly the array of potential candidates was lengthy, whatever the actual nominees, and our account of the short-term forces affecting the electorate would be quite incomplete without consideration of the emotions with which the public regarded the dramatis personae in 1968. Just after the election, respondents in our national sample were asked to locate each of twelve political figures on a "feeling thermometer" running from zero (cold) to 100° (warm), with a response of 50° representing the indifference point. Table 2 summarizes the mean values for the total sample, as well as those within relevant regional and racial partitions.

Numerous well-chronicled features of the campaign are raised into quantitative relief by this tabulation, including Wallace's sharply regional and racial appeal, Muskie's instant popularity and near upstaging of Humphrey, and the limited interest that McCarthy seemed to hold for Negroes compared to other Democratic candidates. At the same time, other less evident comparisons can be culled from these materials, although the reader is cautioned to keep in mind that these scores refer to the period just after the election, and not necessarily to the period of the spring primaries or the summer conventions.[1] This may be of particular importance in the case of the ratings of Eugene McCarthy. When respondents were asked before the election which candidate from the spring they

---

[1] The reader should also keep in mind several other things about Table 2. The "South" here refers, as it will throughout this paper, to the Census Bureau definition of the region that includes 15 states and the District of Columbia. Hence such border states as Maryland or West Virginia are included along with the deeper southern states of the old confederacy. Presumably, for example, George Wallace's rating among whites of a more hard-core South would be correspondingly higher. Secondly, it should be remembered for some of the lesser candidates that respondents knowing so little about a candidate as to be indifferent to him would end up rating him "50°." Thus it would be questionable to conclude from Table 2 that LeMay was more popular than George Wallace, except in a very limited sense. Actually, three times as many respondents (nearly one-third) left LeMay at the indifference point as did so for Wallace. Thus lack of visibility helped to make him *less unpopular*. But among those who reacted to both men, LeMay was less popular than Wallace. Similarly, Wallace's low rating must be understood as a compound of an admiring minority and a hostile majority. The variance of Wallace ratings is much greater than those for other candidates, even in the South.

Table 2 · Average Ratings of Major 1968 Political Figures by a National Sample, November–December, 1968

	TOTAL SAMPLE	NON-SOUTH		SOUTH	
		White (N's of 785–843)	Black (N's of 54–64)	White (N's of 315–340)	Black (N's of 55–66)
Robert Kennedy	70.1	70.4	94.1	60.5	91.2
Richard Nixon	66.5	67.7	53.0	67.8	56.6
Hubert Humphrey	61.7	61.2	86.1	53.4	85.8
Lyndon Johnson	58.4	56.6	81.9	53.7	82.7
Eugene McCarthy	54.8	56.5	59.1	49.8	54.0
Nelson Rockefeller	53.8	54.4	61.6	50.7	53.5
Ronald Reagan	49.1	49.6	42.9	50.0	41.8
George Romney	49.0	50.4	48.3	45.6	50.2
George Wallace	31.4	27.7	9.4	48.2	13.2
Edmund Muskie	61.4	62.7	71.0	54.7	68.9
Spiro Agnew	50.4	50.9	37.7	52.9	42.4
Curtis LeMay	35.2	33.6	21.2	43.9	22.9

had hoped would win nomination, over 20 percent of Democrats and Independents recalling some preference mentioned McCarthy. However, many of these citizens gave quite negative ratings to McCarthy by November, so it appears that some disenchantment set in between the primaries and the election.

The question of timing poses itself acutely as well where Robert Kennedy is concerned.

Taken at face value, the data of Table 2 imply that aside from the tragedy at Los Angeles, Kennedy should have been given the Democratic nomination and would have won the presidential election rather handily. Yet how much of this massive popularity is due to some posthumous halo of martyrdom? It seems almost certain that at least some small increment is of this sort, and that the harsh realities of a tough campaign would have eroded the bright edges of Kennedy appeal. Nevertheless, both in contested primaries and poll data of the spring period, as well as in the retrospective glances of our autumn respondents, one cannot fail to be impressed by the reverberations of Kennedy charisma even in the least likely quarters, such as among Southern whites or among Republicans elsewhere. And rank-and-file Democrats outside the South reported themselves to have favored Kennedy for the nomination over Humphrey by two-to-one margins, and over McCarthy by nearly three-to-one. Clearly a Kennedy candidacy could not have drawn a much greater proportion of the black vote than Humphrey received, although it might have encouraged higher turnout there. But there is evidence of enough edge elsewhere to suggest that Robert Kennedy might have won an election over Richard Nixon, and perhaps even with greater ease than he would have won his own party's nomination.

As it was, Humphrey received the mantle of party power from Lyndon Johnson and, with Robert Kennedy missing, captured the Democratic nomination without serious challenge. At that point he faced much the same dilemma as Adlai Stevenson had suffered in 1952: without gracelessly biting the hand that fed him, how could he dissociate himself from the unpopular record of the preceding administration? In 1952, Stevenson did not escape public disgust with the Truman administration, and was punished for its shortcomings. The 1968 data make clear in a similar manner that Humphrey was closely linked to Lyndon Johnson in the public eye through the period of the election. For example, the matrix of intercorrelations of the candidate ratings presented in Table 2 shows, as one would expect, rather high associations in attitudes toward presidential and vice presidential candidates on the same ticket. Thus the Humphrey-Muskie intercorrelation is .58, the Nixon-Agnew figure is .59, and the Wallace-LeMay figure is .69. But the highest intercorrelation in the whole matrix, a coefficient of .70, links public attitudes toward Lyndon Johnson and those toward Hubert Humphrey. Humphrey was highly assimilated to the Johnson image, and his support came largely from sectors of the population for which the administration had not "worn thin."

When we consider the relative strength of Kennedy enthusiasts as opposed to loyal Humphrey-Johnson supporters among identifiers with the Democratic Party within the mass public, the line of differentiation that most quickly strikes the eye is the noteworthy generation gap. As we have seen above, Kennedy supporters enjoy a marked overall plurality. However, this margin comes entirely from the young. For Democrats under thirty, only about one in five giving a pre-convention nomination preference picks Humphrey or Johnson, and Kennedy partisans outnumber them by nearly three to one. Among Democrats over fifty, however, Humphrey-Johnson supporters can claim a clear plurality. The "wings" of the Democratic Party that emerged in the struggle for the nomination had an "old guard" and "young Turk" flavor, even as reflected in a cross-section sample of party sympathizers.

This completes our summary of the setting in which the 1968 election took place. We have seen that despite great continuity in party loyalties and a surprising constancy in policy positions of the public, there was an unusual degree of change in partisan preference at the presidential level by comparison with 1964. This change occurred in part as a response to increased salience of some issues, such as the question of "law and order," and in part because of the way in which contending leadership cadres had come to be identified with certain policies or past performance. The Democratic party lost, as quickly as it had won, its perceived capacity to cope with international affairs and the exacerbating war in Vietnam. Hubert Humphrey, long a major figure in his own right, could not move swiftly enough to escape his links with a discredited regime.

Let us now pursue some of the more obvious analytic questions posed by the general discontent among voters in 1968, and by the Wallace movement in particular. We shall first consider influences on the actual partitioning of the vote on Election Day, and then examine some of the attitudinal and social bases underlying the outcome.

II. Hypothetical Variations on the Vote Outcome

IMPACT OF THE WALLACE TICKET

There were signs of some concern in both the Nixon and Humphrey camps that the success of George Wallace in getting his name on the ballot might divert votes and lower their respective chances of success. Nixon was more alarmed by the prospective loss of the electoral votes in the Deep South that Goldwater had won in 1964, while Humphrey was alarmed in turn by intelligence that Wallace was making inroads outside the South among unionized labor that had been customarily Democratic since the New Deal. At the very least, the Wallace ticket was responsible for the injection of unusual uncertainty in a game already replete with unknowns. Now that the dust has settled, we can ask more systematically how the election might have been affected if Wallace had been dissuaded from running.

Numerous polls made clear at the time of the election that Wallace voters tended to be quite disproportionately nominal Democrats, and data from our sample are congruent with this conclusion, although the differences were more notable in the South than elsewhere. For the South, 68% of Wallace voters considered themselves Democrats, and 20% Republicans.

Outside the South, proportions were 46% Democratic and 34% Republican. Yet these proportions taken alone do not address in any satisfying fashion what might have happened if Wallace had not run. In the first place, these partisan proportions among Wallace voters do not differ very markedly from those which characterize the regional electorates taken as a whole. Indeed, as we shall see, the overall association between partisanship and attitudes toward Wallace (the rating scale) shows Republicans slightly more favorable across the nation as a whole, although this fact is faintly reversed with blacks set aside, and the main lesson seems to be that the "true" correlation is of utterly trivial magnitude (.05 or less). More important still, however, is the obvious fact that Democrats voting for Wallace were repudiating the standard national ticket, as many as a third of them for the second time in a row. If Wallace had not run, we can have little confidence that they would have faithfully supported Humphrey and Muskie.

It is clear that the crucial datum involves the relative preferences of the Wallace voters for either Nixon or Humphrey, assuming that these preferences would have been the same without Wallace and that these citizens would have gone to the polls in any event. This information is available in the leader ratings used for Table 2. In Table 3 we have arrayed the total sample according to whether Humphrey or Nixon was given the higher rating, or the two were tied, as well as by the respondent's party identification. Within each cell so defined, we indicate the proportion of the vote won by Wallace, and the number of voters on which the proportion is based. The latter figures show familiar patterns. Of voters with both a party and a candidate preference, more than four-fifths prefer the nominee of their party. And while Democrats are in a majority, it is clear that the tides are running against them since they are suffering the bulk of defections.

It is interesting how the Wallace vote is drawn from across this surface. While the numbers of cases are too small to yield very reliable estimates in some of the internal cells, it is obvious that Wallace made least inroads among partisans satisfied with their party's nominee, and showed major strength where such partisans were sufficiently disgusted with their own

Table 3 · Distribution of the Wallace Vote, by Traditional Parties and Candidates

| | | PARTY IDENTIFICATION | | |
		Democratic	Independent	Republican
RATING OF TWO MAJOR CANDIDATES	Humphrey over Nixon	4% (347)	26% (23)	21% (24)
	Tied	24% (79)	9% (11)	6% (17)
	Nixon over Humphrey	26% (132)	15% (53)	7% (314)

The percentage figure indicates the proportion of all voters in the cell who reported casting a ballot for Wallace. The number of voters is indicated between parentheses.

party nominee actually to prefer that of the opposing party. Conceptually, it is significant that these protestors included Republicans unenthusiastic about Nixon as well as the more expected Democrats cool to Humphrey. Practically, however, Nixon Democrats so far outnumbered Humphrey Republicans that while Wallace drew at nearly equal rates from both groups, the majority of his votes were from Democrats who otherwise preferred Nixon rather than from Republicans who might have given their favors to Humphrey.

This in turn provides much of the answer to one of our primary questions. While the data underlying Table 3 can be manipulated in a variety of ways, all reasonable reconstructions of the popular vote as it might have stood without the Wallace candidacy leave Nixon either enjoying about the same proportion of the two-party vote that he actually won or a slightly greater share, depending on the region and the detailed assumptions made. In short, unless one makes some entirely extravagant assumptions about the mediating electoral college, it is very difficult to maintain any suspicion that the Wallace intrusion by itself changed the major outcome of the election.

IMPACT OF THE McCARTHY MOVEMENT

If he was ever tempted at all, Eugene McCarthy decided against mounting a fourth-party campaign for the presidency. At the same time, he withheld anything resembling enthusiastic personal support for Hubert Humphrey. In view of his devoted following, some observers felt that McCarthy's refusal to close party ranks after Chicago cost the Democratic nominee precious votes, and conceivably even the presidency.

In order to understand the basis of McCarthy support at the time of the election, it is useful to trace what is known of the evolution of McCarthy strength from the time of the first primary in the spring. It will be recalled that McCarthy was the sole Democrat to challenge the Johnson administration in the New Hampshire primary. With the aid of many student volunteer campaign workers, he polled a surprising 42% of the vote among Democrats, as opposed to 48% drawn by an organized write-in campaign for President Johnson. Although he failed to upset the president in the vote, most observers saw his performance as remarkably strong, and a clear harbinger of discontent which could unseat Lyndon Johnson in the fall election. This reading was plainly shared by Robert Kennedy, who announced his own candidacy for the nomination four days later, and probably by Johnson himself, who withdrew from any contention less than three weeks later.

Sample survey data from New Hampshire at the time of the primary show some expected patterns underlying that first McCarthy vote, but also some rather unexpected ones as well. First, the vote among Democrats split toward Johnson or McCarthy in obvious ways according to expressions of satisfaction or dissatisfaction with Administration performance in general and its Vietnam policy in particular. The McCarthy vote in New Hampshire certainly reflected a groundswell of anger at the Johnson administration, and an expression of desire for a change which was simply reiterated in November. Surprisingly, however, in view of McCarthy's clear and dissenting "dove" position on Vietnam, the vote he drew in New Hampshire could scarcely be labelled a "peace vote," despite the fact that such a conclusion was frequently drawn. There was, of course, some hard-core peace sentiment among New Hampshire Democrats that was drawn quite naturally to McCarthy. Among his supporters in the primary, however, those who were unhappy with the Johnson administration for not pursuing a *harder* line against Hanoi outnumbered those advocating a withdrawal from Vietnam by nearly a three to two margin! Thus the McCarthy tide in New Hampshire was, to say the least, quite heterogeneous in its policy preferences: the only common denominator seems to have been a deep dissatisfaction with the Johnson administration. McCarthy simply represented the only formal alternative available to registered Democrats. This desire for an alternative was underlined by the fact that most of the 10 percent of the Democratic vote that did not go to Johnson or McCarthy went to Nixon as a write-in candidate on the Democratic ballot.

The entry of Robert Kennedy into the race did provide another alternative and, as we have seen, a very popular one as well. He made major inroads into the potential McCarthy strength, and by the time our autumn sample was asked what candidate of the spring would have been preferred for the Democratic nomination, 46% of those Democrats with some preference cited Kennedy first while only 18% mentioned McCarthy. Nevertheless, even this 18% cannot be thought of as constituting hard-core McCarthy support at the time of the actual election, since almost two-thirds of this group had turned their attention elsewhere, giving at least one of the other presidential hopefuls a higher rating than they gave McCarthy in the responses underlying Table 2. The remainder who reported McCarthy as their pre-convention favorite and awarded him their highest ratings just after the election, make up some 6% of Democrats having some clear candidate preference, or 3% of all Democrats. Along with a handful of Independents and Republicans showing the same reiterated McCarthy preference, these people can be considered the McCarthy "hard-core."

While it is this hard-core whose voting decisions interest us most, it is instructive to note where the other two-thirds of the pre-convention McCarthy support among Democrats went, over the course of the campaign. If these migrations are judged according to which presidential aspirant among the nine hopefuls of Table 2 was given the highest rating in

November, one discovers that a slight plurality of these erstwhile McCarthy backers found George Wallace their preferred candidate in the fall. Slightly smaller groups favored Kennedy and Nixon, and a scatter picked other Republicans like Reagan and Rockefeller, despite their own Democratic partisanship. Very few of these McCarthy Democrats—about one in seven—migrated to a preference for Hubert Humphrey. Where the actual presidential vote was concerned, the choice was of course more constrained.

Since the McCarthy movement was commonly thought of as somewhat to the left of Humphrey and the administration, while Wallace was located rather markedly to the right, a major McCarthy-to-Wallace transfer of preferences may seem ideologically perplexing. Were McCarthy supporters so furious with the Humphrey nomination that pure spite overcame issue feelings and led to a protest vote for Wallace? Although there were rumors of such a reaction at the time, our data suggest a somewhat simpler interpretation. We have already noted the attitudinal heterogeneity of McCarthy voters in New Hampshire. Those in our autumn sample who recall a pre-convention preference for McCarthy are similarly heterogeneous. Indeed, on some issues of social welfare and civil rights, pre-convention McCarthy supporters are actually more conservative than backers of either Humphrey or Kennedy.

This heterogeneity declined markedly, however, as the size of the McCarthy group eroded over the summer to what we have defined as the hard-core. If we compare the attitudes of that hard-core on major issues with those of the professed early backers of McCarthy who subsequently supported Wallace, the differences are usually extreme. The McCarthy-Wallace group was against desegregation, in favor of an increased military effort in Vietnam, and was highly indignant with the situation in the nation where "law and order" was concerned (see Table 4). People supporting McCarthy to the bitter end took opposite positions on all of these major issues. Similarly, the winnowing down of the McCarthy support operated very sharply along demographic lines. Among non-Southern white Democrats who reported a pre-convention McCarthy preference, for example, the hard-core that remained enthusiastic about McCarthy through to the actual election were 60% of college background, whereas, of those whose ardor cooled, only 18% had had any connection with college.

In short, then, it is evident again that among Democrats particularly, McCarthy was an initial rallying point for voters of all policy persuasions who were thoroughly displeased with the Johnson administration. When the Wallace candidacy crystallized and his issue advocacies became more broadly known, that portion of the discontented to whom he spoke most directly flocked to him. Hence it seems very doubtful that Humphrey would have won many votes from this group even if McCarthy had lent the Vice President his personal support in a whole-hearted fashion. The

Table 4 · Issue Differences among Whites Preferring McCarthy as the Democratic
Nominee, According to November Preferences
for McCarthy or Wallace

		McCARTHY "HARD CORE"[a]	VOTED WALLACE[b]
"Are you in favor of desegregation, strict segregation, or something in between?"	*Desegregation*	79%	7%
	in Between	21	50
	Segregation	0	43
		100%	100%
		(24)	(14)
"Do you think the (Chicago) police (at the Democratic Convention) used too much force, the right amount of force, or not enough force with the demonstrators?"	*Too Much Force*	91%	0%
	Right Amount	9	50
	Not Enough	0	50
		100%	100%
		(23)	(14)
"Which of the following do you think we should do now in Vietnam: pull out of Vietnam entirely, keep our soldiers in Vietnam but try to end the fighting, or take a stronger stand even if it means invading North Vietnam?"	*Pull Out*	50%	7%
	Status Quo	50	7
	Stronger Stand	9	86
		100%	100%
		(24)	(13)

[a]This column is limited to whites whose pre-convention favorite was Eugene McCarthy and who continued to give him their top rating after the November election.

[b]It is to be emphasized that this column includes *only* those Wallace voters who said that in the spring of 1968 they had hoped Eugene McCarthy would win the Democratic nomination. This fact explains the small case numbers. However, in view of the relative homogeneity of respondents in the table—all are whites who reported a pre-convention McCarthy preference and most happen in addition to be nominal identifiers of the Democratic Party—the disparities in issue position are the more impressive.

main motivation of this group was to register its disgust with incumbent leaders concerning civil rights advances, timidity in Vietnam and outbreaks of social disorder. It may well be that by September, with the far more congenial candidacy of Wallace available, Senator McCarthy would already have become a relatively negative reference point for this two-thirds of his early support, especially if he had joined forces with Humphrey. Therefore if we are to search for votes withheld from Humphrey because of the kinds of discontent McCarthy helped to crystallize, they are much more likely to be found among the McCarthy hard-core.

We persist in looking for such withheld votes, not simply because of rumors they existed, but also because there are rather tangible signs in the data that they were present in 1968. Such votes could take any one of four major alternative forms: they could be located among citizens who went to the polls but did not vote for president; they could be reflected in votes for minor party candidates; they could involve staying at home on election day; or they could take the form of votes spitefully transferred to Humphrey's chief rival, Mr. Nixon. Easiest to establish as "withheld votes" are the first two categories. Although their incidence is naturally very limited, both types can be discerned in the sample and do occur in conjunction with strong enthusiasm for McCarthy. Projected back to the nation's electorate, perhaps as much as a half-million votes are represented here, lying primarily outside the South. This is only a faint trace when sprinkled across the political map of the nation, however, and taken alone would probably have made little or no difference in the distribution of votes from the electoral college.

It is more difficult to say that specific instances of abstinence from any voting in 1968, or "defection" to Richard Nixon, reflect an abiding loyalty to McCarthy that Humphrey could not replace, and would not have occurred but for the McCarthy intrusion. There is a faint edge of non-voting that looks suspiciously of this sort, but it is again very limited: most ardent McCarthy fans were too politically involved to have thrown away a chance to vote at other levels of office. Far more numerous are the defections to Nixon on the part of voters of liberal and Democratic predispositions, who reported sympathy toward McCarthy. Here, however, it is difficult to be confident that McCarthy made any necessary contribution to the decision equation: the situation itself might have soured these people sufficiently, McCarthy or no. Nevertheless, when one begins to add together putative "withheld votes" from the preceding three categories one does not need to factor in any very large proportion of these defectors to arrive at a total large enough to have provided Humphrey with a tiny majority in the electoral college, without requiring any gross maldistribution of these new-found popular votes outside the South.

We should reiterate, of course, that any such hypothetical reconstructions must be taken with a grain of salt. If McCarthy had embraced Humphrey on the final night in Chicago, not all of his most fervent supporters would necessarily have followed suit, and Humphrey would have needed most of them for victory. Or if Humphrey had catered more dramatically to the McCarthy wing in terms of Vietnam policy after the election, he might have suffered losses of much greater proportion to Wallace on his right, for there is simply no question but that Democrats sharing the circle of ideas espoused by Wallace outnumbered the Democrats attuned to McCarthy by a very wide margin—perhaps as great as ten to one. Moreover, it is appropriate to keep in mind our earlier suggestion that the Wallace intrusion hurt Nixon's vote more than Humphrey's: if we now remove Wallace as well as McCarthy from the scene, the net result might remain a Nixon victory.

However all this may be, it seems probable that the entire roster of prominent Democratic candidates—McCarthy, Wallace, Kennedy, Mc-Govern—who were in their various ways opposing the administration, must have contributed cumulatively to Humphrey's problem of retaining the loyalty of fellow Democrats in the electorate. Certainly the failure of liberal Republican leaders to rally around the Goldwater candidacy in 1964, itself an unusual departure from tradition, had contributed to the Republican disaster of that year. 1968 provided something of a mirror image, and the result was an inordinate movement of the electorate between the two consultations.

III. The "Responsible Electorate" of 1968

In describing the current of discontent that swirled around the Democratic party and the White House in 1968, we indicated that disgruntled Democrats rather indiscriminately supported McCarthy in the earliest primaries, but soon began to sort themselves into those staying with McCarthy versus those shifting to Nixon or Wallace, according to their more precise policy grievances on the major issues of Vietnam, civil rights, and the problem of "law and order." By the time of the election, the sorting had become remarkably clean: in particular, differences in issue position between Wallace supporters and what we have called the McCarthy hard-core are impressive in magnitude.

Even more generally, 1968 seems to be a prototypical case of the election that does not produce many changes of policy preferences but does permit electors to sort themselves and the candidates into groups of substantial homogeneity on matters of public policy. This trend over the course of the campaign calls to mind the posthumous contention of V. O. Key, in *The Responsible Electorate,* that the mass electorate is a good deal less irrational, ill-informed or sheep-like than it had become fashionable to suppose. He presented empirical materials to develop a counter-image of "an electorate moved by concern about central and relevant questions of public policy, of governmental performance, and of executive personality." He argued that in a general way voters behaved rationally and responsibly, or at least as rationally and responsibly as could be expected in view of the pap they were frequently fed by contending politicians, while recognizing in the same breath that contentions of this unequivocal nature were necessarily overstatements.

To our point of view, Key's general thesis represented a welcome corrective on some earlier emphases, but his findings were hardly as discontinuous with earlier work as was often presumed, and the "corrective" nature of his argument has itself become badly exaggerated at numerous points. We cannot begin to examine here the many facets of his thesis that deserve comment. However, several features of the 1968 campaign seem to us to demonstrate admirably the importance of the Key corrective, while at the very same time illustrating vividly the perspective in which that corrective must be kept.

It is obvious, as Key himself recognized, that flat assertions about the electorate being rational or not are of scant value. In New Hampshire, as we have observed earlier, Democrats exasperated at Johnson's lack of success with the Vietnam War voted for Eugene McCarthy as an alternative. The relationship between this disapproval and the vote decision is exactly the type of empirical finding that Key musters in profusion from a sequence of seven presidential elections as his main proof of voter rationality and responsibility. In the New Hampshire case, however, we might probe the data a little farther to discover that more often than not, McCarthy voters were upset that Johnson had failed to scourge Vietnam a good deal more vigorously with American military might, which is to say they took a position diametrically opposed to that of their chosen candidate. This realization might shake our confidence somewhat in the preceding "proof" of voter rationality. But then we push our analysis still another step and find that many of the New Hampshire people fuming about Vietnam in a hawkish mood voted for McCarthy without having any idea of where he stood on the matter. Hence while they may have voted directly counter to their own policy preferences, they at least did not know this was what they were doing, so the charge of irrationality may be a bit ungenerous. In the most anemic sense of "rationality," one that merely implies people have perceived reasons for their behavior, these votes perhaps remain "rational."

However, when we reflect on the rather intensive coverage given by the national mass media to Eugene McCarthy's dissenting position on Vietnam for many months before the New Hampshire primary, and consider how difficult it must have been to avoid knowledge of the fact, particularly if one had more than the most casual interest in the Vietnam question, we might continue to wonder how lavishly we should praise the electorate as "responsible." Here, as at so many other points, pushing beyond the expression of narrow and superficial attitudes in the mass public to the cognitive texture which underlies the attitudes is a rather disillusioning experience. It is regrettable that none of the data presented in *The Responsible Electorate* can be probed in this fashion.

Key was interested in showing that the public reacted in a vital way to central policy concerns, at least as selected by the contending political factions, and was not driven mainly by dark Freudian urges, flock instinct, or worse still, the toss of a coin. With much of this we agree wholeheartedly. In addition, to put the discussion in a slightly different light, let us imagine, in a vein not unfamiliar from the literature of the 1950's, that voting decisions in the American electorate might be seen as a function of reactions to party, issue and candidate personality factors. Let us imagine furthermore that research suggests that these determinants typically have relative weights in our presidential elections of 60 for the party factor, and 40 divided between the issue and candidate determinants. The exact figures are, of course, quite fanciful but the rough magnitudes continue to be familiar. Since classical assumptions about voting behavior have attributed overwhelming weight to the issue factor, it is scarcely surprising that investigative attention shifts heavily away from that factor to the less expected party and candidate influences. If the issue factor draws comment at all, the finding of greatest interest is its surprisingly diluted role.

It is at this point that the Key volume exerts its most useful influence. Key points out that there *is*, after all, an issue factor, and he develops an analytic format which dramatizes the role that issue reactions do play. This dramatic heightening is achieved by focussing attention on voters who are shifting their vote from one party to the other over a pair of elections. If we set for ourselves the explanatory chore of understanding why the change which occurs moves in the direction it did, it is patently evident that the party factor—which merely explains the abiding finding that "standpatters" persistently outnumber "changers" by factors usually greater than four—is to be set aside as irrelevant. If this in turn leaves candidate and issue factors sharing the explanatory burden, our sense of the relative importance of the issue factor is, of course, radically increased, even though it is our question that has changed, rather than anything about the empirical lay of the land. Key was quite explicit in his desire to explain movement and change in the electorate, rather than voting behavior in a more general sense, and there is no gainsaying the fact that from many points of view it is indeed the change—marginal gains and losses— which forms the critical part of the story of elections.

In our analyses of such changes in the national vote over the course of presidential elections in the 1950's and 1960's we have been impressed with the magnitude of the effects introduced as new candidates focus on different issues of public policy, and as external events give particular candidate-issue intersections greater salience for the nation. However, 1968 provides an opportunity to examine relative weights of party, candidate and issue factors under more varied circumstances than United States presidential elections usually proffer. We have talked above for illustrative purposes as though there were "standard" relative weights that would pertain for these three factors in some situation-free way. This is of course not the case: we can imagine many kinds of elections which would vastly shift the weights of such factors, if indeed they can be defined at all.

The Wallace movement is a good case in point. By Key's definition nobody who voted for Wallace could have been a "standpatter": all must be classed as "changers." Therefore party identification as a motivating factor accounting for attraction to Wallace is forced back to zero, and any variance to be understood must have its roots distributed between Wallace's attraction as a personality and the appeal of the issue positions that he advocated.

In point of fact, the Wallace candidacy was reacted to by the public as an *issue* candidacy, a matter which our data make clear in several ways. For example, about half of the reasons volunteered by our respondents for favorable feelings toward Wallace had to do with positions he was taking on current issues; only a little more than a quarter of the reactions supporting either of the two conventional candidates were cast in this mode. Still more noteworthy is the relative purity of the issue feelings among the Wallace clientele where the major controversies of 1968 were concerned. Among the *whites* who voted for one of the two major candidates, only 10% favored continued segregation rather than desegregation or "something in between;" among Wallace voters, all of whom were white, almost 40% wanted segregation. Where the issue of "law and order" was concerned, a substantial portion of the voters felt that Mayor Daley's police had used about the right amount of force in quelling the Chicago demonstrations. However, among white voters for Nixon or Humphrey, the remainder of the opinion was fairly evenly split between criticizing the police for using too much force or too little, with a small majority (55%) favoring the latter "tough line." Among Wallace voters, the comparable ratio was 87–13 favoring a tougher policy. Or again, 36% of white voters for the conventional parties felt we should "take a stronger stand (in Vietnam) even if it means invading North Vietnam." Among Wallace voters, the figure was 67%. Much more generally speaking, it may be observed that all Wallace voters were exercised by strong discontents in at least one of these three primary domains, and most were angry about more than one. Wallace was a "backlash" candidate, and there is no question but that the positions communicated to the public and accounted for his electoral support in a very primary sense. The pattern of correlations between issue positions and the vote for these "changers" would support Key's thesis of a "rational" and "responsible" electorate even more impressively than most of the data he found for earlier elections.

Another way of organizing these preference materials helps to illuminate even more sharply the contrast between the bases of Wallace support and those of the conventional candidates. It will be recalled that all respondents were asked to give an affective evaluation of each of the three candidates taken separately, along with other aspirants. If we examine the pattern of correlations between issue positions and the ratings of Humphrey, Nixon and Wallace, we capture gradations of enthusiasm, indifference and hostility felt toward each man instead of the mere vote threshold, and we can explore the antecedents or correlates of the variations in sentiment toward the individual candidates.

Where the ratings of Wallace given by whites are concerned, patterns vary somewhat between the South and non-South, but substantial correlations with issue positions appear everywhere. In the South, the most generic question of civil rights policy shows a relation of .49 (gamma) with Wallace reactions; the most generic question on "law and order" shows a .39; and the central Vietnam policy question shows a relationship of .30. Party identification, however, shows a relation of only .04. Other ancillary questions probing more specific aspects of policy feelings in these areas vary around the most generic items somewhat, but tend to show fairly similar magnitudes of relationship. Outside the South, patterns are a little less sharp but remain unequivocal. Instead of the above correlations of .49, .39, and .30 in the main issue domains, the figures are .25 (civil rights), .27 (law and order), and .25 (Vietnam). The relationship of party identification to Wallace ratings among whites, however, is .01. Thus it is true in both regions that party identification is entirely dwarfed by any of several issue positions in predicting reactions to Wallace among whites, and in terms of "variance accounted for" the differences between issues and party would best be expressed in terms of *orders of magnitude*.

Differences that are almost as sharp turn up in the relationships surrounding the ratings of Nixon and Humphrey. Here, however, everything is exactly reversed: it is *party* that towers over all other predictors, and the central 1968 issues tend to give rather diminutive relationships. Thus comparable correlations (gammas) between partisanship and candidate ratings all run between .36 and .44, varying only slightly by region and man. Where Nixon is concerned, the average correlation values for issue items in the three main domains emphasized in the 1968 election never get as high as .10, and fall as low as .01, with the central tendency about .05. Where Humphrey is concerned, somewhat higher values are observed, varying between .05 and .25 according to the region and the domain. Moreover, there is another issue domain not hitherto cited in which average values over three items for Humphrey considerably outstrip the Wallace correlation in both North and South. Significantly, this is the domain of items concerning governmental social welfare activities that one might associate with the period running from the New Deal through the 1950's. Nevertheless, averaging correlations across all of these issue domains (the obsolescing as well as the three most salient in 1968) suggests that party identification still accounts for three to five times as much variance in Humphrey ratings as does the average issue among the 18 issues posed in the study. These correlation patterns are summarized by region in Table 5.

Such dramatic comparisons between types of support for Wallace on one hand and the conventional candidates on the other may be perplexing to the casual reader who is keeping the thesis of V. O. Key in mind. After all, it is the pattern of Wallace support that shows the kind of strong issue orientation Key sought to demonstrate, whereas evaluations of both Humphrey and Nixon seem to show a strong factor of traditional party allegiance suffocating most issue concerns into relative obscurity. Yet the span of time Key's data covered limited him almost completely to observa-

Table 5 · Correlations Between Issue Positions, Partisanship and Affective Ratings of the Major Candidates (Whites Only)[a]

ISSUE DOMAIN:	NON-SOUTH			SOUTH		
	Humphrey	Nixon	Wallace	Humphrey	Nixon	Wallace
A. Civil Rights (6 or 7 items)[b]	.17	.09	.27	.24	.08	.41
B. Law and Order (2 items)	.25	.05	.27	.19	.01	.35
C. Vietnam (2 items)	.05	.03	.23	.14	.02	.26
D. Cold War (4 items)	.12	.11	.15	.16	.05	- .28
E. Social Welfare (2 or 3 items)[b]	.22	.20	.09	.26	.13	.10
F. Federal Gov't Too Powerful? (1 item)	.37	.18	.17	.49	.13	.15
Sum: 18 issue items	.19	.10	.20	.22	.07	.31
Sum: Three Major 1968 Issue Domains (A,B,C)	.16	.07	.26	.22	.07	.37
Partisanship: (3 items)	.47	.47	.04	.39	.36	.03

[a]Cell entries are average absolute values of gamma ordinal correlations between items of the types listed in the rows and affective ratings of the candidates noted in the columns.

[b]An item having to do with the role of the federal government in aid to local education was considered a social welfare item outside the South, but a civil rights issue within that region.

tion of races of the routine Humphrey-Nixon type. Did these earlier two-party races look more like the Wallace patterns for some unknown reason?

The answer, of course, is very probably not. However, if we set the Wallace phenomenon in 1968 aside and limit our attention in the Key fashion to two contrasting groups of "changers" between the 1964 and 1968 election (Johnson to Nixon; Goldwater to Humphrey) we can show correlations with issue differences which look very much like those presented in cross-tabulations by Key for earlier elections: some strong, some weak, but nearly always "in the right direction." There are, to be sure, other problems of interpretation surrounding such correlations that one would need to thrash out before accepting the Key evidence fully. But our principal point here is the simple one that even with Wallace analytically discarded from the 1968 scene, the rest of the 1968 data seem perfectly compatible with the data Key used. The only reason there may seem to be a discontinuity, then, is due to the different nature of the question being asked by Key which, by focussing on marginal change from election to election, effectively defines party loyalty out of the explanation and correspondingly opens the way for greater orienting weight for issues.

It is because the change in vote division from election to election is so critical that V. O. Key's contribution is a welcome corrective. On the other hand, the configurations of 1968 data we have summarized here help to put the contribution into perspective. The patterns of Wallace support show how empirical data *can* look when issues play a strongly orienting role. The contrasts between these patterns and those generated by routine two-party politics may help to suggest why investigators have tended to be more impressed by the feeble role of issues than by their strength.

The lessons to be drawn are several. One is a simple point of methodology. It has been suggested upon occasion in the past that relationships between issue positions and voting choice turn out to be as pallid as they usually are because investigators fail to ask the right questions or word them in confusing ways. We feel that improvement in these matters is always possible. However, we have seen that exactly the same issue items which continue to look pallid in accounting for assessments of Humphrey and Nixon blaze forth into rather robust correlations where Wallace is concerned. Hence we conclude that poor item choice scarcely accounts for past findings.

Another lesson is more substantive. Some past findings have been to our mind "overinterpreted" as implying that issues are poorly linked to voting preferences because of innate and hence incorrigible cognitive deficiencies suffered by the mass electorate in the United States.[2] Merely the

[2] We much prefer an interpretation which hinges on a general inattention which is endemic because information costs are relatively high where little information is already in hand, and the stakes are rarely seen as being very large. While such a "condition" is likely to persist in mass electorates, there is nothing about it which is immutable given the proper convergence of circumstances.

Wallace data taken alone would suffice to show, exactly as Key argued, that the public can relate policy controversies to its own estimates of the world and vote accordingly. The fact that it does not display this propensity on any large scale very often invites more careful spelling out of the conditions under which it will or will not.

It seems clear from the 1968 data that one of the cardinal limiting conditions is the "drag" of inertia represented by habitual party loyalties: as soon as features of the situation limit or neutralize the relevance of such a factor, issue evaluations play a more vital role. Much research has shown that partisanship is fixed early in life and tends to endure. As the individual moves through the life cycle, old political controversies die away and new ones arise toward which at least some individuals crystallize opinions. While the parties try to lead this new opinion formation among their faithful, and probably succeed on a modest scale, there are many independent sources of such opinion for the citizen. The average citizen either does not know his party's position well enough to be influenced on many matters, or if he knows, frequently resists the influence. As a result, policy opinions are very loosely or anachronistically linked to party preference at any point in time. But in the moment of truth in the polling booth, party allegiance seems the most relevant cue for many voters *if conditions permit it to be used.*

Another type of condition which mediates the links between citizen position on issues and voting choice is the "objective" degree of difference between parties or candidates with respect to policy controversy, or the clarity with which any objective difference gets communicated to the populace. In every United States election there are accusations from one quarter or another that the two conventional parties provide no more than "tweedledee" and "tweedledum" candidates. However, these accusations as aired in the public media rose to something of a crescendo in 1968 from both the Wallace and the McCarthy perspectives. And even as measured a source as the *New York Times* noted wryly that it would take no more than the deletion of two or three codicils to make the official 1968 campaign platforms of the Democratic and Republican parties into utterly undistinguishable documents. If the main discriminable difference between Humphrey and Nixon began and ended with the party label then it would certainly not be surprising that the public sorted itself into voting camps by party allegiance and little more, save where Wallace was concerned. In this case, the public would be limited to exactly that "echo chamber" role which Key ascribed to it.

As a matter of pure logic, nobody can deny that policy differentiation between parties is likely to be a precondition for meaningful relationships between policy feelings and partisan voting decisions. Our only problem here is to evaluate whether the party/issue data configurations surrounding Humphrey and Nixon are the obvious result of some lack of policy difference peculiar to 1968, or represent instead some more abiding feature of presidential voting in the United States. Unfortunately, there is no obvious way to arrive at an objective measurement of "degree of party difference." Perhaps the closest approximation is to ask the public how clear the differences appear to be. Nevertheless, since some people invariably feel party differences are big and others feel they are non-existent, even this approach leaves one without reference points as to "how big is big" where reports of this kind are concerned, except inasmuch as trends in such reports can be observed over periods of time. In this light, it can be said while reports of "important differences" between the Democrats and the Republicans were slightly fewer in 1968 than in 1964 (the year of Goldwater's "choice, not an echo"), they show a reasonable parity with such reports for 1952 and 1960. Hence in the public eye, at least, differences between what the major parties stand for were not lacking in unusual degree in 1968.

It may be useful to note that whereas we have labelled the Wallace effort in 1968 an "issue candidacy" from the point of view of the electorate, we have not said that it was an ideological candidacy from that same point of view. From other viewpoints of political analysis, it was of course just that: a movement of the "radical right." Moreover, with occasional exceptions, data on issue positions show Wallace voters to differ from Humphrey voters in the same "conservative" direction that Nixon voters do, only much more so. Therefore by customary definitions, not only the leadership of the radical right, but the rank-and-file espoused clearly "rightist" positions of a sort which were frequently extreme, on highly specific questions of public policy.[3]

Yet there was an element of ideological self-recognition present among Goldwater voters in 1964 that was simply lacking among Wallace voters in 1968. One measure of ideological location which we use involves the respondent in rating the terms "liberal" and "conservative." If the respondent gives the highest possible score to the stimulus "liberal" and the lowest possible score to "conservative," he is rated as the most extreme liberal, with a score of 100. In the reverse case, the extreme conservative receives a score of zero. At 50 are clustered individuals who either do not recognize these terms, or give the same affective rating to both. In 1964 there was a rather considerable relationship between such a measure and response to Goldwater, in the expected direction. In 1968, the same scale showed only a very limited correlation with reactions toward Wallace (gammas of .13 and .09 among whites within the South and outside,

---

[3]This was not true across every issue domain. The most notable exception was in the area of social welfare issues such as medicare and full employment guarantees, on which issues Wallace voters were significantly more "liberal" than Nixon voters, and almost matched the liberalism of Humphrey voters. This admixture was of course familiar in Wallace's frequent appeals to the underdog and the working man, in the tradition of Southern populism.

Table 6 · Ideological Responses of White Voters for Different Presidential
Candidates in 1964 and 1968[a]

	1964		1968		
	Johnson	*Goldwater*	*Humphrey*	*Nixon*	*Wallace*
Non-South	51.8	39.9	51.8	43.4	44.9
South	49.6	35.9	49.5	40.7	41.9

[a]The cell entry registers the mean value shown on the ideological scale described in the text for white
voters for each of the candidates listed. A high value indicates that liberalism is held in relative favor: a low
value means that conservatism is preferred.

respectively). Indeed, as Table 6 shows, in both political regions of the
country Wallace voters were more favorable to the "liberal" label than
Nixon voters! Thus while Wallace supporters were entirely distinctive in
their "backlash" feelings on public policy, they were much less ideologically attuned to a left-right spectrum than their Goldwater predecessors.

Although Wallace supporters did not seem anywhere nearly as distinctive in terms of ideological measures as they did on specific issues, they did
show some moderate trends in terms of other more generic political attitudes. In particular, various measures bearing on discontent with the re-
sponsiveness and probity of government show correlations with ratings
given by whites to Wallace, and are related but with opposite signs to
ratings of the "establishment" candidates, Humphrey and Nixon. Since
Wallace was more of a mainstream candidate in the South than in the rest of
the country, it might be thought that his appeal in that region might depend
less strictly on this syndrome of political alienation than it would elsewhere.
However, these relationships are stronger and more pervasive in the South,
and seem only weakly mirrored in other parts of the nation. Within the
South, white attitudes toward Wallace are quite sharply associated with our
scales of political efficacy and cynicism about government. People drawn to
Wallace tended to feel they had little capacity to influence government, and
expressed distrust of the morality and efficiency of political leadership.
These correlations reach a peak on items where the referent is most explicitly "the federal government in Washington," and it is plain that Southern
voters felt more or less attracted to Wallace in the degree that they responded to his complaints that Washington bureaucrats had been persistently and unjustly bullying the South with particular respect to civil rights.
Since there is no methodological need for it to be true, it is of particular
interest that ratings of Humphrey show as substantial correlations in the
opposing direction, in the South and other regions as well: people responding warmly to Humphrey had quite sanguine views of government.

All told, then, a sense of political alienation was a rather visible correlate of a sorting of the citizenry away from the conventional candidates
toward Wallace, as was certainly to be expected and necessary if terms

such as "backlash" are relevant. At the same time, it is worth keeping the apparent temporal sequences clear. The data suggest that Southern whites have become alienated with government because prior attitudes, particularly racial ones have been contradictory to national policy for nearly twenty years. Thus there is a readiness to condemn government on a much broader front, and Wallace appealed in obvious ways to this readiness in the South. Outside the South Wallace also articulated the same array of specific grievances and received a clear response. However, the evidence suggests that any resonance he might have achieved in terms of a more generic condemnation of government, while present, was relatively limited.

IV. The Social Bases of Wallace Support

A variety of facts already cited about the Wallace movement of 1968 makes clear that while there was some modest overlap in support for Goldwater in 1964 and Wallace in 1968, it was at best a weak correlation and the Wallace clientele differed quite notably from Goldwater's. Thus, for example, almost exactly half of our 1968 Wallace voters who had participated in the 1964 election reported that they had voted for Johnson. Or again, we have seen that the majority of Wallace voters, like the electorate as a whole, was identified with the Democratic party, while it is obvious that most Goldwater voters were Republican identifiers. Similarly, we have just noted that the Wallace movement had a much less clear ideological focus among its sympathizers than marked Goldwater supporters in 1964.

This discrepancy in clientele may seem perplexing. After all, in the terms of conventional analysis in political sociology both candidates were "darlings of the radical right." Yet the limited degree of overlap between Goldwater and Wallace voters is confirmed in equally impressive fashion when one compares their social backgrounds or even their simplest demographic characteristics. Among Goldwater voters, for example, women both South and non-South showed the same slight majority they enjoy in the electorate; Wallace voters in the South showed a similar balance, but elsewhere were rather markedly (almost 60–40) male. The Goldwater vote had been much more urban, while the Wallace vote was relatively rural small-town, particularly in the South. Outside the South, the age distribution of Wallace voters departed markedly from that shown by Goldwater in 1964, with the proportion under 35 being about twice as great and that over 65 only half as large.

The well-publicized appeal of Wallace to the unionized laboring man is clearly reflected in our data: outside the South, the proportion of white union members preferring Wallace over the other major candidates was more than three times as great as it was within households having no unionized members (19% to 6%); even in the South, where other appeals were present and the unionization of labor is more limited, the contrast between the preferences of union members and non-union households remains dramatic (52% to 28% giving top preference to Wallace over the conventional candidates). Indeed, in both regions the occupational center of gravity of Wallace popularity was clearly among white skilled workers. Nationwide, only about 10% of the Wallace vote was contributed by the professional and managerial strata, whereas persons of these occupations had given Goldwater almost half of his vote (46%). Needless to say, the proportion of unionized labor supporting Goldwater was very low. Along with these class differences, marked discrepancies in educational background can be taken for granted. In the South, one-third of Wallace's support came from whites with no more than grade school education, while the national figure for Goldwater was 13%. The proportion of voters of college experience backing Goldwater was about double that found voting for Wallace either in the South or elsewhere.

All of these comparisons help to underscore the major disparities in the social bases of support for Goldwater and Wallace, despite the apparent common policy ground of the relatively extreme right. While one should not lose track of the fact that there was a small and systematic overlap in clientele, it is abundantly clear that neither candidate exhausted the potential support for a severely conservative program in matters of civil rights, law and order or Vietnam. In a very real sense, it can be seen that Wallace was a poor man's Goldwater. As we suggested at the time, Goldwater pitched his campaign on an ideological plane which rather escaped some members of the electorate who might otherwise have found his positions congenial. Wallace's perfectly direct appeal to citizens of this latter description, along with the undercurrent of populism alien to the Goldwater conservatism, apparently sufficed to put off some of the Arizona senator's more well-to-do supporters. The Goldwater support was drawn from a relatively urbane and sophisticated conservatism; Wallace appealed to many similar instincts, but the style was folksy and tailored to the common man.

In a significant way, too, Wallace remained a regional candidate despite his discovery that he could win more than scattered votes in the North and his consequent presence on every state's ballot. Over half of his popular votes came from the states of the Confederacy. Everything, from his lack of political experience at a federal level to his marked Southern accent, suggested a parochial relevance that had rarely been salient where Goldwater was concerned. While electoral maps leave no doubt as to the regional nature of the response, sample survey data show that even these visible effects have been diluted by inter-regional migration. Thus, for

Table 7 · Reactions of Whites to Wallace by Region of Socialization and Residence

		RESPONDENT NOW RESIDES . . .		
		Outside the South	Within the South	Total
RESPONDENT GREW UP . . .	Outside the South	26.2[a] (757)	26.5 (51)	26.2 (808)
	Within the South	34.7 (53)	50.0 (281)	48.5 (334)
	Total	26.7 (810)	46.3 (332)	

[a]Cell entries are mean values of ratings on a scale from 0 (hostility) to 100 (sympathy) accorded to George Wallace by white respondents of the types indicated.

example, while much has been written about the Wallace appeal in various European ethnic communities of Northern cities, little has been said about the "American ethnic group" of Southern white migrants, most of whom are blue-collar and frequently in a position to take special pleasure in the spectacle of a Southern compatriot coming north to give the Yankees what for. Our data indicate that Wallace drew over 14% of the vote from these migrants, and less than 7% otherwise outside the South. On the other hand, the significant stream of migration of Yankees into the South, the political implications of which we have described elsewhere, provided something of a barrier to further Wallace successes. Heavily Republican in a non-Southern sense and now constituting better than one-seventh of white voters in the region, these migrants were even less interested in voting for Wallace than were Southern whites in the North, and gave the former Alabama governor only 10% of their vote while their native Southen white colleagues were casting almost one vote in every three for him.

Table 7 summarizes the affective ratings given Wallace by our respondents according to the region in which they grew up as well as their current region of residence. It is rather clear that the region of socialization is a more critical determinant of these assessments of Wallace than is the region of current residence. Moreover, it is easy to show that regional differences in correlates of Wallace preference also follow lines of socialization rather than those of current residence. For example, we have noted that Wallace's appeal to women outside the South was rather limited. For white women of Southern background living outside the South, the response was much as it was in the South. Setting the migrants aside, the ratio among white Wallace enthusiasts outside the South is even more sharply masculine.

It is not our purpose here to do more than briefly summarize the social and demographic correlates of Wallace preferences, for numerous other essays are being prepared to treat the subject in detail. However, one correlate which has frequently surprised observers deserves more extended discussion, both because of its practical significance and because of its high relevance to some of the theoretical issues uniquely illuminated by the 1968 election. We speak of the relationship between the Wallace movement and the generational cleavages so evident at other points in data from the presidential campaign.

It would seem self-evident that Wallace's primary appeal to traditional and even obsolescing American values, as well as his caustic treatment of the rebels of the younger generation, would have brought him votes that were even more heavily clustered among the elderly than those drawn by Goldwater in 1964. We have already noted that Wallace took issue positions that were communicated with unusual clarity, and that these positions determined in unusual degree the nature of his clientele. On almost every issue of nearly a score surveyed, the position characteristic of Wallace voters in our sample is also the position associated with older citizens, where there is any age correlation at all. Hence it is somewhat surprising to discover that among white Southerners there is actually a faint *negative* correlation between age and a Wallace vote. And it is perplexing indeed to discover that outside the South voting for Wallace occurred very disproportionately among the young. For example, Wallace captured less than 3% of the vote among people over 70 outside the South, but 13% of those under 30, with a regular gradient connecting these two extremes. One of the major ironies of the election, then, was that Wallace made his appeal to the old but mainly received the vote of the young.

However, a whole cluster of empirical theory has grown up in recent years which, without any particular knowledge of the Wallace platform, would predict that such a third-party candidate would draw votes primarily from the young in just this way. It is established, for example, that repeated commitments of votes to a political party tend to increase the strength of psychological identification with that party, and it is an immediate corollary that voters of the older generation are more fixed in their party loyalties than are relatively new voters. It follows with equal logic that when some new candidate or *ad hoc* party arises to challenge the conventional parties of a system, it should have relative difficulty making headway among the older generation, even though it might have natural appeals to such voters.

We have never had a chance to test this somewhat non-obvious expectation, although reconstructions of the fall of the Weimar Republic have always suggested that voters for the Nazi Party in its culminating surge were very disproportionately drawn from the youngest cohorts of the German electorate. Therefore the age distribution of Wallace support has been of uncommon interest to us. When issue appeals of a rather vital sort conflict with long-established party loyalties, as they must have in Wallace's case for many older voters, which factor is likely to exert most influence on the voting decision? The apparent difficulties older people had in voting for Wallace, particularly outside the South where he was a less "legitimate" Democrat and hence a less conventional candidate, seem to provide a rather clear answer.

However, if this interpretation is correct a variety of ancillary effects should be discernible in the 1968 data. For example, if prior party identification is truly the critical source of resistance to a Wallace vote simply because of the disloyalty implied, the prediction that the young would vote more heavily for him need not mean the young have any monopoly on admiration for him. Indeed, one could almost predict that the older generation should have shown more warmth of feeling toward Wallace per vote allotted him than would be true of the younger generation, simply because of the "artificial" inhibition on the vote represented by greater loyalty to a conventional party. Moreover, since strength of identification is measured explicitly in this study, it is of importance to show that it does indeed vary positively as in times past with age; that such identification with a conventional party is indeed negatively associated with voting for Wallace; and that the tendency of young persons to vote for Wallace did co-occur with weak conventional loyalties.

All of these empirical expectations are borne out, and usually in rather handsome fashion. First while the young voted more heavily for Wallace, the correlation between age and affective rating of him as a political figure is non-existent. Second, the old in 1968 were, as always, much more strongly identified with one of the two conventional parties than the young. Third, defection from a conventional party to vote for Wallace was indeed strongly related to degree of party identification, particularly outside the South: the probability of a Wallace vote doubles there as one moves each step from strong through weak to "independent" or leaning identifiers. And finally, when strength of partisanship is controlled, the sharp inverse correlation between age and a Wallace vote outside the South is very nearly wiped out; within the South where it was a somewhat ragged relationship to begin with, it completely disappears or if anything, shows a slight reversal as though Wallace might in fact have had some extra drawing power for the older voter, aside from the complications posed by other allegiances.

This nest of relationships holds more than detached clinical interest in several directions. The reader concerned about the future of the Wallace movement as an electoral force on the American scene is likely to be interested in the fact that the clientele was young rather than aging. In one sense this is a pertinent datum and in another it is not. It is unquestionable that a Wallace candidacy in 1972 has a brighter future than it would have if its 1968 legions were dying out of the population. Nonetheless, the whole thrust of our argument above is that the Wallace movement is not in any special good fortune to have drawn young voters: this will be true of virtually any new party entering the lists in an old party system, and but for the habits which kept older voters with the conventional parties, the initial Wallace vote would probably have been significantly larger. Still more to the point, we would hazard that the future of the Wallace movement as a third party will be determined more by Wallace's personal plans and the organizational aspirations of his entourage on one hand, and by the evolution of events affecting national frustrations on the other, than by the age level of its 1968 voters.

Nevertheless, the youthful nature of Wallace's clientele provides a further irony to the backdrop of generational cleavage reflected in the 1968 campaign. For while such a cleavage was genuine and intense, as some of our earlier data have witnessed, one of the most important yet hidden lines of cleavage split the younger generation itself. Although privileged young college students angry at Vietnam and the shabby treatment of the Negro saw themselves as sallying forth to do battle against a corrupted and cynical generation, a more head-on confrontation at the polls, if a less apparent one, was with their own age mates who had gone from high school off to the factory instead of college, and who were appalled by the collapse of patriotism and respect for the law that they saw about them. Outside of the election period, when verbal articulateness and leisure for political activism count most heavily, it was the college share of the younger generation—or at least its politicized vanguard—that was most prominent as a political force. At the polls, however, the game shifts to "one man, one vote," and this vanguard is numerically swamped even within its own generation.

This lack of numerical strength is no intrinsic handicap: any cadre of opinion leadership is small in number. However, it must successfully appeal to some potential rank and file, and it certainly cannot risk becoming a negative reference point for large numbers of people if it expects to operate in a medium involving popular elections. In part because of collegiate naiveté concerning forms of dissent that maintain sympathy,[4] and in part because the public image of constructive efforts by the many can be so rapidly colored by a few whose needs are mainly to antagonize as much of society as possible, this vanguard became a negative reference point for

---

[4]The American public seems to have a very low tolerance for unusual or "showy" forms of political dissent. Responses to an extended set of items in the 1968 study on the subject are appalling from a civil libertarian point of view. At the most acceptable end of the continuum of "ways for people to show their disapproval or disagreement with governmental policies and actions" we asked about "taking part in protest meetings or marches *that are permitted by the local authorities*" (italics not in original question). Less than 20% of all respondents, and scarcely more than 20% of those giving an opinion, would approve of such subversive behavior, and more than half would disapprove (the remainder accepted the alternative presented that their reaction "would depend on the circumstances"). In view of such assumptions, the overwhelmingly negative reaction to the Chicago demonstrations despite sympathetic media treatment (cited earlier) is hardly surprising.

most Americans. The result at the election thus had a different coloration from what went before: McCarthy did not run and Wallace captured a proportion of the vote which was historically amazing. Indeed, it was probably the political stodginess of the older generation so decried by campus activists which kept the vote of "people over 30" within the channels of the conventional parties and prevented the Wallace vote from rising still higher. Certainly it is true that in several major metropolises of the United States where party loyalty has been nullified in primary election settings in the spring of 1969, candidates of relative Wallace coloration have surprised observers with their mounting popularity.

There can be no question but that dramatic and persistent displays of dissent on the campuses between 1964 and 1968 helped to place question marks around "consensual" national policies which might otherwise have continued to be taken for granted by most of the citizenry. At the same time, disregard for the occasional junctures of electoral decision when the mass public has some say in the political process may mean that a battle was won but a war was lost. For some few, this *politique de pire* is quite intentional, being thought to help "radicalize" the electorate in ways that can be controlled and manipulated. For most student activists, however, success in raising questions is of little value if one is helping in the same stroke to elect "wrong people" to answer them. And quite apart from the nature of the leadership elected in 1968, it is obvious to any "rational" politician hoping to maximize votes in 1970 or 1972 that there are several times more votes to be gained by leaning toward Wallace than by leaning toward McCarthy.

If these facts were inevitable consequences of "raising the issues" from the campuses, the dilemma would be severe indeed. It is not clear to us, however, that any intrinsic dilemma is involved. Much of the backlash expressed in the 1968 voting received its impetus less from irreconcilable policy disagreement—although on civil rights there is more than a modicum of that—than from resentment at the frequency with which the message of dissent from the campuses was clothed to "bait" conventional opinion. In the degree that the feelings and opinion reflexes of the common man, including age peers of lower circumstances, were comprehended at all by campus activists, they tended to be a subject for derision or disdain. Strange to say, such hostile postures communicate with great speed even across social gulfs, and are reciprocated with uncommon reliability. Fully as often, of course, there was simply no comprehension of the dynamics of public opinion at all.

Whether one likes it or not, the United States does retain some occasional elements of participatory democracy. A young and well-educated elite-to-be that is too impatient to cope with this bit of reality by undertaking the tedium of positive persuasion may find its political efforts worse than wasted.

·C·

Predicting 1980

Jimmy Carter's Problem

BY RICHARD M. SCAMMON
& BEN J. WATTENBERG

It is the thesis of this piece that the nature and implementation of President Carter's victory in 1976 has within it the seeds of a very great problem for him as he moves now into the second year of his term and begins, inevitably, to look ahead to his own 1980 reelection prospects.

Much of the recent talk has focused on the possibility of Carter becoming a "one-term President," on "his need for victories," the alleged ineptitude of his Georgia staff, the alienation of specific groups because of specific reasons, his attempt to "do too much," and so on. But missing from the discussion so far have been certain structural and ideological factors which may ultimately prove more troublesome to Mr. Carter than—as they say in the polling business—"all of the above."

Mr. Carter's problems are, at once, familiar and national ones, and in a more intense key, regional and peculiar ones: He won by capturing the votes of centrist switchers; he is in trouble, and may get into deeper trouble if he is perceived to be moving from the center toward the left. In his case, these not-so-unusual presidential afflictions are magnified by Carter's remarkable showing in the South in 1976.

Accordingly, it may be useful to look at that Southern regional situation first—critically important in and of itself—because it sheds light on the broader issue as well.

I

Why did Carter win in 1976?

It is, of course, customary after a close election for almost every group to claim that it was their specific group, their hard work, their support

Richard M. Scammon and Ben J. Wattenberg, "Jimmy Carter's Problem," *Public Opinion*, March/Arpil 1978, pp. 3–8. Cartoons deleted. Copyright 1978 American Enterprise Institute.

that "elected" the winner. When the winner in question is the President of the United States, such claims are made with particular vigor.

The aftermath of President Carter's victory has been no exception. Blacks have claimed the credit—although Gallup data show that Carter actually got a slightly lesser proportion of the black vote than did McGovern in 1972 or Humphrey in 1968. Jews have claimed the credit—although their voting precentages for Carter—73 precent according to an NBC election-day poll—were actually slightly less than in so-called "normal" years (it being understood that within the election observing trade, "normal" years have become rare enough to be called "abnormal"). Labor has claimed the credit with somewhat greater justification: They "came back" from a 1972 Republican vote to go solidly with Carter—but at a rate not really greater than pre-1972 years—and they provided him with massive financial and organizational help.

In a sense, they are *all* correct. Carter could not have won *without* their support. But that is the very nature of a close election. A close election is close. (You may quote that.) When it gets close enough our psephological favorite, the Maltese-Americans, can also claim credit for victory.

But saying "you couldn't have won *without* us" is not quite the same as saying "you won *because* of us." It may be said that the latter claim can properly be made by a group that not only provides a margin of difference, but votes *away from traditional patterns* to provide the margin of difference.

A simple analysis of recent presidental elections shows that there is one most obvious major group of voters who can lay claim to that formula for 1976. That grouping is "The South."

As the data [in the table below] show, in recent years "The South" had been trending steadily away from the Democrats in presidential elections—until 1976.

DEMOCRATIC PERCENTAGE OF SOUTHERN*
VOTE IN PRESIDENTIAL ELECTIONS,
1960–1976

1960	50.5
1964	49.5
1968	30.9
1972	28.9
but . . .	
1976	54.1(!)

*Eleven states of the Confederacy.

This trend has also been reflected in the electoral vote count:

ELECTORAL VOTES WON BY DEMOCRATIC
PRESIDENTIAL CANDIDATE IN THE SOUTH,[*]
1960–1976

1960	81
1964	81
1968	25
1972	0
but . . .	
1976	118(!)

---

[*]Eleven states of the Confederacy.

There is another way of putting the 1976 Southern story: *Carter ran best in that area of the country where recent Democratic presidential candidates had been running worst.* That was the great paradox of the 1976 election.

There is a sub-tabulation available that is of particular relevance. The 1976 break with voting patterns in the South occurred almost exclusively among *white* Southerners. It was the sharpest break in that group in three decades. Here is a trend line for Southern white Protestants voting Democratic in recent presidential years, showing a dramatic decline—and a dramatic revival in 1976 (see graph, page 554).

The percentage of Southern blacks voting Democratic has been much higher than Southern whites—but it remained constant in 1976.

The big change came among white Southerners. Had they not switched to Carter in large numbers in 1976 he would not have won. If those switchers do not—for any reason—vote for him in 1980, it is unlikely that he will win again.

White Southerners. Aside from the fact that about half voted for Carter, enabling him to capture the South, what else do we know about them?

We know that despite all of the talk about the "New South"—a term which has a cicada-like rhythm in American politics—white Southerners are still more conservative than most voters in America. Pollster Lou Harris reported in a release last summer: "The South is easily the most conservative part of the country."

If white Southerners were the hinge of the Carter victory, and if white Southerners are more conservative than most American voters, it behooves us to ask: Was Jimmy Carter the more conservative of the presidential candidates in 1976?

The answer is no. Notwithstanding Carter's basic traditionalism (re-

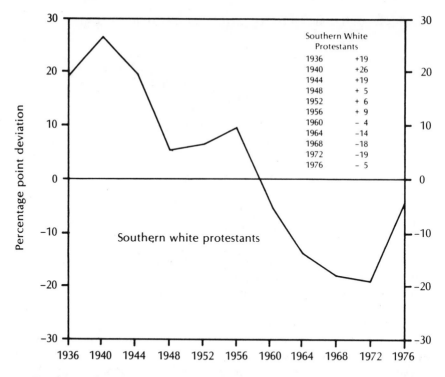

Southern White Protestants: Percentage Point Deviation from the National
Democratic Presidential Vote, 1936–1976

Source: American Institute of Public Opinion Surveys and Everett Ladd, *Transformations of the American Party System.*

ligious, ex-naval officer, small town, moral, businessman, and so on), Ford was generally seen as more conservative by the voters. A nationwide Harris poll taken in early September 1976, asked:

"How would you describe the political philosophy of (Gerald Ford, Jimmy Carter)—conservative, middle of the road, liberal or radical?"

And this was the clear response:

POLITICAL PHILOSOPHY	FORD %	CARTER %
Conservative	36	17
Middle of the road	36	31
Liberal	5	26
Radical	3	4
Not sure	20	22

The most conservative part of the country voted for the more liberal candidate.

Well, then, why did so many white Southerners vote for Carter? Obviously, because he was a Southerner—and in spite of their ideological leanings. Southerners felt, with good reason, that the idea that "a Southerner couldn't be elected President" was an idea whose time had come—and gone. And so, millions of white Southerners, who in other years would likely vote for the more conservative candidate, voted for the Southern candidate.

With all that extra help, Carter managed to carry the South narrowly. Slightly more than half of the white Southerners still voted *against* him. But that was better by far than any recent Democratic candidate had done, as the tabulations above show.

So: looking to the future, we can say that if a relatively few Southern conservatives perceive Carter as a liberal in 1980 and vote conservative instead of Southern, Carter could be in serious trouble

II

There may be a recent analogue to this tale of cross-rippling electoral tides, and it is an analogue that should be of great interest to Carter strategists.

In 1960, John F. Kennedy also won a close election when a large bloc of voters abandoned ideological and/or party-oriented behavior to vote along the axis of an external factor. The "externality" then was not that "a *Southerner* couldn't be elected President," but that "a *Catholic* couldn't be elected President." And millions of Catholics, who would normally have voted Republican, switched to vote for Jack Kennedy in a successful attempt to smash that outrageous religious axiom of our politics.

The big question, in both the Kennedy and the Carter situations, and for election pundits generally, is this: Having once voted on an externality—Catholicism or Southernism—is a voter likely to vote that way again *once his point has been proved?* Would Catholics keep voting for a Catholic President, against their ideological bent, even after it had been demonstrated that a Catholic *could* be elected President? Will Southerners have to prove a point about the South, again, after they proved it once in 1976?

Of course, we don't know the answer to the Southern question yet, but we have an idea about the Catholic question. John Kennedy, tragically, did not live to run for reelection in 1964. But since 1964, many Catholics have run for either President or Vice President in general elections and primaries: William Miller, Eugene McCarthy, Robert Kennedy, Edmund Muskie, Thomas Eagleton, Sargent Shriver, Jerry Brown—to name a few. *In no instance is there evidence that Catholicism became a major voting issue.*

It is as if the external issue, once settled, disappears, much as Prohibition, child labor, and free coinage of silver disappeared as issues once they were resolved.

Let us assume that the Catholic-Kennedy situation is indeed analogous to the Southern-Carter situation. With Southernism no longer a factor (as Catholicism is no longer a factor), President Carter would have to compete in 1980 along only the normal modes of voter reaction. These include: incumbency, personality, state of the nation, state of the world, record in office—*and ideology.*

Question: Under such circumstances, could Carter do well in the still-conservative white South? Surely he *could.* If the country is at peace and inflation rates are low, unemployment rates are low, and economic growth rates are high, Carter would not only carry the South, he'd sweep the nation. On the other hand, if you change the "lows" for "high" and the "high" for "lows," he might not carry Plains. But in a mixed and mottled real-world situation so common in recent years, the critical question is this: Is Carter *likely* to do as well as he needs to in the white South?

Well, he would have a good shot at it so long as he is not perceived to be wholly out of touch with mainstream Southern ideology (which remains more conservative than that of the rest of the nation).

So far—if one accepts the reportage of President Carter's administration—he has managed to maintain and even strengthen his image as a moderate. Enormous publicity is generated when black leaders denounce Carter for not spending enough. He wins more plaudits when he still says he will balance the budget. He denies federal aid for abortion. He promises the new welfare program will not hike welfare costs. He is attacked by organized labor for a variety of slights. He makes a tough-minded, vigorous defense of human rights and tough SALT proposals. And, as a result, public opinion polls show that fewer Americans regard Carter as "a liberal" than when he was elected.

On the other hand—less often reported, or less stressed for their political impact—have been a series of other acts that would, or should, or likely will, persuade more and more people that there is a "liberal" in the White House. ("Liberal," remember, is what liberal Morris Udall described in 1976 as a "worry word" when he asked the political press to please describe him as a "progressive.")

Many moderates and even more conservatives, viewing political developments through their own prisms, have noted with dismay: that Carter has signed the Panama treaties, that his welfare program ended up calling for substantially more spending, that he axed the B-1, that he condemns America's fear of communism as "inordinate" (neglecting to describe the ordinate parameter of such fear, which leads him to ask for a $10 billion increase in the defense budget), that he has taken mini-steps to recognize Cuba and Vietnam, that his energy program is widely assailed as pro-environmental and anti-production, that he backs down on SALT and human rights, that he deals the Soviets back into the Middle East, that it has become increasingly apparent this his budget will not come close to balance, that he goes public with Ralph Nader for a Consumer Protection Agency, that he allows his administration to be characterized as pro-quotas, and so on.

It could be said that these two lists are not a bad mix. Many voters' views would conform with some items in Group A and some in Group B.

But the key tactical question is this one: How vulnerable would President Carter be in his home region if he can readily be depicted as pro-Panama "giveaway," pro-quotas, pro-welfare, anti-growth, pro-Cuba, and so on. Not to put too fine a point on it, how would you like to carry that record into the South in 1980 running against a candidate who disagreed with all those positions—and perhaps had his own Southern credentials as well? (Several names come to mind.)

Well, some will say, what Carter may lose in the conservative South, he will make up in the liberal non-South.

But there is no liberal non-South. There is no clearer datum in modern American politics. Remember: It was Ford, not Carter, who carried the nation outside of the old confederacy, in both popular and electoral votes. And even if there were a liberal non-South, that's not how or why Carter won in 1976. Carter carried what he did outside of the South for the same reason he was able to carry the South: his opponents tried, but were not quite able to tag him as "Southern-Fried McGovern." Carter thus regained many Democratic "switchers," those voters who went to Nixon in 1972 because they found the perceived hyper-liberalism of the McGovernites unpalatable, indeed repugnant. Who were those switchers? Union men and women, Catholics, ethnics, Jews, "inner city peripherals," suburbanites, and on and on. Many, many voters of all stripes; voters able in many instances to identify with a traditional muscular, bread-and-butter, pocket-book liberalism—but wholly against anything perceived as "far-out."

Looking ahead to 1980, then, it can be postulated that much of what has been advanced here about Southern votes may be wholly applicable to the non-South, albeit in lower intensity and without the special minus (from Carter's point of view) of possibly no longer having his "Southern-ness" as quite so potent an issue.

Public opinion polls are clear: quotas, Panama, environmentalism, Russians-in-the-Middle-East are not the issues that endear the non-Southern non-liberals to the Democratic Party or its candidate, even if he is President.

III

As this is written President Carter has served just a year of his first term. The issues of today will not necessarily be the issues of 1980. He has plenty of time to shift course gently, almost imperceptibly, if he feels politically threatened in the South or anywhere else for that matter.

Indeed, that may prove to be exactly what Carter tries to do—all quite properly within the general presidential rubric of "doing what's best for the country." (After all, one of his jobs is to represent the voters, isn't it?) But there is still this question: Will he be able to make such a shift even if he wants to?

To think about that question, one must look at the nature of the presidential appointments—to those men and women who generate presidential policies and who inevitably shape the presidential image.

At the cabinet level one gets a sense of a political outlook that is, at once, technocratic and slightly left-of-center—which is about proper for a Democratic administration.

But quite a different picture emerges when one examines the sub-cabinet and sub sub-cabinet appointments. Perhaps unwittingly, perhaps wittingly, it is not moderate technocrats who most prominently populate these slots. Ideologues live there—ideologues from every one of the activist movements of the last decade. Environmentalists, consumerists, civil rights and women's activists, veterans of the peace movement have moved en masse from their ginger groups to large federal offices controlling massive budgets and armies of bureaucrats. A recent *Fortune* article names *sixty* high-level appointments made from activist groups; beneath them are a small army of their cohorts. And Senator McGovern, after a list of the Carter State Department appointees was completed late in 1976 remarked that those were the same people *he* would have picked. Senator Jackson did not make a similar statement. Columnist John Roche recently quoted a high-level State Department official saying, "I voted for Carter to get rid of Kissinger, and I got McGovern."

(This story is told: A young woman executive, formerly with the Sierra Club, now with the Department of the Interior at a salary about five times higher than the $10,000 per year she previously made, has suggested that all former Movement-niks tithe 10 percent of their salaries to their previous organizations! Imagine the public reaction if in an earlier administration a business-man recruited to government service suggested tithing back to Exxon!)

It is not the purpose of this short article either to praise or condemn the attitudes and views of those remnants of the Movement who now hold high federal office. Nor is the purpose here to suggest that all the ex-activists-now-in-government are reacting the same way to their present high eminence. Some are of the opinion that they work for the elected executive and should represent his views, some feel that ideology reigns and that it is their job to seek an outlet for their ideology.

Still, agree with them or disagree with them, a great many of these once-young ex-activists can be said to represent a general point of view. We can say several things about that point of view. It tends to be activist about the proper role of the federal government. It is often anti-establishment: anti-business, anti-defense, anti-labor to name a few. In the age-old argument, it tends to stress equality somewhat more than liberty. It tends to be somewhat ashamed of America's role in shaping the modern world. It has a know-it-all elitist quality, probably reinforced by President Carter's insistence that all he did was hire the best people with the most merit—apparently without considering just what substantive policies these apparatchiks would be meritorious at initiating. It is a point of view not only well to the left on the American political spectrum but well to the left in the Democratic Party. It takes positions that, as perceived, tend to be "out of sync" with mainstream American attitudes—which remain opposed to quotas, a lower defense posture, ecology-over-growth, and so on.

The President apparently feels that his activists, to use the old Washington phrase, are "on tap not on top." The theory is that the moderates can balance the activists, and one may speculate that is the reason President Carter appointed at the top rung men of moderate reputations—the Schlesingers, Strausses, Lances, Vances, and Schultzes. Ideally, these senior moderates could channel the energies and ideas of the activists into courses sympathetic to the President's own views and synergistic to his political interests.

Well, maybe. We shall see. But many veteran bureaucracy-watchers are dubious. This dubiety stems from several sources. First, in Washington, if you ever have a choice of choosing the cabinet or the sub-cabinet, pick the latter. The men and women whose names are pre-fixed with "Sec." spend a great deal of time testifying, traveling, and giving speeches. Their underlings tend to make policy. Bureaucrats sense that more ideas bubble up than trickle down. Second, winning half the battles isn't nearly enough. As the bubbling-up process ensues, some—most—ideas and rhetoric (and a candidate can get hung on a phrase as well as a program) that are not in keeping with the President's views are surely screened out. No matter. Some are not. If and as they become policy or doctrine, the President must live with them and defend them—all over the country. The hard-liners may win on an I.L.O. decision. Fine. But down in the ranks someone wrote a sentence for the President's Notre Dame speech about the "inordinate fear of Communism," and that may be a subject of attack even if the attackers approve of the I.L.O. position.

As this is written, President Carter is on the griddle for a number of policies that seem clearly to derive from the New Politics bias of his government-by-sub-cabinet apparatchik.

- True to that bias, his energy program was heralded as an ecology program. "The age of abundance is over," crowed the environmentalists after its promulgation last spring. True to that bias, a score and more dams were axed. In each instance, the Congress thought otherwise.

- True to that bias, ideological environmentalists within the government have recently sought to apply American ecological standards to export goods, irrespective, apparently, of the wishes of the buying countries and with scant regard for the economic chaos that might be generated in American.

- True to that bias, the Government's *amicus* brief on Bakke was open to interpretation as pro-quota or at least not anti-quota: "Minority-sensitive" is the new obfuscatory phrase. The President will be politically lucky if the Nixon-dominated Court goes against his brief, bails him out, thereby mooting the issue. It it does not oblige, the President can look forward to a campaign where he is described as Jimmy Quoter.

- True to that bias, Carter seemingly dealt the Soviets a plum in the Middle East, managing in a stroke to politically unite those sympathetic to Israel with those unsympathetic to the Soviets. It was only Anwar Sadat's bold effort that was able to rectify that error.

- True to that bias, early indications show a SALT treaty destined to cause an historic Senate confrontation.

Are these chance occurrences? Will the pattern of a leftward tilt continue? Does it represent the views of "the real Carter"? Is the GOP wise enough, and unified enough, to capitalize on it? If this pattern is perceived in the Washington political community but not around the country, will a ripple effect spread the perception? Credibly? Can Carter control his apparatchiks if he wants to? Has he already begun to try? Do his State of the Union and budget messages already presage that attempt? Will his I'll-never-tell-a-lie personality, which a majority of Americans still trust according to the polls, be enough to override these problems?

In all truth, no one knows. It is a situation without precedent. The last time the Democrats took the White House from the Republicans a very different cast of characters took over. JFK's New Frontiersmen were described as "pragmatic" and "tough." They were men very much from the center of the political spectrum.

Today it is different. The Democratic Party now has a large and militant flapping left wing, nurtured by activists who are veterans of a decade-and-a-half of civil rights, anti-war, environmental, consumerist, and feminist causes. In a party that is slightly to the left of the people on most issues, the activists are to the left of the party and the apparatchiks are often to the left of the activists. They are part of the Carter coalition, they have moved into government and no one knows what their long-range effect will be. It is fair to ask, however, "upon what meat doth this our Caesar feed?"

The circumstance being a new one, it is fair to speculate about it. How much political indigestion have the activists caused Carter so far? Considerable, the authors feel. What will happen in the future? Our speculations vary in degree, not in kind. Mr. Scammon thinks Mr. Carter will not lose control of his government, and a majority of the apparatchiks in question will be co-opted. Mr. Wattenberg acknowledges that possibility, sees some evidence of it, hopes to see more, but remains somewhat more concerned: for him there is a recurring image of the President as the Sorcerer's Apprentice, trying desperately and honorably to gain control of what proves to be uncontrollable.

World Series Winner Key to the Presidency?

BY NORMAN SIEGEL

The 1976 World Series ended with the National League team, the Cincinnati Reds, beating the American League team, the New York Yankees. As an enthusiastic supporter of Jackie Robinson, the Brooklyn Dodgers and consequently the National League, I, of course, was happy that "my team" had won. However, this year, in addition to viewing the World Series as strictly a sports event, there were important national political consequences as a result of the outcome.

At a Bicentennial celebration in New York on the Fourth of July, I was explaining that if someone grew up on the streets of Brooklyn in the early 50's and was a baseball fan, he could tell their politics from the team they rooted for among the Dodgers, Giants, and Yankees. One listener, Jon Margolis, who turned out to be a Washington correspondent for The Chicago Tribune and an avid baseball fan, threw back to me a more startling and perhaps more important political-sports theory. Jon claimed that if in a Presidential election year the National League team beat the American League team in the World Series, the Democrats would win the election. If the American League team won, then the Republicans would win.

Norman Siegel, "World Series Winner Key to the Presidency?", *The New York Times*, October 31, 1976, Section IV, p. 31. © 1976 by The New York Times Company. Reprinted by permission.

Just Watch the Series

It sounded right. The National League—the league of Jackie Robinson, the Dodgers, Ebbets Field—seemed more in tune with the philosophy and make-up of the Democratic Party than the Republican Party. Likewise, the American League—the league of Mickey Mantle, the Yankees, Yankee Stadium—seemed more in tune with the philosophy and make-up of the Republican Party.

If Margolis's theory was correct, then we would not have to wait till Election Day to find out who our next President and Vice President would be. Just think, no need for campaigning and debates. All we would have to do is watch the Series and find out who would win.

The next thing to do was to check out the theory.

Since 1903, the year of the first World Series, there have been 18 Presidential elections. In the 18 elections the theory is correct 12 times. Since 1940, the theory is correct every time except in 1948, when the American League team, the Cleveland Indians, beat the National League team, the Boston Braves, and Harry Truman, a Democrat, edged the Republican Thomas Dewey. (You could explain 1948 by recognizing it as the exception or that it was a "fluke year." Remember how many people, especially Margolis's newspaper, *The Chicago Tribune*, thought Dewey would win.)

You Could Look It Up

You might also argue that the differences between the National League and the American League did not begin to show until the Dodgers, a National League franchise, broke the racial barrier with Robinson in 1947. Therefore, the analysis should begin from 1947. This being the case, then, except for 1948, the theory is 100 per cent. Since 1952, every time the National League team won the Series, the Democratic ticket won. Every time the American League team won, the Republicans won the Presidency.

Just think: 1952, Yankees beat the Dodgers, Eisenhower wins; 1956, Yankees beat the Dodgers, Eisenhower wins; 1960, Pirates beat the Yankees, Kennedy wins; 1964, Cardinals beat the Yankees, Johnson wins; 1968, Tigers beat the Cardinals, Nixon wins; 1972, Athletics beat the Reds, Nixon wins.

Thus, in our last six Presidential elections the theory holds.

So, "my fellow Americans," I am pleased to announce that the winner of the 1976 Presidential election will be Jimmy Carter.